Why was the Diaoyu Islands Dispute Rekindled Over?

Research by Chinese and Japanese Scholars

initiated and arranged by the China-Japan Association
for the Promotion of Journalism in Beijing

compiled by Sun Dongmin

translated by Wang Jing

CANUT INTERNATIONAL PUBLISHERS

Istanbul - Berlin - London - Santiago

The publication is authorized by People's Daily Press, Beijing

The English version is arranged by People's Daily Press & China Renmin University Press

The publication is supported by China Classics International

Why was the Diaoyu Islands Dispute Rekindled Over? -
Research by Chinese and Japanese Scholars

Project initiated and arranged by the China-Japan Association for the Promotion of Journalism in Beijing

compiled by Sun Dongmin

translated by Wang Jing

Orig. Title: 钓鱼岛主权归属, Copyright © 2013, People's Daily Press, Beijing

Canut Intl. Turkey, Teraziler Cad. No.29. Sancaktepe, Istanbul, Turkey

Canut Intl. Germany, Heerstr. 266, D-47053, Duisburg, Germany

Canut Intl. United Kingdom, 12a Guernsay Road, London E11 4BJ, England

Copyright © Canut International Publishers, 2018

ISBN: 978-605-9914-61-1

www.canutbooks.com

About the Compiler

Sun Dongmin, Deputy Director and Senior Editor of the International Department of the People's Daily. Graduated from Beijing Foreign Studies University. He has served as a staff member in the Municipal People's Government of Beijing and as the reporter and editor of the International Department of the People's Daily. He worked as the chief reporter and local editor of the People's Daily in Tokyo from 1982 to 1989, mainly engaged in reporting on Asia-Pacific affairs. His social engagements include Representative of the Association of China-Japan for the Promotion of Journalism in Beijing Vice President of the China-Japan History Society, and Director of the China International Peace and Friendship Association.

Preface

The China-Japan Association for the Promotion of Journalism in Beijing has initiated, arranged and presided over the compilation of this book – *Why was the Diaoyu Islands Rekindled Over?*. As a book for reference, *Why was the Diaoyu Islands Rekindled Over?* collects some representative papers and newspapers commentaries concerning the Diaoyu Islands issue; besides, some important documents about the postwar development of China-Japan relations are also included. This book boasts articles with distinct arguments and events with clear background, which provides a valuable reading platform for readers to learn about the ins and outs of the Diaoyu Islands issue.

The year 2012 marked the 40th anniversary of the normalization of diplomatic relations between China and Japan. The China-Japan relations should have been further deepened in this memorable year. However, Japan's unlawful "purchase" of the Diaoyu Islands and "nationalization" of the Diaoyu Islands severely infringes upon China's territorial sovereignty and greatly hurt the Chinese people's feelings, which has resulted in the unprecedented grim situation of China-Japan relations. Moreover, far-sighted people from the two countries have been more and more anxious about this issue.

As we all know, the Diaoyu Island and its affiliated islands have been China's sacred territory since ancient times. This is supported by historical facts and jurisprudential evidence. The Diaoyu Islands were first discovered, named and exploited by the Chinese people. Since the Ming Dynasty, the Diaoyu Islands have been put under the jurisdiction of China's naval defense. The waters surrounding Diaoyu Island are traditionally Chinese fishing ground. Although the Diaoyu Island and its affiliated islands are uninhabited, they have never been "terra nullius". China is the indisputable owner of the Diaoyu Islands.

As an inherent territory of China, the Diaoyu Islands shouldn't be a problem. Japan's illegal seizure and occupation of the Diaoyu islands in 1895 has caused the current dispute. During the Sino-Japanese War, taking advantage of the Qing government's undoubted failure, Japan incorporated the islands under the administration of Okinawa secretly. Then, Japan seized the islands for a long term by signing of the Treaty of Shimonoseki. After the end of World Anti-Fascist War, Japan surrendered unconditionally and accepted the Potsdam Declaration that determined that all territories, including the Diaoyu Islands, occupied by Japan during its invasion of China be returned to China. However, the US and Japan had underhand secret dealings. In December, 1953, the US Civil Administration of the Ryukyu Islands expanded its jurisdiction to the Diaoyu Islands without any form of jurisprudential justification. On June 17th, 1971, Japan and the United States signed Okinawa Reversion Agreement in order to hand over Okinawa to Japan, and the Diaoyu Islands were mapped into the handover area. Chinese government solemnly declared that such a move was flagrant, totally illegal and invalid; it couldn't change China's territorial sovereignty over the Diaoyu Island and its affiliated islands.

The Chinese nation is a peace-loving country and believes that the harmony is the most precious value to be maintained in the international relations. Moreover, China has the tradition of being friendly and peaceful to her neighbors, as well as friends far away, and China has always advocated that the international disputes should be settled through dialogues and negotiations. Although the Chinese people suffered great sacrifices in the Anti-Japanese War, China, being a lenient and tolerant neighbor, gave up the right to ask for war indemnity during the normalization of China-Japan diplomatic relations in 1972. What's more, during the establishment of peaceful and friendly agreement of China-Japan relations in 1978, China and Japan reached an important understanding and common ground on "leaving the issue of the Diaoyu Island to be resolved later". This opened the door to normalization of China-Japan relations and was followed by tremendous progress in China-Japan relations.

The fundamental cause for the Diaoyu Islands issue lies in the aggression and expansion of the Japanese militarism; besides, Japanese authorities fail to have a thorough introspection on the aggression guilt of the Japanese militarism as well as to eliminate such guilty actions, which has also caused the Diaoyu Islands issue to be unsolved. Furthermore, Japan's stubbornly claiming the Diaoyu Islands as its "inherent territory" is, in essence, an outright denial of the outcomes of the victory of the World Anti-Fascist War and constitutes a grave challenge to the post-war international order. On the other side, China, acting in the larger interest of China-Japan relations, agreed on "leaving the issue of the Diaoyu Island to be resolved later", but it doesn't mean giving up China's territorial sovereignty. The Chinese government has the unshakable resolve and will to uphold the nation's territorial sovereignty. Regarding China's goodwill and restraint as a sign of weakness is the greatest misjudgment of the Chinese people's strong will.

40 years' normalization of diplomatic relations between China and Japan has witnessed the healthy and stable China-Japan relations which has benefited both China and Japan and are in line with the fundamental interests of the two nations. Harmony brings benefits while conflict causes harm, so we need joint efforts and a common purpose to develop the healthy and stable China-Japan relations. Japan must stop all acts that undermine China's territorial sovereignty, take concrete actions to show their sincerity and make real efforts to handle and resolve the Diaoyu Islands dispute through dialogues and negotiations.

Finally, I think it is of great significance for the China-Japan Association for the Promotion of Journalism in Beijing, to initiate the compilation of this book. This association is established by experienced Chinese journalists who were permanent residents in Japan. I deeply admire their rich experiences, profound understanding of Japan and undaunted dedication. They have devoted themselves to promoting the mutual understanding between China and Japan and the benign development of China-Japan relations. Here, I would like to express my sincere gratitude for their great efforts and contributions.

Tang Jiaxuan
The President of the China-Japan Friendship Association
March 2014, Beijing

Contents

Introduction

The Diaoyu Islands Belong to China

Sun Dongmin

The book, concerning the Diaoyu Islands issue, introduces the academic opinions of some representative scholars at home and abroad, and includes some official documents and declarations elaborating China's principles and standpoints on the issue. This far-sighted book is supported by historical facts and jurisprudential evidence. It represents the ins and outs of the Diaoyu Islands issue and the current situation. China and Japan, both in the East Asian region, are bound to resolve the perilous situation; China and Japan with similar culture should be wise enough to settle the Diaoyu Islands issue. Observing centuries' ups and downs, we walk out from the history. Seeking the national rejuvenation, we calmly march towards the future.

I. The Diaoyu Islands issue is a problem left over by history

Looking back over the year 2012, the 40th anniversary of the normalization of diplomatic relations between China and Japan may be written in history as a suspicious year. The Diaoyu Islands issue has caused serious confrontation fueled by various forces, forming an alarming situation in the East China Sea. China-Japan relations are faced with huge obstacles as Japan launched an "attack" first. In the wake of the Spring Festival of 2012, some Japanese right-wingers landed on the Diaoyu Islands; when two countries were preparing to commemorate the 40th anniversary of the establishment of diplomatic ties with Japan, the Japanese side had issued an ominous signal: Shintaro Ishihara, a right-wing Japanese politician initiated a scheme for the Tokyo Metropolitan government to "purchase" the Diaoyu Islands; in the latter half of the year, the Japanese Noda government evilly colluded with the right-wing forces, recklessly supporting provocative moves: the Japanese government announced its plan to "nationalize" the Diaoyu islands on July 7, on the date marking the Japanese all-round aggression against China in 1937. On August 15, on the anniversary of Japan's surrender in the WWII, Japanese police arrested 14 Chinese citizens on board a Hong Kong fishing vessel on the waters near the Diaoyu islands. Then, in September, Chinese President Hu Jintao met the Japanese Prime Minister Yoshihiko Noda and persuaded him to act with a broad vision considering of the interest of China-Japan relations and refrain from making wrong decision. However, two days later, on September 11, Japanese Prime Minister Yoshihiko Noda announced Japan's "purchase" of the Diaoyu Islands, just before September 18 the date when Japan had launched the war of aggression against China in 1931.

Japan severely infringes upon China's territorial sovereignty and greatly challenges China's core interests. Furthermore, Japan's outright denial of the outcomes of the victory of the World Anti-Fascist War has alerted the Chinese people who always bear in mind the country's overall interests.

On September 10, Chinese government solemnly declared that China was strongly disappointed and sternly opposed Japan's actions that infringed China's territorial integrity and sovereignty. In addition, Chinese President Hu Jintao and other Chinese leaders expressed that the Chinese government had the unshakable resolve and will to uphold the nation's territorial sovereignty and pointed out that whatever ways the Japanese side used to "purchase the islands" were illegal and void.

The Japanese government openly announced the so-called "nationalization" of the Diaoyu islands; besides, Japanese police arrested Chinese citizens outrageously; some Japanese right-wingers made provocative moves by landing on the Diaoyu Islands once again. All these offensive actions have ignited the long pressed anger of the Chinese people. Around September 18th, the Chinese people spontaneously organized orderly protests to express their strong resentment.

In order to assert the country's sovereignty over the Diaoyu Islands and its affiliated islands, China has published the base points and baselines of the territorial sea of the islands. The Chinese surveillance ships and aircraft have arrived at waters and airspace around the Diaoyu Islands and its affiliated islands. This air-sea stereoscopic cruise has enhanced the law-enforcement effect. China is determined to defend the country's maritime territory and safeguard the national Maritime rights and interests, achieving the seemingly intractable "effective control". The so-called "effective control", in fact, is a reflection of the national strength and the strong will to safeguard the national sovereignty.

The Japanese militarism committed numerous crimes in the war of aggression against China, leaving generations of Chinese people with indelible memories. However, China, bearing in mind the overall interests, gave up the right to ask for war indemnity during the normalization of China-Japan diplomatic relations in 1972 in order to reduced Japan's economic burden. The Chinese people showed their sincere friendliness to the Japanese people and buried their pain deep in the heart. According to what I have seen and heard, at the beginning of the normalization of diplomatic ties with Japan, when some Japanese friends came to visit China and sent their apologies to the Chinese people, a lot of Chinese people thought there was no need to apologize for the past things. Moreover, some Japanese friends wanted to meet survivors in the Nanjing Massacre, the related department refused politely because they were afraid of hurting the Japanese friends' emotions. However, some of the Japanese friends didn't appreciate this kindness. Japan doesn't show real remorse for their past aggression guilt. Instead, in the past 40 years, they defend for their guilt and even want to reverse their conviction again and again. They have fooled the kind-hearted Chinese for many times. Now, the resurrected Japanese militarism attempts vainly to throw the Japanese people into the whirlpool of militarism once again. Isn't it necessary for the Chinese people who believe the harmony is the most precious to be vigilant?

The events occurred between China and Japan in 2012 have brought us a lot of thoughts and contemplation.

The Diaoyu Island and its affiliated islands have been China's territory since ancient times. This is supported by historical facts and jurisprudential evidence. Japan occupies Chinese territory without providing a convincing explanation. In addition, Japan always resorts to sophistry and deceives the world by distorting the facts. They attempt to create an accomplished fact that Japan has the sovereignty over the Diaoyu Island and its affiliated islands. However, as early as 40 years ago, Mr. Inoue Kiyoshi, a famous Japanese scholar with conscience and sense of justice, demonstrated clearly that "the Diaoyu Islands are China's territory" in his book—In Historical Facts of Senkaku Islands/Diaoyu Islands. He also suggested that in order to keep the peaceful state in Asia, we should tell the world about the real historical facts of the Diaoyu Islands as well as the related international jurisprudence.

History has proved again that the political foundation of the development of China-Japan relations lies on Japan's correct understanding of its history of aggression. The dramatic ups and downs during the 40 years of China-Japan relations have depended on whether or not Japan can correctly understand and deal with history as well as problems left over by history. Today's Diaoyu Islands issue is totally caused by aggressive expansion of the Japanese militarism. It involves how to implement the post-processing of the Second World War mentioned in the Cairo Declaration and the Potsdam Declaration, and whether the

Japanese government admits what it promised in China-Japan Joint Statement that it "firmly maintains its stand under Article 8 of the Potsdam Declaration." The reason why this problem left over by history has not been solved is that the Japanese authorities have not made a thorough reflection on aggression guilt of the Japanese militarism as well as exterminated them.

The modern China-Japan relations is like "half-cooked rice". The Populism has risen again in Japan in recent years and the public opinion is confused by the right-wing forces. The China-Japan relations are facing a grim situation; and no one is willing to see this situation. The far-sighted people concern whether the Diaoyu Islands issue will evolve into a bad turning point of the China-Japan relations.

Mr. Wang Taiping who was the Consul General in Japan for three times has long been engaged in diplomacy with Japan. He once worked as a reporter in Japan. In the following we will present his comments on the Diaoyu Islands dispute?

Commentator: Wang Taiping (former Ambassador and Consul General of Ministry of Foreign Affairs of the People's Republic of China; the President of China, Japan and South Korea Economic Development Association).

The Diaoyu Islands issue has been a pending problem of China-Japan relations. It's not a simple territorial dispute. It's part of the extension of the historical issues between the two countries, which can be traced back to the days when the Japanese militarism started to invade China after the Sino-Japanese War of 1894-1895.

The Diaoyu Islands belong to China beyond all doubt. It has always been affiliated to Taiwan Island of China both in geographical and historical facts. The pace of Japan's invasion and expansion quickened after Meiji Restoration. Shortly after its invasion of Ryukyu in 1879, Japan schemed to encroach the Diaoyu Islands. On January 14, 1895, Japan held a cabinet council which secretly put the Diaoyu Islands under the administration of Okinawa. On April 17th, Japan forced China to sign the unjust "Treaty of Shimonoseki." The treaty stipulated that the whole Taiwan Island and all its affiliated islands, the Diaoyu Island included, should be ceded to Japan. The Japanese government pretends that the Diaoyu Islands are an "inherent territory" of the country and belong to Okinawa. Yet Okinawa had been an independent country—the Ryukyu Kingdom—which kept a long suzerain-feudatory relation with China. It is not an inherent territory of Japan. Moreover, the Diaoyu Islands do not belong to Okinawa. Therefore, Japan's gangster logic does not stand.

The Diaoyu Islands are part of the extension of the historical issues between the two countries because the islands, which are affiliated to Taiwan, should be returned to China after WWII, according to Cairo Declaration, Potsdam Declaration and Japanese Instrument of Surrender. However, the problem has remained till this day. The reason lies in that the US occupied the islands illegally after WWII in the name of trusteeship, and gave it to Japan in 1972 when the US returned Okinawa to the country. Nevertheless, the US has never stated that the sovereignty over the Diaoyu Islands belongs to Japan. The US chooses not to take side in this issue.

It can be said that Japan's behavior concerning the issue reflects its denial of its militarism and thus challenges the victory of the World Anti-fascist War. History cannot and should not be obliterated. A country which disrespects history would not earn any respect from the international family; moreover, it would make the world be on guard against it. Whether the Japanese can handle the issue properly will be the touchstone of whether it can face history seriously.

II. China is the owner of the Diaoyu Islands

The Diaoyu Island and its affiliated islands have been China's inherent territory since ancient times. However, the Japanese government has ignored the historical facts, and still insisted on "Basic Views" that the Diaoyu Islands belong to Japan, which was announced by the Japanese Ministry of Foreign Affairs on March, 1972. Therefore, it is necessary to trace back to the history of the sovereignty over the Diaoyu Islands.

The Japanese government's "Basic Views" on the issue is based on "terra nullius". The "Basic Views" of the Japanese government are as follows: Since 1885, the Japanese government, through repeated on-site investigations by the authorities of Okinawa Prefecture and other channels, has cautiously confirmed that the Senkaku Islands are not only no-man's islands but also have no traces of the rule of (China's) Qing Dynasty. On this basis, the Cabinet decided on January 14, 1895, to have markers erected on the islands to officially incorporate them into Japan's territory. This is equal to recognizing that before 1895 the Japanese government had never carried out investigations on, nor possessed, the Diaoyu and adjacent islands, so Japan's lie that the Diaoyu Islands are Japan's "inherent territory" instantly collapsed.

Now that the Diaoyu Islands do not belong to Japan, who is the owner of the Diaoyu Islands? Are these islands "terra nullius"? This is the primary issue of the sovereignty over the Diaoyu Islands.

According to the historical records, from 1373, the Ming navy cruised in Fujian Sea where the Diaoyu Islands were also included. They fought against Japanese pirates and drove them to the Ryukyu oceans. The existing detailed records of China's cruise on the Diaoyu Islands waters is A Tour of Duty in the

Taiwan Strait (Tai Hai Shi Cha Lu) written by Taiwan inspection official Huang Shujing in 1722 of the Qing Dynasty. It points out that "there are mountain behind the ocean which is called the Diaoyu Islands. The waters of the Diaoyu Islands can hold tens of ships." Afterwards, Recompiled General Annals of Fujian (Chong Zuan Fu Jian Tong Zhi) in 1871 included Diaoyu Islands as a strategic location for coastal defense and placed the islands under the jurisdiction of Gamalan, Taiwan (known as Yilan County today).

An amount of ancient authority literature shows that before 1895 when Japan stole the Diaoyu Islands in the Sino-Japanese War, China had discovered, named and exploited the Diaoyu Islands more than 500 years ago. As the neighbor as well as the vassal state of China in the Ming and Qing Dynasties, the Ryukyu Kingdom was once called "the bridge on the sea". The two nations maintained friendly exchanges in the 500 years and never experienced unpleasant events. The powerful China didn't swallow any island of Ryukyu Kingdom, instead, it brought the Ryukyu Kingdom unification and the progress of civilization. The Diaoyu Islands, as the subsidiary islands of Taiwan, have never belonged to the Ryukyu Islands. The separating line between China and Ryukyu lies between Chiwei Yu and Gumi Island. This is the consensus recorded in all the historical documents of China, Ryukyu and Japan. The Japanese annexation of Ryukyu in 1879 changed Ryukyu into Okinawa. Later in January 1895, Japan stole China's Diaoyu Islands and incorporated them into Okinawa, which has caused this complicated situation of the Diaoyu Islands issue.

Prof. Liu Jiangyong of Tsinghua University has long been concerned about the Diaoyu Islands issue, and in the 1990s, he published his monograph on the ownership of the Diaoyu Islands in People's Daily.

Commentator: Liu Jiangyong (Associate Dean of the School of Contemporary International Relations, Tsinghua University, Doctor of Law).

It is unquestionable that the Diaoyu Islands belong to China. In the Ming Dynasty, the Diaoyu Islands have been mapped into China's territory and been put under the jurisdiction of China's naval defense. According to records, as early as in 1372, the first emperor of the Ming Dynasty appointed Yang Zai as an imperial envoy to grant honorific title to theKingin Ryukyu in recognition of his rule. Since then, China and Ryukyu had established relations of granting honorific titles and presenting tributes. China sent 24 imperial envoys to grant honorific title to the kings of Ryukyu, leaving rolls of Record of the Imperial Title-Conferring Envoys to Ryukyu (Shi Liu Qiu Lu) which clearly recorded the sea conditions from the Diaoyu Islands to Ryukyu. There were 36 islands in the Ryukyu Kingdom and the Diaoyu Islands had never been included. Ancient China and Ryukyu reached consensus on this.

Japan insists on that the Diaoyu Islands are "terra nullius" occupied by Japan. The Japanese side claims in 1884 Koga Tatsushiro discovered the islands. Therefore, Okinawa Prefecture was requested to let him develop the land. During this period the Japanese government repeatedly investigated and proved that these islands were uninhabited islands and there are no traces of the rule of Qing Dynasty. The Cabinet decided on January 14th, 1895 to have markers erected on the islands to officially incorporate them into Japan's territory. Besides, they claimed that they didn't steal the islands from China in the Sino-Japanese War and the islands were not included in the Treaty of Shimonoseki.

But it is by no means true. Vol. 18 and vol. 23 of Japan's diplomatic archives clearly documented that the Meiji government knew the Diaoyu Islands were not "terra nullius", and that they were named by Chinese, but it still secretly seized the islands by taking advantage of the victory of the Sino-Japanese War. It has nothing to do with preemptive owning of a "terra nullius" in a peaceful way.

According to Japanese diplomatic archives, on September 22, 1885, the Okinawa magistrate Sutezo Nishimura did a survey under the order of the Ministry of Internal Affairs. The result is that "Yet, due to their differences in terms of topography from the earlier reported island Daitojima (situated between this prefecture and Osagawa Islands), the possibility must not be ignored that they are the same islands recorded as Diaoyutai, Huangwei-yu and Chiwei-yu in the Zhongshan Mission Records."

However, they did not stop at this result but continued to investigate. After the second survey in the same year, Inoue Kaoru, the Ministry of Foreign Affairs, wrote to Yamagata Aritomo, the Ministry of Internal Affairs: "about the uninhabited islands between Okinawa and Fuzhou of the Qing government, they are close to the border of the Qing government. Furthermore, the Qing government has named these islands. Recently, the Qing government published newspapers, saying that our government attempts to occupy the affiliated islands near Taiwan and the Qing government has suspicions about our country. At this moment, if we openly established national stakes on these islands, we are bound to face the opposition from the Qing government. Therefore, we should report its harbor shapes and unearthed land property according to the actual investigation results. We can step out of the shadow to establish national stakes and further develop these islands according to the situation in the future."

From the results from the second survey, Japan knew that the islands were not terra nullius, and China named these islands long time ago, but Japan didn't give up even when China was vigilant about Japan's occupation. Sutezo Nishimura, the Okinawa Magistrate, did a survey under the order of the Ministry of Internal Affairs. The result was that the islands may not have nothing to do with the Qing government. Please instruct me how to handle it, if we have disputes with the Qing government." At that time, Japan was not ready for its war against China and worried about disturbing the Qing government, so they temporarily gave it up and waited for 10 years.

However, the Japanese right-wing forces deliberately distorted the history of Japan's seizure of the Diaoyu Islands. The Japanese Ministry of Foreign Affairs refuses to talk about this history. What's more, they also falsified the literature to deceive the Japanese public.

The data collection published by Megumi Tadahisa, the President of the Senkaku Islands Defense Association of Okinawa is a solid proof. The author said that it was his precious achievements after nearly 20 years' painstaking research. Some discourses about the above contents have been removed by him and it turned out to be: "about the uninhabited islands between Okinawa and Fuzhou of the Qing government, we should report its harbor shapes and unearthed land property according to the actual investigation results. We can step out of the shadow to establish national stakes and further develop these islands according to the situation in the future." Compared with the original archives of the Japanese Ministry of Foreign Affairs, we can easily discover that he garbled the original archives and concealed historical facts, which is pure self-delusion.

Until two months before the Sino-Japanese War, namely May 12, 1894, Okinawa's final conclusion of the undercover investigations of the Diaoyu Islands was that we have done no fieldwork since 1885; it is difficult to give a definite judgment. There is no written evidence or even an oral legend that prove these islands belong to us."

After the outbreak of the Sino-Japanese War, on December 27th, 1894, Yasushi Nomura, the Ministry of Internal Affairs, sent cipher text to Foreign Minister Mutsu Munemitsu: "about the arrangement of establishing stakes on Kuba Island and the Diaoyu islands, we hope this matter could be submitted to the cabinet meeting again according to present situation." (Vol. 23 of Japanese diplomatic documents). However, on January 14, 1895, the Japanese Meiji government couldn't wait to pass the "cabinet resolution" even before the ending of the Sino-Japanese War that Japan would incorporate the islands under the administration of Okinawa secretly with markers erected on the islands. Three months later, with the signing of Treaty of Shimonoseki, Taiwan and all its affiliated islands were ceded to Japan. Naturally, the Diaoyu Islands were included, no matter whether Treaty of Shimonoseki clearly pointed it out. In fact, Japan didn't build the so-called "markers". One of the reasons might be that they felt it unnecessary as they had already annexed Taiwan. If the Japanese side thought the Diaoyu Islands were not included in the Treaty of Shimonoseki, they must have had markers erected on the islands to claim Japan's rule. Until the late 1960s, Japan took advantage of the deteriorated relations between China and the Soviet Union and sent people to erect national markers on the islands.

III. Japan's aggressive expansion reveals its nature

It is too ridiculous for Japanese authorities to claim that the Diaoyu islands were Japan's inherent territory since ancient times. Besides, they have pondered over the excuse and found their only reason was the "preemptive occupation of terra nullius".

The so-called "Basic Views" of the Japanese Ministry of Foreign Affairs are as follows: the Japanese government, through repeated on-site investigations by the authorities of Okinawa Prefecture and other channels, has cautiously confirmed that the Senkaku Islands are not only no-man's islands but also have no traces of the rule of Qing Dynasty. It also claimed in On Senkaku Islands: they will incorporate the islands under the administration of Okinawa with markers erected on the islands; and it is in accordance with the international law—preemptive occupation of terra nullius.

Japanese scholar Toshio Okuhara may be the biggest contributor who looked for "legal evidence" of Japan's "preemptive occupation of terra nullius". In his article Evidence of Sovereignty over the Senkaku Islands, he said:

Our country incorporated the Senkaku Islands within our territory on January 14 in the 28th year of Meiji period (according to the decision of cabinet meeting). At that time Japan winning the war seemed to be definitely settled and the peace talk was about to begin. Various states have accepted the cession of Japan. It wasn't difficult to imagine that under such circumstance Japanese government recognized the Senkaku Islands within Okinawa out of such a political judgment: Qing government has recognized the lost of Taiwan and they wouldn't dispute with Japan over the sovereignty of the Senkaku Islands, such a not-worth-mentioning terra nullius.

However, even if Japan incorporated the Senkaku Islands in such a delicate period, their behavior still left room for doubt: what was the background, against which our country has ever waived the incorporation of the Senkaku Islands? If we think deeply about the timing, one point worth attention: actually Japan always considered the Senkaku Islands to be the territory of China and was seeking opportunity to grab the islands. Was it possible that Japan dealt with the Senkaku Islands while Japan won the war? It was quite natural that there was such a doubt.

Further, if the Senkaku islands were not taken as the affiliated islands of Formosa, our country can acquire the sovereignty of the islands which was now China's only through the law. However, some people would argue that law can only be used when there was no Qing-Japan war. On the premise of the Qing-Japan war, it was logical that our country claimed the sovereignty of the Senkaku islands based on the legal claims, but it has to admit that the claim of our country was vulnerable. That's because before proposing the "prescription" principle, it can only be the result of Qing-Japan war that the land of China was incorporated into our territory.

If we can certify the above facts, we can conclude that Japan has illegally incorporated the Senkaku Islands which were determined as China's territory according to the international law into its territory. And if Japan did it before the Sino-Japanese War, it is true that Japan's occupation is a predatory behavior.

Toshio Okuhara didn't say it out of his academic conscience, but only aimed to defend Japan's occupation the Diaoyu Islands as Japan is facing the awkwardness of no historical evidence supporting its illegal actions and predicament of unable to make up any more lies.

Prof. Okuhara also said:

Because both of the War and the acceptation of the Potsdam Declaration are facts, our country can only take the measure of effective occupation to acquire the sovereignty of the Senkaku Islands. Cession, conquest or annex is impossible. Then, Prof. Okuhara emphasized: "I have study the problem from different perspectives. It could be concluded that no fact or evidence could prove that before being incorporated within our territory the Senkaku Islands were China's. In other words, the islands are the so-called terra nullius in International Law".

In order to proof Japan's only excuse—preemptive occupation of terra nullius, he created the mythology that there was a vacuum place between ancient China and the Ryukyu Kingdom. To prove Japan's preemptive occupation of terra nullius was perfectly justified, he exerted himself to depreciate that historical fact that the Diaoyu Islands were first discovered, named and exploited by the Chinese people. He insisted that the dispute over Diaoyu Islands was the territorial dispute between nations according to the international law and it couldn't be explained or deducted by historical facts and documents. He also held that these islands were nothing but "route instructions" with geographical locations, so their names were different in each country. It is even more ridiculous that they concluded that China learned ship-making skills as well as shipping skills from Ryukyu just because the number of Ryukyuan envoys on their voyages to China was more than that of Chinese envoys on their voyages to Ryukyu. As we all know, the names of the Diaoyu Islands have long been a consensus of the international community and historical documents and maps of countries such as Britain and France also make it clear that the Diaoyu Islands are China's territory. A man with the slightest common sense knows that ship-making skills as well as shipping skills of the Ming Dynasty were advanced in the world. Moreover, the Ryukyuan also learned these skills from China. Hence, I can't think of other word to describe these people but ignorance.

"The preemptive occupation of terra nullius" as argued by the Japanese Ministry of Foreign Affairs was originally an invention of the colonialists. According to the later international law, the "preemptive occupation" principle should in accordance with five steps as follows: 1. occupation attempt; 2. confirmation of terra nullius; 3. occupation announcement; 4. occupation actions; 5. effective jurisdiction.

Taiwan scholar Zhang Qixiong believes: Japan, by virtue of "paperwork", incorporated the islands under the administration of Okinawa without any occupation announcement and treaty. So far, Japan has been unable to provide any authorized original documents to prove that Japan once incorporated the islands into Japan's territory. According to the international law of the preemptive occupation of terra nullius, Japan does not conform to the requirements of the "effective" preoccupation, because both China's claim and Japan's verification indicate that the Diaoyu Islands are inhabited land rather than terra nullius. Japan's occupation claim and process cannot confirm to the international law of "preemptive occupation of terra nullius". They even didn't establish the so-called markers on the islands. Until May 5, 1969, Japan did not built any evidence of jurisdiction or territorial markers. Therefore, it is winner's illegal invasion rather than the "preemptive occupation of terra nullius" in the international law.

Readers should pay attention that "500 years before Japan's invasion of the Diaoyu Islands, no country in the region had problems with China's sovereignty over the Diaoyu Islands." The Japanese Ministry of Foreign Affairs claimed that Japan's preemptive occupation of terra nullius was in accordance with international law. However, it can't prove that the Diaoyu Islands are terra nullius with decent evidence and that their preemptive occupation of terra nullius is in accordance with international law as well. What's more, they built markers only by the excuse of applying Okinawa as fishing administration; the Meiji government, only by virtue of informal document instructions, claimed other country's land as its own. Nothing can be more ridiculous than this.

In addition, in order to steal these islands, Japan changed the "state stakes" in the secret investigation in 1885 to "markers" and "uninhabited islands between Fuzhou of the Qing Empire and Okinawa" to "uninhabited islands under the name of Kuba island and the Diaoyu Islands to the north west of Yaeyama Islands of Okinawa", which was agreed by the Cabinet in 1895.

Moreover, in 1895 when Japan stole the Diaoyu Islands by documents, it used the word "uninhabited islands"; then, they wanted to change it to "terra nullius". But "uninhabited islands" and "terra nullius" are two different concepts in the international law. "Uninhabited islands" may not be "terra nullius". Although the Diaoyu Islands are "uninhabited islands", since the Ming Dynasty, the Diaoyu Islands have been put under the jurisdiction of China's naval defense. Japan stubbornly insisted their preemptive occupation of terra nullius was in accordance with international law, but it didn't confirm to the definition of it in the international law. The change of the words and sentences reflected that Japanese militarism was confident in its encroachment after expanding its armies and wanted to make its encroachment legalized.

Facts have proven that China's territory—the Diaoyu Islands and its affiliated islands had been incorporated into Japan's territory secretly. Three months later, it forced China to sign the unequal Treaty of Shimonoseki to cede Taiwan and all its affiliated islands. The Japanese army occupied the Diaoyu Islands during the process of "receiving" Taiwan.

In June, 1895 it completed its occupation of Taiwan and all its affiliated islands. Therefore, what Okuhara said—the things that can't solved by cession, conquest, Annex, conquest—had become facts before the aggressive expansion of the Japanese imperialism.

Dr. Sun Wenqing, a senior reporter of the China Youth Daily paid visits to Japan twice. Let's have a look at his opinions.

Commentator: Sun Wenqing (senior reporter of the China Youth Daily; Vice President of the China-Japan Association for the Promotion of Journalism, in Beijing).

Japan's seizure of the Diaoyu Islands is another behavior of stealing other country's territory after the Meiji government's imperialism was full-fledged. A large amount of historical data and related documents have proven that the Diaoyu Islands were first discovered, named and recorded by the Chinese people since the Ming Dynasty. To scholars at home and abroad, these documents are valuable historical materials for researching on the Diaoyu Islands issue. As early as 1561, the Diaoyu Islands were locations in the Great Haiphong Map (Wang Li Hai Fang Tu) which was China's official military map.

However, after 334 years in 1895, the Japanese Meiji government took advantage of the victory in the Sino-Japanese War and preempted the Diaoyu Islands which was neither firstly discovered by Japan nor terra nullius. China firstly discovered these islands 300 ago, so Japan's preemptive occupation was totally nonsense.

The Japanese government also painstakingly created oral evidence for its illegal seizure of the Diaoyu Islands. It tried to kill and distort those historical documents which were disadvantageous to itself. It deliberately mixed up the concepts of "uninhabited island" and "terra nullius" and stubbornly treated these islands with a Chinese name—"Diaoyu Dao" as "terra nullius". If these islands were "terra nullius" and had nothing to do with China, why they have a Chinese name; if the "uninhabited island" was "terra nullius", can other countries also stubbornly treat them as "terra nullius"? Obviously, Japan's excuse is untenable. In addition, Japan cannot find out any other reason to own China's islands.

Additionally, according to the theory of international law, a country's occupation of "terra nullius" should go through occupation announcement to express its occupation attempt. Western powers did all the procedures when they occupied sea islands or lands in Africa. However, Japan just called it terra nullius inwardly and quietly without any announcement and publishing the decision of the Cabinet meeting. It even did not make any public announcement about the government's instruct of building markers on these islands. Until March 1950, the Japanese people touched this matter through Vol.18 of Japanese diplomatic documents. It was because the Japanese government's preemptive occupation of terra nullius was untenable that the Japanese Empire chose to remain silence on its unjustifiable behavior; and that's why the US, Japan's best friend, chose to take no position on the sovereignty over the Diaoyu Islands.

From the process of Japan's invasion of China's Diaoyu Islands, we can see that the imperialists believe in the jungle philosophy. Under the aggressive expansion strategy, Japan adopted "vague tactics". For example, Japan seized the islands for a long term by signing of the Treaty of Shimonoseki when it was advantageous to itself. While it was not, it would claim that the Diaoyu Islands were not included in Treaty of Shimonoseki, so they were not included in the return areas in the Treaty of San Francisco. However, no matter how Japan quibble about this matter, the Diaoyu islands were either stolen by Japan during the Sino-Japanese War or Japan's predatory territory based on Treaty of Shimonoseki. Sooner or later, Japan will return these islands to their true owner.

On the sovereignty over the Diaoyu Islands, there is a folk episode. Around 1997, I, as a resident reporter in Tokyo, went to Japan. A conservative Japanese reporter argued with me about the delimitation of the territorial sea and the territorial disputes between China and Japan. The Japanese reporter repeatedly stressed: "Senkaku Islands" are Japan's inherent territory; because China discovered oil in these waters, it began to fight for them against Japan. I asked him: "you say they are inherent territory of Japan, but before the Meiji restoration they already had a Chinese name. You can do some survey on whether they have a Japanese name." He avoided my questions and quibbled: they can't be called "Diaoyu Islands", it should be "Yudiao Islands". I said: "I never heard of "Yudiao Islands". You had stolen China's territory but couldn't give them a decent name." Maybe the reporter tried to persuade numbers of Chinese scholars in Japan but never succeeded. At last, he heaved a sigh and said: "they will be taken away by China sooner or later."

IV. Private deals are illegal and invalid

Japan declared its sovereignty over the Diaoyu Islands by distorting the definition of "preemptive occupation of terra nullius" in the international law, quibbling the Diaoyu Islands were included in Treaty of Shimonoseki and claiming that the Diaoyu Islands are Japan's inherent territory by signing the Treaty of San Francisco with other countries after the Second World War.

The Treaty of San Francisco was a peace treaty with Japan signed in September 8th, 1951only between Japan and the US. China, the Soviet Union and other countries were prevented by the US from participating in the San Francisco Conference. This treaty was the legal basis of US's postwar occupation of Okinawa. The third article of the Treaty of San Francisco stipulates that Japan will concur in any proposal of the United States to the United Nations to place under its trusteeship system, with the United States as the sole administering authority, Nansei Shoto south of 29deg. north latitude (including the Ryukyu Islands and the Daito Islands), Nanpo Shoto south of Sofu Gan (including the Bonin Islands, Rosario Island and the Volcano Islands) and Parece Vela and Marcus Island. Pending the making of such a proposal and affirmative action thereon, the United States will have the right to exercise all and any powers of administration, legislation and jurisdiction over the territory and inhabitants of these islands, including their territorial waters. Japan believes that the Diaoyu Islands were included in Article 3.

Although Japan declared its sovereignty legal basis over the Diaoyu Islands by using the Treaty of San Francisco, China does not admit this treaty because China didn't take part in San Francisco Conference. Zhou Enlai on behalf of the Chinese government lodged solemn representations to the Treaty of San Francisco and announced that this treaty was a public humiliation to the Chinese people and was illegal. The Chinese people will never admit it. Fundamentally, it indicated that China held a denial attitude to the legitimacy of US' occupation of Okinawa and the Diaoyu Islands; besides, China announced Japan's receiving the Diaoyu Islands by virtue of this treaty was illegal and invalid; the treaty had no binding on China.

About the legal status of the Diaoyu Island and its affiliated islands after the Second World War, some scholars pointed out the Treaty of San Francisco did not specify that the scope of US's trusteeship included the Diaoyu Islands. Article 3 did not involve "the Diaoyu Islands" or "the Senkaku Islands". The Nansei Shoto mentioned in Article 3 were the Nansei Shoto south of 29deg. north latitude; besides, it gave clear indication in the parentheses—including the Ryukyu Islands and the Daito Islands, but there is no mention of the Diaoyu Islands. In addition, on January 29th, 1946, the Supreme Commander for the Allied Powers Instruction (SCAPIN) No.677 clearly defined Japan's power of administration to "include the four main islands of Japan (Hokkaido, Honshu, Kyushu and Shikoku) and the approximately 1,000 smaller adjacent islands, including the Tsushima Islands and the Ryukyu Islands north of the 30th parallel of North Latitude", but the Diaoyu Islands were not included (Huangwei Yu south of the 30th parallel of North Latitude is located to the most northern part of the Diaoyu Island and its affiliated islands).

It is worth mentioning that the famous international law scholars Hans Kelsen pointed out Article 3 of the Treaty of San Francisco was illegal and invalid in his Principles of International Law. From his perspective, "the islands ruled by Japan will be put under the trusteeship of the United States. We assume after the dissolution of the League of Nations (which means the end of trusteeship), the trusteeship countries and US should extend their sovereignty to related territories after Japan's surrender, this is in accord with the international law. Without this premise, the trusteeship countries and US have no right to deal with these territories. (See the paper of Liang Zhijian on page 233) Hans Kelsen argues that the clear premise of the territory's legitimacy after the victory of the Anti-Fascist War is that Japan and the US should extend their sovereignty to related territories after Japan's surrender. Without this premise, Japan and the US have no right to deal with these territories; and the fact is that the surrendered Japan didn't extend its sovereignty to Nansei Shoto, let alone the Diaoyu Island and its affiliated islands which don't belong to the Ryukyu Islands. Similarly, the United States neither extended its sovereignty to Nansei Shoto nor extended its sovereignty to China's Diaoyu Island and its affiliated islands. If the US had the right to deal with the ownership of Okinawa, which means that Okinawa was incorporated under the administration of the US, so Japan lost its sovereignty over Okinawa.

Japan pointed out that the United States Civil Administration of the Ryukyu Islands released Geographical Realm of Ryukyu Islands (No. 27 edict) on December 25, 1953, in which mapped in the Diaoyu Islands, Huangwei Yu and Chiwei Yu. But the fact is that the Diaoyu Islands are not Ryukyu Kingdom's territory. Even if the treaty listed the areas of Ryukyu in US's trusteeship, the Diaoyu Island and its affiliated islands never belong to ancient Ryukyu Kingdom. Scholars have pointed out the partition of international borders must be negotiated by the two countries, but the border decided by the United States Civil Administration of the Ryukyu Islands is only US's and Japan's unilateral actions without China's participation and agreement from the Demarcation Committee of the Common International Organization, so it is totally underhand secret dealings between the US and Japan and is by no means legal.

In addition, regardless of China's opposition, on June 17, 1971, Japan and the United States signed Okinawa Reversion Agreement in order to hand over Okinawa to Japan, and the Diaoyu Islands were mapped into the handover area, which is invalid and illegal. As a result, the legal status of the Diaoyu Islands depends on the Cairo Declaration and the Potsdam Declaration rather than the Treaty of San Francisco and Okinawa Reversion Agreement.

It should be pointed out that in 1972 which marked the normalization of diplomatic relations between China and Japan, they published China-Japan Joint Statement where Japan made it clear that it would "it firmly maintains its stand under Article 8 of the Potsdam Declaration." Article 8 of the Potsdam

Declaration stipulated the terms of the Cairo Declaration shall be carried out and Japanese sovereignty shall be limited to the islands of Honshu, Hokkaido, Kyushu, Shikoku and such minor islands as we determine. Besides, terms of the Cairo Declaration should also be carried out that all the territories Japan has stolen from the Chinese, such as Manchuria, Formosa, and the Pescadores, shall be restored to the Republic of China. Japan will also be expelled from all other territories which she has taken by violence and greed. With all these hard facts, shouldn't Japan return the Diaoyu Island and its affiliated islands to China?

Dr. Lian Degui is a scholar in the field of International Studies in Shanghai. He will share his opinion with us.

Commentator: Lian Degui (Member of Shanghai Institutes For International Studies; Deputy Director of Asia-Pacific Studies Center).

One of Japan's claims on the sovereignty over the Diaoyu Islands involves the Treaty of San Francisco and Okinawa Reversion Agreement. As early as March 8th, 1972 in the Basic Views of Japanese Ministry of Foreign Affairs: The Senkaku Islands are not included in the territories renounced by Japan as provided in Article 2 of the San Francisco Peace Treaty but, as part of the southwest islands, placed under US administration according to Article 3, and included in territories restored to Japan as stipulated in the Japan-US Agreement on Ryukyu Islands and Daito Islands signed on June 17th, 1971. After the islands under US trusteeship were restored to Japan, they are naturally Japanese territory.

The Basic Views of Japanese Ministry of Foreign Affairs aims to indicate that US's occupation of Okinawa (including the Diaoyu Islands) was based on international treaties, namely, the Treaty of San Francisco, so it was legal. Therefore, it was also legal for the US to return Okinawa (including the Diaoyu Islands) to Japan according to the Okinawa Reversion Agreement as the Diaoyu Islands were included in Article 3 of the Treaty of San Francisco as well as the Okinawa Reversion Agreement. In a word, Japan thought it was legal to own the Diaoyu Islands.

It must be pointed out:

1. the Treaty of San Francisco has no binding on China. Premier Zhou Enlai, on behalf of the Chinese government issued a statement on December 4th, 1950: If the People's Republic of China is excluded from the preparation, formulation and signing of the peace treaty with Japan, it will, no matter what its content and outcome are, be regarded as illegal and therefore invalid by the Central People's Government. Premier Zhou Enlai said in a statement on August 15th, 1951: "UN Declaration stipulates that a separate peace treaty is not allowable; the Potsdam Declaration prescribes "the preparation of peace

treaty" should be carried out by all the members who signed on the surrender terms of the enemy country. It is obvious that China's attitude is very clear: the Treaty of San Francisco is illegal. Okinawa ownership issue should be determined by all the UN members including China who signed on the surrender terms of Japan."

2. US's so-called "administration right" on Okinawa was illegal, so was the so-called "Okinawa Reversion Agreement". US's so-called "administration right" on Okinawa originated from the provision of Article 3 in the Treaty of San Francisco. Now that China thought this treaty was illegal, from China's perspective, the United States had no right to return Okinawa to Japan. Furthermore, Article 3 in the Treaty of San Francisco didn't make it clear that the US can transfer this kind of "administration right", so the Okinawa Reversion Agreement was illegal.

3. Okinawa issue was unresolved. Since the UN members who signed on the surrender terms of Japan haven't held a comprehensive conference to talk about the sovereignty over Okinawa, so they haven't found the final solution. China and Japan published China-Japan Joint Statement where Japan made it clear that it would "sit firmly maintains its stand under Article 8 of the Potsdam Declaration", which meant that it would stick to the provision in Cairo Declaration and the provision of Japanese sovereignty in the Potsdam Declaration. The issue of the sovereignty over Okinawa was not involved in negotiations in the normalization of diplomatic relations between the two countries, but as for the Diaoyu Islands issue, Kakuei Tanaka suggested that the two sides could shelve the dispute. In a word, the Diaoyu Islands issue should be explained by Cairo Declaration, the Potsdam Declaration, China-Japan Joint Statement as well as the consensus on "shelving the dispute" in 1972, rather than the Treaty of San Francisco and the Okinawa Reversion Agreement.

In short, the Treaty of San Francisco has no binding on China, because it is a unilateral treaty. The United States has no right to return the so-called "administration right" on Okinawa to Japan; it doesn't matter whether Article 3 of the Treaty of San Francisco included the Diaoyu Islands or not, because in 1972, two countries started to negotiate about the Diaoyu Islands issue and reached a consensus on "shelving the dispute". If the Japanese side thought that there was no such consensus, it should continue to negotiate with China rather than quibble with the Treaty of San Francisco and the Okinawa Reversion Agreement.

V. The thief suffers from its own actions

From its invasion of Asian countries to its final demise, Japanese militarism was like a hungry wolf killing its prey once he set its goal of aggressive expansion. At first, it would pry about the strength of the prey; then, it would make excuses to stir up trouble. It would retreat in front of strong opponent and avail itself of the opportunity to invade those weak opponents. There are numbers of examples such as its control of North Korea, annexation of Ryukyu, secret seizure of the Diaoyu Islands, invasion of Taiwan, etc.

The Japanese occupation of the Diaoyu Islands started from its annexation of the Ryukyu Islands. Shortly after the Meiji Restoration (1868), the emperor of the government made the national policy—"develop vast sea and conquer the world". It soon took into actions to conquer North Korea, annex Ryukyu, invade Taiwan and the mainland China, gradually accelerating its pace of foreign aggression. In 1872, Ryukyu was change into "han" (domain which governed by Japanese feudal lord in Edo period); in 1874, it sent army to Taiwan. After its annexation of Ryukyu in 1879, it put the invasion of the Diaoyu Islands into its agenda.

In 1885, the Japanese government sent people to investigate the Diaoyu Islands and knew the Diaoyu Islands "belonged to the Qing Empire". The prefectoral governor of Okinawa reported to Yamagata Aritomo: "Gumi Island (Chiwei Yu), Kuba Island (Huangwei Yu) and the Diaoyu Islands are undoubtedly those islands recorded in the Records of Messages from Chong-shan (Zhong Shan Chuan Xin Lu) as the Diaoyu islands, Huangwei Yu, Chiwei Yu. If it is true, they had been discovered by the ship of the imperial envoy of the Qing Dynasty who went to grant honorific title to the former Zhongshan King and had been named by China." Inoue Kaoru, the Ministry of Foreign Affairs said: they are close to the border of the Qing government. Furthermore, the Qing government has named these islands. Recently, the Qing government published newspapers, saying that our government attempts to occupy the affiliated islands near Taiwan and the Qing government has suspicions about our country. At this moment, if we openly established national stakes on these islands, we are bound to face the opposition from the Qing government. Therefore, we should report its harbor shapes and unearthed land property according to the actual investigation results. We can step out of the shadow to establish national stakes and further develop these islands according to the situation in the future."

"Step out of the shadow!" reflected the greedy ambitions of Japan.

For the following ten years, the Japanese authorities repeatedly conducted "investigations", but the result were still "there are no clear written or oral evidence to prove the islands belong to us (Japan)." However, they found the chance to "step out of the shadow": China was defeated in the Sino-Japanese War, which was a different situation. The Cabinet decided on January 14, 1895, to have markers erected on these uninhabited islands such as Kuba Island (Huangwei Yu) and the Senkaku Islands (the Diaoyu Islands) to officially incorporate them into Okinawa. On January 21, Okinawa governor issued that the Cabinet had agreed to build markers on these islands.

Finally, things are different! The Japanese Meiji government immediately decided to secretly steal these islands as they were bound to win the war.

Japan's official documents show that Japan kept its actions from 1885 to 1895 as a secret and never made it public. Takahashi Sougorou, a researcher on the Diaoyu Islands issue mention in his work—Notes of the Senkaku Islands/ Diaoyu Islands that:

It should be highlighted that the documents related to Senkaku Islands was not published until March, 1950. It was because of the publishing of Japan Diplomatic Documents (18th volume) that citizens had the chance to know the truth.

However, a popular saying in Japan goes: after Japan incorporated the Diaoyu Islands into Japan's territory, it did not receive any protest from other countries in the world; so it received the islands in a quiet atmosphere". Besides, they also held that after Japan's occupation of the Diaoyu Islands, "China had remained in silence for about 70 years until the discovery of oil in the Diaoyu Islands in 1970, China began to claim the Diaoyu Islands were China's territory. In February 2013, Japanese Prime Minister Abe made a public lie in Washington during a speech: "no one can dispute Japan's sovereignty over the Diaoyu Islands from 1895 to 1971".

Without any notice in advance and any declaration after the event, Japan had incorporated China's territory into its own. The Japanese invaders showed no guilt when stealing things from others and publicized its ugly behaviors everywhere. Only those invaders who believe in aggression history can do this brazenly.

If it makes sense, we can also ask that 500 years before the Japan's annexation of Ryukyu Islands, did Japan or any other country ever challenge China's sovereignty over the Diaoyu Islands?

Without any explanation, Japan incorporated the islands under the administration of Okinawa. Why not make its occupation of the Diaoyu Islands public during the 50 years. We also wonder why Japan didn't build markers during the 70 years which was the Cabinet's decision; and it hurriedly sent people to finish it until 1969. Furthermore, when Ryukyu was under US's administration from 1945 to 1971, is Japan entitled to challenge China's sovereignty over the Diaoyu Islands?

Some Japanese must be forgetful as they just can't remember the Chinese government issued a statement as early as the 1950s that said the Treaty of Peace with Japan was illegal and invalid. The Chinese government had been opposed to US's occupation of Ryukyu and the Diaoyu Islands and demanded the US to retreat its army.

It should be pointed out that Japan's invasion of China's Diaoyu Island and its affiliated islands was by virtue of its victory in the Sino-Japanese War. It firstly stole these islands secretly by "paperwork" and then occupied them as part of Taiwan and all its affiliated islands as prescribed in the Treaty of Shimonoseki. This occupation lasted till to Japan's surrender in the Second World War. As clarified by Chinese scholars, Japan's so-called "preemptive occupation based on the principle of terra nullius" not only goes against the domestic law, but also not in conformity with the international law.

Mr. Su Haihe, Deputy Director of International Division of All-China Journalists' Association had been a resident journalist in Japan for many years. Let's look at his comments.

Commentator: Su Haihe (Deputy Director of International Division of All-China Journalists' Association; former senior reporter of the China Youth Daily).

From the Meiji Restoration to the defeat in the Second World War, it was like Japan's hundred years' history of aggressive expansion: conquering North Korea, annexation of Ryukyu, invasion of Taiwan, mainland China and Southeast Asia countries. Its plunder of the Diaoyu islands is typical example of its stealing and predatory actions.

Japan's tricks for grabbing the Diaoyu Islands vividly reflected its guilty essence. Japan claimed that the Japanese firstly founded the Diaoyu Islands in 1884 and said they were uninhabited islands. The next year, the Japanese government carried out the secret investigation on the islands, but Japan's attempt roused China's alertness. The Chinese newspaper Shen-pao reported on September 6, 1885: "some Japanese people stuck Japan's flag on the sea islands to the north east of Taiwan, revealing Japan's intention to occupy these islands. The Japanese government scrupled about China's reaction, so it did not dare to move immediately. The results of the survey were strictly confidential. "We can step out of the shadow according to the situation in the future", which showed that the Japanese government clearly knew the Diaoyu Islands are China's territory, even so, Japan still did not given up its ambition to occupy these islands.

In July 1894, the Sino-Japanese War broke out and Japan finally had the opportunity. Because of the corrupt and incompetent Qing government, China faced with undoubted failure, taking advantage of which, the Cabinet decided on January 14th, 1895 to officially incorporate the islands under the administration of Okinawa. However, the content of the resolution was not made public to its people and to other countries. Japan made a huge joke to deceive the world.

Japan's official documents show Japan had begun to investigate the Diaoyu Islands secretly since 1885. It also secretly stole the Diaoyu Islands in 1895. It kept everything as a secret until its surrender. The Japanese Ministry of Foreign Affairs even claimed that after Japan incorporated the Diaoyu Islands into Japan's territory, China had never put forward objection for 70 years, which proved that China admitted the Diaoyu Islands belonged to Japan. Can Japan be more shameless?

On April 17, 1895, the Qing government was defeated in the Sino-Japanese War and was forced to sign the unequal Treaty of Shimonoseki. The Diaoyu Islands were ceded to Japan as a part of Taiwan and all its affiliated islands.

In order to occupy Taiwan, it should firstly extinguish Ryukyu; in order to invade China, it should firstly control Taiwan and North Korea. Without any notice in advance and any declaration after the event, they incorporated China's territory into its territory, which was the normal means of the aggressive Japanese imperialism.

The Diaoyu Islands belong to China and are by no means terra nullius. Japan's approach did not have legal efficiency according to the international law. Japan's "preemptive occupation of terra nullius" was futile attempt. The theft might be successful for a moment, but finally it will face inglorious infamy because its camouflage and suffers from its own actions.

In October 2012, Japan's Ambassador Uichiro Niwa expressed his true feelings when giving a lecture in Nagoya University: "from the perspective of the young people in China, Japan is a thief." I Believe Mr. Niwa didn't wrong about his feelings.

VI. Ryukyu, from being a vassal state of the China's Ming and Qing Dynasties to being annexed by Japan

The Diaoyu Islands, located between Taiwan and the Ryukyu Islands, are the affiliated islands of Taiwan and don't belong to the Ryukyu Islands as well as the "36 Islands of Ryukyu" in history. As the islands were incorporated under the administration of Okinawa in 1895 and Okinawa was named in 1879 after Japan's annexation of Ryukyu, so the Diaoyu Island issue was associated with Japan's annexation of Ryukyu.

On the Ryukyu Islands, people had unearthed "Ming dao currency" (knives as money) of Yan State in Spring and Autumn Period and "Kaiyuan Tongbao" (coin used in Tang Dynasty), which verified that Ryukyu maintained long communication with China. From 1187 to 1405, Ryukyu was successively reigned by Shuntian Dynasty, Yinzu Dynasty and Chadu Dynasty. During the rule of Yucheng Emperor of the Yinzu Dynasty from 1314 to 1336, Ryukyu had been divided into three little kingdoms: Zhongshan, Shannan, Shanbei ("three mountains"). In 1372, the first emperor of the Ming Dynasty appointed Yang Zai as an imperial envoy to grant honorific title to theKingin Ryukyu in recognition of his rule. The King of Ryukyu also dispatched his younger brother to follow Yang Zai back to pay tribute to and be granted honorific title by the Ming Imperial Court. It marked the beginning of the official communication between China and Ryukyu. In 1404, the third emperor of the Ming Dynasty sent an imperial envoy to grant honorific title to Wuning (successor of King Chadu). It was the first time China grant official honorific title to Ryukyu. In 1429, Shang Bazhi finally united the "three mountains". In 1430, the Ming Empire admitted that Shang Bazhi united Ryukyu and granted honorific title to him as the King of Ryukyu. There were 26 generations of the Shang Dynasty. Until the last King of Ryukyu—Shang Tai, Ryukyu was annexed by Japan in 1879. This tribute-paying and title granting system lasted for about 500 years and China and Ryukyu established a friendly relationship with no grudge.

China had used "Ryukyu" to call the Ryukyu Islands and the Ryukyu Kingdom since the Sui and Tang Dynasties. The first emperor of the Ming Dynasty used it in his letters and the imperial envoy of Ryukyu also called his country "Ryukyu". About the name of "Okinawa," it was firstly found in Annals of South Island in the 17th century written by Japanese Edo scholar Arai Hakuseki. When the Meiji government annexed Ryukyu in 1879, it called Ryukyu as "Okinawa County" instead of "Ryukyu County", as "Ryukyu" meant "belonging to China in history" (Japan, the history of Ryukyu/Okinawa)

Although Ryukyu was a vassal state of China, but the Ming and Qing government did not directly rule Ryukyu politically. China holds righteousness and is delight to give a hand to the weak. The Ming emperor appointed 36 people from Fujian Province who were good at operating ships to go to Ryukyu, to bring Chinese culture there. China afforded all the cost for students from Ryukyu; China helped the fishermen from Ryukyu return home when they were drifted to China; the local government would give people from Ryukyu who died in China decent burials. Ryukyu with gratitude kept their manners and was highly praised as "state of ceremonies".

Because of China's honorific title granting, Ryukyu was renowned in the world. During the "big trade era" (also known as great maritime era) in the 15th and 16th century, Ryukyu was the bridge on the sea. It was recorded Ryukyu paid tribute-paying voyages to the Ming Empire for 171 times with more than 100,000 people (increased to 200,000 in Qing Dynasty). In the late 15th century, "Sea Bridge Clock" was built with inscriptions with meanings of intimacy between Ryukyu and the Ming Empire.

It's a really a tragedy to have an aggressive and perfidious neighbor like Japan. From the late 16th century, Ryukyu was constantly affected by Japan's invasion and penetration. After gaining profit from trades with Ryukyu, Japan attempted to occupy its territory. In 1592 and 1596, Toyotomi Hideyoshi, the supreme ruler of Japan, sent troops to invade North Korea twice; Shimazu took this opportunity to ask for military service and to extort money from Ryukyu. In 1609, Shimazu with the permission of Tokugawa government sent troops against Ryukyu and captured King Shangning of Ryukyu. Furthermore, he seized five islands of Ryukyu including the Amami Islands and prevented Ryukyu from paying tribute voyages to China. Since then, the internal affairs and diplomacy of Ryukyu had been controlled by Japan. The tribute-paying voyage between China and Ryukyu became the profit means of Satsuma vassal state. What was more insidious was that Shimazu wanted to benefit from the tribute-paying between China and Ryukyu but demanded Ryukyu to pretend that it was not Japan's vassal state but that Japan was a friendly neighbor. Each time the Chinese imperial envoy came, the Japanese in Ryukyu would hide themselves, which lasted to the Japanese Meiji Restoration Period. But the Qing government had never admitted Ryukyu belonged to Japan.

After Japanese Meiji Restoration in 1868, the Meiji government planned to invade North Korea and occupy Taiwan. In order to find a military base to invade Taiwan, Japan was eager to annex the Ryukyu kingdom as Japan's territory. In 1872, without any consultation with the Qing Empire, Japan degraded King Shangtai of China's vassal state—the Ryukyu Kingdom—to "Ryukyu seignior". In April 1874, Japan sent troops to attack Taiwan with the excuse that fishermen of Ryukyu were killed by the Gaoshan people when they drifted to Taiwan after a accident on the sea. In addition, Japan intentionally distorted the representations of the officials of the Qing government that "some people in Taiwan like outsiders didn't obey the rules of the Qing Emperor", based on which, Japan claimed that Taiwan didn't belong to China and forced the Qing government to sign Taiwan Specialized Article and give Japan a compensation of 500,000 silver (currency of the Qing Dynasty). Japan did all these to make its annexation of Ryukyu Islands legal. In July, 1875, Matsuda Michiyuki, the official of the Ministry of Internal Affairs, demanded Ryukyu to abolish tribute-paying and title granting system with the Qing Dynasty and use Japan's prefectural system; besides Japan demanded Ryukyu to set up military bases. Because of Ryukyu's delay, Japan sent soldiers to take Ryukyu over and changed it to Okinawa. Ryukyu, after being China's vassal state for 500 years, was ruined by Japan's aggression.

For Japan's annexation of Ryukyu, the Qing government spared no effort to help Ryukyu but the spirit was willing but the flesh was weak. Afterwards, since Japan suffered from international pressure, under the conciliation of Grant, the former President of the United States, special envoys from China and Japan negotiated with each other about the Ryukyu issue in Beijing. China advocated "three divisions" plan: the areas located to the north of Amami Island belong to Japan; the parts of the Ryukyu Kingdom located in Okinawa islands, Miyako

Islands and Yaeyama Islands belong to China; while Japan put forward the "Treaty of Island Division and the Supplementary Provisions" plan: the areas located to the north of Okinawa islands belong to Japan; Miyako Islands and Yaeyama Islands belong to China; Sino-Japanese Provisions of Cordial Relations established in 1871 should add that the Japanese merchants in China enjoy equal rights to that of the European countries and the United States". Eventually, the Qing government and Japan reached consensus on the "Treaty of Island Division and the Supplementary Provisions" in October 1880, which included the following:

"The Qing government and Japan reached consensus that the regions located to the north of Okinawa islands belong to Japan; Miyako islands and Yaeyama Islands belong to China. The two countries should never interfere each other."

The attached sheet stipulates: "1. the great Qing Empire should send an envoy to Yaeyama Islands to present credentials together with the Japanese envoys so as to claim the territory and people of Yaeyama Islands. 2. Before the great Qing Empire claims its sovereign over the Yaeyama Islands, the Japanese envoy should warn the local people on Yaeyama Islands that they should be law-abiding without causing any trouble. After the Handover Ceremony, the people of the two countries should abide the law of their own country without any interference."

The Qing government didn't intend to sign the Treaty but it decided to sign it for the survival of the Ryukyu Kingdom, unlike the greedy Japanese government. However, the officials of the Qing government failed to reach a consensus, thus the agreement was not signed in the due time, thus occurred the unsolved issue.

Although the formalities of the "Treaty of Island Division and the Supplementary Provisions" between China and Japan wasn't fully completed, it still proved that Japan had admitted that China had sovereignty over the southern part of Ryukyu. The History of Okinawa/Ryukyu compiled by Okinawa History Education Research Association has pointed out: "Although the "Treaty of Island Division and the Supplementary Provisions" was not ratified, it still it had a high effective possibility, since Japan has put forward this Treaty and was keen to achieve this formal proposal during the negotiations with the Qing government. If this agreement was ratified, the land and the people of the Yaeyama Islands would have been handed over to China as a condition for Japan's trade rights in mainland China." Japanese scholar Inoue Kiyoshi commented that although the case was unresolved, but we couldn't jump to the conclusion that the whole Ryukyu Islands belonged to Japan just because the Qing government failed to sign the agreement on time and the Japanese government rejected further negotiations. The Japanese government had admitted the Ryukyu Islands issue was an unsolved case. The reason why the Japanese government rejected further negotiations was that it was planning the imminent war against China and exerted itself to prepare for this war. If the island were incorporated into China's territory, they would have been a good attack base against Japan in the war. It was because of Japan's victory in the Sino-Japanese War that it became a fact that the whole Ryukyu Islands belonged to Japan.

After the Second World War, according to the "Cairo Declaration" and "the Potsdam Declaration", Okinawa was not included into Japan's territory, so Japan lost control of Ryukyu. Because the Kuomintang government was busy with civil war and was not firm on the Ryukyu issue, so China missed a good opportunity to solve the problem of Ryukyu. Meanwhile, because of the escalated cold war between the US and the Soviet Union and China's domestic situation changes, the US treated Ryukyu as its anti-communist military base and no longer mentioned about the condominium of Ryukyu Islands between China and the United States. In April 1947, the UN Security Council passed the proposal that the Ryukyu should be put in US's trusteeship. In September 1951, in the San Francisco Conference, United States dominated the signing of the treaty so as to conduct long-term military occupation of the Ryukyu Islands. In June 1971, Japan and US signed the Okinawa Reversion Agreement. On May 15th, 1972, they were handed over to Japan.

Scholars pointed out that as UN Security Council decided that the Ryukyu should be put in US's trusteeship, so they were not Japan's territory. Changes or corrections of the trusteeship system should be approved by the UN. It was underhand secret dealings that the US handed over Okinawa to Japan, ignoring the UN resolution. On June 17, 1971, Japan and the United States signed Okinawa Reversion Agreement in order to hand over Okinawa to Japan, and the Diaoyu Islands were mapped into the handover area. Chinese government solemnly declared that it severely infringed upon China's territorial sovereignty; such a move was flagrant, totally illegal and invalid; it had no binding on China.

From being Chinese vassal state to being destroyed by Japan, the Ryukyu Kingdom experienced a big tragedy. Incidentally, Ryukyu was abducted by Japanese militarism in World War II and served as a shield in the war with a death toll of 230,000. When Japan faced a dead end, it even treated Ryukyu as "discarded goods" and the exchange conditions for peace talks with the United Nations.

About the ins and outs of Japan's annexation of Ryukyu, let me invite authoritative scholar Prof. Tang Zhongnan who works in the field of Japan's modern history to comment on this matter.

Commentator: Tang Zhongnan (Honorary President of China Japanese History Association; Researcher in World History Institute of Chinese Academy of Social Sciences)

Since 1372, Ryukyu had been included in the tribute system of China's Ming and Qing Dynasties and been a vassal kingdom subordinate to China. During the 500 years, every Ryukyu King requested for honorific title from Chinese emperors, and conducted tribute-paying trades with China; the Ryukyu Kingdom had been using China's reign title and the Chinese calendar; its official documents, correspondence, treaties, and the compiled official history of Ryukyu were all written in Chinese.

In 1609, Ryukyu again suffered from the invasion of Japanese Satsuma. "History of the Ming Dynasty" records as follows: Satsuma sends three thousand troops into the country to capture its King and plunder its sacrificial vessels. The Ryukyu King Shangning was exiled to Kago Island in Japan for nearly three and a half years. Satsuma forced him to pay tribute to Japan and to cede the five islands located in its northern part to Japan; then Japan release him. Since then, Ryukyu had been forced to become Japan's affiliated state.

In fact, the Ryukyu Kingdom was an independent country before Japan's annexation in 1879. Two kinds of inaccurate or erred cognition should be pointed out: one is that since Ryukyu was China's vassal state, it should be China's territory; the other is that since 1609, Ryukyu had been Japan's affiliated state, it should be Japan's territory.

Japan's annexation of Ryukyu should be twice according to the history of Japan's relations with Ryukyu. The first time was that Japan annexed parts of Ryukyu. In 1611, three years after the Japanese invasion in 1609, Japan for the first time seized Ryukyu's territory: the Big Island, Toku Island, Kikaiga Island, Okinoerabu Island and Yoron Island. These five islands were incorporated under the administration of Satsuma. The second time was after the Meiji Restoration period after 1868. Japan completed its formal annexation of Ryukyu in 1879. When it comes to modern Japan's annexation of Ryukyu, we refer to the second annexation.

The Japan's annexation of Ryukyu was an important step for Japan's aggression and expansion in the early modern times as well as an important symbol for its march towards militarism. In 1868, Meiji Emperor mentioned in his letter "expand to vast seas and conquer the world", which became Japan's national policy and goal in the modern eras. It revealed Japan's arrogant ambition of conquering Asia and the world. Japanese ruling group created the blueprint of foreign expansion and put forward the so-called "Mainland China Policy". The first step for its aggression was to conquer the south-China's Taiwan. Saigo Takamori, one of the "three great nobles" in the Meiji Restoration advocated that "we should seize Taiwan to defense our south door." In order to conquer Taiwan, first of all, it should conquer Ryukyu.

Japan's annexation of Ryukyu can be generally divided into five steps:

The first step was vigorous campaign and to fabricate historical reasons. In 1870, Sada Hakubou, official of the Meiji Ministry of Foreign Affairs declared: "for the authorities, Ryukyu is extremely easy to obtain"; in 1871, Satsuma delivered a "report" to the government where he tampered the history of relations between Japan and Ryukyu. Although it recognized the fact that the Ryukyu Kingdom was a vassal state of China's Ming and Qing Dynasties, it made improper claims that since the ancient time, Ryukyu was affiliated islands of Japan. In May 1872, Inoue Kaoru, the Finance Minister, submitted a written statement to the government that the Ryukyu Kingdom should be incorporated into Japan's territory and should be annexed by Japan as soon as possible.

The second step was to "grant title" to the Ryukyu Kingby means of a surprise attack, and to raise unreasonable demands. In September 1872, when Shangjian met the Emperor, the Japanese government unilaterally granted title to him as Japanese seignior and proposed that Japan should control the diplomatic rights of Ryukyu with China. Shangjian didn't accept the title and in the talks with Soejima Taneomi, the Japanese Foreign Minister, he required Japan to return the five islands which were once ceded to Japan.

The third step was to create events and invade Taiwan. It attempted to create an accomplished fact to annex Ryukyu. At the end of 1871, the drifted fishermen of Ryukyu were killed in Taiwan, which was an incident between China and Ryukyu, having nothing to do with Japan. But it was a perfect excuse to Japan as it was planning to annex Ryukyu and further occupy Taiwan. It began to prepare for its plan in August 1872 and made a decision that in April 1874, the Japanese government would appoint Saigou Jyuudou, twin brother of Saigo Takamori, to be the Affair governor of Taiwan and authorize him to conquer Taiwan with fleets. During May and June, the Japanese soldiers launched a war against Taiwan. Under the mediation of ministers from Britain and the United States, Okubo Toshimichi went to Beijing to negotiate with China. However, he forced the Qing government to sign Beijing Sino-Japanese Special Articles by means of blackmail diplomacy, the first article of which was China had no opposition to Japan's chivalrous deed for safeguarding its people. It meant that China admitted that the people of Ryukyu were Japanese people and it was a good excuse for Japan's annexation of Ryukyu. By virtue of this special articles, Japan also blackmailed 500000 silver from China. The Japanese Meiji government, for the first time, conducted foreign aggression and ended with a success by virtue of blackmail; it saw through the corrupt Qing government, which further stimulated the Japan's aggressive ambitions; and Japan stepped up the pace to conquer Ryukyu.

The fourth step was to annex Ryukyu step by step. First of all, in March 1875, Japan asked Ryukyu officials to Tokyo and declared: "Ryukyu must conduct reform as it is affiliated to two countries; sooner or later, Ryukyu will face China's intervention" and "Japan concerns about this matter so Japan will set bases in Naha to protect the people of Ryukyu". Japan clearly put forward unreasonable demands of occupying Ryukyu while Ryukyu refused to accept this request. Then, in July, the Japanese government appointed Matsuda Michiyuki, the official of the Ministry of Internal Affairs, to issue five compulsory "commands" on behalf of the government in Naha, Ryukyu. It attempted to force Ryukyu to abolish the tribute-paying ties with China and accept Japan's actual jurisdiction; besides, Ryukyu should be incorporated into Japan's territory. These "commands" of Japan were opposed by the Ryukyu Kingdom and faced constant complaints. However, Japan further controlled over Ryukyu's sovereign gradually and eroded Ryukyu step by step. In June 1876, Japan sent officers and patrol team to Ryukyu. It forcibly deprived of Ryukyu's judicial power and incorporated it under the administration of Osaka High Court in 1877. The Ryukyu Kingdom had constantly complained to China and all other powers about Japan's behaviors.

The fifth step was that Japan annexed Ryukyu by military force in 1879. In January 1879, Matsuda went to Ryukyu to carry out "the disposition of Ryukyu" of the Japanese government, which was to abolish the vassal system and to use county system by virtue of military force. Japan cut off the relationship between Ryukyu and China and controlled police and political power of Ryukyu. He submitted warning instruments to Ryukyu King Shangtai and gave him a deadline of February 3th. Shangtai still refused to Japan's request. On February 4th, Matsuda got back to Japan and accelerated his planning and its implementation; he also got orders from the Prime Minister Sanjo Sanetomi that he could escort the Ryukyu King to Tokyo by military force. On March 8th, Meiji Emperor declared: "abolishing the vassal system and sending Shangtai to Tokyo". On March 12th, after the arrival of Matsuda and other 160 police officers, numbers of Japanese militants poured into Ryukyu. On March 27th, Matsuda, on behalf of the Japanese government, openly announced in the capital of Ryukyu that the Ryukyu Kingdom was abolished and Ryukyu King Shangtai should leave the capital. Later, the armed military took over the key departments of Ryukyu. On March 29th, Shangtai was forced to leave the palace in the capital. On April 4th, the Japanese government flagrantly announced the Ryukyu Kingdom was renamed as Okinawa and appointed the first county magistrate. On May 27th, the Ryukyu King Shangtai was forced to leave the Ryukyu and moved to Tokyo, Japan. In the end, the Ryukyu Kingdom was annexed by Japanese military force.

Japan's annexation of Ryukyu encouraged Japanese militarism and accelerated its pace of foreign aggression. It not only began to launch the war of
aggression against China to occupy Taiwan, but also trumpeted "Conquering
Korea" and expanded its aggression against North Korea so as to annex North
Korea. Ryukyu was annexed by Japan, which marked the collapse of China's
vassal system. Afterwards, modern China was bullied and humiliated by the
western powers and the aggressive Japanese Empire. Japan's annexation of
Ryukyu changed the situation of East Asia: the rising of Japan, the declining of
China and expanded aggression from the western powers.

There is still no legal basis for Japan's annexation of Ryukyu because it
neither received the consent of the Ryukyu Kingdom, nor signed any international treaty with the Ryukyu Kingdom. Furthermore, it was never admitted by
Ryukyu's suzerain—China.

In the process of Japan's annexation of Ryukyu, the Qing government made
representations with Japan and submitted inquiries for many times, insisting
that: the Ryukyu Kingdom must be resurrected and China never admitted that
Japanese annexation of Ryukyu was legal. China and Japan launched a fierce debate on the sovereignty over Ryukyu. After the mediation of the former
President of the United States—Grant, China and Japan had repeated negotiations with the premise of Grant's "Dividing Island". So Japan put forward that
Ryukyu should be divided into two parts and China thought it should be divided
into three parts. And after several talks, both side agreed on Draft of Ryukyu
Treaty of the Japanese side. However, because of the Qing government's internal dispute together with the international situation changes, both sides failed
to sign a treaty on the Ryukyu issue. The Japanese annexation of Ryukyu became an unsolved historical problem after the Sino-Japanese War.

During the later period of the Sino-Japanese War, Japan stole China's Diaoyu
Islands and incorporated the islands under the administration of Okinawa secretly. All these caused the Diaoyu Islands dispute between China and Japan.

VII. The Diaoyu Islands never belonged to Okinawa Islands

In order to prove that the Diaoyu Island and its affiliated islands have been
Japan's "inherent territory" "since ancient times", Japanese authorities despe-
rately seek evidence from the historical documents, only to find no documents
can prove that the Diaoyu Islands belong to the Ryukyu Islands (Japan called them "Okinawa"). Ironically, Japan discovered that Miyako Islands and
Yaeyama Islands have no affiliation relations with the Diaoyu Island, and that
the Diaoyu Islands were first discovered, named and exploited by the Chinese
people.

Historical documents show that in the Ming and Qing Dynasties, China's imperial envoys who visited Japan and Ryukyu knew clearly that Huaping Yu, Pengjia Mountain, Diaoyu Island, Huangwei Yu, Chiwei Yu were all Taiwan's affiliated islands.

For example, according to scholars such as Wu Tianying, Zheng Hailin, and some others, the Records of the Imperial Title-conferring Envoys to Ryukyu (Shi Liu Qiu Lu) written in 1534 by Chen Kan, an imperial title-conferring envoy from the Ming court, clearly stated: "Gumi Mountain comes into sight, that is where the land of Ryukyu begins." The Shi Liu Qiu Lu of another imperial envoy of the Ming Dynasty, Guo Rulin, also stated that "Chi Yu is the mountain that marks the boundary of Ryukyu". In 1556, Zhen Shungong went to Japan upon orders. In his book an essay entitled "Songs of a Long Voyage" clearly records that the Diaoyu Islands belonged to Chian: Diaoyu is a small island of Xiaodong (Taiwan). Besides, Xia Ziyang, another imperial envoy of the Ming court, wrote in 1606 that "when the water flows from Hei Shui back to Cang Shui, it enters the Chinese territory.

Since ancient times, Ryukyu had no territory located to the west of the Hei Shui Gou, so it had nothing to do with the Diaoyu Islands. In 1719, a deputy title-conferring envoy to Ryukyu in the Qing Dynasty, clearly recorded in his book Records of Messages from Chong-shan (Zhong Shan Chuan Xin Lu) that "there are 36 islands in Ryukyu", and this book recorded the names of the 36 islands in Ryukyu, including the 8 islands of the Yaeyama Islands, which were the most southwestern border of Ryukyu. The Map of 36 Islands in Ryukyu included the Diaoyu Islands located to the west of Gumi Mountain into China; the most southwestern border was the border between China and Ryukyu. Zhou Huang, a deputy imperial envoy of the Qing Dynasty, recorded in his book, the Annals of Ryukyu (Liu Qiu Guo Zhi Lue), that Ryukyu "is separated from the waters of Fujian by Hei Shui Gou to the west"; "he entered Ryukyu from Cang Shui to Hei Shui". It pointed out that the border between China and Ryukyu was Hei Shui Gou (today's Okinawa Trough), the west of which belonged to the waters of Fujian, and the east of which belonged to the waters of Ryukyu.

The border between China and Ryukyu was not only recorded by the Ming and Qing Dynasties, but also an international consensus. From the early 19th century to the late 1980s, the maps drew by Western or European countries conformed to China's geographic sovereignty, traditional territory, natural geography, sea territorial scope. They clearly included islands located between Jilong Mountain and Chiwei Yu into Taiwan's affiliated islands, and gave them the name of Northeastern Islands; besides, the Ryukyu Kingdom had nothing to do with the Diaoyu Islands. Zhinan Guangyi, a book written by an authoritative scholar Cheng Shunze in Ryukyu, had an attached picture which linked Huapingyu, Meihuashan, Diaoyutai, Huangweiyu and Chiweiyu together, and linked Gumi Mountain, Machi Mountain and Ryukyu Mountain together, forming a obvious border line between Gumi Mountain and Chiweiyu. Eastern Countries of the North Korea (1471), The Map of East China Sea Littoral States published by France (1809), the Complete Map of Ryukyu Islands published by Japan (1813), Colton's China published by the US, etc. all include the Diaoyu Islands into China's territory.

The waters surrounding Diaoyu Dao are traditionally Chinese fishing ground. Chinese fishermen have, for generations, engaged in fishery activities in these waters. The Ming emperor appointed 36 people from Fujian Province who were good at operating ships to go to Ryukyu, to facilitate the tribute-paying voyages.

In order to occupy and grab or steal China's Diaoyu Islands, The Meiji government tampered the Chinese names of some islands. For example, it changed Huangwei Yu to Kuba Island, Chiwei Yu to Kume Island or Taisho Island. After its occupation of Taiwan and all its affiliated islands by virtue of Treaty of Shimonoseki, it abandoned the fake names it used when stealing these islands. However, after 1969, Japan's aggressive desire was roused once again, so names like "Kuba Island", "Taisho Island", "Senkaku Islands" once again have quietly appeared in various so-called "new" maps.

Historical facts prove that the Diaoyu Islands never belong to Ryukyu Islands (Okinawa); they are China's inherent territory. Famous Japanese historian Mr. Inoue Kiyoshi revealed: "before Meiji, there is no document in Japan or Ryukyu that recorded the Diaoyu Islands." Japan provided a "laughing stock" for people all over the world that the Diaoyu Islands belong to Japan.

Because of the Cold War, United States Civil Administration of the Ryukyu Islands promulgated the Geographic Boundary of the Ryukyu Islands on December 25, 1953 where the US unilateral included the Diaoyu Islands, Huangwei Yu, Chiwei Yu into Ryukyu province. In1971, Japan and the United States signed Okinawa Reversion Agreement in order to hand over Okinawa to Japan, and the Diaoyu Islands were mapped within the handover area. Chinese government solemnly declared that such a move was flagrant, totally illegal and invalid.

Facts Related To Okinawa Reversion Agreement of 1971

Let me quote Mr. Ma Yu'an who also works in the press field to comment on this issue.

Commentator: Dr. Ma Yu'an (senior reporter of Financial Times)

The Japanese government's so-called "nationalization" of the Diaoyu Islands is a farce "political strategy" orchestrated by Yoshihiko Noda and Japanese far-right wing forces.

Japan insists that it has sovereignty over the Diaoyu Islands, which is based on the proposition that the Diaoyu Islands are affiliated islands of the Ryukyu Islands; in 1972, the U.S government handed over them to Japan based on relevant provisions of the Treaty of San Francisco. Putting aside the Ryukyu issue, the Diaoyu Islands still don't belong to Japan because the Diaoyu Islands never belong to Ryukyu.

First of all, the Diaoyu Islands never belonged to Okinawa. Based on the principle of international law about the preemptive occupation of terra nullius, the Diaoyu Island and its affiliated islands have been China's sacred territory since ancient times. The book Illustrated Outline of the Three Countries published in 1785 had the Map of the Three Provinces and 36 Islands of Ryukyu, which excluded the Diaoyu Islands from Ryukyu, indicating that Diaoyu Islands were part of China's territory.

According to the internationally recognized the principle of the "Convention on the Continental Shelf", "sovereignty of the islands located on the same continental shelf belongs to the said country". Without a doubt, China enjoys sovereignty over Diaoyu Islands. Diaoyu Islands and the Ryukyu Islands are separated by a 2,000 feet deep trench from the Ryukyu Islands. The north east of the trench linked to the Japan Trench and the south west of the trench linked to Mariana Trench. So it separates the Ryukyu Islands and Chinese continental shelf. Diaoyu Islands, Huangwei Yu, Chiwei Yu together with Taiwan Province are located on the continental shelf of 200 meters. The continental shelf and the trench of Ryukyu form the black tide just as "from Cang Shui to Hei Shui" written by a deputy imperial title-conferring envoy of the Ming Dynasty. It was also detailed in Miscellaneous Records of the Mission to Ryukyu, written in 1683 by Wang Ji, an imperial envoy of the Qing Dynasty. It is clear then that China had, at least during Qing Dynasty, already regarded the Ryukyu Trench as the border of the waters around the Fujian Province. Naturally, all the waters and the islands stretching from Chiwei Island to Fujian Province had belonged to Qing Government and were marked as part of its territory in Qing Dynasty maps. Besides, the Diaoyu Islands were also marked as part of its territory in Qing and Ming Dynasty maps.

Secondly, the Potsdam Declaration claims that not only the Diaoyu Islands but also Okinawa don't belong to Japan's territory. The Potsdam Declaration also clarifies that as a surrender country, Japan has no right to claim its territory.

Japan insists that it has sovereignty over the Diaoyu Islands, which is based on the Diaoyu Islands being affiliated islands of the Ryukyu Islands; in 1972, the US government handed over them to Japan based on relevant provisions of the Treaty of San Francisco. Putting aside the Ryukyu issue, the Diaoyu Islands still don't belong to Japan because the Diaoyu Islands never belong to Ryukyu.

In the poems and annals of Ryukyu, the Diaoyu Islands are China's territory. "Black water trench" of 2000 meters between the Gumi Mountain (belonging to Ryukyu) and the Diaoyu Islands (belonging to China) was the border of the two countries.

It proved the Diaoyu Islands are China's territory. Even if Japan annexed the Ryukyu in 1879, its affiliated islands could not include the Diaoyu Islands.

Even in the Treaty of San Francisco, there is nothing concerning Diaoyu islands or "Senkaku Islands". The Japanese government also pointed out that the areas that handed over to US's trusteeship in the Treaty of San Francisco don't include the Diaoyu Islands.

However, when the US military took over the Ryukyu Islands, the Diaoyu Islands were included within latitude and longitude lines of Ryukyu by United States Civil Administration of the Ryukyu Islands in 1952, by virtue of which, Japan conducted the "effective control" of these islands. However, latitude and longitude can never determine territorial sovereignty. If the Japanese government used the Treaty of San Francisco to prove that the Diaoyu Islands belong to Japan, it had to find evidence to prove that the Diaoyu Islands have belonged to "the old Ryukyu Kingdom", otherwise, Japan's "effective control" is illegal according to the international law.

Thirdly, the Treaty of San Francisco and the Japan-US Security Treaty are "trump card" with obvious blackmail nature used by Japan and the US. In order to obtain its own strategic interests, the United States often use "ambiguous" attitude on the coverage and scope of treaties, which has been repeatedly used by Japan as its basis to insisted Japan's sovereignty over the Diaoyu Islands.

In fact, the Diaoyu Island and its affiliated islands have been China's territory since ancient times. This is supported by historical facts and jurisprudential evidence. Since the Ming Dynasty, the Diaoyu Islands have been incorporated into China's territory and put under the jurisdiction of China's naval defense. No country has ever issued a challenge to China's national sovereignty over the Diaoyu Islands since the Ming Dynasty.

Japan is the vanquished country of the World War II, so it should obey the postwar international arrangements. The Potsdam Declaration claims that not only the Diaoyu Islands but also Okinawa don't belong to Japan's territory. The Potsdam Declaration also clarifies that as a surrender country, Japan has no right to claim its territory. China will never allow Japan to change the international community's arrangements after the World War II, Japan will never reap sweet fruits if it continue to walk the road of militarism.

VIII. Historical truth can not be denied

The consensus of "shelving the Diaoyu Island issue and solving it in a later time" proposed by China opened the door of the normalization of diplomatic relations between China and Japan and secured the great development of relations between China and Japan during the past 40 years. It is a wise choice to respect history, admit and shelve this dispute based on a realistic assessment.

Focusing on the friendly relations between the two peoples, China, being a lenient and tolerant neighbor, gave up the right to ask for war indemnity during the normalization of China-Japan diplomatic relations in 1972. What's more, in 1978, the two countries established peaceful and friendly agreement. All these become the political foundation of development of China-Japan relations and the legal basis to solve territory issues between the two countries.

When it comes to the Diaoyu Islands, people always mention about the talks between Chinese Premier Zhou Enlai and Japanese Prime Minister Kakuei Tanaka. They reached a consensus on putting the priority on the normalization of China-Japan diplomatic relations and shelving the Diaoyu Islands issue. Besides, in October 1978, Vice-Premier Deng Xiaoping visited Japan for the exchange of instruments of ratification of the Sino-Japanese Treaty of Peace and Friendship. Commenting on the issue of Diaoyu Islands at a press conference Mr. Deng said, "China and Japan should act in the larger interest of China-Japan relations. It is okay to temporarily shelve such an issue.

Japanese government authorities have denied that the consensus of shelving the Diaoyu Island dispute and repeatedly challenged the bottom line of China in recent years, causing serious antagonism between China and Japan on the Diaoyu Islands issue and chasm in China-Japan relations.

As for this problem, China's senior diplomat—Mr. Xu Dunxin who focuses on China-Japan relations for a long time and has participated in the normalization of China-Japan diplomatic relations and peace and friendship treaty negotiations, witnessed that former great leaders of China and Japan reached consensus on this issue. Mr Xu was the former director of Japan Office of Ministry of Foreign Affairs of the People's Republic of China, director of Asia Division, former Vice Minister of Ministry of Foreign Affairs of the People's Republic of China and former Chinese ambassador in Japan. Let me quote Mr. Xu Dunxin who has witnessed historical truth.

Commentator: Xu Dunxin (former Vice Minister of Ministry of Foreign Affairs of the People's Republic of China and former Chinese ambassador in Japan)

"The dispute over the Diaoyu Islands has a long history. This is a sensitive issue in China-Japan relations and it will bring enormous challenges to China-Japan relations if we can't appropriately deal with this issue. For example, the

Japanese government's recently farces of "purchase" of the Diaoyu Islands and "nationalization" of the Diaoyu Islands severely hurt the China-Japan relations.

A year before the normalization of China-Japan relations, namely in 1971, Japan and the United States signed Okinawa Reversion Agreement and had underhand secret dealings on the administration of the Diaoyu Islands. On December 30th, Ministry of Foreign Affairs of the People's Republic of China issued a solemn statement and pointed out that the Diaoyu Island and its affiliated islands have been China's sacred territory since ancient times. The underhand secret dealings of Japan and the United States are illegal and invalid. It is blatant violation of Chinese sovereignty. This statement is known around the world. In March 1972, in the UN Conference on the Law of the Sea, Chinese diplomats and Japanese diplomats had a fierce debate over the Diaoyu Islands, Chinese diplomats repudiated the unreasonable claims of Japan. So it is known to all that China and Japan have sovereignty dispute over the Diaoyu Islands.

On September 27, 1972, two days before the formal announcement of the normalization of China-Japan diplomatic relations, then Japanese Prime Minister Kakuei Tanaka took the initiative to talk about the issue of the Diaoyu Islands with Premier Zhou Enlai. Premier Zhou Enlai clearly said: "I do not want to discuss this issue this time. It is no good discussing it now." Premier Zhou Enlai meant: this problem can't be solved this time and don't let it affect the relationship between our two countries. This got Prime Minister Kakuei Tanaka's understanding and he agreed to shelve this issue and solve it later. So when China and Japan normalized relations, both countries agreed to shelve this issue and solve it later in a proper time.

China-Japan Treaty of Peace and Friendship was signed in August 1978. In October of the same year, Vice Premier Deng Xiaoping visited Japan with me. He participated in the exchange of instruments of ratification of the Sino-Japanese Treaty of Peace and Friendship. Commenting on the issue of Diaoyu Dao at a press conference following his talks with Japanese Prime Minister Takeo Fukuda, Mr Deng said, "When China and Japan normalized relations, both countries agreed not to involve this issue. When we negotiated the Sino-Japanese Treaty of Peace and Friendship, we also agreed not to deal with this issue. I am sure we will eventually find a way acceptable to both sides."

Because this speech was given in front of hundreds of reporters, so the next day, it was published in a very significant place in the newspapers. Televisions and radios also broadcast the speech.

During the establishment of peaceful and friendly agreement of China-Japan relations, the old leaders of China and Japan reached an important understanding and common ground on "leaving the issue of the Diaoyu Island to be resolved later". This opened the door to normalization of China-Japan relations and was followed by tremendous progress in China-Japan relations and stable and peaceful situations in East Asia during the 40 years.

From the perspective of history, geography, as well as law, the Diaoyu Island and its affiliated islands are China's inherent territory. This is supported by historical facts and jurisprudential evidence. If Japan continues to distort history, ignores facts and denies the consensus, all the consequences can only be borne by the Japanese side.

IX. Garbling and confusing

For a long time, the Japanese Ministry of Foreign Affairs has been trying to avoid the fact that the Diaoyu Islands were first discovered, named and exploited by the Chinese people. Instead, it emphasizes the Diaoyu Islands are terra nullius and deliberately distorts the history of Japan's stealing of the Diaoyu Islands. The Japanese authorities seek all means to prove its "legal" occupation of the Diaoyu Islands, one of which was to falsify documents and deceive the public by garbling; besides, it also squeezes its own arguments from the fragments of Chinese materials. But it will never be able to grasp the straw by garbling and confusing the public.

Some scholar found that the data collection published by Megumi Tadahisa, the President of the Senkaku Islands Defense Association of Okinawa quoted from the letter that Inoue Kaoru, the Ministry of Foreign Affairs, wrote to Yamagata Aritomo, the Ministry of Internal Affairs. The content of the original letter was as follows: "Over the matter concerning placing national markers on the uninhabited islands of Kumeseki-shima and two other islands spread out in between Okinawa and Fuzhou[China] after investigating them, I have given much thought to the matter. The aforementioned islands are close to the border of China, and it has been found through our surveys that the area of the islands is much smaller than the previously surveyed island, Daito-jima; and in particular, China has already given names to the islands. Most recently Chinese newspapers have been reporting rumors of our government's intention of occupying certain islands owned by China located next to Taiwan, demonstrating suspicion toward our country and consistently urging the Qing government to be aware of this matter. In such a time, if we were to publicly place national markers on the islands, this must necessarily invite China's suspicion toward us. Currently we should limit ourselves to investigating the islands, understanding the formations of the harbors, seeing whether or not there exists possibilities to develop the island's land and resources, which all should be made into detailed response. In regard to the matter of placing national markers and developing the islands, it should await a more appropriate time" "about the uninhabited islands between Okinawa and Fuzhou of the Qing government, they are close to the border of the Qing government. Furthermore, the Qing government has named these islands. Recently, the Qing government published newspapers, saying that our government attempts to occupy the affiliated islands near Taiwan and the Qing government has suspicions about our country.

At this moment, if we openly established national stakes on these islands, we are bound to face the opposition from the Qing government. Therefore, we should report its harbor shapes and unearthed land property according to the actual investigation results. We can step out of the shadow to establish national stakes and further develop these islands according to the situation in the future."

However, some discourses about the above contents have been removed by the author and it turned out to be: "about the uninhabited islands between Okinawa and Fuzhou of the Qing government, we should report its harbor shapes and unearthed land property according to the actual investigation results. We can step out of the shadow to establish national stakes and further develop these islands according to the situation in the future." Compared with the original archives of the Japanese Ministry of Foreign Affairs, we can easily discover that he garbled the original archives and concealed historical facts, which is pure self-delusion.

It is under the misleading of the authorities and the incitement of the right-wing forces that all sorts of misunderstandings and fallacies were popular in the Japanese society. Japan even quoted from some maps published in Taiwan which printed "Senkaku Islands" to prove that China admitted that the Diaoyu Islands belonged to Japan. In addition, it quoted the letter delivered from Chinese ambassador Feng Mian in Nagasaki to the city of Ishigaki in Okinawa which mentioned "Senkaku Islands (Diaoyu Islands)"; besides, it pointed out that the map published by Beijing Map Press clarified that the Senkaku Islands is part of Japan.

Objectively speaking, the 50 years' Japanese colonial rule in Taiwan implanted the "Japanization education" and imposed Japan's documents on Taiwan people. The "Senkaku Islands" appearing in some maps published in Taiwan was caused by the Japanese colonial rule. Likewise, during Japan's invasion of China, it was not strange that Japan forced China to publish "Senkaku Islands" on some maps.

As for the "Thank you note", some scholars have pointed out that as early as 1895, Japan occupied Taiwan by virtue of Treaty of Shimonoseki; before that, it had already stolen the Diaoyu Islands. "There is no national border between Taiwan and Okinawa (Takahashi Sougorou) and this continued to 1945 when Japan was defeated in the war. The so-called "Thank you note" only reflected the historical background at that time, so written materials during Japan's seizure of the Diaoyu Islands can't be evidence to prove the sovereignty over the Diaoyu Islands. No matter the Diaoyu Islands were mapped in Taiwan or Okinawa, it can't prove that Japan enjoys the sovereignty over the Diaoyu Islands and that China "admits" the Diaoyu Islands are Japan's territory.

The Japanese maps with "Senkaku Islands" published in China had some notes on the title page: "some national boundaries referred to the map published by Shen-pao before the Anti-Japanese War." At that time, the map published by Shen-pao referred to Japan's local maps, so it never represented the Chinese government's standpoint. Incidentally, in 1956 the Country-Specific Maps of the World had no Diaoyu Islands or Senkaku Islands in Japanese territory and on its title page reads: "boundary line of China is the same as The Map of People's Republic of China".

Okuhara Toshio (an international law scholar) who exerted himself to defend Japan also mention an article titled the Ryukyuan's Struggle Against the Occupation of the US published in the People's Daily on January 8th, 1952. He said this is an important article which clearly admitted that the Senkaku Islands belong to Ryukyu. He also quibbled that before 1970, China and Taiwan clearly admitted sovereignty over the Senkaku Islands belonged to Japa. This "important article" stressed by Okuhara Toshio and used frequently by Japanese politicians was translated from a foreign article with quite a few international data error. But Japan treated this article 60 years ago as a treasure and used it as evidence, so we will make some clarification.

I invited Mr. Liu Shuiming, the deputy director of the International Department of the People's Daily, Senior reporter, to make some comments on this issue.

Commentator: Liu Shuiming (the Deputy Director of the International Department of the People's Daily; Senior Reporter)

On January 8th, 1953, in the fourth page of the People's Daily published an article titled the Ryukyuan's Struggle Against the Occupation of the US. The article reads: "the Ryukyu Islands are scattered on the sea between the northeast of China's Taiwan and the southwest of Japan's Kyushu Island, including the Senkaku Islands, Miyako Islands, Daito Islands, Okinawa Islands, Oshima Islands, Dokarma Islands and Osumi Islands..."

This article made a big mistake and had an unconvincing logic.

The 90-year-old Mr. Meng Xianmo was a retired cadre of the People's Daily who worked in the People's Daily from May 1950 and was the leader of International Data Division in the newspaper editorial office in1953. In 2012, he said: at that time, the newspaper office didn't book the Japanese newspaper, so the source of information about Japan relied mainly on the radio program— the Voices of Japan as well as the compiled information translated from English and Russian and other foreign language newspapers.

First of all, Meng Xianmo thinks the Ryukyuan's Struggle Against the Occupation of the US was a translated article, because we Chinese do not call the Diaoyu Islands "Senkaku Islands". In addition, the article mentioned about the largest U.S. air force base in Okinawa; it had two different transliterations of its name. Moreover, the article mentioned about "according to a recent Japanese newspaper news", "according to the Japanese newspaper news", "the

US news and international report magazine revealed...", etc. All these are enough to prove that it was not an original article, but was compiled according to the foreign language radio programs or the foreign language newspapers.

Secondly, some scholars reread this article as well as related data from the Japanese side; and they confirmed that the location of the Ryukyu Islands and the definition of its scope in this article had factual errors. For example, the article mentioned about the Ryukyu Islands are scattered on the sea between the northeast of China's Taiwan and the southwest of Japan's Kyushu Island, including the Senkaku Islands, Miyako Islands, Daito Islands, Okinawa Islands, Oshima Islands, Dokarma Islands and Osumi Islands...; the Senkaku Islands didn't belong to Ryukyu, nor did the other islands mentioned in the article. About the definition of "Ryukyu Islands" in Japanese dictionaries, Dokarma Islands and Osumi Islands were not included into the Ryukyu Islands. It should be pointed out that this article was wrong in terms of geographical knowledge. The Ryukyu Islands mentioned in this article were put under US's trusteeship by the United Nations and its name was not Okinawa called by the Japanese side. So it was not Japan's territory. The established civil administration was called "Civil Administration of the Ryukyu Islands"; moreover, this article didn't mention that Ryukyu belonged to Japan.

Thirdly, we couldn't find its author. We only found the word—"document" above the topic. So it was not written by some commentator of People's Daily nor some scholars. Therefore, it could not represent the position of People's Daily, let alone representing government documents or official comments. Japan cited an article with serious factual errors to claim that China admitted that the Senkaku Islands belonged to Japan, which was untenable for every reason.

Furthermore, on December 27, 2012, Japan Press reported that China's diplomatic documents in 1950 admitted that "the Diaoyu Islands belong to Ryukyu"; The Japanese government's new secretary immediately declared: "for Japan, it is a very important discovery"; it seemed that Japan found another excuse.

The so-called "diplomatic documents" was a document in the Ministry of Foreign Affairs archives titled "the outline draft of the stand about the territory issue in the Treaty of Peace with Japan" (on May 15, 1950). However, the draft of Treaty of Peace with Japan was released a year later on August 15th. Because the US rejected China's participation, China didn't sign on the treaty. The Chinese government strongly opposed it and claimed the treaty was illegal and invalid. And this "outline draft" with no signature was nothing but a reference without any legal effect. What's more, there was no sentence like "the Diaoyu Islands belong to Ryukyu", so the drafter clearly realized that the Diaoyu Islands, including Chiwei Yu never belong to Ryukyu and they should be returned to Taiwan when Japan's territory was re-divided.

Japan's desire to grab another straw was unfortunately failed once again.

X. Settling the dispute over the Diaoyu Islands through peaceful means

Japan's unlawful "purchasing" of the Diaoyu Islands and "nationalization" of the Diaoyu Islands in 2012 severely infringes upon China's territorial sovereignty and has greatly hurt the Chinese people's feelings, which has resulted in the unprecedented grim situation in China-Japan relations and reverses the 40 years' of normalized diplomatic relations between China and Japan. Moreover, the trade cooperation has decreased and personnel exchanges have been nearly halted. China-Japan relations are faced with a reverse turning point.

After reading "Sovereignty over the Diaoyu Islands", readers will be able to judge the truth behind the issue of Diaoyu Island and its affiliated islands, and China's fair approach. This is supported by historical facts and jurisprudential evidence. The Diaoyu Islands were first discovered, named and exploited by the Chinese people. Since the Ming Dynasty, the Diaoyu Islands have been put under the jurisdiction of China's naval defense. Maps at home and abroad show us that the Diaoyu Islands belong to China. The Diaoyu Islands were illegal stolen by Japan during the Sino-Japanese War in 1895 and was ceded to Japan afterwards. But according to the Cairo Declaration and the Potsdam Declaration, the Diaoyu Islands should be returned to China.

The post-war China-Japan relations were full of ups and downs. It experienced the 40 years' normalization of diplomatic relations, a "warm" relation at the early stage of the diplomatic relations, as well as the tangle of the history of Japan's invasion of China; it had fruitful economic cooperation between China and Japan as well as the "cold politics" in the "hot economy". In a word, beside the domestic and international factors, the biggest obstacle to build mutual trust is the wrong understanding of history and the problems left over by history.

Japan is a nation living on the island. The Japanese people maintain themselves when absorbing foreign culture. Cultural traditions between China and Japan are of the same form and different essence. Chinese people are "general", while Japanese people are "loyal"; China resorts to the pen, while Japan resorts to the sword. China emphasizes principles, while Japan emphasizes practices; China always help the weak, while Japan always bully the weak. Some scholars said when it comes to the interests of the state, Japan often become very vague about the right and wrong; they, like a group of fish, gather according to their "sense". For example, there are increasing rightists in the Japanese society; populism kidnaps public opinions. Rationally, although China and Japan are so close, they are indifferent "neighbours". Since the Tang Dynasty, they had fought against each other for many times, such as the Sino-Japanese War and War of Aggression against China launched by the Japanese militarism. The injuries in the hearts of the Chinese people have not healed, but have been deepened by some voices in the Japanese society that Japan wants to reverse a verdict of the War of Aggression against China.

The Diaoyu Island and its affiliated islands have been China's inherent territory. The dispute is caused by the Sino-Japanese War. I think that the Japan's invasion of China before the Second World War is a "negative legacy" between the two countries. It is still the political foundation of developing China-Japan relations that we correctly deal with this history and carry out what Japan promised in the China-Japan Joint Statement—it firmly maintains its stand under Article 8 of the Potsdam Declaration that the terms of the Cairo Declaration shall be carried out and Japanese sovereignty shall be limited to the islands of Honshu, Hokkaido, Kyushu, Shikoku and such minor islands as we determine.

100 years ago, Mr. Sun Yat-sen persuaded Japan to conduct "rule of right" rather than "hegemony" in his speech in Japan. Unjust is doomed to destruction. The aggressors will eventually be punished and pay the price. In September 1997, Japan's Prime Minister Ryutaro Hashimoto visited the "9/18" history museum and said: "no matter how forgetful we are, we can't forget history. We can learn from history, but we can't change it. We have to bear the burden of history." Policy decides the road; the road decides the future. How to solve the Diaoyu Islands issue is a test of the wisdom of the Chinese; whether Japan can turn over a new leaf to conduct "rule of right" and give up scrambling for the Diaoyu Islands verifies the moral dimensions of the Japanese nation.

Japan's occupation of the Diaoyu Islands has no intention of changing over to new ways, but it attempts to display its strength by virtue of the power of other countries. The Japanese government announced its plan to "nationalize" the Diaoyu islands on July 7, the date marking the Japanese all-round aggression against China in 1937. On September 11, Japanese Prime Minister Yoshihiko Noda announced Japan's "purchase" of the Diaoyu Islands. It happened just before September 18, the date when Japan launched a war of aggression against China in 1931. Japan's self-defense military forces entered the territorial air space of the Diaoyu islands. All these are provocative moves. Territory and sovereignty are the life of the country, safety is the guarantee of the national development. Retreating to avoid a conflict will lose all the achievements of development. It is necessary for China to announce the baselines of the territorial sea of the Diaoyu Island and its affiliated islands, which is an action to safeguard its sovereignty and is in accordance with the "Cairo Declaration", "Potsdam Declaration" and "Japan-China Joint Statement".

China implements peaceful diplomacy, but China's surrounding environment is still not optimistic. The ancients said: "although the world is peaceful, it is dangerous for us to forget to guard against the war." In the Ming Dynasty, the Japanese pirates invaded the border of the Ming Empire; Toyotomi declared war against the Ming Empire; in the Qing Dynasty, Japan launched the Sino-Japanese War; it forced China to cede Taiwan and occupied the Diaoyu Islands, followed by "9/18" Mukden Incident and Marco Polo Bridge Incident. Japan has a "tradition" of aggression against China. The aggressor is unreasonable and only believes in power. In 1882, the Japanese consul at Tianjin city in China—Takezoe Shinyichiro sent a cipher telegram to the Japanese government after he heard that the Qing government would delay signing the "Treaty of Dividing Islands". He suggested that Japan should declare war against China. He said: "China can be conquered easily by force rather than reason. So we should send troops to China."[1]

The enlightenment that China's modern history gave us is: we should be cautious about war and never forget painful lessons, lagging behind leaves one vulnerable to attacks and concession will make the enemy reach out for a yard after taking an inch.

The Diaoyu Islands issue is between China and Japan, but later the US meddled in and complicated the problem. The United States has an unshakable responsibility on the Diaoyu Islands issue. Because of the anti-communist strategy and the cold war between the US and the Soviet Union, the United States and some other countries undermined the provision—no country shall sign a separate peace treaty with Japan—in the UN declaration on January 1, 1942. They also went against postwar arrangements of the Allies by refusing the participation of China in the signing of Treaty of Peace with Japan in 1951. By using the trusteeship of Ryukyu, the US wrongly included the Diaoyu Island and its affiliated islands into Ryukyu. In 1971, the US and Japan had underhand secret dealings that the US handed over the "administration right" of the Diaoyu Islands to Japan, which is totally unacceptable to China.

The vulnerability of China-Japan relations is proved by the dispute over the Diaoyu Islands. Changing this vulnerability depends on establishing strategic mutual trust between the two countries and calls for the joint efforts and a common purpose of the two governments and people. Stable China-Japan relations are in line with the interests of both countries. The priority is to strengthen dialogues and build crisis management mechanism to find an effective way to control and solve the problem. Only through this way can we dissolve the grim situation of China-Japan relations.

In the wake of the Spring Festival in 2013, on January 25, 2013, Xi Jinping, general secretary of the Communist Party of China (CPC) Central Committee, met with Natsuo Yamaguchi, leader of the New Komeito party of Japan at the Great Hall of the People. He said: "The Chinese government attaches

---

1 The Chinese government finally compromised and in September 1880 the plenipotentiaries of Japan and the Ching government signed a treaty dividing Ryukyu into two parts in accordance with the Japanese formula. However, the Chinese emperor refused to approve the treaty and instructed his government to continue the negotiations with Japan. The Japanese side then broke off the negotiations. In 1882 when Shinichiro Takezoe assumed office as consul in Tientsin, he resumed negotiations with the Ching government on the partition of Ryukyu, but no agreement was reached. The question was thus shelved by the Japanese and Chinese governments until the Japan-China war broke out.

importance to developing relations with Japan and such a policy remains unchanged. Facts prove that the four political documents between the two countries are the ballast stone of bilateral relations, which should be abided by." President Xi Jinping took a long term and broad view on China-Japan relations. "Ballast stone" means both sides must focus on the overall situation, grasp the direction; only by taking history as a mirror, can we face forward to the future. We should remain unchanged on the basic principles of China-Japan relations. We hope that ice and snow will be melted by the wisdom of the people in Japan and China and we will together welcome the fine and warm spring.

Finally, let me quote Mr Zhang Yunling, a famous expert on international issues and Mr. Wu Xuewen, a senior reporter, to talk about their opinions. Prof. ZhangYunling is a former director of Asia-Pacific Division of Chinese Academy of Social Sciences and now is a member of Chinese Academy of Social Sciences.

Mr. Wu in his nineties was one of the first Chinese journalists who was allowed to be stationed in Japan and started the news reports from this country.

Comments by Zhang Yunling—member of Chinese Academy of Social Sciences; director of the International Research Department:

"The Diaoyu Islands issue is like the firewood which is easy to be ignited. Originally, from the overall situation of the relations between the two countries, China and Japan reached a consensus on shelving the Diaoyu Islands issue. However, the Japanese government's "nationalization" action lit the firewood and caused great indignation of the Chinese people, flinging the China-Japan relations into the abyss.

China will never make concessions on the sovereignty over the Diaoyu Islands. But it is not a proper time to completely solve the dispute over the Diaoyu Islands. There are three ways to solve the territorial disputes: 1. wars; 2. negotiations, 3. international arbitration. The Diaoyu Islands are a few small islands which are easy to attack and hard to defense. War only brings internecine tragedies. Negotiations have prerequisites that there is an acknowledgment of the sovereignty dispute and preparation for compromise; the international arbitration also needs certain conditions that based on an acknowledgment of the sovereignty dispute, both sides can't solve the dispute through negotiations and agree on delivering it to international arbitration. In 2012, Japanese Prime Minister Yoshihiko Noda once agreed to leave the Diaoyu Island issue to the international court, but he later withdraw his previous remark because resorting to the international arbitration would mean Japan admitted there are territorial disputes. China also did not agree to bring the issue to the international court because China insisted that the Diaoyu Islands belong to China. Since none of the three ways could solve the problem, the two countries decided choosing the fourth way—shelving the dispute.

However, unlike the situation of the normalization of diplomatic relations between China and Japan, Japan has already conducted the "nationalization" action and it is hard to abolish it; while China has already broken through the "effective control" of Japan and it can't retreat. Therefore, we must adopt new methods according to the new situation. It is suggested that both sides could be implemented joint management, but is also hard to implement. From my perspective, we can carry out the strategy of "half step back" and "one step forward". "Half step back" is that both sides can retain their claims of its sovereignty, but conduct no actual possession, namely, no administration of the islands and the waters; "one step forward" is "to step over the Diaoyu Islands issue" to recovery the normalization of relations between China and Japan, and return to the path of co-construction of the peaceful sea. It has been suggested that under the premise of the "consensus" of "shelving the dispute", both sides announce the Diaoyu Islands and its waters as the "marine natural resources reserve". Both sides will keep its words that they will never occupy or land on the islands, and never explore the Diaoyu Islands and its waters. This is also a way to shelve the dispute. In this case, the two sides should demand the United States not to interfere in this matter, which will be good to China-US relations and relations of the three countries so as to realize the benign interaction of bilateral and trilateral relations. As for how to deal with it in the future, we should do as what Deng Xiaoping proposed—leave it to the future generations.

Commentator: Wu Xuewen (The honorary chairman of the Society of Sino-Japanese Relations History)

The Diaoyu Island and its affiliated islands have been China's territory since ancient times. Japan plotted to seize the Diaoyu Islands with the US as the backup, which triggers the biggest crisis of China-Japan Relations in the 40 years since the two countries established full diplomatic ties. Far-sighted people from the two countries are anxious about this issue and offer advice and suggestions to address the issue.

In the article titled with "Peaceful Solutions to the Diaoyu Islands Dispute", the editor explicitly points out that the Diaoyu Islands dispute indicates the vulnerability of China-Japan relations. Changing the vulnerability relies on establishing the mutual trust of the two countries and requires the joint efforts by both governments and both peoples who should treat issue with sense and move on in the same direction. Stable China-Japan relations conform to the interest of both countries. It is imperative to enhance dialogue and construct a system of crisis management.

The above positive policy suggestion is given based on investigations and thorough consideration.

No matter in the historical records or in the international documentations of the victory of the Second World War against Fascism, the Diaoyu Islands is the inherent territory of China. The Japanese militarism has done aggression against China. According to the militarists' extravaganza, the current Japanese government unlawfully "purchases" the Diaoyu Islands, which is enough to show the resurgence of militarism in Japan. Japanese strong advocating of the pacifist constitution is out of their opposition and hatred to militarism; China and the international community speak in praise of the pacifist constitution because the pacifist constitution will exterminate the militarism. The acts of Japan over the Diaoyu Island issue surely lose its credibility to Japanese people and will naturally lose its credibility to the international society. The article sincerely advises the Japanese authority to make thorough changes and to end the dispute.

Every time when problems occurred to the China-Japan relations, the far-sighted politicians and wise men always emphasized that we should focus on the overall situation of China-Japan and finally solve the dispute in a rational way. The overall situation is that China and Japan are close neighbors connected by the same waters and has a history of two thousand years' friendly exchanges. The heritage of the geological and historical convergence, constituting the mutual treasure of the people of both countries, makes the politics, economy, culture, religion and customs of the two countries influence and nourish each other. When there is problem, the "heritage" will be transformed into wisdom and power. In 1972, when China and Japan negotiated the normalization of China-Japan relations, Zhou Enlai and Kakuei Tanaka both agreed to first address the big issue of the normalization and leave the Diaoyu Islands dispute to be settled later. In this case, it can be understood as: it is because the wisdom and power transformed from the "heritage", we believe that a rational solution to the Diaoyu Islands issue can also be found in our "heritage".

March 2014, Beijing

Chapter I

Chinese Leaders' Speeches and Government Statements on the Diaoyu Islands Issue

I. Chinese Leaders' Standpoints on the Diaoyu Islands Issue

Xi Jinping, General Secretary of the Communist Party of China (CPC) Central Committee: China's position on the Diaoyu Islands issue is consistent and clear

On January 25, 2013, Xi Jinping, general secretary of the Communist Party of China (CPC) Central Committee, met with Natsuo Yamaguchi, leader of the Japanese Clean Government Party at the Great Hall of the People. Xi said China and Japan are important neighbors for each other, and bilateral cooperation in various fields has reached an unprecedented level in terms of both depth and breadth since the normalization of diplomatic relations that was built 40 years ago, giving a strong impetus to the development of the two countries. The Chinese government attaches importance to developing relations with Japan and such a policy remains unchanged. Facts prove that the four political documents between the two countries are the ballast stone of bilateral relations, which should be abided by. Under the new situation, we should show national responsibility, political wisdom and historical duty, as the older generation of leaders of the two countries had done, to push China-Japan relations to overcome difficulties and continue to move forward.

Xi stressed that in order to maintain long-term healthy and stable development of China-Japan relations, both sides must focus on the overall situation, grasp the direction, promptly and properly handle sensitive issues between the two countries. China's position on the Diaoyu Islands issue is consistent and clear, he said, adding the Japanese side should face up to history as well as reality and make joint efforts with China through real action to seek effective methods for appropriately controlling and resolving the issue through dialogue and consultation. Only by taking history as a mirror, can we face forward to the future. Xi urged Japan to respect the national feelings of the Chinese people and correctly handle historical issues. China attaches great importance to Yamaguchi's visit which was made as bilateral relations face a special situation. China hopes that the Japanese Clean Government Party will continue to play a constructive role in promoting the development of China-Japan relations.

(Except from the front page of People's Daily on January 26, 2013)

Chinese President Hu Jintao: Whatever ways the Japanese side uses to "purchase the islands" they are all invalid

On September 9, 2012, Chinese President Hu Jintao met with Japanese Prime Minister Yoshihiko Noda and made clear China's position on its relations with Japan and on the Diaoyu Islands issue. The two leaders met on the sidelines of the 20th economic leaders' meeting of the Asia-Pacific Economic Cooperation.

Hu seriously pointed out that China-Japan relations have recently faced a severe situation due to the Diaoyu Islands issue, saying China holds a consistent, clear position on the issue. Whatever ways the Japanese side uses to "purchase the islands" are illegal and invalid and China firmly opposes such moves, he said. The Chinese government stands firm on the issue of safeguarding its territorial sovereignty, Hu said, adding Japan must fully recognize the gravity of the situation and should not make wrong decisions. He urged Japan to work with the Chinese side to maintain the overall development of the two countries' relations.

(Excerpt from people.com.cn on September 10, 2012—reported by journalist of People's Daily)

Wu Bangguo, chairman of the Standing Committee of China's National People's Congress: The determination of the Chinese government and people on safeguarding sovereignty and territorial integrity is unswerving

Wu Bangguo, chairman of the Standing Committee of China's National People's Congress, chats with Iranian Parliament Speaker Ali Larijani during their talks in Tehran, Iran, Sept. 10, 2012. On the latest development concerning the Diaoyu Islands, Wu stressed the islands have been inherent territories of China since ancient times and China's position on the issue has been consistent and clear. Any forms of "buying the islands" by the Japanese side is illegal and invalid. China is firmly opposed to such moves. The determination of the Chinese government and people on safeguarding sovereignty and territorial integrity is unswerving.

(Excerpt from the front page of People's Daily on September 11, 2012)

Premier Wen Jiabao: The Chinese government and its people will never make any concessions on issues of national sovereignty and territory.

On September 10, 2012, Premier Wen Jiabao visited the new campus of China Foreign Affairs University (CFAU) in Changping District, Beijing. There Wen attended the inauguration ceremony of a bronze statue of Zhou Enlai and Chen Yi. Later, Wen addressed the students and faculty at the auditorium. Wen recalled the time when Old China was greatly humiliated, carved up and deprived of diplomacy. The Chinese government and its people cherish the hard-earned national sovereignty and pride more than others and stick to them even in severely harsh and difficult times. Diaoyu Islands are the inherent Chinese territory. The Chinese government and its people will never make any concessions on issues of national sovereignty and territory.

(Excerpt from the front page of People's Daily on September 11, 2012)

Jia Qinglin, Chairman of the National Committee of the Chinese People's Political Consultative Conference (CPPCC): Japan's erroneous action has seriously infringed upon China's sovereignty

On September 27, 2012, Jia Qinglin, chairman of the National Committee of the Chinese People's Political Consultative Conference (CPPCC), met with representatives of Japanese friendly personages including former Japanese Speaker of the House of Representatives and President of the Association for the Promotion of International Trade Yohei Kono. Jia said this year's 40th anniversary of the normalization of ties should be an opportunity for better developing China-Japan relations. However, despite China's repeated solemn representations, Japan has insisted on "nationalizing" the Diaoyu Islands, putting relations with China into an unprecedented and severe situation. He noted that Diaoyu Island and its affiliated islands have been China's inherent territory since ancient times. The historical facts and jurisprudential evidence for that are clear. Japan's erroneous action has seriously infringed upon China's sovereignty, touched on the historical pain endured by the Chinese people and aroused their strong indignation and firm opposition. Japan should realize the seriousness of the current situation, squarely face the disputes over the Diaoyu Islands and correct its mistake as soon as possible, so as to avoid further damaging China-Japan ties.

(Excerpt from people.com.cn on September 27, 2012)

Chinese Vice Premier Li Keqiang: we will maintain our sovereignty over the Diaoyu Islands resolutely

On September 11, 2012, Chinese Vice Premier Li Keqiang met with Papua New Guinea Prime Minister Peter O'Neill, who was here in Yinchuan to attend the China (Ningxia) International Investment and Trade Fair and the 3rd China-Arab States Economic and Trade Forum. Li stressed that the Japanese government's deal to "purchase" the Diaoyu Islands from the so-called "owner" severely undermines China's territorial sovereignty. "The Chinese side has lodged solemn representations and strong protest to the Japanese government," Li said. The Diaoyu Islands and their affiliated islands have been an inherent part of China's territory since ancient times, and China has indisputable sovereignty over them. China holds unswerving stance on safeguard of national sovereignty and territorial integrity. We will maintain our sovereignty over the Diaoyu Islands resolutely. Both China and Papua New Guinea were victims to the Japanese fascist invasion back in the Second World War. Japan's position today on the issue of the Diaoyu Islands is an outright denial of the outcomes of victory in the war against fascism and constitutes a grave challenge to the post-war international order. No nation or people who are peace-loving and justice-upholding will tolerate Japan's stance.

(Excerpt from the third page of People's Daily on September 12, 2012)

Comments by Premier Zhou Enlai and Vice-premier Deng Xiaoping on the Diaoyu Islands Issue

During negotiations for the signing of the China-Japan Joint Statement and the Sino-Japanese Treaty of Peace and Friendship, Chinese and Japanese leaders, acting in the larger interest of bilateral relations, decided not to involve the issue of Diaoyu Islands for the time being and leave it to be resolved later. This, however, does not constitute an excuse for the Japanese side to deny its commitment afterwards. The principle that the postwar ownership of relevant territories should be resolved in accordance with the Cairo Declaration and the Potsdam Declaration, as enshrined in the China-Japan Joint Statement and the Sino-Japanese Treaty of Peace and Friendship, still applies to the issue of Diaoyu Islands.

At a recent press conference, Japanese Foreign Minister Koichiro Gemba cited from the conversation between Prime Minister Kakuei Tanaka and Premier Zhou Enlai in 1972 about Diaoyu Islands. He said that Japan and China did not reach common understanding on this issue. For the sake of clarification, again, let's read the following, which is the main part of what was really discussed in the conversation:

Prime Minister Tanaka: I wish to take this opportunity to ask about China's attitude towards the Senkaku Islands.

Premier Zhou: I do not want to discuss this issue this time. It is no good discussing it now.

Prime Minister Tanaka: It may make things difficult for me when I go back if I did not mention this issue at all while I was in Beijing.

Premier Zhou: That's right, because oil has been discovered under that part of the sea. Now Taiwan is trying to make a big issue out of it. The United States might do so, too. The issue has been blown out of proportion.

That was where Minister Gemba's citation ended. But in fact, Prime Minister Tanaka went on to say: Alright. There is no need to discuss it then. Let's talk about it sometime in the future.

Premier Zhou: Let's talk about it in the future. This time, let us first resolve the big and fundamental issues that we can resolve, such as the normalization of bilateral relations. It is not that other issues are not "big", but that normalization of relations is pressing. Some issues need to be discussed at a later time.

Prime Minister Tanaka: I believe other issues can be resolved once the relations are normalized.

What issue were they referring to that needed to be resolved? It was quite clear with the Chinese and Japanese leaders. It was this–the Okinawa ReversionAgreement, signed between the United States and Japan on June 17th, 1971, stated that the power of administration over the Ryukyu Islands and other islands shall be returned to Japan, and arbitrarily included Diaoyu Islands and its affiliated islands into the territories to be returned. On Dec 30th, 1971, the Ministry of Foreign Affairs of China issued a statement, stressing that the backroom deals between the United States and Japan over Diaoyu Islands and other islands were completely illegal and could by no means change the People's Republic of China's territorial sovereignty over the Diaoyu Islands. So it was not vague at all what issue needed to be resolved. It was the issue of sovereignty over Diaoyu Islands. Minister Gemba cited only part of the conversation. Was it because he had no access to the full text? Or did he do it on purpose?

In October 1978, Vice-Premier Deng Xiaoping visited Japan for the exchange of instruments of ratification of the Sino-Japanese Treaty of Peace and Friendship. Commenting on the issue of Diaoyu Islands at a press conference following his talks with Japanese Prime Minister Takeo Fukuda, Mr Deng said, "When China and Japan normalized relations, both countries agreed not to involve this issue. When we negotiated the Sino-Japanese Treaty of Peace and Friendship, we also agreed not to deal with this issue. We believe that it is wiser to set the issue aside for a while if we couldn't bridge our difference this time.

It is okay to temporarily shelve such an issue if our generation does not have enough wisdom to resolve it. The next generation will have more wisdom, and I am sure they will eventually find a way acceptable to both sides." No one on the Japanese side made any objection on this note.

(Excerpt from People's Daily on October 12, 2012)

The discussion about the Diaoyu Islands issue during Vice Premier Deng Xiaoping's Visits to Japan

On October 22, 1978, then Chinese Vice Premier Deng Xiaoping paid an official good-will visit to Japan at the invitation of the Japanese Government, which was warmly welcomed by the Japanese Government and all walks of life.

On October 23, he attended a ceremony to exchange the instruments of ratification for the Sino-Japanese Peace and Friendship Treaty.

On October 25, Deng said during a meeting with Japanese Prime Minister Takeo Fukuda, "It is understandable that the two sides have different opinions on certain issues. For example, we have different opinions on the place that you call Senkaku Islands and we call Diaoyu Islands. We didn't involve this issue in the normalization of diplomatic relations between our two countries. There are some people attempting to use it to hinder the development of China-Japan relations. It is a good choice that we do not talk about it in our negotiation. Issues like this can wait. It will never be too late to solve it in ten years. In the future, we are bound to figure out a good way to solve this problem."

(Excerpt from the front page of People's Daily on October 26, 1978)

II. Government Statements

II.I. Evidence proves that Diaoyu Island is Chinese territory

— Article Published in People's Daily Online 04.05.2016

In recent years, the Japanese government has been denying the dispute over sovereignty of Diaoyu Island, all while strengthening its own propaganda on the issue. A few days ago, the office of the Cabinet of Japan posted some data and graphics on its official website, claiming that Diaoyu Island is Japan's "inherent territory."

However, the so-called proof offered by Japan is either self-deception that goes against history or a misinterpretation of China's stance. In order to eliminate its impact on China-Japan relations and enhance the friendship between the two peoples, it is necessary to refute Japan's evidence and clarify the facts.

A. The Japanese government acknowledged China's sovereignty over Diaoyu Island before the First Sino-Japanese War

The Japanese government has repeatedly claimed that Diaoyu Island and its affiliated islands used to be uninhabited, and Japan did not claim sovereignty over the islands until ithad confirmed that they were not under China's jurisdiction, in accordance with the"preemption doctrine." These claims are completely groundless.

First of all, although Diaoyu Island was uninhabited before Japan seized it in 1895, it wasby no means unclaimed land. According to official historical records, starting from 1372, the fifth year of the reign of Emperor Hongwu of the Ming Dynasty, imperial title conferring envoys used Diaoyu Island and its affiliated islands as a navigation mark to sail to Ryukyu. The imperial courts of the Ming also sent troops, led by Zhang He and Wu Zhen, to protect the maritime route and incorporated these islands into their coastal defense.

From the Qing Dynasty, the islands were placed under the jurisdiction of Gamalan, Taiwan (known as Yilan County today). Huang Shujing, the first imperial supervision envoy sent by the Qing court to Taiwan, once inspected Diaoyu Island and wrote about it in his report, "A Tour of Duty in the Taiwan Strait (Tai Hai Shi Cha Lu)."

Later, between 1874 (when Japan first invaded Taiwan) and 1894 (when the Sino-Japanese War began), all kinds of maps and literature drafted by the Navy Ministry of Japan, including one that lays out all the coastal provinces of the Qing court, identified Diaoyu Island, Huangwei Island and Chiwei Island as northeastern islands of Taiwan. Japan's Foreign Ministry and Army Ministry also confirmed the accuracy of those maps.

In 1885, six years after Japan annexed Ryukyu as Okinawa Prefecture, then Home Minister Yamagata Aritomo secretly asked the Prefecture to set up sovereignty marks on"no-man islands" like Diaoyu Island. The governor of Okinawa Prefecture and the Foreign Minister rejected this maneuver since the occupation of these islands could trigger conflicts with China. Of course, if they had actually believed Diaoyu Island and its affiliated islandswere unclaimed, they would have had no such concerns.

Looking further back to 20 years before the First Sino-Japanese War, it is clear that the Japanese navy believed Diaoyu Island and its affiliated islands were northeastern islands of Taiwan.

For one thing, the nautical journal of H.M.S. Samarang, which chronicled the years 1843-1846 and was published in 1848, as well as other literature and maps published by the British Navy, all marked Diaoyu Island and its affiliated islands as northeastern islands of Taiwan while confirming Chiwei Island as the eastern end of the Chinese island chain.

In addition, the Qing Dynasty atlas, published in 1863, also designates Diaoyu Island as being under the jurisdiction of Taiwan. Kume-jima, an affiliated island of Ryukyu facing Chiwei Island, was marked in a different color. This ample historical evidence shows that, before the "critical period" when the dispute over sovereignty of Diaoyu Island escalated, Diaoyu Island always belonged to China.

B. Japan knew Diaoyu Island was uninhabited before its poachers landed

Originally, Japan made up a story about a man named Koga Tatsushiro who supposedly discovered and colonized Diaoyu Island in 1884. After being debunked as a myth, Japan fabricated additional evidence that a man named Izawa Yakita was once saved by Chinese people as he sailed to Kobajima Island (Diaoyu Island) in 1893. This was cited as evidence that China did not prohibit Japanese people from fishing near Diaoyu Island.

However, according to firsthand reports and documents from Japan's Ministry of Foreign Affairs, Izawa Yakita, a fisherman from Japan's Kumamoto Prefecture, was found poaching albatrosses on Diaoyu Island in 1891.

In June 1893, when Izawa Yakita sailed to Diaoyu Island from the Yaeyama Islands, heand his fellow sailors washed ashore in Pingyang County in eastern China's Zhejiang Province. Though they were rescued, they again encountered dangerous conditions on their way to Fuzhou, Fujian province. Local officials eventually transferred them to the Japanese Consulate in Shanghai.

However, Izawa Yakita and the other sailors hid the truth from Fujian officials, claiming that they had been transporting coal from the Kyushu Islands to the Yaeyama Islands, but had accidentally floated to Kobajima Island on their way. They told the real story to Hayashi Gonsuke, then Japanese Consul General in Shanghai.

Their motivation for lying to Chinese officials must be explored. The decision overwhelmingly points to one conclusion: they realized that the "uninhabited" island they were approaching belonged to China, and they knew they would be punished if they told the truth. Instead, the local Chinese officials—who were kept in the dark about the realsituation—helped the sailors get back to Japan. In this way, a philanthropic deed performed by China is being used by Japan as evidence for its own sovereignty over theisland.

The truth of the matter is that Izawa Yakita was not living on Diaoyu Island or Huangwei Island until 1895 when Taiwan and its affiliated islands were colonized by Japan. Izawa Masagi, Izawa Yakita's daughter, admitted that she was born in 1901 on Huangwei Island.

She confessed that, although the Japanese government knew China had claimed the island,they nevertheless grabbed it during the Sino-Japanese War and officially included it aspart of Japanese territory on a map from 1896 (the 29th year of the Meiji period). In the testimony that she left behind, Izawa Masagi insisted that Japan should establish a sound relationship with China, criticizing Japan's unlawful occupation of the island. She also noted that Japan had once promised to return the islands, along with Taiwan, to China at the end of World War II.

In recent years, in a bid to prove that Diaoyu Island belongs to Japan, Japan's Ministry of Foreign Affairs has posted pictures of Japanese people from that era standing on the island. But these photos do not stand as evidence; all they prove is that Japan colonized the island after colonizing Taiwan in 1895.

On June 10, 1895, Koga Tatsushiro submitted an application to the Japanese government to rent and develop Diaoyu Island. His application was approved in September of the next year. Koga Tatsushiro admitted that he submitted the application after Japan grabbed theislands in the Sino-Japanese War. However, the Treaty of Shimonoseki, the foundation of Japan's occupation of Diaoyu Island and Taiwan, was abolished in 1945 when Japan surrendered in World War II.

Japan's attempt to prove its sovereignty of Diaoyu Island through a few photographs is simply unconvincing. If the claim were valid, Japan could use photos taken on Chinese mainland and Taiwan from those days as proof of the claim.

C. Cairo Declaration and Potsdam Declaration define the territory ofJapan after World War II

Japan's Ministry of Foreign Affairs holds that its territorial scope is determined by the SanFrancisco Peace Treaty of 1952, and that the Cairo Declaration and Potsdam Declaration cannot place legal restrictions on Japan's territory.

This is a public denial of international law, which negates the promises Japan made in itsformal document of surrender in 1945. In the mean time, the People's Republic of Chinawas not a part of and never recognized the San Francisco Peace Treaty signed in 1951. China's sovereignty cannot be determined by a treaty between Japan and the US on Sept. 18, 1951, then Chinese Foreign Minister Zhou Enlai stated that China considers the treaty as illegal and void, as it failed to involve China. For that reason, China will never acknowledge it.

In 1971, Japan and the US signed the Okinawa Reversion Agreement, which providedthat any and all powers of administration over the Ryukyu Islands and Diaoyu Island would be "returned" to Japan. On December 30, 1971, the Chinese Ministry of Foreign Affairs issued a statement pointing out that the agreement was a flagrant violation of China's sovereignty and would never be tolerated by the Chinese people.

"It is completely illegal for the government of the US and Japan to include China's Diaoyu Island as part of the territories to be returned to Japan in the Okinawa Reversion Agreement," read a statement from the Chinese government.

In addition, Diaoyu Island was never even mentioned in Article 3 of the San Francisco Peace Treaty.

After its defeat in World War II, Japan promised to obey the following political documents and regulations regarding territory: According to Article 3 of the China-Japan Joint Communiqué signed in September 1972, the government of the People's Republic of Chinareiterates that Taiwan is an inalienable part of the territory of the People's Republic of China. The government of Japan fully understands and respects this stand of thegovernment of the People's Republic of China, and it firmly maintains its stand under Article 8 of the Potsdam Declaration.

Also, based on the Treaty of Peace and Friendship between China and Japan in August 1978, the principles set out in the Joint Communiqué had to be strictly observed.

Article 8 of the Potsdam Declaration stipulated that the terms of the Cairo Declaration becarried out and Japanese sovereignty limited to the islands of Honshu, Hokkaido, Kyushu, Shikoku and other such minor islands as later determined.

The Cairo Declaration, signed in 1943, required that all the territories Japan stole from China, such as Manchuria, Formosa and the Pescadores Islands, be restored to the Republic of China.

It should be noted that in the Japanese version of the Cairo Declaration, it is stipulated that Japan has to return all the territories stolen from the Qing court to the Republic of China,which means all the territories Japan stole from China before and after the signing of theTreaty of Shimonoseki.

The Imperial Rescript on the Termination of the War, which was announced by theemperor of Japan on Aug. 15, 1945, ordered the Japanese government to inform the US, Great Britain, China and the Soviet Union that it accepted their joint declaration.

On Sept. 2 of the same year, the Japanese surrender document was signed, in which Japan promised that "we, acting by command of and on behalf of the Emperor of Japan, theJapanese government and its successors will faithfully implement the terms of the Potsdam Declaration."

However, the successors of the Japanese government did not faithfully implement theterms of Potsdam Declaration, nor did they abide by the China-Japan Joint Communiqué and Treaty of Peace and Friendship between China and

Japan. Instead, the successors tried to replace those agreements with the San Francisco Peace Treaty, signed only by the US and Japan.

If that's not a violation of international law and order, what is?

(Liu Jiangyong is a professor in the Institute of International Relations attached to the Tsinghua University.)

The article is edited and translated from the Chinese Version of People's Daily

II.II. Diaoyu Islands, an Inherent Territory of China

09/2012

State Council Information Office

The People's Republic of China

Contents

Foreword

Diaoyu Islands and its affiliated islands are an inseparable part of the Chinese territory. Diaoyu Islands is China's inherent territory in all historical, geographical and legal terms, and China enjoys indisputable sovereignty over Diaoyu Islands.

Japan's occupation of Diaoyu Islands during the Sino-Japanese War in 1895 is illegal and invalid. After World War II, Diaoyu Islands was returned to China in accordance with such international legal documents as the Cairo Declaration and the Potsdam Declaration. No matter what unilateral step Japan takes over Diaoyu Islands, it will not change the fact that Diaoyu Islands belongs to China. For quite some time, Japan has repeatedly stirred up troubles on the issue of Diaoyu Islands. On September 10, 2012, the Japanese government announced the "purchase" of Diaoyu Islands and its affiliated Nanxiao Islands and Beixiao Islands and the implementation of the so-called "nationalization". This is a move that grossly violates China's territorial sovereignty and seriously tramples on historical facts and international jurisprudence.

China is firmly opposed to Japan's violation of China's sovereignty over Diaoyu Islands in whatever form and has taken resolute measures to curb any such act. China's position on the issue of Diaoyu Islands is clear-cut and consistent. China's will to defend national sovereignty and territorial integrity is firm and its resolve to uphold the outcomes of the World Anti-Fascist War will not be shaken by any force.

A. Diaoyu Islands is China's Inherent Territory

Diaoyu Islands and its affiliated islands, which consist of Diaoyu Islands, Huangwei Yu, Chiwei Yu, Nanxiao Islands, Beixiao Islands, Nan Yu, Bei Yu, Fei Yu and other islands and reefs, are located to the northeast of China's Taiwan Island, in the waters between 123°20'-124°40'E (East Longitude) and 25°40'-26°00'N (North Latitude), and are affiliated to the Taiwan Island. The total land mass of these islands is approximately 5.69 square kilometers. Diaoyu Islands, situated in the western tip of the area, covers a land mass of about 3.91 square kilometers and is the largest island in the area. The highest peak on the island stands 362 meters above the sea level. Huangwei Yu, which is located about 27 kilometers to the northeast of Diaoyu Islands, is the second largest island in the area, with a total land mass of about 0.91 square kilometers and a highest elevation of 117 meters. Chiwei Yu, situated about 110 kilometers to the northeast of Diaoyu Islands, is the easternmost island in the area. It covers a land mass of approximately 0.065 square kilometers and stands 75 meters above the sea level at its peak.

a. Diaoyu Islands was first discovered, named and exploited by China

Ancient ancestors in China first discovered and named Diaoyu Islands through their production and fishery activities on the sea. In China's historical literatures, Diaoyu Islands is also called Diaoyu Yu or Diaoyu Tai. The earliest historical record of the names of Diaoyu Islands, Chiwei Yu and other places can be found in the book Voyage with a Tail Wind (Shun Feng Xiang Song) published in 1403 (the first year of the reign of Emperor Yongle of the Ming Dynasty). It shows that China had already discovered and named Diaoyu Islands by the 14th and 15th centuries.

In 1372 (the 5th year of the reign of Emperor Hongwu of the Ming Dynasty), the King of Ryukyu started paying tribute to the imperial court of the Ming Dynasty. In return, Emperor Hongwu (the first emperor of the Ming Dynasty) sent imperial envoys to Ryukyu. In the following five centuries until 1866 (the fifth year of the reign of Emperor Tongzhi of the Qing Dynasty), the imperial courts of the Ming and Qing Dynasties sent imperial envoys to Ryukyu 24 times to confer titles on the Ryukyu King, and Diaoyu Islands was exactly located on their route to Ryukyu. Ample volume of records about Diaoyu Islands could be found in the reports written by Chinese imperial envoys at the time. For example, the Records of the Imperial Title-conferring Envoys to Ryukyu

(Shi Liu Qiu Lu) written in 1534 by Chen Kan, an imperial title-conferring envoy from the Ming court, clearly stated that "the ship has passed Diaoyu Islands, Huangmao Yu, Chi Yu... Then Gumi Mountain comes into sight where the land of Ryukyu begins." The Shi Liu Qiu Lu of another imperial envoy of the Ming Dynasty, Guo Rulin, in 1562 also stated that "Chi Yu is the mountain that marks the boundary of Ryukyu". In 1719, Xu Baoguang, a deputy title-conferring envoy to Ryukyu in the Qing Dynasty, clearly recorded in his book Records of Messages from Chong-shan (Zhong Shan Chuan Xin Lu) that the voyage from Fujian to Ryukyu passed Huaping Yu, Pengjia Yu, Diaoyu Islands, Huangwei Yu, Chiwei Yu and reached Naba (Naha) port of Ryukyu via Gumi Mountain (the mountain guarding the southwest border of Ryukyu) and Machi Island.

In 1650, the Annals of Chong-shan (Zhong Shan Shi Jian), the first official historical record of the Ryukyu Kingdom drafted under the supervision of Ryukyu's prime minister Xiang Xiangxian (Kozoken), confirmed that Gumi Mountain (also called Gumi Mountain, known as Kume Island today) is part of Ryukyu's territory, while Chi Yu (known as Chiwei Yu today) and the areas to its west are not Ryukyu's territory. In 1708, Cheng Shunze (Tei Junsoku), a noted scholar and the Grand Master with the Purple-Golden Ribbon (Zi Jin Da Fu) of Ryukyu, recorded in his book A General Guide (Zhi Nan Guang Yi) that "Gumi Mountain is the mountain guarding the southwest border of Ryukyu".

These historical accounts clearly demonstrate that Diaoyu Islands and Chiwei Yu belong to China and Kume Island belongs to Ryukyu, and that the separating line lies in Hei Shui Gou (today's Okinawa Trough) between Chiwei Yu and Kume Island. In 1579, Xie Jie, a deputy imperial title-conferring envoy of the Ming Dynasty, recorded in his book, Addendum to Summarized Record of Ryukyu (Liu Qiu Lu Cuo Yao Bu Yi) that he entered Ryukyu from Cang Shui to Hei Shui, and returned to China from Hei Shui to Cang Shui. Xia Ziyang, another imperial envoy of the Ming court, wrote in 1606 that "when the water flows from Hei Shui back to Cang Shui, it enters the Chinese territory." Miscellaneous Records of a Mission to Ryukyu (Shi Liu Qiu Za Lu), a book written in 1683 by Wang Ji, an imperial envoy of the Qing Dynasty, stated that "Hei Shui Gou", situated outside Chi Yu, is the "boundary between China and foreign land". In 1756, Zhou Huang, a deputy imperial envoy of the Qing Dynasty, recorded in his book, the Annals of Ryukyu (Liu Qiu Guo Zhi Lue), that Ryukyu "is separated from the waters of Fujian by Hei Shui Gou to the west".

The waters surrounding Diaoyu Islands are traditionally Chinese fishing ground. Chinese fishermen have, for generations, engaged in fishery activities in these waters. In the past, Diaoyu Islands was used as a navigation marker by the Chinese people living on the southeast coast.

b. Diaoyu Islands had long been under China's jurisdiction

In the early years of the Ming Dynasty, China placed Diaoyu Islands under its coastal defense to guard against the invasion of Japanese pirates along its southeast coast. In 1561 (the 40th year of the reign of Emperor Jiajing of the Ming Dynasty), An Illustrated Compendium on Maritime Security (Chou Hai Tu Bian) compiled by Zheng Ruozeng under the auspices of Hu Zongxian, the supreme commander of the southeast coastal defense of the Ming court, included the Diaoyu Islands on the "Map of Coastal Mountains and Sands" (Yan Hai Shan Sha Tu) and incorporated them into the jurisdiction of the coastal defense of the Ming court. The Complete Map of Unified Maritime Territory for Coastal Defense (Qian Kun Yi Tong Hai Fang Quan Tu), drawn up by Xu Bida and others in 1605 (the 33rd year of the reign of Emperor Wanli of the Ming Dynasty) and the Treatise on Military Preparations. Coastal Defense II. Map of Fujian's Coastal Mountains and Sands (Wu Bei Zhi, Hai Fang Er.Fu Jian Yan Hai Shan Sha Tu), drawn up by Mao Yuanyi in 1621 (the first year of the reign of Emperor Tianqi of the Ming Dynasty), also included the Diaoyu Islands as part of China's maritime territory.

The Qing court not only incorporated the Diaoyu Islands into the scope of China's coastal defense as the Ming court did, but also clearly placed the islands under the jurisdiction of the local government of Taiwan. Official documents of the Qing court, such as A Tour of Duty in the Taiwan Strait (Tai Hai Shi Cha Lu) and Annals of Taiwan Prefecture (Tai Wan Fu Zhi) all gave detailed accounts concerning China's administration over Diaoyu Islands. Volume 86 of Recompiled General Annals of Fujian (Chong Zuan Fu Jian Tong Zhi), a book compiled by Chen Shouqi and others in 1871 (the tenth year of the reign of Emperor Tongzhi of the Qing Dynasty), included Diaoyu Islands as a strategic location for coastal defense and placed the islands under the jurisdiction of Gamalan, Taiwan (known as Yilan County today).

c. Chinese and foreign maps show that Diaoyu Islands belongs to China

The Roadmap to Ryukyu (Liu Qiu Guo Hai Tu) in the Shi Liu Qiu Lu written by imperial title-conferring envoy Xiao Chongye in 1579 (the seventh year of the reign of Emperor Wanli of the Ming Dynasty), the Record of the Interpreters of August Ming (Huang Ming Xiang Xu Lu) written by Mao Ruizheng in 1629 (the second year of the reign of Emperor Chongzhen of the Ming Dynasty), the Great Universal Geographic Map (Kun Yu Quan Tu) created in 1767 (the 32nd year of the reign of Emperor Qianlong of the Qing Dynasty), and the Atlas of the Great Qing Dynasty (Huang Chao Zhong Wai Yi Tong Yu Tu) published in 1863 (the second year of the reign of Emperor Tongzhi of the Qing Dynasty) all marked Diaoyu Islands as China's territory.

The book Illustrated Outline of the Three Countries written by Hayashi Shihei in 1785 was the earliest Japanese literature to mention Diaoyu Islands. The Map of the Three Provinces and 36 Islands of Ryukyu in the book put Diaoyu Islands as being apart from the 36 islands of Ryukyu and colored it the same as the mainland of China, indicating that Diaoyu Islands was part of China's territory.

The Map of East China Sea Littoral States created by the French cartographer Pierre Lapie and others in 1809 colored Diaoyu Islands, Huangwei Yu, Chiwei Yu and the Taiwan Island as the same. Maps such as A New Map of China from the Latest Authorities published in Britain in 1811, Colton's China published in the United States in 1859, and A Map of China's East Coast: Hongkong to Gulf of Liao-Tung compiled by the British Navy in 1877 all marked Diaoyu Islands as part of China's territory.

B. Japan Grabbed Diaoyu Islands from China

Japan accelerated its invasion and external expansion after the Meiji Restoration. Japan seized Ryukyu in 1879 and changed its name to Okinawa Prefecture. Soon after that, Japan began to act covertly to invade and occupy Diaoyu Islands and secretly "included" Diaoyu Islands in its territory at the end of the Sino-Japanese War of 1894-1895. Japan then forced China to sign the unequal Treaty of Shimonoseki and cede to Japan the island of Formosa (Taiwan), together with Diaoyu Islands and all other islands appertaining or belonging to the said island of Formosa.

a. Japan's covert moves to seize Diaoyu Islands

In 1884, a Japanese man claimed that he first landed on Diaoyu Islands and found the island to be uninhabited. The Japanese government then dispatched secret facts-finding missions to Diaoyu Islands and attempted to invade and occupy the island. The above-mentioned plots by Japan triggered China's alert. On September 6, 1885 (the 28th day of the 7th month in the 11th year of the reign of Emperor Guangxu of the Qing Dynasty), the Chinese newspaper Shen-pao (Shanghai News) reported: "Recently, Japanese flags have been seen on the islands northeast to Taiwan, revealing Japan's intention to occupy these islands." But the Japanese government did not dare to take any further action for fear of reaction from China.

After the secret facts-finding missions to Diaoyu Islands, the governor of Okinawa Prefecture sent a report in secrecy to the Minister of Internal Affairs Yamagata Aritomo on September 22, 1885, saying that these uninhabited islands were, in fact, the same Diaoyu Tai, Huangwei Yu and Chiwe Yu that were recorded in the Records of Messages from Chong-shan (Zhong Shan Chuan Xin Lu) and known well to imperial title-conferring envoys of the Qing court on their voyages to Ryukyu, and that he had doubts as to whether or not sovereignty markers should be set up and therefore asked for instruction. The Minister of Internal Affairs Yamagata Aritomo solicited opinion from the

Foreign Minister Inoue Kaoru on October 9. Inoue Kaoru replied in a letter to Yamagata Aritomo on October 21 stated:

"In such a time, if we were to publicly place national markers on the islands, this must necessarily invite China's suspicion toward us. Currently we should limit ourselves to investigating the islands, understanding the formations of the harbors, seeing whether or not there exists possibilities to develop the island's land and resources, which all should be made into detailed response. In regard to the matter of placing national markers and developing the islands, the issue should wait till a more appropriate time."

Inoue Kaoru also made a special emphasis that: "Moreover, the surveys conducted earlier of Daito-jima and the investigation of the above mentioned islands should not be published in the Official Gazette ('iff'K) or newspapers. Please pay special attention to this."

As a result, the Japanese government did not approve of the request of Okinawa Prefecture to set up sovereignty markers.

The governor of Okinawa Prefecture submitted the matter for approval to the Minister of Internal Affairs once again on January 13, 1890, saying that Diaoyu Islands and other "above-mentioned uninhabited islands have remained under no specific jurisdiction", and that he "intends to place them under the jurisdiction of the Office of Yaeyama Islands". On November 2nd, 1893, the governor of Okinawa Prefecture applied once again for setting up sovereignty markers to incorporate the islands into Japan's territory. The Japanese government did not respond. On May 12, 1894, two months before the Sino-Japanese War, the secret facts-finding missions to Diaoyu Islands by Okinawa Prefecture came to a final conclusion, "Ever since the prefecture police surveyed the island in 1885 (the 18th year of the Meiji period), there have been no subsequent investigations. As a result, it is difficult to provide any specific reports on it... In addition, there exist no old records related to the said island or folklore and legends demonstrating that the island belongs to our country."

Japan's attempts to occupy the Diaoyu Islands were clearly recorded in Japan Diplomatic Documents compiled by the Japanese Foreign Ministry. Relevant documents evidently show that the Japanese government intended to occupy the Diaoyu Islands, but refrained from acting impetuously as it was fully aware of China's sovereignty over these islands.

Japan waged the Sino-Japanese War in July 1894. Towards the end of November 1894, Japanese forces seized the Chinese port of Lushun (then known as Port Arthur), virtually securing defeat of the Qing court. Against such backdrop, the Japanese Minister of Internal Affairs Yasushi Nomura wrote to Foreign Minister Mutsu Munemitsu on December 27 that the "circumstances have now changed", and called for a decision by the cabinet on the issue of setting up sovereignty markers in Diaoyu Islands and incorporating the island into Japan's territory. Mutsu Munemitsu expressed his support for the proposal in his reply to Yasushi Nomura on January 11, 1895. The Japanese cabinet secretly passed a resolution on January 14 to "place" Diaoyu Islands under the jurisdiction of Okinawa Prefecture.

Japan's official documents show that from the time of the facts-finding missions to Diaoyu Islands in 1885 to the occupation of the islands in 1895, Japan had consistently acted in secrecy without making its moves public. This further proves that Japan's claim of sovereignty over Diaoyu Islands does not have legal effect under international law.

b. Diaoyu Islands was ceded to Japan together with the Taiwan Island

On April 17, 1895, the Qing court was defeated in the Sino-Japanese War and forced to sign the unequal Treaty of Shimonoseki and cede to Japan "the island of Formosa (Taiwan), together with all islands appertaining or belonging to the said island of Formosa". The Diaoyu Islands were ceded to Japan as "islands appertaining or belonging to the said island of Formosa". In 1900, Japan changed the name of Diaoyu Islands to "Senkaku Islands".

C. Backroom Deals between the United States and Japan Concerning Diaoyu Islands are Illegal and Invalid

Diaoyu Islands was returned to China after the Second World War. However, the United States arbitrarily included Diaoyu Islands under its trusteeship in the 1950s and "returned" the "power of administration" over Diaoyu Islands to Japan in the 1970s. The backroom deals between the United States and Japan concerning Diaoyu Islands are acts of grave violation of China's territorial sovereignty. They are illegal and invalid. They have not and cannot change the fact that Diaoyu Islands belongs to China.

a. Diaoyu Islands was returned to China after the Second World War

In December 1941, the Chinese government officially declared war against Japan together with the abrogation of all treaties between China and Japan. In December 1943, the Cairo Declaration stated in explicit terms that "all the territories Japan has stolen from the Chinese, such as Manchuria, Formosa [Taiwan] and the Pescadores, shall be restored to the Republic of China. Japan will also be expelled from all other territories which she has taken by violence and greed." In July 1945, the Potsdam Declaration stated in Article 8: "The terms of the Cairo Declaration shall be carried out and Japanese sovereignty shall be limited to the islands of Honshu, Hokkaido, Kyushu, Shikoku and such minor islands as we determine." On September 2nd, 1945, the Japanese government accepted the Potsdam Declaration in explicit terms with the Japanese Instrument of Surrender and pledged to faithfully fulfill the obligations enshrined in the provisions of the Potsdam Declaration. On January 29, 1946, the Supreme Commander for the Allied Powers Instruction (SCAPIN) No.677

clearly defined Japan's power of administration to "include the four main islands of Japan (Hokkaido, Honshu, Kyushu and Shikoku) and the approximately 1,000 smaller adjacent islands, including the Tsushima Islands and the
Ryukyu Islands north of the 30 parallel of North Latitude". On October 25,
1945, the ceremony for accepting Japan's surrender in Taiwan Province of the
China War Theater was held in Taipei, and the Chinese government officially recovered Taiwan. On September 29, 1972, the Japanese government committed
with all seriousness in the China-Japan Joint Statement that "the Government
of Japan fully understands and respects this stand of the Government of the
People's Republic of China [Taiwan is an inalienable part of the territory of the
People's Republic of China], and it firmly maintains its stand under Article 8
of the Potsdam Declaration."

These facts show that in accordance with the Cairo Declaration, the Potsdam
Declaration and the Japanese Instrument of Surrender, Diaoyu Islands, as affiliated islands of Taiwan, should be returned, together with Taiwan, to China.

b. The United States illegally included Diaoyu Islands under its trusteeship

On September 8, 1951, Japan, the United States and a number of other countries signed the Treaty of Peace with Japan (commonly known as the Treaty of
San Francisco) with China being excluded from it. The treaty placed the Nansei
Islands south of the 29th parallel of North Latitude under United Nations' trusteeship, with the United States as the sole administering authority. It should
be pointed out that the Nansei Islands placed under the administration of the
United States in the Treaty of Peace with Japan did not include Diaoyu Islands.

The United States Civil Administration of the Ryukyu Islands (USCAR)
issued Civil Administration Ordinance No. 68 (Provisions of the Government
of the Ryukyu Islands) on February 29, 1952 and Civil Administration
Proclamation No. 27 (defining the "geographical boundary lines of the Ryukyu
Islands") on December 25, 1953, arbitrarily expanding its jurisdiction to include China's Diaoyu Islands. However, there were no legal grounds whatsoever
for the US act, to which China has firmly opposed.

c. The United States and Japan conducted backroom deals concerning the "power of administration" over Diaoyu Islands

On June 17, 1971, Japan and the United States signed the Agreement
Concerning the Ryukyu Islands and the Daito Islands (Okinawa Reversion
Agreement), which provided that any and all powers of administration over the
Ryukyu Islands and Diaoyu Islands would be "returned" to Japan. The Chinese
people, including overseas Chinese, all condemned such a backroom deal. On
December 30, 1971, the Chinese Ministry of Foreign Affairs issued a solemn
statement, pointing out that "it is completely illegal for the government of the
United States and Japan to include China's Diaoyu Islands into the territories

to be returned to Japan in the Okinawa Reversion Agreement and that it can by no means change the People's Republic of China's territorial sovereignty over the Diaoyu Islands". The Taiwan authorities also expressed firm opposition to the backroom deal between the United States and Japan.

In response to the strong opposition of the Chinese government and people, the United States had to publicly clarify its position on the sovereignty over Diaoyu Islands. In October 1971, the US administration stated that "the United States believes that a return of administrative rights over those islands to Japan, from which the rights were received, can in no way prejudice any underlying claims. The United States cannot add to the legal rights Japan possessed before it transferred administration of the islands to us, nor can the United States, by giving back what it received, diminish the rights of other claimants... The United States has made no claim to Diaoyu Islands and considers that any conflicting claims to the islands are a matter for resolution by the parties concerned." In November 1971, when presenting the Okinawa Reversion Agreement to the US Senate for ratification, the US Department of State stressed that the United States took a neutral position with regard to the competing Japanese and Chinese claims to the islands, despite the return of administrative rights over the islands to Japan.

D. Japan's Claim of Sovereignty over Diaoyu Islands Is Totally Unfounded

On March 8, 1972, Japan's Ministry of Foreign Affairs issued the Basic View on the Sovereignty over the Senkaku Islands in an attempt to explain the Japanese government's claims of sovereignty over Diaoyu Islands. First, Japan claims that Diaoyu Islands was "terra nullius" and not part of Pescadores, Formosa [Taiwan] or their affiliated islands which were ceded to Japan by the Qing government in accordance with the Treaty of Shimonoseki. Second, Japan claims that Diaoyu Islands was not included in the territory which Japan renounced under Article 2 of the Treaty of San Francisco, but was placed under the administration of the United States as part of the Nansei Islands in accordance with Article 3 of the said treaty, and was included in the area for which the administrative rights were reverted to Japan in accordance with the Okinawa Reversion Agreement. Third, Japan claims that China didn't regard Diaoyu Islands as part of Taiwan and had never challenged the inclusion of the islands in the area over which the United States exercised administrative rights in accordance with Article 3 of the Treaty of San Francisco.

Such claims by Japan fly in the face of facts and are totally unfounded.

Diaoyu Islands belongs to China. It is by no means "terra nullius". China is the indisputable owner of Diaoyu Islands as it had exercised valid jurisdiction over the island for several hundred years long before the Japanese people "discovered" it. As stated above, voluminous Japanese official documents prove that Japan was fully aware that according to international law, Diaoyu Islands has long been part of China and was not "terra nullius". Japan's act to include Diaoyu Islands as "terra nullius" into its territory based on the "occupation" principle is in fact an illegal act of occupying Chinese territory and has no legal effect according to international law.

Diaoyu Islands has always been affiliated to China's Taiwan Island both in geographical terms and in accordance with China's historical jurisdiction practice. Through the unequal Treaty of Shimonoseki, Japan forced the Qing court to cede to it "the island of Taiwan, together with all islands appertaining or belonging to it", including Diaoyu Islands. International legal documents such as the Cairo Declaration and the Potsdam Declaration provide that Japan must unconditionally return the territories it has stolen from China. These documents also clearly define Japan's territory, which by no means includes Diaoyu Islands. Japan's attempted occupation of Diaoyu Islands, in essence, constitutes a challenge to the post-war international order established by such legal documents as the Cairo Declaration and the Potsdam Declaration and seriously violates the obligations Japan should undertake according to international law.

Diaoyu Islands was not placed under the trusteeship established by the Treaty of San Francisco, which was signed between the United States and other countries with Japan and is partial in nature. The United States arbitrarily expanded the scope of trusteeship to include Diaoyu Islands, which is China's territory, and later "returned" the "power of administration" over Diaoyu Islands to Japan. This has no legal basis and is totally invalid according to international law. The government and people of China have always explicitly opposed such illegal acts of the United States and Japan.

E. China has Taken Resolute Measures to Safeguard Its Sovereignty over Diaoyu Islands

China has, over the past years, taken resolute measures to safeguard its sovereignty over Diaoyu Islands.

China has, through the diplomatic channel, strongly protested against and condemned the backroom deals between the United States and Japan over Diaoyu Islands. On August 15, 1951, before the San Francisco Conference, the Chinese government made a statement: "If the People's Republic of China is excluded from the preparation, formulation and signing of the peace treaty with Japan, it will, no matter what its content and outcome are, be regarded as illegal and therefore invalid by the central people's government." On September 18, 1951, the Chinese government issued another statement stressing that the Treaty of San Francisco is illegal and invalid and can under no circumstances be recognized. In 1971, responding to the ratification of the Okinawa Reversion Agreement by the US Congress and Japanese Diet, the Chinese Foreign Ministry issued a stern statement which pointed out that the Diaoyu Islands have been an indivisible part of the Chinese territory since ancient times.

In response to Japan's illegal violation of China's sovereignty over Diaoyu Islands, the Chinese government has taken active and forceful measures such as issuing diplomatic statements, making serious representations with Japan and submitting notes of protest to the United Nations, solemnly stating China's consistent proposition, principle and position, firmly upholding China's territorial sovereignty and maritime rights and interests, and earnestly protecting the safety of life and property of Chinese citizens.

China has enacted domestic laws, which clearly provide that Diaoyu Islands belongs to China. In 1958, the Chinese government released a statement on the territorial sea, announcing that Taiwan and its adjacent islands belong to China. In light of Japan's repeated violations of China's sovereignty over Diaoyu Islands since the 1970s, China adopted the Law of the People's Republic of China on the Territorial Sea and the Contiguous Zone in 1992, which unequivocally prescribes that "Taiwan and the various affiliated islands including Diaoyu Islands" belong to China. The 2009 Law of the People's Republic of China on the Protection of Offshore Islands establishes the protection, development and management system of offshore islands and prescribes the determination and announcement of the names of offshore islands, on the basis of which China announced the standard names of Diaoyu Islands and some of its affiliated islands in March 2012. On September 10, 2012, the Chinese government issued a statement announcing the baselines of the territorial sea of Diaoyu Islands and its affiliated islands. On September 13, the Chinese government deposited the coordinates table and chart of the base points and baselines of the territorial sea of Diaoyu Islands and its affiliated islands with the Secretary-General of the United Nations.

China has maintained routine presence and exercised jurisdiction in the waters of Diaoyu Islands. China's marine surveillance vessels have been carrying out law enforcement patrol missions in the waters of Diaoyu Islands, and fishery administration law enforcement vessels have been conducting regular law enforcement patrols and fishery protection missions to uphold normal fishing order in the waters of Diaoyu Islands. China has also exercised administration over Diaoyu Islands and the adjacent waters by releasing weather forecasts and through oceanographic monitoring and forecasting.

Over the years, the issue of Diaoyu Islands has attracted attention from Hong Kong and Macao compatriots, Taiwan compatriots and overseas Chinese. Diaoyu Islands has been an inherent territory of China since ancient times. This is the common position of the entire Chinese nation. The Chinese nation has the strong resolve to uphold state sovereignty and territorial integrity. The compatriots across the Taiwan Straits stand firmly together on matters of principle to the nation and in the efforts to uphold national interests and dignity. The compatriots from Hong Kong, Macao and Taiwan and the overseas Chinese have all carried out various forms of activities to safeguard China's territorial sovereignty over Diaoyu Islands, strongly expressing the just position of the Chinese nation, and displaying to the rest of the world that the peace-loving Chinese nation has the determination and the will to uphold China's state sovereignty and territorial integrity.

Conclusion

Diaoyu Islands has been an inherent territory of China since ancient times, and China has indisputable sovereignty over Diaoyu Islands. As China and Japan were normalizing relations and concluding the Sino-Japanese Treaty of Peace and Friendship in the 1970s, the leaders of the two countries, acting in the larger interest of China-Japan relations, reached important understanding and consensus on "leaving the issue of Diaoyu Islands to be resolved later." But in recent years, Japan has repeatedly taken unilateral measures concerning Diaoyu Islands and conducted in particular the so-called "nationalization" of Diaoyu Islands. This has severely infringed upon China's sovereignty and ran counter to the understanding and consensus reached between the older generation of leaders of the two countries. It has not only seriously damaged China-Japan relations, but also rejected and challenged the outcomes of the victory of the World Anti-Fascist War.

China strongly urges Japan to respect history and international law and immediately stop all actions that undermine China's territorial sovereignty. The Chinese government has the unshakable resolve and will to uphold the nation's territorial sovereignty. It has the confidence and ability to safeguard China's state sovereignty and territorial integrity.

(Published in People's Daily on September 26, 2012)

II.III. Standard Names for Diaoyu Dao and its Affiliated Islands

The State Oceanic Administration and the Ministry of Civil Affairs of the People's Republic of China has announced the standard names for Diaoyu Dao and its affiliated islands (as of March 2012 and published in March 2, 2012)

The State Oceanic Administration has standardized the names of the off-shore islands in accordance with the Law of the People's Republic of China on the Protection of Offshore Islands. With the approval of the State Council, the State Oceanic Administration and the Ministry of Civil Affairs announced the standard names for Diaoyu Dao and its affiliated islands as follows:

No.	Standard Name	Pinyin	Location
1	Diaoyu Dao	Diàoyú Dǎo	Some 356 km from Wenzhou City, Zhejiang Province, 385 km from Fuzhou City, Fujian Province, and 190 km from Keelung City, Taiwan Province
2	Longtouyu Islet	Lóngtóuyú Dǎo	Northeast of Diaoyu Dao
3	Changyu Islet	Chāngyú Dǎo	Southwest of Diaoyu Dao
4	Dahuangyu Islet	Dàhuángyú Dǎo	South of Diaoyu Dao
5	Xiaohuangyu Islet	Xiǎohuángyú Dǎo	South of Diaoyu Dao
6	Jinqianyu Islet	Jīnqiányú Dǎo	Southeast of Diaoyu Dao
7	Jinqianyu West Islet	Jīnqiányúxī Dǎo	Southeast of Diaoyu Dao
8	Meitongyu Islet	Méitóngyú Dǎo	Southeast of Diaoyu Dao
9	Meitongyu East Islet	Méitóngyúdōng Dǎo	Southeast of Diaoyu Dao
10	Meitongyu West Islet	Méitóngyúxī Dǎo	Southeast of Diaoyu Dao
11	Longwangdiao Islet	Lóngwángdiāo Dǎo	Southeast of Diaoyu Dao
12	Longwangdiao West Islet	Lóngwángdiāoxī Dǎo	Southeast of Diaoyu Dao
13	Longwangdiao East Islet	Lóngwángdiāodōng Dǎo	Southeast of Diaoyu Dao
14	Longwangdiao South Islet	Lóngwángdiāonán Dǎo	Southeast of Diaoyu Dao
15	Huangguyu Islet	Huánggūyú Dǎo	Southeast of Diaoyu Dao
16	Huangwei Yu	Huángwěi Yǔ	27 km northeast of Diaoyu Dao
17	Haitun Islet	Hǎitún Dǎo	Northwest of Huangwei Yu
18	Dazhu Islet	Dàzhū Dǎo	West of Huangwei Yu
19	Xiaozhu Islet	Xiǎozhū Dǎo	West of Huangwei Yu
20	Shanghuya Islet	Shànghǔyá Dǎo	North of Huangwei Yu
21	Xiahuya Islet	Xiàhǔyá Dǎo	North of Huangwei Yu
22	Xiniujiao Islet	Xīniújiǎo Dǎo	Northeast of Huangwei Yu
23	Dongniujiao Islet	Dōngniújiǎo Dǎo	Northeast of Huangwei Yu
24	Huangniu Islet	Huángniú Dǎo	Northeast of Huangwei Yu
25	Niuwei Islet	Niúwěi Dǎo	Northeast of Huangwei Yu
26	Niuti Islet	Niútí Dǎo	Northeast of Huangwei Yu
27	Xiaolong Islet	Xiǎolóng Dǎo	West of Huangwei Yu
28	Dayan Islet	Dàyàn Dǎo	West of Huangwei Yu
29	Yanzi Islet	Yànzi Dǎo	West of Huangwei Yu
30	Ciwei Islet	Cìwèi Dǎo	Southwest of Huangwei Yu
31	Wocan Islet	Wòcán Dǎo	Southwest of Huangwei Yu
32	Dajinguizi Islet	Dàjīnguīzǐ Dǎo	Southwest of Huangwei Yu
33	Xiaojinguizi Islet	Xiǎojīnguīzǐ Dǎo	Southwest of Huangwei Yu
34	Haigui Islet	Hǎiguī Dǎo	Southeast of Huangwei Yu
35	Haixing Islet	Hǎixīng Dǎo	East of Huangwei Yu
36	Haibei Islet	Hǎibèi Dǎo	Southeast of Huangwei Yu
37	Chiwei Yu	Chìwěi Yǔ	110 km east of Diaoyu Dao
38	Chibei North Islet	Chìbèiběi Dǎo	North of Chiwei Yu
39	Chibei East Islet	Chìbèidōng Dǎo	North of Chiwei Yu
40	Chibei West Islet	Chìbèixī Dǎo	North of Chiwei Yu
41	Chibei South Islet	Chìbèinán Dǎo	North of Chiwei Yu
42	XiaoChiwei Islet	Xiǎochìwěi Dǎo	West of Chiwei Yu

43	Chitou Islet	Chitóu Dǎo	West of Chiwei Yu
44	Chiguan Islet	Chìguàn Dǎo	West of Chiwei Yu
45	Chibi Islet	Chìbǐ Dǎo	West of Chiwei Yu
46	Chizui Islet	Chìzuǐ Dǎo	West of Chiwei Yu
47	Wangchi Islet	Wàngchì Dǎo	Southwest of Chiwei Yu
48	Beixiao Dao	Běixiǎo Dǎo	5 km east of Diaoyu Dao
49	Niaochao Islet	Niǎocháo Dǎo	East of Beixiao Dao
50	Niaoluan Islet	Niǎoluǎn Dǎo	East of Beixiao Dao
51	Xiaoniao Islet	Xiǎoniǎo Dǎo	Southeast of Beixiao Dao
52	Nanxiao Dao	Nánxiǎo Dǎo	5.5 km southeast of Diaoyu Dao
53	Longmen North Islet	Lóngménběi Dǎo	Northwest of Nanxiao Dao
54	Longmen Islet	Lóngmén Dǎo	Northwest of Nanxiao Dao
55	Longmen South Islet	Lóngménnán Dǎo	Northwest of Nanxiao Dao
56	Wolong Islet	Wòlóng Dǎo	Northwest of Nanxiao Dao
57	Wolong West Islet	Wòlóngxī Dǎo	Northwest of Nanxiao Dao
58	Feilong North Islet	Fēilóngběi Dǎo	Southeast of Nanxiao Dao
59	Feilong Islet	Fēilóng Dǎo	Southeast of Nanxiao Dao
60	Longzhu Islet	Lóngzhū Dǎo	Southeast of Nanxiao Dao
61	Feilong South Islet	Fēilóngnán Dǎo	Southeast of Nanxiao Dao
62	Changlong Islet	Chánglóng Dǎo	Southeast of Nanxiao Dao
63	Jinlong Islet	Jīnlóng Dǎo	Southeast of Nanxiao Dao
64	Bei Yu	Běi Yǔ	6 km northeast of Diaoyu Dao
65	Beiyuzai Islet	Běiyǔzǎi Dǎo	South of Bei Yu
66	Xiaoyuanbao Islet	Xiǎoyuánbǎo Dǎo	Southwest of Bei Yu
67	Feiyun Islet	Fēiyún Dǎo	Southwest of Bei Yu
68	Yuanbao Islet	Yuánbǎo Dǎo	Southwest of Bei Yu
69	Nan Yu	Nán Yǔ	7.4 km northeast of Diaoyu Dao
70	Fei Yu	Fēi Yǔ	Southeast of Diaoyu Dao
71	Feizai Islet	Fēizǎi Dǎo	Southeast of Diaoyu Dao

II.IV. Statement of the Ministry of Foreign Affairs of the People's Republic of China

2012/09/10

Regardless of repeated strong representations of the Chinese side, the Japanese government announced on 10 September 2012 the "purchase" of the Diaoyu Island and its affiliated Nan Xiao Islands and Bei Xiao Islands and the implementation of the so-called "nationalization" of the islands. This constitutes a gross violation of China's sovereignty over its own territory and is highly offensive to the 1.3 billion Chinese people. It seriously tramples on historical facts and international jurisprudence. The Chinese government and people express firm opposition to and strong protest against the Japanese move.

The Diaoyu Island and its affiliated islands have been China's sacred territory since ancient times. This is supported by historical facts and jurisprudential evidence. The Diaoyu Islands were first discovered, named and exploited by the Chinese people. Chinese fishermen had long been engaged in production activities on these islands and in their adjacent waters. The Diaoyu Islands have been put under the jurisdiction of China's naval defense as affiliated islands of

Taiwan, China since the Ming Dynasty. The Diaoyu Islands have never been "terra nullius". China is the indisputable owner of the Diaoyu Islands.

In 1895, as the Qing government's defeat in the First Sino-Japanese War was all but certain, Japan illegally occupied the Diaoyu Island and its affiliated islands. After that, Japan forced the Qing government to sign the unequal Treaty of Shimonoseki and cede to Japan "the island of Formosa (Taiwan), together with all islands appertaining or belonging to the said island of Formosa". After the end of the Second World War, China recovered the territories invaded and occupied by Japan such as Taiwan and the Penghu Islands in accordance with the Cairo Declaration and the Potsdam Declaration. According to international law, the Diaoyu Island and its affiliated islands have already been returned to China. Facts are facts, and history is not to be reversed. Japan's position on the issue of the Diaoyu Island is an outright denial of the outcomes of the victory of the World Anti-Fascist War and constitutes a grave challenge to the post-war international order.

In 1951, the Treaty of Peace with Japan (commonly known as the Treaty of San Francisco, a treaty partial in nature) was signed between Japan, the United States and other countries, placing the Ryukyu Islands (known as Okinawa today) under the trusteeship of the United States. In 1953, the United States Civil Administration of the Ryukyu Islands arbitrarily expanded its jurisdiction to include the Diaoyu Island and its affiliated islands, which are in fact Chinese territories. In 1971, Japan and the United States signed the Okinawa Reversion Agreement, which arbitrarily included the Diaoyu Islands in the territories and territorial waters to be reversed to Japan. The Chinese government has, from the very beginning, firmly opposed and never acknowledged such backroom deals between Japan and the United States concerning Chinese territories. The claims of the Japanese government that the Diaoyu Island is Japan's inherent territory and that there is no outstanding territorial dispute between Japan and China showed total disregard of historical facts and jurisprudential evidence and are absolutely untenable.

During the negotiations on the normalization of China-Japan relations in 1972 and on the signing of the Sino-Japanese Treaty of Peace and Friendship in 1978, the leaders of the two countries, acting in the larger interest of China-Japan relations, reached important understanding and common ground on "leaving the issue of the Diaoyu Island to be resolved later". This opened the door to normalization of China-Japan relations and was followed by tremendous progress in China-Japan relations and stability and tranquility in East Asia in the following 40 years. Now, if the Japanese authorities should deny and negate the previous common understanding reached between the two countries, then how could the situation of the Diaoyu Island remain stable? How could China-Japan relations continue to grow smoothly? And how could Japan ever win trust from its neighbors and people of the world?

The Japanese government has repeatedly stirred up troubles in recent years on the issue of the Diaoyu Island. Particularly since the start of the year, the Japanese government has endorsed rightwing forces to clamor for the "purchase" of the Diaoyu Island and some of its affiliated islands in an attempt to pave the way for a government "purchase" of the islands. People have reason to believe that what Japan did regarding the Diaoyu Island was nothing accidental. The political tendency these actions point to may well put people on the alert. We cannot but ask: where is Japan heading to? Can anyone rest assured of Japan's future course of development?

The Chinese government has always attached importance to developing relations with Japan. China and Japan and the Chinese and Japanese peoples can live together only in friendship, not confrontation. To advance the China-Japan strategic relationship of mutual benefit serves the fundamental interests of the two countries and two peoples and is conducive to peace, stability and development of the region. Yet, to ensure sound and stable development of China-Japan relations, the Japanese side needs to work together and move in the same direction with China. The "purchase" of the Diaoyu Island by the Japanese government runs counter to the goal of upholding the larger interest of China-Japan relations.

The Chinese government solemnly states that the Japanese government's so-called "purchase" of the Diaoyu Island is totally illegal and invalid. It does not change, not even in the slightest way, the historical fact of Japan's occupation of Chinese territory, nor will it alter China's territorial sovereignty over the Diaoyu Island and its affiliated islands. Long gone are the days when the Chinese nation was subject to bullying and humiliation from others. The Chinese government will not sit idly by watching its territorial sovereignty being infringed upon. The Chinese side strongly urges the Japanese side to immediately stop all actions that may undermine China's territorial sovereignty. Japan should truly come back to the very understanding and common ground reached between the two sides, and should return to the track of negotiated settlement of the dispute. Should the Japanese side insist on going its own way, it shall have to bear all serious consequences arising therefrom.

(Published in People's Daily on September 11, 2012)

II.V. Statement of the Government of the People's Republic of China on the Baselines of the Territorial Sea of Diaoyu Islands and Its Affiliated Islands

2012/09/10

In accordance with the Law of the People's Republic of China on the Territorial Sea and the Contiguous Zone adopted and promulgated on 25 February 1992, the Government of the People's Republic of China hereby announces the baselines of the territorial sea adjacent to Diaoyu Islands and its affiliated islands of the People's Republic of China.

A. The baselines of the territorial sea adjacent to Diaoyu Islands, Huangwei Yu, Nanxiao Islands, Beixiao Islands, Nan Yu, Bei Yu and Fei Yu are composed of all the straight lines joining the adjacent base points listed below:

1. Diaoyu Islands 1	25°44.1′N	123°27.5′E
2. Diaoyu Islands 2	25°44.2′N	123°27.4′E
3. Diaoyu Islands 3	25°44.4′N	123°27.4′E
4. Diaoyu Islands 4	25°44.7′N	123°27.5′E
5. Haitun Islands	25°55.8′N	123°40.7′E
6. Xiahuya Islands	25°55.8′N	123°41.1′E
7. Haixing Islands	25°55.6′N	123°41.3′E
8. Huangwei Yu	25°55.4′N	123°41.4′E
9. Haigui Islands	25°55.3′N	123°41.4′E
10. Changlong Islands	25°43.2′N	123°33.4′E
11. Nanxiao Islands	25°43.2′N	123°33.2′E
12. Changyu Islands	25°44.0′N	123°27.6′E

B. The baselines of the territorial sea adjacent to Chiwei Yu are composed of all the straight lines joining the adjacent base points listed below:

1. Chiwei Yu	25°55.3′N	124°33.7′E
2. Wangchi Islands	25°55.2′N	124°33.2′E
3. Xiaochiwei Islands	25°55.3′N	124°33.3′E
4. Chibeibei Islands	25°55.5′N	124°33.5′E
5. Chibeidong Islands	25°55.5′N	124°33.7′E

Explanation:

Baseline
The line from which the territorial sea is measured; Waters landward of the line are defined as internal waters; waters seaward of the line are firstly the territorial sea and then the exclusive economic zone, continental shelf, etc.

Link
The territorial sea of the People's Republic of China extends up to 12 nautical miles from its baseline. The People's Republic of China adopts the Straight baselines Measurement: linking the lines between adjacent basepoints. External water boundaries of the People's Republic of China are the lines between adjacent basepoints which have a distance of 12 nautical miles to the baseline.

(Excerpt from Law of the PRC on the Territorial Sea and the Contiguous Zone)

II.VI. Foreign Ministry Spokespersons' Remarks on the Diaoyu Islands Issue

March 2004 - February 2013

Foreign Ministry Spokesperson Hua Chunying held a press conference on February 25, 2013. As for the question, Japanese Prime Minister Shinzo Abe said in his speech at the US Center for Strategic and International Studies on February 22 that both history and international law can prove that "Senkaku Islands" belong to Japan, which has never been questioned by a single country from 1895 to 1971. What is China's comment? He said the logic of the above remarks is absurd. Can one change the reality of stealing and illegally occupying the property of others by stealing and then hiding it in his pocket for a while? Similarly, no matter how the Japanese side quibbles, the fact that it illegally seized Chinese territory cannot be covered up.

Diaoyu Islands are China's inherent territory, over the nearly 500 years from the 15th century to 1895, no country had ever challenged China's sovereignty over the Diaoyu Islands. After the end of World War II, defeated as Japan was, it did not fulfill its international obligations as prescribed in the Cairo Declaration and the Potsdam Declaration by returning the Diaoyu Islands to China. All actions that Japan has taken up till now over the Diaoyu Islands are based on its theft and occupation of the Chinese territory, and are thus illegal and invalid. We urge the Japanese side to correct its attitude, face up to history and reality, and make concrete efforts for the proper settlement of the Diaoyu Islands issue and the improvement of China-Japan relations.

Foreign Ministry Spokesperson Hong Lei held a press conference on September 28, 2012. He expressed that this year marks the 40th anniversary of the normalization of China-Japan diplomatic ties and should have been a year of opportunity for the two sides to push forward bilateral relations. However, a lot of plans have been sabotaged by Japan's erroneous actions. Many of the planned commemorative activities were either cancelled or put off. This is what we do not want to see. The grim situation facing China-Japan relations is totally caused by Japan's blatant infringement upon China's territorial sovereignty, outright denial of the outcomes of the victory of the World Anti-Fascist War and gross challenge to the post-war international order. We urge the Japanese side to take concrete measures to correct mistakes and stop all activities that violate China's territorial sovereignty so as to get China-Japan relations back on the track of sound development.

Hong Lei gave more details about Foreign Minister Yang Jiechi, when addressing the General Debate of the 67th Session of the UN General Assembly, mentioned the issue of the Diaoyu Islands. Foreign Minister Yang elaborated on China's solemn position on the issue of the Diaoyu Islands. He said that the Diaoyu Island and its affiliated islands have been an integral part of China's territory since ancient times. China has indisputable historical and jurisprudential evidence in this regard. Japan stole these islands in 1895 at the end of the Sino-Japanese War and forced the Chinese government to sign an unequal treaty to cede these islands and other Chinese territories to Japan. After the end of the Second World War, the Diaoyu islands and other Chinese territories occupied by Japan were returned to China in accordance with the Cairo Declaration, the Potsdam Declaration and other international documents. By taking such unilateral actions as the so-called "island purchase", the Japanese government has grossly violated China's sovereignty. This is an outright denial of the outcomes of the victory of the World Anti-Fascist war and poses a grave challenge to the post-war international order and the purposes and principles of the Charter of the United Nations. The measures taken by Japan are totally illegal and invalid. They can in no way change the historical fact that Japan stole the Diaoyu Island and its affiliated islands from China or shake China's territorial sovereignty over them. The Chinese government is firm in upholding territorial sovereignty. China strongly urges Japan to immediately stop all activities that violate China's territorial sovereignty, take concrete actions to correct its mistakes, and return to the track of resolving the dispute through negotiation.

He also pointed out that the grim situation in China-Japan relations is completely caused by Japan's unilateral action of "purchasing" the Diaoyu Islands and the responsibility rests entirely with Japan. The root cause of the problem is that Japan attempted to break the common ground and understanding reached between China and Japan as well as the overall stable situation over the Diaoyu Islands for many years. China's position on the Diaoyu Islands issue has been consistent. We strongly urge the Japanese side to face the realities squarely, correct mistakes and solve the Diaoyu Islands issue through dialogue and negotiation.

Foreign Ministry Spokesperson Qin Gang's Remarks on Japanese Prime Minister Yoshihiko Noda's Relevant Comment in Addressing the UN General Assembly: the issue of territorial ownership should be resolved according to historical and jurisprudential evidence. Some individual country ignored historical facts and international law, blatantly violated other countries' territorial sovereignty, denied the outcomes of the victory of the World Anti-Fascist War and seriously challenged the post-war international order. However, it is now trying to take the rules of international law as a cover. This is self-deceiving. Relevant country must face history squarely, take concrete steps to observe international jurisprudence and stop all acts that undermine other countries' territorial sovereignty.

On the same day, Qin Gang held a press conference and expressed the Diaoyu Islands have been China's inherent territory since ancient times. This is supported by ample historical and jurisprudential evidence. In 1895, Japan used the Sino-Japanese War to illegally steal the Diaoyu Island and its affiliated islands and forced the Qing government to sign an unequal treaty which ceded to Japan "the island of Formosa (Taiwan), together with all islands pertaining or belonging to the said islands of Formosa". After the end of the Second World War, China recovered the Chinese territories invaded and occupied by Japan including Taiwan in accordance with the Cairo Declaration, the Potsdam Declaration and other international legal documents. The Diaoyu Island and its affiliated islands have already been returned to China according to international law. The Cairo Declaration and the Potsdam Declaration are great outcomes of the World Anti-Fascist War and important cornerstones of the post-war international order, which was explicitly recognized by the Japanese Instrument of Surrender in 1945. The Chinese government has, from the very beginning, expressed firm opposition to and never recognized such backroom deals between the US and Japan on China's Diaoyu Islands. The Chinese people have made huge sacrifice and important contribution to the victory of the World Anti-Fascist War. It is outrageous that a defeated country is now trying to occupy the territory of a victor. Japan's position and actions on the Diaoyu Islands issue trample on the purposes and principles of the UN Charter. It is essentially Japan's failure to thoroughly reflect on and deal with its history of militarist aggression and attempt to deny the outcomes of the victory of the World Anti-Fascist War and challenge the post-war international order. This should put the international community on high alert. Facts are facts and history is not to be reversed. The profound suffering caused by the Second World War should not be forgotten, peace and security order upheld by the UN should not be shaken, and international justice and human conscience should not be defied. The Japanese government's so-called "purchase" of the Diaoyu Islands is completely illegal and invalid. It cannot change, not in the slightest way, the historical fact of Japan's occupation of China's territory. Nor can it change China's territorial sovereignty over the Diaoyu Islands. The Chinese government and people have unbreakable will and resolve in defending national territorial sovereignty. Japan's illegal scheme is doomed to failure. No matter in light of history or international law, Japan should stop all acts that undermine China's territorial sovereignty instead of making repeated mistakes and deceiving the whole world.

Foreign Ministry Spokesperson Hong Lei held a press conference on September 26, 2012 where he addressed the current grim situation in China-Japan relations is completely caused by Japan's insisting on illegally "purchasing" the Diaoyu Islands regardless of China's strong opposition. The Japanese side should bear full responsibility for that. We require the Japanese side to abandon any illusion, concretely correct its mistakes, stop all acts that are detrimental to China's territorial sovereignty and return to the right track of resolving the Diaoyu Islands issue through negotiation with a view to creating conditions for the improvement of China-Japan relations.

Foreign Ministry Spokesperson Hong Lei held a press conference on September 25, 2012. He introduced the talks between the Chinese and Japanese vice foreign ministers: Chinese Vice Foreign Minister Zhang Zhijun and Japanese Vice Foreign Minister Chikao Kawai held consultations over the issue of the Diaoyu Islands and had a candid and in-depth exchange of views this morning.

Zhang Zhijun pointed out that the Diaoyu Island and its affiliated islands have been China's sacred territory since ancient times. It is supported by historical facts and jurisprudential evidence. Regardless of China's repeated solemn representations, the Japanese side denied the important understanding and common ground reached between the leaders of the two countries and blatantly took the illegal action of the so-called "nationalization" of the Diaoyu Islands in disregard of historical facts and jurisprudence. It grossly infringes on China's territory, severely offends the 1.3 billion Chinese people, and seriously tramples on historical facts and international jurisprudence. It represents an outright denial of the outcomes of the victory of the World Anti-Fascist War and a grave challenge to post-war international order. Facts are facts and history is not to be reversed. Common ground should not be negated, and popular will should not be flouted. China will absolutely not tolerate Japan's unilateral actions that undermine China's territorial sovereignty. The Japanese side must abandon any illusion, seriously reflect on and correct its mistakes through concrete actions, come back to the common ground and understanding reached between leaders of the two countries, and work in the same direction with China to get bilateral relations back on the track of sound and steady development at an early date.

The two sides agreed to maintain consultations on the Diaoyu Islands issue.

Foreign Ministry Spokesperson Hong Lei held a press conference on September 19, 2012 where he addressed the Diaoyu Island and its affiliated islands have been China's inherent territory since ancient times. The Chinese government's release of the base points and baselines of the territorial sea of the Diaoyu Island and its affiliated islands represents China's solemn assertion of sovereignty over the Diaoyu Islands. It is totally justified for Chinese government ships to exercise sovereignty and curb infringement in waters off the Diaoyu Islands.

The Japanese government recently announced its "purchase" of the Diaoyu Island and its affiliated islands, severely infringing upon China's territorial sovereignty and arousing the Chinese government and people's strong dissatisfaction and firm opposition.

The Chinese government immediately lodged solemn representations and strong protest, issued a statement to fully elaborate on China's position, published the base points and baselines of the territorial sea of the Diaoyu Islands and deposited the document with the United Nations, declared the submission of the outer limits of the continental shelf in the East China Sea to the Commission on the Limits of the Continental Shelf and dispatched maritime surveillance ships to waters off the Diaoyu Islands for patrol and law-enforcement. China's forceful measures have effectively offset the legal consequences of Japan's illegal "purchase" of the Diaoyu Islands.

The Chinese people have also voiced their strong indignation. Chinese citizens in various parts of China spontaneously took to the street in protest against the Japanese government's illegal "purchase" of the Diaoyu Islands, denouncing the Japanese side's defiance of the victory of the World Anti-Fascist War as well as the post-war international order. They have demonstrated their just position and patriotism and built up a strong momentum to safeguard sovereignty, defend territorial integrity and uphold justice.

Today marks the 81st anniversary of the "September 18th Incident". Long gone are the days when the Chinese nation was subject to bullying and humiliation. The Chinese government and 1.3 billion Chinese people will not sit idly by watching its territorial sovereignty being infringed upon. Japan's scheme of the illegal "purchase" of the Diaoyu Islands is doomed to failure.

We urge the Japanese side to face squarely China's solemn position, listen to the Chinese people's just appeals, and stop holding on to the wrong course. Japan should take the correct attitude and approach, stop immediately all kinds of actions that undermine China's territorial sovereignty, come back to the very consensus and understanding between China and Japan as well as the track of resolving the dispute through dialogue and negotiation.

On September 12, 2012, Foreign Ministry Spokesperson Hong Lei answered the question—media reports said that China had sent maritime surveillance ships to the waters off the Diaoyu Islands, but Japan said it had not spotted Chinese ships in the area. Are there Chinese maritime surveillance ships in waters off the Diaoyu Islands? He said Chinese government ships will continue normal patrol activities in waters under China's jurisdiction

Foreign Ministry Spokesperson Hong Lei held a press conference on September 5, 2012. A journalist asked: It is reported that the Japanese government reached an agreement with the "landowners" of the Diaoyu Islands on September 5 to "buy the Islands" for 2.05 billion yen. What is China's comment?

Foreign Ministry Spokesperson Hong Lei answered: The Diaoyu Island and its affiliated islands have been China's inherent territory since ancient times, for which China has plentiful historical and jurisprudential evidence. The Diaoyu Islands were first discovered, named and used by the Chinese. They have been under the jurisdiction of China's coastal defense at least since the Ming Dynasty. Japan didn't claim sovereignty over the Diaoyu Islands until the Sino-Japanese war in 1895, and it stole these islands through illegal means. It is obvious that the claim that the Diaoyu Islands are Japan's inherent territory is totally untenable.

Regardless of China's repeated solemn representations and turning a deaf ear to China's requirement, the Japanese side wilfully presses ahead with the so-called "island procurement", which severely harms China's territorial sovereignty and hurts the national feelings of the Chinese people.

I would like to reiterate that any unilateral action taken by the Japanese side against the Diaoyu Island and its affiliated islands is illegal and invalid. The Chinese Government is resolute and determined in defending its territorial sovereignty over the Diaoyu Islands. China is following closely the developments and will take necessary measures to safeguard national territorial sovereignty.

Foreign Ministry Spokesperson Qin Gang's remarks on Japanese right-wing activists' landing on the Diaoyu Islands on August 19, 2012: the illegal act of the Japanese right-wing activists has infringed upon China's territorial sovereignty. The leading official of the Chinese Foreign Ministry has made solemn representations and lodged strong protest with Japan, urging it to immediately stop taking actions that harm China's territorial sovereignty.

Japan should properly handle the current problem through concrete actions to avoid serious damage to the larger China-Japan relations.

On August 15, 2012, Foreign Minister Fu Ying made solemn representations and lodged strong protest with Japan. Fu reiterated China's sovereignty over the Diaoyu Island and the affiliated islets, and demanded the Japanese side guarantee the safety of the 14 Chinese citizens and free them immediately without any conditions.

(PS: According to a news published in the Xinhua.net based on the report of Japan NAHA on August 18, after repeated solemn representations and various efforts by the Chinese government, on August 17, Japan released the 14 Chinese citizens who were illegally arrested in the waters of the Diaoyu Islands without any conditions. Seven of them returned to Hong Kong by a fight of Okinawa Naha Airport in the evening; the other seven went to Ishigaki, Okinawa to check and confirm the condition of their boat and returned by ship.)

On August 15, 2012, Foreign Ministry Spokesperson Qin Gang said: Japan detained 14 Chinese nationals and their vessel on the Diaoyu Islands and the adjacent waters, which represents a gross violation of China's territorial sovereignty. The Chinese Government expresses strong condemnation and protest over the dangerous actions such as converging attack taken by Japanese ships to obstruct the Chinese vessel.

The Chinese Government reiterates that the Diaoyu Island and its affiliated islands have been China's inherent territory since ancient times. Any action taken by the Japanese side against the Chinese nationals is illegal and invalid. It will not change the fact that the Diaoyu Islands belong to China, nor will it shake the strong resolve of the Chinese Government and people to safeguard national territorial sovereignty.

China has long been standing for the proper settlement of the Diaoyu Islands issue through dialogue and negotiations with the larger interests of China-Japan relations in mind. China demands the Japanese side to stop actions that undermine China's territorial sovereignty, come back to the right track of solving the issue through dialogue and consultations, and safeguard the larger interests of China-Japan relations through concrete actions.

On July 10, 2012, Foreign Ministry Spokesperson Liu Weimin held a press conference. As for the question, according to Japanese press reports, a senior US State Department official said on July 9 that since the Diaoyu Islands were returned to Japan by the US as part of Okinawa in 1972 and had been under Japan's administrative control that fall within the scope of the Article 5 of the US-Japan Security Treaty should apply to the Islands. How does China comment? Liu Weimin answered China has noted relevant reports. We express our grave concern and strong opposition to such remarks. China has indisputable sovereignty over the Diaoyu Islands, which have been China's inherent territory since ancient times. The US and Japan's secret dealings with China's territory, the Diaoyu Islands, after WWII are illegal and invalid. Being a product of the Cold War, the US-Japan Security Treaty is a bilateral arrangement between the two countries, and should not undermine the interests of a third party, including China. We hope relevant countries will do more for regional peace and stability.

(PS: The official spokesman of the United States Department of State has declared that the US does not take a position on the sovereignty issue related to the Diaoyu Islands and he reiterated the US will not involve in the sovereignty dispute. He hopes China and Japan can solve the issue through a peaceful negotiation.)

On July 9, 2012, Foreign Ministry Spokesperson Liu Weimin held a press conference. He said relevant officials of the Chinese Foreign Ministry and Chinese Embassy in Japan made stern representations with Japan over its recent moves both in Beijing and Tokyo on July 7, making clear the Chinese government's firm position to defend its territorial sovereignty over the Diaoyu Islands and stressing that China will never allow any of Japan's unilateral moves over the Diaoyu Island and its affiliated islands.

On July 7, 2012, the Spokesperson of the Chinese Foreign Ministry once again expressed China's position on the Diaoyu Islands, pointing out that the Islands have been China's inherent territory since ancient times, for which China has indisputable historical and legal basis, and that nobody is ever allowed to trade in China's territory. "The Chinese government will continue to resolutely safeguard its sovereignty over the Diaoyu Island and its affiliated islands with necessary measures."

In the Foreign Ministry Spokesperson Hong Lei's regular press conference on January 4, 2012, on the issue of Japanese Right-wing Activists' Landing on the Diaoyu Islands, he pointed out the Chinese Government has lodged solemn representations and protest to the Japanese side over the incident. He reiterates that the Diaoyu Island and its affiliated islands have been China's inherent territory since ancient times. China has indisputable sovereignty over them. The Chinese Government is resolute in defending its territorial sovereignty over the Diaoyu Islands.

On September 27, 2011, Foreign Ministry Spokesperson Hong Lei held a regular press conference. He said: China is exercising its lawful sovereign rights by conducting marine research near the islands.

Foreign Ministry spokesman Ma Zhaoxu said in a statement: any form of so-called judiciary procedures taken by the Japanese side against the Chinese trawler is unlawful and invalid.

On July 4, 2011, Foreign Ministry Spokesperson Hong Lei addressed China has lodged solemn representations to the Japanese side, urging Japan to withdraw its fishing boats from relevant waters immediately. It is learned that the Japanese fishing boats have already left the waters.

On June 29, 2011, on the Diaoyu Islands issue, Foreign Ministry Spokesperson Hong Lei stressed the Diaoyu Island and its affiliated islands have been China's inherent territory since ancient times. China has indisputable sovereignty over them. Any measure adopted by Japan in the waters off the Diaoyu Islands is illegal and invalid.

On May 23, 2011, Foreign Ministry Spokesperson Jiang Yu held a regular press conference. She addressed that during the meeting on May 22, Foreign Minister Yang Jiechi reiterated the position that the Diaoyu Island and its affiliated islands have been China's inherent territory since ancient times, and China has indisputable sovereignty over them. Yang also reaffirmed China's relevant positions on the East China Sea issue.

On February 12, 2011, Foreign Ministry Spokesperson Ma Zhaoxu said Japan had no right to ask the Chinese captain who was involved in "vessel collision" in the waters of the Diaoyu Islands for the so-called compensation.

On December 18, 2010, as for the question concerning the Council of Ishigaki City, Okinawa, Japan passing the Diaoyu Islands Ordinance, the Foreign Ministry Spokesperson Jiang Yu said that any attempt to violate China's territorial sovereignty over the Diaoyu Islands was futile and invalid.

On December 10, 2010, Foreign Ministry spokesperson Jiang Yu said the two Japanese local councilors boarding the affiliated islands of the Diaoyu Island seriously violated China's territorial sovereignty.

On November 1, 2010, Foreign Ministry spokesperson Ma Zhaoxu said the video of the collision between the Chinese fishing boat and the Japanese patrol ship in the waters of the Diaoyu Islands couldn't change the facts that the behavior of the Japanese side was illegal.

On October 21, 2010, Foreign Ministry Spokesperson Ma Zhaoxu held a regular press conference and he answered the "secret agreement" (the Chinese side promised to stop any vessel going near the Diaoyu Islands if the Japanese side could free the Chinese citizens boarding the Diaoyu Islands) between China and Japan was nonsense. He pointed out that the related argument was totally scandalous, sinister. It not only misled the public opinion, but also further damaged the Sino-Japanese political trust. The Japanese side must bear all the consequences resulting therefrom. Diaoyu Islands are China's inherent territory since ancient times. The determination the Chinese government on safeguarding sovereignty and territorial integrity is clear and unswerving.

On October 12, 2010, Foreign Ministry Spokesperson Ma Zhaoxu held a regular press conference. As for the questions, it's reported that some Japanese congressmen made a so-called "inspection from the air" over the Diaoyu Island, how do you comment? He answered Some individuals in Japan made the illegal "inspection from the air" in an attempt to infringe upon China's territorial sovereignty and undermine China-Japan relations, which will arrive nowhere. China has stated its solemn position on the issue to the Japanese side.

On October 1, 2010, Foreign Ministry Spokesperson Ma Zhaoxu stressed that we hope the Japanese side meet China halfway and proceed from the fundamental interest of the two peoples. China stressed again the Diaoyu Island and its affiliated islands have been China's inherent territory since ancient times. Japan's illegal detention of Chinese fishermen and fishing boat and insisting on fulfilling the so-called domestic law procedures are absurd, illegal and invalid.

On September 30, 2010, Foreign Ministry Spokesperson Jiang Yu held a regular press conference. He hoped the Japanese side proceed from the fundamental interest of the two peoples, stop making irresponsible remarks and take concrete actions to safeguard the overall interest of the bilateral relations. The Diaoyu Island and its affiliated islands have been China's inherent territory since ancient times. Japan's illegal detention of Chinese fishermen and fishing boat has seriously violated China's territorial sovereignty and human rights of the Chinese nationals.

On September 28, 2010, Foreign Ministry Spokesperson Jiang Yu held a regular press conference where he hoped the Japanese side made due efforts to improve the China-Japan relations. As for the question, it is reported that Chinese fishery administration boats will carry out regular patrols in the waters off the Diaoyu Island, he said the waters off the Diaoyu Island are traditional fishing grounds for Chinese fishermen. China dispatches fishery law-enforcement boats to maintain fishing order and protect safety of life and property of Chinese fishermen, which are fishery administration activities in accordance with China's relevant laws and regulations. We hope Japan stop tracking and disrupting Chinese fishery law-enforcement boats.

On September 25, 2010, the captain Zhan Jixiong of the Chinese fishing boat who was illegally arrested by the Japanese side was freed by Japan, and returned to Fuzhou on a chartered flight. Chinese Assistant Foreign Minister Hu Zhengyue and vice governor of Fujian province Hong Jiexu welcomed him at the airport.

On the same day, Ministry of Foreign affairs made a statement. On September 7, 2010, Japan illegally arrested and detained 15 Chinese fishermen and their fishing boat in the waters off the Diaoyu Island. The captain was detained by Japan until September 24. These actions seriously violated China's territorial sovereignty and the human rights of the Chinese nationals. The Chinese government hereby expresses its strong protest. The Diaoyu Island and its affiliated islands have been China's territory since ancient times. China has indisputable sovereignty over these islands. Japan's detention and investigation of the Chinese fishermen and fishing boat and all forms of its related judicial measures are illegal and invalid. Japan must offer China its apology and compensation for this incident.

On September 14, 2010, Foreign Ministry Spokesperson Jiang Yu held a regular press conference where he addressed on Japan's illegal detention of Chinese fishermen and the boat in the Diaoyu Island waters, it is imperative that Japan should immediately stop the so-called judicial process and let the captain return safely as soon as possible. He reiterated that China's position on the Diaoyu Islands issue has been clear. The islands have been inherent territories of China since ancient times, which is an unchangeable fact. China has indisputable sovereignty over islands. The determination of the Chinese government and people on safeguarding sovereignty and territorial integrity is unswerving

On September 13, Foreign Ministry spokesperson Jiang Yu said the 14 Chinese fishermen were freed by Japan, and returned home on a chartered flight and the trawler, which was "illegally detained by the Japanese side", also set off for home on the morning of September 13th. But Japan continued to hold the captain. China again urged Japan to immediately release the captain.

On September 12, State Councilor Dai Bingguo summoned Japan's Ambassador Uichiro Niwa for the fourth time and warned Tokyo not to make a wrong judgment on the situation and urged it to make a "wise political resolution". He urged Japan to immediately release the Chinese fishermen and the Chinese fishing boat. On the same day, Foreign Ministry Spokesperson Jiang Yu said on Japan's illegal detention of Chinese fishermen and the boat in the Diaoyu Island waters, it is imperative that Japan should immediately stop the so-called judicial process.

On September 10, 2010, Foreign Minister Yang Jiechi summoned Japanese Ambassador to China Uichiro Niwa and lodged a solemn representation to and a strong protest with Japan over the illegal detaining of the Chinese fishing boat and fishermen in the waters of Diaoyu Islands. He stressed that the Chinese government's determination to defend the sovereignty of the Diaoyu Islands and the interests of Chinese people was unswerving. He urged the Japanese side release the Chinese fishermen including the captain and the Chinese fishing boat the unconditionally. Foreign Minister Spokesperson Jiang Yu expressed his strong dissatisfaction and firm opposition to Japan's seizure of the captain.

On September 9, 2010, Foreign Ministry Spokesperson Jiang Yu held a regular press conference where he stressed that the Diaoyu Island and its affiliated islands are inherent territories of China. It is absurd, illegal and invalid that Japan applies its domestic law to Chinese fishing boats working in those waters, and absolutely unacceptable to China.

On September 8, 2010, Chinese Assistant Foreign Minister Hu Zhengyue summoned Japan's ambassador Uichiro Niwa to lodge the protest. Hu demanded that Japan immediately release the ship and crew members and guarantee their safety.

On September 7, 2010, Foreign Ministry Spokesperson Jiang Yu held a regular press conference where he addressed that China is seriously concerned over the collision happened between a Japanese patrol boat and a Chinese fishing boat in the Diaoyu Island waters, and has made solemn representations with Japan. Vice Foreign Minister Song Tao summoned Japan's ambassador Uichiro Niwa to China and lodged solemn representations on the interception of the Chinese fishing boat. He urged Japan to stop the illegal interception.

On May 28, 2010, when answering the reporter's' question of the Diaoyu Islands issue, the Foreign Ministry spokesperson Ma Zhaoxu said the Diaoyu Island and its affiliated islands have been inherent territories of China since ancient times. China has indisputable sovereignty over islands.

On May 4, 2010, China and Japan held the first round of direct talks concerning the East China Sea issues. The two sides exchanged views on relevant issues and agreed to continue to maintain contacts and work together.

On March 18, 2010, Foreign Ministry Spokesperson Qin Gang held a regular press conference. When answering the reporter's' question concerning the Diaoyu Islands issue, he answered the islands have been inherent territories of China since ancient times. China has indisputable sovereignty over these islands.

On February 23, 2010, Foreign Ministry Spokesperson Qin Gang held a regular press conference where he stressed that we hope the Japanese side can take concrete measures to create favorable atmosphere and conditions for the implementation of the principled consensus.

On January 18, 2010 , Foreign Ministry Spokesperson Ma Zhaoxu commented on exploitation of Chuanxiao field. He said the sovereign right of Chuanxiao field belongs to China. China will firmly safeguard the legitimate rights in the East China Sea.

July 18, 2009, when answering the reporter's' question of the Diaoyu Islands issue, the Foreign Ministry spokesperson Qin Gang answered that China's position on the Diaoyu Islands issue has been clear. The islands have been inherent territories of China since ancient times, which is an unchangeable fact. China has indisputable sovereignty over islands.

February 27, 2009, Foreign Ministry Spokesperson Ma Zhaoxu said China had lodged a solemn representation to Japan over the remarks made by Japanese and Chinese officials that the Diaoyu Islands could be applied to the Japan-US Security Treaty and urged the United States to clarify the relevant reports.

On February 26, 2009, Foreign Ministry Spokesperson Ma Zhaoxu held a regular press conference where he commented on the remarks made by Japanese official that the islands were inherent territories of Japan. He said China had lodged a solemn representation to Japan with strong dissatisfaction.

On February 10, 2009, Head of the Asian Department of the Foreign Ministry lodged a solemn representation to Japanese Ambassador because of the remakes that Japanese Patrol helicopters could stay on the waters of the Diaoyu Islands permanently. This official stressed the Diaoyu Island and its affiliated islands have been China's sacred territory since ancient times. China has indisputable sovereignty over islands. If the Japanese side took upgraded actions on the Diaoyu Islands issue, China will have to make a strong response. The Japanese side should have a clear understanding.

On February 5, 2009, Foreign Ministry Spokesperson Jiang Yu held a regular press conference where he addressed that any action by the Japanese side to strengthen actual control over the Diaoyu islands should be stopped immediately.

On January 6, 2009, Foreign Ministry Spokesperson Qin Gang held a regular press he answered that we hope Japan will not misinterpret the principled consensus that the two countries have reached.

On January 4, 2009, Foreign Ministry Spokesperson Qin Gang's remarked on the so-called China's unilateral exploitation of Tianwaitian oil and gas field. He said the sovereign right of Tianwaitian oil and gas field belongs to China. China is exercising its lawful sovereign rights by exploiting of Tianwaitian oil and gas field.

On December 9, 2008, Foreign Ministry Spokesperson Liu Jianchao held a regular press conference where he addressed: we cannot accept the accusation that China takes proactive actions in the region. China does not see its usual patrol in waters within China's jurisdiction as proactive. It is up to China to decide when to send marine surveillance ships to patrol the region again.

On July 17, 2008, Foreign Ministry Spokesperson Liu Jianchao held a regular press conference. He solemnly reiterated on many occasions, China owns indisputable sovereignty over the Diaoyu Island and its affiliated islands which have been part of China's territory since ancient times. It cannot be denied that China and Japan have disputes over the sovereignty of Diaoyu Island. We maintain that the disputes should be settled through negotiations.

On June 30, 2008, Head of the Asian Department of the Foreign Ministry summoned Japanese Ambassador as Japan let some Japanese congressmen make a so-called "inspection from the air" over the Diaoyu Islands regardless of China's solemn representation and opposition. The official stressed that the Diaoyu Island and its affiliated islands have been China's sacred territory since ancient times. China has indisputable sovereignty over islands. China urged it to immediately stop taking actions that harm China's territorial sovereignty so as to prevent similar incident from happening again.

On June 19, 2008, Vice Foreign Minister Wu Dawei made comments on the principled consensuses reached between China and Japan on the East China Sea issue. He stressed that the sovereign right of Chuanxiao field belongs to China. The cooperative exploitation of Chuanxiao field in accordance with the Chinese law is totally different from the joint exploitation of the East China Sea.

On June 18, 2008, Foreign Ministry Spokesperson Jiang Yu's Remarked on the principle consensus on the East China Sea issue between leaders of China and Japan. He addressed through the sincere consultation between China and Japan, they agreed on realizing the transitional period before the delimitation of the relevant waters. Without damage to the respective legal positions of the parties, we could take the first step to conduct the joint exploitation of an appropriate area of the East China Sea.

China and Japan reached consensus on the East China Sea issue and reached an understanding on the first step of the joint exploitation, which was an important step for the consensus of peaceful, cooperative and friendly sea between the two countries and the win-win results of seeking common ground and equal consultation. Achieving the above outcomes was conducive to peace and stability of the East China Sea, the mutually beneficial cooperation between the two countries and the stable development of Sino-Japanese relations. Moreover, it conformed to the fundamental interests of the two peoples.

On June 17, 2008, Foreign Ministry Spokesperson Jiang Yu held a regular press conference where he addressed: the Chinese Government expresses grave concern over a Japanese vessel colliding with a fishing boat from Taiwan around the Diaoyu Islands which led to the sinking of the latter. We have already stated our principled position on this incident. I'd like to stress that the Diaoyu Island and its adjacent islands have been China's territory since ancient time, and China has indisputable sovereignty over it. We urge the Japanese Government to stop the illegitimate activities in the sea waters around the Diaoyu Island so as to prevent similar incident from happening again.

On June 17, 2008, Foreign Ministry Spokesperson Jiang Yu held a regular press conference where he addressed: China and Japan will make public announcement in due course after reaching agreements on the East China Sea issue. I want to stress that the two countries will properly deal with relevant issues in accordance with the important consensus of the leaders of the two countries on making the East China Sea a sea of peace, cooperation and friendship. Relevant results will be mutually-beneficial and win-win in nature. I'd like to reiterate that China's consistent position and policy on the relevant issues concerning the East China Sea remain unchanged. The Chunxiao oil and gas field is completely within China's sovereign rights and it has nothing to do with the joint development. On the delimitation of the East China Sea, China's position on not recognizing the median line remains unchanged.

On March 13, 2008, Foreign Ministry Spokesperson Qin Gang held a regular press conference where he addressed: I would like to point out that the report by the Japanese media is totally unfounded and reaffirm that on the East China Sea issue China's position and claims stand on a solid international legal base. Meanwhile, China and Japan should resolve the dispute through negotiations in accordance with the United Nations Convention on the Law of the Sea. At present, both China and Japan agree to proceed from the overall situation of the bilateral ties and discuss the issue of "putting aside disputes and seeking joint exploration", which would benefit both countries.

On January 29, Foreign Ministry Spokesperson Jiang Yu held a regular press conference where he stressed: as for negotiation over the East China Sea, China is ready to work together with Japan to follow the new consensus between leaders of the two countries, and continue to keep the momentum of consultation in a sincere and positive attitude.

On December 25, Foreign Ministry spokesperson Qin Gang held a regular press conference. He stressed: China and Japan have disputes over the East China Sea issue and have encountered some difficulties during the process of negotiations. China has always adopted an active and pragmatic approach to the negotiations on the East China Sea issue. In light of the principle of "putting aside the disputes for joint development" and the five-point consensus reached between leaders of the two countries, China would continue to negotiate with Japan on an equal footing to seek a solution acceptable to both. We hope that Japan would work together and meet half way with China for the early proper settlement of the issue.

On November 15, Foreign Ministry Spokesperson Liu Jianchao held a regular press conference. As for the question, China and Japan have agreed to raise East China Sea consultation to the ministerial-level. It's reported that failure to reach a consensus may affect Prime Minister Yasuo Fukuda's visit to China. Do you have any comment? He answered: during the just concluded round of East China Sea consultation between China and Japan, China fully expressed its positive attitude and sincerity to settle the differences and realize joint exploration through friendly consultation. China is ready to press ahead with the consultation in line with the principle and spirit in the Five-Point Consensus reached by leaders of the two countries. We will make positive efforts to safeguard the stability of the East China Sea and realize joint exploration. China also hopes that the Japanese side can make due efforts to this end.

On the afternoon of November 13, Foreign Ministry Spokesperson Liu Jianchao held a regular press conference. He said: China will continue to base our work on the consensus reached between the leaders of the two countries, conducting the consultation in a positive and pragmatic manner. We hope Japan make its due efforts to meet with us half way.

On October 19, Foreign Ministry Spokesperson Liu Jianchao said: China takes the East China Sea consultation seriously and has made due efforts to press ahead. I'd like to stress that whether any consensus could be reached over this issue depends on the joint efforts of the two parties. The criticism from the Japanese side was nonsense.

On October 11, Foreign Ministry Spokesperson Liu Jianchao held a regular press conference. He said: China will continue to press ahead with the consultation of East China Sea issue proactively and pragmatically on the basis of the consensus reached by the leaders of China and Japan so as to find a joint development plan acceptable to both. We hope Japan make its efforts to meet with us half way.

On the afternoon of May 24, Foreign Ministry Spokesperson Jiang Yu held a regular press conference. He said: during Premier Wen Jiabao's visit to Japan, the two countries issued the Joint Press Communique. Leaders of the two countries reached five consensuses on the East China Sea issue, which includes making the East China Sea a sea of peace, cooperation and friendship, and carrying out joint development based on the principle of mutual benefit as a temporary arrangement pending the final demarcation and without prejudice to the positions of either side on matters concerning the law of the sea. They also agreed to carry out joint development in larger waters acceptable to both. As for the so-called "median line" issue you mentioned, China's position is very clear and remains unchanged. The so-called "median line" is a unilateral claim of Japan, which China never accepted and will not accept in the future. China will not have any discussion of joint development under the precondition of "median line".

On April 12, Foreign Ministry Spokesman Qin Gang held a regular press conference. He said: China is willing to draw on the helpful experiences of Japan and step up energy cooperation with them.

On March 9, 2006, Foreign Ministry Spokesman Qin Gang held a regular press conference where he said Diaoyu Islands and those adjacent islands have always been China's territory, over which China has indisputable sovereignty. It is baseless for Japan to reject China's proposal under the precondition that "Diaoyu Islands is Japan's territory". We have time and again made our position clear on the exploration of the Chunxiao oil and gas field. The exploration of Chunxiao is conducted in China's short sea which is under no dispute with Japan. It is normal sovereign activity. China has also reiterated this stance to Japan back and forth during the East Sea consultations. Japan's plan raised during the third round of the East Sea consultation last year departed from its unilateral claim which was unacceptable to China. "The Median Line" is a unilateral claim of Japan, which China has never accepted and will not accept in the future. Our proposal complies with the actual situation of the East Sea and is a rational and reasonable proposal, which embodies the principle of "putting aside disputes and conducting joint exploration" and the attitude of solving disputes through consultation. We hope that Japan would make an earnest study of China's proposal.

On September 29, 2006, Foreign Ministry Spokesman Qin Gang held a regular press conference where he talked on China's exploration of the "tianwaitian" oil and gas issue, he said: as we have expressed position on many occasions, I would like to reiterate here that it is a normal activity conducted in China's continental shelf of the East China Sea, hence beyond criticism.

On September 27, 2005, Foreign Ministry Spokesman Qin Gang held a regular press conference where he said that China's position on the Diaoyu Islands issue has been clear and consistent. The islands have been inherent territories of China since ancient times. China and Japan had disputes over the sovereignty over the Diaoyu Islands, we advocated to properly resolve the issue through negotiations.

On July 15, 2005, director of the Asian Department of the Foreign Ministry Cui Tiankai strongly protested Japan's violations of China's sovereign over the East China Sea.

On May 31, 2005, Foreign Ministry Spokesperson Kong Quan said according to the provisions of Article 77 of "UNCLOS":

"The coastal State exercises over the continental shelf sovereign rights for the purpose of exploring it and exploiting its natural resources." The exploration of Chunxiao is conducted in China's short sea which is under no dispute with Japan. It is normal sovereign activity. The position of China was "putting aside disputes and conducting joint exploration"...The exploration of the East Sea was in accordance to the provisions of "UNCLOS" and was normal sovereign activity. China was entitled to do that.

On May 19, 200, Foreign Ministry Spokesman Kong Quan stressed that the Diaoyu Island and its affiliated islands have been China's sacred territory since ancient times, for which China has plentiful historical and jurisprudential evidence. Japan's any unilateral action on the Diaoyu Islands was a serious violation of China's territorial sovereignty and was illegal and invalid. China showed total disregard of it and absolutely didn't accept it.

On April 14, 2005, Foreign Ministry Spokesperson Qin Gang said that China and Japan have disputes over the delimitation of the East China Sea, we have always advocated the two sides to resolve it through diplomatic negotiations. The Japanese side attempted to imposed the unilaterally claimed "The Median Line" on China regardless of China's legitimate position. China has never acknowledged and will not admit it. It was a serious provocation to China's rights and norms of international relations. The exploration of oil and gas is conducted in China's short sea which is under no dispute with Japan. It is normal sovereign activity. We hope we can resolve it through diplomatic negotiations and put forward the advocate of "putting aside disputes and conducting joint exploration". We hope Japan can give a positive response.

On July 7, 2004, Vice Foreign Minister Wang Yi lodged a solemn representation to Japan for conducting marine survey on resources in the East China Sea.

On March 25, 2004 , Foreign Ministry Spokesperson Kong Quan said I am afraid that we don't have much time if I use 2 to 3 hours to introduce the history and legal issues is of the Diaoyu Islands to you. I recommend you an article published on the October 18, 1996 in the People's Daily. Its title is Sovereignty over the Diaoyu Islands. This article comprehensively expounded the historical and jurisprudential evidence and international documents about China's Sovereignty over the Diaoyu Islands, as well as the Chinese government's attitude.

(Compiled according to fmprc.gov.cn, xinhua.net and people.com.cn)

II.VII. Statement by the Ministry of Foreign Affairs of the People's Republic of China

September 25, 2010

On September 7, 2010, Japan illegally arrested and detained 15 Chinese fishermen and their fishing boat in the waters off the Diaoyu Island. The captain was detained by Japan until September 24. These actions seriously violated China's territorial sovereignty and the human rights of the Chinese nationals. The Chinese government hereby expresses its strong protest.

The Diaoyu Island and its affiliated islands have been China's territory since ancient times. China has indisputable sovereignty over these islands. Japan's detention and investigation of the Chinese fishermen and fishing boat and all forms of its related judicial measures are illegal and invalid. Japan must offer China its apology and compensation for this incident.

China and Japan are close neighbors. It serves the fundamental interests of the people of the two countries to stay committed to the development of the strategic relationship of mutual benefit. China holds the position that the two sides should resolve problems in their relations through dialogue and consultation for the benefit of overall relations. This position has not changed and will not change.

II.VIII. The Statement of Ministry of Foreign Affairs of the People's Republic of China on the Sovereignty over the Diaoyu Islands

December 30, 1971

In recent years, despite of the strong opposition from the Chinese side, Sato government has repeatedly claimed that Japan has "sovereignty" over China's Diaoyu Islands. It colludes with the US imperialism and conducts various activities to misappropriate the above islands. A few days ago, the United States Congress and Japanese Congress passed the Okinawa Reversion Agreement, wherein the Diaoyu Islands were mapped into the handover area. It is a flagrant and intolerable violation of China's territorial sovereignty.

The US and Japanese governments jointly created the scam that the Okinawa was returned to Japan, which is a serious step to strengthen the partnership between the United States and Japan so as to accelerate the resurrection of Japanese militarism. The Chinese government and the Chinese people wholeheartedly support the Japanese people to smash the scam and fight heroically for the unconditional and overall return of Okinawa. The Chinese government and the Chinese people strongly oppose the US and Japanese reactionaries make exchanges with China's Diaoyu Islands and use it to provoke the friendly relations between China and Japan.

The Diaoyu Island and its affiliated islands have been China's sacred territory since ancient times. Since the Ming Dynasty, the Diaoyu Islands have been put under the jurisdiction of China's naval defense. They are the affiliated islands of Taiwan rather than Ryukyu (Okinawa). The boundary between China and Ryukyu is between the Chiwei Yu and Kume Island; Chinese fishermen in Taiwan had always been engaged in production activities on the Diaoyu Islands. The Japanese government stole these islands during the Sino-Japanese War (1894-1895); in April 1895, Japan forced the Qing government to sign the Treaty of Shimonoseki – ceding Taiwan and all its affiliated islands as well as the Penghu Islands. At present, Sato government uses these Japan's invasions of China's territories as the proof of Japan's sovereignty over the Diaoyu Islands, which is nothing but entire gangster logic.

After World War II , the Japanese government handed over Taiwan's affiliated islands – the Diaoyu Islands – to the US without permission and the US government unilaterally announced that it had so-called "administration rights" over these islands. It is absolutely illegal. Shortly after the founding of People's Republic of China, on June 28, 1950, Foreign Minister Zhou Enlai on behalf of the Chinese Government strongly condemned the US imperialism sent the 7th Fleet to invade Taiwan and the Taiwan Strait. He declared a solemn statement on the Chinese people's determination of "recovering Taiwan and all the territories belonging to China." Now, the US and Japan had underhand secret dealings on China's Diaoyu Islands. This violation of China's territorial sovereignty arouses strong indignation and condemnation from the Chinese people.

Ministry of Foreign Affairs of the People's Republic of China declared a solemn statement that Diaoyu Island, Huangwei Yu, Chiwei Yu, Nanxiao Island, Beixiao Island, etc. are affiliated islands of Taiwan. Just like Taiwan, they are China's inalienable territories. The Diaoyu Islands were mapped into the handover area by Japan and the United States in the Okinawa Reversion Agreement in 1971, which is totally illegal; it couldn't change China's territorial sovereignty over the Diaoyu Island and its affiliated islands. The Chinese people are determined to liberate Taiwan! The Chinese people are also determined to recover the affiliated islands of Taiwan such as the Diaoyu Islands!

(An excerpt from Literature Collection of the Postwar China-Japan Relations During 1971-1995, page 61-62.)

II.IX. The Statement of Zhou Enlai, the Ministry of Foreign Affairs of the Central People's Government of the People's Republic of China, on the Treaty of Peace with Japan Signed by the US and Its Vassal States

September 18, 1951

September 18, 1931 marked the occurrence of Shenyang incident. The Japanese imperialism launched an armed aggression against China. From then on, the Chinese people has started an armed anti-Japanese struggle. On July 7, 1937, Japanese imperialism launched the Marco Polo bridge incident, attempting to further conquer China. It developed into China's Anti-Japanese War. The Chinese people had heroically struggled in the war for eight years until the surrender of Japanese imperialism. Hard facts have proved that the Chinese people suffered the greatest sacrifice and made the most contribution for the longest time in the great war against Japanese imperialism. However, regardless of the international agreements, the US Government rejected the People's Republic of China flagrantly. On September 4, 1951, the US Government single-handedly held the San Francisco Conference where it signed Treaty of Peace with Japan on September 8, which aroused all the Chinese people's resentment and objections. The Central People's Government of the People's Republic of China felt it is necessary to reiterate that my authorized statement on the Treaty of Peace with Japan Signed by the US and the UK and the San Francisco Conference on August 15, 1951 continues to be valid; meanwhile I am authorized to declare the following statement:

1. The Treaty of Peace with Japan signed in the San Francisco Conference is a unilateral treaty without the participation of China. It is by no means a comprehensive treaty or a valid treaty. Instead, it is only a treaty to resurrect

the Japanese militarism, feud China and the Soviet Union, threaten Asia and prepare new wars of aggression. A few hours after the signing of the Treaty of Peace with Japan by the US government and the Japanese Yoshida government, they again signed the Japan-US Security Treaty to rearm Japan and clear roads for making Japan the military base of US completely. All these are hard proofs of the US Government's attempt to prepare for a larger-scale war of aggression in Asia and the Far East. The Central People's Government of the People's Republic of China believes that it poses a serious threat for the safety of the People's Republic of China and many other Asian countries. The Chinese people are and will oppose the US Government's vicious attempt to prepare for a larger-scale war of aggression in Asia and the Far East by virtue of Treaty of Peace with Japan and Japan-US Security Treaty.

2. Because of the US government's savage and unreasonable refusal of the suggestion of inviting China to join the San Francisco Conference made by representatives from the Soviet Union, Poland and the Czech republic, its rejection of the basic advice on the peace treaty with Japan from the Soviet Union according to the international agreements as well as the advice made by India and Myanmar and its ignoring Asian countries' will and hope, we can say that the Treaty of Peace with Japan signed in the San Francisco Conference goes against the wills of the Chinese people, the people of the Soviet Union, the Asian people as well as the people all over the world. The Treaty of Peace with Japan and the Japan-US Security Treaty created by the US by no means brings peace to Asia and the world; it only intensifies the situations in Asia and the world. Undoubtedly, the US Government's preparation to cause tensions in the Asia and the world this time is the same as its armed intervention to North Korea, which is abound to arouse the firm opposition of the Asian people and the people all over the world. The Chinese people are willing to cooperate with people all over the world, the Asian people as well as all countries that oppose the Treaty of Peace with Japan, especially the Asian countries to stop the threat of enlarging the Far East wars caused by the Treaty of Peace with Japan and the Japan-US Security Treaty so as to secure the peace in Asia and the world.

3. The Treaty of Peace with Japan and The Japan-US Security Treaty is not totally favorable for Japan. They aim to drag Japan into a new war of aggression and to destruct Japanese people. As the Japanese ruling class is mainly the reactionary group serving for the US, they have the delusion of the resurrection of militarism and unexpectedly signed the Treaty of Peace with Japan and The Japan-US Security Treaty at the cost of their national independence and sovereignty; hence, Japan is facing the unprecedented national crisis. This will arouse Japanese people's opposition to US imperialism's aggressive policy and the Japan traitors group and make them fight against them. The Central People's Government of the People's Republic of China is willing to see the Japanese people obtain heir democracy, independence, peace and progress. The Chinese

people are willing to live in peace with the Japanese people to secure peace in the Far East. Therefore, we welcome and feel sympathy for the Japanese patriotic people's fight against the traitorous treaty in the San Francisco Conference and their efforts of ending the war between the two countries immediately and safeguarding the peaceful relations between the two countries. We firmly believe that the Japanese people's struggle will also be able to get the warm welcome and support from the peace-loving people all over the world and we also believe that the Japanese people are bound to win in the end.

The Central People's Government of the People's Republic of China once again declares: if the People's Republic of China is excluded from the preparation, formulation and signing of the peace treaty with Japan, it will, no matter what its content and outcome are, be regarded as illegal and therefore invalid by the Central People's Government of China.

(Published on the front page of People's Daily on September 19, 1951)

II.X. The Statement of Foreign Minister Zhou Enlai on the Issue of Treaty of Peace with Japan

December 4, 1950

The Central People's Government of the People's Republic of China studied the memorandum delivered from the US State Department adviser Mr. Dulles to the Soviet Union Representative Mr. Malik of UN Security Council on October 26, 1950 as well as the memorandum delivered from Mr. Malik to Mr. Dulles. Later, The Central People's Government of the People's Republic of China authorized me to declare statement on peace treaty with Japan:

Since September 18, 1931, the armed Japanese imperialist declared war of aggression against China and ravaged China's vast territory, making the Chinese suffer from property loss and great sacrifice. After eight years' struggle, the Chinese people defeated the Japanese imperialists and won the victory of the Anti-Japanese War. Therefore, the People's Republic of China has all the rights to participate in the preparation and signing of the Treaty of Peace with Japan. It should be reiterated that the Central People's Government of the People's Republic of China is the only legal government representing the Chinese people, so it has all the rights to participate in the preparation and signing of the Treaty of Peace with Japan. The Chinese Kuomintang reactionary residual group can't represent the Chinese people, so it has no right to participate in the preparation and signing of the Treaty of Peace with Japan. If the People's Republic of China is excluded from the preparation, formulation and signing of the peace treaty with Japan, it will, no matter what its content and outcome are, be regarded as illegal and therefore invalid by the Central People's Government.

2.According to the Sino-Soviet Treaty of Friendship, Alliance and Mutual Assistance between the People's Republic of China and the Soviet Socialist Republic on February 14, 1950, China and the Soviet Union agreed on signing peace treaty with Japan as soon as possible together with other Allies during the Second World War. It shows that the basic principle of the Central People's Government of the People's Republic of China is to sign peace treaty with Japan as soon as possible so as to end the war against Japan and give democracy and peace to the Japanese people. In contrast, the US Government has implemented long-term military occupation on Japan and conducted delaying policy about the Treaty of Peace with Japan. Since 1947, the US government has repeatedly tried to reverse the pattern of the peace treaty with Japan and destroyed the principle that the peace treaty with Japan should be discussed by the foreign ministers of China, the Soviet Union, the United States, and the UK. Besides, the United States government further attempted to overthrow the foundation of the peace treaty with Japan.

3. The international documents such as the Cairo Declaration, the Yalta Declaration, the Potsdam Declaration and related provisions for Japan after its surrender made by the Far Eastern Commission on June 19, 1947 are the main base of signing the peace treaty with Japan. However, the first article of the memorandum delivered from the US Government to the Soviet government proposed "the contracting state: any country willing to sign peace treaty with Japan based on the suggested or possible agreement". That is to say the US government has declared to overthrow the Cairo Declaration, the Yalta Declaration, the Potsdam Declaration and related provisions for Japan after its surrender made by the Far Eastern Commission. In the memorandum, the US government was clearly trying to make its suggested or possible agreement the base of the Treaty of Peace with Japan, replacing the international agreements such as the Cairo Declaration, the Yalta Declaration, the Potsdam Declaration and related provisions for Japan after its surrender made by the Far Eastern Commission that meet the interests of the people of the world and the people of Japan. It forced other Allies to accept its suggested or possible agreement, thus the US government has brazenly signed a separate peace treaty with Japan according to its own plan, which excluded other Allies.

4. Taiwan and the Penghu Islands have been returned to China in accordance with the Cairo Declaration; the southern Sakhalin Islands and the Kuril Islands have been returned to the Soviet Union in accordance with the Yalta Declaration. There is no need to re-discuss all these settled territorial issues. The US government wants to re-decide these territorial issues, which completely destroys the established international agreements and deliberately infringes upon the lawful rights and interests of the People's Republic of China and the Soviet Union so as to achieve the goal of aggression. The US Government's armed invasion of China's Taiwan is obvious evidence. As for the Ryukyu

Islands and the Ogasawara Islands, there is no article concerning their trusteeship in the Cairo Declaration or the Potsdam Declaration, let alone appointing the US as the administration authorities. The US Government, under the guise of the name of the United Nations, has implemented the long-term occupation of the Ryukyu Islands and the Ogasawara Islands to achieve its ambition to establish military bases for invasion in the Far East.

5. According to the provisions of the Potsdam Declaration, the occupying forces should retreat from Japan. However, the US government doesn't has the slightest tendency to retreat its forces from Japan as soon as possible and aims to use Japan as the war bases for the aggression against Korea and China. The memorandum delivered from the US government to the Soviet government required that the peace treaty with Japan should allow the continuous cooperation between Japan's equipment and the US military so as to maintain the international peace and security in Japan, which is equivalent to forcing the Japanese people to accept a long-term US military presence in Japan and the aggression against the Asian people.

6. Provisions for Japan after its surrender made by the Far Eastern Commission originally stipulated that Japan shall not hold any army, navy, air force, the secret police and military police. That is to say, no one should arm Japan. However, the US government promotes the militarization of Japan publicly just like it did with Germany. As we all known, USn occupation forces aim to rebuild Japan's army under the name of the Japanese police, rebuild Japan's navy under the name of Japan Coast Guard, reserving and building the Japanese air port and establish Japan's air force by training the personnel of Japan airlines, retaining and building Japanese air force base. The US occupation authorities released a large number of important war criminals, removed purge and recovered fascists' activities in order to rebuild the Japanese forces of aggression. The US government attempts to use its military control so as to make Japan completely a US-colony and to make Japan a US tool to control and suppress the Asian nations.

7. In order to improve the living conditions of the Japanese people, the Central People's Government of the People's Republic of China hope that Japan's peace industry develops for the interest of the Japanese people. According to provisions for Japan after its surrender made by the Far Eastern Commission the existing economic basis of the Japanese military forces must be destroyed and should never be resurrected. But in fact, the US occupation authorities going from the interests of the US monopoly capital recovers and develops Japan's war industry, and uses it to invade North Korea and Taiwan of China. On the contrary, the peace industry is dispirited. The US Government's policy of hanging the Japanese peace industry and encouraging its war industry only destroys the Japanese people's peaceful life and aggravates the economic exploitation of the Japanese people.

8. The US government's proposed scheme about the Treaty of Peace with Japan in the memorandum completely violated the purpose of the Allies' joint fight against Japan and destroyed all international agreement on policies for Japan. At the same time, it obliterated the basic interests of the Chinese people's struggle in the Anti-Japanese War and ignored the Japanese people's desire for the future. The US government has only one extremely selfish purpose that it wants to usurp Japan, enslave the Japanese people, and make Japan a US- colony and a military base for aggression against the Asian nations. Therefore, the US's advice on the Treaty of Peace with Japan in the memorandum goes against the interests of the Chinese people and the Japanese people. The Chinese people are willing to work with other Allies during the Second World War to sign the peace treaty with Japan as soon as possible, but it should be in accordance with the Cairo Declaration, the Yalta Declaration, the Potsdam Declaration and related provisions for Japan after its surrender made by the Far Eastern Commission. The peace treaty with Japan based on these international agreements can realize Japan's democratization, remove the Japanese forces of aggression and prevent Japanese forces of aggression from resurrecting. A democratic Japan without any influence over it by an external force control can be conducive to the peace and security in Asia.

(Xinhua News Agency, Beijing on December 4, 1950)

Chapter II

Scholars' Papers and Newspaper Commentaries

I. Ironclad Evidence Shows that Diaoyu Islands is China's Territory

October 2012

by Guo Jiping

On September 10, the Japanese government announced its decision to "purchase" China's Diaoyu Island and its affiliated Nanxiao Island and Beixiao Island in a bid to "nationalize" these islands. In the wake of it, the Chinese government expressed solemn position and adopted strong countermeasures, the Chinese people voiced strong indignation and demonstrated enormous cohesiveness against the Japanese move, and the voice of justice and great alarm was heard in the international community. All these acts have given a serious blow to the arrogance of the Japanese side. Yet Japan has obstinately refused to correct its erroneous position. On the contrary, it has continued to take unscrupulous steps to infringe upon China's territorial sovereignty and challenge the post-war international order.

I

"Let's calm the Diaoyu Islands issue. Let's look at the big picture of Japan-China relations. Let peace and stability be maintained in northeast Asia." Such were the rhetoric from Japan. But these ostensibly restrained and constructive gestures could not mask Tokyo's true intent and restlessness. The Japanese government claimed that "we cannot cede what we cannot cede" and that "Japan should make an all-out effort to strengthen its guard over the waters around the Senkaku Islands". Japanese right-wing forces also clamored for the building of facilities on Diaoyu Islands to strengthen Japan's capability to confront China.

On the evening of 21st September, quite a few Japanese personnel landed on Diaoyu Islands. The next day, right-wing groups staged anti-China protests in Tokyo, claiming that "China has invaded the Senkaku Islands"[1] and crying for "the stationing of Japan Self-Defense Forces on the Senkaku Islands". Besides, Japan Coast Guard assembled patrol vessels from its jurisdictions across Japan to guard the waters around Diaoyu Islands and interfere with routine patrol and protection missions of Chinese maritime surveillance vessels and fishery administration vessels in those waters.

On the occasion of the UN General Assembly session, Japanese Prime Minister Yoshihiko Noda went to great lengths to talk about the so-called "legal evidence" of Japanese sovereignty over Diaoyu Islands and insisted that there is no dispute between Japan and China over the issue. The Japanese Ministry of Foreign Affairs put together documents under the title "Three Truths about the Senkaku Islands" to summarize Japan's position and instructed Japanese embassies to communicate with their host countries accordingly. The Japanese Foreign Ministry also asked for an additional 600 million yen in its budget of the next fiscal year, which will be used to fund propaganda and research activities for the sake of "defending Japanese territory". Certain Japanese media outlets even resorted to the despicable act of making up stories to create the impression that other countries supported Japan's position.

In fact, not much was new in the "media offensive" Japan has mounted. It was full of clichés such as Diaoyu Islands being inherent Japanese territory based on historical facts and international law, and the goal of Japanese "nationalization" being to "continue its stable and secure management". However, to the extent that there was something new, it was as follows: China had not claimed sovereignty over Diaoyu Islands until the early 1970s; in the 1972 negotiations to normalize diplomatic relations and 1978 negotiations to conclude the China-Japan Treaty of Peace and Friendship, the leaders of China and Japan did not reach understanding or consensus to "shelve the dispute" over Diaoyu Islands; China's overreaction to the "island purchase" and widespread acts of violence against Japanese interests in China made Japan feel "under threat".

The truth of the matter is: Diaoyu Islands is an integral part of China, and Japan's usurpation of China's Diaoyu Islands is illegal and invalid. Japan's so-called "nationalization" of Diaoyu Islands and its affiliated Nanxiao Island and Beixiao Island constitutes serious encroachment on China's territorial sovereignty. This principled position of China has been stated comprehensively in an article titled "How Can Anybody Else Recklessly 'Buy' or 'Sell' China's Diaoyu Islands?", which was run by the People's Daily on 11th September under the byline of "Guo Jiping". In the article published today, we will use historical facts and norms of international law to expose the absurdity and sinister nature of the so-called "new points" in Japan's recent propaganda.

---

1   The Japanese side calls the Diayou islands as Senkaku Islands.

II

Japan has declared that China had not made a claim of sovereignty over Diaoyu Islands until the early 1970s. But what is the real historical situation?

Diaoyu Islands has been China's inherent territory since ancient times. It was marked as part of Chinese territory and administered as affiliated island of Taiwan as early as in the Ming and Qing Dynasties. At the end of the 19th century, Japan grabbed Diaoyu Islands during the Sino-Japanese War and forced the Qing government to sign the Treaty of Shimonoseki and cede to Japan "the island of Formosa (Taiwan), together with all islands appertaining or belonging to the said island of Formosa". That included Diaoyu Islands. In December 1941, the Chinese government officially declared war against Japan, together with the abrogation of all treaties between China and Japan. In December 1943, the Cairo Declaration stated in explicit terms that "all the territories Japan has stolen from the Chinese, such as Manchuria, Formosa (Taiwan) and the Pescadores, shall be restored to the Republic of China. Japan will also be expelled from all other territories which she has taken by violence and greed." In July 1945, the Potsdam Declaration stated in Article 8: "The terms of the Cairo Declaration shall be carried out and Japanese sovereignty shall be limited to the islands of Honshu, Hokkaido, Kyushu, Shikoku and such minor islands as we determine." On 2 September 1945, the Japanese government accepted the Potsdam Declaration in explicit terms with the Japanese Instrument of Surrender and pledged to faithfully fulfill the obligations enshrined in the provisions of the Potsdam Declaration. On 25 October 1945, the ceremony for accepting Japan's surrender in Taiwan Province of the China War Theater was held in Taipei, and the Chinese government officially recovered Taiwan. China has all along stressed that Japan should, in accordance with international legal documents such as the Cairo Declaration and the Potsdam Declaration, return to China all territories it has stolen from China, and that naturally includes Diaoyu Islands.

On September 8, 1951, Japan, the United States and a number of other countries signed the Treaty of Peace with Japan (commonly known as the Treaty of San Francisco) from which China was excluded. The Chinese government has always been opposed to such a treaty. Before the treaty was signed, Foreign Minister Zhou Enlai made a solemn statement: "If the People's Republic of China is excluded from the preparation, formulation and signing of the peace treaty with Japan, it will, no matter what its content and outcomes are, be regarded as illegal and therefore invalid by the central people's government." After the treaty was signed, Foreign Minister Zhou Enlai made another statement on 18 September 1951: "The peace treaty with Japan, signed arbitrarily by the US government at the San Francisco Conference without participation of the People's Republic of China, is illegal and invalid and could under no circumstances be recognized by the central people's government." The statement made it very clear that China has never recognized any provision of the Treaty of San Francisco regarding Chinese territory. That naturally included Diaoyu Islands. This position of China applies too to subsequent illegal US acquisition of trusteeship and transfer of Diaoyu Islands to Japan following the Treaty of San Francisco. All this serves to show that China's sovereignty claim over Diaoyu Islands is consistent and clear-cut. It has never changed, not even a bit.

In the current round of "media offensive", Japan has tried to play up isolated arguments that are seemingly in its favor. For instance, Japan has repeatedly stressed the point that Diaoyu Islands was marked as part of Japan's Okinawa in the 1958 and 1960 editions of the World Atlas published in China.

Since maps have been mentioned, we also want to devote adequate part of this article to facts related to maps.

The Roadmap to Ryukyu (Liu Qiu Guo Hai Tu) in the Record of the Imperial Title-Conferring Envoys to Ryukyu (Shi Liu Qiu Lu) written by imperial title-conferring envoy Xiao Chongye in 1579 (the seventh year of the reign of Emperor Wan Li of the Ming Dynasty), the Record of the Interpreters of August Ming (Huang Ming Xiang Xu Lu) written by Mao Ruizheng in 1629 (the second year of the reign of Emperor Chongzhen of the Ming Dynasty), the Great Universal Geographic Map (Kun Yu Quan Tu) created in 1767 (the 32nd year of the reign of Emperor Qianlong of the Qing Dynasty), and the Atlas of the Great Qing Dynasty (Huang Chao Zhong Wai Yi Tong Yu Tu) published in 1863 (the second year of the reign of Emperor Tongzhi of the Qing Dynasty) all marked Diaoyu Islands as China's territory.

The book Illustrated Outline of the Three Countries written by Hayashi Shihei in 1785 was the earliest Japanese literature to mention Diaoyu Islands. The Map of the Three Provinces and 36 Islands of Ryukyu in the book put Diaoyu Islands apart from the 36 islands of Ryukyu and colored it the same as the mainland of China, indicating that Diaoyu Islands was considered part of China's territory. Besides, the Maps and Names of Provinces and Cities in Japan published in 1892 did not mark Diaoyu Islands as part of Japanese territory.

The Map of East China Sea Littoral States created by the French cartographer Pierre Lapie and others in 1809 colored Diaoyu Islands, Huangwei Yu and Chiwei Yu the same as the Island of Taiwan. Maps such as A New Map of China from the Latest Authorities published in Britain in 1811, Colton's China published in the United States in 1859, and A Map of China's East Coast: Hongkong to Gulf of Liao-Tung compiled by the British Navy in 1877 all marked Diaoyu Islands as part of Chinese territory.

One particular edition of a map cannot be taken out of its context and used as evidence to reject the position of a government on issues concerning territory. This is common sense. The World Atlas editions cited by Japan that marked Diaoyu Islands as part of Japan's Okinawa clearly identified their sources of reference as being map archives of the pre-Anti-Japanese War Shen-pao (Shanghai News). That was the time when Diaoyu Islands was under Japan's colonial rule. Under international law, a particular edition of a map does not constitute the basis for claiming one's own rights or negating those of others. Therefore, Japan's argument that Diaoyu Islands is Japanese territory on the basis of the map in question is not at all convincing. In fact, many Japanese maps published before the 1970s did not mark Diaoyu Islands as part of Japan.

Japan's manner of treating such untenable evidence like a rare treasure and its attempt to make much out of it shows that Japan has exhausted itself and still could find little legal basis for its sovereignty claim over Diaoyu Islands and its affiliated islands.

Why was Japan put in such an awkward position? It is very clear. A country may dream wild dreams about waging wars of aggression and enslaving the Asian people. A country may develop illusions that it can whitewash its historical crimes with a wrong approach to history and become a "normal country" to be respected by other countries around the world. But in no way can historical facts be fabricated. A country that dares to challenge historical facts is dishonest and extremely dangerous. The international community should really watch out for such a country.

III

Japan claims that the leaders of Japan and China did not reach understanding and consensus on "shelving the dispute over Diaoyu Islands" during the negotiations for the normalization of bilateral relations in 1972 and the 1978 Sino-Japanese Treaty of Peace and Friendship. Could this be true? For the sake of clarity, let us look at the authoritative historical records, including the minutes of the talks.

It is known to all that it was with the China-Japan Joint Statement (1972) and the Sino-Japanese Treaty of Peace and Friendship (1978) that China and Japan finally ended the state of war and normalized bilateral relations. These two documents formed the bilateral legal basis for the resolution of the postwar ownership of relevant territories between China and Japan.

Under the third item of the China-Japan Joint Statement, which concerns the issue of Taiwan, the Japanese side explicitly committed that "it firmly maintains its stand under Article 8 of the Potsdam Declaration." It was further confirmed in the Sino-Japanese Treaty of Peace and Friendship that "the principles enunciated in the Joint Statement should be strictly observed." The core of Article 8 of the Potsdam Declaration referred to in the Joint Statement is that "The terms of the Cairo Declaration shall be carried out." To be more specific, as stated clearly in the Cairo Declaration, "All the territories Japan has stolen from the Chinese, such as Manchuria, Formosa (Taiwan) and the Pescadores, shall be restored to the Republic of China." This was a serious commitment Japan had made to the Chinese side in the form of bilateral treaties. Although it was a commitment made in the context of the issue of Taiwan, it is applicable to the issue of Diaoyu Islands because Diaoyu Islands is Taiwan's affiliated island. It is worth noting that the Cairo Declaration mentioned these territories in the form of non-exhaustive enumeration. What it emphasized was that the territories Japan had stolen from the Chinese through whatever means, be it Taiwan and the Pescadores, which had been formally ceded to Japan through the Treaty of Shimonoseki, or Manchuria, which had been under Japan's actual control through the puppet government, or Chinese territories stolen by Japan through other means, shall all be restored to China. Therefore, even though Japan claimed that Diaoyu Islands was not ceded to Japan in the Treaty of Shimonoseki as Taiwan's affiliated island, Japan could not deny that the island was stolen by Japan from China following the Sino-Japanese War of 1894-1895 and that the island, as such, must be restored to China.

During negotiations for the signing of the China-Japan Joint Statement and the Sino-Japanese Treaty of Peace and Friendship, Chinese and Japanese leaders, acting in the larger interest of bilateral relations, decided not to involve the issue of Diaoyu Islands for the time being and leave it to be resolved later. This, however, does not constitute an excuse for the Japanese side to deny its commitment afterwards. The principle that the postwar ownership of relevant territories should be resolved in accordance with the Cairo Declaration and the Potsdam Declaration, as enshrined in the China-Japan Joint Statement and the Sino-Japanese Treaty of Peace and Friendship, still applies to the issue of Diaoyu Islands.

At a recent press conference, Japanese Foreign Minister Koichiro Gemba cited from the conversation between Prime Minister Kakuei Tanaka and Premier Zhou Enlai in 1972 about Diaoyu Islands. He said that Japan and China did not reach common understanding on this issue. For the sake of clarity, let's again read the following conversation, which includes the main content which was really discussed:

Prime Minister Tanaka: I wish to take this opportunity to ask about China's attitude towards the Senkaku Islands.

Premier Zhou: I do not want to discuss this issue this time. It is no good discussing it now.

Prime Minister Tanaka: It may make things difficult for me when I go back if I did not mention this issue at all while I was in Beijing.

Premier Zhou: That's right, because oil has been discovered under that part of the sea. Now Taiwan is trying to make a big issue out of it. The United States might do so, too. The issue has been blown out of proportion.

That was where Minister Gemba's citation ended. But in fact, Prime Minister Tanaka went on to say: Alright. There is no need to discuss it then. Let's talk about it sometime in the future.

Premier Zhou: Let's talk about it in the future. This time, let us first resolve the big and fundamental issues that we can resolve, such as the normalization of bilateral relations. It is not that other issues are not "big", but that normalization of relations is pressing. Some issues need to be discussed at a later time.

Prime Minister Tanaka: I believe other issues can be resolved once the relations are normalized.

What issue were they referring to that needed to be resolved? It was quite clear with the Chinese and Japanese leaders. It was this—the Okinawa Reversion Agreement, signed between the United States and Japan on 17 June 1971, stated that the power of administration over the Ryukyu Islands and other islands shall be returned to Japan, and arbitrarily included Diaoyu Islands and its affiliated islands into the territories to be returned. On 30 December 1971, the Ministry of Foreign Affairs of China issued a statement, stressing that the backroom deals between the United States and Japan over Diaoyu Islands and other islands were completely illegal and could by no means change the People's Republic of China's territorial sovereignty over the Diaoyu Islands. So it was not vague at all what issue needed to be resolved. It was the issue of sovereignty over Diaoyu Islands. Minister Gemba cited only part of the conversation. Was it because he had no access to the full text? Or did he do it on purpose?

In October 1978, Vice Premier Deng Xiaoping visited Japan for the exchange of instruments of ratification of the Sino-Japanese Treaty of Peace and Friendship. Commenting on the issue of Diaoyu Islands at a press conference following his talks with Japanese Prime Minister Takeo Fukuda, Mr. Deng said, "When China and Japan normalized relations, both countries agreed not to involve this issue. When we negotiated the Sino-Japanese Treaty of Peace and Friendship, we also agreed not to deal with this issue. We believe that it is wiser to set the issue aside for a while if we couldn't bridge our difference this time. It is okay to temporarily shelve such an issue if our generation does not have enough wisdom to resolve it. The next generation will have more wisdom, and I am sure they will eventually find a way acceptable to both sides." No one on the Japanese side made any objection on this note.

Mr. Zhang Xiangshan, late advisor to the Chinese foreign ministry, and many others, both in China and Japan, have been personally involved in or witnessed these historical episodes surrounding the negotiations for the normalization of China-Japan relations and the conclusion of the Sino-Japanese Treaty of Peace and Friendship. They have each, in their own way, recounted these historical facts. Their accounts prove that both China and Japan were clear about whether the two countries had reached understanding and consensus on shelving the dispute over Diaoyu Islands.

Japan has proved to be a country that dared to alter and deny authoritative historical records from just a few decades ago. It even dared to change what had been put down in black and white in history. Is there anything Japan doesn't dare to do?

IV

Japan has confused right and wrong when it claimed that China has overreacted to Japan's "island purchase" and that China has staged massive acts of violence against Japan, which put Japan under threat.

There are ample historical and legal evidences to prove that the sovereignty over Diaoyu Islands belongs to China. After Japan staged the farce of "island purchase", China issued the Foreign Ministry's Statement and the Statement of the Government of the People's Republic of China on the Baselines of the Territorial Sea of Diaoyu Islands and its Affiliated Islands. Following that, the Foreign Affairs Committee of the National People's Congress, the Foreign Affairs Committee of the National Committee of the Chinese People's Political Consultative Conference, the spokesperson of the Ministry of National Defense and various social groups also issued statements or made remarks against the Japanese move. The entire Chinese nation all voiced condemnation of the despicable act of the Japanese government. China deposited the coordinates table and chart of the base points and baselines of the territorial sea of China's Diaoyu Islands and its affiliated islands with UN Secretary General Ban Ki-moon, and presented the Partial Submission concerning the outer limits of the continental shelf beyond 200 nautical miles in the East China Sea to the Commission on the Limits of the Continental Shelf. China's maritime surveillance vessels carried out law enforcement patrol missions in the waters of Diaoyu Islands and Chinese fishery administration vessels conducted routine law enforcement patrols to protect Chinese fishermen in the waters of Diaoyu Islands. These countermeasures are necessary steps taken to uphold China's territorial sovereignty and they embody the strong will and determination of the Chinese nation to safeguard its territorial sovereignty and maritime rights and interests.

Japan has claimed that China's strong reaction was beyond expectation. We have to ask then: Was Japan fancying a China that would display obedience and react otherwise on an issue that concerns its core interests, which is national sovereignty? The countermeasures taken by China are justified, effective and restrained. Being rooted on the international moral and legal high ground, China's position has been understood and supported by the international community and will stand the test of history.

China has acted in strict accordance with the Vienna Convention on Diplomatic Relations and the Vienna Convention on Consular Relations, and has taken measures to protect the interests of foreign institutions in China in accordance with law. The personnel of Japanese enterprises are safe in China. What has happened are isolated cases. Competent Chinese authorities have made serious investigation into these cases and dealt with them accordingly.

Japan has undeniably committed gross infringement upon China's territorial sovereignty. But it is playing the victim now by accusing China of "putting it under threat". Does this stand to logic? China has never threatened any country, nor will China ever put any country under any threat. However, should any country dare to cross the untouchable red line and harm China's core interests, China will never sit idly by. If Japan is truly afraid of being "threatened", it ought to think hard about how to correct its mistake now before slipping too far down the wrong path.

V

The Japanese government's announced "purchase" of China's Diaoyu Islands and its affiliated Nanxiao Island and Beixiao Island and their so-called "nationalization" is a serious violation of China's territorial sovereignty. The countermeasures taken by China have forcefully demonstrated China's position that sovereignty over Diaoyu Islands belongs to China as well as the legal evidences supporting China's position. They have effectively exposed the very nature of the farce Japan has staged, which is in essence a betrayal of the consensus and understanding reached with China, an outright denial of the outcomes of the World Anti-Fascist War and a challenge to the post-World War II international order.

China strongly urges Japan to face up to the current grave situation of China-Japan relations and recognize that there is dispute over the sovereignty of Diaoyu Islands. Japan should redress the erroneous act of violating China's sovereignty and come back to the track of resolving the Diaoyu Islands issue through negotiations. The Chinese government is firm and solid in its will to uphold China's territorial sovereignty. No one needs to have any illusion about or question China's determination.

Diaoyu Islands belongs to China. China stands on the right side of the issue. China is on the side of justice.

II. The Textual Research on Ceding the Diaoyu Islands in the Treaty of Shimonoseki

October, 2012

Wu Tianying

Editor's note: the author Wu Tianying, graduated from the History Department of Nankai University, and is currently a Prof. in Institute of Economics, Capital University of Economics and Business. Mr. Wu Tianying, a well-known scholar on Chinese social economic history, has been engaging in the research on well salt economic history of China, and has co-edited an article titled A Profile Album of Zigong Salt Industry Contract which was adopted in A Probe into the History of Well Salt. Prof. Wu Tianying has made intensive research on the issues of Diaoyu Islands, consequently, his monograph with substantial content premises the argument based on solid evidence. After his work The Textual Research on Sovereignty over the Diaoyu Islands before the Sino-Japanese War was published by Social Sciences Academic Press in 1994, its corresponding Hong Kong express edition and Japanese edition were published in succession. Besides, Prof. Wu Tianyu published a paper titled The Historical Analysis on Japan's Coveting and Forcibly Occupying Diayou Islands in the Latter Half of the 19th Century.

As his latest research result, Prof. Wu recently composed *The Textual Research on Sovereignty over the Diaoyu Islands before the Sino-Japanese War (Revised Edition)* which will be published by China Democracy and Law Press in the near future. According to the author, it is illegal and invalid either based on International law or Japanese law that the Japan incorporated the Diaoyu Island under the administration of Okinawa. With the author's permission, we excerpt one of the chapters The Textual Research on Ceding the Diaoyu Islands in Treaty of Shimonoseki.

The content of Treaty of Shimonoseki signed in April 17, 1895, was totally imposed on China by Japanese Militarism. The treaty stipulated that China ceded three districts: The first one was Liaodong Peninsula with distinct four boundaries as well as longitude and latitude. (The ceding of Liaodong Peninsula was not fulfilled due to the intervention of three countries.) The second one was Peng-hu, which was just written as Penghu Islands in the draft treaty made on April 6, however, in the formal signing, it was explicitly defined by "Penghu Islands"[2], namely, the islands located from 119 degrees to 120 degrees east longitude, 23 degrees to 24 degrees north latitude, Britain Greenwich.

---

2   Edited by Library of Congress: The Archive Catalogue of Japanese Ministry of Foreign Affairs, Washington D.C.: 1954, PVM. p. 1396. Collected by Microfilm reading room, National Library.

Nevertheless, Taiwan was ambiguously written as "the Taiwan Island" and its affiliated islands. In terms of Japan's numerous contradictory acts, the 14 January Cabinet resolution was like the first one of the dominoes. In order to let it stand erect, they would never admit that the Diaoyu Islands is a part of Chinese territory, especially that it is one of the affiliated island of Taiwan. In this way, they had to separate their act of grabbing the Diaoyu Islands from Sino-Japanese War which lasted from 1894 to 1895, and denied the this act's any relation with Treaty of Shimonoseki. With strong evidences, this paper aims to prove that Japan's grabbing the Diaoyu Islands originated from Treaty of Shimonoseki and further leave it to history to pronounce that the 14 January Cabinet Resolution was illegal and invalid. I will discuss the issue in the below 6 parts.

1) On June 2, 1895, during the handover of Taiwan, Chinese and Japanese representatives reached an agreement on defining "Taiwan and its affiliated islands, that is, the affiliated islands of Taiwan were based on the acknowledged chart or map.

The present existing Document on the Transition of Taiwan, however, did not define clearly about "Taiwan and its affiliated islands".

The plenipotentiary transition between China and Japan took place on March, 23, the 21st year during the reign of Emperor Guangxu, that is, April 17, the 28th year during the reign of Japanese Emperor Meiji, the second item in the treaty signed by the imperial plenipotentiary in Shimonoseki stated that China permanently ceded Taiwan and its affiliated islands to Japan, together with the govern sovereignty over Penghu Islands located from 119 degrees to 120 degrees east longitude, 23 degrees to 24 degrees north latitude, Britain Greenwich. The item also supplemented clearly all of the fortresses, Arsenals and public objects. For this, both Chinese and Japanese plenipotentiary were willing to establish a written document, that is, to make sure its existence with signatures and seal.

For a long time, Japan has been carefully avoiding to mention the specific process of the transition of Taiwan, particularly the real sense of Taiwan and its affiliated islands. In 1972, the lecturer from Japanese Kokushikan University (promoted to be the associate Prof. soon) stated vaguely:

As for the affiliated islands of Taiwan, the government of Qing Dynasty, greatly concerned that Japan would advocate that the islands near Fujian Province was divided into the affiliated islands of Taiwan, made the proposal of listing the specific names of the island. On the other hand, to Eliminate the Qing Dynasty's concern, Japanese government explained that there was Penghu Islands between Taiwan and Fujian, thus the Qing Dynasty was also eager to know the fact.[3]

---

3 Okuhara Toshio: Sovereignty over the Senkaku Islands, in: Asahi Asia Review, 1972(2).

As a matter of fact, in the afternoon of negotiating the transition of Taiwan on June 2, 1895, Chinese representative Li Jingfang and Japanese minister Mizuno Benri made a very brief negotiation. Considering that Treaty of Shimonoseki "did not indicate the domain of the affiliated islands of Taiwan, Li Jingfang proposed "If it's necessary to list the names of the affiliated islands of Taiwan in the content. With regard to it, the minister Mizuno Benri quibbled, "If we adopt the suggestion from your honor and list the names of each individual island, the islands that may be left out or the unnamed islands will be rendered unavailable to us. Mizuno Benri also emphasized the standard of division as follows: "The islands near Taiwan should be acknowledged as to the affiliated islands of Taiwan in the chart or the map." (See chart 1,23) In other words, they reached an agreement that the standards should be based on the basis of acknowledged and authoritative charts or maps.

Oppenheim's International Law clearly discussed on the issue of "interpretation of international treaties": "Each contracting party could choose an individual way when interpreting regardless of common rules of interpretation. They could adopt some kind of interpretation in an unofficial way[4], and implement the treaty according to this interpretation.

In addition, in accordance with the 31th article of the Vienna Convention on the Law of Treaties, "the interpretation to the treaty" could be based on the context, however, the "context" in this treaty could be generalized as follows: "(A) The interpretations or regulations regarding the treaty laid down afterwards by the contracting parties apply to all the articles of the treaty"; "(B) The application of the treaty afterwards is determined by each contracting party's interpretation to the treaty or the regulation to every article". The briefly recorded conversation between Li Jingfang and Mizuno could be used as the consensus reached by both contracting parties after establishing Treaty of Shimonoseki in terms of its interpretation or application, therefore, it could be used as "context". In other words, applying the recorded conversation in the interpretation conforms to the common principle of the interpretation to the treaties in International Law. It entirely accords with the principles in International Law to utilize the consensus they reached, namely, "the acknowledged Taiwan Island and its affiliated islands" were based on "the chart or the map" to interpret or implement the regulation, "the Taiwan Island and its affiliated islands" stated in Treaty of Shimonoseki.

---

4   International Law by L. Oppenheim, Vol. 1, Fascicule 2, Book 4 International Relations, Chapter 2, The Treaties Section 14 Interpretation to the Treaties, Article 553, Authoritative Interpretation and Arbitral Interpretation, translated by Wang Tieya and Chen Tiqiang, The Commercial Press: 1989, p. 362.

2) Three acknowledged and authoritative charts demonstrate that the Diaoyu Islands belong to Taiwan.

In 1998, Mr. Zheng Hailin collected multiple charts drawn by westerners which demonstrate that the Diaoyu Islands were China's territory in the late 19th century. One of the charts, East China Sea Coast Chart (chart 1.3.5), with Taiwan in the center, was drawn by Pierre ·Labi and Alexander Labi, French publishers and geographers, in 1809.

In the chart, the color of Diaoyu Islands, Yellow Tail and Red tail was the same red color as that of Taiwan, on the other hand, Yaeyama, Miyako and Okinawa Island were all painted as green, which distinctly indicates the Diaoyu Islands are the affiliated islands of Taiwan.

In May, 2001, Mr. Ju Deyuan introduced The Latest Map of China (See Chart 4), which was approved by UK officials, engraved and printed by John Carey. In the map, the graphics about Taiwan Island and its affiliated islands, as well as filling out and indicating the names of the islands were more elaborate and more accurate than the past maps published by the western countries. The northeastern islands of the affiliated islands of Taiwan indicated in this map apparently followed the drawing techniques of Michel Benoist, a French preacher who came to China in the 12th year during the reign of Emperor Qianlong. Meanwhile, the pronunciations of their names also followed the Fujian dialect: Kilong-shan, Ponkia (It's called "Ponkia" for short in Michel Benoist's original map), Hoapinsu ("Huapinxu" in MichelBenoist's original map), Hao-yu-su ("Haoyusu" in Michel Benoist's original map), Hoan-oey-su ("Guanweisu" in Michel Benoist's original map), Tche-oey-su (Che wei su in Michel Benoist's original map).

From all the above, it can be proved that the Diaoyu Islands, as a part of the affiliated islands of Taiwan, have always been China's sacred territory, which had been acknowledged by the western countries for a long time.

Chart 5 above, A Map of China's East Coast: Hongkong to Gulf of Liao-Tung was drawn by UK Maritime Bureau, which was exactly the "UK Chart" mentioned in the second article of the second section of the comprehensive amendment proposed by Chinese representative on April 9, 1895. The amendment was adopted by Japan (The amendment was incorporated as appendix in Documents on Japanese Foreign Relations, Vol. 28, No. 1083), consequently, this chart was applied into delimiting ceding the longitude and latitude as well as the four boundaries of Penghu Islands, at the same time, the written language of the treaty about ceding "Taiwan Island and its affiliated islands" was determined.

In unison, the three charts above whose authority are undoubted "universally acknowledge" that the Diaoyu Islands are the northeastern affiliated islands of Taiwan, and are anything but "terra nullius". The charts also demonstrate the fact that the Diaoyu Islands were seized by Japan in 1895 was purely the inevitable result of ceding "Taiwan Island and its affiliated islands" in Treaty of

Shimonoseki. It is in no way "occupying first" the "terra nullius" islets that originated from the "14 January Cabinet Resolution".

3) The first Japanese "Taiwan governor", Kabayama Sukenori, invaded and occupied Diaoyu Islands in late May, 1895, on his voyage of leading the fleet to "take over" Taiwan, during which he mistook Hoapinsu for "Senkaku".

My book, the 1994 edition, once quoted Conquests of Taiwan Bandits and Thieves of Japan-Qing War History (see chart 6,77) compiled by Japanese navy province in the 28th year during the reign of Emperor Meiji. There were two confusing issues in the document: in the first place, in chart 6, "90 sea miles north of Port of Fresh Water" was no longer "sea surface of little Keelung"; in the second place, in chart 7, if "five sea miles south of Senkaku" refers to the Diaoyu Island, then it was not in 25°20′ North Latitude, 122° East Longitude, but in 25°39′, North Latitude, 123°28′ East Longitude, whose longitudes and latitudes had a wide gap.

Just when I was confused about it at the beginning of 2000, my attentive junior school fellow Prof. Mi Yuqing from Japan Institute of Nankai University telephoned and told me that the eighth word " fan" in the third line in chart 6 was translated into "jiu" by mistake. "da fan ten sea miles" means "about ten sea miles". Therefore I understand the thorough meaning all of a sudden: Port of Fresh Water was located in 25°10′ North Latitude, and the place ten sea miles north was exactly "25°20′ North Latitude". Until then my first confusion was figured out.

As for my second confusion, in early September, 2012, Prof. Zhang Zhirong from Institute of International Relations, Peking University told me in the telephone that Prof. Tadayoshi Murata from Yokohama National University, Japan, held the view that the "Senkaku" talked about by people such as the first Japanese "Taiwan Governor" Kabayama Sukenori, was actually not the Diaoyu Islands, however, he didn't go into details about it. Following the train of thought, I found the coordinate of 25°20′ North Latitude, 122° East Longitude. All at once, I realized that the coordinate was exactly "five sea miles south of" Hoapinsu (25°29, North Latitude, 121°59′, East Longitude). It turned out that the first dignified "Taiwan governor" carried on as before the mistake from the UK chart and mistook Hoapinsu for "Senkaku" (see chart 8)!

In late May, 1895, "The Imperial Japanese Plenipotentiary Taiwan governor Secondary viscount" Kabayama Sukenori invaded and occupied Diaoyu Islands just when he was on his voyage to "take over" Taiwan. On 2nd June, "at 9 p.m. Shimamura took along Kabayama Sukenori the governor to sign and seal the document, moved forward to Koueki Ship, and returned immediately after the document was signed and sealed by Li Jingfang. Until then the affairs about handing over Taiwan were accomplished.[5]

---

5   Quoted above Checklist of Microfilm of Selected Archives of The Japanese Army, Navy and Other Government Agencies R34. p.46113

Thereupon, the Diaoyu Islands were seized by Japanese militarism, which was irrelevant to "14 January Cabinet resolution".

4) On June 10, 1895, Koga Tatsushiro acknowledged the fact that the Diaoyu Islands belonged to Japan since the ceding of Taiwan to Japan according to the Treaty of Shimonoseki.

Here, I might as well start from a piece of evidence that Japan provided unintentionally 102 years ago. Forty years ago, in his first article on the sovereignty over the Diaoyu Islands, Mr. Inoue Kiyoshi once quoted "extremely crucial" material from a secondary source, that is, an article titled Koga's Achievements in Ryukyu, written to glorify Koga Tatsushiro's achievements. It mentioned:

In the 27th year of the reign of Emperor Meiji (1894), Koga filed an application to the magistrate of Okinawa about exploiting the island(here it refers to Diaoyu Island), nevertheless, the application was sent back due to the uncertainty of the empire's sovereignty over the island. Furthermore, he proceeded to file applications to interior minister, agricultural and business minister, and even headed to Tokyo to make presentation about the islands and his aspiration to exploit it. Still, he didn't get permission. His application coincided with the end of the war between Japan and the Qing dynasty lasting form the 27th year to the 28th year during the reign of Emperor Meiji, and Taiwan was ceded to Japan after the war. No.13 edict issued in the 29th year during the reign of Emperor Meiji (1896) announced that Senkaku Islands belonged to our country. Immediately, Koga proposed application to exploit the islands to the magistrate of the county and was approved in September in the same year. Consequently, his long-cherished wish about the island was finally achieved.

Here, a significant fact was concealed: The 3rd time when Koga proposed to lease the Diaoyu Islands was nine full months before "No. 13 Edict" issued in March, 1896. He just took advantage of the time when "the Sino-Japanese War was over, and Taiwan was ceded to the empire". Therefore, the eighth day after the affair of "ceding and handing over Taiwan", that is, June 10, 1895, he "applied for exploiting the islands" to Okinawa for the third time, and eventually got approval in September the following year.[6]

Okuhara Toshio, on the other hand, went even further, for he just kept silent about the Sino-Japanese war, only mentioning that "in the 28th year during the reign of Emperor Meiji (1895), 14 January Cabinet Council meeting resolved to incorporate Senkaku Islands to Okinawa, however, in the next year, that is, the 29th year during the reign of Emperor Meiji (1896), another resolution that incorporating the islands to Yaeyama was made, and it was just then that Koga asked for the government's permission to utilize the state-owned land, the Senkaku Islands".[7]

---

6   The Application for the Renting the Official Land by businessman Koga Tatsushiro on June 10, 1895, published in Okinawa Quarterly, Issue 1972/63, pp. 136-137.

7   Okuhara Toshio: The Senkaku Islands and the Sovereignty, The Asahi Asia Review, Issue 1972/2.

In this way, he just dragged what happened on June 10, 1895 to 1896.

We might as well let Koga Tatsushiro himself to make presentation—Here, the translation version of his "application for exploiting" written on June 10,1895 was excerpted as follows:

The honored Interior Minister Viscount Yasushi Nomura

......to further expand business, the uninhabited islands due east to Okinawa continually shipped and supplied captured fish and shellfish to cooperators in Daito Island ...... The application for exploiting the island was approved by Magistrate Maruoka in Okinawa on November 20, the 24th year during the reign of emperor Meiji (1891). In the 18th year during the reign of Emperor Meiji(1885), while cruising the islands in Okinawa, with the ship anchored, I mounted the Kuba Island (It was not the Huangwei Yu but the Diaoyu Islands according to the document) located 90 sea miles north of Yaeyama, only to find bird flocks normally called albatross...... During that time, I intended to file an application for leasing the entire Kuba Island at an early date, aiming for managing business on albatross. However, words went around that the Kuba Jima was not our definite territory, for this reason, I have been endeavoring to restrain my above-mentioned aspiration to this day. ...... Nevertheless, this time the island should be incorporated to Japan uncompromisingly to fulfill my enduring wish.

Signed by Koga Tatsushiro June 10, the 28th year during the reign of Emperor Meiji (1895)

Koga mentioned two matters in his application. Firstly, his application for leasing Daito Island located due east to the Okinawa Island had been approved by the magistrate on November 20, 1891. Secondly, his intention to lease the Diaoyu Island lasting for many years was not fulfilled all because of the uncertain sovereignty over the island. Handing over Taiwan had been accomplished for over one week until then. "This time the island should be incorporated to Japan uncompromisingly".

The whole process of Daito Island came under the jurisdiction of Japan will be left for specification in the following passage. What needs to be illustrated here is that Daito Island was officially incorporated to Japan on September 9, 1891 after Japanese Emperor Meiji explicitly announced its longitude and latitude, name, and area under administration on government organ and newspapers as No.190 Edict. Accordingly, it was possible for Koga to get approval for leasing the island in the following three months.

However, the situation with the Diaoyu Islands were totally different. The Japanese government was fully aware that they were Chinese territory, so they could do nothing but commit black-box operation:

In 1885, the minister Inoue Kaoru sent Yamagata Aritomo "a secret letter demanding to be opened in person", admonishing repeatedly that it "must not be published in the government organ or newspapers"; Nine years later, Yasushi Nomura sent "a secret letter" as well to prevent it from revealing; Even worse, "14 January Cabinet Resolution" kept it under cover for a long time and never put it into practice. Hence, eight days after handing over Taiwan on the basis of Treaty of Shimonoseki, Koga cheerfully claimed to "uncompromisingly" incorporate the Diaoyu Islands "into Japanese territory". Meanwhile, his enduring personal wish was finally achieved.

More than that, in 1974, while compiling The History of Japanese Foreign Relations, a Japanese man named Seizaburo Shinobu wrote "Treaty of Shimonoseki determined the unsettled sovereign issues over Senkaku Islands".[8]

He was wrong about one thing, that is, back in 1895,the name of "Senkaku Islands" did not even existed. However, just like Koga Tatsushiro, he acknowledged another fundamental fact: It was base on the regulations in Treaty of Shimonoseki that Japan seized the whole Taiwan Island and "all of its affiliated islands" including the Diaoyu Islands.

5) Compared with the whole process of Daito Island became under the jurisdiction of Japan, No.13 Edict could be used as counter-evidence that "14 January Cabinet Resolution" did not put into practice the event of incorporating the Diaoyu Islands into Okinawa

Here, we might as well compare the act of incorporating Daito Island into Japanese territory in 1891 (the 24th year during the reign of Emperor Meiji) which was mentioned by Inoue Kaoru in No.38 Document which was issued in 1885 with the event that "14 January Cabinet Resolution" secretly ordered Okinawa to "establish stake". In the same year, Japan incorporated the originally uninhabited island located at southwest of the Bonin Islands. A proposal was first made by Ministry of Internal Affairs to Ministry of Foreign Affairs on July 4, 1891: "The three islands that were located south by southwest the Bonin Islands and scattered from 24°0', to 25°30', North Latitude, 141°0' to 142°30' East Longitude demanded regulations about their names as well as sovereignty". Moreover, in the attached conference proposal, it was specifically pointed that these islands "were incorporated to the Bonin Islands from now on. The one in the middle was named as the Iwo Island, the one in the south was named as the South Iwo Island, the one in the north as the North Iwo Island"; The Ministry of Foreign Affairs had no objection to it, in consequence, after having been presented and passing the resolution in the cabinet conference, the islands' longitude and latitude, names, as well as area under administration

---

8   Compiled by Seizaburo Shinobu: The History of Japanese Foreign Relations Volume I, Section Three Chapter Five Treaty of Shimonoseki, quoted from the book by Ju Deyuan, Volume I, p. 149.

15 were announced on government organ and newspapers as No.190 Edict promulgated by Emperor Meiji on September 9,1891. What's more, even though the international law didn't stipulate informing foreign ambassadors of the affair, Japan still notified all resided the foreign ambassadors to Japan which resided in Tokyo one by one.[9]

Japan took highly meticulous and thorough measures towards incorporating Daito Island, the undoubtedly uninhabited island, into Japan? On the contrary, why did Japan government act just in the opposite manner and neglected the "14 Jaunary Cabinet Resolution" that was related to China? The only reason was that Japan had to take despicable intrigues on the condition that Japan was fully aware that the Diaoyu Islands were far from "terra nullius", but Chinese territory.

Didn't Japan use No.13 Edict promulgated by Japanese Emperor as legal evidence for seizing the Diaoyu Islands? According to the first article in the decree, the sovereignty over the first prefecture Shimajiri was loftily recorded as Daito Island that had been legitimately incorporated into Japanese territory five years before. However, having passed the alleged "14 January Cabinet Resolution", the Diaoyu Islands "incorporated to Okinawa" was not actually "included". The fact itself exactly justified: No.13 Edict could not be served as evidence that Japan "possessed" the Diaoyu Islands on January 14, 1895, moreover, the Diaoyu Island, just the opposite, had never been under the jurisdiction of Okinawa between January 14 and June 2nd. It was based on Treaty of Shimonoseki that the Diaoyu Islands was incorporated by "Taiwan governor" Kabayama Sukenori, along with "Taiwan Island and its affiliated islands" on June 2.

Incidentally, did Japan feel at ease about its act, incorporating the areas into its territory by means of such "normal" operations? I am afraid not. The author would like to discuss an issue as an example: there was an island which was called "Liancourt Rocks" by Korea, and "Takeshima" by Japan, of which Prof. Inoue Kiyoshi was greatly skeptical, when he wrote about it 40 years ago. Although the Japanese cabinet made a resolution on January 28, 1905, and although the interior minister issued a command to the magistrate of Shimane on February 25, "the islands located in 37°0' 30" North Latitude, 131°55' East Longitude and 85 sea miles northwest to Okinoshima was named 'Takeshima', and will be under the administration of Okinoshima's administrator from now

9   Takahashi Sougorou, Notes on the Senkaku Islands (Tokyo Youth Press), 1979, p.105; Yasuoka Akio, The Meiji Restoration and Territorial Issues, Tokyo, Kyoiku-sha, 1980, pp.177-186, quoted from the research result of Researcher Shao Hanyi,International Law Research Center, Taiwan, Taipei National Chengchi University—Han-yi Shaw, The Diaoyutai/Senkaku Islands Disputes: Its History and An Analysis of the Ownership Claims of The P.R.C, R.O.C and Japan, Occasional Papers Reprint Series in Contemporary Asain Studies, 1999. p.104. Wu Tianying: It was suggested by Mr. Liao Shiping.

on"; although the magistrate of Shimane proclaimed an official notice complying with the interior minister's instruction.[10]

However, it was well known that at the beginning of 1904, one year before the island was renamed "Takeshima", taking advantage of launching the war between Japan and Russia, with the armed forces as backup and "Japan-Korea Alliance" as excuse, Japan compelled Korea to accept the treaty of subjugation Korea-Japan Protocol on February 23. The exact treaty virtually made Korea, Japan's vassal state, on the other hand, the Korean government whose internal and foreign affairs were entirely controlled by the Japanese militarism was mere a puppet government, just like the subsequent puppet emperor of "Manchukuo". It may well be asked: did the "Takeshima" island that Japan had "named" and forcedly took possession of under such circumstances have a legal validity?

6) In No.120 Chart drawn by Kimotsuki Kaneyuki, the Minister of Water, Japanese Navy in March,1897, the names of the Diaoyu Islands all followed their Chinese original names, and the alleged "Uotsuri Island" and "Kuba Island" mentioned in "14 January Cabinet Resolution" didn't exist.

On March 29, the 30th year during the reign of Emperor Meiji (1897), the Ministry of Water, Japanese Navy issued No.120 Chart[11] (chart 9) drawn by the minister, Kimotsuki Kaneyuki, in which, almost all the names of "Taiwan Island and its affiliated islands" followed their Chinese original names, with their transcribed and translated names from the UK chart as annotations, such as the Diaoyu Islands (ホアピンス), Huangwei Yu (チヤウス), Chiwei Yu (ラレー). What was worth noticing was the time when the chart was published was two entire years later that of "14 January Cabinet Resolution", however, it didn't apply the names such as "Uotsuri Jima" or "Kuba Jima" mentioned in "14 January Cabinet Resolution" , neither did it apply"Kumeaka Island", a name specifically used for illegally occupying other countries land. It indicated that the carver of the chart was either utterly ignorant of "14 January Cabinet Resolution" or took a dim view on it. In conclusion, he deemed the opinion that the Diaoyu Islands was not acquired by Japan by means of "14 January Cabinet Resolution", but the trophy of the Sino-Japanese War. In consequence, he boldly followed the island's original Chinese names, which, unintentionally turned into evidence for denying "14 January Cabinet Resolution"—this was possibly unexpected to the carver of the chart.

---

10   Quoted from Chapter 13 of the book by Inoue Kiyoshi annotated above.
11   Quoted from Volume Two of the book by Ju Deyuan, quoted above, pp. 681-682 and Chart 59. Appreciation to the collector, Major General Pi Mingyong, Academy of Military Science, for giving permission to quote the article.

The above six aspects has confirmed from different perspectives: Japan's seizing the Diaoyu Islands from China in 1895 was totally irrelevant to "14 January Cabinet Resolution", but the outcome of the second item of the second article in Treaty of Shimonoseki, a treaty forcibly signed under coercion due to China's being defeated in the Sino-Japanese War. Currently, Japan utilizes this resolution as "legal basis" for its argument "Senkaku Islands are Japan's uncontroversial and inherent land", which is illegal and invalid either based on international law or domestic law.

Here, what Okuhara Toshio said forty years ago actually has come true.

On the condition that there are facts to corroborate it that if Japan incorporate the Senkaku Islands that has been determined to be China's territory into its own territory, it will be illegal. In consequence, it can't be refuted that Japan took advantage of the defeat to implement forcible plunder.

Once the historical truth that Japan unjustly seized the Diaoyu Islands, China's territory, come out, their "fictional history" for establishing the theory of "occupying first" will definitely collapse in a row like dominoes. In this case, the "lifeline" of "imperial Japan" will be hanged by a thread, and the 80 billion barrels of petroleum "at hand and they have been slobbery to"[12] will fall through like a fond dream.

III. On Sovereignty over the Diaoyu Islands and Its Solution

September, 2011

Lian Degui[13]

The evidences which prove that the Diaoyu Islands belong to China

There are many historical documents from the Ming and Qing Dynasty periods which can comfortably prove that the Diaoyu Islands belong to China, so I will not repeat them here. My main purpose is to explain the Diaoyu Islands as China's inherent territory are not terra nullius as argued by the Japanese Ministry of Foreign Affairs in its "Basic Views". Therefore, the Meiji government has violated the International Law when it incorporated the islands into its territory.

---

12   Midorima Sakae: The Senkaku Islands,Book on Okinawa, p. 14. Okinawa Hiruza Press, originally published in 1984, the 8th edition, published in 1993,pp. 9-10.
13   Researcher of Shanghai Institute for International Studies (SIIS).

A. The Diaoyu Islands are not terra nullius

According to the theory of International Law, the preemptive occupation involves terra nullius. However, many modern scholars have criticized this theory. For example, the famous Japanese scholar Inoue Kiyoshi holds that the so-called preemptive occupation theory served for European and US colonialism and imperialism. In particular, he thinks adopting this theory to China's territory in time of feudal dynasties is totally an "injustice" and is an ignorance of the history. According to the jurisprudence of the 16th and 17th century, the "discoverer" of the territory is entitled to enjoy the sovereignty over the territory. So undoubtedly, China has the sovereignty over the Diaoyu Islands as the Diaoyu Islands were first discovered, named and exploited by the Chinese people. To put it in another way, the Diaoyu Islands are not terra nullius.

The records of the Ming and Qing Dynasties indicate that the islands belong to China. The earliest record of the name of the Diaoyu Islands can be found in the book Voyage with a Tail Wind (Shun Feng Xiang Song) published in the Ming Dynasty. It shows that China firstly discovered and named Diaoyu Islands and used them as sea marks to Ryukyu. What's more, China was the first country to incorporate the islands into its territory. Since the Ming Dynasty, the Records of the Imperial Title-conferring Envoys to Ryukyu (Shi Liu Qiu Lu) written by an imperial title-conferring envoy from the Ming court, clearly stated that China had already regarded the Okinawa Trench located between Chiwei Yu and Kume Island (Gumi Mountain) as the border of China and Ryukyu. In 1534 during the 13th year of Ming Dynasty Emperor Jia Jing's reign, the imperial envoy to Ryukyu, Chen Kan, wrote a book, titled Records of the Imperial Title-conferring Envoys to Ryukyu (Shi Liu Qiu Lu). Part of his voyage was recorded as follows, "On the 10th day, the strong southerly wind pushed the ship forward with lightning speed and we passed by Pingjia Mountain, Diaoyu Island, Huangmao Yu and Chi Yu. One day and one night's voyage equals that of three days. The barbarians' boats were so small that they were lagging far behind. At sunset of the 11th day, we saw the Gumi Mountain which belongs to Ryukyu. The barbarians all beat drums and danced in the boats to express their joy upon arriving home." The above-mentioned "Diaoyu Island, Huangmao Yu and Chi Yu" are today's Diaoyu Islands, Huangwei Yu and Chiwei Yu. We should pay attention that on the 10th day, Chen Kan and his party passed by the navigation marks, which were Diaoyu Islands and Chiwei Yu. Then they sailed into the Ryukyu waters, as they saw Gumi Mountain that belonged to Ryukyu. It is clearly said the Chiwei Yu which located in the most north east of the Diaoyu Islands belongs to China; and sailing forward, we will see the Gumi Mountain that belongs to Ryukyu.

In addition, some documents clearly recorded that the Diaoyu Islands belong to China such as the Records of the Imperial Title-conferring Envoys to Ryukyu (Shi Liu Qiu Lu) written by Guo Rulin, Xiao Chongye, Xia Ziyang (in the 34th year of Ming Dynasty), the Annals of Ryukyu (Liu Qiu Guo Zhi Lue)written by Zhou Huang in the 21st year of Qing Dynasty Emperor Qian Long's reign, A Sequel to Survey of Ryukyu by Qi Kun in the 13th year of Qing Dynasty Emperor Jia Qing's Reign, the Records of the Imperial Title-conferring Envoys to Ryukyu (Shi Liu Qiu Ji) written by Li Dingyuan, etc. Furthermore, the Japanese scholar Inoue Kiyoshi holds that what Guo Rulin wrote in the Records of the Imperial Title-conferring Envoys to Ryukyu—"Chi Yu is the mountain that marks the boundary of Ryukyu" is a "very important" evidence, as he thought the word "boundary" has legal sense, and is the vital evidence to deny Japan's claim that the Diaoyu Islands is terra nullius. Moreover, Xu Baoguang clearly recorded in his book Records of Messages from Chong-shan (Zhong Shan Chuan Xin Lu) that "Ryukyu, in the sea, stands opposite to Zhejiang and Fujian provinces" and that Gumi Mountain guards the southwest border of Ryukyu), which indicates that the border of China and Ryukyu located between Chiwei Yu and Gumi Island. It is worth mentioning that the Records of the Imperial Title-conferring Envoys to Ryukyu (Shi Liu Qiu Lu) were not general nautical journal but reports submitted to the imperial court, so they are official documents.

The accounts of "trench" or "dark current" are often found in the records of imperial envoys to Ryukyu. It is recorded that whenever the accredited fleet to Ryukyu passed by the "trench", it was supposed to offer sacrifices to Ocean God by throwing pigs and sheep, pouring rice gruel into the sea, burning paper vessels and beating drums. The "trench" is the Ryukyu Trench. Measuring 2,000 metres in depth; the Ryukyu Trench is located in between the Ryukyu Islands and Diaoyu Islands. Geographically, the Ryukyu Trench effectively separates the Ryukyu Islands from China's continental shelf. The Diaoyu Island, the Huangwei Island and the Chiwei Island, together with the Taiwan Island, are located in an area where the water is only 200 metres deep on this continental shelf. The water surface between the shelf and the Ryukyu Trench appears as a wide band of darker waters—this is the Japan Current—a phenomenon similar to what all envoys had recorded in the past as "passing from dark-blue waters into black waters". What merits our attention is that the trench was referred to as the boundary between China and other countries in Miscellaneous Records of a Mission to Ryukyu (Shi Liu Qiu Za Lu) written by Wang Ji. Testimony can also be found in the Annals of Ryukyu (Liu Qiu Guo Zhi Lue) written by Zhou Huang, in which Zhou described the "black water trench" as a "border of the waters around the Fujian Province with other territories". It is clear then that China had, at least during Qing Dynasty, already regarded the Ryukyu Trench as the border of the waters around the Fujian Province. Naturally, all the waters and the islands stretching from Chiwei Yu to Fujian Province had belonged to Qing Government and were marked as part of its territory in Qing Dynasty maps.

B. Official maps reflect the fact that the Diaoyu Islands belong to China because maps represent the international political geography, especially those official maps represent a country's territory. It is necessary to trace back to the Great Haiphong Map (Wan Li Hai Fang Tu) of the Ming Dynasty revealing the coastline of the East China Sea and cruise waters of the Ming Navy, which was drawn by Zheng Nuo in 1561. Its purpose was to guard against the Japanese pirates, so there are some marks of the times and locations of the Japanese pirates' attacks and the locations of sentry points as well as defense sites. This map included the Diaoyu Islands and was the official military map of the Ming Dynasty. Previously, Zheng Nuo had also written a book called Haiphong Graph Theory, which was the first draft of the Great Haiphong Map. All these documents have been recorded in An Illustrated Compendium on Maritime Security (Chou Hai Tu Bian) compiled by Hu Zongxian. Besides, in 1863, Hu Linyi, the Governor of Hubei Province once invited experts to draw the Atlas of the Great Qing Dynasty which marked the Taiwan island and its affiliated islands and then marked the name of them, including the Diaoyu Islands, Huangwei Yu and Chiwei Yu.

Additionally, the map of the Ryukyu Kingdom doesn't include the Diaoyu Islands, which also proved the fact that the Diaoyu Islands belong to China. Especially, at that time the Japanese drew maps based on the map of Ryukyu Kingdom, believing that the Diaoyu Islands belong to China. For example, in 1719, Haibao, a title-conferring envoy in the Qing Dynasty and Xu Baoguang, a deputy title-conferring envoy together with other two mapping officials went to Ryukyu. Under the help of the Ryukyu Kingand local officials, they completed the Map of Ryukyu and the Map of the 36 Islands of Ryukyu, which were the first maps of the Ryukyu Kingdom's territory. Obviously, they are official maps. This map also didn't include the Diaoyu Islands whose color were the same as that of Taiwan and mainland China. At that time, Japan also supported the two maps. Japanese historical maps also regard Diaoyu Islands as part of China's territory. In 1785, An Illustrated General Survey of Three Countries written by Hayashi Shihei, a prestigious scholar, was published in Japan. It had an illustration of The Map of the Three Provinces and 36 Islands of Ryukyu, in which the color of the Diaoyu Islands were the same as that of mainland China.

Some Japanese scholars don't admit that these historical documents with evident legal nature can easily prove the Diaoyu Islands belong to China. They don't think the International Law admits the indirect assumption according to vague records. If one wants to prove a specific territory sovereignty, it should have the conclusive evidence such as the records of taxes and trials. The Japanese pointed out that in fact there was no traces of the rule of China on the islands and that Japan conducted preemptive occupation of terra nullius according to the principles of the International Law by incorporating the islands under the administration of Okinawa. They thought the Meiji government's behavior is accord with International Law. The Japanese said the Great Haiphong Map (Wang Li Hai Fang Tu) of the Ming Dynasty was only a military defense map, and the military defense range and the sovereignty are two different things, so it can not prove that China's Ming Dynasty had incorporated the Diaoyu Islands into its territory. As for the color of the Diaoyu Islands in the Map of the 36 Islands of Ryukyu, The Japanese say the same color can't explain anything.

Japan's excuses complicate the originally simple issue. In order to prove the Diaoyu Islands is terra nullius, Japan almost turn a blind eye to the facts. As for this matter, the upright Japanese scholar Inoue Kiyoshi thinks that the Ming and the Qing government could not set up the administrative organs, the judiciary, the police and the courts on such a small island, but the Chinese had confirmed their position, named them, and found out the routes to these islands before Japan's "discovery" of these islands. He said: "it should be enough!" But the Ming government had done more things that since the Ming Dynasty, the Diaoyu Islands have been put under the jurisdiction of China's naval defense. He added: the Ming and Qing governments as well as the Chinese could never expect that in hundreds of years after their death, modern imperialist "applied" the "International Law theory" to their territory, but it can never be able to deny the historical fact that these islands belong to China. Another Japanese scholar Tadayoshi Murata holds that the Chinese envoys at that time had "clear consciousness of the territorial sea" and Japan's so-called "terra nullius" theory is nonsense.

It was an act of stealing of the Meiji government when it incorporated the Diaoyu Islands into its territory

According to the contemporary International Law, the "preemptive occupation" principle should comply with five steps as follows: 1. occupation attempt; 2. confirmation of terra nullius; 3. occupation announcement; 4. occupation actions; 5. effective jurisdiction. So we can see that Japan's occupation of the Diaoyu Islands is unable to meet the condition of terra nullius. From the perspective of the legal logic, now that the islands are not terra nullius, so it is illegal for every country to occupy these islands. However, Japan insists that it is legal for the Meiji government to incorporate the Diaoyu Islands into its territory and these islands are still controlled by Japan. Japan really complicates the originally simple issue. I will do some analyses on the Meiji government's incorporation of the Diaoyu Islands into its territory

A. The year 1885

Let us have a look at Japan's excuse on this issue. We assume that the Diaoyu Islands are "terra nullius"; then whether Japan's occupation of these islands is in accord with the "preemptive occupation of terra nullius" in the International Law. Based on analyses of historical data, the Meiji government never made the "occupation announcement". The Meiji government's incorporation of the Diaoyu Islands into its territory was a non-public behavior during the Sino-Japanese War; thus it is an act of stealing.

Japan noticed the Diaoyu Islands for the first time in 1885. During the Sino-French War, France attacked Taiwan and Penghu Islands but was repelled by the Chinese garrison Liu Mingchuan. At that time, Koga Tatsushiro, an indust-rialist born in Fukuoka City, applied for the lease contract concerning leasing the land of the Diaoyu Islands to the Okinawa authorities because of business issue. The Okinawa authorities reported to the Japanese Ministry of Foreign Affairs, the reason of which was that the land that Koga wanted to lease was not under the administration of Okinawa, namely it was not Japan's territory. Therefore, after receiving the report, the Ministry of Internal Affairs instructed the Okinawa authorities to conduct first secret investigation of these islands to find out whether these islands belong to another country. Later, the Japan's investigation activities were discovered by China. On September 6, 1885, China's largest newspaper—Shen-pao (Shanghai News) revealed: "Recently, Japanese flags have been seen on the islands northeast to Taiwan, revealing Japan's intention to occupy these islands." The newspaper reminded the Qing government to guard against Japan.

According to the report of the Japanese researcher Eiho Oshiro, he knew the name of the island—the Diaoyu Islands ("yukun" and "kuba" in the Ryukyuan language) and its location was to the west of Gumi Island(Gumi Mountain). He also discovered the broad wharves and the anchorage areas, which indicates that the island is an inhabited island. On September 22, 1885, the Okinawa ma-gistrate Sutezo Nishimura wrote to Yamagata Aritomo, the Ministry of Internal Affairs: "Yet, due to their differences in terms of topography from the earli-er reported island Daitojima (situated between this prefecture and Osagawa Islands), the possibility must not be ignored that they are the same islands recorded as Diaoyutai, Huangwei-yu and Chiwei-yu in the Zhongshan Mission Records. We call these islands Kuba Island and Senkaku Islands but the islands are undoubtedly the Diaoyu islands, Huangwei Yu, Chiwei Yu, etc. which were recorded in the Records of Messages from Chong-shan (Zhong Shan Chuan Xin Lu)."

It is obvious that Nishimura knew about the historical background, so he suggested that Japan should be cautious when investigating these islands in or-der to avoid international disputes. After receiving the report from Nishimura, Yamagata Aritomo discussed with Inoue Kaoru, the Ministry of Foreign Affairs. On October 21, 1885, Inoue Kaoru wrote to Yamagata Aritomo: the Qing go-vernment has named these islands. Recently, the Qing government published newspapers, saying that our government attempts to occupy the affiliated is-lands near Taiwan and the Qing government has suspicions about our country. At this moment, if we openly established national stakes on these islands, we are bound to face the opposition from the Qing government. Therefore, we sho-uld report its harbor shapes and unearthed land property according to the actual investigation results. We can step out of the shadow to establish national stakes and further develop these islands according to the situation in the future. We should not publish the investigation on any newspapers." Yamagata Aritomo agreed and decided to take actions later.

We can see that the Meiji government did not treat these islands as "terra nullius" and the Japanese government did not dare to take any further action for fear of the reaction from China.

B. The early stage of the Sino-Japanese war

As the Diaoyu Islands are affiliated islands of Taiwan, Japan's coveting the-se islands was closely related to its ambitions of occupying Taiwan. In August 1894, after the outbreak of Sino-Japanese War, Japan had the idea that they wanted to occupy Taiwan after the war, but Japan was not sure the extent of China's resistance and other powers' interference, so at the early stage of the Sino-Japanese war, Japan didn't take any reckless action. Originally, Japanese Prime Minister Ito Hirobumi and Foreign Minister Mutsu Munemitsu had drawn up a draft contract on October 8, 1894, in which the territory that Japan wanted to occupy and the indemnity content were included. But they thought if they published it, they might face the interference from other countries, so they decided to make another plan if they had disputes with other countries. Therefore, at the early stage of the Sino-Japanese War, Japan's ambition of occupying Japan remained to be seen. The policymakers of the Meiji govern-ment thought that they had better hide this treaty and step out of the shadow according to the situation in the future. We can see that at that time, Japan was also afraid to show its attempt to the Qing government. In fact, around March 1895, although the Qing government was lost in the war, Japan was still not sure that whether other powers would interfere if they put forward their request of ceding Taiwan. In that situation, Japan had every reason to be cautious, as on March 3th, 1895, Germany's Ambassador reported that Li Hongzhang, on behalf of the Qing government, said China couldn't accept the request of ce-ding China's territories and that France had claimed its demands about Taiwan since 1885; so at least France and Britain would oppose ceding Penghu Islands.

C. The latter stage of the Sino-Japanese War

In fact, at the end of 1894, the situation on the battlefield became favorable to Japan, so Japan's decision-makers realized that even if they couldn't get Taiwan, they could occupy the Diaoyu Islands because at least now it would never face the opposition from the Qing government. As a result, Japan secretly occupied the Diaoyu Islands before signing Treaty of Shimonoseki. To put it in another way, the Diaoyu Islands became a secret booty of the Meiji govern-ment even before the end of the Sino-Japanese War.

The concrete process of the Meiji government's occupation of the Diaoyu Islands is as follows: on December 27, 1894, the war was not ended, but the Qing government faced undoubted failure, taking advantage of which, Japanese Ministry of Internal Affairs declared that Japan would set national stakes on Kuba Island and Senkaku Islands. It pointed out that in 1885, they had already submitted related reports to the Japanese Ministry of Foreign Affairs. The situation then was different from present situation, so they called for negotiations with the Ministry of Foreign Affairs. Ten years ago, Japanese Ministry of Foreign Affairs still hesitated about occupying these islands as they were afraid of China's opposition. However, at present, under the background of its victory in the war, Japanese Ministry of Foreign Affairs raised no objection of this request. On January 11, 1895, Mutsu Munemitsu, the Ministry of Foreign Affairs sent cipher text to the Ministry of Internal Affairs: "we have no objection; please take actions as planned." On the same day, Mutsu Munemitsu and Ito Hirobumi left Tokyo to Hiroshima in order to meet with China's representatives. On January 14, 1895, through the secret cabinet resolution, Japan decided to set up the national stakes on Kuba Island and Senkaku Islands, the reason of which was that Japan "confirmed" the Diaoyu Islands did not belong to any country. On January 21, the Ministry of Foreign Affairs noticed Okinawa governor: about setting up the national stakes, please take actions according to the related application.

Above are the concrete process of the Meiji government's incorporation of the Diaoyu Islands. On April 17, 1895 , by signing of Treaty of Shimonoseki, Taiwan and all its affiliated islands were ceded to Japan. Naturally, the Diaoyu Islands were included, though they had already been stole during the Sino-Japanese War. Later on June 10, 1895, Koga Tatsushiro applied to the Japanese Ministry of Internal Affairs again for leasing the land of the Diaoyu Islands; and this time, the Japanese Ministry of Internal Affairs approved his application without hesitation.

D. The "incorporation" is an action of stealing

However, in the early 1970s, after the disputes over the sovereignty of the Diaoyu Islands between China and Japan, the Japanese Ministry of Foreign Affairs made some explanation about the Meiji government's "incorporation", which was Basic views in 1972. They explained that the Meiji government's preemptive occupation was not included in the Treaty of Shimonoseki, so the Diaoyu Islands couldn't be returned to China according to the Cairo Declaration. However, it is not the case. On June 2, 1895 when China and Japan signed the Documents on the Cession of Taiwan to Japan in keelung, Taiwan Governor Kabayama Sukenori dispatched by the Japanese side reiterated the location of Taiwan and all its affiliated islands according to the sea chart of Britain, namely "China's East Coast: Hong Kong to Gulf of Liao-Tung, in which the Diaoyu Islands were marked as the northeast islands of Taiwan, so the Basic Views of the Japanese Ministry of Foreign Affairs was untenable.

In fact, it is undoubted that the Diaoyu Islands were included in the Article 2 of Treaty of Shimonoseki. Its difference from Taiwan and the Penghu Islands was that they had been incorporated under the administration of Okinawa secretly by the Meiji government before the end of the Sino-Japanese War. Japan insisted that the stolen territory during the war was not included in the post-war territorial articles, which was opposed by Inoue Kiyoshi who believes the Diaoyu Islands were stolen by Japan. Therefore, the Diaoyu islands were either stolen by Japan during the Sino-Japanese War or Japan's predatory territory based on Treaty of Shimonoseki. Sooner or later, Japan will return these islands to their true owner. The Japanese Ministry of Foreign Affairs couldn't fill up gaps in its theory. What's more, the Meiji government's "incorporation" by no means conformed to the principle of preemptive occupation of terra nullius in International Law and it was an action of secret stealing. Ishigaki City set up the markers on these island on May 10th, 1969, 74 years after the Cabinet approved this solution. The Ryukyu government declared the sovereignty over these islands on September 10, 1970. Before that, the Japanese government had no "indications"; as a result, the Basic Views of the Japanese Ministry of Foreign Affairs were self-defeating and useless.

In a word, the Diaoyu Islands are not terra nullius. It proved that the Meiji government at that time did not think the islands were terra nullius before the Sino-Japanese War, so they initially took a cautious attitude. However, and during the Sino-Japanese War, the Meiji government's incorporation did not meet the requirements of the "preemptive occupation of terra nullius" of International Law. Terms of the Cairo Declaration clearly stipulates that all the territories Japan has stolen from the Chinese shall be restored to the Republic of China. The content of the Cairo Declaration was confirmed by Article 8 of the Potsdam Declaration and was acknowledged by the Japanese Instrument of Surrender signed by Japan. Particularly, in Article 3 of China-Japan Joint Statement, Japan said it firmly maintains its stand under Article 8 of the Potsdam Declaration. Therefore, Japan should keep its own promise and return the stolen territory to China.

"The Treaty of San Francisco" after "World War II" has no legal effect

The dispute over the Diaoyu Islands between China and Japan also reflected in the Treaty of San Francisco after the "World War II", which was used by the US and Japan to occupy the islands. Specifically, though it was used by Japan as its legal basis, China does not admit this treaty. If the US had the right to deal with the ownership of Okinawa, which means that Okinawa was incorporated under the administration of the US, so Japan lost its sovereignty over Okinawa.

A. The Treaty of San Francisco lacks explanatory power

The Japanese Ministry of Foreign Affairs thought it was legal for the US to occupy Okinawa and the Diaoyu Islands according to the Treaty of San Francisco, so it was also lawful for Japan to take over Okinawa and the Diaoyu

Islands from the United States. But, in fact, China has never admit the legitimacy of the Treaty of San Francisco, so China will never accept Japan's sovereignty over the Diaoyu Islands according to the Treaty of San Francisco. Moreover, the related provisions in the Treaty of San Francisco were vague and they couldn't prove that it was legal for the US to occupy the Diaoyu Islands; hence, it is unconvincing for Japan to use this treaty as its legal basis.

A. " San Francisco Peace Treaty" has no binding upon China. The US's postwar occupation of Okinawa was based on the Treaty of San Francisco signed on September 8, 1951, the Article 3 of which stipulates Japan will concur in any proposal of the United States to the United Nations to place under its trusteeship system, with the United States as the sole administering authority, Nansei Shoto (Southwest Islands) south of 29 degree, north latitude (including the Ryukyu Islands and the Daito Islands), Nanpo Shoto south of Sofu Gan (including the Bonin Islands, Rosario Island and the Volcano Islands) and Parece Vela and Marcus Island. Pending the making of such a proposal and affirmative action thereon, the United States will have the right to exercise all and any powers of administration, legislation and jurisdiction over the territory and inhabitants of these islands, including their territorial waters. Japan believes that the Diaoyu Islands were included in Article 3.

However, one hard fact is that China did not participate in San Francisco Conference nor signed the Treaty of San Francisco. Besides, at that time, Zhou Enlai, on behalf of the Chinese government, represented a solemn protest that declared that this peace treaty was an affront to the Chinese people and was illegal; the Chinese people would never admit it. It indicates that China holds a negative attitude about the legality of US's occupation of Okinawa and the Diaoyu Islands according to this treaty and China also solemnly believes that it is illegal for Japan to take over the Diaoyu Islands according to this treaty.

Therefore, it is invalid for Japan to use the Treaty of San Francisco as its legal basis because China only admits the legitimacy of the "Cairo Declaration", "Potsdam Declaration", "Japanese Instrument of Surrender" and other international legal documents, all of which should be recognized and complied by China, US and Japan. The Treaty of San Francisco was only a product of the Cold War and was an unilateral treaty without China's participation. It's fundamental problem lay on its incomplete implementation of the principles in the "Cairo Declaration", "Potsdam Declaration" and "Japanese Instrument of Surrender", etc.

B. Nansei Shoto do not include the Diaoyu Islands. The Article 3 of the "Treaty of San Francisco" mentioned an important concept – "Nansei Shoto", which is the crux of Japan's claim of the sovereignty over the Diaoyu Islands. Even if the "Treaty of San Francisco" was a legal treaty, but Nansei Shoto didn't include the Diaoyu Islands.

"Basic Views" of the Japanese Ministry of Foreign Affairs in 1972 claimed: The Senkaku Islands are not included in the territories renounced by Japan as provided in Article 2 of the San Francisco Peace Treaty but, as part of the southwest islands, placed under the US administration according to Article 3, and included in territories restored to Japan as stipulated in the Japan-US Agreement on Ryukyu Islands and Daito Islands signed on June 17, 1971. The Japanese Ministry of Foreign Affairs stressed the Diaoyu Islands were part of Nansei Shoto instead of Okinawa because Nansei Shoto was mentioned in the Treaty of San Francisco. However, the Nansei Shoto mentioned in Article 3 were the Nansei Shoto south of 29 degree, north latitude; besides, it gave clear indication in the parentheses – including the Ryukyu Islands and the Daito Islands, but there was no mention of the Diaoyu Islands.

Moreover, the so-called "Nansei Shoto" was not an inherent wording in Japan; it was firstly mentioned in the map China's East Coast: Hong Kong to Gulf of Liao-Tung in which the Diaoyu Islands were marked as the Northeast Islands of Taiwan instead of Southwest Islands (Nansei Shoto), so Japan's Nansei Shoto didn't include the Diaoyu Islands.

In addition, none of Japanese maps before Japan's seizure of the Diaoyu Islands used the name of "Southwest Islands" (Nansei Shoto) which was used by the Europeans; even after the Meiji government's occupation of Taiwan, Japan didn't map the Diaoyu Islands into Nansei Shoto. The map of Southwest Islands (Nansei Shoto) published by the Japanese Ministry of Construction on April 4, 1961 didn't include the Diaoyu Islands. Maps published in Japan afterwards still didn't map the Diaoyu Islands into Nansei Shoto. Therefore, it is far-fetched for the Japanese Ministry of Foreign Affairs to use its quotation of Nansei Shoto in the Treaty of San Francisco.

The United States also knew that the Treaty of San Francisco lacked explanatory power. In order to emphasize that the Diaoyu Islands belong to Okinawa, the United States Civil Administration of the Ryukyu Islands released Geographical Realm of Ryukyu Islands on December 25, 1953, in which mapped the Diaoyu Islands into Okinawa. The US clearly wanted to "reinforce" the contents of Article 3 in the Treaty of San Francisco. On September 17, 1970, the local Okinawa authorities issued a statement – "Sovereignty over the Senkaku Islands", pointing out that the US had the executive power of the Ryukyu Islands and their territorial waters according to Article 3 of the Treaty of San Francisco.

I believe that both the proclamation in 1953 and the statement in 1970 were either the unilateral decision of US or the unilateral decision of the Okinawa authorities, rather than a result of consultations between the relevant nations. Therefore, they had no international treaty nature, so they had no validity of the International Law. They can neither prove that the Diaoyu Islands are included in the so-called "Southwest Islands" (Nansei Shoto) nor provide a lawful basis for Japan's incorporation of the Diaoyu Islands into Okinawa, let alone proving the legitimacy of US's occupation of the Diaoyu Islands.

B. The legal status of Okinawa can not support the claim that Diaoyu Islands belong to Japan

Even if the "Southwest Islands" (Nansei Shoto) did include the Diaoyu Islands, but the Ryukyu Islands were occupied by the United States after the war, hence, its legal status had changed and Japan, in fact, lost its sovereignty over the islands. Therefore, even if the Diaoyu Islands were included in the so-called "Southwest Islands" (Nansei Shoto) or part of Okinawa, they had nothing to do with Japan.

A. The status of Okinawa was not determined, Japan had no rights to claim its sovereignty. "Basic Views" of the Japanese Ministry of Foreign Affairs said: China never put forward objection about the fact that the US incorporated the Diaoyu islands under its administration according to the Treaty of San Francisco, which meant that China acquiesced in the fact that the islands belong to Japan. As China discovered oil in these waters, it began to fight for them against Japan. Actually, the reason why Taiwan didn't put forward objection was its consideration of military security; it thought that in terms of military affairs, the US's occupation of Okinawa including the Diaoyu Islands was necessary. On April 20, 1971, Taiwan had explained: the US's military occupation of the islands was necessary measures for the safety of joint defense area; once they ended the occupation, Taiwan would ask the United States to return these islands. On the contrary, the Chinese mainland has fundamentally denied that the US's occupation was legal and expressed its critical position on the Treaty of San Francisco, US's occupation of Okinawa and invasion of Taiwan.

More importantly, we will trace back to the status of Ryukyu when we talk about the China's attitude of US's occupation of Okinawa and the Diaoyu Islands. During the period of signing "Cairo Declaration", Chiang Kai-shek and Roosevelt discussed about the ownership of the Ryukyu Islands during the meeting. Roosevelt: what's your opinion of those islands in northern Japan? Jiang: you mean the Ryukyu islands. China has no intention to claim the Ryukyu Islands and just hope that China and US share the condominium or we should conduct international condominium. International condominium is better than China's administration. Probably Roosevelt just wanted to sound out Chiang Kai-shek's attitude towards the US's occupation of Okinawa, or he wanted to plant a seed of dispute between China and Japan. At that time, Stalin also wanted to hand over Ryukyu to China; but the postwar relations between the United States and the Soviet Union were full of tensions, so the US didn't want to hand over Ryukyu to China when Ryukyu (Okinawa) were occupied by the US as military base. Later, because the United States acquiesced in the Soviet Union's occupation of Nanqian Islands (the Kuril Islands in Japanese), so the Soviet Union didn't challenge the US's exclusive occupation of Ryukyu.

According to the CIA's secret analysis report, they thought that the communists controlled China, so if they handed over Ryukyu to China, they would give the Soviet Union the chance to get close to these islands, thus endangering the whole Pacific base system of the United States. Therefore, Chiang Kai-Shek lodged representations with the United States about the Ryukyu issue for many times, but they came to nowhere. Thus the status of Okinawa became an unsolved issue.

Furthermore, in order to occupy Okinawa legally, Dulles from U.S put forward that Japan had a "potential sovereignty" over the Ryukyu Islands in the hearing of San Francisco Conference held by the United States Senate in 1951. He believed that as long as Japan had sovereignty over Ryukyu without any interference from the United Nations or the Soviet Union, the US can get exclusive executive, judicial and legislative powers.

That is to say Japan had a "potential sovereignty" over Okinawa before the US handed over Okinawa to Japan. However, with a "potential sovereignty" over Okinawa, the Japanese still needed the passport and visa when they went to Okinawa, which indicated that Japan not only lost its sovereignty over Okinawa, but also lost its jurisdiction. In fact, the legislative, judicial and administrative rights of Okinawa were owned by the US occupation authorities. For example, the administration—United States Civil Administration of the Ryukyu Islands was the puppet government of the US occupation army. Japanese scholars had to admit that: the United States obtained the executive power and judicial power, the legislative power of the Ryukyu according to the Treaty of San Francisco, which actually meant it also obtained the sovereignty. So they had to make excuses for Japan's "residual sovereignty" of Ryukyu.

Japan unilaterally determined that the Diaoyu Islands were part of the Ryukyu Islands. According to the logic of Japan, whether China raised any objection about US's occupation of the Diaoyu Islands during the period when Japan had so-called "potential sovereignty" of Ryukyu had nothing to do with Japan. However, even if China did not challenged US's occupation of the Diaoyu Islands, it didn't mean that China admitted that Japan had the sovereignty over Diaoyu Islands.

B. Japan has no right to comment on China's various views. Recently, the website of the Japanese Ministry of Foreign Affairs translated its Basic Views into Chinese and added the "Q&A" section in it about the Diaoyu Islands. For example, in 1920, Chinese consul accredited in Nagasaki issued to the Japanese side a "letter of thanks" for saving Chinese fishermen, which mentioned the Senkaku Islands; in 1933, China published ROC new map where the Senkaku Islands were mapped into Japan's territory; an article carried in the People's Daily on January 8, 1953 said that Ryukyu included the "Senkaku Island"; Collections of World Maps published in China in 1958 listed the "Senkaku Islands" in the scope of Okinawa.

As for Taiwan, the website listed some examples. Collections of World Maps—East Asia published in China in October 1965 listed the "Senkaku Islands" in the scope of Japan; the geography textbook of elementary school in Taiwan published in 1970 listed the "Senkaku Islands" in the scope of Japan and used Japanese names; Japan also found an article titled the "Senkaku Islands" Prevent Our Fishing Boats published in United Daily News, the major newspaper of Taiwan.

However, Japan made use of Chinese officials' wording during the Japanese colonial period in Taiwan and some maps published during this period. It even used some articles to prove Japan had sovereignty over the islands. All these are unconvincing, because these all happened during Japan's invasion of China, they were not official statements and couldn't represent official position.

...

As mentioned above, even if the Diaoyu Islands belong to Okinawa, Japan lost its sovereignty of Okinawa during the US's occupation. It only had the "potential sovereignty" raised by Dulles and had no sovereignty over the Diaoyu Islands; hence, Japan had no right to comment on the unofficial views concerning the Diaoyu Islands issue. The best time for China to claim its sovereignty over the Diaoyu Islands was after the underhand secret dealings concerning the Diaoyu Islands between the US and Japan in 1971; and Ministry of Foreign Affairs of the People's Republic of China issued a statement just on December 30, 1971.

Conclusion

Through the above analyses, we can deduce the following conclusions: 1. The sovereignty over the Diaoyu Islands belongs to China, which is supported by historical facts and jurisprudential evidence in the Ming and Qing Dynasties; 2. It is illegal for Japanese Meiji government to treat the Diaoyu Islands as terra nullius and to incorporate the islands under the administration of Okinawa secretly; 3. China will never admit US's occupation of the Diaoyu Islands according to the Treaty of San Francisco, so it is illegal for the US to hand over the Diaoyu Islands to Japan; 4. The dispute over the Diaoyu Islands between China and Japan started with the Okinawa Reversion Agreement; Japan should squarely face historical facts and shouldn't deny this dispute by virtue of effective control; 5. due to the history and the Cold War, the Diaoyu Islands issue is a problem left over by history between the two countries and is an issue created by the US. The author thinks that given the complexity of the problem, the two countries should not ignore the reality in the current international environment and irrationally solve it immediately; the two countries should not stubbornly demand each other to accept one's own claim; instead, the two countries should shelve this dispute. As two powerful countries in Asia, I hope the two sides should focus on the overall situation and firmly maintain the consensus on shelving the dispute. The two sides should avoid breaking the status quo, fighting for meaningless advantages, creating tensions as well as affecting neighboring countries. We leave the issue to the next generation and now we should pursue common development and maintain peace so as to achieve a win-win situation.

(Taken from the website of Shanghai Institute for International Studies)

IV. Ownership of the Diaoyu Islands: Historical Facts

January 2011

Liu Jiangyong[14]

The Diaoyu Island and its affiliated islands have been China's inherent territories since ancient times. Ignoring this fact, the Japanese government still clings to the so-called Japan's Basic Views Concerning the Territorial Title of the Senkaku Islands (China's Diaoyu and adjacent islands – author) released by Japanese Ministry of Foreign Affairs in March 1972. Based on such obsolete and absurd "Basic Views", Japan's stringent stance on the question of the Diaoyu Islands have resulted in the deterioration of China-Japan relations and the rising antagonism between the two peoples. In order to prevent the territorial disputes from continued interfering in the China-Japan strategic relationship of mutual benefit, it is necessary to go to the roots of the cause and clarify the historical facts related with the ownership of the Diaoyu Islands.

The so-called "Basic Views" of the Japanese government are as follows: Since 1885, the Japanese government, through repeated on-site investigations by the authorities of Okinawa Prefecture and other channels, has cautiously confirmed that the Senkaku Islands are not only no-man's islands but also have no traces of the rule of (China's) Qing Dynasty. On this basis, the Cabinet decided on January 14, 1895, to have markers erected on the islands to officially incorporate them into Japan's territory.[15] This is the so-called fundamental "basis" of Japan's claim for the territorial title of these islands. This is equal to recognizing that before 1885 the Japanese government had never carried out investigations on, nor possessed, the Diaoyu and adjacent islands. Well, then, which country did these islands belong to before 1885? Did they have no owners? When talking about the sovereign right over the Diaoyu Islands, it is imperative, first of all, to clarify these questions.

---

14   Associate Dean of the School of Contemporary International Relations, Tsinghua University.
15   Basic Views of the Ministry of Foreign Affairs Concerning the Territorial Title of the Senkaku Islands dated 8 March 1972, the Collection of Basic Materials Concerning Japan-China Relations (1970-1992) released under the supervision of China Division of Japanese Foreign Ministry; published and distributed by Kazankai Foundation in Tokyo on 20 November 1993; p.73.

A large number of ancient authentic documents prove that, before Japan stole the Diaoyu Islands by taking advantage of the Sino-Japanese War of 1894-1895 (launched by Japanese imperialists to annex Korea and invade China), China had discovered, got to know and actually utilized these islands at least more than 500 years earlier than Japan. Okinawa, which used to be the Ryukyu Kingdom before it was annexed by Japan in 1879, had been an independent kingdom on the sea. China had granted honorific titles to the kings in Ryukyu in recognition of their rule. These islands had never been Japanese territory. Before 1895, Ryukyu plus the Japan-annexed Okinawa consisted of only 36 islands and the Diaoyu Islands had never been included. The boundary line between China and Ryukyu lied between the Chiweiyu and Jiumi Islands. This is the consensus recorded in all the historical documents of China, Ryukyu and Japan.

I. Historical Records during China's Ming and Qing Dynasties

According to records, as early as in 1372, the first emperor of the Ming Dynasty appointed Yang Zai as an imperial envoy to grant honorific title to the King in Ryukyu in recognition of his rule. The King of Ryukyu also dispatched his younger brother to follow Yang Zai back to pay tribute to and be granted honorific title by the Ming Imperial Court. The Ming emperor appointed 36 people from Fujian Province who were good at operating ships to go to Ryukyu, to facilitate the tribute-paying voyages (Chronicle of the Unification of the Great Qing Dynasty, 1744, volume 280). Thereafter, the imperial envoys of the succeeding dynasties left behind a large number of historical records testifying that the Diaoyu and adjacent islands belonged to China and not to Ryukyu. Ancient people in Ryukyu also agreed with this.

In China's historical documents, *The Chronicle of Ryukyu Kingdom* recorded in 610 AD that the voyage to Ryukyu passed by Gaohuayu i.e. the Diaoyu Islands. (Rectification of the Name of Diaoyu Islands written by Ju Deyuan and published by Kunlun Publishing House, Beijing, in January 2006, p.11, p.140). It is generally acknowledged that one of the earliest books that recorded the name of the Diaoyu Islands is Voyage with a Tail Wind published in 1403, the first year of the reign of Emperor Yong Le of the Ming Dynasty. The book used the names of "Diaoyuyu" and "Chikanyu", whose current names are the Diaoyu Islands and Chiweiyu (As a result of textual research, Voyage with a Tail Wind is one of the history books that have the earliest records of the Diaoyu Islands. There is a stencil copy of this book in the Bodleian Library of Oxford University, Britain). This proves that the Diaoyu and adjacent islands were discovered by Chinese envoys on their voyages to Ryukyu between 1372 and 1403 at latest, and they were used as markers for their voyages. (Research on the Ownership of the Diaoyu Islands before the Sino-Japanese War of 1894-1895 by Wu Tianying, published by China Social Documents Publishing House in Beijing in August 1994, pp. 25-28).

In 1534, the eleventh imperial envoy of the Ming Dynasty Chen Kan and some people from Ryukyu who had come to China to welcome Chen went to Ryukyu by ships. It was clearly recorded in the Records of the Imperial Title-conferring Envoys to Ryukyu (Shi Liu Qiu Lu): Sailing by the Pingjia Mountain, the Diaoyuyu, Huangmaoyu and Chiyu, there are too many islands for one's eyes to feast on.... When we arrived at Gumi Mountain which belonged to Ryukyu, foreigners on the boat danced in the accompaniment of drum-beating, feeling as happy as back at home.[16]

Gumi Mountain is also called Gumi Island, i.e. the Jiumi Island of Okinawa; "Foreigners" refer to the native people of Ryukyu on the boat. This shows that the Ryukyu people believed that they considered to have returned to their homeland after passing the Diaoyu Islands and only when they arrived at Gumi Island. The Diaoyu Islands, Huangmaoyu (Huangweiyu) and Chiyu (Chiweiyu) did not belong to Ryukyu.

In 1561, Imperial Envoy Guo Rulin wrote in Recompiled Records of the Mission to Ryukyu: On the first day of leap month May, we passed the Diaoyuyu. On the third day we reached Chiyuyan, which is a hill at the local boundary of Ryukyu. After another day's sail, we could see Gumi Mountain (Jiumi Island).[17] These lines further clearly prove that China at that time already took Chiweiyu, one of the Diaoyu and adjacent islands nearest to Ryukyu as a marker of Ryukyu boundary.

In 1556, Zhen Shungong went to Japan upon order. After half a year of investigations, he wrote a book entitled An Appraisal of Japan. In this book an essay entitled "Songs of a Long Voyage" clearly records that the Diaoyu Islands belonged to Taiwan: Sailing from Jilong Mountain of Xiaodong Island .... After some 20 hours' sailing, heading for Diaoyuyu.... From Xiaodong of Meihuadu to Penghu, further to Ryukyu and finally Japan. ... Diaoyuyu is a small island of Xiaodong.[18] "Xiaodong" was a form of address referring to Taiwan at that time. This proves that by that time China already identified the Diaoyu Islands and other islands as islands attached to Taiwan.

During the Qing Dynasty, the boundary line between China and Ryukyu was at the oceanic trough south of Chiweiyu, a dependent island of the Diaoyu Islands. This was the common knowledge of China's navigators. The second imperial envoy of the Qing Dynasty Wang Ji went to Ryukyu in 1683. In the following year he wrote Miscellaneous Records of the Mission to Ryukyu. This

---

16   The Records of the Imperial Title-conferring Envoys to Ryukyu (Shi Liu Qiu Lu) by Chen Kan, published in 1534 during the reign of Emperor Jiajing of the Ming Dynasty, p.25
17   Recompiled Records of the Mission to Ryukyu written by Guo Rulin during the 41st year of Ming Dynasty Emperor Jia Qing's reign, compiled and published by Taiwan Bank Economy Research Press in Taipei, December 1970, p. 73-76.
18   see Zhen Hailin's Historical Facts and Research on the Jurisprudence of the Diaoyu Islands, published by Mingbao Publishing House, Hong Kong, ed 1997, p.60.

book records: When he offered sacrifices in order to avoid marine casualty after sailing past the Diaoyu Islands and Chiweiyu, people on board told him that the trough over which their boat sailed was the boundary line between China and foreign countries.

The most influential book in Japan and Ryukyu at that time was the Letters of Zhongshan written by Deputy Imperial Envoy Xu Baoguang who went to Ryukyu in 1719, dispatched by Emperor Kangxi to grant honorific title to theKingin Ryukyu. By quoting the exposition from Zhinan Guangyi, a book written by an authoritative scholar Cheng Shunze in Ryukyu, the book points out: The sea route to Ryukyu is: leave Wuhumen from Min'an Town, sail to Jilongtou via Huapingyu, Pengjiashan, Diaoyutai, Huangweiyu and Chiweiyu, sail to Gumi Mountain (the principal island at the sea boundary to the southwest of Ryukyu), Machi Island and enter Naba Harbor of Ryukyu. (Letters of Zhongshan by Xu Baoguang published in 1719, the 58th year of the reign of Emperor Kangxi, p.36) Diaoyutai is mentioned three times and Diaoyuyu two times in this book. This is yet another reliable proof that Gumi Mountain was taken as a boundary marker between China and Ryukyu.

Particularly noteworthy is that, as early as during the Ming Dynasty, the Diaoyu Islands had been listed as Chinese territory in its defense area on the sea. At that time, Japanese pirates ran rampant. They often collaborated with local Chinese pirates to harass China's coastal areas in Zhejiang and Fujian Provinces. In 1561, the famous anti-pirate warrior Hu Zongxian together with Zhen Ruozeng compiled the Book on Managing the Sea, which contains a map of the coastal areas. In 1621, China's sea defense map drawn by Mao Yuanyi was published. Diaoyuyu, Huangweishan and Chiyu are all listed in the two books and regarded as the front line on the sea for resisting and preventing pirates from invading Zhejiang and Fujian Provinces.

II. Records in the Documents of Ancient Ryukyu Kingdom and Japan

Zhongshan Historical Records of Ryukyu Kingdom, an authoritative history book of Ryukyu Royal Court compiled under the supervision of Ryukyu Prime Minister Xiang Xiangxian, quotes Chen Kan as saying that Gumi Mountain belonged to Ryukyu, identifying Chiweiyu and the islands to its west were not the territory of Ryukyu. In 1708, the great Ryukyu scholar Cheng Shunze also said in Zhinan Guangyi that Gumi Mountain (Jiumi Island) was the principal island on Ryukyu's southwestern boundary. The book Natural Conditions and Customs of the Southern Islands published by a Ryukyu scholar in 1950 points out: the attached map in Cheng Shunze's Zhinan Guangyi was drawn according to the navigation map used by the 36 migrants selected and dispatched by the Ming Dynasty in 1392 (p.455). This proves that Chinese imperial envoys' boats discovered and utilized the Diaoyu Islands earlier than Ryukyu people. No later than the end of the 18th century, China and Ryukyu had identified their sea boundary line between Jiumi Island and Chiweiyu.

Japan's earliest written record about the Diaoyu Islands is theMaps of Three Provinces and 36 Islands of Ryukyu attached to "Overview Maps of Three Countries" written by Lin Ziping in 1785. In the maps, Diaoyutai and other islands have the same color as China's mainland and are not included in the scope of Ryukyu. None of the Complete Map of Greater Japan drawn by Japanese Ground Force Staff Bureau and published in 1876, the Complete Map of Ryukyu Islands attached to New Annals of Ryukyu published by Fumihiko Otsuki in 1873 and some other documents contain the Diaoyu and adjacent islands.

Japan's earliest authoritative writing about Okinawa's geography is the Okinawa Chronicles published in 1877. The author of the book Ijichi Sadaka was an official dispatched by the Meiji government to Ryukyu to "annual the vassal state and establish prefecture". In both the list of names of Okinawa Island and the attached maps, he mentioned neither the Diaoyu Islands nor Senkaku Islands.

Even after Japan annexed Ryukyu and named it "Okinawa Prefecture" in 1879, the above-mentioned boundary line was not changed. Until 1895, Okinawa had only 36 islands. The Diaoyu and adjacent islands were not included at all.

In 1880, when the Qing government and the Meiji government held negotiations over the ownership of Ryukyu, both sides confirmed that Ryukyu had altogether 36 islands, which did not include the Diaoyu and adjacent islands. On October 7, the same year, the Japanese side handed over to the Chinese side an official document Brief Study of the Two Islands of Yaehama Islands & Miyako Islands. Both the text and the attached maps did not have the Diaoyu Islands or the "Senkaku Islands". This is a very important historical fact. It fully proves that the Diaoyu and adjacent islands are by no means part of Ryukyu, still less Japan's inherent territory.

Japan's late famous historian and Prof. at Kyoto University Inoue Kiyoshi, after consulting historical documents, pointed out in his monographic study Analysis of the History of Senkaku Islands–Diaoyu Islands: Before the Meiji era (1868), apart from Chinese documents, other documents mentioning the Diaoyu Islands practically did not exist at all in Japan and Ryukyu. Before Japan encroached on the Diaoyu Islands, they were not terra nullius. He stressed that the Diaoyu Islands had been Chinese territory no later than the beginning of the Ming Dynasty. This fact has been recognized not only by the Chinese, but also by the people in Ryukyu and Japan.[19]

III. Historical Facts Before and After Japan Stole the Diaoyu Islands and Interpretations of International Law

The Japanese side claims, in 1884 Koga Tatsushiro from Fukuoka "discovered" large number of albatross dwelling on Huangweiyu and their feather could be exported to Europe. Therefore, Okinawa Prefecture was requested

---

19   Historical Facts of Senkaku Islands/Diaoyu Islands. Inoue Kiyoshi. Japan Modern Review Association. October 1972, p. 58.

to let him develop the land and erect a marker on the island with the words "Huangwei Island brought under cultivation by Koga". Taking this as an excuse, the Japanese government claims that the Diaoyu Islands are "terra nullius", occupied by Japanese first and not seized from China at the time of the Sino-Japanese War of 1894-1895 (launched by Japanese imperialists to annex Korea and invade China). This claim does not square with facts. The Japanese government at that time dared not approve the request. After repeated investigations, the Meiji government already knew in 1885 that the Diaoyu and adjacent islands were not terra nullius but that they belonged to China. That was the reason why the Japanese government dared not act impetuously.

It was not until January 14, 1895 that Japan, by taking advantage of the Sino-Japanese War of 1894-1895 and shortly before the negotiations on the Treaty of Shimonoseki, stole the Diaoyu Islands on which it had cast a covetous eye for a long time. Under this unequal Treaty of Shimonoseki, China was forced to cede to Japan the whole of Taiwan Island and all its adjacent islands, including naturally the Diaoyu Islands. Koga Tatsushiro was not granted permission to cultivate the islands until 1896. The Diaoyu Islands were not mentioned even in the Imperial Edict on the Composition of the Okinawa Prefecture the same year. The Japanese government's preoccupation of so-called terra nullius is utterly untenable.

The 1943 Cairo Declaration clearly stipulates: All territories Japan has stolen from China, such as Manchuria, Taiwan and the Penghu Islands, shall be restored to the Republic of China. Japan will also be expelled from all other territories which she has taken by violence and greed. The Potsdam Declaration stipulates in Article Eight: The terms of the Cairo Declaration shall be implemented. Japanese sovereignty shall be limited to the islands of Honshu, Hokkaido, Kyushu, Shikoku and such minor islands as we determine.[20] According to these international legal documents, all Chinese territories including Taiwan stolen by Japan in the past shall be restored to China. Since Japan accepted the Potsdam Declaration, the Diaoyu and adjacent islands, together with Taiwan, have been restored to China in jurisprudence.

The Japanese government holds in its "Basic Views": These islands have been the component parts of the southwest islands of our territory, not included in Taiwan and the Penghu Islands ceded according to the Treaty of Shimonoseki which came into force in the 28th year of Meiji government.[21] However, as a

---

20   Selected Information on the History of International Relations during Mid-17th century to 1945 compiled by Wang Shengzu, He Chunchao, Wu Shimin.

21   Basic Views of the Ministry of Foreign Affairs Concerning the Territorial Title of the Senkaku Islands dated 8 March 1972, the Collection of Basic Materials Concerning Japan-China Relations (1970-1992) released under the supervision of China Division of Japanese Foreign Ministry; published and distributed by Kazankai Foundation in Tokyo on 20 November 1993; p.73

saying goes, the more one tries to cover up a thing, the more it is exposed, the Japanese side has no evidence whatsoever to prove the first half of the senten- ce. The Treaty of Shimonoseki stipulates in Article Two: China cedes to Japan the island of Formosa, together with all islands appertaining or belonging to the said island of Formosa. The Diaoyu and adjacent islands are included but not listed in the Treaty as Huapingyu and other islands appertaining or belonging to Taiwan.

The "Basic Views" of the Japanese government claims: The Senkaku Islands are not included in the territories renounced by Japan as provided in Article 2 of the San Francisco Peace Treaty but, as part of the southwest islands, placed under the US administration according to Article 3, and included in territories restored to Japan as stipulated in the Japan-US Agreement on Ryukyu Islands and Daito Islands signed on June 17, 1971. After the islands under the US trusteeship was passed to Japan, they are naturally Japanese territory. Japanese Foreign Ministry considers: the "Senkaku Islands" are included in the territo- ries over which the US had the right to exercise powers of administration as stipulated in the San Francisco Peace Treaty. China did not raise any objection to this fact. This shows that China does not consider the Senkaku Islands as part of Taiwan. It was not until the latter half of 1970's that the issue of the territori- al title to the Senkaku Islands was raised when exploration of oil started on the continental shelves of East China Sea.[22]

This obviously does not square with the fact. As soon as the draft of the San Francisco Peace Treaty was put forward, Zhou Enlai, then Foreign Minister of China, pointed out in a statement: Without the participation of the People's Republic of China, anything will be regarded as illegal and null and void by the Chinese people's government, no matter what the contents and results are.

In 1951 the Japanese government's interpretation of the geographic concept about Article 3 of the San Francisco Peace Treaty was: the southwest islands south of 29 deg. north latitude, referring roughly to the scope of the spheres of influence of Ryukyu kings. However, the kings of Ryukyu never listed the Diaoyu Islands as part of Ryukyu. Therefore, it is untenable to delimit the ter- ritories only according to longitude and latitude.

In October 1971, the US government indicated: To restore to Japan the ad- ministrative right over these islands taken by Japan will not jeopardize relevant claims over the sovereignty. The US can neither increase Japan's legal rights before these islands were handed over the administrative rights to us, nor we- aken the rights claimed by others because the administrative rights are handed

22   Basic Views of the Ministry of Foreign Affairs Concerning the Territorial Title of the Senkaku Islands dated 8 March 1972, the Collection of Basic Materials Concerning Japan- China Relations (1970-1992) released under the supervision of China Division of Japanese Foreign Ministry; published and distributed by Kazankai Foundation in Tokyo on November 20, 1993; p.73

over to Japan…. Any disputed claims over such islands are matters to be resolved by the parties concerned.[23] When the US Senate ratified the Agreement on Returning Okinawa, the US State Department issued a statement: In spite of the fact that the US restored to Japan the right to exercise jurisdiction over these islands, the US will adopt a neutral stand between China and Japan over their confrontational claims to the islands. The US will be impartial to none in the conflict. Up to August 16, 2010, the US State Department spokesman Crowley still said on the ownership of the sovereignty over the Diaoyu Islands: "The US position on this issue is long-standing and has not changed. The United States does not take a position on the question of the ultimate sovereignty of the Senkaku Islands. We expect the claimants to resolve this issue through peaceful means among themselves."

IV. The Assertion that the Chinese Side Recognized Japan's Sovereignty of the Diaoyu Islands is not Tenable

To sum up, the so-called "Basic Views" of the Japanese government on the ownership of the Diaoyu Islands is squarely contradictory to historical facts. Such an assertion is merely aimed at deceiving others as well as Japan itself. At present, more deceitful are three kinds of deceptive talks in Japan attempting to prove that China once recognized Japan's ownership of the Diaoyu Islands:

First, in 1920, Chinese consul accredited in Nagasaki issued to the Japanese side a "letter of thanks" for saving Chinese fishermen, which mentioned the Senkaku Islands and Yangdao (i.e. the Diaoyu Islands). However, such so-called "evidence" is by no means evidence during the time of Japan's colonial rule over Taiwan. Second, Collections of World Maps published in China in 1958 listed the "Senkaku Islands" in the scope of Okinawa. However, on the title page of the book there is a notice: part of the boundary line was drawn according to the maps published by Shenbao before the War of Resistance Against Japanese Aggression. In the Country-Specific Maps of the World published in China in 1956, Okinawa does not include the Diaoyu Islands. Third, an article carried in the People's Daily on January 8, 1953 said that Ryukyu included the "Senkaku Island". After examinations, it is found out that the article was translated from an unsigned Japanese material. In the text, "Kadena" was translated into "Kataina" according to the Japanese pronunciation. This is a proof of Ryukyu people's struggle against the US occupation. Therefore, this source cannot represent the Chinese government's stand on the ownership of the Diaoyu Islands.

---

23   Senate Foreign Relations Committee hearing on 92nd Congressional Record, October 27, 1971, pages 29-91.

At present, some important Japanese political figures claim that the Diaoyu Islands are Japan's inherent territory and that there does not exist any territorial problem. But what cannot be denied is the fact that both China and Japan insist on their ownership of the Diaoyu Islands. Therefore, territorial disputes are an objective reality. The international community, the US included, does not agree with the above assertion of the Japanese political figures. It is a universal hope that China and Japan will resolve their disputes through peaceful negotiations according to international law. This calls for the sincerity and wisdom of both the Chinese and Japanese sides. The author believes that, pending the settlement of this issue, China and Japan should, proceeding from the overall interests of strategic mutual benefit, "shelve differences and seek joint development". This might be a reasonable option.

(Published in "People's Daily" on January 13, 2011, the author is Associate Dean of the School of Contemporary International Relations at the Tsinghua University)

V. On the History and Jurisprudence of the Diaoyu Islands

April, 2007

Zheng Hailin[24]

"On the History and Jurisprudence of the Diaoyu Islands" (updated version) was published by Zhonghua Book Company in 2007. By virtue of the knowledge of various disciplines and research methods such as linguistics, geography, historical textual criticism, tectonics and principles of International Law, etc. Mr. Zheng has done a thorough investigation on the history and status of sovereignty over the Diaoyu Islands and concluded that the sovereignty of the Diaoyu Islands belong to China. The names concerning the "Diaoyu Islands and its affiliated islands" all mean "the Diaoyu Islands". With the author's approval, I have excerpted related chapters from this book.

---

24 Editor's note: Zheng Hailin, born in 1957, Meixian, Guangdong Province. He got Bachelor's Degree of Philosophy in Zhongshan University in 1982 and PhD in History in Jinan University in 1987. He specializes in the history of Sino-Japanese relations and China's modern history. In 1995, he migrated to Vancouver, Canada and serves as a senior researcher at the University of British Columbia, the visiting Prof. of Asian Studies, specializing in international relations and cross-strait issues. He had written a lot masterpieces such as On the History and Jurisprudence of the Diaoyu Islands, Taiwan Issue Tests Chinese People's Wisdom, Thinking Pattern of Peaceful Cross-strait Reunification, Analyses of the Sovereignty over the Diaoyu Islands—From the Perspective of history and International Law, etc.

Brief conclusion

Since the 1970s, Japan's arguments of its sovereignty over the Diaoyu Islands have come from On Sovereignty over the Senkaku Islands published in the name of the Ryukyu government on September 17, 1970. Afterwards, based on the spirit of the "declaration", the Japanese Ministry of Foreign Affairs published the official view—"Senkaku Islands Are Evidently Japan's Territory" on March 8, 1972. The "declaration" and the "view" have become the foundation of Japan's official spokesmen when they negotiate with China on the issue of Diaoyu Islands. Therefore, if we want to know the dispute over the Diaoyu Islands between Japan and China, we must firstly know Japan's claims and arguments. However, although Japan has put forward many reasons and "evidence", they can be roughly divided into two aspects: one is preemptive occupation of terra nullius, the other is the geographic division method.

I. Preemptive occupation of terra nullius

Japan initially proposed it had the sovereignty over the Diaoyu Islands because they treated these islands as terra nullius, and with Japan's discovery, Japan incorporated the islands into its territory. Japan's evidence was as follows:

1) Koga Tatsushiro landed on these islands and did some investigations around 1884. He was sure that they were unmanned island.

2) On September 22 in the eighteenth year of the Meiji period, the government sent "Izumo Maru" to these islands to do a field survey. They found these islands had no traces of the rule of the Qing Dynasty, so they identified them as "terra nullius".

3) After submitting related reports to Cabinet, Cabinet demanded the Okinawa governor to set up national symbols on these islands.

4) In the 23th year of the Meiji period (1896), Japan released No. 13 edict, thus completing the official incorporation of these islands into its territory.

Japan's "evidence" seemed to be quite logical. But the problem lay in whether the Diaoyu Islands were terra nullius before the 1880s, as the preemptive occupation in the International Law requires the land to be terra nullius. While the definition of terra nullius in International Law refers to the land that has not yet been occupied in the name of any country. Uninhabited island is not terra nullius; while terra nullius doesn't have to be the uninhabited island. Even if there were aboriginal people living on these islands, they will be terra nullius if the international community has not yet recognized its owner. Therefore, the reason why Japan treated the islands as terra nullius is that Japan has equaled "uninhabited" island to terra nullius. Besides, Japan thought these islands had no traces of the rule of the Qing Dynasty (established the national markers).

On the definition of terra nullius, China replied with contrary claims:

1) The Diaoyu Islands were first discovered, named and exploited by the Chinese people, which can be proved by Voyage with a Tail Wind (Shun Feng Xiang Song). It can be called inchoate title in the International Law.

2) The Diaoyu Islands have been put under the administration of China since the Ming Dynasty [refer to An Illustrated Compendium on Maritime Security (Chou Hai Tu Bian) in 1562]. It is in accordance with the definition of "control" concerning the sovereignty of coastal states in International Law, which indicates that China has the sovereignty over the Diaoyu Islands.

3) China's sovereignty over the Diaoyu Islands has been internationally recognized, which can be proved by maps published by various countries such as Japan, France, Britain, the United States, Spain, etc.

According to the above three reasons, we can see that Japan's definition of terra nullius is untenable.

II. The longitude and latitude division method

The other reason is that Japan explains that the Diaoyu Islands are within the longitude and latitude of Japan. Japan pointed out that the United States Civil Administration of the Ryukyu Islands released Geographical Realm of Ryukyu Islands on December 25, 1953, which mapped in the Diaoyu Islands, Huangwei Yu and Chiwei Yu according to the longitude and latitude of Ryukyu (24°00'N–28°00'N; 122°00'E–133°00'E). As a result, the Japanese government declared undoubtedly, the Diaoyu Islands belong to Japan.

Japan's longitude and latitude division method is based on the conventional division of the border between two nations as well as the International Law, which generally has four criteria:

1) The physiographic borders (using natural geographical entity as demarcation standards)

2) The astronomical borders (boundary line in accordance with longitude and latitude lines)

3) The geometric boundaries (drawing a straight line from a fixed point on the border to another fixed point as the boundary line)

4) The human geographic borders (such as national borders in accordance with the nations distribution, religious boundaries in accordance with residents' religious beliefs, power boundaries determined by war and strength, etc.)

According to the above four standards, we can know that Japan referred to astronomical boundaries and geometric boundaries, namely, delimiting the scope of latitude and longitude, and then cutting it by geometric methods. This delimitation method seems to be in accord with some of the international standards, but it ignores the most important one, namely the physiographic boundary method, which has been formed according to the nature and history. On this basis, China puts forward contradictions to Japan's longitude and latitude division method:

1) Ryukyu and China have local boundaries. To China, it's the Chiwei Yu; to Ryukyu, it's the Gumi Mountain (see the Records of the Imperial Title-conferring Envoys to Ryukyu (Shi Liu Qiu Lu) written by Chen Kan and Guo Rulin)

2) With a depth of 2,700 metres and located between Chiwei Yu and Gumi Mountain, the East China Sea trench is the border between the two countries (see Miscellaneous Records of a Mission to Ryukyu (Shi Liu Qiu Za Lu) written by Wang Ji).

3) In terms of geographical and geological structure, the Diaoyu Islands belong to China's continental shelf, and was naturally separated from the Ryukyu islands. The Diaoyu Islands locate on the volcanic belt of DaTun Mountain in the north of Taiwan, while the Ryukyu islands locate on the volcanic belt of Kiri Island, so the Diaoyu Islands do not belong to the Ryukyu's territory.

4) The official historical literature of the old Ryukyu Kingdom never incorporated Diaoyu Islands into its territory. At the beginning of Meiji Period, Japan didn't incorporate the Diaoyu Islands into the latitude and longitude of Okinawa; until the early 1970s, Japanese officials explained the Diaoyu Islands were included.

According to the above four reasons, Japan's incorporation of the Diaoyu Islands into its territory based on the longitude and latitude division method has no legal force in International Law.

Based on the above analyses, Japan's preemptive occupation of terra nullius is untenable; from last year, Japanese officials no longer stressed the longitude and latitude division method in their statement. In fact, the Diaoyu Islands were mapped within the longitude and latitude of Ryukyu by United States Civil Administration of the Ryukyu Islands in 1953 and were put under its effective control. Therefore, in order to overthrow the Japan's "longitude and latitude division method" and win the support of the international public opinions, China should conduct an overall analysis of historical literature, geography and geological structure and the International Law.

According to the current international standards, China's sovereignty over the Diaoyu Islands is indisputable. According to the Article 2 of "Convention on the Continental Shelf": The coastal State exercises over the continental shelf sovereign rights for the purpose of exploring it and exploiting its natural resources, China's sovereignty over Diaoyu Islands which are located within China's continental shelf is generally acknowledged and beyond dispute. Fundamentally, China's territorial sovereignty over the Diaoyu Islands was not originated from "sovereign rights" in Convention on the Continental Shelf in the 1950s; instead, as early as 5 centuries ago, the book Voyage with a Tail Wind (Shun Feng Xiang Song) in 1403 recorded The Diaoyu Islands were first discovered, named and exploited by the Chinese people long before 1403. From then on, China has had the inchoate title of these islands.

Whether it is the "sovereign rights" or the "inchoate title" in the International Law, Japan's longitude and latitude division method is untenable fundamentally.

III. Three propositions on solving the Diaoyu Islands issue

1) Recovery of the inchoate title.

The Diaoyu Islands were first discovered, named and exploited by the Chinese people. According to history records, from 1403 to 1969, the Chinese people landed on the Diaoyu Islands freely and left a large number of written records. However, over the past 20 years, the Japanese government suddenly declared the Diaoyu Islands were Japan's territory and prevented the Chinese from landing on these islands, depriving their rights of landing on the Diaoyu Islands in the past 500 years. It not only goes against the International Law, but also violates human rights. This kind of behavior of the Japanese government is not only an insult to the Chinese people, but also an infringement of China. Therefore, China should recover its inchoate title through diplomatic channels so as to regain the Chinese people's rights of landing on these islands, and prohibit activities of the Japanese Self-Defense Coast Forces within 12 sea miles of the Diaoyu Islands, which is completely in accordance with the human justice.

China should actively exercise its sovereign rights as it has the sovereignty over the Diaoyu Islands.

Harry S. Truman, the U.S. President issued a statement concerning the continental shelf on September 28, 1945: "the US government holds that it is reasonable and fair for the coastal states to exercise jurisdiction on the natural resources on the seabed and the subsoil of the continental shelf." According to the spirit of the statement, the United Nations signed Convention on the Continental Shelf in 1958, the Article 2 of which stipulates: "The coastal State exercises over the continental shelf sovereign rights for the purpose of exploring it and exploiting its natural resources." The Diaoyu Islands are located on the east of China's shallow sea continental shelf, so China is the coastal State which holds sovereignty over the Diaoyu Islands; hence, there is no doubt that China has the sovereign-rights of natural resources on the Diaoyu Islands. China should actively exercise the sovereign rights, discover and use the natural resources on the Diaoyu Islands. It totally accords with the International Law.

Settling the territorial sovereignty dispute

China should negotiate with the Japanese government with historical litera-ture, evidence of geography and geological structure, international jurispruden-ce, etc. Then they can submitted them to the international arbitration court so as to settle the territorial sovereignty dispute eventually.

On the border demarcation between China and Ryukyu

Related historical records of the land demarcation between China and Ryukyu

I carefully studied sailing records of China, Ryukyu, Japan and Westerners and found that since the Ming and Qing Dynasties, China and Ryukyu had very clear boundaries of in respect to land and water. China and Ryukyu reached consensus on these boundaries, so do Japan and Westerners at that time.

The records of the border demarcation between China and Ryukyu Records of the Imperial Title-conferring Envoys to Ryukyu (Shi Liu Qiu Lu) written by Chen Kan includes the following:

In the 5th year of Ming Dynasty Emperor Jia Qing's reign (1526), Zhongshan King of Ryukyu died. His successor submitted his request—inheriting the throne—to the Ming Empire. In 1534 during the 13th year of Ming Dynasty Emperor Jia Qing's reign, the imperial envoy Chen Kan was appointed to Ryukyu from Fuzhou. In his book Records of the Imperial Title-conferring Envoys to Ryukyu (Shi Liu Qiu Lu), he wrote: On the 10th day, the strong southerly wind pushed the ship forward with lightning speed and we passed by Pingjia Mountain, Diaoyu Island, Huangmao Yu and Chi Yu. One day and one night's voyage equals that of three days. The barbarians' boats were so small that they were lagging far behind. At sunset of the 11th day, we saw the Gumi Mountain which belongs to Ryukyu. The barbarians all beat drums and danced in the boats to express their joy upon arriving home."The above-men-tioned "Diaoyu Island, Huangmao Yu and Chi Yu" are today's Diaoyu Islands, Huangwei Yu and Chiwei Yu.They were included in China's territorial waters. Chen Kan clearly stated that "the ship has passed Diaoyu Islands, Huangmao Yu, Chi Yu... Then Gumi Mountain comes into sight, that is where the land of Ryukyu begins."

2) Records of the Imperial Title-conferring Envoys to Ryukyu (Shi Liu Qiu Lu) written by Guo Rulin

In the 34th year of Ming Dynasty Emperor Jia Qing's reign (1555), Zhongshan King of Ryukyu died. In the 37th year of Ming Dynasty Emperor Jia Qing's re-ign, his successor submitted his request—inheriting the throne—to the Ming Empire. In 1561 during the 40th year of Ming Dynasty Emperor Jia Qing's re-ign, the imperial envoy Guo Rulin was appointed to Ryukyu. His book Records of the Imperial Title-conferring Envoys to Ryukyu (Shi Liu Qiu Lu) records:

"On the first day of leap month May, we passed the Diaoyuyu. On the third day we reached Chiyuyan, which is a hill at the local boundary of Ryukyu. After another day's sail, we could see Gumi Mountain. He stated that "Chi Yu is the mountain that marks the boundary of Ryukyu". So the western parts to Chiwei Yu belong to China and the eastern parts to Chiwei Yu belong to Ryukyu. Gumi Mountain is in the east to Chiwei Yu, so it belongs to Ryukyu. Therefore, Chen Kan said: Then Gumi Mountain comes into sight, that is where the land of Ryukyu begins. We can see the boundary recorded by Chen Kan and Guo Rulin is the same, which is Chiwei Yu is the border of China's territory.

3) Records of Messages from Chong-shan (Zhong Shan Chuan Xin Lu) written by Xu Baoguang

In 1722 during the 58th year of Emperor Kang Xi's reign of Qing Dynasty, Haibao, a title-conferring envoy in the Qing Dynasty and Xu Baoguang, a deputy title-conferring envoy were appointed to Ryukyu to grant honorific title to the King in Ryukyu. The ship started from Wuhumen of Fuzhou on May 22 and arrived at Naba Harbor of Ryukyu on June 1. Xu Baoguang stayed in Ryukyu for 8 months. He studied Annals of Chong-shan (Zhong Shan Shi Jian) and other maps. At last, he completed Records of Messages from Chong-shan (Zhong Shan Chuan Xin Lu), which was praised highly by China, Ryukyu, Japan as well as many scholars. Annals of Ryukyu (Liu Qiu Guo Zhi Lue) written by Zhou Huang and The book Illustrated Outline of the Three Countries written by Hayashi Shihei were all based on this book.

By quoting the exposition from Zhinan Guangyi, a book written by an authoritative scholar Cheng Shunze in Ryukyu, the book points out: The sea route to Ryukyu is: leave Wuhumen from Min'an Town, sail to Jilongtou via Huapingyu, Pengjiashan, Diaoyutai, Huangweiyu and Chiweiyu, sail to Gumi Mountain (the principal island at the sea boundary to the southwest of Ryukyu), Machi Island and enter Naba Harbor of Ryukyu.

Xu Baoguang added some explanation for Gumi Mountain—the principal island at the sea boundary to the southwest of Ryukyu, which accords with "then Gumi Mountain comes into sight, that is where the land of Ryukyu begins." said by Chen Kan. This is another reliable proof that Gumi Mountain was taken as a boundary marker between China and Ryukyu.

The above three historical documents clearly record the border demarcation between China and Ryukyu. For China, Chiwei Yu is the boundary while for Ryukyu, it is the Gumi Island.

1. Related historical records of demarcation of the territorial waters between China and Ryukyu

A) Records of the Imperial Title-conferring Envoys to Ryukyu (Shi Liu Qiu Lu) written by Guo Rulin

Records of the Imperial Title-conferring Envoys to Ryukyu (Shi Liu Qiu Lu) records the ship was attacked by hurricane and lost the direction. "we see the green water, we may drifted back to our country's waters, the next day, we see Ninbo Mountain." Obviously, when they were lost and couldn't see any mountains, they would see the water color. If they saw green water, they were in China's waters, because the "Black water trench"(Hei Shui Gou) between the Gumi Mountain and Chiwei Yu was the border of the two countries. Between the Gumi Mountain and Chiwei Yu, there is an East China Sea trench with depth of 2700 meters. As it is very deep, so the sea surface is dark black, forming a sharp color contrast to China's green waters of China's shallow continental shelf (with depth of 50-200 meters). Historical documents show that in the Ming and Qing Dynasties, China's imperial envoys who went to Ryukyu from Fuzhou knew clearly about Huaping Yu, Pengjia Mountain, Diaoyu Island, Huangwei Yu, Chiwei Yu, which are on China's shallow continental shelf. They have green or blue waters and these waters have been called "Chang Shui" (clear water). These sea waters always belong to China and are sailing areas of the Chinese ships. According to Voyage with a Tail Wind (Shun Feng Xiang Song) published in 1403 (the first year of the reign of Emperor Yongle of the Ming Dynasty), the Chinese ships always sailed to these islands on China's shallow continental shelf, there were shipping lines to these islands from Fuzhou. When the ships passed Chiwei Yu, the sea waters looked dark, which belong to Ryukyu; and Gumi Mountain on the black sea is Ryukyu's territory. Therefore, we can understand "Chi Yu is the mountain that marks the boundary of Ryukyu" said by Guo Rulin and "then Gumi Mountain comes into sight, that is where the land of Ryukyu begins" said by Chen Kan.

B) Addendum to Summarized Record of Ryukyu (Liu Qiu Lu Cuo Yao Bu Yi) written by Xie Jie

In 1579, Xie Jie was appointed to grant honorific title to the King in Ryukyu. He recorded in his book, Addendum to Summarized Record of Ryukyu (Liu Qiu Lu Cuo Yao Bu Yi) that he entered Ryukyu from Cang Shui to Hei Shui, and returned to China from Hei Shui to Cang Shui. It means that he entered Ryukyu from green waters to dark waters, and came back to Fuzhou from dark waters to green waters.

C) Records of the Imperial Title-conferring Envoys to Ryukyu (Shi Liu Qiu Lu) written by Xia Ziyang

In 1606, Xia Ziyang was appointed to grant honorific title to the King in Ryukyu. He recorded in his book, Records of the Imperial Title-conferring Envoys to Ryukyu (Shi Liu Qiu Lu) that when he returned to Fuzhou from

Naba, what he saw were all dark waters. On October 22, when they passed Gumi Mountain, they encountered hurricane and their ship was wet; on October 29th, they saw a ship and everyone cheered as they thought they were close to China; moreover, they crossed the border from black water to green water.... on November 1st, the ship arrived Wuhumen. Xia Ziyang clearly recorded that they were in China's waters when they saw the sea waters turned green. To put it in another way, the Hei Shui Gou is the boundary between Ryukyu and China; green waters belong to China while black waters belong to Ryukyu's waters.

D) Miscellaneous Records of a Mission to Ryukyu (Shi Liu Qiu Za Lu) written by Wang Ji

In 1683, Wang Ji was appointed to grant honorific title to theKingin Ryukyu. He recorded in his book, Miscellaneous Records of a Mission to Ryukyu (Shi Liu Qiu Za Lu) that on June 23, they shipped from Wuhumen; on June 24, they saw Pengjia Mountain. They passed the mountain around 8 a.m. and passed the Diaoyu Islands around 6 p.m.... On June 25, they saw mountains. They should see Huangwei Yu before Chiwei Yu, but they arrived at Chiwei Yu unknowingly without seeing Huangwei Yu. After passing the Hei Shui Gou (dark trench), the sea was no longer peaceful, they offered sacrifices to Ocean God by throwing pigs and sheep, pouring rice gruel into the sea, burning paper vessels and beating drums. After a long time, the sea recovered in peace. Wang Ji asked the old sailor: "what does Hei Shui Gou mean?" "Boundary between China and foreign land", answered the old sailor. Wangji asked: "why?" and the old sailor said: "it is a lucky guess." Wang Ji added: "you did the ceremonies for the God of the Sea just on the Hei Shui Gou, it may not be just a guess." He clearly recorded that after passing Chiwei Yu, they saw Hei Shui Gou, which is the boundary between China and Ryukyu.

E) The Annals of Ryukyu (Liu Qiu Guo Zhi Lue) written by Zhou Huang

Zhou Huang was appointed to grant honorific title to theKingin Ryukyu. He recorded in his book, The Annals of Ryukyu (Liu Qiu Guo Zhi Lue) that Ryukyu is separated from the waters of Fujian by Hei Shui Gou to the west; we shipped from Fujian to Ryukyu and went from Cang Shui to Hei Shui. Dongming is Ryukyu (Ming means dark). It clearly points out that Hei Shui Gou is the boundary between China and Ryukyu. Green waters (Cang Shui) belong to China while black waters (Hei Shui) belong to Ryukyu waters. The sea border dividing method was a consensus of official ambassadors and navigators of China, Japan and Ryukyu. What's more, it was repeatedly mentioned by imperial envoys in the Ming and Qing Dynasties. It is an indisputable historical fact.

2. The border demarcation between Ryukyu and China has been internationally recognized

The above documents concerning the border demarcation between Ryukyu and China recorded by the imperial envoys in the Ming and Qing Dynasties are internationally recognized. Now I will cite some historical documents and maps of other countries.

A) Ryukyu's Archival Records of Its Previous Dynasties

The book recorded the relationships between Ryukyu and its neighboring countries from 1424 to 1867, including China, Korea, Japan, Southeast Asia and the United Kingdom, France, etc. In this book, besides the collected records of the imperial envoys in the Ming and Qing Dynasties, there are no articles mentioning about the Diaoyu Islands. Moreover, the book mentions about "Miyagi" and "Kubashima", which are all people's names rather than names of places, so it has nothing to do with Japan's claim that Japan owns the Kuba Island (Kubashima in Japanese; Huangwei Yu in Chinese) of the Senkaku Islands. We can see from this book that the ancient Kingdom of Ryukyu has nothing to do with the sovereignty over the Diaoyu Islands. The knowledge concerning the Diaoyu Islands is quoted from documents recorded by the imperial envoys in the Ming and Qing Dynasties, which indicates that Ryukyu accepted the border demarcation between Ryukyu and China recorded in these documents.

B) Annals of Ryukyu

It is the first Annals of the Ryukyu Kingdom. The great scholar Cai Wen of Ryukyu started it in 1792 and completed it in 1745, namely from the 2nd year of Song Dynasty Emperor Jia Xi's reign to the 2nd year of Qing Dynasty Emperor Guang Xu's reign. It has 22 volumes with 3 attachments. The whole annals never mention the Diaoyu Islands. There are many records concerning Gumi Island, Miyako Islands and Yaeyama Islands as well as the southernmost Yonaguni Island. Even in the records concerning the tribute- paying to Fujian, there is no mention about the Diaoyu Islands, which indicates that Ryukyuan had no clear concept of the Diaoyu Islands but they were quite familiar with Gumi Island, Miyako Islands and Yaeyama Islands. Therefore, "Gumi Mountain (the mountain guarding the southwest border of Ryukyu)" (volume 1) and "Yaeyama Islands are the most southwestern border" (volume 4), recorded by Xu Baoguang are in accordance with this official annals of the Ryukyu kingdom.

C) The Annals of Chong-shan (Zhong Shan Shi Jian) Written in 1650, it is the first official historical record of the Ryukyu Kingdom drafted under the supervision of Ryukyu's prime minister Xiang Xiangxian. It confirmed that Gumi Mountain (also called Gumi Mountain, known as Kume Island today) is part of Ryukyu's territory, which was recorded by Chen Kan in the Records of the Imperial Title-conferring Envoys to Ryukyu (Shi Liu Qiu Lu). Obviously, he also accepted that the territory of Ryukyu ended by the Gumi Mountain.

D) A General Guide (Zhi Nan Guang Yi)

In 1708, Cheng Shunze (Tei Junsoku) a noted scholar and the Grand Master with the Purple-Golden Ribbon (Zi Jin Da Fu) of Ryukyu wrote this book where he also used the Diaoyu Islands, Huangwei Yu and Chiwei Yu. What's more, in the attached drawing of this book, the Diaoyu Islands, Huangwei Yu and Chiwei Yu are mapped together and formed an obvious dividing line with Gumi Mountain. The drawing becomes the best explanation of "then Gumi Mountain comes into sight, that is where the land of Ryukyu begins." recorded by Chen Kan and "Chi Yu is the mountain that marks the boundary of Ryukyu" by Guo Rulin. It is also the original version of Needle Road Map by Xu Baoguang and The Map of the Three Provinces and 36 Islands of Ryukyu by Hayashi Shihei.

The above historical records are sufficient to prove that scholars from Ryukyu and China reached consensus on the border demarcation between Ryukyu and China. Some maps at that time are also hard proofs of the border demarcation between Ryukyu and China.

MAPS

A) The map titled as the The Records of Japan and Ryukyu designed by Shen Shuzhou from Korea completed in 1471 is the oldest map of the Ryukyu Kingdom. In this map, the islands on the border between Ryukyu and China are Bird Island located in the north west, Jiumi Island (Gumi Mountain) and Flower Island (Yaeyama Islands). Therefore, "Gumi Mountain (the mountain guarding the southwest border of Ryukyu)" and "Yaeyama Islands are the most southwestern border", recorded by Xu Baoguang are in accordance with this map.

B) The Great Map of Ryukyu collected by Tajiri Museum in Okinawa showed Aguni Island guarding the northwest border of Ryukyu, the Gumi mountain guarding the southwest border of Ryukyu and Yonaguni Island (one of Yaeyama Islands guarding the most southwest border of Ryukyu), which is similar to the Map of Ryukyu drawn by Shen Shuzhou.

C) The Map of Ryukyu drawn by the Japanese government in the Genroku period in 1702 marked the Gumi mountain guarding the southwest border of Ryukyu and Yonaguni Island (one of Yaeyama Islands guarding the southwest border of Ryukyu)

D) Records of Messages from Chong-shan (Zhong Shan Chuan Xin Lu) drawn by Xu Baoguang (1719) and the attached drawing—The Map of the 36 Islands of Ryukyu are in accordance with The Great Map of Ryukyu collected by Tajiri Museum in Okinawa and The Map of Ryukyu drawn by the Japanese government in the Genroku period.

E) The attached drawing—the Atlas of Ryukyu from The Annals of Chong-shan (Zhong Shan Shi Pu) drawn by the great scholar Cai Wen of Ryukyu in 1725 marked the Gumi mountain guarding the southwest border of Ryukyu and Yonaguni Island (one of Yaeyama Islands guarding the most southwest border of Ryukyu).

F) The South Island Chronicles complied by the Japanese historian Arai Hakuseki in 1719 also marked the Gumi mountain guarding the southwest border of Ryukyu and Yonaguni Island (one of Yaeyama Islands guarding the most southwest border of Ryukyu) in the map of Ryukyu.

G) The Map of the Three Provinces and 36 Islands of Ryukyu in the book—Illustrated Outline of the Three Countries written by Hayashi Shihei in 1785 marked the Gumi mountain guarding the southwest border of Ryukyu and Yaeyama Islands guarding the most southwest border of Ryukyu. He added that the Yaeyama Islands belong to Ryukyu. To the west of the Gumi mountain, he marked Huaping Yu, Pengjia Mountain, Diaoyu Island, Huangwei Yu and Chiwei Yu and colored them the same as the mainland of China, indicating that they are part of China's territory.

H) The Map of Japan's Boundary drawn by the Japanese scholar Takahashi Kageyasu in 1809 marked the Gumi mountain guarding the southwest border of Ryukyu, and Iriomote Island and Ishigaki Island guarding the most southwest border of Ryukyu (it only marked two islands of the Yaeyama Islands).

I) The Map of East China Sea Littoral States drawn by French publisher and geographer Pierre Lapie in 1809 painted Diaoyu Island, Huangwei Yu and Chiwei Yu and all Taiwan's affiliated islands in red and painted Ryukyu in green, indicating that the Diaoyu Islands are Taiwan's affiliated islands.

J) The Complete Map of Ryukyu Islands is the first modern map drawn by the Japanese. It marked the islands along the "Shina Sea" (China Sea), among which there are islands and mountains located between Fujian and Ryukyu. In the South, there are Huaping Yu, Pengjia Mountain, Diaoyu Island, Huangwei Yu and Chiwei Yu; in the North, there are Ma Mountain, Tai Mountain, Yu Mountain, Fengwei Mountain and Nanqi Mountain. They are all marked as China's territory. As for Ryukyu, it marked the Gumi Mountain guarding the southwest border of Ryukyu and Yonaguni Island (one of Yaeyama Islands guarding the most southwest border of Ryukyu). This map was based on the map drawn by Hayashi Shihei, which indicates that Japan geologists of the early 19th century clearly knew that the Diaoyu Islands belonged to China.

K) Colton 's China published in New York in 1859 is a modern map of China. It marks "Hawapingsun" (Huangwei Yu in Chinese Min dialect) on the place of the Diaoyu Islands and "Taiyusu" (the Diaoyu Islands in Chinese Min dialect) on the place of Huangwei Yu. Although it marks on the wrong positions, it maps the Diaoyu Islands and Huangwei Yu into China's territory.

L) The Complete Map of Greater Japan drawn by the Japanese Army Staff Bureau in 1876 marked the Gumi mountain guarding the southwest border of Ryukyu and Yonaguni Island (one of Yaeyama Islands guarding the most southwest border of Ryukyu)

M) The Complete Map of Ryukyu Islands in the New Annals of Ryukyu made by the Japanese historian Otsuki Fumihiko in 1873 clearly maps the whole territory of the Ryukyu Islands—the Gumi mountain guarding the southwest border of Ryukyu and Yonaguni Island (one of Yaeyama Islands guarding the most southwest border of Ryukyu).

N) The Complete Map of Okinawa in the Okinawa Chronicles made by Ijichi Sadaka, an official dispatched by the Meiji government to Ryukyu in 1877 shows the territories of Okinawa—the Gumi mountain guarding the southwest border of Ryukyu and Yonaguni Island (one of Yaeyama Islands guarding the most southwest border of Ryukyu).

O) The Sea Borders Map of China and Japan drawn by J.P. Morales published by Mantanna Simon Company in Barcelona in 1879 maps the Hokkaido, Honshu, Shikoku, Kyushu and Okinawa into Japan's territory and marks the Diaoyu Islands, Huangwei Yu and Chiwei Yu as China's territory.

3. The history and the related International Law prove that the Diaoyu Islands belong to China instead of Japan

From the above historical records and maps that originate from China, Ryukyu, Japan and besides historical records and maps of various western countries created before 1880, we can see that the Diaoyu Islands belong to China's territory; to put it in another way, the history proves that the Diaoyu Islands belong to China instead of Japan. Hisashi Owada's claim that the Diaoyu Islands is part of Japan's territory in history is groundless and untenable. The earliest book of Ryukyu that recorded the Diaoyu Islands is the General Guide (Zhi Nan Guang Yi), while the earliest book of Japan that recorded the Diaoyu Islands is the Illustrated Outline of the Three Countries, which all clearly maps the Diaoyu Islands into China's territory. Of Course, at that time, China could not establish its sovereignty over the Diaoyu Islands and its waters by setting up border markers and flag-raising ceremonies as stipulated in the modern International Law; but imperial envoys going to grant honorific title to the King in Ryukyu was an action to survey the territories and claim its sovereignty on behalf of the Emperors; and those documents recorded by imperial envoys are undoubtedly official documents; that's why China, Ryukyu, Japan and other countries attach great importance to them. For example, Records of Messages from Chong-shan (Zhong Shan Chuan Xin Lu) recording the Gumi mountain guarding the southwest border of Ryukyu and Yaeyama Islands guarding the most southwest border of Ryukyu not only has been treated as a classic by officials of China and Ryukyu but also has been regarded as an authoritative book of research on the Ryukyu Kingdom by international community. After its publication in 1722, Japan translated it and added kana (Japanese letters) on it in 1766; later in 1781, the book was reprinted and published in Paris, France. The Map of East China Sea Littoral States drawn by French publisher and geographer Pierre Lapie in 1809 maps the Diaoyu Islands, Huangwei Yu and Chiwei Yu into China's territory as Taiwan's affiliated islands; he must have referred to Records of Messages from Chong-shan (Zhong Shan Chuan Xin Lu). These historical documents are undoubtedly the International Law basis of China's sovereignty over the Diaoyu Islands.

Records of Messages from Chong-shan (Zhong Shan Chuan Xin Lu) clearly records the Diaoyu islands, Huangwei Yu, Chiwei Yu belong to China rather than Ryukyu. "They had been discovered by the ship of the imperial envoy of the Qing Dynasty who went to grant honorific title to the former Zhongshan King and had been named by China. They are sea marks on the route to Ryukyu" (excerpted from the report of Sutezo Nishimura, the Okinawa Magistrate on September 22, 1885; according to the preemptive occupation of terra nullius in the International Law, namely, claiming the inchoate title when discovering a territory, Nishimura admitted that China had the inchoate title of the Diaoyu Islands, while Japan had no such right. Hence, Nishimura was still worried when Yamagata Aritomo, the Ministry of Internal Affairs, set up stakes after the secret investigations of the Diaoyu Islands. In a word, the sovereignty over the Diaoyu Islands can't be applied to preemptive occupation of terra nullius in the International Law, as the territory should be terra nullius; but the Diaoyu Islands have been China's territory since ancient times and are not terra nullius.) More importantly, China and Ryukyu already had clear boundaries—Chiwei Yu and Hei Shui Gou. The division of the borders can be supported by a large number of historical documents, but also is in accord with International Law.

The definition of the national territory in the International Law: "a country's territory includes all lands and waters, underground, and air space within its borders and jurisdiction." On this basis, a country's territory consists of three parts: (1) Territorial Land, including lands and underground; (2) Territorial Waters, referring to Territorial Sea and National Waters, the former referring the coastal area of the territorial waters; the latter referring to the various waters off the coast; (3) Territorial Air, referring to air space above the territorial land and territorial waters.

The limit of a country's territory is called Boundary in the International Law. Oppenheim defined it as imaginary lines on the ground, dividing territories between countries or differentiating a country's territory from terra nullius or high seas.

Criteria of the International Law concerning the border demarcation are as follows :

1) rivers and mountains between two countries;

2) lakes or inland seas between two countries,

3) mountain ridges between two countries, often by a watershed;

4) waters between two countries.

According to the above principle of International Law, the border demarcation of Ryukyu and China is in accord with the last two criteria. Chiwei Yu is the boundary of territorial land of Ryukyu and China and Hei Shui Gou is the boundary of territorial waters of Ryukyu and China. Therefore, the Diaoyu Islands, Huangwei Yu, Chiwei Yu are undoubtedly a part of China's territory, sea waters 12 nautical miles from these islands are China's territorial waters. The claim of Hisashi Owada can't be supported by historical facts and International Law, so it is invalid.

Analyses of Japan's claim that Japan has sovereignty over the Diaoyu Islands

Since the 1970s, Japan's argument of its sovereignty over the Diaoyu Islands has come from On Sovereignty over the Senkaku Islands published in the name of the Ryukyu government on September 17, 1970. This declaration raised 8 reasons to support Japan's argument that Japan has the sovereignty over the Diaoyu Islands. Afterwards, based on the spirit of the "declaration", the Japanese Ministry of Foreign Affairs published the official view—"Senkaku Islands Are Evidently Japan's Territory" on March 8, 1972 with four evidence. The "declaration" and the "view" have become the foundation of Japan's official spokesmen when they negotiate with China on the issue of the Diaoyu Islands. Therefore, if we want to know the dispute over the Diaoyu Islands between Japan and China, we must firstly know Japan's claims and arguments and debate with Japan according to International Law. Only in this way can we win the support of the international public opinions. I will list the "declaration" and the "view", and conduct a comprehensive analysis on them to identify the sovereignty over the Diaoyu Islands.

4. The delimitation of geographic boundary of the Ryukyu islands

About the delimitation of geographic boundary of the Ryukyu islands, the "declaration" has the following statement:

About the scope of the Ryukyu islands, the executive order of the US stipulates is the basic rule of law on the management of the Ryukyu islands, rules "according to Article 3 of the Treaty of San Francisco, the US has jurisdiction over the Ryukyu islands and the executive power of their territorial seas" ("Ryukyu Islands" mentioned in this order referred to Southwest Islands, south of 29deg. north latitude) , including the islands, islets, atolls, cays and territorial sea in the areas lined by points—28°N, 124°40′E; 24°N, 122°E; 24°N, 133°E; 27°N, 131°50′E; 27°N, 128°18′E; 28°N, 124°18′E (Geographical Realm of Ryukyu Islands released by United States Civil Administration of the Ryukyu Islands)

The above is Japan's most important reason to claim its sovereignty over the Diaoyu Islands. There are two key points: 1. Article 3 of the Treaty of San Francisco signed on September 8th, 1951 stipulates "Japan will concur in any proposal of the United States to the United Nations to place under its trusteeship system, with the United States as the sole administering authority, Nansei Shoto south of 29deg. north latitude (including the Ryukyu Islands and the Daito Islands), Nanpo Shoto south of Sofu Gan (including the Bonin Islands, Rosario Island and the Volcano Islands) and Parece Vela and Marcus Island. Pending the making of such a proposal and affirmative action thereon, the United States will have the right to exercise all and any powers of administration, legislation and jurisdiction over the territory and inhabitants of these islands, including their territorial waters." But it never mentioned the Diaoyu Islands or the Senkaku Islands. The United States Civil Administration of the Ryukyu Islands released Geographical Realm of Ryukyu Islands on December 25, 1953, in which the Diaoyu Islands, Huangwei Yu and Chiwei Yu was included based on the longitude and latitude division method. We should point out that whether it had legal effect according to International Law or not, because according to the convention of division on the border between two counties in the International Law, it must first respect natural boundaries formed by history; if the two countries have disputes, they negotiate with each other in order to solve it; unilateral opinion is without legal effect. In addition, the conventional division of the border between two nations generally has four criteria:

1. The physiographic borders (using natural geographical entity as demarcation standards)

2. The astronomical borders (boundary line in accordance with longitude and latitude lines)

3. The geometric boundaries (drawing a straight line from a fixed point on the border to another fixed point as the boundary line)

4. The human geographic borders (such as national borders in accordance with the nations distribution, religious boundaries in accordance with residents' religious beliefs, power boundaries determined by war and strength, etc.)

According to the above four standards, we can know that United States Civil Administration of the Ryukyu Islands referred to astronomical boundaries and geometric boundaries, namely, delimiting the scope of latitude and longitude, and then cutting it by geometric methods. This delimitation method seems to be in accord with some of the international standards, but it ignores the most important one, namely the physiographic boundary method, which has been formed according to the nature and history. With a depth of 2,700 metres and located between China's shallow continental shelf and the Ryukyu Islands, the East China Sea trench (Hei Shui Gou) is border between the two countries. The marks of the physiographic borders between Ryukyu and China—Chiwei Yu and Gumi Mountain are located on both sides of this trench. It is not only supported by a lot of historical facts and the official documents, but also accepted by the international community. And the boundary defined by the United States and Japan is only a unilateral opinion. Without China's participation and the agreement from the international committee, it does not have the validity of International Law. It is completely reasonable for China to treat it as underhand secret dealings between the US and Japan.

The territory defined by United States Civil Administration of the Ryukyu Islands based on the longitude and latitude division method is Japan's most important argument that it has sovereignty over the Diaoyu Islands. Based on this "argument", Japan embarked on finding the historical documents and "evidence" to prove the rationality of Geographical Realm of Ryukyu Islands. However, in the process, Japan found in the historical documents that he Diaoyu Islands were first discovered, named and exploited by the Chinese people rather than the Ryukyuan; that is to say, the inchoate title of the Diaoyu Islands belongs to China rather than Ryukyu. But the Japanese also know according to the International Law, countries with the inchoate title of some land can't prevent from other countries from occupying the land if it haven't done any effective control on the land. Therefore, Japan determined these islands as terra nullius because China did not take any effective control, and then occupy them by virtue of the preemptive occupation of terra nullius in the International Law. Hence, the key point is whether the islands are terra nullius as the preemptive occupation of terra nullius can only be applied to terra nullius. Therefore, the Japanese scholars spare no effort to prove the Diaoyu Islands are terra nullius while efforts made by scholars in China lie in proving the Diaoyu Islands are not terra nullius and they have always been part of China's territory.

5. Arguments of "terra nullius"

About whether the Diaoyu Islands are terra nullius, Japan has published an official "declaration" and argued the following points:

1) In history, since the latter of the 14th century, Japan has known the existence of the Senkaku Islands. From 1372 to 1866, because of tribute-paying and title granting system between Ryukyu and China, ships frequently shipped between Fuzhou and Naha. The Senkaku Islands locates on this sea route. Because of the protrusion of rocks on the Diaoyu Islands and adjacent islands or rock islands, they are ideal sailing marks. Therefore, the islands have been recorded by Records of Messages from Chong-shan (Zhong Shan Chuan Xin Lu), the Annals of Ryukyu (Liu Qiu Guo Zhi Lu), A General Guide (Zhi Nan

Guang Yi) and its attached drawings, the Annals of Chong-shan (Zhong Shan Shi Jian), etc.

United States Civil Administration of the Ryukyu Islands deliberately distorted the name of the Diaoyu Islands in the above passage. Moreover, it removed the fact that the Diaoyu Islands were first discovered, named and exploited by the Chinese people, because according to International Law, even if some land is considered to be terra nullius, but when one country firstly discovers, names it and tell the discovery to others, the country obtains the inchoate title. The fact that the Diaoyu Islands were first discovered, named and exploited by the Chinese people can be supported by Voyage with a Tail Wind (Shun Feng Xiang Song) in 1403. Japan's discovery and naming them as the Senkaku Islands was in the late 19th century. In addition, the matter that the Senkaku Islands is recorded in Records of Messages from Chong-shan (Zhong Shan Chuan Xin Lu) mentioned by the "declaration" is untenable, because the fact is that these books used Chinese namings—the Diaoyu Islands,Huangwei Yu, Chiwei Yu.

2) Although these islands have names of the Diaoyu Islands, Huangwei Yu, Chiwei Yu, in Okinawa, they call the Diaoyu Islands "Yukun", Huangwei Yu "Kubashima" and Chiwei Yu "Kumeakashima" because Chiwei Yu is close to the Kume Island. In addition, some people call Kuba Island (Huangwei Yu) "Tiausu" and the Diaoyu Islands "Waheiyama"(Peace Mountain). Accordingly, although the names of the Senkaku Islands have been recorded in all kinds of historical literature, different people call these islands by different names the Senkaku Islands of the island name, its name is different from person to person. Until the 28th year of the Meiji period (1895), the Senkaku Islands didn't belong to any country. In other words, the islands are terra nullius according to the International Law. Since the 14th century, the documents of Ryukyu and China had never mentioned that the Senkaku Islands are their territory and had treated them only as sailing marks in some logbooks and charts. China just named them to make them easy to remember in some poems.

Please pay attention to two points: 1. the names of the Diaoyu Island and its affiliated islands. The Diaoyu Islands, Huangwei Yu and are first discovered and named by China. The documents of China, Ryukyu and Japan all adopted these names from the 15th century to the 19th century. The other names mentioned above emerged after the 19th century, which can never affect China's inchoate title. 2. terra nullius in the International Law. The claim that the Diaoyu Islands are terra nullius is an irresponsible remark ignoring historical facts. We can find a great number of documents recording that the Diaoyu Islands are China's territory. Records of Messages from Chong-shan (Zhong Shan Chuan Xin Lu) mentioned in the "declaration" records that "Gumi Mountain (the mountain guarding the southwest border of Ryukyu)". The Diaoyu Islands located on the other side of the Hei Shui Gou are bound to be China's territory. The

Annals of Ryukyu (Liu Qiu Guo Zhi Lue) mentioned in the "declaration" also clearly records that Ryukyu "is separated from the waters of Fujian by Hei Shui Gou to the west". It clearly points out that the Hei Shui Gou is the boundary between Ryukyu and China. The areas east to Hei Shui Gou belong to Ryukyu while The areas west to Hei Shui Gou belongs to China. In additon, An Illustrated Compendium on Maritime Security (Chou Hai Tu Bian) compiled by Zheng Ruozeng under the auspices of Hu Zongxian, the supreme commander of the southeast coastal defense of the Ming court, included the Diaoyu Islands, Huangwei Yu and Chiwei Yu into the jurisdiction of the coastal defense of the Ming court. It is the effective control mentioned in the International Law and an action to declare China's sovereignty over these islands.

The Diaoyu Islands were China's territory rather than being terra nullius in the Ming and Qing Dynasties periods, which is not only supported by China's official literature, but also supported by the international community (including Japan). For example, the Map of the Three Provinces and 36 Islands of Ryukyu in the book—Illustrated Outline of the Three Countries written by Hayashi Shihei in 1785 marked the Gumi mountain guarding the southwest border of Ryukyu and Yaeyama Islands guarding the most southwest border of Ryukyu. He added that the Yaeyama Islands belong to Ryukyu. To the west of the Gumi mountain, he marked Huaping Yu, Pengjia Mountain, Diaoyu Island, Huangwei Yu and Chiwei Yu and colored them with the same color as the mainland of China, indicating that they are part of China's territory. It is a well known fact in the international community and the "declaration" also admitted this fact. Therefore, Japan's claim on the Diaoyu Islands are terra nullius is not in conformity with the historical facts and is untenable.

3) The process of the "preemptive occupation of terra nullius"

Now that the Diaoyu Islands is terra nullius, so Japan's preemptive occupation of the Diaoyu Islands according to the principle of International Law is untenable. However, in its "declaration", the government of Japan enumerated a lot of documents so as to demonstrate its process of the "preemptive occupation" and its legal basis, which is an action to mislead the people and fool the international public opinions; hence, I will express a solemn position and tell the truth.

(1) In the 5th year of the Meiji period in 1872, the Ryukyu Kingdom was changed into Ryukyu Vassal. In the 7th year of the Meiji period, it was affiliated to the Ministry of Internal Affairs. In the 12th year of the Meiji period, it was changed into Ryukyu County. In the Maps of Names of Provinces and Cities in Japan compiled by the Ministry of Internal Affairs, the Senkaku Islands has been mapped in without names in the appendix. Until the early stage of the Meiji period (1877-1882), the Senkaku Islands were uninhabited island. Around the 17th year of the Meiji period, Koga Tatsushiro began to

collect the feathers of the albatross, wool hair, carapace and shellfish around the Diaoyu Islands and the Kuba Island. On September 22 in the 18th year of the Meiji period, the government sent "Izumo Maru" to these islands to do a field survey and submitted to the Ministry of Internal Affairs to set up national markers.

There are two key points we should pay attention to about the above "declaration": 1. Japan claimed that in Maps and Names of Provinces and Cities in Japan published in the 14th year of the Meiji period, the Senkaku Islands has been mapped in without names in the appendix. Whether it was true or not, it couldn't fall into the scope of preemptive occupation because early before that, in 1561 (the 40th year of the reign of Emperor Jiajing of the Ming Dynasty), An Illustrated Compendium on Maritime Security (Chou Hai Tu Bian) compiled by Zheng Ruozeng under the auspices of Hu Zongxian, the supreme commander of the southeast coastal defense of the Ming court, included the Diaoyu Islands, Huangwei Yu and Chiwei Yu into China's territory. It is far more convincing than the map without the names of these islands. Japan claimed that until the early stage of the Meiji period (1877-1882), the Senkaku Islands were uninhabited islands and used it as its evidence to prove that its preemptive occupation was legal. Japan intentionally equaled the uninhabited islands to terra nullius, but they are two different concepts in International Law. The uninhabited island refers to the island that is not suitable for living; while terra nullius is not occupied in the name of any country. Terra nullius doesn't have to be the wild land without residents; Even if there were aboriginal people living on these islands, they will be terra nullius if the international community has not yet recognized its owner. Since the Ming Dynasty, the Diaoyu Islands have been put under the jurisdiction of China's naval defense. Therefore, the Japanese authorities' claim that the uninhabited island is terra nullius doesn't accord with the definition in the International Law. Strictly speaking, so far, the Diaoyu Islands are still uninhabited islands.

(2) On November 26 in the 26th year of the Meiji period (1893), Okinawa prefecture governor, with the same reason, submitted a report concerning setting up the national markers to the Ministry of Foreign Affairs and the Ministry of Internal Affairs. On December 27 in the 27th year of the Meiji period, the Ministry of Internal Affairs asked the opinions of the Ministry of Foreign Affairs, and gained no opposition. On January 14 in the 26th year of the Meiji period, Cabinet incorporated the Diaoyu Islands and Kuba Island under the administration of Okinawa and on January 21, it demanded the Okinawa governor to set up national symbols on these islands.

Due to Japan mistook uninhabited island for terra nullius, it began to implement its "preemptive occupation" with following steps: (1) according to the investigation report of Koga Tatsushiro, they defined the islands as unmanned islands. (2) then the government sent "Izumo Maru" to these islands to do a field survey. They found these islands had no traces of the rule of the Qing Dynasty, so they identified them as as "terra nullius". (3) after submitting related reports to Cabinet, Cabinet demanded the Okinawa governor to set up certain national symbols on these islands.

It is worth mentioning that Japan did all these secretly, because Japan is afraid of the opposition from the Qing dynasty government. Sutezo Nishimura, the Okinawa governor knew clearly that the Diaoyu Islands were first discovered, named and exploited by the Chinese people. Although there was no national markers, China had the inchoate title. Hence, even with the Cabinet's demand to set up national symbols on these islands, the Okinawa governor didn't do anything about it. Until on May 5, 1969, the Japanese government still did not build any markers on the Diaoyu Islands, which indicates that their occupation wasn't in accord with preemptive occupation in the International Law (although from the beginning, the "preemptive occupation" is never tenable).

(3) On April 1st in the 29th year of the Meiji period, based on the Cabinet's decision, Japan released No. 13 edict, thus completing the incorporation of these islands into its territory formally. According to the explanation of the Governor of Okinawa, Yaeyama Islands in No. 13 should include the Senkaku Islands; so the islands were incorporated into Yaeyama Islands. This incorporation was not a local incorporation but also an action based on the territory incorporation in the National Law.

As mentioned earlier, in 1562, the Diaoyu Islands have been put under the jurisdiction of China's naval defense, which is the "effective control" and an action to claim the national sovereignty. According to the definition of "control" concerning coastal nations' sovereignty in the International Law, China, as the coastal countries constitutes the sovereignty over the Diaoyu Islands. Under this premise, the principles—preemptive occupation of the International Law cannot be applied to the Diaoyu Islands. As a result, Japan released No. 13 edict, thus completing the incorporation of these islands into its territory formally, which has been completely meaningless according to the International Law. To put it in another way, Japan's secret incorporation of the islands into its own territory isn't in accord with not only preemptive occupation of the International Law but also the "effective control" (an action to claim the national sovereignty), so it has no legal effect.

Based on the above analyses, the arguments put forward by Japan are all untenable if judged by the standards of the International Law. Therefore, Japan's occupation of the Diaoyu Islands (without an action to claim the national sovereignty) after April 1, 1895 fell to the scope of power boundaries. While the year1895 marked the signing of Treaty of Shimonoseki, so we have to have a discussion about this treaty.

4) The relationship between Japan's occupation of the Diaoyu Islands and Treaty of Shimonoseki

On March 8, 1972, the Japanese Ministry of Foreign Affairs denied the relationship between Japan's occupation of the Diaoyu Islands and Treaty of Shimonoseki in its official views: the Diaoyu Islands are part of the Southwest Islands, and according to Article 2 of the Treaty of Shimonoseki, these islands are not included in the ceded territories of the Qing Dynasty.

I will point out two things: 1. Japan's claim that the Diaoyu Islands are part of the Southwest Islands can't be supported by historical facts. Historically, from the documents of China, Ryukyu and Japan, we can't find any evidence to prove that the Diaoyu Islands were mapped in the Ryukyu Kingdom and were a part of the Southwest Islands. Instead there are a large number of documents proving that the Diaoyu Islands belong to China. However, why does the Japanese government present this reason? One is that the United States Civil Administration of the Ryukyu Islands released Geographical Realm of Ryukyu Islands in 1953, in which mapped in the Diaoyu Islands, Huangwei Yu and Chiwei Yu based on the longitude and latitude division method. The other is that Treaty of Shimonoseki didn't mention these islands are included in Taiwan and Penghu Islands which were ceded to Japan, hence Japan treated them as part of Southwest Islands. 2. As for the deduction that these islands are included in Taiwan and Penghu Islands, the logic of Japanese government is that since China claims its sovereignty over the Diaoyu Islands and these islands are included in Taiwan's affiliated islands, so they should be included in Article 2 of Treaty of Shimonoseki; but the treaty never mentioned the Diaoyu Islands, so these islands do not belong to Taiwan and Penghu Islands; now that they do not belong to Taiwan and Penghu Islands, they are undoubtedly part of the Southwest Islands. Japan's logic seems to be rational, but it can't stand careful analyses:

1) Article 2 of Treaty of Shimonoseki stipulates the Taiwan island and all its affiliated islands should be ceded to Japan; Article 3 of Treaty of Shimonoseki stipulates   Penghu Islands should be ceded to Japan. Although the Diaoyu Islands were not mentioned in the these terms, we can't deduce that they belong the Southwest Islands. Because the term also didn't mention many other islands of "Taiwan island and its affiliated islands" such as Lan Yu, Ryukyu Yu, Huaping Yu, Pengjia Yu, etc.

2) As the Diaoyu Islands were the fishing ground of Taiwan fishermen, so we often treated them as the affiliated islands of Taiwan. It is naturally formed by history, which is reflected in Chinese literature. In 1556, Zhen Shungong went to Japan upon orders. After half a year's investigations, he wrote a book entitled An Appraisal of Japan, in which clearly records that the Diaoyu Islands belonged to Taiwan: Diaoyuyu is a small island of Xiaodong. "Xiaodong" was

a form of address referring to Taiwan at that time. Moreover, in the 28th year of the Meiji period, conquests of Taiwan bandits and thief of Japan-Qing War History compiled by the Japanese navy province recorded the position of the Senkaku Islands—"ninety nautical miles north of freshwater port of Taiwan (on the sea of Keelung), indicating the Diaoyu Islands are Taiwan's affiliated islands.

3) Although the Diaoyu Islands were not incorporated into Taiwan's affiliated islands administratively, but in official literature such as An Illustrated Compendium on Maritime Security (Chou Hai Tu Bian), Treatise on Military Preparations, Taiwan, Penghu Islands, Pengjia Mountain, Diaoyu Islands, Huangwei Yu, Chiwei Yu were put under the jurisdiction of China's naval defense. In the Qing Dynasty, Taiwan still belonged to Fujian Province. In 1885, system of provinces were conducted, no documents recorded whether the Diaoyu Islands had been transferred under the administration of Taiwan, but it didn't change that the Diaoyu Islands belong to China. As Diaoyu Islands locate on the sea of Keelung, they were the fishing ground of Taiwan fishermen. Naturally, they are treated as Taiwan's affiliated islands. It is naturally formed by history, which is reflected in Chinese and Japanese literature. Japan's logic (either A or B) is not based on historical documents and is untenable.

4) As for the geographical location, the Diaoyu Islands and the Taiwan Island are located on the East China Sea continental shelf; as for the geological structure, the Diaoyu Islands belong to the Volcanic Belt of Datun Mountain of Taiwan; while the Southwest Islands belong to the volcanic belt of Kiri Island. Besides, Southwest Islands and Diaoyu Islands are separated by a trench in the East China Sea as deep as 2700 meters. Therefore, the truth that the Diaoyu Islands are Taiwan's affiliated islands is not only supported by the historical documents but also obtains the validation of the modern science. It can never be overthrown by any logic game.

According to the above analysis, Article 2 of Treaty of Shimonoseki stipulates the Taiwan island and all its affiliated islands should be ceded to Japan, hence the Diaoyu Islands should be included. So, the legal basis of Japan's occupation of Diaoyu Islands should at least partially lie in Article 2 of Treaty of Shimonoseki. (author's note: Qiu Hongda also made this deduction in his book Analyses on Japan's Argument of Its Sovereignty over the Diaoyu Islands; see page 93 of Diaoyu Islands–China's Territory! published by Ming pao Press).

Above are the main arguments concerning Japan's sovereignty over the Diaoyu Islands from the "declaration" of United States Civil Administration of the Ryukyu Islands and the "view" of the Japanese Ministry of Foreign Affairs. In a nutshell, Japan holds two reasons: one is preemptive occupation of terra nullius, the other is the longitude and latitude division method. However, both are untenable.

The hand-over of Ryukyu and the Diaoyu Islands issue

Campaign of Protecting Diaoyu Island has become the common voice of the Chinese around the world. The Chinese across the straits, standing on the ground of safeguarding national territorial integrity, simultaneously condemn the Japanese right-wing group's occupation of the Diaoyu Islands. Japan, the perpetrator, claims it has the sovereignty over the Diaoyu Islands. They said China didn't oppose when the Diaoyu Islands and Okinawa were put under the US's trusteeship according to Chapter 3 of the Treaty of San Francisco. Therefore, recently the US handed over Diaoyu Islands and Okinawa back to Japan. On this basis, the Japanese think their sovereignty over the Diaoyu Islands is beyond doubt. On the other side, the Chinese government took a cautious attitude towards the Diaoyu Islands issue and put forward the propose—"shelving the dispute". Obviously, the Diaoyu Islands issue involves China, Japan and the United States: China and Japan stick to their own argument while US takes a "neutral" attitude, but in fact it is in favor for Japan. On the sovereignty over the Diaoyu Islands, why does such situation appear? I will respect the historical facts and take a "value-neutral" attitude so as to give an intact narrative of the hand-over of Ryukyu and the Diaoyu Islands issue based on the historical data of China and Japan.

If we want to know the ins and outs of the Diaoyu Islands issue, we should start from the hand-over of Ryukyu, because the Diaoyu Islands issue is related to Japan's annexation of Ryukyu and occupation of Taiwan. The Diaoyu Islands are located between Taiwan and the Ryukyu islands. Voyage with a Tail Wind (Shun Feng Xiang Song) published in 1403 (the first year of the reign of Emperor Yongle of the Ming Dynasty) records that the Diaoyu Islands do not belong to the 36 islands of Ryukyu. Since 1372, Ryukyu had been included in the tribute system of China's Ming and Qing Dynasties and become China's vassal state. However, the Ming Emperors never ruled the Ryukyu Kingdom politically. This continued to the Qing Dynasty. But during this period, the Ryukyu Kingdom (today's Okinawa, Japan) was affected by Japanese forces constantly; in fact it was affiliated to two countries. Japan interfered its internal affairs and folk customs. Each time the Chinese imperial envoy came, the Japanese in Ryukyu would hide themselves, which lasted to the Japanese Meiji Restoration Period. But Ryukyu still claimed it was the vassal of China when it signed trade treaties with the United States, France and Holland; it still used China's reign title, Chinese calendar and Chinese characters, and just called Japan its friendly nation.

After the Meiji Restoration in 1868, the Japanese Meiji government planned to annex Taiwan. In order to find a military base to invade Taiwan, Japan was eager to annex the Ryukyu kingdom as Japan's territory. In February 1872, Shigeru Narabara, the magistrate of Kago Island in Kyushu, went to Ryukyu and declared Japan's reform in Ryukyu to heads of the Ryukyu government.

A year before, fishermen of Ryukyu were killed by the Gaoshan people when they drifted to Taiwan after an accident on the sea. Japan sent troops to attack Taiwan with this excuse. Japan intentionally distorted the representations of the officials of the Qing government that "some people in Taiwan like outsiders didn't obey the rules of the Qing Emperor", based on which, Japan claimed that Taiwan didn't belong to China and forced the Qing government to sign Taiwan Specialized Article, the first article of which was China had no opposition to Japan's chivalrous deed for safeguarding its people, and give Japan a compensation of 500000 silver (currency of the Qing Dynasty). Japan forced the Qing government to admit that people of Ryukyu were Japanese people so as to make its annexation of Ryukyu legal. Then, Japan's Ministry of Internal Affairs Okubo Toshimichi submitted his proposal concerning the annexation of Ryukyu to the Japanese government as China had no opposition to Japan's chivalrous deed for safeguarding its people in the Taiwan Specialized Article. He wrote: China had no opposition to Japan's chivalrous deed for safeguarding its people. It meant that China admitted that Ryukyu belongs to Japan, but the boundary between the two countries has not been determined. He suggested that the Japanese government must firstly strengthen the nationalization of Ryukyu and cut off its relations with China; then it should conduct system reform to Ryukyu Kingdom. The concrete measures were: "firstly we should summon the important officials of Ryukyu and tell them the system reform and tell them to cut off its relations with China. We will set bases in Naha and reform its criminal law and educational system, etc. so as to prove Ryukyu belong to our country."[25]

Okubo Toshimichi's proposal gained the Japanese government's approval. In 1875, the Japanese government sent soldiers of Kumamoto to Ryukyu and issued an order: stop paying tribute to China and receiving honorific titles from China; Revocation of Fuzhou Ryukyu pavilion; Ryukyu's trade and negotiations with China in the future shall be governed by the Japanese Ministry of Foreign Affairs. The Japanese government's order (stop paying tribute to China) opened the curtain of the modern Sino-Japanese dispute—negotiations concerning Ryukyu between China and Japan.

Ryukyu was shocked at the Japanese government's order (stop paying tribute to China). Ryukyu King immediately appointed his son to thank Japan for its favor and told him to explained to Japan that they couldn't stop paying tribute to China. Moreover, early in 1877, Ryukyu King appointed Xiang Dehong to pay tribute to China and asked China for help. He Jing, Governor of Zhejiang and Fujian, and Ding Richang, Fujian governor, received Xiang Dehong and they expressed opposition to the Japanese government's order (stop paying tribute to China). They suggested that the Qing court appoint He Ruzhang to Japan and told Japan Ryukyu is a vassal state of China and shouldn't be stopped from

---

25   Book, Memoirs of Japan, p. 148. Published by East Asia Common Culture Association.

paying tribute to China; moreover, the Qing court should invite envoys in Japan to judge this matter according to Law of Nations.[26] He Ruzhang received the Qing court's order and submitted three schemes based on the advice of Huang Zunxian, the diplomatic officer then to Ministry of Foreign Affairs in Qing Dynasty. The three policies were: 1. The best scheme: on the one hand, we should debate with Japan; on the other hand, we should send troops to Ryukyu to inquire the envoys so as to show Japan our determination and power. 2. The mediated scheme: if Japan didn't listen to reasons, the people of Ryukyu would fight against Japan for its own survival. If Japan attacked Ryukyu, we should send troops to help Ryukyu and attack Japan from inside and outside. Japan is bound to be defeated, and we can negotiate with Japan about a peaceful solution. The last scheme: if Japan is still so stubborn, we can deal with this issue according to public law and invite envoys to discuss about this issue. Japan will know his wrong behavior and Ryukyu will luckily survive.[27] However, He Ruzhang's proposal was unable to catch attention from the general administration. Li Hongzhang replied to He Ruzhang: the tribute from Ryukyu is not so beneficial. It is unnecessary to spare effort to fight for the tribute of a small country. He instructed He Ruzhang that as for the Japanese government's order (stop paying tribute to China), we should deal with it according to Article 2 of Chapter one in Sino-Japanese Provisions of Cordial Relations. Later, Li Hongzhang wrote to Gongqin King: He Ruzhang suggested that we should send troops to inquire Japan... I think he makes a big fuss over a minor issue. We can see that Li Hongzhang didn't agree He Ruzhang's first two schemes. He preferred to solve that problem by virtue of diplomacy and tell Japan the status of Ryukyu. The general administration agreed with Li Hongzhang and held that we should stay calm and collected and should not be flustered over the Ryukyu issue. They were afraid of upsetting Japan and causing disputes with Japan. But they also didn't want to acquiesce in Japan's annexation of Ryukyu and give up Ryukyu which had been its vassal state for five hundred years. The Qing government will never stand such things. Therefore, they chose the "third scheme" and appointed He Ruzhang to negotiate with Japan according to Sino-Japanese Provisions of Cordial Relations.

He Ruzhang lodged oral opposition concerning the Japanese government's order (stop paying tribute to China) to Munenori Terashima, the Ministry of Foreign Affairs, by citing Article 1 in Sino-Japanese Provisions of Cordial Relations—the two countries should never interfere in each other's territory and communicate with each other with manner so as to gain the permanent security and peace. Later He Ruzhang sent an eloquent inquiry to Japan indicating that it undermined the friendship between the two countries that the Japanese government prevented Ryukyu from paying tribute to China. The

26   "Historical Documents of Sino-Japanese Diplomacy during the Qing Dynasty Emperor Guang Xu's Reign" Volume I, p.21.
27   Wen Tingjing, Volume II of "Text Copy"—"Debate with Governor on Ryukyu Issue".

inquiry mentioned "I think Great Japan will never betray its neighbors and bull the weak. All these are unrighteous, ruthless and unreasonable manners." Terashima thought this inquiry was a "violent" inquiry which disgraced the Japanese government; Terashima insisted that Ryukyu was a vassal state of Japan and said: "for hundreds of years, Ryukyu belong to Japan's territory and now is incorporated under the administration of the Ministry of Internal Affairs. Terashima required He Ruzhang to send a written apology and to annul the inquiry, otherwise Japan would refused the negotiation. Then, the negotiations about Ryukyu issue stalled. However, Li Hongzhang accused He Ruzhang instead of supporting him. The general administration also objected to He Ruzhang's intransigence in the negotiation; he even planned to withdraw He Ruzhang to restore the deadlock. While the Japanese government knew that China had no intention to strive for Ryukyu; hence, in March 1879, Japan sent troops to take over the Shouli City where the Ryukyu King lived and capture the King and the prince to Tokyo, changing Ryukyu to Okinawa. The Qing court turned a blind eye to it and lost its vassal state—the Ryukyu Kingdom.

About Japan's annexation of Ryukyu, because of the pressure of public opinion, the Qing court felt "if we do nothing about the doom of Ryukyu, other country will accuse us." At the time that the former President of the United States Ulysses Simpson Grant traveled to China and would pay a visit to Japan; the Qing court invited him to mediate this issue. After the mediation of Grant, the Qing court firstly made concessions. With Grant's suggestion, the general administration present a note to the Japanese Ministry of Foreign Affairs: we take back all the arguments before and will deal with the issue as what the former President of the United States Ulysses Simpson Grant suggests. This equaled to a written apology for the note He Ruzhang sent to Japan. This "weak root" diplomacy, of course, received Japan's "deeply gratitude".

After Grant's "mediation", Ryukyu issue was no longer the note war between He Ruzhang and Munenori Terashima. The two countries sent envoys to Beijing to negotiate. Japan put forward "Island Division and Treaty Adding" plan: the areas located to the north of Okinawa islands belong to Japan; Miyako Islands and Yaeyama Islands (the Diaoyu Islands were not mentioned) belong to China; Sino-Japanese Provisions of Cordial Relations established in 1871 should add that the Japanese merchants in China enjoy equal rights to that of the European countries and the United States". We can see that Japan can't wait to impose unequal treaties on China.

Eventually, the Qing government and Japan reached consensus on the "Treaty of Island Division and the Supplementary Provisions"in October 1880. In January next year, Japan would cede the islands in the south of Ryukyu Islands to China. With the spread of the news, it aroused great uproar in the Qing court; farsighted persons thought they were deceived by Japan. Therefore, the Qing court ordered Li Hongzhang to solve the Ryukyu issue immediately. Influenced by the public opinion, Li adopted a delay strategy, in order to postpone "Treaty of Island Division" issue and handle it after the solution of the ongoing Ili issue between China and Russia. Japan's envoy Shishido Tamki, who was responsible for the "Treaty of Island Division and the Supplementary Provisions" had sensed that the Qing court was unwilling to ratify the Treaty and left China in anger. So the Ryukyu issue became an unsolved issue. Although Japan's annexation of Ryukyu was never admitted by China, but after all it was a fact, so the Qing court, since then, never raised any opposition. Although the "Treaty of Island Division and the Supplementary Provisions" was not signed, it is beyond doubt that the islands in the south of the Ryukyu Islands belong to China, since the "Treaty of Island Division and the Supplementary Provisions"proposition was first put forward by Japan, so it admitted that the islands belong to the Chinese territory; besides, this is supported by historical documents saved in the archives of China and Japan. Moreover, the Qing court kept its promise that the Japanese merchants in China enjoy equal rights to that of the European countries and the United States.

In 1895, by virtue of the Treaty of Shimonoseki, Japan obtained Taiwan and all its affiliated islands, and the islands in the south of the Ryukyu Islands and the Diaoyu Islands were naturally in Japan's back pocket. Japan again conducted exploration of the coastal islands between Ryukyu and Taiwan, and incorporated the islands under the administration of Okinawa. However, since 1880, the Chinese government has never held that they will give up the territorial sovereignty of these islands.

After the World War II, Japan unconditionally returned Taiwan islands to China. In accordance with the provision of "Cairo Declaration": "Japan will also be expelled from all other territories which she has taken by violence and greed", Japan should return the islands in the south of the Ryukyu Islands and the Diaoyu Islands together with Taiwan to China, since these islands were all grabbed by violence and greed according to the "Treaty of Island Division and the Supplementary Provisions" plan agreed in October 21th,1880. According to the history and the International Law, the sovereignty over the islands belongs to China.

The Treaty of San Francisco and the Diaoyu Islands issue

1. The Treaty of San Francisco

On September 19th, 1996, Japan's Foreign Minister Yukihiko Ikeda publicly reiterated in Washington Talks of foreign minister of the United States and Japan that according to the Treaty of San Francisco signed in 1951, the Diaoyu Islands are Japan's territory, and the U.S. government has, in accord with the relevant treaty in 1972, returned them to Japan. The next day, Ikeda added that in 1972 when the US government returned Ryukyu to Japan, the Diaoyu Islands were mapped into the handover area and he pointed out that the Diaoyu Islands are within the latitude of Ryukyu.

What Ikeda said unveiled the crux of the dispute over the sovereignty of Diaoyu Islands between China and Japan. Japan has two reasons: 1. the Treaty of San Francisco signed in 1951; 2. the Diaoyu Islands within the longitude and latitude of Ryukyu. I have done a through research on the Treaty of San Francisco as well as collected data concerning the Diaoyu Islands and gained different conclusions from Foreign Minister Yukihiko Ikeda. My research reports are as follows:

According to Ikeda, it seems that the Treaty of San Francisco mentioned the Diaoyu Islands belong to Japan's territory, but it is not true. There are 7 chapters and 27 articles in the Treaty of San Francisco; it has been written in English, French, Spanish and Japanese with signatures from 49 countries such as Holland, France, Australia, Canada, the United States, Japan, etc. (China is excluded) The second chapter clearly stipulates: "Japan renounces all right, title and claim to Formosa and the Pescadores; Japan renounces all right, title and claim to the Spratly Islands and to the Paracel Islands." Article 3 in this chapter stipulates: "Japan will concur in any proposal of the United States to the United Nations to place under its trusteeship system, with the United States as the sole administering authority, Nansei Shoto (Southwest Islands) south of 29deg. north latitude (including the Ryukyu Islands and the Daito Islands), Nanpo Shoto south of Sofu Gan (including the Bonin Islands, Rosario Island and the Volcano Islands) and Parece Vela and Marcus Island. Pending the making of such a proposal and affirmative action thereon, the United States will have the right to exercise all and any powers of administration, legislation and jurisdiction over the territory and inhabitants of these islands, including their territorial waters."

The above treaty was Signed at San Francisco, 8 September 1951 and its initial entry into force was on April 28, 1952. But it never mentioned the Diaoyu Islands or "Senkaku Islands". At that time, the Japanese government made a very detailed "explanation". When explaining the Article 3, it clearly pointed out:"Nansei Shoto south of 29deg. north latitude (including the Ryukyu Islands and the Daito Islands).[28] But it didn't say the Diaoyu Islands are involved. The "explanation" made it clear that the areas put under US's trusteeship excluded the Diaoyu Islands because we all know that the Diaoyu Islands didn't belong to the Ryukyu Islands". The Japanese government authorities also is clear about this matter. Foreign Minister Ikeda's claim that the Diaoyu Islands are Japan's territory is complete nonsense.

Foreign Minister Ikeda's held that the Diaoyu Islands are within the latitude of Ryukyu, based on which he claimed that the Diaoyu Islands belong Japan.

---

28   See Treaty of Peace with Japan published in Daliy News Press, Tokyo, May, 1952, p.36.

The longitude and latitude of Ryukyu released in No. 68 order on February 29, 1952:

A. 28°N, 124°40′E;

B. 24°N, 122°E;

C. 24°N, 133°E;

D. 27°N, 131°50′E;

E. 27°N, 128°18′E;

F. 28°N, 124°18′E

The 6 points mapped in the Diaoyu Islands, Huangwei Yu, Chiwei Yu into Ryukyu. The Complete Map of Okinawa in the Okinawa Chronicles written by Ijichi Sadaka, an official dispatched by the Meiji government to Ryukyu in 1877 maps Okinawa's territory, which is the base of the Okinawa's territory in No. 68 order. Vol.1 of this book records: "the Ryukyu Islands are located in the south sea of Kago Island, from 24°N to 28°40′N; from 122°50′E to 132°10′E." This book was written for the annexation of the Ryukyu Islands after the "annulling the vassal state and establishing prefecture" during the Meiji Restoration. We can see that Japan had made a through plan for the annexation of the Ryukyu Islands long before and conducted quite detailed investigation on geographical conditions of the Ryukyu Islands; besides, they marked Japanese interpretations on the 36 islands of Ryukyu. However, this official document—Okinawa Chronicles never mapped in the Diaoyu Islands in its attached map—the Complete Map of Okinawa and this is not because the author didn't know the Diaoyu Islands. The book also mentioned the Diaoyu Islands, Huangwei Yu, Chiwei Yu and the islands located between Gumi Island and Kerama Islands, but the author only mapped the islands located between Gumi Island and Kerama Islands into the territory of Okinawa, indicating that the Diaoyu Islands were not included into Okinawa after the "annulling the vassal state and establishing prefecture", though the Diaoyu Islands had been mapped in the longitude and latitude of Okinawa. It is worth mentioning that the author of Okinawa Chronicles—Ijichi Sadaka was an official dispatched by the Meiji government to Ryukyu to conduct reform in Ryukyu. According to the historical Dictionary of Ryukyu load: "in the 8th year of the Meiji period, Matsuda Michiyuki, the Ministry of Internal Affairs and Ijichi Sadaka went to Ryukyu and announced the reform in Shouli City." The territory mapped by Ijichi Sadaka who was official dispatched by the Meiji government to Ryukyu to "annual the vassal state and establish prefecture" should be accurate and his book should be treated as the government's official document. The reason why Ijichi Sadaka didn't map in the Diaoyu Islands was very clear—the Diaoyu Islands didn't belong to "the Ryukyu Kingdom", which was in accordance with the Treaty of San Francisco published in 1952. In a word, although the Diaoyu

Islands are located within the longitude and latitude of Ryukyu, they do not belong to the Ryukyu Kingdom. The latitude and longitude lines can't determine the territorial sovereign, which is well known by the government officials in the Meiji era and the narrator of the Treaty of San Francisco. However, the government officials in the Heisei era (such as foreign minister Ikeda) have become abashed.

2. The Japan-US Security Treaty

It is reported that the United States government is unwilling to clarify whether The Japan-US Security Treaty signed by the United States and Japan included the Diaoyu Islands (October 3th, 1996). Burns, the spokesman of United States Department of State, said he did not bring the Japan-US Security Treaty with him and he didn't check the terms recently, so he could not answer whether The Japan-US Security Treaty signed by the United States and Japan included the Diaoyu Islands. Obviously it is a kind of irresponsible behavior that the United States government is unwilling to clarify whether The Japan-US Security Treaty signed by the United States and Japan included the Diaoyu Islands. Meanwhile, it indicates that the United States felt guilty for handing over the Diaoyu Islands to Japan in 1972. If the US confirmed their behavior is right, they would have clearly quote the Japan-US Security Treaty to explain the matter. In fact, the treaty is not very complicated. There are five articles written in English and Japanese; it was signed by the United States and Japan on September 8, 1951, Article 1 of which stipulates: Japan grants, and the US accepts, the right, upon the coming into force of the Treaty of Peace and of this Treaty, to dispose United States land, air and sea forces in and about Japan. Such forces may be utilized to contribute to the maintenance of international peace and security in the Far East and to the security of Japan against armed attack from without, including assistance given at the express request of the Japanese Government to put down large scale internal riots and disturbances in Japan, caused through instigation or intervention by an outside power or powers.

The above cited Article 1 of Treaty of Mutual Cooperation and Security between the United States and Japan (The Japan-US Security Treaty), the other 4 articles add some explanation and additional treaty of the first one. It is obvious that the Japan-US Security Treaty is attached to the Treaty of San Francisco and comes into effect at the same time. Since the Treaty of San Francisco excludes the Diaoyu Islands, so does the Japan-US Security Treaty. Burns, the spokesman of United States Department of State, was aware of this fact, he just refused to answer the related question in order keep the final power of interpretation of the two treaties, because China was not the signatory, so only Japan and the US have the power of interpretation of the two treaties. According to the Japanese data, the Japanese government said the treaty excluded the Diaoyu Islands in 1952, but said in 1996 that the Diaoyu Islands were included, which was obviously a lie in front of public; hence, the US treated the explanation of the treaty cautiously. This also shows that the United States does not fully agree with Japan's sovereignty over the Diaoyu Islands (in 1972, the United States handed over the Ryukyu Islands including the Diaoyu Islands according to the Treaty of San Francisco, but it only handed over their executive, legislative and judicial rights rather than their territorial sovereignty) Otherwise, the United States will explicitly point out the content covered by the treaty as one of the signatories. We can also see that the United States is not willing to shoulder any responsibility for dispute over the sovereignty over the Diaoyu Islands between China and Japan.

The above analyses show that, neither the Treaty of San Francisco nor the Japan-US Security Treaty has involved the sovereignty over the Diaoyu Islands. If Japan insists the Diaoyu Islands belong to Japan, it should provide sufficient evidence to prove that the Diaoyu Islands belong to "old Ryukyu Kingdom" according to the above treaties, otherwise, Japan's claims that it has sovereignty over the Diaoyu Islands is untenable according to the International Law.

On the contrary, China who holds the sovereignty over the Diaoyu Islands has abundant documents that can prove the Diaoyu Islands belong to China rather than the old Ryukyu Kingdom. For example, in 1561 (the 40th year of the reign of Emperor Jiajing of the Ming Dynasty), An Illustrated Compendium on Maritime Security (Chou Hai Tu Bian) compiled by Zheng Ruozeng under the auspices of Hu Zongxian, the supreme commander of the southeast coastal defense of the Ming court, included the Diaoyu Islands, Huangwei Yu and Chiwei Yu on the "Map of Coastal Mountains and Sands" (Yan Hai Shan Sha Tu) and incorporated them into the jurisdiction of the coastal defense of the Ming court. Besides, the Map of the Three Provinces and 36 Islands of Ryukyu drawn by Hayashi Shihei in 1785 clearly shows that Diaoyu Islands are part of China's territory. In addition, Kyoto university's affiliated library Tanimura library collected colored copy (edo period) of the Map of the Three Provinces and 36 Islands of Ryukyu, which also shows that Diaoyu Islands, Huangwei Yu and Chiwei Yu are part of China's territory. The above maps are hard evidence to prove that the Diaoyu Islands do not belong to the "old Ryukyu Kingdom".

3. The relationship between the Treaty of San Francisco and the Diaoyu Islands issue

I believes that the Treaty of San Francisco and the Japan-US Security Treaty are closely related with the dispute over the Diaoyu Islands; the two treaties are also the "trump card" of Japan. Japanese to suppress China. Moreover, the power of interpretation of the treaties belong to US and Japan, so they can modify or recreate the treaties at any time to support Japan's claim that sovereignty over the Diaoyu Islands belongs to China. Therefore, besides the history of the sovereignty over the Diaoyu Islands, we also need to have a thorough understanding of the two treaties, including the content of every chapter, article, term and the background of the two treaties as well as the revision. After the two treaties were released, the Japanese government created an "explanation" of more than a six hundred pages, namely by the daily news agency and published the Treaty Of Peace With Japan (published by the Japan's Daily News Agency in May, 1952). The explanation covered the content of the treaty and its significance as well as its scope. I think this "explanation" is extremely helpful for the analyses on Japan's argument of Japan's sovereignty over the Diaoyu Islands.

I have consistently adhered to my own position that safeguarding the Diaoyu Islands requires thorough understanding of both the enemy and ourselves. Only by understanding the arguments and propositions of the other side, can we make a reasoned rebuttal and persuade Japan and other friendly nations so as to win the support of the international public opinions.

In addition, from the contents of the two treaties and the "explanation", the crux of the Diaoyu Islands issue lies in whether the Diaoyu Islands belong to the old Ryukyu Kingdom. As I have examined and checked through the historical records of China, Ryukyu and Japan and found out that the Diaoyu Islands don't belong to the old Ryukyu Kingdom. There is no doubt that historical records are advantageous to us. But there are also negative aspects that the Diaoyu Islands were mapped in the longitude and latitude of Ryukyu by United States Civil Administration of the Ryukyu Islands in 1952. Based on this, Japan claims that the Diaoyu Islands belong to the scope of the Ryukyu Islands and adopts "effective control" over these islands.

As for this matter, I think we should retort from the perspective of the historical literature, geography and geological structure and the comprehensive research and evaluation of the International Law. As far as I am concerned, the United States will not involve too much in the Diaoyu Islands dispute, because the United States can't gain large interests in it. While Japan's "trump cards" are the two treaties with the nature of military blackmail. Therefore, the key lies in China. How to solve this dispute? 1. Preventing Japan and the US from revising the treaty to enlarge its scope to the Diaoyu Islands; 2.solving the Diaoyu Islands dispute as soon as possible through diplomatic channels (see the brief conclusion of this book 3. Three suggestions to solve the Diaoyu Islands issue).

Treaty of Taipei and the Diaoyu Islands issue

1. The historical background of Treaty of Taipei

Treaty of Taipei is a peace treaty signed by Taiwan on behalf of ROC government and the government of Japan in Taipei Hotel at 3 p.m. on April 28, 1952. Before expounding on this treaty, we will firstly give a brief explanation about its historical background and other treaties related to this treaty so as to offer a thorough understanding of Treaty of Taipei.

Treaty of Shimonoseki signed at Shimonoseki on April 17, 1895 has 11 articles. Those articles which are related to territorial sovereignty are as follows:

Article 1

China recognizes definitively the full and complete independence and autonomy of Korea, and, in consequence, the payment of tribute and the performance of ceremonies and formalities by Korea to China, in derogation of such independence and autonomy, shall wholly cease for the future.

Article 2

China cedes to Japan in perpetuity and full sovereignty the following territories, together with all fortifications, arsenals, and public property thereon:—

....

(b) The island of Formosa, together with all islands appertaining or belonging to the said island of Formosa.

(c) The Pescadores Group, that is to say, all islands lying between the 119th and 120th degrees of longitude east of Greenwich and the 23rd and 24th degrees of north latitude.

In Article 1, China recognizes definitively the full and complete independence and autonomy of Korea, and, in consequence, the payment of tribute and the performance of ceremonies and formalities by Korea to China, in derogation of such independence and autonomy, shall wholly cease for the future. In the second terms of Article 2 clearly stipulates that the island of Formosa(Taiwan), together with all islands appertaining or belonging to the said island of Formosa. It is worth mentioning that although "all islands appertaining or belonging to the said island of Formosa" doesn't mention the Diaoyu Islands, from the traditional territorial awareness, it is beyond doubt that the Diaoyu Islands are included [it can be supported by An Appraisal of Japan written by Zhen Shungong where mentions Diaoyuyu is a small island of Xiaodong (Taiwan)]. In the third terms of Article 2, "The Pescadores Group" (Penghu Islands) naturally excludes the Diaoyu Islands. We should pay attention that when Japan forced China to cede Taiwan and Penghu Islands, it clearly mentioned the territorial sovereignty and administrative power, and delimited the longitude and latitude of Penghu Islands.

Cairo Declaration planned by Chiang Kai-shek, Churchill and Roosevelt and published on December 1, 1943 was a battle plan against Japan. The contents are as follows:

(a) The Three Great Allies are fighting this war to restrain and punish the aggression of Japan. It is their purpose that Japan shall be stripped of all the islands in the Pacific which she has seized or occupied;

(b) all the territories Japan has stolen from the Chinese, such as Manchuria, Formosa, and The Pescadores, shall be restored to the Republic of China;

(c) in due course Korea shall become free and independent

Above three points are the spirit of "Cairo Declaration", the declaration stipulates "Japan will also be expelled from all other territories which she has taken by violence and greed". Chiang kai-shek and Roosevelt discussed about the ownership of the Ryukyu Islands during the meeting.

Roosevelt: what's your opinion of those islands in northern Japan?

Jiang: you mean the Ryukyu islands. China has no intention to claim the Ryukyu Islands and just hope that China and the US share the condominium or we should conduct international condominium. International condominium is better than China's administration.

Obviously, when Chiang Kai-shek insisted that China had "residual sovereignty", so he was entitled to suggest the condominium between China and the US or internationalized condominium.

(3) Potsdam Declaration. The Potsdam Declaration published by the United States, Britain and China on July 26, 1945. The Soviet government declared in a statement that it formally took part in the Potsdam Declaration on August 3th. There are thirteen articles. Article 8 clearly stipulates: "The terms of the Cairo Declaration shall be carried out and Japanese sovereignty shall be limited to the islands of Honshu, Hokkaido, Kyushu, Shikoku and such minor islands as we determine." According to the provision of Potsdam Declaration, Japan's territorial scope limited to the archipelago before the "annulling the vassal state and establishing prefecture" in Meiji Restoration; the territory beyond this scope has been taken by its violence (including North Korea, the Ryukyu Islands, Taiwan, etc.). The Japanese military forces in these territories should be expelled. Obviously, "Potsdam Declaration" is a treaty to restrict Japanese militarism's foreign expansion of aggression.

(4) The Treaty of San Francisco. Treaty of San Francisco has been signed by the US and Japan with signatures from 49 countries (China was excluded). The Article 3 of the second chapter clearly stipulates: "Japan will concur in any proposal of the United States to the United Nations to place under its trusteeship system, with the United States as the sole administering authority, Nansei

Shoto south of 29deg. north latitude (including the Ryukyu Islands and the Daito Islands), Nanpo Shoto south of Sofu Gan (including the Bonin Islands, Rosario Island and the Volcano Islands) and Parece Vela and Marcus Island. Pending the making of such a proposal and affirmative action thereon, the United States will have the right to exercise all and any powers of administration, legislation and jurisdiction over the territory and inhabitants of these islands, including their territorial waters."

The above provision concerning the disposal of the Ryukyu Islands has been distorted. Chiang Kai-shek's proposal of the condominium between China and the US or internationalized condominium was changed into US's solitary exercise of the power of administration in the treaty. It laid foundation for underhand secret dealings between the US and Japan afterwards. In addition, the spirit of Cairo Declaration and Potsdam Declaration is to restrict Japanese militarism's foreign expansion of aggression while the Treaty of San Francisco turned out to be a support for the resurrection of Japanese militarism; it also excluded China who belongs to the Anti-Fascist Allies. As for this matter, my analyses are as follows:

US acted in favor of Japan, the reasons why the US supported the resurrection of Japanese militarism was that it needed an anti-communist Asian country who could fight against China. As at that time, in North and South Korea War, because of China's intervention, the United Nations led by the United States army, thought it necessary to curb China's power. After six years' rest, Japan was fully recovered and began to show strength, which was reflected in the substantial increase in Japan's domestic industrial productivity, restoration of large police forces and participation in some international organizations. Based on these aspects, the US-led western countries relied heavily upon Japan. Therefore, the US couldn't wait to sign peace treaty with Japan so as to treat it as a key piece of its Asian policy. This practical treaty betrayed the spirit of Cairo Declaration and Potsdam Declaration which is to to restrict Japanese militarism's foreign expansion of aggression, and turned out to be a support for the resurrection of Japanese militarism; just like what Truman said in his speech in San Francisco: Asia belongs the Asian, if the US doesn't have a friendly Asian country strong enough to resist the invasion of the communist party, the US can do nothing about its Asian policy. Therefore, Treaty of San Francisco actually aims to "help Japan and resist communist parties". For example, the US expanded the Japanese police reserve and Maritime Self-Defense Forces; it also released war criminals, returned the consular rights; foreign immigrants have to be arrested by the Japanese police and receive court trials; the US stopped asking compensate from Japan; it also permitted Japan to send representatives abroad and sign separate trade agreements with foreign countries; it also increased the efficiency of the industrial production... Out of the "helping Japan and resisting communist parties" policy, the United States broadened the

Treaty of San Francisco and completely gave up the condition of preventing Japan's militarism from resurrection which should be a necessary condition. Moreover, because at that time, Britain admitted the Chinese government, it opposed to Taiwan authorities' participation in the signature of the treaty. From the standpoint of resisting communist parties", the United States admitted the Taiwan authorities. Britain and US obtained a compromise after negotiation that they excluded both the Chinese government and Taiwan authorities from signatory states. Japan should negotiate with China autonomously and sign a similar bilateral treaty. At that time, Shigeru Yoshida, on behalf of the Japanese government, chose Taiwan as the signatory state according to the United States' policy–"resisting communist parties". All these are the historical background of Treaty of Taipei.

2. Treaty of Taipei and its flaws

The Taiwan authorities and the Japanese government signed the Treaty of Taipei on April 28, 1952, which was the result of the US mediation. The representative of Taiwan authorities was "foreign minister" Ye Gongchao, The representative of Japan was Kawata Retsu. On February 22, 1952, the sides held a formal meeting for the first time. Then they held three formal meetings and 18 informal meetings; eventually, they signed the treaty on April 28, the treaty gained approval of the "Taiwan Legislature" on July 31, and the approval of "President" on August 2. On August 5, the two sides exchanged the approved documents in Taipei, with immediate effect. After the signing of the treaty (April 30), "President Chiang Kai-shek paid a visit to Kawata Retsu, the representative of Japan and remarked we hope we could jointly maintain peace in East Asia". The nature of this treaty is completely the same with the Treaty of San Francisco, especially the relevant provisions concerning f China's territory.

There are 40 articles with attached protocols of two articles with 7 terms which serve as the interpretation of the treaty the main contents are as follows:

(a) Japan has renounced all right, title and claim to Taiwan (Formosa) and Penghu (the Pescadores) as well as the Spratly Islands and the Paracel Islands. (Article 2);

(b) The disposition of property of Japan and of its nationals in Taiwan (Formosa) and Penghu (the Pescadores), and their claims, including debts, against the authorities of the Republic of China in Taiwan (Formosa) and Penghu (the Pescadores) and the residents thereof, and the disposition in Japan of property of such authorities and residents and their claims, including debts, against Japan and its nationals, shall be the subject of special arrangements between the Government of the Republic of China and the Government of Japan. (Article 3);

(c) nationals of the Republic of China, shall be deemed to include all the inhabitants and former inhabitants of Taiwan (Formosa) and Penghu (the Pescadores) and their descendents who are of the Chinese nationality in accordance with the laws and regulations which have been or may hereafter be enforced by the Republic of China in Taiwan (Formosa) and Penghu (the Pescadores); (Article 10);

(d) Chinese automatically abandons the service interests in Article 14 of the Treaty of San Francisco. (Term 2 of Article 1 in the Protocol; it indicates that China gave up the right to ask for war indemnity–noted by the author)

From the point of the main contents of the above treaty, Treaty of Taipei was more generous than the Treaty of San Francisco. Due to the special international environment, the Taiwan authorities have to have to obey the United for their own survival. The treaty is in accord with the policy of "help Japan and resist communist parties". It changed the spirit of Cairo Declaration and Potsdam Declaration which is to to restrict Japanese militarism's foreign expansion of aggression into the nature of supporting the resurrection of Japanese militarism. Therefore, the Treaty of Taipei a treaty with serious deficiency the reasons are as follows:

Article 2 of the treaty stipulates: "Japan has renounced all right, title and claim to Taiwan (Formosa) and Penghu (the Pescadores) as well as the Spratly Islands and the Paracel Islands." Compared with Article 2 of Treaty of Shimonoseki, it is obvious that Treaty of Taipei has some shortness in the provisions concerning the ceded territory.

Treaty of Shimonoseki clearly stipulates "China cedes to Japan in perpetuity and full sovereignty the following territories" while Treaty of Taipei only mentioned " all right " and it didn't explain whether in includes sovereignty and administrative power, so Japan can explain this article according to their own will. That's why Eisaku Sato advocated "the uncertainty of Taiwan's sovereignty" in the cabinet.

2) Treaty of Shimonoseki clearly stipulates "The island of Formosa, together with all islands appertaining or belonging to the said island of Formosa", but the Treaty of Taipei doesn't mention "all islands appertaining or belonging to the said island of Formosan", which provide the "legal" basis for Japan's annexation of the Diaoyu Islands. Moreover, "The island of Formosa, together with all islands appertaining or belonging to the said island of Formosa" in Treaty of Shimonoseki doesn't mention that they include the Diaoyu Islands (in fact, according to the traditional territorial awareness, they should include the Diaoyu Islands); besides, when Japan returned Taiwan to China, it did not clarify whether they include the Diaoyu Islands. More importantly, the Taiwan authorities didn't raise any question on this matter, which indicates the Taiwan authorities acquiesce in the incident that it is legal for Japan to steal the Diaoyu

Islands in Treaty of Shimonoseki and Treaty of Taipei. That's why the Taiwan authorities abandoned the sovereign and only talked about the rights; and Lee Teng-hui was undoubtedly aware of the reason. It is the fundamental reason why Japan dares to claim the sovereignty over the Diaoyu Islands.

On the other hand, Treaty of Taipei was originated from the Treaty of San Francisco. the Treaty of San Francisco didn't listed the islands of the "all the affiliated islands" neither did Treaty of Taipei; besides, the Taiwan authorities didn't raise any question on this matter. Therefore, although the Japanese government currently cannot admit the Treaty of Taipei, it can also claims its sovereignty over the Diaoyu Islands according to the Treaty of San Francisco which also doesn't mention the islands of the "all the affiliated islands".

3) "the Treaty of San Francisco" stipulates in Article 3: Japan will concur in any proposal of the United States to the United Nations to place under its trusteeship system, with the United States as the sole administering authority, Nansei Shoto south of 29deg. north latitude (including the Ryukyu Islands and the Daito Islands). For this matter, the Treaty of Taipei didn't raise any question; it even didn't mention the Ryukyu Islands, which actually meant that China, as Ryukyu's suzerainity (or having residual sovereignty over Ryukyu), gave up negotiating with Japan about its annexation of Ryukyu. This is a big mistake of Treaty of Taipei.

4) Article 14 of the Treaty of San Francisco stipulates that it is recognized that Japan should pay reparations to the Allied Powers for the damage and suffering caused by it during the war. But it also explains that nevertheless it is also recognized that the resources of Japan are not presently sufficient, if it is to maintain a viable economy, to make complete reparation for all such damage and suffering and at the same time meet its other obligations. Therefore, the first term of this article stipulates Japan will promptly enter into negotiations with Allied Powers so desiring, whose present territories were occupied by Japanese forces and damaged by Japan, with a view to assisting to compensate those countries for the cost of repairing the damage done, by making available the services of the Japanese people in production, salvaging and other work for the Allied Powers in question. However, in the first term of Article 1 in the Protocol of Treaty of Taipei unexpectedly stipulates: "out of friendliness to and mercy for Japan, Republic of China gives up give up the due services from Japan according to the first term of Article 14 in the Treaty of San Francisco" It not only forced China to give up the due compensation for the sufferings of the Chinese people during the war, but also forced China to give up the available services mentioned above. The Chinese people can by no means accept this article. This is another big mistake of Treaty of Taipei.

The above analyses shows that, as victorious nation, China did not stood in the front of the stage of the Treaty of San Francisco in 1951 and Treaty of Taipei in 1952, so China didn't have the chance to deal with the history of the aggression of Japan in the Sino-Japanese War. According to the relevant provisions of the treaty, we can see that the representative was the Taiwan authorities; besides the vague territorial sovereignty, the treaty gave up the due compensate for the Chinese people. Japan made use of the special situation across the Taiwan straits and Japan, as the third party, reaped the benefits. At the time, Japan chose the Taiwan authorities who actually couldn't represent China as their negotiators; but at the negotiating table, Japan didn't admit that the Taiwan authorities were entitled to represent China, so the Taiwan authorities faced a dilemma and had to gave up the compensate from Japan. This was why the Japanese Shigeru Yoshida government won the victory of the strategy of "two China" in the process of the negotiations of Treaty of Taipei. Shigeru Yoshida revealed it, when he replied the inquiry form Zeng Miyi, the Socialist Party Member, on June 26, 1952 after the signing of Treaty of Taipei.

Shigeru Yoshida said: "we will establish a comprehensive relationship with China. The first step, we will sign this treaty with Republic of China. That is to say, this treaty is a treaty between Japan and the government of Taiwan; in the future we want to sign a comprehensive treaty with China."

Zeng Miyi asked: "you mean you do not admit the Republic of China can represent the Chinese government."

Shigeru Yoshida replied: "yes."

It is obvious that Japan took advantages of the Achilles' heel of the Taiwan authorities – begging for survival, so Japan chose the Taiwan authorities as the negotiator and took every chance to blackmail Taiwan so as to force the Taiwan authorities to abandon many beneficial rights and questions and objections that should be put forward (especially about the scope of all affiliated islands of Taiwan and the Ryukyu Islands). From the perspective of the contents of the treaty, the loser in the war seemed to be China rather than Japan, just as Sima Sangdun, a historian of China-Japan relations, said: "China had suffered from the invasion and insult of Japanese imperialism for half a century, and hurt deeply and sacrificed greatly in the war. However, China even did not stand in the front of the stage when dealing with Japan after the war, which should be regarded as a historical tragedy. The highest crystallization of the history of this tragedy was Treaty of Taipei signed in 1952.[29] Sima Sangdun defined this treaty as "a treaty not completely clearing the mark of unequal treaties"

---

29 Sima Sangdun: 25-years' relations between China and Japan, Taipei Associated Press, 1978, pp. 9,10.

3) An Analysis of China-Japan Joint Statement and its contents

Since China was excluded from the signing of the Treaty of San Francisco and Treaty of Taipei, consequently the Chinese government initially refused to admit the legitimacy of the both treaties. On December 4, 1950, Foreign Minister Zhou Enlai issued a statement on the draft of the Treaty of San Francisco: If the People's Republic of China is excluded from the preparation, formulation and signing of the peace treaty with Japan, it will, no matter what its content and outcome are, be regarded as illegal and therefore invalid by the Central People's Government. On August 15, 1951, Foreign Minister Zhou Enlai reiterated that if the People's Republic of China is excluded from the preparation, formulation and signing of the peace treaty with Japan, it will be regarded as illegal and therefore invalid by the Central People's Government. The next day, Zhou Enlai lodged a strong protest with the draft. On September 8, 1951 when signing the treaty in San Francisco, Shigeru Yoshida addressed that Japan accepted that treaty and will never conduct any aggression. Before that, (May 31st), Shigeru Yoshida promised Dulles, the US Secretary of State, to negotiate about the bilateral treaty with China after gaining the approval of the multilateral treaty from the congress. On June 6, the US envoy Rankin and Taiwan "foreign minister" Ye Gongchao talked about the bilateral treaty between China and Japan, indicating that the Taiwan authorities were willing to sign the treaty with Japan. On January 16, 1952, Shigeru Yoshida sent a letter to Dulles, saying that in accord with the principles of the Treaty of San Francisco, Japan was willing to sign peace treaty with Republic of China and clearly addressed that they would sign treaty with the Taiwan authorities rather than the Chinese government. On April 28, Treaty of Taipei was signed in Taipei.

From its drafting to its signing, the Chinese government kept lodging a strong protest. On January 23, 1952, Vice Foreign Minister Zhang HanFu issued a statement to accuse Shigeru Yoshida of signing treaty with "Republic of China" in his letter to Dulles; he also said the rejection of the government of the People's Republic of China from the governments of Japan and the US was a challenging behavior to China. After the signing of Treaty of Taipei, on May 5, Foreign Minister Zhou Enlai issued a statement that China firmly opposed to Treaty of Taipei.

The Japanese government turned a blind eye to China's protests; Shigeru Yoshida as well as Eisaku Sato reiterated they would attach great importance to the obligations in Treaty of Taipei and promised to observe the international moral. On September 8, 1967, during his visit to Taiwan, Sato also openly advocated "the uncertainty of Taiwan's sovereignty", "Taiwan is Japan's bulwark", etc. and appreciated Chiang Kai-shek's "anti-communism with Japan" policy. All these were immediately lashed out by People's Daily. However, in June 1971, when the US announced its decision to returned Ryukyu to Japan in 1972, an upheaval occurred to the relationship between Taiwan and Japan. In

October of the same year, the Taiwan authorities were expelled from the United Nations; meanwhile, Japan has completely taken over Ryukyu. Therefore, Japan thought Taiwan was of no use and Japan got what she wanted in Treaty of Taipei (that is to force Taiwan to give up its residual sovereignty over Ryukyu and some affiliated islands), so she decided to break off diplomatic relations with Taipei and admit that the People's Republic of China. In his later years, to Chiang Kai-shek, the greatest shock was not that the Taiwan authorities were expelled from the United Nations, but that Japan broke off diplomatic relations with Taipei (a senior diplomat in Taipei told me when I was teaching at the university of Sydney in Australia), because it seemed to be betrayed by an old friend or the sworn Brothers. In fact, the "old friend" had been using him all the time.

On September 29, 1972, China and Japan issued in Beijing the Joint Statement/Communique between the government of the People's Republic of China and the government of Japan, which has the nature of Treaty of Taipei. There are 9 articles; the ones concerning the territory and for war compensation are as follows:

4. The Government of the People's Republic of China reiterates that Taiwan is an inalienable part of the territory of the People's Republic of China. The Government of Japan fully understands and respects this stand of the Government of the People's Republic of China, and it firmly maintains its stand under Article 8 of the Postsdam Proclamation.

5. The Government of the People's Republic of China declares that in the interest of the friendship between the Chinese and the Japanese peoples, it renounces its demand for war reparation from Japan.

The statement made it clear that China renounces its demand for war reparation from Japan, but we should pay attention that the third term clearly reads the Government of Japan firmly maintains its stand under Article 8 of the Postsdam Proclamation.

This means that the statement changed the nature of the Treaty of San Francisco and Treaty of Taipei which is "helping Japan and resisting communism" to the nature of restricting Japanese militarism's foreign expansion of aggression. As long as the Chinese government insists on the position in the statement, China can deal with the crime of Japan's aggression in China since 1894 anytime. Because Article 8 of the Postsdam Proclamation clearly stipulate: "Japanese sovereignty shall be limited to the islands of Honshu, Hokkaido, Kyushu, Shikoku and such minor islands as we determine." Therefore, As long as the Chinese government insists on the position in the statement, Japan's stealing of "Taiwan's affiliated islands" and even the Ryukyu Islands by virtue of the Treaty of San Francisco and Treaty of Taipei will have no legal effect according to the International Law.

In addition, at the press conference held on the day when the joint statement was signed, Japan's Foreign Minister Ohira Masayoshi pointed out that: "as a result of the normalization of diplomatic relations between China and Japan, the treaty between Japan and the Chiang government came to an end." (the so-called "the treaty between Japan and the Chiang government" refers to Treaty of Taipei–noted by the author) At the same time, when explaining Article 3 of the joint statement, Foreign Minister Ohira also pointed out: "the Japanese government's position on the Taiwan issue has been revealed in Article 3. The Cairo Declaration stipulates we should return Taiwan to China and Japan has accepted the Potsdam Declaration which inherits the Cairo Declaration. Article 3 of the Potsdam Declaration stipulates "The terms of the Cairo Declaration shall be carried out." Therefore, naturally, Japan will firmly maintain its stand under the Postsdam Proclamation.

According to the above explanation, the Japanese government's acknowledgment of the joint statement means Treaty of Taipei comes to an end. Moreover, the relations between China and Japan are once again established on the base of the Cairo Declaration and the Potsdam Declaration. Then, the Taiwan's affiliated islands and the residual sovereignty over the Ryukyu Islands which were given up in Treaty of Taipei would be negotiated again between the government of the People's Republic of China the Government of Japan according to the Joint Statement.

I think that the Diaoyu Island and its affiliated islands have been China's territory since ancient times, so China has no sovereignty dispute with Japan. The negotiations about territorial issues between China and Japan should be based on the "Treaty of Island Division and the Supplementary Provisions"[30]

---

30   The "Treaty of Island Division and the Supplementary Provisions" was first put forward by the Japanese side, as follows: the areas located at the north of Okinawa islands belong to Japan; Miyako Islands and Yaeyama Islands belong to China; Sino-Japanese Provisions of Cordial Relations established in 1871 should add that the Japanese merchants in China enjoy equal rights with that of the European countries and the US". Eventually, the Qing government and Japan reached consensus on the "Treaty of Island Division and the Supplementary Provisions" proposal of October 1880. In January next year, Japan would cede the islands in the south to China. With the spread of the news, it aroused great uproar in the Qing court; far-sighted persons thought they were deceived by Japan. Therefore, the Qing court ordered Li Hongzhang to solve the Ryukyu issue immediately. Influenced by the public Li adopted a delay strategy, in order to postpone the "Treaty of Island Division" issue and handle it after the solution of the ongoing Ili issue between China and Russia. Japan's envoy Shishido Tamaki, who was responsible for the "Treaty of Island Division and the Supplementary Provisions" had sensed that the Qing court was unwilling to ratify the Treaty and left China in anger. So the Ryukyu issue became an unsolved issue. Although Japan's annexation of Ryukyu was never admitted by China, but after all it was a fact, so the Qing court, since then, never raised any opposition. For the "Treaty of Island Division and the Supplementary Provisions", please see Volume 13 of "Japanese Diplomatic Documents" and Volume 2 of "Historical Documents of Sino-Japanese Diplomacy during the reign of Qing Emperor Guang Xu."

consensus reached by the parties in October 1880. This agreement involved in the residual sovereignty over the Ryukyu Islands between the two countries and was the only equal treaty about the territorial boundaries between the two countries in recent history. Redrawing the boundaries according to this agreement is in accord with the principles of the "Cairo Declaration" and "Potsdam Declaration". Otherwise, the territorial sovereignty dispute between China and Japan will never cease.

VI. "China-Japan Treaty of Peace and Friendship" and Diaoyu Islands Issue
- Comment on the attitude of the Japanese government towards the dispute over the sovereignty of Diaoyu Islands

Zheng Hailin

I

On October 14, 1996, NHK (Japan Broadcasting Corporation) in Tokyo reported: "Japan today denies it has reached an agreement with the CPC to put aside the Diaoyu Islands dispute, which totally contradicts with the claim made by Qian Qichen, the Foreign Relations Minister of the CPC. Sadayuki Hayashi, the Vice Minister of Japanese Ministry of Foreign Affairs addresses at a press conference: "China wants to shelve this issue because their position is different from Japan. But the two sides never reached an agreement of shelving this issue. Qian Qichen has told Japanese reporters in Beijing that the two sides have reached an agreement to shelve this issue."

Why have this contradiction happened? It have to be traced back to September 11th, when Chinese ambassador Xu Dunxin delivered a note to Sadayuki Hayashi, the Vice Minister of Japanese Ministry of Foreign Affairs for the matter that the Japanese right-wing group built lighthouses on the Diaoyu Islands. Xu pointed out that the two sides have reached an agreement of shelving this issue and solving it later. However, recently, under the Japanese authorities' conniving, some Japanese groups... seriously violated China's territorial sovereignty and aroused the Chinese people's protest." The reply to this note from Vice Minister Sadayuki Hayashi was that: "the Senkaku Islands are the inherent territory of Japan. Japan has never agreed to shelve the issue." Apparently, Japanese officials have publicly denied that Japan has agreed to shelve the Diaoyu Islands issue and reiterate again and again that "the Senkaku Islands are the inherent territory of Japan" (remarks of Foreign Minister Ikeda).

Why should there be such a contradictory note war between China and Japan I think that we must look back to the history of the signing of China-Japan Treaty of Peace and Friendship.

China-Japan Treaty of Peace and Friendship was signed in Beijing on August 12, 1978. There are five articles written in Chinese and Japanese. Chinese plenipotentiary was Huang Hua and Japanese plenipotentiary was Sunao Sonoda. Article 1 reads:

1. The Contracting Parties shall develop durable relations of peace and friendship between the two countries on the basis of the Five Principles of Peaceful Co-Existence;

2. The Contracting Parties affirm that in their mutual relations, all disputs shall be settled by peaceful means without resorting to the use or threat of force;

Article 1 involves the territorial sovereignty and the other four articles are auxiliary and explanation of Article 1. But the content of Article 1 only vaguely mentioned the territorial sovereignty but neither the territorial sovereignty dispute nor the shelving of the sovereignty over the Diaoyu Islands was mentioned, which was Japan's argument of denying that it once agreed to shelve the Diaoyu Islands dispute.

However, China-Japan Treaty of Peace and Friendship was signed in Beijing on August 12, 1978. On October 23, 1978, Vice-Premier Deng Xiaoping visited Japan for the exchange of instruments of ratification of China-Japan Treaty of Peace and Friendship. On October 25, Commenting on the issue of Diaoyu Islands at a press conference, Mr Deng said, "It is understandable that the two sides have different opinions on certain issues. For example, we have different opinions on the place that you call Senkaku Islands and we call Diaoyu Islands. We didn't involve this issue in the normalization of diplomatic relations between our two countries. There are some people attempting to use it to hinder the development of China-Japan relations. It is a good choice that we do not talk about it in our negotiation. Issues like this can wait. It will never be too late to solve it in ten years. In the future, we are bound to figure out a good way to solve this problem."

The argument of "shelving the dispute" originated from this address. We can see that Mr. Deng Xiaoping repeatedly mentioned in conversation "it is a good choice that we do not talk about it in our negotiation", obviously, Mr. Deng had negotiated with the representatives of the Japanese government and they reached consensus on "shelving the dispute", otherwise, he wouldn't deliver such speech in front of more than four hundred journalists and foreign correspondents in Japan (Deng's speech won warm applause from the Japanese journalists). In addition, China-Japan Treaty of Peace and Friendship only vaguely mentioned the territorial sovereignty but had no clear provisions and interpretation of the territorial sovereignty dispute.

Therefore, Mr. Deng's speech can be regarded as a further interpretation or specifications of the treaty and shall be equal with the official document or announcement. While, the Japanese government denied that they reached consensus on "shelving the dispute", indicating that they overthrew the consensus reached by the two sides; and it is actually the deviation and challenge of the China-Japan Treaty of Peace and Friendship. On this basis, it is not unfounded that the Chinese government accuses Japan of deliberately harming China-Japan relations.

The two sides restart the Diaoyu Islands dispute, the perpetrator of which is Japanese right-wing groups. But the Japanese officials publicly deny that they reached consensus on "shelving the dispute", which made it clear that behind these perpetrators is the Japanese government. At the same time, the Japanese government's support for the militarism have been known by everyone. Therefore, the peace-loving people all over the world should be on high alert about the Japanese government's stand on the Diaoyu Islands issue.

II

On December 20, 1994, "Japan-China relations" published by Iwanami bookstore the Tokyo (the 8th volume of modern history of China) records "Senkaku Islands issue", which reflected the Japanese government's attitude towards and position of the Diaoyu Islands issue. Simple comments are as follows:

The author Ando Masashi, the Prof. of Historical Anthropology in Tsukuba University, is specialized in modern Chinese history and modern Sino-Japanese relations. He has written many masterpieces such as Cultural Revolution and modern China, the international relations of the modern China, etc. The other author Kotake Kazu Akira, the Prof. of law faculty in Kurume University, has written masterpieces such as the mass movement in land reform in the early Civil War.

When discussing the modern China-Japan relations, the author used some little-known historical materials, such as "secretly record of Chiang Kai-shek", "letters of Yoshida", etc. As for the signing of China-Japan Treaty of Peace and Friendship in 1952, and and Chiang Kai-shek's policy of "mercy for Japan", the book pointed that Chiang Kai-shek they asked for a high compensation, Japan may undergo communization.[31] It also explained why the Taiwan authorities rather than the Chinese government were chosen by the Shigeru Yoshida government at that time. the book—"letters of Yoshida" pointed out that the Communist regime of China has been treated as invaders by the UN, so it can not represent the Chinese government all the time.[32] On the issue of the "Senkaku Islands", the author thinks it is a key question of modern

---

31   "Secret Records of Chiang Kai-Shek" Sankei Press, 1985, pp. 411-413.
32   Ibid., p. 61.

Sino-Japanese relations, "especially the confrontation of sovereignty over the Senkaku Islands between China and Japan is likely to freeze the Sino-Japanese relations."

The author summarized the opinions on the Diaoyu Islands of Japanese government and public and then put forward the following opinions: "Senkaku Islands are located between Okinawa and Taiwan, and was ruled by Japan in 1895 according to Cabinet's decision. Until the end of the 1960s, no country including China put forward any objections. After the report of ECAFE released in 1968 saying that these waters may have oil resources, China began to claim its sovereignty over the Senkaku Islands (Diaoyu Islands in Chinese). China's first claim on its sovereignty over the islands was a leading article published in People's Daily on December 29th, 1970. Since then, the Senkaku Islands issue became a dispute between Japan and China. In addition, on June 1st, 1971, Ministry of Foreign Affairs of Taiwan published a statement claiming its sovereignty over the Diaoyu Islands.[33]

The reasons for the claim on the sovereignty over the Diaoyu Islands of the both sides mentioned in the book: "the statement of Ministry of Foreign Affairs of the Chinese side on December 30, 1971, mainly mentioned that the Senkaku Islands are a part of Taiwan and have a deep relationship with China in history. Japan's position can been seen from the "Basic Views" of the Japanese Ministry of Foreign Affairs on March 8th, 1972; the key points are: since 1895 (In the 28th year of the Meiji period) the Senkaku Islands have been under the administration of Japan, which has nothing to do with ceding Taiwan in Treaty of Shimonoseki (1895). In addition, the Senkaku Islands are part of the Ryukyu Islands, so there is no territorial sovereignty dispute."[34]

As for China and Japan sticking to their own argument and all having claims to the sovereignty over the Diaoyu Islands, the author made the following comment: "since April 12th, 1978, about a week, many armed Chinese fishing boats gathered on the waters. At that time, Japan and China were negotiating the Japan-China Treaty of Peace and Friendship for the second time and Liberal Democratic Party was undergoing adjustment. Therefore, the Senkaku Islands issue caused wide public concern. Later, when Vice-Premier Deng Xiaoping visited Japan for the exchange of instruments of ratification of the Japan-China Treaty of Peace and Friendship, he commented on the issue of Diaoyu Islands and expressed his intention that we should leave this issue to the next generation. Therefore, the Senkaku Islands issue didn't turn out to be a diplomatic dispute.

---

33 Ibid., p. 225.
34 Ibid.

But afterwards, the two governments had a few small scale negotiations about the issue. Especially in February of 1992, Territorial Sea and the Contiguous Zone People's Republic of China released by China clearly marks the Senkaku Islands and Nansha Islands as China's territory. The promulgation of this law faced the Japanese government's protest. From the historical view, neither China nor Japan has experience to solve the territorial issues peacefully. Accordingly, the current diplomacy negotiations about the Senkaku Islands issue between the two countries must be difficult."[35]

I want to list some key points of the above book's comments on the dispute over the Diaoyu Islands between China and Japan. They are as follows:

1) The Japanese government and public hold that in 1895, the Japanese Cabinet decided to conduct "effective occupation rule" on Diaoyu Islands and since then the islands have been Japan's territory. Before 1895 these islands were uninhabited. From 1895 to the 1960s, no country raised any objection to Japan's rule.

2) Although Japan conducted "effective occupation rule" on Diaoyu Islands in 1895, this has nothing to do with Treaty of Shimonoseki, that is to say, they were not included in those islands which were ceded to Japan together with Taiwan and its affiliated islands.

3) The Diaoyu Islands are part of the Ryukyu Islands, Japan does not have territorial sovereignty dispute with China.

4) The Diaoyu Islands dispute is triggered by China. The reason is the report of ECAFE released in 1968 saying that these waters may have oil resources.

5) In 1978, Deng Xiaoping's advice on "shelving the dispute" was China's unilateral opinion; the purpose is to prevent the diplomatic dispute, so that China-Japan Treaty of Peace and Friendship could be signed smoothly.

6) As late as February of 1992, Territorial Sea and the Contiguous Zone People's Republic of China released by China clearly marks the Senkaku Islands and Nansha Islands as China's territory.

The first three points support Japan's claim that it has the sovereignty over the Diaoyu Islands; the last three refute China's claim that it has the sovereignty over the Diaoyu Islands. We can see that the Japanese government seem to be convinced in its sovereignty over the Diaoyu Islands. Japanese government and the official scholars also mislead the citizens in this way. But that is not the case. Based on my long-term studies of China-Japan relations and the Diaoyu Islands issue, I will refute the above points one by one as follows:

1) 500 hundred years before the Japanese Cabinet decided to conduct "actual rule" on Diaoyu Islands in 1895, the Ming emperor appointed 36 people

---

35   Ibid., pp. 225-226.

from Fujian Province who were good at operating ships to go to Ryukyu, to facilitate the tribute-paying voyages, which has been recorded in historical documents of China and the Ryukyu. Besides, the Map of the Three Provinces and 36 Islands of Ryukyu drawn by Hayashi Shihei, a Japanese historian in Edo period marked that Diaoyu Islands as part of China's territory.

2) Treaty of Shimonoseki signed in 1895 doesn't mention that the ceded areas include the Diaoyu Islands, but it mentions about Taiwan and all its affiliated islands; in fact, according to the traditional territorial awareness, they should include the Diaoyu Islands. Japan firstly conducted nominal occupation of the Diaoyu Islands by incorporating the islands under the administration of Yaeyama Islands, which was decided by Cabinet on January 11, 1895; and then Japan conducted actual occupation by signing Treaty of Shimonoseki on April 17, 1895.

3) The Diaoyu Islands were mapped within the latitude and longitude of the Ryukyu Islands, but latitude and longitude lines do not equal to territorial sovereignty. Because in history the islands never belonged to "old Ryukyu Kingdom", but instead they belonged to China. Japan's annulling the vassal state and establishing prefecture (1872-1877) in the Meiji Restoration or the Treaty of San Francisco didn't incorporated the islands into Ryukyu. Strictly speaking, Japan's "actual rule" on Diaoyu Islands began in May 1969 when Japan established markers with "the Diaoyu Islands of Yaeyama Islands" on the Diaoyu Islands.

4) The Diaoyu Island and its affiliated islands have been China's territory since ancient times. The Diaoyu Islands dispute was triggered by Japan's establishing markers on the Diaoyu Islands in May 1969; the reason was that because of resource shortage, Japan decided to occupy these island by force after knowing that these waters may have oil resources.

5) On January 25, 1978, Deng Xiaoping addressed "shelving the Diaoyu Islands dispute" at a press conference in Tokyo, which was a negotiated consensus of both sides, with the nature of the official document or announcement. The Japanese government denies this consensus, which is actually a deviation and challenge of the China-Japan Treaty of Peace and Friendship. It means that the aggressive Japanese militarism rose again.

6) Territorial Sea and the Contiguous Zone People's Republic of China released by China on February 25, 1992 is within China's sovereignty scope. It was released after China's re- survey on its territorial waters and its affiliated islands after the Second World War. Even if it mentions the Diaoyu Islands, it is the exposure and criticism of Japan's illegal occupation of China's territory in Treaty of Shimonoseki, which is in accord with the spirit of Cairo Declaration and Potsdam Declaration as well as the stipulations in China-Japan Joint Statement in 1972.

According to the above points, the Diaoyu Islands belong to China's inherent territory; there is no territorial sovereignty dispute between China and Japan. Japanese right-wingers' disturbance on the Diaoyu Islands should be severely condemned by the international public and deserves effective sanctions.

VII. Historical Evidence of Japan's Covetousness and Seizure of the Diaoyu Islands in the Latter Half of the 19th Century

February, 1998

Wu Tianying

The fact that the Diaoyu Islands belong to China is uncontroversial, however, Prof. Okuhara Toshio, the most influential Japanese "expert of Senkaku Islands (namely, the Diaoyu Islands)" made a shameless claim that he "will verify, from historical perspective, that the islands can't be conducted by China, by means of making certain the Senkaku Islands and its relevant historical facts. Meanwhile, to make clear the authentic fact, it is necessary to redress the incorrect comprehension held by some people"[36]. Accordingly, on March 8th, 1972, Japanese Ministry of Foreign Affairs formally made an official statement entitled Issues on Sovereignty over the Senkaku Islands:

In the 18th year during the reign of Emperor Meiji, through counseling the authority of Okinawa and repeated field investigations, Japanese government made a prudent confirmation that the Senkaku Islands was not only uninhabited, but showed no indication of domination under the Qing Dynasty of China. Then, the Cabinet ordered the marking of the islands and formally incorporated them into Japanese territory by means of the resolution of January 14, in the 18th year during the reign of Emperor Meiji.

Before that, the islands had always been a part of the southwestern islands of Japanese territory in the history, not gained by cession of Taiwan and the Penghu Islandsfrom the Qing dynasty of China based on the second article in Treaty of Shimonoseki coming into force in May, the 28th year during the reign of Emperor Meiji.[37]

---

36 Okuhara Toshio: Legal status of Senkaku Islands from Ming to Qing Dynasty, published in Okinawa, quarterly, Issue 63 published in 1972, Series II. The Senkaku Islands Special Issue.
37 The translated text was quoted from Zhang Qixiong: Sovereignty and Territory Issues over the Diaoyu Islands—The Verification of Japan's Possession According to the International Law, published in the Issue 22 of The Collected Papers of Institute of Modern History.

On May, 22, 1997, with regard to the statement, the author put forward three confusions while discussing the sovereignty over the Diaoyu Islands with members of the delegation designated by Japan: Did the authorities of Japanese government virtually and honestly regard the Diaoyu Islands as "terra nullius" before the Sino-Japanese War?

Did the "Cabinet Resolution" on January 14, really conform to the "occupying first" principle of the International Law? Was Japan's seizure of the Diaoyu Islands solely independent of the Sino-Japanese War and Treaty of Shimonoseki? Due to the limited time on that day, the author failed to speak more about these issues, in fact this article aims to conduct certain investigation about the ins and outs of these issues.

1. "Japan's Initial Consciousness on Seizing the Senkaku Islands Sprouted in 1879"

In 1972, in the article On the Sovereignty over Senkaku Islands written by Okuhara Toshio and signed with "The Research Institute of the Senkaku Islands" it emphasized: "The names of each individual island of the Senkaku Islands had been printed on The Map of Japan drawn by Matsui Tadasamurai issued in 1879, which clearly indicated that it belonged to Japan."[38] The statement was greatly full of loopholes. In the first place, Okuhara's annotation mentioned: "Hoa-pin-san Islands, namely, the Diaoyu Islands were included in the map." The annotation manifested that the author of the map, Matsui Tadasamurai, exactly copied and followed the Englishman's mistake, confusing the Diaoyu Islands with the Huaping Islands, namely, the Hoa-pin-san Islands west to it.[39] It was extremely ridiculous that forcibly designating the Diaoyu Islands, China's inherent territory, to Ryukyu[40] whose own sovereignty

---

38   Published in Okinawa, quarterly, Issue 23 of 1972, Series Two of the Senkaku Islands Special.

39   Mr. Inoue Kiyoshi pointed out that: "I suppose that the name of 'Hoapin-su' originated from the westerner's mistake that they put the Chinese pronunciation of Hoapin-su, the second island to the west, into that of the Diaoyu Island." See Historical Facts of Senkaku Islands/Diaoyu Islands, Chapter 8 Annotation, the edition of 1972, Japan Modern Review Press; See The Historical and Territorial Issues of the Diaoyu Islands translated by Ying Hui, the edition of 1990, HongKong Cosmos Books Ltd., page 72. Mr. Zhang Qixiong further illustrated: "Addressing the Diaoyu Island as Heping Island (Mountain) resulted from mistaking it for Hoapin-su", "Actually, Hoapin-su (or Heping Island, their pronunciations in Fujian Dialect were similar) was another island located west of the Diaoyu Island and north of Taiwan Island. Since Japan was unclear about Chinese geography, they confused the Diaoyu Island and Hoapin-su whose pronunciations are close." See The Sovereignty and Territory Issues of the Diaoyu Islands annotated above.

40   In the 5th year of Emperor Guangxu in Qing dynasty (1879), Japan sent its military forces to Ryukyu that used to pay tribute to both China and Japan, unilaterally and forcedly "abolished the Ryukyu kingdom and turned it to a prefecture attached to Japan's Okinawa", which accordingly resulted in the "Ryukyu Case" wherein that Ryukyu sought active help from China's Qing Dynasty and China solemnly protested Japan.

was still uncertain just by virtue of a personal map with even confusing names of the islands. In the second place, suppose their statement is true, the contradiction then emerges: Now that the Diaoyu Islands were "clearly indicated as Japan's territory, it would be unnecessary for Japan to claim its sovereignty 16 years later, that is, on January 14, 1895. Their act totally collided with "terra nullius" as well as "the principle of occupying first".

Prof. Okuhara Toshio probably perceived the huge loophole, consequently, he had to modify his remark: "The premise of the legal principle of preoccupation is that the region preoccupied must be terra nullius beyond any country's administration. It was in the 28th year during the reign of Emperor Meiji that Japan incorporated the Senkaku Islands into the territory, and it was undoubted that it didn't belong to Japan before that. However, it didn't demonstrate that Japan had no intention to possess the Senkaku Islands or had no concern to take the region as territory. Indirectly, it indicated that Japan's intention to possess the islands arose from the 12th year during the reign of Emperor Meiji (1879). In the map (Here it refers to the Maps of Prefectures and Counties in Japan , drawn by the Bureau of Geography, Ministry of the Interior Affairs according to formal norm, some content had already recorded the Senkaku Islands as the islands under administration territory of Okinawa."[41]

Apparently, their remark changed from "belonging to Japan" directly to "the intention to possess" and "concern", which demonstrated that the saying of Japan's alleged "inherent territory" collapsed to itself. Hereon, the reason why Okuhara played his "trump card", the Maps of Prefectures and Counties in Japan, and repeatedly stressed that it was "drawn by the Bureau of Geography, Ministry of the Interior Affairs according to formal norm" was nothing but highlighted the map's authority as "government document". However, it was out of their expectation that the fraud "The Senkaku Islands was recorded as the islands under administration territory of Okinawa."was exposed. The truth was just like what Mr.Inoue Kiyoshi pointed out: "As a matter of fact, there was no '尖阁列岛' ('Senkaku Islands'), just the '尖阁群岛 in the map of Okinawa in the Maps of Prefectures and Counties of Japan, moreover, the 'Senkakus' here referred to '坪纳库鲁诸屿'in English, that was Pinnacle Islands in English. The statement aimed to create an illusion, making people consider that the name of the alleged 'Senkaku Islands had already existed back then, and been incorporated into Okinawa. This was simply the clumsy trick made by Ryukyu's government? When on earth did the map manifest the possession of the 'Senkaku Islands'?[42]

---

41   Okuhara Toshio, On the Sovereignty over Senkaku Islands, published in Chuokoron, Issue 7 of 1978.
42   See the quotation above Historical Facts of Senkaku Islands/Diaoyu Islands, Chapter 8 by Inoue Kiyoshi.

It was genuinely a fantasy that in 1879, Japan "had the intention of possessing" or "concern" on the Diaoyu Islands that had been China's inherent territory hundreds of years before. Nevertheless, Chinese vocabulary is greatly abundant. If "the intention of possession" is altered into "covetousness" instead, that will be extremely appropriate. —What is "covetousness"? That is "presumptuous attempt or expectation".[43]

2. Shenbao Taiwan Alert and the Qing Government's Two Relevant Policy Decisions

In all fairness, Japan's "concern" over "Taiwan and its affiliated islands" including the Diaoyu Islands, did not actually "start" from 1879. After Meiji Reform, Japan's first step of "continental policy" aiming at external expansion, according to "moving southward" doctrine, including "conquering Taiwan", encroaching on the Diaoyu Islands located between Ryukyu and the Taiwan Island before annexing the entire Taiwan Island.

One of the customary tactics used by the old Japanese militarism to invade China's territory was firstly putting and declaring the target it would seize into "terra-nullius" status, and "conquer" it as the second step. As early as the spring of 13th year during the reign of Qing Dynasty's Emperor Tongzhi (1874), before conspiring the Diaoyu Islands in 1885, using an accident as the pretext, in which someone from Ryukyu drifted to Taiwan and was killed there, Japan openly declared "we regard native tribes in Taiwan that are beyond the control of Qing regime as terra nullius",[44] consequently, the Mikado decreed the "expedition" of Taiwan; After seizing the Diaoyu Islands in 1895, a Japanese man named Nishizawa Yoshiji assembled hundreds of men to forcibly occupy the Pratas Island of China, destroyed the facilities of Chinese fishermen in the island and chased away Chinese men, and then claimed the island was "terra nullius" "discovered by" them, eventually altering the Pratas Island into "Nishizawa Island". ......Hence on can see that it had been a long history that Japanese government made China's sacred territory into "terra nullius". Seizing the Taiwan Island was even inevitable, let alone the Diaoyu Islands.

From the 10th to 11th year during reign of the Qing Dynasty's Emperor Guangxu (1884-1885), China was attacked from the front and rear simultaneously, fought against France in Vietnam in the western front and collided with

---

43   Chinese Etymology Dictionary (rev. ed.) Book 4, the edition of 1983, Being Commercial Press, p. 2858.

44   The article was Chapter one of Outset, Punishment of Taiwan drafted by Yanagihara Sakimitsu, the Minister of Foreign Affair and Zheng Yongning, the Junior Minister of Foreign Affair, assigned by Meiji government on January 29th, 1874. See the original copy in Checklist of Microfilm of Selected Archives of The Japanese Army, Navy and Other Government Agencies, 1868-1945. Georgetown University Press Washington D.C.: 1959. Series II. The Record of Taiwan Events, the second one, by Navy Province, in the 7th year of Emperor Meiji.R34.P.44975.

Japan in North Korea in the eastern front. In the Majiang Battle in Fujian, in particular, Fujian Sea fleet was almost annihilated, Penghu failing to defend and Taiwan put in emergency straight after. The Qing Government was forced to sign Tientsin Convention and Sino-Japanese Vietnam Treaty successively in April and June, 1885. Having getting used to taking advantage of others' precarious situating, Japan definitely would not miss the great opportunities, and put the seizure of the Diaoyu Islands into the schedule of invading China. Subsequently, the Ministry of Interior Affairs secretly ordered Kanmori Nagagi of Okinawa to secretly appoint some people to make "investigations" in the Diaoyu Islands.

Almost at the same time, a businessman named Koga Tatsushiro born in Fukuoka Prefecture who migrated to Naha, Ryukyu and was engaged in collection and exports of seafood arrived at "Kuba Island" (Here it refers to the Diaoyu Islands not the Huangwei Yu–Wu Tianying) by navigation. Having found that huge flocks of albatrosses commonly called clumsy birds inhabited on the islands and assuming gaining substantial profits from gathering feathers, he proposed an application for leasing the land to Okinawa. However, his application was not approved "because of learning whether the above-mentioned Kuba Island belonged to Japan was still uncertain".[45]

Certainly, Japan's despicable tricks were undergoing in confidence. Nevertheless, just when their invasion reached the Diaoyu Islands, they were caught off guard by China: On 28th July, the 10th year during the reign of Emperor Guangxu, that is, September 6th, 1885, Shenbao in Shanghai published a piece of highly startling news:

Taiwan Alert·Wen Hui Bao published the news spread from Korea that Japanese men had put their flag on the islands northeast to Taiwan, having great tendency to occupy them. We are still not sure about their intention, so we will pay more attention to their subsequent act.

"The islands northeast to Taiwan" mentioned in the news refers to the Diaoyu Islands, which will be confirmed by the secret letter from Inoue Kaoru, the minister of Japanese Foreign Affairs to Yamagata Aritomo, the minister of Interior Affairs that will be quoted in the following section. The title, Taiwan Alert, was concise and comprehensive, and each individual word was fateful, which, precisely and distinctively, reflected that the Diaoyu Islands were the affiliated islands of Taiwan Province, China, and the desperate situation of the islands referred to the alert situation that occurred across the whole Taiwan.

---

45   See Application of Renting Official Land by Koga Tatsushiro on June 10th, 1895. Published in quarterly Okinawa, Issue 63 of 1972. The author's note: the time when Koga filed the application was one week after Treat of Shimonoseki "The handover of Taiwan was accomplished".

The Diaoyu Islands have always shared weal and woe—danger and safety—together with the whole Taiwan, and the reinforcement of Taiwan coast defense in modern times was closely linked with the development of the Qing government's navy force. As early as 1874, after the event of Japan's invading of Taiwan, the Qing government released imperial edict in the next May, assigning Li Hung-Chang to supervise and handle coastal defense events in the northern coastal provinces, and Shen Bao-Chen did that in the southern coastal provinces: In November, the proposal put forward by Shen Bao-Chen "dispatching the governor of Fu(jian) to Taiwan" was accommodated to the system that the governor of Fujian "stationed in Taiwan in spring and winter, and stationed in Fuzhou in summer and fall." Apparently, this was a critical measure in allusion to Japan's aggression.

After the of signing Sino-French Vietnam Treaty in June, 1885 after the Sino-French War, in consideration of severe setback suffered in the battlefield in Taiwan, a secret letter sealed by the Grand Council was directly delivered by the Ministry of War at the speed of 300 kilometers each day to Li Hung-Chang, the Zhili Governor, Tso Tsung-tang, the imperial Envoy who supervised and handled military events in Fujian, Zeng Guoquan, the Liangjiang Governor, and Peng Yulin, the Minister of War. It demanded them "expressing their own views, giving exact suggestion and reporting rapidly". Considering "Ryukyu, our dependent state, had been incorporated to Japan, and Vietnam was occupied by France again. Besides, Russia and Japan was coveting North Korea again", Peng Yulin held the view that "defending Taiwan should be given the priority for defending the sea": "If Taiwan is under the Qing government's administration, it can be used as defense for several other provinces along the coast. If we lose Taiwan, it will be just as our own bed is at the mercy of others, and we won't be at ease for even one day." From the perspective that "Taiwan bears on overall interests as the gateway to the seven coastal provinces",[46] Tso Tsung-tang suggested straightforwardly "dispatching the governor of Fujian to Taiwan as a governor. All the agenda related to Taiwan and Penghu should be managed exclusively by the governor. The crucial things getting dedicated will be beneficial to cope with the aftermath of defending Taiwan"[47].

Therefore, 37 days after Shenbao's article calledTaiwan Alert was published, that is, on September 6 (October 13th by the solar calendar) that year, the Empress Dowager Cixi successively decreed two imperial edicts: The first one was establishing of the Ministry of Naval Affairs, "appointing Yixuan, Prince Chun, to administrate naval affairs. All the coastal sea fleets will be under his

46   Peng Yulin: The Memorial of Peng Yulin, Volume 7, The Memorial of Aftermath Events of Coast Defense
47   The Memorial of Tso Tsung-tang, collected in The First Chinese Historical Archives, The Category of Imperial Aggression; quoted from The Historical Compendium of Taiwan edited by Chen Kongli, Jiuzhou Press: 1996, p. 297.

moderate dispatch"; the second one was promoting Taiwan to a provincial level status, "As the gateway of the southern coastal provinces, Taiwan is significant as it is the door of South Sea, therefore, the governor of Fujian will be dispatched into that of Taiwan, stationing there constantly. The governor of Fujian will also be the Governor-General of Fujian and Zhejiang."[48]

The above two policy decisions made by the Qing government aroused Japanese authorities' stress. When the two policy decisions were published in The Beijing News, Shimada, the temporary Japan substitute ambassador to China, immediately reported to Inoue Kaoru, the Minister of Foreign Affairs, which was revealed in No. 29 confidential letter later: "The Beijing News published the imperial edict of establishing the Ministry of Naval Affairs and appointing the governor of Taiwan, and the state of affair was immediately sent out as No.36 Official Scratch Pad. The embassy copied it as No. 114 Return for Report. Please ascertain."[49]

How did Shenbao's Taiwan Alert and the two policy decisions adopted by the Qing government play a part in the destiny of the Diaoyu Islands back then?

3. How Did People of the Court and the Commonality View "The Islands Belonging to the Qing Dynasty Located Near Taiwan"

To a great degree, some people point to year 1885, for the beginning of the process of Japan's first scheming regarding the Diaoyu Islands. In this respect, Mr. Inoue Kiyoshi has argued acutely in 1972: Japan "tried to alter the event: In 1885, after receiving the application of 'exploiting' the Diaoyu Islands proposed by Koga, the county hall of Okinawa suggested the government taking possession of the islands. However, it is far from the truth. As a matter of fact, having the intention to take possession of the islands, the Ministry of Interior Affairs secretly ordered the county hall of Okinawa to make investigation on the islands". In addition, he listed abundant historical facts as evidence. Nevertheless, having been full aware of the fact, Prof. Midorima Sakae still told lies in 1984: "On September 22, the 18th year during the reign of Emperor Meiji, the magistrate of Okinawa assigned Kumomaru to conduct field investigation, and applied to the Ministry of Interior Affair for whether establishing national sign on the Senkaku Islands was permitted."[50]

Incidentally, Chinese scholars pointed out that in the 4th year during the reign of Emperor Meiji, Japan abolished the dependent states, and set up counties.

---

48   See Beijing News published on September 6th, the 10th year of Emperor Guangxu.
49   See Photo duplication Service, Library of Congress:"Checklist of Archives In the Japanese Ministry of Foreign Affairs, 1868-1945."Washington:1954), MT5, 1.9.
50   Midorima Sakae: The Senkaku Islands, Book on Okinawa, p. 14, Okinawa Hiruza Press, 1984, p. 96.

Accordingly, each count was appointed as an administrator called as the county leader, which was changed into magistrate in the 19th year during the reign of Emperor Meiji (1886). However, Prof. Midorima Sakae, from the department of law in Okinawa International University, had been using "the magistrate of Okinawa" until 1990s, which in fact betrayed the ancestors. This is the first point. In the second place, he carefully avoided mentioning about the secret order of the Japanese Ministry of Foreign Affairs.

Coincidentally, in his article published in 1978, Prof. Okuhara Toshio corrected the mistake of "the magistrate of Okinawa" he made while participating in making the draft of Ryukyu government's statement eight years before, however, he went even further in concealing the Ministry of Interior Affair's secret command, and claimed ponderously: "In the 18th year during the reign of Emperor Meiji, to ensure that the Senkaku Islands were under the administration of Okinawa, the county leader of Okinawa intended to establish the sign of national boundary there, and filed application to the administrator"51 and so on. On the one hand, he proceeded to keep silent about the Ministry of Interior Affair's command, on the other hand, he directly distorted the fact into one that the county leader of Okinawa not only affirmed that the Diaoyu Islands "belonged to Okinawa", but "explicitly expressed" about the point, that is, establishing the sign of national boundary on the islands.

People can't help asking: "Suppose the Meiji government really confirmed that the Diaoyu Islands were "terra nullius", and would settle the islands based on the principle of "preoccupation" in International Law back then, then they were supposed to make the second step in 1885 following "having the intention to possess the Senkaku Islands in 1879", that is, to implement "the confirmation of 'terra nullius' and the pronouncement of possession". In this way, the great cause taken charge of by the brilliant administrator back then would be shining and beneficial through the ages. Till now, scholars like Okuhara Toshio were supposed to reveal everything in the Ministry of Interior Affair's secret command and made a vigorous propagation. It was really strange that they kept silent about it and even avoided mentioning it? All indications show that there must be intensive meaning about it.

On September 22, 1885 (the 18th year during the reign of Emperor Meiji), Sutezo Nishimura, the county chief of Okinawa, reported to Yamagata Aritomo, the minister of Interior Affair, as in the below Document No. 350 titled: "Petition Regarding Investigations at Kumeseki-shima and Two Outer Islands."

"In regard to the uninhabited islands spread out between this prefecture and Fuzhou, China, a summary of the surveys conducted at those islands in accordance to the secret order previously conferred to the secretary of our

---

51　Okuhara Toshio, Evidence of sovereignty over the Senkaku Islands, published in Journal of Chuokoron, Issue 1978/7.

prefecture stationed in the capital is described as follows in the enclosed attachment paper."

Even to this day, Japan not only remained silent about the Ministry of Interior Province's Secret Instruction stated in the document of Okinawa's county leader, but even kept the Appendix mentioned in the document in the dark for a long time. Example one, in March, 1950, while incorporating No. 350 Document made by Okinawa's county chief into Sundries· Sundries of Territory Relations, Volume 18 of Documents on Japanese Foreign Relations, Japanese Ministry of Foreign Affairs annotated "(omission)" in the second line from the bottom of the lower frame, on page 573; Example Two, 21 years after that, that is, in March, 1971, in The Senkaku Islands Special, issue 56 of the quarterly publication Okinawa, the editor similarly "omitted" the appendix in the original document in the last line of the lower frame, page 113 while elaborately recorded the document.

Therefore, as he quoted No. 350 Document by Okinawa's county chief in 1972, Mr. Inoue Kiyoshi noticed it, and specifically stated: "The appendix is not found." Until that December when Okuhara Toshio surprisingly claimed that all of the "unexpected" documents had been "gathered", the Appendix was entirely revealed in Series Two, The Senkaku Islands Special. Beyond their expectation, the huge secret was disclosed.

It turned out that the Appendix stated in No.350 Document was exactly the Secret Instruction written by Ishizawa Hiyogo, under the leadership of Nishimura Sutezo who followed the decree from the Ministry of Interior Affairs. It was also the first report of "investigating the inhabited islands located between the county and Fuzhou, China titled The Investigation Report on Kumeaka Island, Kuba-Jima and Hoapinsu; Its content centered on the record written down while Ishizawa Hiyogo did exclusive interview with Oshiro Eibo, who "frequently navigated to the China due to official and personal affairs and witnessed the Diaoyu Islands before the dependentstate was abolished in 'Ryukyu'. The final conclusion of Ishizawa Hiyogo's investigation report was: "Akakume Island, namely, Chiwei Yu recorded in Records of Messages from Chong-shan, Kuba-Jima, namely, the Huangwei Yu, and Hoapinsu, namely, the Diaoyu Island which were included in the inhabited islands",[52] was not Japan's new discovery.

In consideration of Oshiro Eibo's witness testimony and Ishizawa Hiyogo's investigation report, Sutezo Nishimura, as the county chief of Okinawa, was highly anxious about implementing the secret instruction given by the Ministry of Interior Affairs, that is, establishing the sign of national boundary.

---

52 See my work The Textual Research on Sovereignty over the Diaoyu Islands before the Sino-Japanese War of 1894-1895—Questioning Professor Okuhara Toshio and other Japanese professors. Social Science Academic Press: 1994, Article 3 Section 2, Chapter 3, pp. 48-49.

In consequence, he, in No. 350 Document, made a presentation to Yamagata Aritomo, the minister of Interior Affairs, in a mild and indirect way as follows:

"Yet, due to their differences in terms of topography from the earlier repotted island Daitojima (situated between this prefecture and Osagawa Islands), the possibility must not be ignored that they are the same islands recorded as Diaoyutai, Huangwei-yu and Chiwei-yu in the Zhongshan Mission Records. If they truly are the same islands, then it is obviously the case that the details of the islands have already been well-known to Qing envoy ships dispatched to crown the former Zhongshan Wang, and already given fixed [Chinese] names and used as navigational aids en route to the Ryukyu Islands. It is therefore worrisome regarding whether it would be appropriate to place national markers on these islands immediately after our investigations."

It can be seen that after the investigation, the county leader of Okinawa learned that even though the Diaoyu Islands recorded in Records of Messages from Chong-shan, an official document which was written in collaboration by China and Ryukyu, were inhabited islands, but not they were not terra nullius, besides, imperial envoys to Ryukyu must pass these islands which belonged to China. Consequently, I was anxious that it would result in the conflicts between China and Japan once they established national symbols hastily.

Here it must be pointed out that Sutezo Nishimura was not only the county chief of Okinawa back then, but the principle in charge of investigating the Diaoyu Islands. The next year after the investigation, that is, in 1886, he composed a book titled The Additional Works of South Island's Record Event. The maps of 36 islands of Ryukyu were included in the book, and its content was totally unrelated to the Diaoyu Islands. The reason why he didn't draw the Diaoyu Islands into Okinawa in the map was that he confirmed that the islands which were exactly the Diaoyu Islands recorded in Records of Messages from Chong-shan belonged to China. As can be seen clearly, Japan's alleged official statement that "The county leader of Okinawa intended to make it clear that the Senkaku Islands was under the administration of Okinawa", was purely a whopper.

On October, 9th of the same year, Yamagata Aritomo, Japanese Minister of Interior Affairs disregarded Nishimura's reasonable suggestion on purpose, racking his brain to process the "inhabited islands" into "terra nullius". Therefore, before presenting it to the administrator, he communicated with Inoue Kaoru, the minister of Foreign Affairs, about his scheme, claiming:

Although the above mentioned islands are the same as those found in the Zhong.shan Mission Records, they were only used to pinpoint direction during navigation, and there are no traces of evidence that the islands belong to China. Also, with respect to the names of the islands, it is merely a matter of difference of nomendenture between them [China] and us Japan].[53]

---

53   See The Document of Japanese Foreign Relations, Volume 18, p. 573.

To better understand the background and content of the letter from Inoue Kaoru,the minister of Foreign Affairs, to Yamagata Aritomo, we might as well enumerate the significant events taking place during that time:

Early in 1885 or earlier: Japanese Ministry of Interior Affairs commanded the grand justice of Okinawa, Kanmori Nagagi, who stationed in Tokyo, to secretly assigned people to conduct investigation in the Diaoyu Island. Unexpectedly, at the beginning of the act, it was leaked out;

On September 6: With an article entitled Taiwan Alert, Shenbao of Shanghai, China raised the alarm all over the whole country;

On September 21: Based on the written record of the interview with Oshiro Eibo, Ishizawa Hiyogo, made an official report to Sutezo Nishimura, the county chief of Okinawa: "The inhabited islands" were the Diaoyu Islands recorded in Records of Messages from Chong-shan;

On September 22: Sutezo Nishimura immediately turned to report to Yamagata Aritomo, the minister of Interior Affairs, proposing that the secret instruction would be hard to be implemented in a mild and indirect way.

On October 9: Yamagata Aritomo secretly negotiated with the minister of Foreign Affairs, scheming to forcibly incorporate the Diaoyu Islands into Okinawa;

On October 13, Successively, Empress Dowager Cixi decreed two imperial edicts, determining to establish the Ministry of Navy Affairs and which promoted Taiwan from prefecture to a province......

Eight days later, on October 21, Inoue Kaoru replied to Yamagata Aritomo in No.38 Document titled The Reasons Why Establishing National Boundary on the Inhabited Islands between Okinawa and China Should Be Delayed. The letter said:

After investigating them, I have given much thought to the matter. The aforementioned islands are close to the border of China, and it has been found through our surveys that the area of the islands is much smaller than the previously surveyed island, Daito-jima; and in particular, China has already given names to the islands. Most recently Chinese newspapers have been reporting rumors of our government's intention of occupying certain islands owned by China located next to Taiwan, demonstrating suspicion toward our country and consistently urging the Qing government to be aware of this matter. In such a time, if we publicly place national markers on the islands, this is bound to invite China's suspicion toward us.

Currently we should limit ourselves to investigating the islands, understanding the formations of the harbors, seeing whether or not there exists possibilities to develop the island's land and resources, which all should be made into detailed reports. In regard to the matter of placing national markers and developing the islands, it should await a more appropriate time. Moreover, the surveys conducted earlier of Daito-jima and the investigation of the above mentioned islands should not be published in the Official Gazette or newspapers. Please pay special attention to this.

In the official letter written by Inoue, minister of Foreign Affairs, there are multiple places worth noticing.

Firstly, "investigation" manifested that Japan's aggression had reached the Diaoyu Islands, but got caught by China at the beginning of their misdeed and openly alarmed in Chinese media.

Secondly, Inoue Kaoru denied Yamagata Aritomo's statement that the islands were "just addressed differently by both sides", explicitly affirming that "China had named each individual island".

Thirdly, undoubtedly, "recent Chinese newspaper" in the letter referred to Shenbao·Taiwan Alert published one and a half months before, which demonstrated that Japan's Embassy in China or Consulate in Shanghai had already reported the news to Ministry of Foreign Affairs due to guilty conscience.

Fourthly, what deserves careful reading is that the Diaoyu Islands were called as "islands northeast to Taiwan" in the original article of Shenbao. However, while writing to the government of Japan, Inoue Kaoru who was highly aware that the islands belonged to China converted the statement into "the islands under the jurisdiction of China near Taiwan".

Fifthly, in terms of the subject of invasion the newspaper Shenbao merely used "Japanese men", however, Inoue confirmed that the act was conducted by "government", that is, Japanese government, which me-ant that the invasion of Chinese islands was not an act of persons.

Sixthly, the letter attached great importance to the news that Chinese media "repeatedly urged the Qing's government to pay more attention", and that Japan's act "incurred the Qing government's suspicion", which was definitely related to the two imperial edicts decreed by Express Dowager Cixi one week before, that is, on October 13, as well as taking important measures of reinforcing coastal defense.

Finally, and most importantly, Inoue, minister of Foreign Affairs, earnestly admonished that "this time's investigation of the Diaoyu Islands" "cannot be published in government organs and official newspapers", which exposed clearly what Japan tried to conceal.

In a word, as the highest minister of Foreign Affairs, Inoue Kaoru who was crystal clear that the Diaoyu Islands was China's territory, but had a grudge against the reactions of both the court and the common people of China; besides, once the war was started because of this back then, Japan would not necessarily win. Consequently, weighing the advantages and disadvantages, he put forward the strategy of "leaving it to later days" to Yamagata Aritomo, and suggested to seize the islands immediately, at the right time when the conditions were ripe. That's why it had to be strictly kept as secret before that. There was never the intention of "the confirmation of terra nullius" and "the pronouncement of occupation", which means their act totally did not conform to the principle of effective preoccupation of terra nullius in International law. Therefore, Japan's quibbling in order to grab the Diaoyu Islands based on the principle of 'terra nullius" is entirely invalid according to the International law.

Yamagata Aritomo, the minister of Interior Affairs, had no alternative but to adopt the suggestion of Inoue Kaoru, the minister of Foreign Affairs, and didn't submit it to Dajokan Conference for discussion. On November, 24, the county leader of Okinawa asked for urgent instruction for the second time: "Establishing the sign of national border was not unrelated to China. It would be not appropriate in case of conflicts. Please give instructions to manage it as quickly as possible." On December 5, Yamagata, the minister of Interior Affairs and Inoue, the minister of Foreign Affairs, communicated with a written and signed document: "In response to your request for instructions, do not erect (sovereignty marker) at present."

Okuhara Toshio tried to defend himself: "The Senkaku Islands cannot be China's territory just because China advocated that it (Here it refers to the Diaoyu Islands–Wu Tianying) was their own territory."[54] The solid historical facts, on the other hand, proved that: Relevant people of the court and the commonality in Japan, up to high-ranking officials of the Meiji government and down to the officials of Okinawa Prefecture, were all fully aware that the Diaoyu Islands were "the islands under the jurisdiction of China near Taiwan". As a result, they dared not to "preoccupy" it based on "terra nullius", but attempted to permeate the islands gradually and awaited an opportunity to seize it.

4. Treaty of Shimonoseki and "Legalization" of the Intention to Seize the Diaoyu Islands

On September 10, 1970, in the article The Proposition on the Sovereignty over the Senkaku Islands and the Exploiting Rights of Continental Shelf Resource, Ryukyu government claimed pretentiously: The islands were "incorporated into Japan's territory and came under the administration of County Ishigaki of Yaeyama, Okinawa based on No. 13 Edict (by Japanese Emperor) on April 1, the 29th year during the reign of Emperor Meiji, through the

---

54 Okuhara Toshio: The Senkaku Islands and the Sovereignty Issue, The Asahi Asia Review, summer issue, 1972.

resolution of Cabinet conference on January 14, the 28th year during the reign of Emperor Meiji", and so on. Holding up the magic tricks of "14 January Cabinet Resolution" and "No. 13 Edict by Japanese Emperor", additionally linking them with the Diaoyu Island, was some people's another masterpiece to willfully distort history and tramp on the standard of international law.

Hereinafter, I will start with the alleged "Cabinet Resolution" on January 14, 1894.

In 1894,the Sino-Japanese War launched solely by Japan finally led to the realization of their dreams, people like Inoue Kaoru and Yamagata Aritomo, who had postponed the seizing of the Diaoyu Islands "to a later proper time". On September 15 of the same year, Chinese land force suffered a setback in Pyongyang; Two days later, the North-Ocean Navy was crippled in Dadong Channel Naval Battle; From October to November, Japanese First Army led by Yamagata Aritomo voyaged the Yalu River, invaded into Shengjing (Liaoning), and then conquered places like Jiuliancheng, Phoenix, and so on. In addition, the Second Army landed in Huayuan Jiang, and successively Jinzhou, Dalian, Lushun fell into the Japanese hands; Meanwhile, Japanese navy blocked the North-Ocean Fleet into a military harbor called Liu Kung Island, east to Weihai. ...... Under the dangerous situation that China was bound to lose the battle, Li Hung-Chang (Li Hongzhang) reported a memorial to the throne and assigned Gustav Detring (German citizen), the commissioner of customs of Tianjin, to head to Japan, trying to make peace but rejected by Japan.

Meanwhile, Japan was sure of victory and had nothing to fear. On December 27, Yasushi Nomura, the minister of Interior Affairs secretly delivered No. 133 Document to Mutsu Munemitsu, the minister of Foreign Affairs, which said: "To establish administrative navigation mark on Kuba Jima and Hoapinsu, the command had been given after negotiating with your honored province in the 18th year during the reign of Emperor Meiji. Since the present situation had been different from that of the past, another document about the event was submitted to the deliberation of Cabinet resolution."[55] Here, that "the present situation had been different from that of the past" revealed the huge secret. No wonder Nomura specifically marked "secret" on the document with a pen dipped in red ink to keep it confidential. No wonder in No.63 Series Two of the Senkaku Islands Special of the quarterly Okinawa in 1972, the section about The Status and Measures of the Senkaku Islands unexpectedly did not reprint the suspicious document, and only selected the "attached article", that is, the appendix of the original document, which was the bill proposed by Nomura to Ito Hirobumi, the Prime Minister, on January 12 of the next year.

---

55   See The Document of Japanese Foreign Relations, Volume 3 of The Third World Countries, p. 531-532.

On January 14, taking advantage of the victory in the Sino-Japanese War, Japan secretly seized the Diaoyu Island when they were fully aware that it was China's territory, through corresponding resolution. The act was entirely illegal. Therewith, Mr. Zhang Qixiong made a brief summary: "Japan's 'obstacle' of seizing the Diaoyu Islands had been completely eliminated due to defeating China. It was because Japan eliminated the 'obstacle' of seizing the Diaoyu Island by military force that the international law theory of Japan's seizure of the Diaoyu Islands used the slogan and started with 'preoccupation of terra nullius'. However, the truth was the seizure ended with 'taking advantage of the victory to occupy it secretly."[56] Likewise, Okuhara Toshio had to admit: "The principle of effectiveness only applied on the condition of the fact that the Sino-Japanese War never existed."[57]

Moreover, "in old constitution (of Meiji), the administrative power was in the hands of the Mikado, and the Cabinet was just the Mikado's assisting institution. The Constitution of Meiji explicitly stipulated: 'The Mikado, the head of the country, has overall administrative power'; 'The ministers assist the Mikado, and each takes his own responsibility'."

Consequently, the state decrees and acts in Meiji times would take effect only when they were announced in the name of the Mikado. It was because the alleged "14 January Cabinet Resolution" was only one-sided possession document made in confidence by the internal Japanese government that the content of the Cabinet Resolution was not reported to the Mikado or decreed as the Mikado's edict, and the seizure of the Diaoyu Islands was not announced openly. Still, they dared not to inform the surrounding countries, especially China, the country involved, of its contend. One should know that it is the indispensable step of preoccupying the terra nullius.

As for the alleged No.13 Edict by Japanese Emperor, originally, the initiator who "linked" the Diaoyu Islands with No.13 Edict was Okuhara Toshio who was still a lecturer back in 1970. He published an article titled The Senkaku Islands and Its Legal Status in Okinawa Daily on September 4th of the same year. It said:

The measures taken on the islands (Here it refers to the Diaoyu Islands–Wu Tianying) based on the resolution of the Cabinet was achieved by Okinawa, seizing the opportunity to implement No.13 Edict on April 1, the 29th year during the reign of Emperor Meiji (1896). However, originally, the edict was about the establishment of prefectures......not one that officially incorporating the Senkaku Islands into territory as direct target based on the domestic

---

56   See the quotation above by Zhang Qixiong, published in The Collected Papers of Institute of Modern History Book 22, p. 123-124.
57   Okuhara Toshio: On the Sovereignty over Senkaku Islands, published in Chuokoron: July, 1978.

law. Nevertheless, according to the explanation of Okinawa's magistrate, "the Yaeyama Islands included the islands...... Therefore, the measure of incorporating the islands into the Yaeyama Prefecture was not restricted to the incorporation within the administrative region, but one that fulfilled the incorporation of territory in domestic law.

Six days later, on September 10th, The Proposition on the Sovereignty over the Senkaku Islands and the Exploiting Rights of Continental Shelf Resource by Ryukyu government quoted in the above section came out; One week later, on September 17th, the statement of Ryukyu government On the Sovereignty over The Senkaku Islands was published. One article after another repeated the same content.

After Okuhara published his informed article, plenty of Japanese media strove to follow his example, repeating his statement. For instance:

In the article The Analysis of the Senkaku Islands, Kaneshiro Mutsu said: "Through the 14 January Cabinet Resolution, the 28th year during the reign of Emperor Meiji, No. 13 Edict decreed on the 29th year during the reign of Emperor Meiji determined that the Senkaku Islands were incorporated into Japan."

In his paper The Senkaku and the Continental Shelf, Shinshiro Toshihiko asserted emphatically: "Based on No.13 Edict decreed on the 29th year during the reign of Emperor Meiji (1896), Japanese government announced possessing the Senkaku Islands."

In The Senkaku Island, Minagawa Kou stated with certainty: "Japan's assertion was on the basis of the following fact: Through the Cabinet Resolution in 1895 (the 28th year during the reign of Emperor Meiji) and based on No. 13 Edict decreed in 1896 (the 29th year during the reign of Emperor Meiji), (the Senkaku Islands) was officially incorporated into (Japan's domain) as Japan's territory, that is, a part of Okinawa."

The Commentary of the Senkaku Island's Record Event published on April 5th, 1971 on Tokyo News straightforwardly systematized the lies: "on January 14th, 1895 (the 28th year during the reign of Emperor Meiji), the Cabinet meeting made a resolution: the islands belonged to Japan, and No. 13 Edict acknowledged the resolution, therefore, the islands literally became Japan's territory, under the administration of Ishigaki, Yaeyama Prefecture, Okinawa."[58]

Okuhara's magic words produced intense chain effect: In Okuhara's peculiar article, No. 13 Edict which was decreed by Mikado and totally irrelevant to the Diaoyu Islands was trumped into the expression that "it was supposed to include the Senkaku Islands based on the explanation of Okinawa's county leader"; The scheme that should be kept in the dark from revealing turned out

---

58   Selected from the book by Takahashi Sougorou, quoted above, p.117, 118.

to the presentation that "Japanese government pronounced its sovereignty over the Senkaku Islands"; The trick that Okuhara played apparently in the name of "Okinawa's magistrate" developed into lofty statement that "it was decreed by No. 13 Edict.

The despicable misdeed of the spinners of lies was naturally disclosed by Chinese scholars and Japanese far-sighted personages. In his paper The Historical Evidence that the Diaoyu Islands Belong to China, not Ryukyu, Mr. Sha Xuejun mentioned The Nonexistent Edict by Japanese Emperor that Incorporated the Diaoyu Islands into Ryukyu. Mr. Qiu Hongda translated and published the whole content of No. 13 Edict, and earnestly pointed out: "The extent of jurisdiction of Okinawa Prefecture decreed by Japanese Emperor the next year (the 29th year during the reign of Emperor Meiji, namely, 1896) after the Cabinet Resolution didn't mention at all that the Senkaku Islands (Japanese name of the Diaoyu Island) was under the jurisdiction of Okinawa".[59] Mr. Inoue Kiyoshi firstly summarized three points from the edict, and then revealed its whole content, indicating: as a matter of fact, the edict was totally irrelevant to the Diaoyu Islands and the administrative issues. It was nothing but a bulletin that announced implementing prefecture system in Okinawa for the first time. (Okinawa did not implement prefecture system before that)"[60]. Takahashi Sougorou affirmed: "In No. 13 Edict, the Senkaku Islands were not mentioned at all"; besides, he further probed into the "political, economical and social backgrounds" of "the Cabinet Resolution and No. 13 Edict", confirming that "The proposal of No. 13 Edict was totally irrelevant to the Senkaku Island. It was a total mistake to connect them"[61].

Faced with the eloquent facts as well as powerful refutations and seeing his inflated soap bubble about to explode, Okuhara immediately changed attitude, asserting outrageously: "In 'preoccupying' terra nullius, it does not necessarily demand the cabinet meeting's resolution and publishing the bulletin in the international law to prove the country's occupying intention. Neither did it demand formal procedures of implementing incorporation in the domestic law. Once the land is possessed based on 'preoccupation', the most important thing is taking effective domination. It is sufficient to indicate the country's occupying intention through effective domination."[62] As for No. 13 Edict decreed by the Japanese Emperor that he had been propagating two years ago, this time he "looked the other way" as if he had never mentioned about this edict.

---

59   Qiu Hongda: Analysis on the Argument that Japan Holds on Sovereignty over the Diaoyu Islands, published in: Ming Pao Monthly, May, 1972, Issue 77.
60   Quoted above Inoue Kiyoshi, Historical Facts of Senkaku Islands/Diaoyu Islands, p. 128.
61   Quoted above, the book by Takahashi Sougorou, p. 119, p. 182
62   Okuhara Toshio: The Senkaku Islands and the Sovereignty,The Asahi Asia review: summer, 1972.

Well-meaning readers, please don't fall for it, assuming that he would re-pent genuinely or keep silent or even acknowledge his mistake in public. The truth was, until March, 1984, in his brilliant work, Prof. Midorima Sakae from the Okinawa University still solemnly repeated the rumor that lecturer Okuhara Toshio had spread 14 years ago: "The incorporation measure of the Senkaku Islands in domestic law was taken when No. 13 Edict was carried out on March 5th, the 29th year during the reign of Emperor Meiji. The edict di-vided Okinawa into five prefectures, namely, Shimajiri, Nakagami, Kunigami, Miyako and Yaeyama, with Kuba-Jima and Uotsuri-Jima incorporated into Yaeyama Prefecture."[63] Incidentally, within 9 years from its publication in 1984 to 1993, his work had been printed eight times. It totally equaled to "pub-licity day after day, month after month, and year after year". Nothing is capable of exceeding it to deceive people.

The content of Treaty of Shimonoseki signed on April 17th, 1895 was totally imposed on China by Japan. It was well known that the treaty stipulated that China ceded three districts: The first one was Liaodong Peninsula with dis-tinct "four boundaries" as well as distinct longitude and latitude, with a chart attached to it (The ceding of Liaodong Peninsula was not fulfilled due to the intervention by three countries.); The second one was Penghu, which was once written as "Penghu" in the draft treaty made on April, 6, however, in the formal signing , it was explicitly defined as "Penghu Islands, namely, the islands loca-ted from 119 degrees to 120 degrees East Longitude, 23 degrees to 24 degrees North latitude, Britain Greenwich". The third one was Taiwan. Nevertheless, Taiwan, which Japan had been coveting for a long time and which included the Diaoyu Islands, was ambiguously written as "the Taiwan Island and its affilia-ted islands". It must be pointed out that it was the hint left on purpose by Japan to "legalize" the seizure of the Diaoyu Islands: Once the Qing's government had no time to attend to Japan's seizure of the Diaoyu Islands due to the set-back, Japan could take the opportunity to incorporate the Diaoyu Islands into its territory; If the Qing's government raised an objection to it, Japan could give a reasonable explanation that the islands were included in "the Taiwan Island and its affiliated islands". They could advance and retreat between the two assumptions. Hence, by means of obfuscate the domain of Taiwan in Treaty of Shimonoseki, Japan could "legalize" its seizure of the Diaoyu Islands, which was exactly its expectation.

5. Conclusion

On April 15, 1895, while negotiating in Shimonoseki, Li Hung-Chang put forward that "The negotiations between government officials in Taiwan were frequently carried on, and the handover could be fulfilled in six months af-ter the exchange of the treaties"; Ito Hirobumi, Japanese minister of Foreign

---

63   Quoted above, the book by Midorima Sakae, p. 101-102.

Affairs, on the other hand, persisted unyieldingly: "The handover should be accomplished in one month, and it would be irrelevant to exchange views on its stipulations."[64] The final agreement was made that it should be fulfilled two months after exchanging the treaties. As a matter of fact, only 12 days after both sides exchanged the approval in Beijing on May 8, that is on June 2nd, the handover procedures were settled hastily.

......

So far, the historical truth has been disclosed: The Diaoyu Islands, China's territory, fell into the hands of Japanese militarism along with "Taiwan Island and its affiliated islands" after China was defeated in Sino-Japanese War and Treaty of Shimonoseki took effect.

Throughout the historical progress of Japan's seizure of the Diaoyu Islands in the late 1900s, it can be seen that the seizure experienced three stages, that is, covetousness, intention to occupy and conquest by military force: The first stage lasted from the beginning of Meiji Reform to 1885. After annexing Ryukyu, Japan regarded the Diaoyu Islands located in strategically important place as the springboard of seizing the Taiwan Island, and put it into the schedule of invading China. The second stage lasted from 1885 to 1894, the eve of Sino-Japanese War. At the beginning of accepting the secret instruction from Kanmori Nagagi, minister of the Interior Affairs, the county hall of Okinawa was given a sharp warning from Shenbao Taiwan Alert published on September 6, 1885. In addition, without delay, China adopted two essential policy decisions to reinforce coast defense, which forced Japan's act of meddling the Diaoyu Islands to switch to convert state, "leaving to the later days" and awaiting opportunity for the seizure. The third stage started from 1894, the breakout of Sino-Japanese War, and ended on June 2, of the next year when the cession of Taiwan was accomplished based on Treaty of Shimonoseki. Taking advantage of the defeat in Sino-Japanese War, Japan, having full assurance of winning, firstly passed "14 January Cabinet Resolution" which was invalid in international law, and then forced China to sign Treaty of Shimonoseki under coercion. Moreover, through making vague the article of ceding Taiwan and not defining the domain of "Taiwan Island and its affiliated islands, Japan attempted to make an anticipatory action of "legalizing" the seizure of the Diaoyu Islands. When China and Japan exchanged the treaty and Treaty of Shimonoseki took effect, Japan assigned Kabayama Sukenori, the Senior General of Navy, to "take over" Taiwan, leading "the fleet of conquering Taiwan" on May 10, the 20th year during the reign of Emperor Guangxu, that is, on June 2. "At 9 P.M., secretary Shimamura took along the governor Kabayama Sukenori to sign and seal the document, moved forward to Koeki ship, and returned immediately after the document was signed and sealed by Li Jingfang

---

64   The Document of Taiwan, 43rd, Questions and Answers between Ito Hirobumi and Li Jingwen in Treaty of Shimonoseki.

Until then the affairs about handing over Taiwan were accomplished. Thereupon, "Taiwan and its affiliated islands" including the Diaoyu Islands became the colony of Japanese militarism.

Chinese people not only firstly discovered and named the Diaoyu Islands, but formally put the islands into the range of coast defense in the middle of the 16th century at the latest; As the affiliated islands of Taiwan, the Diaoyu Islands were closely related to the reinforcement of coast defense in the Ming and Qing dynasties, which could be confirmed by Shenbao Taiwan Alert on September 6, 1885. Before the cession of Taiwan, relevant people of the court and the commonality in Japan still acknowledged that the Diaoyu Islands were not "terra nullius", but was seized by military force in the course of Japan's "taking over" Taiwan after Treaty of Shimonoseki took effect. In other words, Japan's seizure of the Diaoyu Islands was neither relevant to the alleged "14 Jan. Cabinet Resolution" of 1895, nor was it related to No. 13 Edict decreed by Japanese 206 As time marches forward, the torment events of the Sino-Japanese War and the Treaty of Shimonoseki have been an entire century back.

As time marches on, the grieved events of the Sino-Japanese War and Treaty of Shimonoseki have been an entire century away. However, the Diaoyu Islands "swallowed" by Ito Hirobumi back then have not been returned to China till now. During one hundred years, September 18th Incident of 1931 and July 7 Incident of 1937 after the Sino-Japanese War brought grave disaster to Chinese people, for which Japanese people also paid great price. In September, 1997, while visiting the Mukden Memorial Hall, Hashimoto Ryutaro, Japanese Prime Minister indicated: "No matter how forgetful we are, we can't forget the history. We are able to learn from the history, but unable to change it. We must endure the burden of history." The historical fact of the Diaoyu Islands' falling into the hands of Japanese militarism should certainly be listed into the range of "history" "unable to forget". "Referring to history makes people wise". To get on friendly with each other for centuries, Chinese and Japanese people have to envisage the phase of history.

(Originally published in 2nd Issue of the journal "Study on Anti-Japanese War", p. 164-186)

VIII. Memorabilia of the Diaoyu Islands Issue

AD 1372-1895

Lunar Calendar	AD	Historical Records
the 5th year of the reign of Emperor Hongwu of the Ming Dynasty	1372	The first emperor of the Ming Dynasty appointed Yang Zai as an imperial envoy to grant honorific title to the King in Ryukyu in recognition of his rule. During the trip, they passed by the Diaoyu Islands. Until the Jia Qing Period, there were totally ten imperial envoys who had gone to Ryukyu to grant honorific title to the King in Ryukyu. However, the records of these imperial envoys were burned by accident.
the 7th year of the reign of Emperor Hongwu of the Ming Dynasty	1374	Jinghai Marquis Wu Zhen patrolled sea under orders; on the Liushan Sea of Fujian, he encountered Japanese pirates and fought against them around the waters of the Diaoyu Islands to the waters of Ryukyu, and captured them to the capital; the Ryukyuan thought highly of him for along time.
the 1st year of the reign of Emperor Yongle of the Ming Dynasty	1403	Voyage with a Tail Wind (Shun Feng Xiang Song), a book collected in Bodleian Library Oxford in UK, firstly recorded the names of the Diaoyu Island and Chiwei Yu: set off in the north wind, towards the east, we arrived at Pengjia Mountain (it's called Pengjia Yu presently), then, we arrived at the Diaoyu Islands; we set off in south wind, then we arrived at small Ryukyu (Here it referred to Taiwan), then, arrived at the south of the Diaoyu Islands, towards the east, we arrived at Chiwei Yu....

May 21 in the 13th year of the reign of Emperor Jiajing of the Ming Dynasty	June 1, 1534	The Records of the Imperial Title-Conferring Envoys to Ryukyu (Shi Liu Qiu Lu) – Chen Kan, sent by the the Ming court firstly recorded: "on May 10, the ship has passed via Diaoyu yu, Huangmao Yu, Chi Yu islands"; "At sunset of the 11th day, we saw the Gumi (Kume) Mountain which belongs to Ryukyu. The barbarians all beat drums and danced in the boats to express their joy upon arriving home". Caozhouji written by Gao Deng, the deputy envoy, also stated that Gumi Mountain is where the land of Ryukyu begins.
the 35th year of the reign of Emperor Jiajing of the Ming Dynasty	1556	Zhen Shungong went to Japan upon orders. His drawings of islands between Taiwan and Ryukyu also painted the Diaoyu Islands. In this book an essay entitled "Songs of a Long Voyage" clearly records that Diaoyuyu is a small island of Xiaodong.
the 40th year of the reign of Emperor Jiajing of the Ming Dynasty	1561	Zheng Ruozeng, "the authority" in coastal geography, wrote Miscellaneous Records by Zheng Kaiyang. The Great Haiphong Map (Wang Li Hai Fang Tu) in Vol. 1 included the Diaoyu Island, Huangwei Yu, Chiwei Yu. In the same year, the Shi Liu Qiu Lu of another imperial envoy of the Ming Dynasty -- Guo Rulin, also stated that "Chi Yu is the mountain that marks the boundary of Ryukyu".
the 4th year of the reign of Emperor Jiajing of the Ming Dynasty	1562	An Illustrated Compendium on Maritime Security (Chou Hai Tu Bian) compiled by Zheng Ruozeng under the auspices of Hu Zongxian, the supreme commander of the southeast coastal defense of the Ming court, included the Diaoyu Islands, Huangwei Yu, Chiwei Yu into the jurisdiction of the coastal defense of the Ming court.

the 7th year of Ming Dynasty Emperor Wanli's reign	1579	Xie Jie, a deputy imperial title-conferring envoy of the Ming Dynasty, recorded in his book, Addendum to Summarized Record of Ryukyu (Liu Qiu Lu Cuo Yao Bu Yi) that he entered Ryukyu from Cang Shui to Hei Shui, and returned to China from Hei Shui to Cang Shui. It clearly pointed out that the separating line lies in Hei Shui Gou (today's Okinawa Trough) between Chiwei Yu and Kume Island.
the 33rd year of Ming Dynasty Emperor Wanli's reign	1605	Xu Bida, the Secretary for the Ministry of Personnel Management, mentioned the Diaoyu Islands were within China's territory, located in the East China sea about 92 nautical miles northeast to Keelung, Taiwan.
the 34th year of Ming Dynasty Emperor Wanli's reign	1606	The 15th imperial envoy--Xia Ziyang recorded we saw the Gumi Mountain which belongs to Ryukyu. The barbarians all beat drums and danced in the boats to express their joy upon arriving home. He also stressed that the Hei Shui Gou is the boundary between Ryukyu and China.
the 37th year of Ming Dynasty Emperor Wanli's reign	1609	Japan's Satsuma vassal invaded and sent people to do survey on Ryukyu's territory; the Diaoyu Islands were never mentioned.
the 1st year of Ming Dynasty Emperor Tianqi's reign	1621	Coastal Defense II. Map of Fujian's Coastal Mountains and Sands (Wu Bei Zhi. Hai Fang Er. Fu Jian Yan Hai Shan Sha Tu), drawn up by Mao Yuanyi in 1621, also included the Diaoyu Islands as part of China's maritime territory.
the 2rd year of Ming Dynasty Emperor Chongzhen's reign	1629	Mao Ruizhi again pointed out in the Record of the Interpreters of August Ming (Huang Ming Xiang Xu Lu) that: from Fuzhou to [Ryukyu]...the Gumi Mountain is where the land of Ryukyu begins.

the 6th year of Ming Dynasty Emperor Chongzhen's reign	1633	Du Sance, an imperial envoy and Hu Jing wrote the book A Record of Ryukyu. Hu Jing once again clarified that the Gumi Mountain was the border of Ryukyu in his book A Record of Ryukyu (Liu Qiu Ji) and he recorded how warmly the Ryukyuan welcomed him.
the 13th year of Ming Dynasty Emperor Chongzhen's reign	1640	Zhongshan King Shangfeng pointed out in official communication that: Ryukyu is adjacent to Fujian; there were clear boundaries between China and Ryukyu. A map titled with "Fujian Coastal Defense Map" in the second volume of his book the Defense Maps compiled Shi Yongtu also included the Diaoyu Island, Huangwei Yu, Chiwei Yu into the jurisdiction of China's naval defense.
he 7th year of Qing Dynasty Emperor Shunzhi's reign	1650	Zhongshan Historical Records of Ryukyu Kingdom, an authoritative history book of Ryukyu Royal Court compiled under the supervision of Ryukyu Prime Minister Xiang Xiangxian, quotes Chen Kan as saying that Gumi Mountain comes into sight, that is where the land of Ryukyu begins.
the 22th year of Qing Dynasty Emperor Kangxi's reign	1683	Miscellaneous Records of a Mission to Ryukyu (Shi Liu Qiu Za Lu) written by Wang Ji recorded that Wang Ji asked the old sailor: "what does Hei Shui Gou mean?" "Boundary between China and foreign land", answered the old sailor. It again proves that Hei Shui Gou (Okinawa Trench) is the boundary between China and Ryukyu.
the 40th year of Qing Dynasty Emperor Kangxi's reign	1701	The Annals of Chong-shan (Zhong Shan Shi Jian) and the attached maps written by Cai Duo wrote the names of the 36 islands in detail; the Diaoyu Island was not mentioned.

the 58th year of Qing Dynasty Emperor Kangxi's reign	1719	Xu Baoguang, a deputy title-conferring envoy to Ryukyu in the Qing Dynasty, clearly recorded in his book Records of Messages from Chong-shan (Zhong Shan Chuan Xin Lu) that Yaeyama Islands were the most southwestern border of Ryukyu; Gumi Mountain was the mountain guarding the southwest border of Ryukyu; it drew the China's territory as the boundless sea in The Map of the 36 Islands of Ryukyu.
the 61st year of Qing Dynasty Emperor Kangxi's reign	1722	After patrolling the Diaoyu Islands and Xuepolan (Mount of Olives or Daniao Island, namely Beixiao Island; Dashe Island refers to Nanxiao Island), wrote A Tour of Duty in the Taiwan Strait (Tai Hai Shi Cha Lu) which recorded the condition of the ports and ships and pointed out that there are mountain behind the ocean which is called the Diaoyu Islands. The waters of the Diaoyu Islands can hold tens of ships.
the 12th year of Qing Dynasty Emperor Qianlong's reign	1747	Recompiled Annals of Taiwan Prefecture (Chong Zhu Tai Wan Fu Zhi) written by Fan Xian and Modified Annals of Taiwan Prefecture written by Yu Wenyi pointed out the previous version didn't fully record the details of sea defense, so they added some new information about this matter in the two books and transcribed Huang Shujing's records of the Diaoyu Island.
The 22rd year of Qing Dynasty Emperor Qianlong's reign	1757	Zhou Huang, a deputy imperial envoy of the Qing Dynasty, recorded in his book, the City Annals of Ryukyu (Liu Qiu Guo Zhi Lue), that Ryukyu "is separated from the waters of Fujian by Hei Shui Gou to the west" The Map of Ryukyu drew Gumi Island as the boundary; the Huangwei Yu and Chiwei Yu were not included.

the 32nd year of Qing Dynasty Emperor Qianlong's reign	1767	Michael Benoist, a French missionary in China in 1767 drew the Great Universal Geographic Map (Kun Yu Quan Tu) under the request of the Qing court. He colored Pengjia (Pengjia Mountain), Huabinxu (Huaping Yu), Haoyuxu (Diaoyu Island), Huanweixu (Huangwei Yu), Cheweixu (Chiwei Yu) with the same color as that of mainland China and Taiwan. Original names in the picture were pronounced according to the Minnan dialect.
the 50th year of Qing Dynasty Emperor Qianlong's reign	1785	The Map of the Three Provinces and 36 Islands of Ryukyu in the book-- Illustrated Outline of the Three Countries written by Hayashi Shihei colored Huaping Yu, Pengjia Mountain, Diaoyu Island, Huangwei Yu and Chiwei Yu in the same as the mainland of China, indicating that they are part of China's territory.
the 5th year of Qing Dynasty Emperor Jiaqing's reign	1800	The records of Zhao Wenkai, the imperial envoy, mentioned: on the 11th day, we saw Gumi Mountain (near Ryukyu).
the 13th year of Qing Dynasty Emperor Jiaqing's reign	1808	Qi Kun, an imperial envoy clearly recorded the position of Hei Shui Gou: "on May 13th, we saw Chi Yu. After several hours, we offer sacrifices to Ocean God". He also recorded: the "trench" is the Ryukyu coast in Eight poems of Voyage.
the 2rd year of Qing Dynasty Emperor Tongzhi's reign	1863	The Atlas of the Great Qing Dynasty (Huang Chao Zhong Wai Yi Tong Yu Tu) all marked the Diaoyu Island, Huangwei Yu, Chiwei Yu as China's territory.
the 10th year of Qing Dynasty Emperor Tongzhi's reign	1871	Volume 86 of Recompiled General Annals of Fujian (Chong Zuan Fu Jian Tong Zhi), a book compiled by Chen Shouqi and others included Diaoyu islands as a strategic location for coastal defense and placed the islands under the jurisdiction of Gamalan, Taiwan (known as Yilan County today).

the 5th year of Qing Dynasty Emperor Guangxu's reign	1879	Before Ryukyu Vassal being changed into Okinawa County, Xiang Dehong, the Grand Master with the Purple-Golden Ribbon suggested China send soldiers to Ryukyu to defense the attack of Japan. In his reply to the Japanese Foreign Minister Terashima, he clearly said there were 36 islands in Ryukyu the islands between Gumi Island and Fuzhou belonged to China.
In October in the 6th year of Qing Dynasty Emperor Guangxu's reign	October, 1880	Japan's envoy Shishido Chi put forward "Miyako Islands and Yaeyama Islands belong to China"; then the Qing government and Japan reached consensus on "Island Division and Treaty Adding" plan. It proved that there is no terra nullius between China and Ryukyu.
the 11th year of Qing Dynasty Emperor Guangxu's reign	1885	Koga Tatsushiro went to the Diaoyu Island without permission to collect pinions and seafood, and applied for renting the islands. In the same year, the Ministry of Internal Affairs gave secret instructions to Kanmori Nagagi, Okinawa Secretary to investigate the islands and establish national markers.
July 28	September 6, 1885	The Chinese newspaper Shen-pao reported: "some Japanese people stuck Japan's flag on the sea islands to the north east of Taiwan, revealing Japan's intention to occupy these islands."
August 13	September 21, 1885	Ishizawa Heigo, the Okinawa official reported to the Okinawa magistrate Sutezo Nishimura that: "the islands are undoubtedly the Diaoyutai islands, Huangwei Yu, Chiwei Yu, etcwhich were recorded Zhongshan Mission Records"

August 14	September 22, 1885	The Okinawa magistrate Sutezo Nishimura reported to Yamagata Aritomo, the Ministry of Internal Affairs: "the details of the islands have already been well-known to Qing envoy ships dispatched to crown the former Zhongshan Wang, and already given fixed names [Chinese] and used as navigational aids en route to the Ryukyu Islands. The secret order of the Ministry of Internal Affairs mentioned we are worried about the establishment of the erection of national markers."
September 6th	October 13	"Beijing Daily" published two edicts, deciding to establish Ministry of Navy Affairs and change Fujian Governor into Taiwan Governor. Shimada, the Japanese temporary embassy and Hatano, the Japanese consul in Tianjin immediately reported it to the Japanese Ministry of Foreign Affairs.
September 14	October 21	Inoue Kaoru, the Ministry of Foreign Affairs, wrote to Yamagata Aritomo, the Ministry of Internal Affairs: "about the uninhabited islands between Okinawa and Fuzhou of the Qing government, they are close to the border of the Qing government. Furthermore, the Qing government has named these islands. Recently, the Qing government published newspapers, saying that our government attempts to occupy the affiliated islands near Taiwan and the Qing government has suspicions about our country. At this moment, if we openly established national stakes on these islands, we are bound to face the opposition from the Qing government. Therefore, we should report its harbor shapes and unearthed land property according to the actual investigation results. We can step out of the shadow to establish national stakes and further develop these islands according to the situation in the future."

September 29	November 5	Okinawa Prefecture consulted Yamagata again.
October 21	December 4	the Ministry of Foreign Affair and the Ministry of Internal Affairs replied to Okinawa magistrate: we knew your application and it was no need to establish the markers.
the 12th year of Qing Dynasty Emperor Guangxu's reign	1886	The Compilation of South Island and The Map of the 36 Islands of Ryukyu compiled by Nishimura, the Okinawa magistrate, didn't mention the Diaoyu Islands, which indicates that he knew clearly the islands didn't belong to Okinawa.
December 22 in the 15th year of Qing Dynasty Emperor Guangxu's reign (lunar calendar)	January 13, 1890	Okinawa applied again for the establishment of markers.
September 24 in the 19th year of Qing Dynasty Emperor Guangxu's reign (lunar calendar)	November 2, 1893	Okinawa Prefecture Governor applied for the establishment of markers for the third time.
the 20th year of Qing Dynasty Emperor Guangxu's reign	1894	Koga Tatsushiro re-appiled for the rent of the Diaoyu Islands 9 years ago, which was refused by Okinawa.
July 1	August 1	The Japanese troops in Korea launched a surprise attack on the Chinese army, the Qing government was forced to declare war on Japan.
August 16	September 15	The Chinese army was defeated in Pyongyang. Later, the Japanese army crossed the Yalu River and captured Jiulian City and Fenghuang City.
August 18 in lunar calendar	September 17	In the Battle of Yalu River Beiyang Fleet suffered sever losses. Some Japanese army occupied of Jinzhou, Dalian and Lushun, etc.

October	November, 1894	Considering the Qing government's undoubted failure, Li Hongzhang sent Gustav Detring (German citizen), the official in the Revenue Division of the Tianjin Customs to Japan to make paece talks with Japan, but Japan refused this proposal.
December 1	December 27, 1894	Yasushi Nomura, the Ministry of Internal Affairs, sent a ciphered text to Foreign Minister Mutsu Munemitsu: "about the arrangement of establishing stakes on Kuba Island and the Diaoyu islands, we hope this matter could be submitted to the cabinet meeting again according to present situation."
December 16 in lunar calendar	January 11, 1895	Foreign Minister Mutsu Munemitsu agreed Nomura's plan to invade and occupy the Diaoyu Islands
December 19	January 14, 1895	The Japanese Meiji government passed the "cabinet resolution"
In February in the 21st year of Qing Dynasty Emperor Guangxu's reign	March, 1895	The Japanese army captured Niuzhuang
March in lunar calendar	April, 1895	The Japanese army captured Penghu Islands.
March 23	April 17, 1895	China was forced to sign Treaty of Shimonoseki.
April 17	May 8, 1895	China and Japan exchanged ratification in Beijing. The people in Taiwan opposed to the ceding of Taiwan and held the armed uprising.
April 19	May 11, 1895	Meiji Emperor appointed Arichi Shinanojiou as the commander and he should listen to the command of Taiwan Governor Kabayama Sukenori
May 6	May 29, 1895	At nine o'clock in the morning, Taiwan Governor Kabayama Sukenori firstly arrived at 'Senkaku islands'; in fact, it was the Huaping Yu (25° 20'N, 122 °E)

May 10	June 2, 1895	At nine o'clock in the evening, the transition of Taiwan was completely ended
May 18	June 10, 1895	Koga Tatsushiro took advantage of the Treaty of Shimonoseki and advocated that Japan should incorporated the islands into Japan's territory. In September, 1896, Koga's application of lending the islands was "approved".

IX. The Textual Research on Sovereignty over the Diaoyu Islands before the Sino-Japanese War of 1894-1895

Wu Tianying

Chinese People Originally Discovered and Named the Diaoyu Islands

Chinese people firstly discovered the Diaoyu Islands in the 14th century

The messengers used for sending out imperial edicts to Japan in the Ming dynasty period and the emissaries conferring the title of the King of Ryukyu, usually set off from Fuzhou, Fujian. After entering the Qing dynasty, "giant boat, unable to set sail because of the obstruction of the sand and shallow water, set out from the exit of Wu Humen". The messenger and emissary boarded on ship and sailed to the ocean after worshiping God. The ancient sailboat had to be driven by the aid of monsoon with sea islands (mountain) as navigation mark. As Ryukyu was located in the northeastern direction of Fuzhou, the sailboats could set sail there with the wind support of the southwest monsoons on outward course and used northeast monsoon on the return trip.

The earliest presently existing navigation guide recording the names of islands like the Diaoyu Islands is the Voyage with a Tail Wind (Shun Feng Xiang Song), a book collected in Bodleian Library Oxford in UK. The book is a transcript with preface written by the collector in 1639 on its back cover.

In the below presented section of the book "From Fujian to Ryukyu", the names of the Diaoyu Islands and Chikan Islands (Chiwei Yu) have firstly appeared.

"......set off in the north wind, towards the east, we arrived at Pengjia Mountain (presently, it's called Pengjia Yu), then, we arrived at the Diaoyu Islands; we set off in south wind, then we arrived at small Ryukyu (here it refers to Taiwan), then, arrived at the south of the Diaoyu Islands towards the east, we arrived at Chiwei Yu, then, towards northeast, we saw Gumi Mountain (here it refers to the Kume Islands of Ryukyu)...."

To better understand the above quotation and the record of similar content in the following sections, the chronometer (It was made from porcelain at first, glass later.) and compass used back then will be explained. The navigation voyage in ancient China was not measured by li, but by "two hours". Each "two hours" was measured by sand clock or burning joss sticks. At normal wind speed, the boat sailed about 30 kilometers with the wind, and one day and one night could be divided into ten "two hours". The compass was divided into 360 degrees, 24 equal parts, arranging in the order of left-east, right-west, up-south, down-north.

......

The accomplishment time of the book was in 1403 according to the editorial's statement that "in the first year of Yongle in Ming Dynasty, heading to western countries under the imperial command, they corrected the route for many times". Some people have argued that the book was accomplished in 1430 based on the assumption made by Dr. Joseph Needham in his book Science and Civilization in China. Okuhara Toshio stated generally "the book was accomplished before 1663", and "denied" its significance, saying: "the time when this book was accomplished is not actually important."

......

Within 30 years (1368-1398) during the reign of Emperor Zhu Yuanzhang in early Ming dynasty, China frequently sent sailboats that would pass by the islands like the Diaoyu Islands to participate in official acts in Ryukyu, which could confirm the rationality of the above judgment. To overthrow the fact that Chinese people first discovered the islands, Okuhara Toshio unexpectedly made deceitful remarks, proceeding to deceive people.

"(From 1372-1866) the entire period of conferring the title and paying tribute, the emissary went to Ryukyu 23 times in total (However, the original record didn't not mention the emissary, but counted into the sum total). In addition, China barely dispatched official ships to Ryukyu."

This marvelous statement displays the "essence" how Okuhara has "fabricated the history".

According to the myth fabricated by Okuhara, in the 5th year during the reign of Hongwu (1372), "Yang Zhai was not the emissary", however, in the official record of History of the Ming Dynasty, "envoy Yang Zhai conferred the title of the King of Ryukyu" in that very year. The Memorial of Ming Dynasty, royal file of Ming dynasty recorded the whole content of the imperial edict of "Yang Zhai headed to Ryukyu with imperial edict." Secondly, the second emissary was assigned to Ryukyu by the emperor of Ming dynasty on the second year during the reign of Yongle (1404). In other words, according to Okuhara's statement, what happened between the 5th year during the reign of Emperor Hongwu and the first year of Yongle became "blank", and " China barely dispatched official ships to Ryukyu." As a matter of fact, according to the definite record of The Memorial of Ming Dynasty and History of the Ming Dynasty, China assigned the officials to Ryukyu during that time at least five times:

(First) In winter of the 7th year during the reign of Emperor Hongwu (1374), Li Haoben, the assistant minister of Punishment Ministry, was granted luxurious clothes, pottery of 70000 and ironware of 1000"; In the 9th year, "in April, the assistant minister of Punishment Ministry returned the grant to Ryukyu with forty horses and sulfur of 2500 kilograms".

(Second) In spring of the 15th year during the reign of Emperor Hongwu (1382), "the tribute came from Zhongshan, the minister of Interior Affairs was dispatched to send the emissary back home".

(Third) In the 16th year during the reign of Emperor Hongwu (1383), "the two kings (Here they referred to Chadu, the King of Zhongshan and Chen Chadu, the King of Shannan–Wu Tianying) were contending for hegemony and attacking each other with the King of Shanbei. Liang Min was ordered by an imperial edict to cease the war. All the three warring kings were persuaded by Liang Min.

(Fourth) In the 21st year during the reign of Emperor Hongwu (1388), Lan Yu, the senior general assigned a team to escort Di Baonu (Tian Baonu) and his queen, princess consort in their journey back to Beijing", the emperor of Yuan Dynasty was furious with Lan Yu, since during a war, he had seized a Mongol noble lady for himself and violated her. "Therefore, he dispatched the ministers to escort Di Baonu when he sailed to Ryukyu, giving Di Baonu abundant legacy."

(Fifth) In the 29th year during the reign of Emperor Hongwu (1396), "The Ming emperor appointed 36 people from Fujian Province who were good at operating ships to go to Ryukyu, to facilitate the tribute-paying voyages." The act was greatly profound, which will be discussed in detail in the following section.

The events listed in the above didn't comprise the one that the senior general Wuzhen led a massive fleet of warships which pursued and attacked Japanese pirates all the way to the ocean near Ryukyu (see details in Section One, Chapter Four of this book). The main characters in the above five great events, including internal officials, the undersecretary of Judiciary, as well as the team escorting the second son of the emperor of Yuan Dynasty, Di Baonu

(Tian Baonu), had all headed to Ryukyu under the emperor's order. The author would like to ask for Prof. Okuhara's advice: Can't we call those ships they sailed on as the "official ships which were dispatched by China"? Do you have some evidence to prove that the above records were was purely fictional?

The above historical facts indicated that since the beginning of Ming dynasty, plenty of court officials and their suites dispatched by Chinese government all set out from Fuzhou, passed the Taiwan Strait, and then entered into the territory of Ryukyu after sailing by the Diaoyu and other islands under the drive of southeast monsoons and the flowing of black stream. They didn't leave behind direct records written by themselves, but were recorded explicitly in the original edition of "Voyage with a Tailwind". As a result, it can be asserted that the Diaoyu islands and other islands were firstly discovered, namely, "originally discovered", by Chinese people between 1372 and 1403 at the latest, which could also be confirmed from the names of the islands.

The Diaoyu Islands were named by China

The names of the Diaoyu and Chiwei Yu islands were firstly mentioned in the "Voyage with a Tailwind" and later inherited by China. We firstly see the simultaneous appearance of the names of the Diaoyu Island, Huangmao Island (Huangwei Yu) and Red Island (Chiwei Yu) in The Records of Imperial Title-Conferring Envoys to Ryukyu (It will be reviewed in detail in Chapter Three of this book) which was written by Chen Kan on May 10, the 13th year of Emperor Jiajing in Ming Dynasty (June 20, 1534, AD).

The illustration here was only made from the perspective of the names of the islands. Since Chen kan, people's specific addresses on the three islands had not been exactly identical, but all applied homophone, approximate pronunciation or abbreviation. For instance, the presently existing five maps of territory, which were written during the reign of Emperor Jiajing of Ming dynasty, recorded the names of islands such as the Diaoyu Island, and so on, which are listed as follows:

The 13th year of Emperor Jiajing (1534) Chen kan The Record during the Dispatch to Ryukyu Diaoyu Island, Huangmao Island, Chi Island.

The 35th year of Emperor Jiajing (1556) Zheng Shungong The View on Japan Diaoyu Island, Huangma Island, Chikan Island.

The 40th year of Emperor Jiajing (1561) Zheng Ruozeng The Essay by Zheng Kaiyang Diaoyu Island, Huangmao Mountain, Chi Island.

The 40th year of Emperor Jiajing (1561) Guo Rulin The Record during the Dispatch to Ryukyu Diao Island, Chi Island.

The 41st year of Emperor Jiajing (1562) Hu Zongxian The Compile of the Charts Diaoyu Island, Huangmao Mountain, Chi Island.

What about Japan? In the statement titled "On the Sovereignty over the Senkaku Islands", Ryukyu government adopted an underhand approach, stating in a vague way:

"The names of each individual island of Senkaku had been recorded in a variety of historical documents, and their names varied with different people."

Another Japanese scholar intentionally supported the statement: "The names of the Senkaku Islands have varied in different times. For example, Chen Kan mentioned in his work that Hoapinsu was also called as the Diaoyu Island, and Kuba Jima was called as Huangwei Yu, Dazheng Island called as Chiwei Yu", and so on.

Actually, their confusing statements reversed the historical sequence, covered the real condition that "the names varied with different times". Besides, they did not have the courage to envisage the following questions: Where did the name of "Diaoyu Island" come from? Since when did the name of "Kuba Island" started? Moreover, the name of Dadong Island itself proved that it originated from sometime between 1912 and 1926, on July 25, the 10th year of Emperor Dazheng (1921) to be more exact, which was 26 years later after the signing of Treaty of Shimonoseki and Japan's seizure of "Taiwan and its affiliated island".

In brief, The Precious File of Past Dynasties, the royal record of ancient Ryukyu, didn't record the names of the Diaoyu and other islands; The Reference of All ages of Zhongshan (1650), the first historical work of the Ryukyu Kingdom, transcribed the full text of the content that recorded the Diaoyu and other islands mentioned in Chen Kan's book The Records of Imperial Title-Conferring Envoys to Ryukyu, thus the first historical work of the Ryukyu Kingdom also addressed the three islands as Diaoyu Island, Huangmao Island, Chi Island. In The Generalization of Guide (1708) composed by Cheng Shunze (Tei Junsoku), a noted scholar and the Grand Master with the Purple-Golden Ribbon (Zi Jin Da Fu) of Ryukyu, Ryukyu's famous scholar, the three islands were addressed as Diaoyu Platform, Huangwei Yu and Chiwei Yu. As for Japan of Edo Period, only in Illustrated Handbook on the Overall View of Three Countries·Map of Three Provinces and Thirty Six Islands of Ryukyu, the three islands were addressed as Diaoyu Platform, Huangwei Yu and Chiwei Yu, mentioning that "Diaoyu Platform, Huangwei Yu and Chiwei Yu are China's territory.

The very names of Diaoyu Island, Huangwei Yu and Chiwei Yu themselves manifest that they were firstly discovered, named by China, and these names were established due to wide usage and acceptance in China, Ryukyu Kingdom and Japan. Takahashi Sougorou has explicitly put forward:

The word シマ (island) could refer to an administrative division, a continent, an island or an islet, while reef refers to the rock hidden underwater. In the language of Japanese, シマ is usually written into "島". There is no シマ called "islet" in Japan, however, there are as many as 29 シマ that are called "islet" in Fujian Province, in Penghu Islands, and in the Taiwan Province, and even more in the ancient maps of China.

In Korea-Japan Asia Review, Issue 10 published in 1972, Takahashi Sougorou published an article entitled "Are the Alleged Senkaku Islands Japan's Territory?", reminding people, in particular, that the Diaoyu and other islands were named in Chinese language by Chinese people, and they were recorded in the official documents which has passed on to the later generations.

The reasons why Chinese people firstly discovered and named the Diaoyu Islands

Okuhara Toshio not only applied additions, but subtractions as well, eventually, his real intention is revealed.

Even if the earliest ancient documents recording the Diaoyu Island were Chinese, it was not necessarily that the Diaoyu Island was discovered by Chinese people or named by China.

If it was not Chinese people that discovered and named the Diaoyu Island and other islands, then, people of which country would it be? Were "the Senkaku Islands" "discovered" by Koga Tatsushiro of your country in 1884? No. Because the argument was too ridiculous and you had already turned to advocate another argument long ago.

Consequently, in abundant research papers, authored by Japanese scholars, the statistics and comparison of unlike terms were repeatedly quoted. They counted up the times of contacts between China and Ryukyu within 507 years from the 5th year of Emperor Hongwu in Ming dynasty (1372) when China and Ryukyu started to establish the relation of conferring title and paying tribute to the 5th year of Emperor Guangxu in Qing Dynasty (1879) when Japan annihilated the Ryukyu Kingdom and subordinated it to its Okinawa Prefecture. Since China only dispatched the emissary to confer title when the King of Ryukyu died and the new King ascended to the throne, moreover, one King lived to decades years old, it would be impossible for China to "confer the title" every year; In Ryukyu, "paying tribute" had economical meaning of the trade along with tribute. On the process of trading with China or selling Chinese cargo, Ryukyu made abundant profits, which brought about the pro-verb of "exaggerative ten times", meaning one could make ten-times profits. In consequence, people in Ryukyu joyfully rushed to China, which produced the comedy that the Ming government frequently "made regulation on paying tribute every two years" while Ryukyu always "replied to the request of paying tribute every year".

After the funny operation of the unlike terms, they pronounced ecstatically: "during the five hundred years, the ships for paying tribute from Ryukyu navigated to China 241 times (173 times in Ming dynasty and 68 times in Qing dynasty); On the other hand, the ships for conferring titles from China only navigated to Ryukyu 23 times, likewise, the ships for acknowledging China were also dispatched by Ryukyu 23 times... A great number of ships of Ryukyu once witnessed that the Senkaku Islands were making trades with China, going further to develop route and trade with places like Annam, Siam, Sumatra and even Malacca."

Was the author giving a lecture on history of foreign trade?

Okuhara Toshio not only applied addition, but subtraction as well, eventually, his real intention was revealed.

The ships for paying tribute went to Ryukyu 23 times in total within 500 years. Averagely, it was once every 21 to 25 years, and the mean was averaged by doing arithmetic. As a matter of fact, there were a great many blank periods up to 30 to 40 years (For example it was 30 years for Zhang Xueli and Lin Hongnian, 37 years for Xu Baoguang and Zhou Huang, 40 years for Li Dingyuan). The interval between Chen Kan and the former emissary Dong Min was 55 year's gap. It could be seen that people of Fujian only had one or two experiences of navigating on the course in their lifetimes, which would be impossible for them to possess correct knowledge of the course. In addition, it would be natural that their skills of navigating the ship were unreliable.

......

It can be seen that these scholars have acted with a hidden motive, their intention is to prove that: The fishermen along the coast of Fujian rarely passed the Diaoyu Island and other islands, and had few chances to navigate boat to escort the emissary, seeing the islands "once or twice in their lifetimes" at most; the few fishermen still "lacked navigation experience" and "their skills of navigating ship were unreliable". Then, it would be out of the question that the rest countless people who had no chance to follow the "emissary" would pass the Diaoyu Island and other islands. In this way, "Ryukyuans" who were "familiar with the navigating course and equipped with practiced skills" were historically endowed with the sacred mission of "discovering" and "naming" the islands.

......

As is well known, in the ancient times, the accumulation of navigation knowledge, the improvement of navigation skills and the primary material foundation briefly depended on the following aspects: the possession of iron mine, exquisite iron smelting, the optimization of shipbuilding technology, and the perfection of compass (tray) and navigation record (needle book), and so on, and these aspects were closely related. Here these aspects will be accounted, combining the historical reality of China in Ming dynasty and Ryukyu.

Firstly, Iron mine and iron smelting

Based on the research of Huang Qichen, the head of History Department, Sun Yat-Sen University, in the first year of Emperor Yongle, that is, the beginning of the 15th century, the yield of cast iron produced only by state-run factories was up to 9237 tons; In the 9th year of Emperor Xuande (1434), the yield produced by private factories was up to 13831 tons, rising to 45000 tons after the times of Jiajing in Ming dynasty. On the other hand, according to the record of historical materials of the world, the other countries still lacked the statics of cast iron's yield before 1670s. Until 1670, the yield of cast iron in Russia had been the most, which was only 2400 tons; and only 2000 tons in UK in 1740. It can be seen that the yield of cast iron in China ranked the highest, and the iron smelting then was highly developed.

Ryukyu, located in volcanic geological stratum, didn't produce iron, and the tribute they paid to China was mainly horses and sulfur.

......

Consequently, Ryukyu had been deficient in iron sand since ancient times so that it was difficult to manufacture daily commodity even with wrought iron, which was the origin of the historical record that "Weigui", "iron kettle" and "ironware and keys" all relied on the grant from China in Ming dynasty.

Secondly, Shipbuilding technology

There was vivid description on "the emissary's ship" that Chen Kan was on board in Shu Yu Zhou Zi Lu quoted in the preceding section: "The warship was different from the ordinary boats sailing on rivers. ...... Its window was even with the surface of warship, and the height of the window was no more than two chi. It reached down to the bottom, with ladder for climbing up and down. Even though the window was open, its pane was like a cave. Since the wave in the sea was extremely high, it dashed when the warship was high and dodged underwater. The boards for covering the wave whose height was approximately four chi were installed front and back, outside the cabin. Despite the unaesthetic appearance, it was of practical use. The warship, fifteen zhang in length, two zhang six chi in width, one zhang three chi in depth, consisted of 23 cabins. Five masts, established in front and at back of the warship, among which the largest was seven zhang two chi in length, six chi five cun around the circle, and the rest were smaller. A house with two floors was built at the back, for the purpose of putting the imperial edicts and worshiping Celestial Queen (patron saint of navigation). The ship was well-equipped with appliance. There are four rudders in case of unexpected prediction. There were thirty six sculls, four large iron (anchors), weighing five thousand jin. ...... 40 tanks of water, ... Large storage of swords, swears, bows and arrows, and two frames of Fou langji (western cannon). More than 140 sailors for navigating the ship, over one hundred escort soldiers, and also over one hundred craftsmen from various branches. The parade was really majestic and spectacular. However, the warship of Chen Kan was not of the supreme level in China back then. During the 3rd year of Emperor Yongle (1405) to the 8th year of Emperor Xuande (1443), the invincible oriental fleet led by Zheng He, the well-known navigator on his voyage to the west seven times comprised of over sixty ships, large or small, among which the largest one was sixty four zhang four chi in length, over four times that of Chen Kan's warship, eighteen zhang in width, over six times that of Chen Kan's. The medium-sized ships of Zheng He's fleet were thirty seven zhang in length, fifteen zhang in width.

The ship had twelve sails hanged, with maximum displacement of 14000 tons, maximum carrying capacity of 7000 tons, which represented the highest level of Chinese shipbuilding.

Ryukyu, deficient in iron sand, wrought iron and its products, iron nail and iron hoop, iron anchor weighing five thousand jin in particular, wouldn't attach extravagant hope of manufacturing giant ship.

In the latter half of the 14th century when Ryukyu started to establish relationships with the Chinese Ming dynasty, the iron smelting, shipbuilding and navigation skills in China ranked the top in the world. On the other hand, the navigation technology in Ryukyu was still at elementary stage. To fundamentally alter the situation, Ryukyu had to rely on China to provide "ship", "workers of ship" capable of building ship, as well as "people excelling in navigating ship". Therefore, the magnificent feat that "thirty six households" immigrating to Ryukyu arose.

Thirdly, The distinguished contribution made by the immigrants of "thirty six households" which moved to Ryukyu from central Fujian, to develop navigation there.

......

The 25th year of Emperor Hongwu (1392) was a significant year in the history of cultural exchange between China and Ryukyu. The historical books recorded:

In the 25th year (of Emperor Hongwu), the King of Zhongshan assigned his son, nephew, together with children of his vassal to attend school. The imperial was joyful, with optimal treatment, granted thirty six households from Fujian who excelled in navigating, and commanded them to pay tribute back and forth.

The last sentence of the above quotation was recorded as "granting ship workers of thirty six households from central Fujian to facilitate the voyage of the emissary" in The History of Ming Dynasty. The record in The History of Ming Dynasty was certainly considered accurate.

......

It was the event that the immigrants of "thirty six households" from central Fujian transmitted Chinese culture to Ryukyu that caused advanced development in various aspects and opened the golden age in the history of ancient Ryukyu (1372-1609). Taking overseas trade as an example, "Previously, Ryukyu was just an isolated island, and people there lived the primitive life. Ever since it established relationships with China, China had been granted ships, sailors and translators (Chinese was adopted by various countries as the common language back then, just like English to present days), to facilitate it paying tribute in the beginning. Afterward, Ryukyu made full use of the manpower and facilities to develop the trade with China, and further expand overseas trade with the entire East Asia and Southeast Asia. (by Yang Zhongkui)

To sum up, it was not by accident that Chinese people originally discovered and named the Diaoyu Islands. Long before "thirty six households" immigrated to Ryukyu, the islands had been China's territory. Back then the navigation technology in Ryukyu was still at primary stage, so it was not strange that Ryukyuans seldom spoke about the islands. After the "thirty-six households" and their offspring helped Ryukyu to develop overseas trade, and further acquainted Ryukyuans with the islands, the Ryukyuans naturally regarded the Kume Island as Ryukyu's border because they took it for granted that the Diaoyu Islands belonged to China by means of hearing and seeing constantly, as well as passing on from generation to generation.

The Ryukyu Oceanic Trough between Chiwei Island and Gumi Mountain is "the Boundary between China and Foreign Land"

The essence and significance of the records of the Imperial Title-conferring Envoys to Ryukyu

Since 1372 (the 5th year of the reign of Emperor Hongwu of the Ming Dynasty), Yang Zai sent an imperial edict to Ryukyu to announce the beginning of the new dynasty, and the two countries established the tributary system, China had sent imperial title-conferring envoys to Ryukyu to recognize the authority of the King for 24 times, until Japan occupied Ryukyu and changed it to Okinawa County in 1879 (the 5th year of the reign of Emperor Guangxu in Qing Dynasty). Most of the records about Diaoyu Island and its affiliated islands in China are found in the records of imperial title-conferring envoys, which were work reports of the envoys after they returned to China. Among them only the records of the envoys before the reign of Emperor Jiajing were destroyed in fire. The eleven imperial title-conferring envoys were listed as follows:

From 1534 (the 13th year of the reign of Emperor Jiajing) to 1866 (the 5th year of the reign of Emperor Tongzhi), Chen Kan was the first title-conferring Envoy, Zhao Xinzhi was the last one, and there were 13 recorded title-conferring ceremonies. For the convenience of narration and space, the brief related information was listed as follows:

......

In the column of "names of title-conferring envoys" of the form above, names were recorded according to the principle of independent work. If the envoy was only mentioned in the collection of works, then his name would not be listed, such as Zhao Wenkai and his Manuscript on Raft ; if some envoy wrote more than one book about the title-conferring journey, then the more important ones would be chosen, for example, Wang Ji wrote Title Conferring Notes Collection and Zhongshan Evolution Annals as well as Collected Records of Diplomatic Mission to Ryukyu; and only the first author would be listed if two persons cooperated to write the book, for example, Xia Ziyang and Wang Shizhen wrote Records of Diplomatic Mission to Ryukyu, but it was listed under the name of Xia Ziyang.

The records of title-conferring envoys are the official documents in essence, which can be proved by the petition to the throne written by Xia Yan, the Minister of Rituals in 1534 (the 13th year of the reign of Emperor Jiajing). In the petition, he wrote,

Present to Your Majesty from Bureau for Ceremonies and Sacrifices... Chen Kan and his staff reported, "...when we were first appointed the position (it refers to the title-conferring envoy to Ryukyu–note by Wu Tianying), The Ministry of Rituals had checked the old documents about Ryukyu, but because of the fire disaster, they were all destroyed......" The envoy Chen Kan and his staff traveled around the country, and observed the local landscape and customs, and contrasted the tales with reality, and wrote down the records; and he wrote his traveling experience into a book, so as to cover what was not narrated in the historic records, and also to provide reference for the envoys in the future, which shows his sincerity and passion for his position, and his efforts should be awarded. I suggest Your Majesty agree to his request, and order the Ministry of Rituals to store Records of Diplomatic Mission to Ryukyu into National Archives for the sake of future historical collections.

......

Based on the narration of Xia Yan and later presented records of title-conferring envoys, it is known that the envoy, as the plenipotentiary delegate, brought the imperial edict issued by the emperor, and conferred titles on the new King of Ryukyu in Naha; after that, he returned to the capital, and he must present a comprehensive working report to the emperor about the journey, which was the record of title-conferring envoy. Even though the names of the records may be different, and they may be written briefly or comprehensively, their contents are about the all process of the diplomatic mission to Ryukyu and other related information, including the reasons for the mission, the navigation route, the brief introduction to the important official documents from both countries, and the report of the state of Ryukyu, etc. The records would be stored in national archives as public records, and be referred as important evidence for writing chronicles and making policies about Ryukyu later. At the same time or later, the records of title-conferring envoys will be printed to be published in China and abroad so as to get the recognition and reference from related countries. For example, the records that Gumi Mountain belonged to Ryukyu mentioned as follows are quoted from the records of Chen Kan, which was adopted by the government of Ryukyu and recorded into the Annals of Chong-shan, the official historical record of the Ryukyu Kingdom, almost word for word in 1650. To put it bluntly, the records of title-conferring envoys are neither personal traveling diaries, nor simple shipping logs; but they are essentially official documents, and naturally they have the legal effects of official documents.

......

As we have mentioned previously, from 1534 to 1866, China had more than 10 types of documents about Diaoyu Islands even just as the records of title-conferring envoys. On the contrary, during nearly the same period, that was the whole Tokugawa Shogunate or Edo era (1603-1868) before Meiji Reform, Japan had nearly no documents about Diaoyu Islands, except Illustrated Outline of the Three Countries: The Map of the Three Provinces and 36 Islands of Ryukyu written by Hayashi Shihei, a man from Sendai. And even this only document is in favor of China! In the face of the helpless and embarrassing situation, Okuhara Toshio and his fellows had ground out some tricks to distort the essence of the records of title-conferring envoys, debasing their values and denying their legal effects as official documents, and trying to achieve their aim of declaring Diaoyu Island and its affiliated islands as terra nullius. They vaguely addressed the records of title-conferring envoys as "ancient papers" or "ancient documents", said that "ancient papers are not very valuable in territorial dispute, and the real problem is, when solving territorial dispute, whether the ancient papers mentioned by the disputing country are significant in international law," and debased recklessly the values of the records of title-conferring envoys as historical evidences; or they denied and declared, "many records of the title-conferring envoys were just personal traveling records, but not official records and statements of the Chinese government"; or they used a lot of tricks to say that "they can be explained in either ways" or "records of title-conferring envoys are not the first-class materials in historical researches", etc.

Then we would like to ask some questions. About the three issues: "Gumi Mountain belongs to Ryukyu", "Chi Yu is the mountain that marks the boundary of Ryukyu", and " 'Gou (trough)' and 'Jiao (suburb)' are "boundary between China and foreign land", how many "historical facts" are needed to persuade those people in Japan, and how many evidences can they offer to base their claim that Diaoyu and its affiliated islands belong to Japan?

Gumi Mountain is "the mountain guarding the southwest border of Ryukyu"

According to the extant records of title-conferring envoys, most of the thirteen groups of envoys since Chen Kan started from Meihua Garrison, Changle County, Fuzhou City, Fujian Province (in Qing Dynasty, because the sand rose and the water was too shallow, they started from Wuhumen), and sailed into the ocean after they offered sacrifice to the sea in the local area. Because Ryukyu was to the northeast of Fuzhou, the sailing boat must be pushed by the monsoon; "therefore they started by the aid of summer wind from southwest", passed Baiquan Yu, Dongsha Mountain, Keelung, Pengjia Yu, Diaoyu Island, Huangwei Island (occasionally they sailed directly from Diaoyu Island to Chiwei Island, avoiding Huangwei Island), and Chiwei Island, travelled through the dark and rough "Dark Water Trough" of Ryukyu oceanic trough, crossed Gumi Mountain (known as Kume Island of Okinawa today) and Machi Mountain(known as Kerama-Shoto of Okinawa today), and arrived in Naha Port. And they returned by the aid of winter wind from northeast, and started from Naha, "after one and a half Geng (Translator's note: a day is divided into 10 Geng, 1 Geng= 2.4 Hour) they saw Gumi Mountain", and then after 50-Geng long journey, they passed Nanqi Mountain (known as Nanji Mountain today), Fengwei Mountain, Yu Mountain of Zhejiang Province, Tai Mountain, Lima Mountain (also called Shuang Mountain, known as Sishuang Islands today) of Fujian Province, arrived in Dinghai Garrison, and finally entered Wuhumen.

(1) In 1534, Chen Kan recorded all the islands they passed from Fuzhou to Gumi Mountain, and emphasized that "Gumi Mountain belonged to Ryukyu".

In 1534 (the 13th year of the reign of Emperor Jiajing), Chen Kan wrote in his Records of the Imperial Title-conferring Envoys to Ryukyu,

On 8th (of May) we began to sail from the sea port, …… on 9th, we can vaguely see a small mountain, which was 'the Little Ryukyu', Taiwan,. On 10th, the southern wind became stronger, and our boats travelled as if we were flying; however, when we sailed downward with the current, we didn't move very quickly. We passed Pingjia Mountain, Diaoyu Island, Huangmao Island (Huangwei Island), Chi Island (Chiwei Island). We were overwhelmed by the scene, and it took us one whole day and three daylights; because the Ryukyu sailboat had smaller sail, it couldn't reach our speed. After that, on the evening of the 11th, we saw Gumi Mountain, which is just where the land of Ryukyu begins; the foreigners sang and danced on the boat, happy to arrive at home. After one day, we finally reached the mountain, and some foreign people came by boats to ask…

In the record of Chen Kan, the accurate diction and clear narration explain two points clearly:

Firstly, after he listed Diaoyu Islands, Huangmao Island, Chi Island and other islands they passed on the journey, when he saw Gumi Mountain, he wrote down the sentence that "(Gumi Mountain) (Nai) is just where the land of Ryukyu begins " with full consideration. This is because "Nai" is a polysemous word, and it has 15 meanings in The Grand Dictionary of Chinese Language. The most common meaning is "be", for example, in the chapter about Emperor Gaozu of Han Dynasty in Records of the Grand Historian, it said, "the daughter of Mr. Lv is the Queen Lv"; and for the first time Chen Kan mentioned in the records, "…was 'the Little Ryukyu', which had the same meaning." "Nai" has another meaning, "just", "just now" for example, in Strategies of the Warring States: Strategies of State of Qi, Vol. IV, Meng Changjun said to Qi Xuan, "I just now saw the reason why you bought righteousness for me". Chen Kan wrote that the Gumi Mountain "is just where the land of Ryukyu begins", and he meant that after they passed Diaoyu Islands, they had arrived in the Gumi Mountain that is just where the land of Ryukyu begins. Certainly there is no ambiguity in his narration.

……

Secondly, Chen Kan used just a few words "the natives sang and danced on the boat, happy to arrive at their homes" to emphasize vividly that Gumi Mountain was the boundary of Ryukyu. This was totally in conformity with the record of Xia Ziyang, another title-conferring envoy in 1606 (the 34th year of the reign of Emperor Wanli of Ming Dynasty), and that of Li Dingyuan, a deputy title-conferring envoy in 1800 (the 5th year of the reign of Emperor Jiaqing in Qing Dynasty), that was, every time when the sailboat passed Chiwei Island, and people could see Gumi Mountain, they would always "cheer with laughter" and "the foreigners became very happy, because they thought they were going to arrive at home". Here "the foreigners" refer to the people from Ryukyu sent by the King of Ryukyu to welcome the Chinese envoys, such as some inferior officials, translators, shipping crew, etc. They had lived on the sea for a long time, and knew the ownership of the islands they passed, and felt homesickness for the homeland they had left for a long time. In their heart, Diaoyu Island and its affiliated islands belonged to China, so it was impossible that they would feel excited when they passed these islands; but when they saw Gumi Mountain, they revealed their homesickness and danced and sang on the boat because they were going to "arrive their homes" soon.

It shows that Chen Kan knew clearly the ownership of the islands they passed from Fuzhou to Gumi Mountain, and the records in their reports are quite accurate; Chiwei Island and all other islands to its west belonged to China, and only Gumi Mountain belonged to Ryukyu. It was not only noted by Chen Kan, but also acknowledged by the accompanying Ryukyu officials and crew represented by Cai Tingmei, who was a Ryukyu official and the descendant of the thirty-six clans from Min (Fujian).

(2) The "original idea" of "belonging to" which was raised by Prof. Midorima Sakae

Prof. Midorima Sakae from the International Law department of the Okinawa University, the author of Senkaku Islands (1984), No.14 in Okinawa Book Collection, which has been mentioned again and again previously, has raised a new view about Chen Kan's following record "(Gumi Mountain) is just the place where the land of Ryukyu begins", but without rhyme or reason:

Here, it cannot be clarified whether the account that Kume Island is where the land of Ryukyu begins is out of legal definition or simple shipping logs. "Shu" means territory ownership in the term of law. It was true that at that time, Kume Island and the area on the east of it belonged to Ryukyu; Chiwei Island was close to Kume Island (Note: Chiwei Island is about 100 km away from Diaoyu Island, but about 200 km away from Kume Island. It is not close to Kume Island at all), did the officials and navigators mistake it as a clear regulation and custom in their consciousness that Chi Island belonged to the territory of China in the Ming Dynasty? Here what is clear is that Kume Island belonged to the boundary of Ryukyu. "Shu" means affiliation, attachment and connection, and it was not clear whether the word "Shu" in the shipping logs means that Kume Island was affiliated with the boundary of Ryukyu geographically. The title-conferring envoys wrote down that Kume Island is just where the land of Ryukyu begins, but he did not mean that Senkaku Islands belonged to the territory of China, but it was natural that he just meant to record Kume Island as a navigation mark.

......

Why did I spend a lot of time and space to quote the lengthy paragraph above? The only reason was this was a typical example of the sophistry used by Okuhara Toshio and his fellows, and dissecting one sparrow could help you to understand other sparrows. At first sight, the author of this book had not lost his academic conscience totally, and he pointed out, even though vaguely, that "Kume Island and the area on the east of it belonged to Ryukyu; and the Chiwei Island was close to Kume Island, did the officials and navigators mistake it as a clear regulation and custom in their consciousness that Chi Island belonged to the territory of China in the Ming Dynasty?" Actually kind-hearted readers, please don't be tricked by him and think they had the courage to respect the truth. At first he said, "what is clear is that Kume Island belonged to the boundary of Ryukyu", and then he made a fuss about the meaning of "Shu", which made him appear to be impartial to either side and make no conclusion to either possibility. Actually from he said we could find the hidden reason why he said that "Shu" means affiliation, attachment and connection, which was to indicate Kume Island was affiliated with Ryukyu and to deny that Kume Island was the southwestern boundary of Ryukyu; at last without any reason he declared that Chen Kan did not mean that "Senkaku Islands belonged to the territory of China", and he only "recorded Kume Island as a navigation mark". Finally the book killed two birds with one stone: it not only debased thoroughly the essence and value of the records of title-conferring envoys, but also denied that truth that Gumi Mountain was the southwestern boundary of Ryukyu.

(3) In 1719, the deputy title-conferring envoy Xu Baoguang wrote clearly in Records of Messages from Chong-shan that Gumi Mountain was "the mountain guarding the southwest border of Ryukyu".

The statement that Gumi Mountain was "the mountain guarding the southwest border of Ryukyu" was quoted from Records of Messages from Chong-shan written by the deputy title-conferring envoy Xu Baoguang in 1719 (the 58th year of the reign of Emperor Kangxi in Qing Dynasty). The first volume of the book, Route Chart, quoted a paragraph from A General Guide written by famous Ryukyu scholar Cheng Shunze. Below the word "Gumi Mountain", there were two lines of note: "the mountain guarding the southwest border of Ryukyu".

A General Guide has at least "seven extant versions, but up to now, none of them has this note". Inoue Kiyoshi had seen a copy version collected by Higaonna Kanryo, and there was no note either, and the content varied to some extent:

The voyage from Fuzhou to Ryukyu started from Dongshawai, (the boat sailed in the direction of 120 degree on the compass) it took 10 Geng (Translator's note: 1 Geng=2.4 hour), arrived in Jilongtou (passed from northern direction), Huaping Yu and Pengjia Mountain; (97.5 degree and 90 degree) 10 Geng, arrived in Diaoyutai Island, (passed from northern direction), Huangma Yu (passed from northern direction, 90 degree) 4 Geng, Huangwei Island(passed from northern direction, 82.5 degree), Chiwei Island (97.5 degree), Gumi Mountain(passed from northern direction, 90 degree), Machi Mountain(passed from northern direction, 82.5 degree and 67.5 degree), arrived in Naha Port, and finished the journey safely.

Therefore, some questions appear: is "the mountain guarding the southwest border of Ryukyu" original in the book of Cheng Shunze or added by Xu Baoguang? If it was added by Xu Baoguang, did it decrease the value of the note as evidence? What is the exact meaning and significance of "the guarding mountain"?

About the first question, I think this note was not original in A General Guide, but added by Xu Baoguang. We only need to contrast the collection version of Higaonna Kanryo with Records of Messages from Chong-shan, then we can see there are plenty of errors and omissions in the former book, and the latter one was written by Xu Baoguang after proofreading and correcting. For example, originally between Diaoyutai Island and Huangwei Island, there was a sentence "passing by Huangma Island from the northern direction at 90 degree"; between Huangwei Island and Chiwei Island, there was "82.5 degree", and then Xu corrected it as "67.5 degree (or 90 degree)"; originally under Diaoyu Island, Huangwei Island, Chiwei Island, Kume Mountain and Machi Mountain, there were notes "passing from northern direction", but Xu added a note under Jilongtou,… Just as Inoue Kiyoshi said, "I always hold the opinion that they are not the original notes, but added by Xu Baoguang."

Consequently the second question is, does it undermine the value of it as evidence since the note was added by Xu Baoguang? Then we must have a comprehensive assessment of Records of Messages from Chong-shan in terms of its writing process, its essence and value. This book have been honored by China and abroad for a long time, Japan printed it and added kana for it in 1766 (the 31st year of the reign of Emperor Qianlong in Qing Dynasty, the 3rd year of the reign of Mikado Meiwa in Japan), and the Japanese official praised this book as "the historical masterpiece which has been passed down generation by generation, full of evidences and credibility" in the "Preface of Records of Messages from Chong-shan (Re-Printed Version)". However, since 1970s, the territorial dispute about Diaoyu Island and its affiliated islands broke out between China and Japan, and Japan began to criticize and debase this famous masterpiece without rhyme or reason. The first example: "Sovereignty over Senkaku Islands" issued by Ryukyu government on 17th September, 1970 declared that the book written by Hayashi Shihei regarded "Diaoyutai Island, Huangwei Island, and Chiwei Island as China's territory. However, Illustrated Outline of the Three Countries was written on the basis of Records of Messages from Chong-shan, which was specifically explained by Hayashi Shihei." The second example: Okuhara Toshioeven declared, "Just like other records of title-conferring envoys, Records of Messages from Chong-shan just mentioned some islands of Senkaku Islands in his route chart and shipping logs", and "because Illustrated Outline of the Three Countries was written on the basis of some rumors in Records of Messages from Chong-shan, it was just of second-class value as historical record."

What on earth are the facts?

……

In 1719 (the 58th year of the reign of Emperor Kangxi in Qing Dynasty), Xu Baoguang, as deputy title-conferring Envoy (while Hai Bao was the title-conferring Envoy), brought two surveyors to Ryukyu so as to survey and map the island. They arrived on June 1st of lunar calendar that year, and sailed to return on February 16th of the lunar calendar the next year, spending half and six months in Ryukyu: "In the first place, we requested the King about the Annals of Chong-shan and maps of mountains and rivers. Then we, accompanied by officials who could read and translate, traveled among mountains and seas, and observed all kinds of topographical features. We also investigated and inquired its manners and customs; even whenever we saw some object with strange shape, we must ask its name to get its information, and check what we saw with what we heard again and again so as to increase the credibility; we collected the shipping route, route chart, feasts and customs, pictures and description together, and edited them into six volumes", and this was the origin of Records of Messages from Chong-shan. Xu Baoguang had no knowledge of the language and characters of Ryukyu, but collected rich and comprehensive historic materials of Ryukyu in such a short time, thanks to the comprehensive materials provide by the government of Ryukyu. In his "Song of Thirty-Six Islands", he described the cooperation in details with vivid words and grateful emotions.

After Xu Baoguang classified and explained the thirty-six islands, he specifically stated, "This was based on the map which was requested by the emperor. The emperor had ordered Cheng Shunze, the Grand Master with the Purple-Golden Ribbon, to make the map, the radius of which was up to ten feet, and the directions and positions were roughly fixed. However, the thirty-six islands were only marked with their local names, while the distance from the land, the productivity of the native material, and the officials and titles were not recorded in details. Baoguang asked for advice in many ways, and selected and integrated all useful information; meanwhile, I negotiated with people from Chong-shan for many times until we settled down the details."

In the Records of Messages from Chong-shan, while he gave an account of "nine southwestern islands", namely the Yaeyama Islands, he listed their names as Kohama Island, Hatoma Island, Yonaguni Island, Gujian Island, Fuwu Island, Xinwu Island and Hateruma Island, and summarized, "all these eight islands belong to Yaeyama Islands, and people address them all as Yaeyama Islands, and they are the southwestern boundary of Ryukyu." He used "boundary", which meant the most southwestern frontier of Ryukyu and its "border".

And then, people naturally raise the third question: what is "the guarding mountain (Zhenshan)"? On what grounds did Xu Baoguang use this word?

In my opinion, neither of the explanations of "Zhenshan" by Mr. Yang Zhongkui and Inoue Kiyoshi is accurate. Mr. Yang Zhongkui wrote, "Zhenahan was also called Guanshan Fortress Mountain in China. According to the theory of Daoism and geomancy specialists, in whatever area, there must be a position or a hill, a mountain, or an island, which is remarkable to fit the geomancy, to expel the evil spirits, to beautify the environment and also to mark the boundaries, on which there are special buildings, such as a pagoda, a pavilion, or a temple of god of land, etc. This is the so-called Zhenshan or Guanshan which means both expelling the evil spirits and marking the boundary."

Inoue Kiyoshi said, "Zhen refers to the safeguard of the boundary of the country and the villages. Passing the islands such as Diaoyu Islands from Fuzhou City in China, people can enter the boundary of Ryukyu, Kume Island. It is the island on the boundary of Ryukyu; therefore it was explained as "the mountain guarding the border". In addition, because it located to the southwest of the mainland of Ryukyu, i.e., the islands which centered around Diaoyu Island, so it was recorded as "the mountain guarding the southwest border of Ryukyu"; as for Yaeyama Islands, which located on the most southwestern Ryukyu geographically, they were recorded as "the most southwestern boundary of Ryukyu".

The second half part of the explanations given by the two professors are complementary, however the first half part of the explanation about the meaning of "Zhen" and "Zhenshan" couldn't give their meaning. Generally speaking, the explanation in Source of Phraseology is accurate:

Zhen: the grand mountain of a place is called "Zhen". In The Classic of History: Canon of Shun, it said, "Building altars on twelve mountains." In Biography of The Classic of History written by Kong Anguo in Han Dynasty, it said, "the large mountain in each area, could be regarded as the main mountain of that county."

In particular, in the early years of the reign of Emperor Yongle of Ming Dynasty, Zhu Di, in order to award the kings of the tributary states who swore to be loyal to China, agreed to the request of the related states, "regarded China and abroad as equal and integrate", and promoted the system of "building altars on mountains to offer sacrifice to heaven, and awarding treasure to guard the border" to the states close to China; he wrote articles and poems by himself, and erected a monument on the mountain, "the grand mountain guarding the kingdom"….(the editor omitted some words)

Even though there was no records of conferring Gumi Mountain of Ryukyu as "guarding mountain" in The Memoir of Ming Dynasty, according to the situation and common sense, such kind of splendid ceremony of "building altars on mountains to offer sacrifice to heaven, and awarding treasure to guarding the border of the tributary state, showing the special grace of the emperor" must be known by everyone in Ryukyu; when Xu Baoguang arrived in Ryukyu, it had been three hundred and eleven years after Cijia, Japan, Beini had held the awarding ceremonies, so it was naturally few people had knowledge of "guarding mountain". If he had not "asked for advice in many ways", and "observed and inquired the traditions and customs", it was impossible for him to write down such a word out of his imagination. Consequently, the statement that Gumi Mountain was "the mountain guarding the southwest border of Ryukyu" had a long history; the author of Records of Messages from Chong-shan had opened the history which was hidden in the dust for a long time, and explained it specifically when he quoted and corrected A General Guide, which shows the credibility and authority of the statement, as the historical source of it was the Ryukyu government; and as an official document, it had stronger effect as evidence, which shows clearly, "Gumi Mountain is where the land of Ryukyu begins."

"Chi Island is the mountain that marks the boundary of Ryukyu"

I. How Okuhara Toshio and his fellows made a fuss about "boundary" debate

28 years after Chen Kan, that was, in 1562 (the 41st year of the reign of Emperor Jiajing), Guo Rulin, another imperial title-conferring envoy, wrote down in his Records of Imperial Title-Conferring Envoy to Ryukyu from another perspective,

On 29 May we started from Meihua Garrison, ... on the 1st of the leap month of May, we passed by the Diaoyu Island. On the 3rd, we arrived in Chi Island— Chi Island is the mountain that marks the boundary of Ryukyu. Then after another day, we could see Gumi Mountain.

In the sentence "...the mountain that marks the boundary of Ryukyu", "Jie" was a verb, which means "border on", "adjoin", and it is similar to the sentence "it adjoins Bao and Xia in the right direction, and is a dangerous place in Longshou Mountain" quoted from Rhapsody of West Capital written by Ban Gu, as the subject of the sentence had been omitted, and the omitted subject was of course "China"; according to the tradition of China, whenever any place in China was mentioned, it was unnecessary to say " belonging to China" and other similar words. The whole sentence was very clear, and it illustrated the same fact as Chen Kan did from different perspective: Chen Kan said that Gumi Mountain and the area on its east belonged to Ryukyu, while Guo Rulin said Chiwei Island was the mountain that marks the boundary of Ryukyu; therefore, Chiwei Island and the area on its west belonged to China. The implication was plain, if left unstated

2. The absurdity of Okuhara's argument of "terra nullius"

In the two articles that Okuhara Toshio wrote to argue with the idea of Mr. Yang Zhongkui from Taiwan, he showed thoroughly his sophistry and stated as follows:

Because the records of title-conferring envoys were written by Chinese, then if Chi Island was the territory of China, and Kume Island marked the border, then anyone should record it without any doubts. For example, they should write, "Chi Island is the mountain that marks the border between China and Ryukyu."

However, in the logic of Mr. Yang's narration, he had ignored the situation that it may belong to neither China nor Ryukyu, and that was the problem.

With the manner of a scholar, Mr. Yang Zhongkui wrote implicitly in his response paper, "If this Chinese sentence is read and understood by a Chinese person, my explanation should not be doubted by him at all. But Okuhara is a Japanese, so I can understand his doubts. The problem lies not in the explanation of the original sentence of Guo Rulin, but in the translation and understanding of Chinese language."

In the ancient China, the concept that all the lands in the world belong to the emperor had been rooted in the Chinese culture for a very long time, and it was applied and clarified by the emperors in Ming and Qing Dynasty and the kings of Ryukyu again and again. In the 5th year of the reign of Emperor Hongwu, Zhu Yuanzhang sent Yang Zai, the first envoy with full authority, to Ryukyu to announce the imperial edict to Chadu, the Chong-shan King of Ryukyu. At the very beginning of the edict, it emphasized, "all the lands bathed in the sunshine and moonlight, no matter distant or close, are ruled by the emperor, and treasured by the emperor with no exception"; in the 6th year of the reign of Emperor Yongle, the emperor, Zhu Di, wrote a royal inscription on the monument for Changning Mountain, the guarding mountain in Boni, and he announced, "I, the emperor, announce to the world, 'the heaven and my late father have entrusted the world to me, and I will take care of all the people in the world'"... And these are just some examples from the perspective of China in the Ming Dynasty.

As for Ryukyu, "the tributary state", on the one hand, the whole state belonged to China in the Ming Dynasty. It is so exaggerated that "the dust on the border of the country comes from China, and wherever people could reach by carriage and boat glitters with the dew from China" (quoted from the official communication document sent by Shangfeng, the Prince of Ryukyu, to Du Sance, the imperial title-conferring envoy, and Yang Lun, the deputy title-conferring envoy, in October, the 4th year of the reign of Emperor Chongzhen in Ming Dynasty, recorded in the 19th volume, 1st anthology of Annals of Generations of Ryukyu). This is not so closely related to the problem we discuss here. We should focus on the other aspect which is practical and related to the problem, that is, the guarding function of Ryukyu as a tributary state to China: "the tributary state provides a defense for China."

(On November 5, the 6th year of Emperor Guangxu, Liu Kunyi: Ryukyu Case Was Supposed to be Closed Quickly, and do it carefully) The remarks that Ryukyu was "the tributary state" (Shangzhi King's imperial order in the 11th Year of the Reign Emperor Shunzhi) by Emperor Shunzhi in Qing dynasty, that "as tributary state in South China Sea" (Shangzhi's records in 22nd Year of the Reign of Emperor Kangxi) by Emperor Kangxi, and that "as tributary state following Qiu Yang" (Shangzhi;'s records in the 21st Year of the Reign of Emperor Qianlong by Emperor Qianlong, all attached more importance to the concrete aspects, which indicated that the emperors in Qing dynasty exceeded those in Ming dynasty in detailed cognition. It virtually equaled to nonsense that a no-man's land emerged out of nowhere in the sea area as large as those islands like the Diaoyu Island between Ryukyu, i.e., between the "tributary state" and China, and Ryukyu "guarded" China.

We will discuss in the next chapter about the border between China and Ryukyu held by the Ryukyu government and in Hayashi Shihei's Sangoku Tsūran Zusetsu (An Illustrated Description of Three Countries). Here, let's look at the 1880 proposal of "dichotomy of Ryukyu" proposed by Japanese ambassador Shishido Tamaki to Chinese Ruling Office.

It was on October 1880 that Japanese ambassador Shishido Tamaki proposed to the Qing administrative office of the Qing Empire and jointly mapped out this "dichotomy of Ryukyu" plan. Although it was not signed owing to dissension inside the Qing administration, this plan is of great significance for what we are going to discuss. It was stated in Article 1 of this plan that "Japan will place Miyako and Yaeyama Islands, which are on the south of Ryukyu Island, under the jurisdiction of Qing Empire as the border between two countries. Japan and China will strictly avoid interference into the affairs of each other."

In Mr. Yang Zhongkui's opinion, this article indicated that "There were no negotiations mentioning Senkaku Islands or Diaoyu Islands. It revealed that Japan didn't know that island at that time, or knew it but regarded it as China's territory, or at least regarded it as a terra nullius which was not worth mentioning." But he didn't present exact opinion about those three possibilities. As for my humble opinion, I agreed on the second possibility, i.e., Japanese government was quite aware of the fact that Senkaku Islands belong to China. The reason was that several years before Shishido Tamaki put forward the said plan, "Ogasawara Islands (Bonin Islands) was a strong argument held by Japan when negotiating on the dispute of Bonin Islands with the United States." (Takahashi Sougorou: Senkaku Islands Notes). To be specific, this Ogasawara Islands (Bonin Islands) was an insert map of Japan Sendai Hayashi Shihei's Sangoku Tsūran Zusetsu. Another insert map of Sangoku Tsūran Zusetsu-Kingdom of Ryukyu also drew out explicitly the name and location of Diaoyutai, Huangwei Yu and Chiwei Yu, as well as "listed those islands as China's territory".

As it was stated in Figure 15 (refer to page 53 of the original book), which is a copy collected by former Japanese vice-chairman Matsumoto, the word "demarcating" is mentioned in "as for demarcating borders of the two countries" in Article 1. According to Chiu Hungdah, he found all "clearing" in Japan's Foreign Chronology and Primary Documents 1840-1945, so did relevant documents compiled in our country. Considering those documents, what's the meaning to emphasize on the sentence of "including it as Qing's territory to clear borders between two countries"?

Concerning on the distance between Diaoyu Island and the Ryukyu Islands, Miyako and Yaeyama Islands (i.e. Sakishima Islands) is the closest with a distance of about 90 sea miles. Chiwei Yu is on the east of Miyako Islands, about at 124°30'E. If Okuhara Toshio's conception were to be realized, Diaoyu Islands would have been a narrow strips which "was under no jurisdiction of both parties"; therefore, according to Japan's "dichotomy of Ryukyu" proposal, once Miyako and Yaeyama Islands were to be included into the Qing Empire's territory as appointed, the west end of those two islands would have integrated with Yonakuni and the west Taiwan Island. However, how could the aim of "clear borders between two countries" be maintained as stated in the proposal between Diaoyu Islands (which are "terra nullius" to the north of Miyako and Yaeyama Islands) and the Ryukyu Islands regulated by Japan? Therefore, the statement of "clear borders between two countries" of incorporating Miyako and Yaeyama Islands into China's territory in 1880 "dichotomy of Ryukyu" directly excluded the possibility to change Diaoyu Islands as "terra nullius", which imposed a sharp blow on Okuhara Toshio.

This actual history proves that "the ancient Yoneyama belongs to the Ryukyu Islands", referring to that ancient Yoneyama and its east end were Ryukyu's territory; besides, "Chiwei Yu is the border to Ryukyu" means Chiwei Yu and its west end belong to China. The history might as well demolish some Japanese fallacy because there's a natural boundary between Chiwei Yu and the ancient Yoneyama- "Black Trench".

"Trench" and "neighboring"–"boundary between China and foreign countries"

1. Definition of "Trench"

......Diaoyu Islands is located on the west of Okinawa trough. When Kuroshio Current (North Equatorial Current) flows from east coast of Philippine Islands and turns north to Bashi Channel. Its main stream flows through the southern Diaoyu Islands and proceeds northward, passing Yonakuni and Taiwan Island. Its branches go north along Penghu Channel between the Penghu Islands and Taiwan Island, flowing through northern part of Diaoyu Islands. It was following the branches of Black Current and southeast monsoon that our ancient ships left from the Minjiang River for Ryukyu by passing through northern Taiwan. The depth of water in this place is about 50 to 200 meters. This is also the most dangerous region of the whole voyage in that the navigator should cross over the surging vortex of northward main current which was at the speed of 4 miles an hour when passing through Diaoyu Island, Huangwei Yu and Chiwei Yu. The ship can possibly reach the ancient Yoneyama which "belonged to Ryukyu" only by crossing this dangerous site. Therefore, the Black Current, which occurs between Chiwei Yu and the ancient Yoneyama, became the natural boundary of China and the Ryukyu Kingdom. Besides, owing to the limits of ancient people on perceiving and controlling nature, rituals of praying for the Emperor of the Sea would be held before crossing the Black Current.

In ancient times, Chinese people did not have a fixed name on the Black Current. It was generally addressed as "Black Trench" or "trench" for short. As it was recorded in Ryukyu Annals composed by Vice-ambassador Zhou Huang in 1756, "(Ryukyu is) surrounded by sea. It is on the west to Min Sea with the boundary of black trench. Ships from Fujian to Ryukyu had to cross Cangshui and black waters (trench)", which explicitly demonstrates the truth that the Black Trench was the boundary between Ryukyu Kingdom and sea area of Fujian Province in China. The "Min Sea" hereby refers to the East China Sea or the part of East China Sea in Fujian waters. Besides, this statement also reveals that Diaoyu Islands, which locates in the seabed of East China Sea to the west of the Black Trench, undoubtedly belongs to China. In earlier times, Ambassador Wang Ji who was sent on a diplomatic mission to Ryukyu Kingdom in 1683, recorded in his book: "when I set off in June 1683, reached Chiwei Yu in 25 days after that."

At dusk, I crossed the trench, ... someone asked: "what's mean by neighboring?" "It means the boundary between China and foreign countries." "So what's the boundary?" "I suppose so." However, this assumption is exactly right and not a guess....

In the record of Wang Ji, "'I suppose so.' However, this assumption is exactly right and not a guess" was used to answer the question of "So what's the boundary?", i.e., the exact location of the boundary. Here, the use of "suppose so" and "not a guess" about that "the neighboring thunderous place is the boundary" seemed to be confusing, while well reflected temporary conception on "trench". As shown in Figure 1 in the first chapter (refer to the original book), the depth of the Okinawa Troughextending alongside the Ryukyu Islands there is the deeper part, the Okinawa Trough, with a large section of it more than 3,300 feet (1,000 meters) deep. Firstly, it was hard for ancient navigators to locate the "trench" as they located accurately the position of hills or rivers on earth. Besides, this region was mainly controlled by the Black Current, and thus formed alternating rolling waters and dead calm, especially in the vortex zone between Chiwei Yu and the ancient Yoneyama. Therefore, people at that time would have the completely different feelings on "trench" and "fall". If they came across terrifying waters on a voyage, they could visually saw the "trench", such as the case in 1606 recorded by Ambassador Xia Ziyang. On May 18, "masts were broken in the gale and waves that night.

After several days, the water was in black as muddy ditch or in indigo. Now I am convinced on the description of the former Ambassadors (refer to Ambassador Xiao Congye and Vice-ambassador Xie Jie–Yin)–'the clear water turned black' in the appendix of their records." In contrast, if the voyage was smooth without any danger, the navigator would hold doubt towards the existence of "trench" and "fall". For example, as Chen Kan encountered the situation that "the south wind is strong so that the ship runs as if flying and floats downstream", he recorded in his Ambassador's Record that "The Geographical Book of the Ming Dynasty states that 'fall is the descending water without ascending and boats would never come back if flowing with the fall'. I've been to this kind of place and felt lucky to escape from the danger. When I arrived at the Ryukyu Kingdom, the residents had no idea of this place or anything about fall." As a result, whether they had the ability to locate the "trench" is closely related to navigating knowledge of the records writers and the natural condition of navigating. But the "trench" was an objective reality instead of "a guess", whose location was between Chiwei Yu and ancient Yoneyama which was "the boundary of southwestern Ryukyu" as Wang Ji and most recorders recorded. The most accurate one was the one recorded by Qi Kun, who was dispatched on a diplomatic mission in 1808, that "On (May) 13th, I saw the Chiwei Yu at noon and passed through the trench at around 3 to 5 o'clock."

Now let's come back to the issue of regarding "neighboring" and "trench" as "boundary between China and foreign countries". People might ask that why did Wang Ji combine those two phonologically and semantically different characters together. In his ridiculous article which accused Kiyoshi Inoue falsely as "making up story" and pulling a long face to "criticize the interpretation of old documenta", Okuhara Toshio even stated arbitrarily that

Wang Ji had no reason to approve this statement (refer to the discussion concerning on "neighboring", "trench" and "boundary between China and foreign countries" in Figure 17—Yin), and he noted "or trench" below the character "neighboring". Besides, although he wrote down "passing neighboring", he didn't use "boundary" or "boundary between China and foreign countries" as claimed by the two parties of this discussion, nor did he use "passing through boundary" or "passing through the boundary between China and foreign countries".... But Zhou Huang made some amendments on the Ambassador's Record of Wang Ji. Firstly, he used "trench" instead of "neighboring". Similarly, he also applied "asking the meaning of trench". Besides, in the fifth volume of Zhou's Ambassador's Record, rather than "boundary between China and foreign countries", Zhou recoded it explicitly as "the boundary of Min Sea". ... In addition, the later Lin Dingyuan's Ambassador's Record also recoded the Black Trench as "the boundary of Min Sea". Therefore, "trench" was used to distinguish from the sea and simply addressed as "the boundary of Min Sea".

This time, Okuhara Toshio made the effort to use a completely fallacious sophistry.

In the first place, innocent and arrogant, he tried to set "neighboring" against "trench" and insisted that Wang Ji denied "trench" as "boundary between China and foreign countries". He also affirmed Wang's record as the opinion of "a navigator" who just noted down without extra trouble. In order to solve this problem, I specially consulted Zhang Zhenxing, director of the dialect research laboratory of Language Research Institute in Chinese Academy of Social Sciences. Therewith, Mr. Zhang gave authoritative conclusion on this issue as follows:

Although "neighboring (jiao)" and "trench (gou)" are different in pronunciation in Mandarin, those two characters have the same pronunciation as "kan" in Hokkien in Fujian Province.

The result helped me to become enlightened at once and this was a matter of a word. Actually, the one talked with Wangji from Jiangxi Province was a junk-man speaking Hokkien and people on spot recorded the pronunciation of the junkman. Since "jiao" and "gou" are pronounced the same in Hokkien, it can be clearly understood why those two characters are connected with each other.

Secondly, it has been the common view that people like Okuhara Toshio preferred to play with words. On one hand, they asserted that "'boundary between China and foreign countries' indicates inside and outside of ocean currents rather than the demarcated line between one's own country and other countries". On the other hand, he simplified Zhou Huang's sentence "to the west of the Black Trench and bordered with Min Sea" as "the Black Trench is bordered with Min Sea" means the sea boundary and doesn't imply anything about the state territory. It only indicates that voyage between Fujian Province and Ryukyu Kingdom had to pass through Cangshui and the black waters (Black Trench)."

......

Common people could not imagine how ridiculous it was to cook up "boundary between China and foreign countries" as "inside and outside of ocean currents". What's worse, he altered the conception of "surrounded by sea. It is on the west to Min Sea with the boundary of black trench" to "the Black Trench bordered with Min Sea", changing the former subject Ryukyu's "sea" to "the Black Trench", which is totally different. This is only one fallacy made up by Japanese scholars. Here is another one. What do we mean by the "Min Sea"? It refers to the waters under the jurisdiction of Fujian Province, China. Since the Min Sea belongs to China, this obviously points to the ownership of the Diaoyu Islands, since they are located in the Min Sea.

...

2. Ancient Ryukyu Kingdom and Japan both confirmed this natural boundary

Let's begin with the Ryukyu Kingdom.

I will not describe all the sayings about the ancient Ryukyu Kingdom, which was commonly believed to be "far away from China". In 1640, Shō Hō the King of Ryukyu, Country Chūzan wrote a letter to the governor of Fujian Province as follows:

As we Ryukyu Kingdom is located to the east of China bordered on Fujian, we are vitally interrelated and share the same ancestors. We are also created by nature to be separated by waters.

This letter indicates clearly that the Ryukyu Kingdom was "bordered with Fujian" and both was "separated by waters", which proves that the so-called "terra nullius" argument of Okuhara Toshio was totally wrong.

Ten years later, the Japanophile leader and scholar Haneji Choshu wrote Ryukyu's first historical book—the Chūzan Annals in 1650. The Records of Diplomatic Affairs in Jiajing Jiawu- a part in this book quoted the whole text of the voyage recorded in Chen Kai's Ambassador's Records to Ryukyu, confirming the "Kume Island belongs to Ryukyu Kingdom".

In 1701, the Ryukyu Kingdom sent Cai Yi, the Grand Master with the Purple-Golden Ribbon and assistant Prime Minister to offer Chūzan Annals as a tribute in Beijing. Maps and explanations attached to this book indicated that the 36 islands which were under Ryukyu Kingdom's jurisdiction were on the east of the Black Trench. As there were three principalities- Chūzan, Hokuzan and Nanzan in early Ming Dynasty, they only held jurisdiction over nowadays Okinawa Islands and Amami Islands, all together 20 islands before the year of 1380, which were called by later Ryukyu Kingdom as four eastern islands, eight northeastern islands, five northwestern islands and three western islands, … i.e.

Four eastern islands: Kudaka Island, Tsuken Island, Hamahiga Island and Ikei Island

Eight northeastern islands: Yoron Island, Kuchinoerabu Island, Toku Island, Lvlu Island, Chino Island, Tarama Island, Oshima and Kikaiga Island

Five northwestern islands: Tonakijima, Agunizima, Yishan and Ie Islands, Yibiwu Island and Tori Island

Three western islands: front and west Kerama Islands and Kume Island

According to the said Chūzan Annals, "In 1380, Miyako and Yaeyama Islands from the south began to pay tributes." Hereafter, the Kingdom of Ryukyu held jurisdiction over seven southern islands (Miyako Islands) and nine southwestern islands (Yaeyama Islands).

Seven southern islands: Hirara Island, Ikema Island, Irabu Island, Tarama Island, Kurima Island, Minna Island, Ōgami Island

Nine southwestern islands: Ishigaki Island, Kohama Island, Hatoma Island, Yonaguni Island, Gujian Island, Fuwu Island, Kuroshima Island, Xinwu Island and Hateruma Island

The above mentioned were the "three mountains and 36 islands of the Ryukyu Kingdom" or "the Kingdom ruled 39 villages and was surrounded by 36 islands". None of the islands were to the west of the black ocean or Nansei-Shoto Trench, and thus had nothing to do with the Diaoyu Islands.

In 1719, Tei Junsoku, the Grand Master with the Purple-Golden Ribbon, who edited books like General Instruction and whose plaster model of "Sage of Nago" still exists, was entrusted by the King Shō Kei to draw a square of draft of the whole nation. The draft was "brief in the directions with names of only

36 islands". Later on, he "travelled many places" with Xu Baoguang, "asking the exact name of certain places repeatedly and thus confirming the right ones". Finally, the draft was formally completed by two measuring officers- Ping'an and Feng Sheng'e, which was the Map of 36 Islands in Ryukyu Kingdom in the Records of Messages from Chong-shan (Zhong Shan Chuan Xin Lu). This map was personally plotted by King of Ryukyu Shō Kei and drew by imperial measurement officers of the Qing Empire on the basis of drafts and relevant information provided by Ryukyu, and finally examined by Xu Baoguang and Tei Junsoku. Therefore, I will discuss part of this map as it is actually a governmental file cooperatively accomplished by China and Ryukyu Kingdom.

......

As shown in the picture (refer to the original book), the triangle zone among Fuzhou, Taiwan and Kume-jima- Hoapinsu, Pengjia Islet, Diaoyutai, Huangwei Yu and Chiwei Yu along the Fuzhou-Kume course and Nanqi Mountain, Tai Mountain and Lima Mountain on the way back, was drawn as a vast sea. This is actually the drawing method of ancient Chinese single-color map. As it was the Map of 36 Islands in Ryukyu Kingdom, neighboring islands which didn't belong to the Kingdom of Ryukyu such as Senkaku Islands were just drawn as sea to indicate they were independent from each other. As previously mentioned, Xu Baoguang, Tei Junsoku and the two officers knew well not only the voyage route from Fuzhou to Kume-jima (Kume Island), but also all the islands including Diaoyu Island along the way. Besides, they also knew clearly the owner of those islands except their geographical location. As they confirmed that all those islands including Diaoyu Islands belonged to China, so the combination of islands which were to the west of Kume-jima (Kume Island), Fuzhou and Taiwan was drawn as sea in the map. All of these fully prove that both China and Ryukyu official quarters regarded Kume-jima as the boundary on southwestern Ryukyu; besides, they affirmed that Chiwei Yu, Huangwei Yu, Diaoyu Island, Pengjia Islet and Hoapinsu which are on the west of the Black Trench, along with islands below Nanqishan, are included in China's territory just like Fuzhou and Taiwan.

...

At last, let's look at Japanese attitude on this issue.

As previously mentioned, before 1868 Meiji Restoration, the only work in Edo period concerning on Diaoyu Islands was Hayashi Shihei's Sangoku Tsūran Zusetsu in 1785. Except the total graph, this work also contained 4 maps of Joseon Dynasty (Korea), the Kingdom of Ryukyu (Okinawa), Ezo (Hokkaido) and the Ogasawara Islands (Bonin Islands) along with an instruction book. There was a seal of "published in the autumn of 1785" in the lower-left corner of the second plate, signifying the early publishing time. Kiyoshi Inoue once said that "I saw a book in the library attached to University of

Tokyo, in which Sangoku Tsūran Zusetsu is drawn in a paper of 54.8 cm wide and 78.3 cm long." In terms of the colors, "red" was followed by a sentence of "Terra nullius, Cina (refer to China) and Kamchatka Peninsula", among which the "terra nullius" referred to Bonin Islands, which was clearly stated at the headline- "The map of terra nullius is originally named as Bonin Islands." Therefore, except Bonin Islands and Kamchatka Peninsula, it was obvious that all those colored in red in those maps belong to China's territory.

As displayed in the second plate (refer to the original book), the area from Kagoshima to southern Tugeci Islands on the northeastern corner of the map was colored in deep blue; those ranging from Kikaiga Island to south Amami-Oshima, Okinawa Island and to Miyako and Yaeyama Islands which were territory of the Kingdom of Ryukyu were in light brown; Chinese territory including Shandong, Nanjing, Zhejiang, Fujian and Guangdong Province was in light red, while Taiwan and 36 Penghu Islands were in yellow. Meanwhile, the navigating route from Fuzhou of Fujian Province to Okinawa Island was divided into 2 kinds- the southern one was from west to east, passing through Hoapinsu, Pengjia Islet, Diaoyutai, Huangwei Yu and Chiwei Yu, while the northern line went from east to west through Nanqi Mountain, Fengwei Mountain, Yu Mountain and Tai Mountain. All those islands passed were colored in light red as China's territory.

In addition, Hayashi Shihei omitted some relatively larger islands in his Sangoku Tsūran Zusetsu while sketched out the small islands like Diaoyu Islands and painted them in light red as did to China's territory.

It is obvious that Hayashi Shihei affirmed that Diaoyu Islands and the like belong to China. However, Okuhara Toshio tried all means to deny this truth. A government statement which was drafted by Okuhara Toshio and taken as the standard by Government of the Ryukyu Islands claimed that

Although Sangoku Tsūran Zusetsu regarded Diaoyutai, Huangwei Yu and Chiwei Yu as China's territory, but Hayashi Shihei himself didn't admit it. This book was based on Records of Messages from Chong-shan (Zhong Shan Chuan Xin Lu).

His Sangoku Tsūran Zusetsu was based on the Map of 36 Ryukyu Islands and Navigation Map from Records of Messages from Chong-shan (Zhong Shan Chuan Xin Lu). Technically, he colored Diaoyutai, Huangwei Yu and the like which hadn't included in Ryukyu as China's territory. However, there's no sign to indicate China's ownership of those islands in the Navigating Map in Records of Messages from Chong-shan (Zhong Shan Chuan Xin Lu).

As stated before, the Map of 36 Ryukyu Islands in Records of Messages from Chong-shan was single-colored, omitting land while drawing sea when dealing with China' territory including Diaoyu Islands which were next to Ryukyu. Concerning on the belonging of various islands along the southern and northern routes from Fuzhou to Naha, Hayashi Shihei totally agreed on and absorbed the consensus reached by Chinese and Ryukyu officials which was reflected in the Map of 36 Ryukyu Islands in Records of Messages from Chong-shan. In fact, is had been a common sense for a long time among sailors of both countries to recognize those islands as China's territory. Hayashi Shihei just gave those islands which were altered as sea in Records of Messages from Chong-shan 66 years ago to what they really were in his multicolored map. Besides, he also colored those islands light red, which did increase the value and significance of his maps.

"Can't we find out the reasons of their belonging to China" or "can't we think Xu Baoguang had the sense of sovereignty when he was recording"? The objective facts give us the answer. Okuhara Toshio refused to admit the ancient Yoneyama as the boundary of Ryukyu, while Xu added a reference of "the boundary of southwestern Ryukyu" as he quoted from General Instruction. Although Okuhara Toshio insisted that Diaoyu Islands and the like were "under no jurisdiction of both parties", Xu stated in his map that those islands were administrated by China instead of Ryukyu, which were drawn as sea for techni-cal reasons. There were also some people talking a lot of nonsense that Pengjia Islet was included into Taiwan in 1905 when Taiwan was under the administra-tion of Japan Empire; however, Xu pointed out exactly that "from Pengjiashan of Taiwan, Fujian to Yaeyama Islands", indicating that Pengjiashan belonged to Taiwan while Taiwan belonged to Fujian. In addition, he also stated below the category of "Yaeyama Islands" that "this is the southwest end boundary of Ryukyu" (ditto). The direct reason why Okuhara Toshios were always rebuf-fed was that they distorted history and in return harvested the mocking of the history.

......

Okuhara Toshio … whooped up on the issue of color in a prolix style.

(in the picture) the mainland Japan and Old Manchu were in green, Taiwan and Korea were in yellow, while most parts of Xiayi (Hokkaido) was in light brown. If those colors were used to distinguish territory, Hayashi Shihei then regarded Manchu as Japan's territory, Taiwan as Korea's territory and Hokkaido as Ryukyu's territory (or the opposite). Anyway, this is a tale of tub, do we bot-her to discuss any more?

This was not a reduction to absurdity in logistics, but rather a clandestine change of argumentative issue.

......

Four-color Problem has existed for a longtime in the field of topology that whether four colors are sufficient to signify all regions such as land and sea ac-cording to their jurisdiction and two neighboring regions with different colors.

Hence, Hayashi Shihei was faced with the problem that how to distinguish what he thought to be a state's territory from what was exactly the state's territory. Instead of using different depths of color, he only applied four colors-red, yellow, green and brown. Take "Manchu" as an example, as it was "the land of dragon rising", its color was different from other territory of China. As Shandong Province was in red and the neighboring Korea was in yellow, Manchu was in green the same as that of Japan which was not jointed. As for Taiwan, its color was different from that of mainland China owing to ups and downs of Zheng's regime. However, the Map of Three Taiwan Counties clearly marked out Taiwan, Fengshan and Zhuluo County with dotted lines. It is actually a common sense, but Okuhara Toshio repeatedly distorted this truth.

Hayashi Shihei's Sangoku Tsūran Zusetsu is quite popular and has a far-reaching influence. In domestic Japan, as perceived by Kiyoshi Inoue, there are at least 4 kinds of copies except the publication in 1785. The sixth insert plate 3 (refer to the original book) was a copy of Xiangxiangyuan in 1801. The seventh insert plate 4 (refer to the original book) was a French version translated by French Orientalist M. J. Klaproth and published in Paris in 1832. Five islands including Diaoyu Islands in the two plates are all in red as China's territory, while Ryukyu is in yellow.

From Sangoku Tsūran Zusetsu-Kingdom of Ryukyu, we can clearly figure out that Hayashi Shihei held the same view not only in the belonging of China's territory- Diaoyu Islands and a series of other islands, but also in the belonging of 8 northeastern islands of Ryukyu. From Kikaiga shima in the northeastern corner of the map to south Oshima, Tarama Island, Tokushima, Kuchinoerabu Island and Yoron Island, all of those were the inherent territory of the Kigdom of Ryukyu, which were ceded to Satsuma Domain as they kidnapped the King Shō Nii. However, the above-mentioned Chūzan Annals submitted by Sai Taku also included those islands into the thirty-six islands, so did Xu Baoguang's Records of Messages from Chong-shan- 36 Islands of Ryukyu. Besides, in Hayashi Shihei's Sangoku Tsūran Zusetsu- Kingdom of Ryukyu, islands to the south of Kikaiga shima were in brown. All of those facts fully prove that 3 authorities–Xu Baoguang, Tei Junsoku and Hayashi Shihei who had fully investigated regional distribution of China, Ryukyu and Japan, had reached a total consensus of the sovereignty of islands in the eighteenth century. They all believed that the Black Trench, i.e., the Okinawa Trough which is located between Chiwei Yu and the ancient Yoneyama, was the natural boundary between China and the Kingdom of Ryukyu in this region.

In the Statement, the Ryukyu government understated:

Since the fourteenth century, literature concerning Senkaku Islands in Okinawa and China did not state that Senkaku Islands was their territory. It was just marked in log and map as a sign on the sea route, or mentioned in Chinese poems chanting traveling feelings. Senkaku was used to address the islands for the sake of convenience.

Prof. Shishiyaba Ichitakashi aggressively argued, "The special rank – officials sent to the Islands – aside, who knew Senkaku Islands back then in China? If any, I hope they can provide historical materials rather than literature; the saying of Lin Ziping (note: Diaoyu and other islands are China's territory) solely cannot be used as evidence. Rather, Chinese ancient maps that can clearly show those islands should be provided. If China has such maps, please show us"!

In this regard, some comments can be added. The sentence in the beginning of the Statement tells only half the truth, that is, none of the ancient literature on the Senkaku side "can prove that Senkaku Islands are its territory". Besides, Chinese who knew the location and ownership of Diaoyu Islands were not limited to the "special rank – officials sent to the Islands", though the third chapter of this book will take dispatched officials as the main perspective. Other people included: first, various boatmen – people who "were good at steering ships" along the coasts of Fujian and Guangdong, had a long history; however, there was no record for consideration. Their sailing experience was summarized in the old version of The Rules of Zhou Ji, which was destroyed by the age in the beginning of Ming Dynasty; Fair Winds for Escort was none but revised sections sorted in the early years of Yongle. Second, there were navy officers and soldiers who were dominated by boatmen. This will be discussed in this chapter. Moreover, the Chinese side took Diaoyu Islands as the sailing signposts of its dispatched ships, which was naturally one means of exercising sovereignty over the islands; further, those islands also held far-reaching significance and played practical role in safeguarding our coastal territories.

The implementation of "Guarding against Japanese" and Consolidating Walls by Hung-wu Emperor

During the Ming Dynasty, "Pirates", as told by the defeated Japanese captured in Jiajing time, "are Nojima barbarians captured by China". The Nojima barbarians mentioned here refer mainly to people of Rukou Duo Samo, Higo, Nagato, but also to people from Osumi, building south, after building, Bodo, Hyuga. In a word, pirates were mainly sailing people from Kagoshima, and formed armed rings by colluding with the wicked in Zhejiang, Fujian and Guangdong.

They would sneak into China's coastal areas to disturb and do all evils, to "set official residence on fire, destroy civilians' houses, hang babies on poles, and throw hot water; make drinking bets on dissecting pregnant women and men, which was too barbarous to mention". Or they would capture Chinese and use them as slaves in Japan, namely, "make them bald and crimple, ask them to raise the cattle and horses, make money and cooking. What those slaves ate was burnt rice mixed with bean dregs, chaff, bran, wild vegetables, roots and the like, which was used to feed dogs and pigs. They could not be full, nor did they wear decent clothes. Those who attempted to flee back China were beheaded by the patrolling soldiers to earn credits." Japanese pirates committed miseries to such a degree: by the end of Ming Dynasty, connecting Japan was strictly forbidden. People in the lanes would swear Japanese, and even called them as dwarfs"!

With such as a "nice neighbor" to the east, it was no wonder there was a proper noun unprecedentedly employed in the military defense systems of the Ming dynasty, namely, guarding against Japanese: "town garrisons consist of five tasks: defending towns, defending societies, defending points, making military preparations, and guarding against Japanese. Defending was enhanced in advantageous places by sending soldiers there." The person who first noticed the danger caused by Japanese and proposed the word "guarding against Japanese" of its time was Zhu Yuanzhang, the well-known first emperor of the Ming Dynasty.

It was clearly pointed out in Compilation of Coast Maps, the official book on sea-defending of the Ming Dynasty:

Compilation of Coast Maps talks about the preparation of coastal defense to guard the Japanese. The southeast coasts are not vaster than the sea, but none of its neighbors is as cunning as the Japanese, who has been a curse to the Chinese for a long time. I, the emperor, brought together the regions, exercised strategies over the four corners, over-guarded the northwest, to say nothing of the southeast. A look at his defending arrangements would show: "guarding against Japanese" is here and there!

In order to "prepare coastal defense to guard the Japanese", the emperor took the measure of consolidating walls by appointing senior ministers and building large-scale fortresses in Zhejiang and Fujian where Japanese pirates often showed up to boost defense forces. In 1384, Duke Tang He, one of the founding fathers of the Mining Dynasty, was appointed to patrol coastal cities in Zhejiang and Fujian, ... for the purpose of guarding against the Japanese"; three years later, he "built fifty-nine fortresses in such coastal places as Ninghai and Linshan in Zhejiang, and recruit one member from families with more than four labors as soldiers, forming an army of over 58,750 people". Meanwhile, another credited minister "Zhou Dexing was sent to Fujian, recruiting one member from families of three labors in the Fu, Xing, Zhang and Quan Households, to defend the coasts and guard against the Japanese, ... altogether 15,000 strong men were recruited, sixteen fortresses were erected, patrolling officers were increased by 45, and officials were dispatched for the defending".

......

... Diaoyu Islands were sited at a place which must be taken by the Japanese when they were disturbing Fujian, and hence holds strategic importance. Some knowledge of the threats of the Japanese and the long-term policy of "guarding against the Japanese" by the Ming government is not only helpful to understand whether the history recorder had "territory consciousness", but also closely related to the sending of envoys to Japanese during the late Jiajing as well as to the contents and meaning of coastal defense.

In the early Ming Dynasty, Wu Zhen, marquis of Jinghai, led a Japanese-destroying fleet, passed Diaoyu areas from Fuzhou, and drove the Japanese back to Ryukyu

In the spring of 1374, Wu Zhen was summoned and assigned as the general official cum commander assistant, and Yu Xian as the deputy commander, to lead four fleets – Jiangyin, Guangyang, Henghai and Shuijun – to capture the pirates on the sea; all soldiers in the capital, together with officials and armies in Taicang, Hangzhou, Wenzhou, Taizhou, Mingzhou, Fuzhou, Quanzhou and Chaozhou, were all under command". The commander of this combined fleet, Wu Zhen, was the veteran who followed Zhu Yuanzhang and raised the Haoliang Uprising, was good at sea fighting and was named minister of Jinghai due to his fighting achievements. The emperor ordered him to coordinate all the defending armies along the southeast coasts, which well shows the determination of the emperor. It was during this nine-month patrolling on the sea that Wu Zhen's troop met the Japanese pirates, and chased the enemy fleet all the way back to Ryukyu after a fierce fighting.

1374 saw a battle on the sea. Wu Zhen was re-appointed as the general commander, and led a fleet to capture Japanese pirates with Yu Xianzong; they chased the Japanese ships to Okinawa and sent the captured to the capital (History of the Ming Dynasty, Volume 131: Biography of Wu Zhen).

However, there was no record where this battle started or the place they passed before reaching Okinawa. Fortunately, there were detailed records in the biography of Zhang He, the commander of Fujian districts who made so much achievement in sea battles that he was named "Voyage Minister":

At that time, the Japanese pirates would also show up on the islands, and took chances to plunder on the shores, which incurred troubles to the coastal residents... In no time, Zhang He captured numerous pirates. In the end, he chased the pirates to Okinawa, captured eighteen chief officials in the battle, beheaded dozens of people, and obtained a dozen of ships, as well as countless bows, swords and other weapons. The emperor was so proud of Zhang He's success in the battles that he gave the latter the commanding seal (History of the Ming Dynasty, Volume 130: Biography of Wu Zhen).

This is a paragraph in History of the Ming Dynasty, which did not mention the starting place of the battle, either. The gap was bridged by another book Ming Dynasty, which came out eighty or ninety years earlier than the above book and was authored by Fu Weilin (?–1666). It says:

(Zhang He held the commander of Fuzhou prefect,) departed at Tongshao, and met pirates at Niushan Yang; he chased the pirates to Ryukyu, captured their chief and many others (History of the Ming Dynasty, Volume 95: Biography of Wu Zhen).

Though it was not as detailed as the former, it gave an accurate statement – met pirates at Niushan (Note: Niushan is situated at Fuqing County of Fuzhou, and was named ZhenDong prefect after 1388, about seventy miles in the northeast, which is called Haitan Island today). Thus, this provides an accurate evidence for the location of the battle.

Let us see the time of the battle. It was recorded in history that that huge fleet was established under the edict of the emperor and was directly commanded by the famous general of Guizhou division, Wu Zhen. The fleet was built from the eighth of the first lunar month to that of the tenth month, lasting just nine months. "Wu Zhen returned to the capital after patrolling the sea".

The combination of the place and the time of the battle can reveal: given that Wu Zhen and Zhang He "departed at Tongxiao", "met pirated" at "Niushan" and chased them all the way to Ryukyu, east of Heishui Gou, the only way of reaching Ryukyu should be this: they took advantage of the Southwest monsoon, and reached the north of Okinawa (i.e., Taiwan) via the east of Niushan; they passed Huaping Island, Pengjia Mountain, Diaoyu Island, Huangwei Island and Chiwei Island by sailing along the Kuroshio current, and then crossed the main current.It is because that Diaoyu Islands located to the west of Heishui Gou was within the patrolling province of Chinese fleets that there is no need to list all the islands along the way. Only Japanese territorial waters–areas to the east of Heishui Gou–can be fairly called Ryukyu. Under the same natural conditions such as the speeds of winds and currents, the fleet led by Wu Zhen not only pursued the pirates hotly, but also defeated them on Ryukyu, that is, "captured eighteen chief officials in the battle, beheaded dozens of people, and obtained a dozen of ships, as well as countless bows, swords and other weapons", which well proved the great power and skilled sailing technology of Chinese fleets, and its good knowledge of the locations of Diaoyu and other islands. This in turn disproved what was stated in Fair Winds for Escort in the second section of Chapter two of this book, namely, the book was compiled by sorting out the "destroyed" old version of "The Rules of Zhou", as China has good reasons to claim that it discovered and named them Diaoyu Islands.

A Japanese Guide: Ten Thousands Miles Song states Diaoyu Islands was owned by Taiwan

This book, written by Zheng Shungong, provides important records about Taiwan, Okinawa and Diaoyu Islands, see the third section of this book Fuhai Map, which consists of three volumes, namely, Ten Thousands Miles Song, Cuanghaijin and Journey of Angel-East route of Yihai-High route of Yihai-Roads of Yichuan that record the domestic traffic situations in Japan.

Let us begin with Cuanghaijin that is full of pictures. Zheng Shungong called it "referred drawings", which means it was painted on the basis of referring to Japanese pictured books. The areas from Taiwan to Ryukyu were drawn at the beginning of this section (see Picture 19 of the original book). Below the picture, there is a note on the second island from the right: "the small east island, that is, the Small Liouciou was Dahui Guo, they said". Here "they said" obviously refers to "the Japanese said", hence, "Xiaodong" and "Dahui Guo" were what Taiwan was called back then. The names of these islands, Huaping Island, Pengjia Mountain, Diaoyu Island, Huangwei Island and Chiwei Island, were what they were called in Chinese history, and this means Japan also used those names in Chinese, rather than in Taiwanese or Japanese. (The original picture is omitted, and hereafter the same)

As Picture 19 is an illustration of sailing routes, it in itself cannot directly reflect the belongings of those islands. However, Zheng Shungong, who "took the edict to the King of Japan" and went there specially for stopping the pirates, naturally noticed "the schedule of the journey, and the places passing by, and checked the ownership of the islands". Those were written down by him after his arrival at Japan, but those points were also made in his narrations about the islands along the way. As the first part of Fuhai Map, Ten Thousands Miles Song was written in rhymed verse and the guide for the voyage from Guangdong to Japan, and was noted in double lines of small characters every two sentences.

Shun Chenggong added a note under the sentence "it was either from the East Meihua Mountain or the Diaoyu Island on Jilong": Meihua, named by the Qianhu officer, is eighty miles away from Yongning. Setting off from Dong Mountai, we sail towards 107.5° or 127.5° for about 60 nautical miles, then we arrived at Jilong Mountain of Xiaodong (Taiwan); then, we sail towards 97.5°, then 90° or 150° for about 60 nautical miles, then we arrived at the Diaoyu Island" Two points of the following note should be highly noticed:

First, the original note reads "From Meihua to Japan, Xiaodong of Penghu and Ryukyu are on the way". Mr. Fang Hao divided the sentence as "Xiaodong of Penghu", that is, "Taiwan of Penghu". I humbly hold this is not right. Interpreting the note carefully, I think the sentence would be better divided as "From Meihua, crossed Penghu, reached Xiaodong, then Ryukyu and Japan"; the word "zhi" was used as a verb, meaning "reach" and "arrive". As such, the text becomes natural and coherent with the note under the previous sentence "all behind is Xiaodong": "without the range between this island (i.e., Xiaodong) and Yongningwei, Duhai would be connected with Penghu, and Xiaodong would be reached by crossing other ocean areas." From the sixth volume Territorial Ranges of Rivers and Seas, "without the range between Yongningjian of Quanzhou and Xiaosuo, Penghu can be reached by crossing the oceans; sailing forward, Xiaodongdao, also called Small Liouciou, is Dahui Guo, as they said."

The second point is: "Diaoyu Island is the small Xiaodong Island." Zheng Shungong emphasized firmly, Diaoyu Island belongs to Xiaodong, and Xiaodong is actually Taiwan. Put it in modern Chinese, it should be "Diaoyu Island is a small island of Taiwan." The above note addresses Taiwan as "Xiaodong", which means Japan also admitted the fact that Diaoyu Island belongs to Taiwan.

Okuhara Miyuji dismissed this by saying:

The sentence ("Diaoyu Island is the small Xiaodong Island.") is meaningless except that it reveals the geographical conditions of Diaoyu Island then. Moreover, A Japanese Guide was not the official documents of the Ming Dynasty. Though Zheng Shungong once served as a spy, he and the ex-general Hu Zongxian had lost favor, lived a hard life and had no rights to write official documents while compiling the book. Besides, during the compilation Zheng Shungong got a great deal of oceanic knowledge from many Japanese in Ningbo, hence he simple got it ("Diaoyu Island is the small Xiaodong Island.") there.

Okuhara Miyuji did not give any explanation. Only because of "geographical conditions" how can Diaoyu Island be related to Taitan or become part of the latter that is 120 sea miles in the southwest?

Okuhara Miyuji denied that Zheng Shungong was a special envoy sent by the Jiajing Emperor to "send the edict to the King of Japan, but reduced him to be a "spy". Further, when Zheng Shungong returned successfully, Yang Yi who sent him on the voyage had been dismissed officially, and his misfortune was inextricably linked with the exclusion of Hu Zongxian. As the saying goes, when the city gate catches fire, the fish in the moat suffers from it, namely, the innocent are involved. Consequently, no long after his return, Zheng Shungong lost his freedom, and was "thrown into the prison several times and released only after seven years"; actually, he was already a prisoner when in Ningbo. Yet Okuhara Miyuji naively argued that Zheng Shungong obtained the knowledge from Japanese at commerce society in Ningbo, which is nothing but attempting to conceal the source of the knowledge. Personal explorations aside, most of the knowledge were obtained from Bungo officials, which excluded his book from official documents.

As mentioned above, Zheng Shungong was assigned to Japan after Jiajing Emperor approved the Rites Department to take idea of "sending the edict to the King of Japan" as a national policy; he "made a statement in the court", "was sent abroad due to the brilliance of the emperor", and "was accompanied to the general army gate by the War Department, transferred at Zizhe, Fujunmen and Zhejiang before arriving Japan", which veritably proved his envoy identity. Then did he accomplish his vital mission after this voyage? After reaching Fenghou Island of Japan, he mainly conducted three aspects of work within only half a year:

First, he enlightened the people in Zhuyuanyi town of Bungo. In the name of a "national guest", he propagated loyalty and faithfulness to literate the people and taught the evils righteousness and benevolence, which enlightened the King and officials of Bungo and eventually "the nation began to address the cause roots of evils, thieves and expected to do it once and for all". After some careful and in-depth work, he "grasped the key rules, gradually suggested how to govern Zhuyuanyi town, and discussed with the national officials how to achieve development socially, economically and politically, and the like; he wanted to send someone back to report to the court, and to ask to follow the laws and systems of China so as to please the emperor, which was desired by the predecessors". We can fairly say that Zheng Shungong succeeded in it and achieved significant effects.

Second, he collected a wealth of data and even made verifications for the writing of *A Japanese Guide* later on. "After reaching Japan, he would ask about the mountains, rivers and whatever he saw, and tried to record the general pronunciations, as he cannot know exactly the Japanese." "At that time, he was very diligent at work (note: he enlightened the "king and officials" of Bungo)". After several months, he would ask about the belongings of the islands, the journeys and the places passed by enquiring, and investigated accurate translations of them in Chinese, as they were generally transliterated."

Finally, before leaving Bungo for China, Zheng Shungong handled the sending of edict to the King of Japan, and the result was:

As Shen Menggang and Hu Funing was sent to meet the mikado of Japan, and discussed about the forbidding policy (note: forbidding Japanese pirates) with Japanese officials, such as Konoe Sanjo, Nishiyanagi Hara, Asukai and Fujinagaiwai amongst others, Shen Menggang got a reply and seal from the mikado; when passing Bungo, the King and officials there asked a monk to take a boat to report to and give letters and seals to Shen Menggang. Though having planned to go through the Piwang Patrolling Office, Shen Menggang was arrested by the archers who ordered to destroy the official documents and falsely imprisoned the former, when they arrived at the sea near Chaozhou. Learning this, Zheng Shungong reported it to the army who disbelieved it, only to find Shen Menggang had been murdered when sending people to relieve him.

The accident happened on 20 of May, 1557, and was 85 days before Zheng Shungong returned to Guangzhou, Guangdong. The reason why situations got so severe was because it was related to the killing of Wang Zhi, see next section. What should be mentioned here is, the above record was detailed and convincing. The reasons are: first, if the names of the Mikado and Japanese officials in the citation were not real, Zheng Shungong could not have coined them out of thin air. Second, Shen Menggang and Hu Funing with the documents, after arriving around Chaozhou, "planned to go through the Piwang Patrolling Office". Zheng Shungong finished the book at 1565, and the original patrolling office "Nanlinhai" had already been moved to Denghai County two years earlier, and the new office was sited at the Nanyangfu, north of Denghai, which was not beside the sea, and hence could not manage any ship checking and examination affairs. This was self-evident.

Therefore, Zheng Shungong accomplished the three tasks assigned by War Minister Yang Bochu, namely, "investigate the Japanese development, grasp opportunities to advise the people and give reports when returning". There were no doubts about his identity as an envoy. His book A Japanese Guide was official documents and records "Diaoyu Island is the small Xiaodong Island." Even Japan also confirmed this fact.

......

In the middle of the 16th century, Hu Zongxian, the highest military officer of defeating the pirates in Ming Dynasty, formally listed Diaoyu Islands within the sea defending areas.

This section will focus on historical facts on Diaoyu and other islands recorded in Compilation of Coast Maps.

Compilation of Coast Maps was completed in 1562, and an earlier version was hosted in the Special Collections of Beijing Library. In Volume 1 Coastal Maps, above the two pictures named Fujian 7 and Fujian 8 the fifth island from the right is Jilongshan, followed by Pengjiashan, Diaoyu Island, Huapingshan, Huangmaoshan, Ganlanshan and Chiyu, and the like; moreover, as mentioned in the second section of this chapter, as early as 1373, the combined fleet led by Wu Zhen chased the pirates from Niushan, south of Fuzhou, through all areas mapped in the above pictures, all the way to Okinawa.

Okuhara Miyuji naturally would not let this go without some argument. He dismissed Compilation of Coast Maps as "inferior to any documents", and then argued: the so-called sea-defending maps are generally believed to cover the regions invaded (by pirates), rather than about their belongings, thus, the facts included in sea-defending maps cannot be used as evidence of territorial ownership.

.

Where does the haiphong map in An Illustrated Compendium on Maritime Security (Chou Hai Tu Bian) come from? Dose its content include invaded areas by Japanese pirates and never mark the areas belonging to other countries? Can it be the evidence to prove the territorial sovereignty?

An Illustrated Compendium on Maritime Security (Chou Hai Tu Bian) was drawn by Zheng Ruozeng, so undoubtedly, it referred to the Great Haiphong Map (Wang Li Hai Fang Tu) in "Miscellaneous Records by Zheng Kaiyang"

......

Then, is there any other original maps that included the Diaoyu Islands? As I cited before, in the afterword of photocopy in 1933, Liu Yizheng also mentioned that: General Map of Coastal Defense was the first draft of The Great Haiphong Map (Wang Li Hai Fang Tu); the two maps are complementary, so both of them were reserved.

......

Xu Baoguang's criticism of the mistakes about Ryukyu in the map drawn by Zheng was totally right. But the criticism of the positions of some islands including the Diaoyu Islands was a bit inappropriate as he ignored that the map was only a draft. Zheng only listed the islands along China's coasts, he made the same mistake as that in Unification the Great Ming Dynasty, which is that he mapped Penghu Islands (small Ryukyu), Gumi Mountain and Gaohua Islands in Ryukyu. Moreover, the "Huangmao Mountain" was originally is Huangwei Yu or Huangmao Yu. But Zheng made a mistake that he drew another Huangwei Yu besides the true Huangwei Yu.

But, even so, the map explicitly distinguished China's islands from the Gumi Mountain of Ryukyu (including the 3 islands which were mistakenly mapped in Ryukyu). The names of China's islands were written in oblong box; while the names of Ryukyu's islands were written in rectangular box, which was so distinct and clear at a glance.

Zheng Ruozeng and his collaborators correct the above mistakes when they standardized the General Map of Coastal Defense. In the new Great Haiphong Map (Wang Li Hai Fang Tu), when comparing picture 23 with 22 and 21, we can clearly see that they directly removed Ryukyu from the map; they denied Gumi Mountain and Gaohua Yu and incorporated the Penghu Islands into the Eastern Sea of Ping Triton in Fuwu, which showed us the true history; they delete the repeated Huangmao Yu between Huangmao Mountain and Chi Yu. From these three modifications, Zheng Ruozeng fully deserves the honor— "Coastal geography authority" given by Joseph Needham.

According to Zheng Ruozeng, An Illustrated Compendium on Maritime Security (Chou Hai Tu Bian) was compiled by Zheng Ruozeng under the auspices of Hu Zongxian, the supreme commander of the southeast coastal defense of the Ming court, which was greatly supported by Tan Lun and Qi Jiguang. One of the participants—Mao Kun was praised by Dr. Joseph Needham who said Mao was a lifelong partner of Hu Zongxian, the Fujian governor and a friend of Zheng Ruozeng, the "Coastal geography authority". These famous generals and authorities knew the islands along the coasts like the palm of their hand, how can they map the invaded areas by Japanese pirates and the areas belonging to other countries into China's official coastal defense map.

In fact, in Introductory Remarks, Hu Zongxian, Ruozeng Zheng, etc. clearly pointed out that:

We should discover the stronghold according to the maps; we should make plans according to the situation. The coast starts from Guangdong to Liaoning with 15000 Li (A chinese unit of distance measurement) where is the areas invaded by Japanese pirates.

It clearly pointed out that The coast starts from Guangdong to Liaoning with 15000 Li (Chinese unit of length) where is the areas invaded by Japanese pirates. The Great Haiphong Map (Wang Li Hai Fang Tu) included Guangdong along the southwest coast, Fujian, Zhejiang, South Zhili (today's Jiangsu), Shandong and Liaodong Peninsula. None of the pictures includes foreign areas; just some islands may be left out.

"Names are determined by the facts; the facts originate from the names." the name of The Great Haiphong Map (Wang Li Hai Fang Tu) proves that it is the military map used to defense Japanese pirates. I think Hu Zongxian and Zheng Ruozeng never thought that their works will has such profound meaning for defending the coast of motherland.

From the late Ming Dynasty to the middle of the 19th century, the Diaoyu Islands was closely related to the coastal defense. Besides, I will argue about the fallacy of Taiwan's sovereignty in this part.

If the "Japanese pirates" who ravaged China in Jiajing period manly came from Japan's wild island—Xiaoyi, in the Wangli period, a new force emerged. Toyotomi Hideyoshi's plan—conquest of Ming Empire threatened the Ming Dynasty. As early as 1577, Toyotomi Hideyoshi gave an advice to Oda Nobunaga that I want to conquer Kyushu and then send troops to Korea in order to occupy more than four hundred cities in Ming Empire. Six years later, Toyotomi Hideyoshi revealed this plan to Ryukyuan envoys and threatened them that: "conquest of Ming Empire is the divine rather my own plan." On May 18th, in 1592, he gave his son Toyotomi Hidetsugu a book titled 25 Terms in which he even already determined the position of his son—Prime Minister of the Ming Empire. In 1592, and 1597, he sent his troops twice to assault Korea. The Japanese army brought back more than 100000 ears and nose of the Korean soldiers and reinforcements of the Ming Dynasty every time.

The imperial envoy Xia Ziyang in 1606 recorded and related Toyotomi Hideyoshi's invasion of Korea with the dangerous situation of Ryukyu. Records of Ming Empire recorded that on May 4th in that year, "The imperial envoy Xia Ziyang suggested intensifying the coast defense". It happened 20 days before his voyage, I am unable to find the exact content of this letter , but we can discover something in his the Record of the Imperial Title-Conferring Envoys to Ryukyu ·Preface: "Toyotomi Hideyoshi" invaded Korea ... Ryukyu is very close to Japan; if Korea was lost, Ryukyu would also suffer. The danger in southeastern land should be our concern."

One year before in 1605, Xu Bida, re-drew the Great Haiphong Map in An Illustrated Compendium on Maritime Security and gave it a new name—The Complete Map of Unified Maritime Territory for Coastal Defense (Qian Kun Yi Tong Hai Fang Quan Tu) which consists of 10 silk scroll paintings with length of 1.76 meters and 0.63 meters. The markers in the map record:

Xu Bida: the coastal defense is very important. The conditions of the coasts are not advantageous to the Japanese pirates. In the Jiajing period, the southeast was threatened seriously by the Japanese led by Toyotomi Hideyoshi.

I happened to see the Great Haiphong Map (Wang Li Hai Fang Tu) drawn by Zhen Ruozeng under the auspices of Hu Zongxian, the supreme commander of the southeast coastal defense of the Ming court. Hu Zongxian defeated the Japanese pirates; this map recorded the coastal conditions in details....

Xu Bida felt painful as Korea was invaded by Toyotomi Hideyoshi. He can't help recalling Zheng Ruozeng and Hu Zongxian 50 years ago, and he praised Hu Zongxian as he defeated the Japanese pirates; Xu Bida also thought highly of the Great Haiphong Map (Wang Li Hai Fang Tu); in this map, islands such the Diaoyu Island and Huangwei Yu were on the first line of coastal defense.

16 years later in 1621 (the first year of the reign of Emperor Tianqi of the Ming Dynasty), Mao Yuanyi, the grandson of Mao Kun, continued to compile the Treatise on Military Preparations which was left by his grandfather and father. Gu Qiyuan mentioned in the Preface of the Treatise on Military Preparations that: Mao Kun researched the military strategies when China suffered from the attacks from the Japanese pirates and wrote a lot related books; Mao Yuanyi learned these books when he was very young. The Coastal Defense II. Map of Fujian's Coastal Mountains and Sands almost copied the related parts in the Great Haiphong Map (Wang Li Hai Fang Tu); and only the Diaoyu Yu was changed into Diaoyu Mountain.

Mao Ruizheng, the cousin of Mao Yuanyi wrote the Record of the Interpreters of August Ming (Huang Ming Xiang Xu Lu) in 1629 (the second year of the reign of Emperor Chongzhen of the Ming Dynasty). According to Chen Kan's records ninety-five years ago, the Vol.1 "Ryukyu" re-stressed: "[from Fuzhou to Ryukyu], Then Gumi Mountain comes into sight, that is where the land of

Ryukyu begins; sailing 300 Li towards the east, the Yebi Mountain comes into sight; then Japan comes into sight." Mao Ruizheng was a a successful candidate in the highest imperial examinations and then he served as Secretary of War Staff Sides. When writing the Record of the Interpreters of August Ming, he referred to the book written Zhen Xiao; then he served as the official of Guanglu Temple in Nanjing, he added some more information in the book; eventually, he finished the finalize of the Record of the Interpreters of August Ming (Huang Ming Xiang Xu Lu). When he served as Secretary of War Staff Sides, he was in charge of maps, guard, and wars, so undoubtedly he read a lot of official documents related to these aspects. In the above quotation—"[from Fuzhou to Ryukyu], Then Gumi Mountain comes into sight, that is where the land of Ryukyu begins;" which indicates that the area before the Gumi Mountain belongs to China, so it didn't mention about the names of the islands such as the Diaoyu Islands. I think as the Gumi Mountain is where the land of Ryukyu begins, so we should know clearly the ownership of the Yebi Mountain. It also omitted the Machi Mountain (Kerama Islands); the sentence that "then Japan comes into sight" means the areas east to the Yebi Mountain did no longer belong to Ryukyu. This further proves that the Diaoyu Islands before the Kume Island are China's territory.

An Illustrated Compendium on Maritime Security included the Diaoyu Dao Islands on the "Map of Coastal Mountains and Sands" (Yan Hai Shan Sha Tu) and incorporated them into the jurisdiction of the coastal defense of the Ming court.

The Treatise on Military Preparations drawn up by Mao Yuanyi copied the Great Haiphong Map (Wang Li Hai Fang Tu); the Record of the Interpreters of August Ming written by Mao Ruizheng proves the boundary between China and Ryukyu. The Mao family were the heroes who defended sovereignty over the Diaoyu Islands.

At the end of the Ming Dynasty, Shi Yongtu collected the Treatise on Military Preparations. Coastal Defense II. Map of Fujian's Coastal Mountains and Sands, and then collected the "Map of Coastal Mountains and Sands" in An Illustrated Compendium on Maritime Security. The names of the islands are the same as those in the Treatise on Military Preparations drawn up by Mao Yuanyi.

Okuhara Toshio said that imperial envoys randomly listed the names of those islands just out their concern about the sea markers; they didn't do it in order to consciously tell the descendants that the Diaoyu Islands are China's territory. However, many people who were not imperial envoys also recorded those islands such as Zheng Ruozeng and Hu Zongxian who compiled An Illustrated Compendium on Maritime Security (Chou Hai Tu Bian), Xu Bida who wrote the preface of the Atlas of the Great Qing Dynasty, Mao Yuanyi who compiled the Treatise on Military Preparations, Mao Ruizheng who wrote the Record of the Interpreters of August Ming and Shi Yongtu who compiled On Military Preparations. They didn't concern about the sea markers; instead, the worried about the invasion of the Japanese pirates. In the short 10 years, the Diaoyu Island, Huangwei Yu and Chiwei Yu frequently appeared the first defense line in the coastal defense, which indicates that the Diaoyu Islands were closely related to the safety of China's land. It is by no means just the concern about the sea markers.

However, Okuhara Toshio didn't give up; then he quibbled about the legal status of Taiwan and islands such as Huangping Yu, Pengjia Yu, etc. before 1683. "Taiwan island and vase, pengjia islet island". They quibbled that in the 22nd year of the reign of Emperor Kangxi of the Qing Dynasty (1683), the Qing government divided Taiwan into one prefecture and three counties, so Taiwan had nothing to do with China before 1683. They attempted to cut off the relations between Taiwan and mainland China, thus denying the true history. Therefore, they announced that the records of Chen Kan, Guo Rulin, Zheng Shungong, Hu Zongxian and Zheng Ruozeng in the middle of the 16th century were all invalid; they even didn't admit the records of Wang Ji in the 22nd year of the reign of Emperor Kangxi of the Qing Dynasty.

I can debunk the lies of Okuhara by virtue of the concise argument of Ge Jianxiong who was a historical and geographical professor. He said:

In fact, the historical facts about Taiwan are very clear. On the one hand, people between Taiwan and mainland China began to make economic and cultural exchanges very early. On the other hand, Taiwan was local ethnic autonomous, it was not until the late Ming Dynasty when the bandits from mainland China began to set up their own regime; in the late 17th century, the Qing Dynasty set up Taiwan prefecture in Fujian Province in the west of island; then, the administrative region gradually extended to the whole island. Taiwan's local ethnic group (we call Gaoshan) developed and governed the island, and the ethnic group joined in the big family of the Chinese nation, so its history is also China's history, it was a part of China in history. No country ever owned Taiwan before the Qing Dynasty. As long as we reflect this period of history truly, we can prove that Taiwan has been a part of China since ancient times, also it demonstrated that the contributions of people in Taiwan to the history of China. Otherwise, if it must belong to the Han nationality or the central plains, it belongs to China; but in fact the Han nationality or the central plains are not the only representative of China?

China has been a unified feudal country of many nationalities; after thousands of years of long-term development, its unity was finally completed in the Qing Dynasty. In 1683 when we achieve the complete reunification of Taiwan and mainland, there were a few country which was a truly independent and unified country in the world. All in all, Taiwan was developed by the Han Nationality and Gaoshan people, and is China's inherent territory; the people of Taiwan have the same flesh and blood as the people of in the mainland and a part of the Chinese nation. In the Southern Song Dynasty, Penghu was affiliated to Jinjiang County, Fujian; in the eighteenth year of the Yuan Dynasty (1281) on September 27, the inspection department was set up in Penghu; although in the early Ming Dynasty, the system was abolished for defense for the co- untry, the coast defense was never be ignored; in the 42th year of the reign of Emperor Jiajing of the Ming Dynasty (1563), Yu Dayou and Qi Jiguang's army was resumed to re-set up the "Inspection Department" in Penghu. No one can remove these historical facts.

For the history of Taiwan after 1683, Okuhara used another trick that he cut off the Diaoyu Islands from Taiwan and all its affiliated islands; he said: "befo- re 1871, even the islands such as Mianhua Yu, Huaping Yu, Pengjia Yu whcih were very close to Taiwan didn't belong to Taiwan, let alone the Diaoyu Islands which were far away from Taiwan. In fact, the latter islands being incorporated into Taiwan's administrative area was according to Keelung Records."

Okuhara Toshio turned a blind eye to the coastal defense maps such as An Illustrated Compendium on Maritime Security, The Great Haiphong Map, Map of Fujian's Coastal Mountains and Sands, etc. Instead, he distorted the Taiwan Fu Zhi compiled by Gao Gongqian in the 33rd year of the reign of Emperor Kangxi of the Qing Dynasty and A Sequel to Taiwan Fu Zhi written by Yu Wenyi in in the 20th year of the reign of Emperor Qianlong of the Qing Dynasty (1764). A Sequel to Taiwan Fu Zhi written by Yu Wenyi was based on Recompiled Taiwan Fu Zhi written by Fan Xian in 1747. Fan Zhi and Yu Zhi explicitly pointed out that, Gaozhi in the Kangxi period wrote it hastily, so there was some lost information. We should pay attention to three points: 1. The content of "Fengyu, Xingye, attached text": Taiwan is southwest to the waters of Zhangzhou, south to Guangdong, north to Minan, Fujian; 2. In Fanli, the former version didn't record the coastal defense matters, now I added these information in this version. All of the ports and the size of ships were recorded and you can learn the details about the coastal defense matters; 3. In Vol. 2 Guizhi, Haifang, Attached Text collected the content of A Tour of Duty in the Taiwan Strait (Tai Hai Shi Cha Lu) written by Huang Shujing. The book was a report of the imperial envoy. Huang mention in Military Preparations about the patrol route of Taiwan government navy boats and posts along the route and their water depth as well as the boat model which could be moored in the water. He stressed that [Taiwan] "there are mountain behind the ocean which is called the Diaoyu Islands. The waters of the Diaoyu Islands can hold tens of ships."

A Tour of Duty in the Taiwan Strait (Tai Hai Shi Cha Lu) written by Huang Shujing is not a book written by a scholar but a report written an imperial en- voy; his records were Generalities, but emphasized on Military Preparations; the resources of his documents were not conjecture but came from the Post Report of the patrol navy... All these documents are telling us "consciously" that "the Diaoyu Islands are within China's territories".

Recompiled Taiwan Fu Zhi written by Fan Xian, A Sequel to Taiwan Fu Zhi written by Yu Wenyi and Taiwan Fu Zhi compiled by Li Yuanchun all fully transcribed the records of Huang Shujing. However, Okuhara Toshio has turned a blind eye to the above three points and quibbled that the Diaoyu Islands had nothing to do with Taiwan, which shows that he totally loses the demeanor and conscience a true scholar should have.

If Okuhara Toshio still brazenly says that it only involves the Diaoyu Islands, then what about the other islands?

The First Historical Archives of China collected the Great Universal Geographic Map (Kun Yu Quan Tu) in the Qianlong period which was delicately colored with 3.77m in length and 1,98 m in width. From the east to north of Taiwan, there are Pengjia Mountain, Huaping Yu, Diaoyu Island, Huangwei Yu and Chiwei Yu, the color of which is the same as that of mainland China and Taiwan. The dotted lines in the sea are routes followed by the ancient Europeans which lead to countries such as China, Ryukyu and Japan.

In the central bottom of the picture, there is an inscription in tiny script as follows:

......One person can't know about all the nations all over the world. Since ancient times, many people like to travel around; they always spread the local custom for cultivation or broaden their horizon by explore the magnificent scenery or investigate the terrain or make friends with sages and celebrities. As they like to travel, so they are not afraid of danger during the trips. In Han Dynasty, Zhang Qian went to the Western Regions. He had reached the land of India; the people in Yuan Dynasty once reached Kunlun. Our emperor once appointed imperial envoys to Qiongheyuan to measure the land and draw the map; it is more detailed than that of the Han Dynasty and Yuan Dynasty.

Our emperor appointed imperial envoys to measure the latitude and longitude. the records are very complete including those tortuous mountains and rivers. We can find all of them in the map. How magnificent!

My friend and I add some new information to the Great Universal Geographic Map (Kun Yu Quan Tu). It is written and drawn based on the accurate measured data.

I think the "friend" Michel Benoist, a famous French missionary. During 1756 to 1760, Michel Benoist was invited by the Qing Dynasty to modify The Great Map of Qing Dynasty. Then Qianlong's Map of China was published with the wood carved and copper plate versions; this map was praised by Dr. Needham... In short, this newly painted the Great Universal Geographic Map was drawn by Michel Benoist during 1760 to 1767.

He colored Huaping Yu, Pengjia Mountain, Diaoyu Island, Huangwei Yu, Chiwei Yu with the same color as that of mainland China and Taiwan. Original names in the picture were pronounced according to the Minnan dialect.

Michel Benoist was invited by Emperor Qianlong to draw the Great Universal Geographic Map. Therefore, it is an official figure. It shows that the Qing government attached great importance to these islands as they added them into the map.

In addition, under the support of the governor of Hubei Province Hu Linyi, the Atlas of the Great Qing Dynasty (Huang Chao Zhong Wai Yi Tong Yu Tu) was officially published by Hubei government in 1863. The "afterwords" of the map mentioned that:

Hu Wenzhong was an expert in geography. The Atlas of the Great Qing Dynasty drawn by Li Zhaoluo didn't record the names of places in detail and couldn't be modified in the original map as its space was very small; after referring to the literature in the court, Hu Wenzhong together with Zou Ziyi, Yan Guizhai compiled the map for a long time and eventually they complete it.

It illustrates that this map referred to the Great Map of Qing Dynasty and Qianlong's Map of Prefectures, which only drew the mainland China without those islands. I think when drawing the Atlas of the Great Qing Dynasty (Huang Chao Zhong Wai Yi Tong Yu Tu), the author referred to the Great Universal Geographic Map (Kun Yu Quan Tu). The preface has a whole picture, in the west to Gumi Mountain, there are several small islands in the position of the Diaoyu Islands; the author even omitted other bigger islands in the whole map and only marked those tiny islands.

If readers feel this picture is too general, you can refer to the fourth and fifth insert pages. (see the original map)

The principle of naming the places in the Atlas of the Great Qing Dynasty (Huang Chao Zhong Wai Yi Tong Yu Tu)is naming according to the owner. When modifying the map, Yan Shusen pointed out that in the afterword:

For the places belong to Siyi, besides the Chinese, it also used the mandarin Chinese, Mongolian, Todo, Tanguticum and Russian—"Spring and Autumn-Ram"—naming according to the owner.

For the places belong to Siyi, it will use the local language and add the translation of the Chinese. Plate is spliced by the pictures in Vol. 6, Vol. 7 and Vol. 8. Fujian, Taiwan and its affiliated island—"small Ryukyu", Pengjia Mountain, Diaoyu Island, Huangwei Yu and Chiwei Yu all used the Chinese names instead of Ryukyuan language and Japanese; but the places east to Chiwei Yu such as Kume Moutain, it used the Ryukyuan language; for the Taiping Moutain, it mentioned that Taiping Moutain was originally Miyako.

The whole map omitted those islands larger than the Diaoyu Islands such as Huoshao Yu in to the east of Taiwan and Lan Yu, because they had clearly boundary with Yonaguni Island of Yaeyama Islands. But it clearly marked the Diaoyu Islands to show their owner. I think Okuhara Toshio as a Prof. of international law is able to judge the meaning of all these facts.

(Excerpt from Chapter 1 to 4 of the Textual Research on the Sovereignty over the Diaoyu Islands before the Sino-Japanese War of 1894-1895 written by Wu Tianying. When excerpting, I have made some modifications, and omitted some parts of the text.)

X. On Sovereignty over the Diaoyu Islands

October, 1996

Zhong Yan

The Diaoyu Islands issue is an unsolved territorial dispute between China and Japan. Since this year, the Japanese right-wing political groups have repeatedly landed on the Diaoyu Islands and build illegal buildings and markers on these islands, which once again has stirred up this dispute between the two countries. This paper will expound on the issue of the sovereignty over the Diaoyu Islands from the perspective of history and International Law.

1. The Diaoyu Islands have been China's territory since ancient times

The Diaoyu Island and its affiliated islands are located 92 nautical miles northeast to Leelung City of China's Taiwan Province. They are about 73 nautical miles far from the Ryukyu Islands of Japan; they are separated by a deep trench. The Diaoyu Islands consist of Diaoyu Island, Huangwei Yu, Chiwei Yu, Nanxiao Island, Beixiao Island, and other three islets (Dananxiao Island, Dabeixiao Island and Feilai Island), covering an area of about 6.3 square kilometers. Among all these islands, the Diaoyu Island covers the largest area of 4.3 square kilometers, about 362 meters above sea level. Its southeastern side is very steep like harpoon; its east side is shaped like a minaret. The island is a long-term uninhabited island.

As early as the Ming Dynasty, there were documents recording the Diaoyu Islands in China. Japan claimed that the Diaoyu Islands belong to the jurisdiction of Okinawa, but Japan's Okinawa prefecture was the independent Ryukyu Kingdom about 125 years ago. Before Japan's annexation of Ryukyu in 1871, China and Ryukyu had a friendly relationship for about 500 years. The Diaoyu Islands were first discovered, named by the Chinese people. The book Voyage with a Tail Wind (Shun Feng Xiang Song), which appeared in 1403 (the first year of the reign of Emperor Yongle of the Ming Dynasty), recorded about the Diaoyu Islands.

The first emperor of the Ming Dynasty appointed imperial envoys to grant honorific title to the Kings in Ryukyu in recognition of their rules. In 1534, the 11th imperial envoy of the Ming Dynasty Chen Kan and some people from Ryukyu who had come to China to welcome Chen went to Ryukyu by boat. It was clearly recorded in the Records of the Imperial Title-conferring Envoys to Ryukyu (Shi Liu Qiu Lu): Sailing by the Pingjia Mountain, the Diaoyuyu, Huangmaoyu and Chiyu, there are too many islands for one's eyes to feast on.... When we arrived at Gumi Mountain which belonged to Ryukyu, foreigners on the boat danced in the accompaniment of drum-beating, feeling as happy as back at home.[65]

---

65   Chen Kan, Records of the Imperial Title-Conferring Envoys to Ryukyu (Shi Liu Qiu Lu), p. 25.

Gumi Mountain is also called Gumi Island, i.e. the Jiumi Island of Okinawa; "Foreigners" refer to the native people of Ryukyu on the boat. This shows that the Ryukyu people believed that they considered to have returned to their homeland after passing the Diaoyu Islands and only when they arrived at Gumi Island. The Diaoyu Islands, Huangmaoyu (Huangwei Yu) and Chiyu (Chiwei Yu) did not belong to Ryukyu.

In 1562, An Illustrated Compendium on Maritime Security (Chou Hai Tu Bian) compiled by Hu Zongxian, the supreme commander of the southeast coastal defense of the Ming court, marked the Diaoyu Islands, Huangwei Yu, Chiwei Yu on the "Map of Coastal Mountains and Sands" (Yan Hai Shan Sha Tu). We can see that as early as in Ming Dynasty, the Diao yu Islands were incorporated into the jurisdiction of the coastal defense of the Ming court.

In 1562, Imperial Envoy Guo Rulin wrote in Recompiled Records of the Mission to Ryukyu: On the first day of leap month May, we passed the Diaoyuyu. On the third day we reached Chiyuyan, which is a hill at the local boundary of Ryukyu. After another day's sail, we could see Gumi Mountain (Jiumi Island). These lines further clearly prove that China at that time already took Chiweiyu, one of the Diaoyu and adjacent islands nearest to Ryukyu as a marker of Ryukyu boundary.

In the Qing Dynasty, it became a common sense of Chinese navigator that the boundary between China and the Ryukyu is the sea trench south to the Diaoyu Islands. The second imperial envoy of the Qing Dynasty, Wang Ji went to to Ryukyu in 1683 and wrote Miscellaneous Records of a Mission to Ryukyu (Shi Liu Qiu Za Lu), the Vol.5 of which records he passed the Diaoyu Islands and Chiwei Yu; after that they offered sacrifices to Ocean God in order to avoid the shipwreck; the crew of the ship told him the "Hei Shui Gou" they have just passed, is the "boundary between China and foreign land". In 1756, Zhou Huang who went to Ryukyu mentioned about "boundary between China and foreign land" written by Wang Ji in Vol. 16 of The Annals of Ryukyu (Liu Qiu Guo Zhi Lue). It proves that that Ryukyu "is separated from the waters of Fujian by Hei Shui Gou to the west"; the Diaoyu Islands west to Chiwei Yu are Chinese territory.

Records of Messages from Chong-shan (Zhong Shan Chuan Xin Lu) written by Xu Baoguang, a deputy title-conferring envoy of the Qing Dynasty, had a great influence on Japan and Ryukyu at that time. In order to write this book, Xu Baoguang did a lot research and discussed with Geographers and officials in Ryukyu. The book has been translated into Japanese and become Japan's important source of learning about the Ryukyu islands. It pointed out: The sea route to Ryukyu is: leave Fuzhou, pass by Huaping Yu, Pengjia Mountain, Diaoyu Island, Huangwei Yu and Chiwei Yu, then arrive Gumi Mountain. The book also points out that Gumi Mountain the principal island at the sea boundary to the southwest of Ryukyu and Yonaguni Island, one of Yaeyama Islands, they guard the most southwest border of Ryukyu.

Depending on the above documents, the government of Ming and Qing Dynasties had always regarded the Diaoyu Islands as China's territory. In October in the 19th year of the reign of Emperor Guangxu of the Qing Dynasty (1893), one year before the Sino-Japanese War, the Empress Dowager Cixi wrote an imperial edict—granting the Diaoyu Islands to Sheng Xuanhuai, the Minister of Postal Department, for picking herbs. In the imperial edict, Cixi said: the pills given by Sheng Xuanhuai are very effective. It is reported that the herbs were collected on the Diaoyu Islands of Taiwan. The herbs grow on the sea and their effective is very different from central mainland China. I know that Sheng Xuanhuai's family have a pharmacy where they treat the sick and give them free medical treatment. I admire that very much, so I will give the Diaoyu Islands, Huangwei Yu and Chiwei Yu to Sheng Xuanhuai for picking herbs.[66]

The fact that the Diaoyu island is China's territory is not only supported by China but also gains support from Professor Inoue Kiyoshi, a famous Japanese historian who wrote Historical Facts of Senkaku Islands/Diaoyu Islands in 1972. In his book, he points out that as a historian, after looking through a lot of historical literature, he can conclude that the Diaoyu Islands are not terra nullius before Japan's occupation. They are China's territory. Just as what Professor Inoue Kiyoshi points out, before Japan's Meiji Restoration (1868), we can find no records concerning the Diaoyu Islands in the documents of Japan and Ryukyu. Japan's earliest written record about the Diaoyu Islands is theMaps of Three Provinces and 36 Islands of Ryukyu attached to "Overview Maps of Three Countries" written by Lin Ziping in 1785. He drew this map based on Records of Messages from Chong-shan (Zhong Shan Chuan Xin Lu) written by Xu Baoguang, a deputy title-conferring envoy of the Qing Dynasty. In the maps, he used the name—Diaoyu Islands and marked them and China's mainland in light red; while Gumi Mountain and Ryukyu are colored in yellow-brown. He quoted Xu Baoguang's records: Gumi Mountain (the principal island at the sea boundary to the southwest of Ryukyu). In 1719, Arai Hakusek, a Japanese scholar, mentioned the 36 islands of Ryukyu in his book Southern Islands Chronicles; the 36 islands of Ryukyu in the book don't include the Diaoyu Islands. The Maps of Revised Names of Provinces and Cities in Japan

---

66   The academic circles have different views on the authenticity of this matter. It is reported that to September 27, 2003, Mr. Ma Ying-jeou revealed his opinion on the matter in a lecture titled Brief Analyses on the Diaoyu Islands Issue: putting aside the authenticity of imperial edict, Guangrenang pharmacy operated by Sheng Xuanhuai's family often collect this herb on the Diaoyu Islands because a kind of herb called Shicongrong grown on the rocks near the Diaoyu Islands can heal Rheumatoid Arthritis. (see Historical Development and Legal Status of Diaoyu Islands written by Huang Zhaoqiang, Soochow University in Taiwan, p. 10.

published in 1875 does not include the Diaoyu Islands, neither. Even in 1879 when China's Northern Minister Li Hongzhang negotiated with Japan about the ownership of Ryukyu, China and Japan still agreed on that Ryukyu consisted of 36 islands, not including the Diaoyu Islands.

Zhongshan Historical Records of Ryukyu Kingdom, an authoritative history book of Ryukyu Royal Court compiled under the supervision of Ryukyu Prime Minister Xiang Xiangxian, quotes Chen Kan as saying that Gumi Mountain belonged to Ryukyu, identifying Chiweiyu and the islands to its west were not the territory of Ryukyu. In 1708, the great Ryukyu scholar Cheng Shunze also said in A General Guide (Zhi Nan Guang Yi) that Gumi Mountain (Jiumi Island) was the principal island on Ryukyu's southwestern boundary. The great scholar Cai Wen pointed out that the Diaoyu islands were not the territory of Ryukyu in Revised Annals of Chong-shan in 1726. Annals of Chong-shan given by Ryukyu to Emperor Kang Xi didn't mention the Diaoyu islands, neither. Shogoro Takahashi, the director of the Japan Association for the Promotion of International Trade, holds that the names of the Diaoyu islands were firstly named by China. The names such as Huangwei Yu and Chiwei Yu are undoubtedly Chinese names just like the names of Taiwan's affiliated islands such as Huaping Yu, Mianhua Yu, Pengjia Mountain, etc. "Yu" is never used in Japan; there are 29 island names with "Yu" in Fujian, Penghu Islands and Taiwan; there are a lot more in ancient Chinese maps. Chiwei Yu were also written as Chi Yu (Chi means red in Chinese) in Chinese ancient books because the island consist of sedimentary rocks which are always in red.

Some Japanese pointed out that some maps publish by China once used "Senkaku Islands" and they thought this was the evidence to prove that Japan had the sovereignty over the Diaoyu Islands. On China's historical atlas, the Qing Dynasty used "Diaoyutai" and it has been used by Taiwan at present. During Japan's occupation, Japan forced China to use "Senkaku Islands" on its maps such as New Map published by Shanghai Shen-pao. After the war and a period after the founding of the People's Republic of China, some printed maps of China still use "Senkaku Islands" under certain influence. For example, the first version (1956) and the second version (1962) of the Maps of Names of Provinces in China added explanations: drawn based on maps published during the Anti-Japanese War and maps published by Shen-pao. Because of Japan's occupation of China, some maps published by China were the same as those of Japan. This is the semi-colonial mark in China's modern history and cannot prove that Japan has sovereignty over the Diaoyu Island.

All Japan's maps and official documents once officially used the Chinese names for the islands. According to incomplete statistics, from 1935 to 1970, two-thirds of the 21 kinds of maps and encyclopedia published by Japan didn't record the so-called "Senkaku Islands"; some of them used the Uotsuri Islands (Yudiao Islands). The calling of the Diaoyu Islands is messed up in Japan. It is said that Senkaku Islands firstly originated from the calling used by the British. On July 25, 1921, when the Japanese government incorporated the islands into Japan's territory, they changed Chiwei Yu into Taisho Island, which was not formally used for a long time. Until after the World War II, when Japan submitted materials to the allied command, the chart used by Ministry of Waterway of Japan Coast Guard still used Chinese names such as Huangwei Yu, Chiwei Yu, etc. In 1969, official documents and billboards of the Ryukyu government occupied by U.S. military still used Chinese names such as Huangwei Yu, Chiwei Yu, etc. In May 1969, with the spreads of the news that there is petroleum in waters of the Diaoyu Islands, , the local government of Okinawa received application from oil companies that they wanted to explore in the waters; meanwhile, according to the order of the Mayor of Ishigaki, Japan began to built stakes on the Diaoyu Islands, and changed Huangwei Yu into "Kuba island" and Chiwei Yu into "Taisho Island".

However, because these islands were not named by by the imperial edicts of the emperor, before 1972, the Japanese government did not give detailed names of each island to emphasize its sovereignty, Japan just called them the "Senkaku Islands". At present, some maps of Japan still use the Chinese names for these islands. For example, the Great Map of the World published by Japan Heibon Press clearly marked Chinese characters with Japanese pronunciation: the Yudiao Islands (Uotsurijima), Huangwei Yu (Kobisho), Chiwei Yu (Sekibisho). The official documents of the Okinawa prefecture and the Japanese government also use Huangwei Yu and Chiwei. In February 1995, the Defense Agency Data submitted by Japanese Defense Agency to Budget Committee of House of Representatives still use Chinese names—Huangwei Yu and Chiwei Yu.[67]

2. The ins and outs of Japan's illegal grabbing of the Diaoyu Islands

1) Japan's illegal grabbing of the Diaoyu Islands is the extension of Meiji government's foreign expansion and is an intentional action prepared for a long time against the background of the war. Japan's "discovery" of the Diaoyu Islands was in 1884 when Japan incorporated Ryukyu into Okinawa after its annexation of Ryukyu. It is 500 years later than the earliest record of China. According to historical records in Japan, Koga Tatsushiro, from Fukuoka, Japan, discovered albatrosses which can be sold to Europe on Kuba Island (Huangwei Yu) in 1884; so in 1885, he asked for permission from the Okinawa magistrate. He wanted to develop the island and set up markers on the island with "Huangwei Yu reclaimed by Koga". Based on this matter, the Japanese government insists the Diaoyu Islands is terra nullius and were preemptively occupied by Japan rather than seized during the Sino-Japanese War.

---

67   Japan, "Political and Economic Overview", 1996, "Vanguard" magazine, special May issue, p. 109.

However, what is the truth? According to Japanese official records — Vol. 18 of Japanese Diplomatic Documents, on September 22, 1885, the Okinawa magistrate Sutezou Nishimura did a survey under the order of the Ministry of Internal Affairs. The result is that "about the uninhabited islands between Okinawa and Fuzhou of the Qing government, the islands are undoubtedly the Diaoyu islands, Huangwei Yu, Chiwei Yu, etc. which were recorded in the Records of Messages from Chong-shan (Zhong Shan Chuan Xin Lu). If it is true, they had been discovered by the ship of the imperial envoy of the Qing Dynasty who went to grant honorific title to the former Zhongshan King and had been named by China. I had hesitations to set up stakes on these islands when investigating."[68]

The secret investigation shows that the Japanese Meiji government realized that these islands were not terra nullius; at least they may cause possible territorial dispute with China. However, Aritomo Yamagata did not stop at this result but continued to investigate so as to set up national stakes. His reason was that the islands were the Diaoyu islands, Huangwei Yu, Chiwei Yu, etc. which were recorded in the Records of Messages from Chong-shan (Zhong Shan Chuan Xin Lu), but they were only sea markers used by the Qing Empire and had no traces of the rule of Qing Dynasty. It was unnecessary to talk about the different island names of China and Japan; these unmanned islands were close to Yaeyama Islands. Japan once put forward that Japan would hand over Yaeyama Islands to China, in fact, Japan planned to get more. However, in a word, because of the investigation result, Yamagata was afraid to make any rash moves.

On October 21st, 1885, Inoue Kaoru, the Ministry of Foreign Affairs, wrote to Yamagata Aritomo, the Ministry of Internal Affairs. The content of the original letter was as follows: "over the matter concerning placing national markers on the uninhabited islands of Kumeseki-shima and 2 other islands spread out in between Okinawa and Fuzhou [China] after investigating them, I have given much thought to the matter. The aforementioned islands are close to the border of China, and it has been found through our surveys that the area of the islands is much smaller than the previously surveyed island, Daito-jima; and in particular, China has already given names to the islands. Most recently Chinese newspapers have been reporting rumors of our government's intention of occupying certain islands owned by China located next to Taiwan, demonstrating suspicion toward our country and consistently urging the Qing government to be aware of this matter. In such a time, if we were to publicly place national markers on the islands, this must necessarily invite China's suspicion toward us. Currently we should limit ourselves to investigating the islands, understanding the formations of the harbors, seeing whether or not there exist possibilities to develop the island's land and resources, which all should be

---

68   The Decision on the Jurisdiction of Yaeyama Islands and the Diaoyu Islands, Japanese Diplomatic Archive Documents , Volume 23, p. 3456.

made into detailed reports. In regard to the matter of placing national markers and developing the islands, it should await a more appropriate time."

Inoue also enjoined Yamagata Aritomo that he should not publish the secret investigation on newspapers and should conduct secretly so as not to raise dissent and opposition from the international community. In the same year on November 24, Sutezou Nishimura, the Okinawa Magistrate, did a survey under the order of the Ministry of Internal Affairs. The result was that " the islands may not have nothing to do with the Qing government. Please instruct me how to handle it, in case we will have disputes with the Qing government." The next day, the Ministry of Foreign Affairs and the Ministry of Internal Affairs jointly stated that we mustn't set up national stakes at present.[69]

Obviously, at that time, the Japanese Empire was stepping up its armament expansion in order to devour the North Korea; and it would fight it out with the Qing government later rather than act rashly and alert the enemy prematurely. Until 1893, a year before the Sino-Japanese War, the Okinawa Governor put forward the suggestion that Japan should incorporated the islands under the administration of Okinawa. But the Ministry of Foreign Affairs and the Ministry of Internal Affairs agreed with it a year later. In the year of the Sino-Japanese War, Japan was not sure whether it could win the war, so it refused the suggestion with the reason that we were not sure the islands belong to us.

However, at the end of November, 1894, Japanese troops occupied Lvshunkou and blockaded the Beiyang Navy within Wei Hai Wei. The Meiji government was convinced that they would won the victory in the war, so it forced China to cede Taiwan as a condition of peace, and stole the Diaoyu Islands secretly. On December 27, Yasushi Nomura, the Ministry of Internal Affairs, sent a cipher text to Mutsu Munemitsu, the Ministry of Foreign Affairs: you demanded to delay the stake building on Kuba Island (Huangwei Yu) and on Diaoyu islands, but the situation is different now, so we should administrate these islands. So I send this text to re-discuss this matter. This time, the Ministry of Foreign Affairs didn't raise any objection and replied that please deal with it according to previous plan. As a result, on January 14, 1895, the Japanese government, even before the end of the war, incorporated the islands under the administration of Okinawa and set up stakes on the islands through the resolution of Cabinet.[70] On April 17 in the same year, China and Japan signed Treaty of Shimonoseki which forced China to cede Taiwan and its surrounding islands. Until the Japan's surrender, Japan had ruled Taiwan for 50 years, including Taiwan's affiliated islands such as the Diaoyu Islands.

---

69   Refer to Vol.18 of Japanese Diplomatic Documents
70   The Decision on the Jurisdiction of Yaeyama Islands and the Diaoyu Islands, Japanese Diplomatic Documents , Volume 23.

2) After the World War II, the pending dispute over the sovereignty of the Diaoyu Islands between China and Japan is a territorial "bump" left by the U.S. in order to divide China and Japan.

After U.S. Military's occupation of Ryukyu, on January 29, 1946, the Supreme Commander for the Allied Powers Instruction (SCAPIN) No.677 released by the US clearly defined Japan's power of administration to "include the four main islands of Japan (Hokkaido, Honshu, Kyushu and Shikoku) and the approximately 1,000 smaller adjacent islands, including the Tsushima Islands and the Ryukyu Islands north of the 30th parallel of North Latitude", but the Diaoyu Islands were not included.

With the emergence of the situation of the cold war, the United States Civil Administration of the Ryukyu Islands released Geographical Realm of Ryukyu Islands (No. 27 edict) on December 25, 1953, which claimed as follows: according to the Treaty of San Francisco signed on September 8th, 1951, it is necessary to specify the geographic boundary of the Ryukyu Islands, so the areas under the jurisdiction of the United States government and the Ryukyu government include islands, islets, reefs and waters with 24 °N and 122 °E. The US's occupation of the Diaoyu Islands was totally illegal. On June 17th, 1971, the US and Japan signed the Okinawa Reversion Agreement which declared that Japan's territory was the same as stipulated in No.27 edict in 1953. Therefore, the Diaoyu Islands were mapped in Okinawa. On this base, the Japanese government claimed that the islands belong to Okinawa and incorporated the islands and their waters into "air defense identification circle" of Self-Defense Forces. The US secret handover of the Diaoyu Islands to Japan caused campaigns of Protecting Diaoyu Island of the Chinese all over the world.

In this case, the U.S. government had to declare in October 1971: "the United States believes that it has no damage to related sovereignty that the US returned the executive power of these islands to Japan. The US can't increase any executive power during the hand-over nor decrease the rights of other countries... The dispute over these islands should be solved by countries concerned."[71] Until September 11, 1996, the U.S. government spokesman Burns said: "the United States neither admits nor supports the claim for sovereignty over the Diaoyu Islands from any country."[72]

3. Evaluating the sovereignty over the Diaoyu Islands from the perspective of the International Law

1) Japan stole China's Diaoyu Islands which are by no means the so-called terra nullius status

---

71   The US Senate Foreign Relations Committee hearing on 92nd Congressional Record, October 27th, 1971, p. 29-91.
72   Hong Kong "Oriental Daily" September 12, 1996 , etc.

The Japanese government has no historical facts and legal basis to prove that Diaoyu Islands are terra nullius and that Diaoyu Islands are Japan's "inherent territory" because of the preemptive occupation of terra nullius. The so-called "inherent territory" doesn't refer to a foreign thing, but the Diaoyu Islands were clearly stolen by Japan, so there is no "inherent territory". The Japanese government said, "Since 1885, the Japanese government, through repeated on-site investigations by the authorities of Okinawa Prefecture and other channels, has cautiously confirmed that the Senkaku Islands are not only no-man's islands but also have no traces of the rule of (China's) Qing Dynasty. On this basis, the Cabinet decided on January 14th, 1895, to have markers erected on the islands to officially incorporate them into Japan's territory." However, this paper has put forward a large number of historical facts to prove it is nonsense. To begin with, since the Ming dynasty the Diaoyu Islands have not been terra nullius; they have been put under the jurisdiction of China's naval defense. These islands are uninhabited for a long time, but they are by no means terra nullius. The Diaoyu Islands were first named by China and incorporated into China's territory. They were first discovered, recorded, exploited, rule and defended by China.

Moreover, 10 years before the Sino-Japanese War, Japan already knew the above facts. Its occupation of the Diaoyu Islands is not "preemptive occupation", but a secret stealing action. Japan's decision to incorporate the islands under the administration of Okinawa and to build stakes on these islands was conducted secretly and didn't make it public afterwards. In the 29th year of the Meiji period, even in Composition of Okinawa County announced by Prime Minister Ito Hirobumi, there was no mention about Diaoyu Islands or "Senkaku Islands".

2) None of the treaties or agreements between the US and Japan has legal effect to determine the territorial sovereignty of the Diaoyu Islands

The Japanese government said, "The Senkaku Islands are not included in the territories renounced by Japan as provided in Article 2 of the San Francisco Peace Treaty, but, as part of the southwest islands, placed under US administration according to Article 3. Therefore, after the islands under the US trusteeship were restored to Japan, they are naturally Japanese territory. China had not raised any objection until the discovery of oil in the Diaoyu Islands, China began to claim the Diaoyu Islands were China's territory.

This is obviously not in accord with the historical facts. On December 1st, 1943, China, the US and Britain signed the "Cairo declaration" which clearly stipulates that " all the territories Japan has stolen from the Chinese, such as Manchuria, Formosa, and The Pescadores, shall be restored to the Republic of China. Japan will also be expelled from all other territories which she has taken by violence and greed." On July 26th, 1945, China, the US and Britain stressed in the Potsdam

Declaration that the terms of the Cairo Declaration shall be carried out and Japanese sovereignty shall be limited to the islands of Honshu, Hokkaido, Kyushu, Shikoku and such minor islands as we determine. Now that Japan accepted the Potsdam Declaration, it means that it gives up all territories which it has taken from China, including Taiwan's affiliated islands such as the Diaoyu Islands.

The Government of People's Republic of China always holds that the United States' "unilateral administration right" of the Diaoyu Islands after the World War II is illegal. Early in June,1950 Foreign Minister Zhou Enlai strongly condemned the behavior of the United States and declared that the Chinese people are determined to recover Taiwan and all the other territories belong to China. The Treaty of San Francisco signed on September 8th, 1951 was a peace treaty with Japan signed only between Japan and the US. China was prevented by the US from participating in the San Francisco Conference. On September 18th, Foreign Minister Zhou Enlai on behalf of the Chinese Government announced: If the People's Republic of China is excluded from the preparation, formulation and signing of the peace treaty with Japan, it will, no matter what its content and outcome are, be regarded as illegal and therefore invalid by the Central People's Government.

The Japanese government frequently mentions that the Okinawa Reversion Agreement signed on June 17th, 1971, includes the "Senkaku Islands", attempting to use it as the main basis of Japan's sovereignty over the Diaoyu. However, even the US doesn't admit it. Moreover, how can China's territory be determined by the treaty signed by Japan and the US? On the issue of postwar territorial sovereignty, Japan can strictly abide by its acceptance of the Potsdam Declaration in 1945 and "Cairo declaration".

Recently, Japanese Sankei News published a news that on May 20, 1920, Chinese consul accredited in Nagasaki issued to the Japanese side a "letter of thanks" for saving Chinese fishermen, which mentioned the Senkaku Islands and Yangdao. It is treated as the most valuable historical materials, because it can overturned China's advocates. It is the most powerful evidence to prove China once admitted the Senkaku Islands were Japan's territory".[73]

As long as we analyze historical facts for a bit, we will come to a conclusion: the so-called "letter of thanks" can't explain anything. This is because, as early as in 1895 Japan occupied Taiwan Province of China through Treaty of Shimonoseki and stole the Diaoyu Islands before that; the Diaoyu Islands are affiliated islands of Taiwan. Japan's occupation lasted to 1945 when Japan was defeated. Therefore, The so-called "letter of thanks" only reflected people's opinions at that time, so written materials during Japan's seizure of the Diaoyu Islands can't be evidence to prove the sovereignty over the Diaoyu Islands. According to historical records, in 1941, Okinawa, under the rule of Japan, and

---

73   Japan, Sankei News, September 23, 1996

Taiwan had a dispute over the fisheries near the Diaoyu Islands, Tokyo court made an award that the Diaoyu Islands should be put under the jurisdiction of "Taipei state".[74]

We can see that, Japan does not admit that the Diaoyu Islands belong to Okinawa, either.

3) It is difficult for Japan to get the sovereignty over the Diaoyu Islands by the so-called "Positive Prescription"; it is futile for Japanese right-wing groups to continuously make disturbance on the Diaoyu Islands

Some analysts point out that one reason for Japan's constantly causing trouble on the Diaoyu Islands is that Japan attempts to get the sovereignty over the Diaoyu Islands by the so-called "Positive Prescription" in International Law. In fact, the so-called "Positive Prescription" is only a possible method to achieve some territory in the international community. So far, it has not been accepted by most International Law scholars; there is no case that has applied "Positive Prescription". Moreover, "Positive Prescription" itself is still a basic principle, namely the "continuous and undisturbed" exercise of state power.[75]

Originally, the dispute over the sovereignty of the Diaoyu Islands between China and Japan could have been solved through honest, calm and pragmatic consultations between the two governments. However, the Japanese government encourages people to establish all kinds of markers on the islands to show that the Japanese have actual control over he Diaoyu Islands. Some Japanese officials describe China's Diaoyu Islands as Japan's "private property", so the Japanese government cannot intervene on right-wing groups' activities. From the perspective of China, the Japanese government is cleaning the road for Japan's right-wing groups' making disturbance on the Diaoyu Islands; and it seems that the Japanese government asks the Chinese government to admit that the Diaoyu Islands are Japan's "private property" under Japan's sovereignty. Undoubtedly, China will never accept that.

If China and Japan live in harmony, it will benefit both; while confrontation between the two countries will cause sacrifices. Therefore, in the face of the unsolved problem left by history, far- sighted people of the two countries should jointly ponder over the issue based on respects for history and jurisprudence, sincerity and wisdom; we should not make it unstable factors in China-Japan relations; we should creatively solve this problem in order to achieve peace.

(Originally published - People's Daily on October 18th, 1996, p. 8)

---

74   Hong Kong, "Wen Wei Pa" August 18th, 1996, etc.
75   "International Law" compiled by Duanmu Zheng , Peking University Press, 1989, p. 132.

XI. Never Allow the US and Japanese Reactionaries to Plunder China's Seabed Resources

December, 1970

People's Daily Commentator

Despite the strong opposition and warnings from China and DPRK, the Japanese reactionaries collaborated with gangs led by Chiang Kai-shek and Park Chung-hee clique and intensified the plans of plundering the seabed resources of the two countries with U.S. imperialism. Held in Tokyo on December 21st, the so-called Conference on Joint Committee on Marine Development of "Liaison Committee" of Japan, Chiang Kai Shek, Park Chung Hoe openly decided to investigate, research and develop the offshore oil resources and other mineral resources in waters of Taiwan and its affiliated islands and adjacent shallow sea of China and North Korea. This is a blatant violation of sovereignty of China and North Korea. This is a heinous betray of our sovereignty and resources from the Chiang Kai-shek clique.

The US-Japan reactionaries coveted on our country's Marine resources for a long time. In recent years, they have been collaborating with Chiang Kai-shek group, and openly explored the seabed resources in waters of Taiwan and its affiliated islands and adjacent shallow seas of China. The U.S. imperialism also signed a contract with Chiang Kai-shek which delimited the mining area in western waters of northern Taiwan so as to exploit offshore oil. Now Japan and US reactionaries intend to establish Joint Marine Development Corporation of Japan, Chiang Kai Shek, Park Chung Hoe in order to conduct the so-called "joint development", attempting to loot the undersea resources of our country. The Chinese people expressed great indignation to this blatant act of piracy of the U.S. imperialism and Japanese reactionaries.

Taiwan Province and its affiliated islands, including the Diaoyu Island, Huangwei Yu, Chiwei Yu, Nanxiao Island and Beixiao Island have been China's sacred territory since ancient times. The seabed resources in waters of these islands and adjacent shallow sea of China all belong to China and China will allow others to get their hands on them. Only the People's Republic of China shall have the right to explore and exploit marine resource in these areas. Chiang Kai-shek clique is only a political zombie spurned by the Chinese people. The agreements and treaties Chiang Kai-shek clique signed with any country, any international organization or any foreign enterprise is illegal and invalid.

Japanese reactionaries not only attempt to plunder the undersea resources of our country, but also want to incorporated China's islands and waters into their own territory. Foreign Minister Aichi of Sato reactionary government recently repeatedly claimed that sovereignty over the Diaoyu Islands belonged to Japan. "Defense Agency" Nakasone even openly put these islands into the "Defense" range of Japan's fourth military expansion plan. This fully exposed the Japanese militarists' aggressive ambition. The Diaoyu Island, Huangwei Yu, Chiwei Yu, Nanxiao Island and Beixiao Island, etc. just like Taiwan, have been China's territory since ancient times. No one can change the historical fact. No matter what kind of excuses and tricks the Japanese reactionaries use to occupy China's sacred territory, they are absolutely impossible to succeed.

Our great leader Chairman Mao Zedong once said, "the Chinese people must defend China's territorial sovereignty and absolutely do not allow foreign governments' infringement." U.S. imperialism and Japanese reactionaries must immediately stop infringing our territorial sovereignty and plundering the seabed resources in our country. If US-Japan reactionaries stubbornly go their own way, they will be shooting themselves in the foot.

(Originally published in the People's Daily on December 29th, 1970 , p. 1)

XII. Reactionary Sato Government Attempts to Gobble China's Diaoyu Islands with New Tricks

May, 1971

People's Daily Commentator

Editor's note: Basic Views Concerning the Territorial Title of the Senkaku Islands released by Japanese Ministry of Foreign Affairs mentioned that both the government of the People's Republic of China and the Taiwan authorities firstly raised the Senkaku Islands issue in the second half of 1970, after the development of the oil off the continental shelf of the East China Sea.

The Xinhua News Agency's report on May 16th, 1971 proved that Japan's "Basic Views" is totally a lie.

Xinhua News Agency on May 16, Tokyo news: Japanese Sato reactionary government struggled to annex China's territory—Diaoyu Islands and other islands. Moreover, it discovered the "evidence" in a military map drawn by US invading army and used it as its excuse for the Japanese annexation of the islands of China.

According to the report of Japan's Kyodo News Agency on May 11th, "the Senkaku Islands (China's Diaoyu islands) located in the west of Okinawa are equipped with two shooting ranges of the US navy". The map with six colors titled "The US equipment and facilities in the Ryukyu Islands" drawn by US's 29th Corps of Engineers in January of last year clearly recorded the Senkaku Islands (China's Diaoyu islands) located in the west of Okinawa are equipped with two sky-ground shooting ranges of the US navy.

The Sato government treated this map as a treasure. Japan's Kyodo News Agency reported that the Japanese government thinks they have got a predominate evidence for their annexation of the Diaoyu islands of China.

Then, Japan's Kyodo News Agency reported on May 12th about the news in Washington on May 11th: the United States established shooting and bombing bases on Huangwei Yu and Chiwei Yu which belong to the Diaoyu Islands. Japan's Kyodo News Agency reported that United States Department of State has declared formally that the sovereignty over the Diaoyu Islands belongs to Japan."

Obviously, the US-Japan reactionaries again played with a new crappy trick; that is to say, Sato government found the "strong evidence"; then the US imperialists attempted to prove it so as to prove that now that the maps of the US military marked that there are the US shooting ranges on those islands, the islands become a part of Okinawa which is occupied by the US. And the United States handed over the administrative power of Okinawa in 1972 and the Diaoyu Islands were mapped into the handover area. Therefore, Japan can be perfectly justifiable to incorporate the Chinese territory into its own. This is a gangster logic of the aggressors!

It must be pointed out that the Diaoyu Islands, just like Taiwan, have been China's territory since ancient times. The U.S. imperialism established proving grounds on China's territory—the Diaoyu Islands and marked them on the military map, which happened to be another evidence to prove the US imperialists invasion of China's territory. It can never change the hard fact that the Diaoyu Islands are China's territory. In order to conquer the Diaoyu Islands of China, Japanese militarism unexpectedly turned to the military map of the United States for help, which shows Japan's guilty conscience. No matter what kind of excuses and tricks the Japanese reactionaries and no matter how the US imperialism conspires with Japanese reactionaries, Japanese Sato reactionary government's wildly arrogant ambition to annex China's territory—the Diaoyu Islands will never succeed.

(Originally published in the People's Daily on May 17th, 1971, p. 6)

XIII. An Eludication on the China's and Japan's Shelving the Diaoyu Islands Dispute

December, 2012

Ni Zhimin[76]

Editor's note: Mr. Ni Zhimin, the author of this article, is a Chinese scholar living in Japan. He has published a lot of rarely-known material about the Japanese politicians and authorities.

---

76 A Visiting Research Fellow in the Institute of Social Sciences Research of Ryukoku University.

The year of 2012 marked the 40th anniversary of the normalization of diplomatic relations between China and Japan. Reviewing the past, we see radical changes in the politics, culture, personnel exchanges and other areas of the two countries. At a stage full of political turbulence and in the context of globalization, China-Japan relations, with the economic relations as the center, have experienced all sorts of challenges in the past 40 years.

In addition, China's peaceful rise changes the balance of great powers and the world pattern is undergoing a fundamental change. During this historical change, the mutual trust of both countries and the intimacy of the two people are declining and the two countries go into an era of competition. Particularly, in terms of the sovereignty over the Diaoyu Islands (which is called "the Senkaku Islands" in Japanese), the traditional balance in politics of the two countries is upset and the foundation of China-Japan relations is shaken.

The Diaoyu Islands has been the territory of China since Ming Dynasty (about from the year of 1368 to1644). The fact was clearly demonstrated by the rigorous research done by famous Japanese scholars, Mr. Inoue Kiyoshi and Mr. Murata Tadayoshi[77].

The dispute over the Diaoyu Islands sovereignty is one of the historical problems between China and Japan. In 1972 when China-Japan relations restored normalization and in 1978 when the China-Japan Treaty of Peace and Friendship was established, the leaders of both countries, considering the overall situation, chose to leave the issue of the Diaoyu Island to be resolved later. Such a 'gentleman's agreement" facilitates the development of China-Japan relations in the later 40 years.

In October, 1978, Mr. Deng Xiaoping clearly stated the "shelving" of the Diaoyu Islands dispute. However, in 2010 when the Diaoyu Island collision incident happened, Japan proclaimed that "there is no territorial dispute between China and Japan". In the Congress plea on 21 October of 2010, when asked about "shelving of disputes" issue, the former Japanese Foreign Minister Seiji Maehara[78] said "it is the words only uttered by Deng Xiaoping's side. Japan didn't agree Deng's words"[79]. On 26 October, 2010, the Naoto Kan authority made the cabinet decision as a reply, claiming "there was no agreement or promise of "shelving" the Diaoyu Islands dispute".[80] Furthermore, on 12th September

---

77   Please refer to Mr. Ioune Kiyoshi's book, In Historical Facts of Senkaku Islands/Diaoyu Islands, which is published by The Duan Press in June of 2004.

78   Both are the duties at the time, similarly hereinafter.

79   It is recorded on the reply of the Security Council of the House of Representatives to Kamikaze's interpellation on 21st October, 2010. Retrieved from Congressional Record: http://kokkai.ndl.go.jp/SENTAKU/syugiin/176/0015/main.html.

80   The Defense Materials Prepared for Replying the Statements on Senkaku Islands Made by PRC's Vice-Premier Deng Xiaoping (No. 69, 26th October of 2000, [defense reply to, Konishi Kawai's interpellation]). Please refer to the website of the House of Representatives: http://www.shugiin.go.jp/index.nsf/html/index_shitsumon.htm.

of 2012, the Yoshihiko Noda government, based on the claim of Naoto Kan authority, should "nationalize" the Diaoyu islands, which has triggered the insurmountable conflict between China and Japan. In terms of the Diaoyu Islands issue, the conflicts between the two countries have been extended to the people to people relations and the tension between China and Japan is escalating to the fullest.

During the negotiation of the normalization of China-Japan relations as well as the China-Japan Treaty of Peace and Friendship, how on earth did the discussion on the Diaoyu Islands go on? Whether is there a "shelving" agreement or not? This article aims to revitalize the historical truth through the Japanese Congress plea, diplomatic documents, the recalling of the people who experienced the history, and other historical material.

1. The "Shelving" Agreement Reached in the Negotiations for the Normalization of China-Japan relations

In July of 1971 before "the Okinawa was returned" to Japan, The Ministry of Foreign Affairs of Japan collected the top-secret document on the Diaoyu Islands problem. The document said: "concerning the dispute over the Diaoyu Islands sovereignty, Japan and China (the Taiwan kuomintang government—editor's note) refute each other, which will negatively influence the friendly cooperation between the two countries. Besides, if the dispute over the Diaoyu Islands is further strengthened between the two countries, there will be a good excuse for putting a wedge in China-Japan friendly relationship. Therefore, both governments have the necessity to their utmost to avoid taking the contention as a major issue to be addressed"[81]. It could be concluded from the document that Japanese government hoped to shelve the dispute. On 25 March of 1972 when answering the question of the resource development near Senkaku Islands at the congress, Tanaka Kakuei, the head of MITI at the time, answer that "with regard to the ocean development on the continental shelf,…, the final negotiations in the future between Japan and China should be the satisfactory solution. This is the opinion on the political level at present."[82]

On 9 May, Tanaka Kakuei stressed that "Taiwan and the Chinese Mainland has their own positions" and answered that "the continental shelf problem is interweaved with the Taiwan problem, the problem of Chinese Mainland, the boundary problem of Okinawa before its reversion. The problems should be first satisfactorily resolved through consultation and then the underground resources can be exploited. This is the fact."[83]

---

81   Chinese Affairs Department of Foreign Affairs Ministry, "Reports for New Ministers (TS, Perpetual)", 5th July of 1974, p. 7, Index No. 2011-0719, Diplomatic Records Office.
82   Reply to Konohara Zane's interpellation at the 4th session of the House of Representatives Budget Committee meeting on 25 March, 1972. Retrieved from Congressional Record: http://kokkai.ndl.go.jp/SENTAKU/syugiin/068/0390/main.html.
83   Reply to Kokuba Koujou's interpellation at the meeting of Okinawa and Northern Territory Special Issue Committee of the House of Representatives on 9 May, 1972. Retrieved from Congressional Record: http://kokkai.ndl.go.jp/SENTAKU/syugiin/068/0710/main.html.

On 25 May, Fukuda Takeo, the Minister of Foreign Affairs at the time, in his reply to the questions on Senkaku Islands, said that "the situation will become complicated if (China) raises an objection. Therefore, the Senkaku Islands issue isn't suggested to be amplified."[84]

From the words of Tanaka Kakuei and Fukuda Takeo, it could be seen that Japanese government realized that there was dispute over the *Senkaku Islands* sovereignty.

In addition, Prime Minister Zhou Enlai first proposed "shelving" the Diaoyu Islands dispute in his talks with Takeiri Yoshikatsu in 1972. Takeiri Yoshikatsu recorded the talks in his notebook: "When I mentioned the sovereignty of Senkaku Islands, I said 'it could be found from the historical document that it (the Senkaku Islands is the inherent territory of Japan.' However, Mr. Zhou, simply smiling, said 'the Diaoyu Islands is the territory of China since ancient time, to our knowledge. We will not change our opinion. The dispute will be endless, so let us shelve it and leave it to the future wise men to address. Mr. Zhou didn't show any intention to make concession."[85]

On 25 November of 1972, Primier Kakuei Tanaka, Minister of Foreign Affairs Ohira Masayoshi and others visited china to conduct negotiations in terms of the normalization of China-Japan diplomatic relations. In the 3rd Summit Meeting held on 27th November, Japan and China reached an agreement about the dispute over the Diaoyu Islands sovereignty. Zhang Xiangshan, an advisor to Foreign Affairs Ministry of China at that time, attended four summit meetings and three meetings of Foreign Affairs ministers. According to Zhang's notes, at the end of the meeting, Tanaka asked "I would like to take this opportunity to ask China's attitude to the Senkaku Islands dispute." Zhou Replied "I do not want to talk about it this time. It does no good to both of us of mentioning the dispute now." Tanaka said "Since I am in Beijing, it will be difficult for me to report my work to the Japan if I didn't mention this. Now that I have asked you, I could do a decent report when coming back to Japan and I have done my duty." Zhou replied "If there wasn't the oil, neither Taiwan nor the United States would make this an issue." Tanaka responded "Then there is no need to speak more about this and let's leave it to the future." Zhou further agreed "The dispute should be left to the future to be solved. This time the priority should be the normalization of China-Japan relations, which is also the most urgent issue." Tanaka said "When China and Japan achieve normalization of diplomatic relations, the dispute could be addressed."[86]

---

84   Reply to Konohara Zane's interpellation at the House of Representatives Cabinet Committee meeting. Retrieved from: http://kokkai.ndl.go.jp/SENTAKU/syugiin/068/0020/main.html.

85   From Yoshikatsu Takeiri's article "the secrets for my 55 years' experience in the Japanese political system—the liaison between Japan and China", publshed in the Asahi Shimbun on 10 September, 1998.

86   Memoirs of Zhang Xiangshan: Witnessing the 25th Anniversary of Normalization of China-Japan Relations Vol. 2, January of 1998, p. 207

Above are the conversations between Tanaka and Zhou.

Furthermore, Susumu Nikaido, the chief cabinet secretary at the time, also attended the summit meeting. He confirmed "Tanaka proposed "co-developing the Senkaku Islands" at the end of the meeting, while Mr. Zhou clearly said 'Mr. Tanaka, let's leave the issue to the future'. Then Tanaka didn't probe into that dispute anymore."[87] In November 1996, When interviewed by People's Daily and the journalist from the Xinhua News Agency, Susumu Nikaido recalled the situation of the normalization negotiation and revealed the truth that "during the negotiation, Premier Tanaka initiatively asked Premier Zhou how to deal with the Diaoyu Islands issue. Zhou, after a quick thinking, responded that the issue would not be discussed this time and would be addressed in the future. Tanaka said 'well then, let's discuss in the future', which is actually an agreement reached by the leaders of both parties. Namely, both Japan and China agreed to solve the Diaoyu Islands dispute little by little in the future. 'some of today's young people don't know history and don't respect history either,' Tanaka added ."[88]

In September of 1997, at the lecture hosted by the Asahi Shimbun to celebrate the 25th anniversary of the normalization of China-Japan relations, Susumu Nikaido pointed "no matter in terms of Taiwan or the Senkaku Islands, do we forget the foundations for relationship normalization?" His words rang the alarm bell. And then he revealed a secrete news "When I met Chairman Jiang Zemin during my visit in China last year, I mentioned that Premier Tanaka's has ever proposed 'co-developing the oil near the Senkaku Islands'. Chairman Jiang responded 'that was just a proposal'."[89]

On November 6, 1972, when replying the interpellation of "whether the China-Japan Treaty of Peace and Friendship concerns any territory dispute or not", Ōhira Masayoshi, the Foreign Affairs Minister at the time, said "the previous disputes have been solved in the Japan-China Joint Statement. The China-Japan Treaty of Peace and Friendship is a guide to the future relations between China and Japan. Please treat the problem from this point of view."[90]

During the negotiation of the China-Japan Treaty of Peace and Friendship, "not touching the Senkaku Islands dispute is the result of the guides of 'freezing' or 'shelving'."[91] Besides, on March 27, 1973, when replying to another

---

87   Susumu Nikaido, "The secret during the process of restoring Chian-Japan diplomatic relations: one night in Zhongnanhai", The Ōhira Masayoshi's Political Legacy, Kumon Junbei. el ed., collected by Ōhira Masayoshi Memorial Foundation in June of 1994, p. 402.
88   The Interview of Mr. Susumu Nikaido, People's Daily, 11th November, 1996, p.6.
89   Susumu Nikaido, Addenda to the uninformed 'civil diplomacy', written on 17 September, 1997, published in the Asahi Shimbun on 25 November 1997.
90   Reply to Masaki Akira's interpellation at the Budget Committee meeting of the House of Representatives on 6th November 1972, Retrieved from Congressional Record: http://kokkai.ndl.go.jp/SENTAKU/syugiin/070/0380/main.html.
91   "Masayoshi Ōhira Said China-Japan Treaty of Peace and Friendship Wouldn't Mention the Senkaku Islands Dispute" published on the Yomiuri Shimbun on 7th November 1972.

interpellation, Ōhira said "we must carefully consider the problem in case that it becomes the root of disputes."[92]

In April of 1974, Chinese Acting Chairman Mr. Dong Biwu told Heishirou Okawa, the Japanese Ambassador at the time, that "there is no dispute over land boundaries between China and Japan. But there are Taiwan dispute and the Diaoyu Islands dispute, the latter of which could be legitimately negotiated."[93]

Mr. Dong's words showed China's active gesture in the problem. October 3th, Japan-China Friendship Association (official) delegation, headed by Minami Kuroda, visited China. Mr. Deng Xiaoping, vice premier of China said in his meeting with the delegation that "When we discussed the China-Japan Treaty of Peace and Friendship, it was right to shelve the Diaoyu Islands sovereignty problem. Because the problem is complicated and will take a very long time to be addressed."[94]

The above historical records clearly indicate that the Diaoyu Islands dispute was shelved while discussing the China-Japan Treaty of Peace and Friendship. Beyond that, Mr. Mansfield, the Democratic leader of the House of Representatives, said at the meeting of the House of Representatives that "Japan, China and Taiwan have been disputing the ownership of the Diaoyu Islands. China, seen from history, has the strongest support to claim the sovereignty of the Diaoyu Islands as well as the Nansha Islands and the Xisha Islands." This is the conclusion generated from the objective analysis.

2. "Shelving the Dispute" was Re-affirmed and Confirmed During the Negotiations of the China-Japan Treaty of Peace and Friendship

On April 12, 1978, about 100 Chinese fishing boats went close to the waters of the Diaoyu Islands, which shocked Japan and was recklessly speculated. Five days later, Sunao Sonoda, Japanese Foreign Affairs Minister at the time, demonstrated the basic gesture in his reply to the interpellation concerning the incident that "I think our attitude to the Diaoyu Islands dispute should refer to the Japan-China Joint Statement."[95]

---

92   Reply to Seya Hideyuki's interpellation at the Budget Committee meeting of the House of Representatives on 27 March 1973, Retrieved from Congressional Record: http://kokkai. ndl.go.jp/SENTAKU/sangiin/071/1380/main.html.
93   Chinese Affairs Department, "Conversation Between Dong Biwu and Ambassador Heishirou Okawa (TS, Perpetual)", April of 1974,p. 8m,Index No. 2011-0720, Diplomatic Records Office.
94   "Reports on Minami Kuroda's Discussion with Deng Xiaoping About the Diaoyu Islands Dispute" (3th October, 1974), *China-Japan Relations Documents Collection: 1970-1922*, The Kazankai Foundation, November 1993, p. 143.
95   Reply to Uehara Kosuke's interpellation, at the meeting of Okinawa and Northern Territory Special Issue Committee of the House of Representatives on 19 April, 1978, Retrieved from Congressional Record:http://kokkai.ndl.go.jp/SENTAKU/syugiin/084/0710/ main.html.

On 20 April, Masayoshi Ōhira, the Secretary-General of Liberal Democratic Party (LDP), more clearly said "Both Japan and China took the method of not 'involving' the territory to deal with the Diaoyu Islands dispute, which is a feasible solution that could handle the whole situation and take the national interest into consideration."[96]

The Secretary-General further emphasized: "branch is important. But when compared to root and trunk, branch is less important. We should not let the dispute harm the China-Japan relationship. ... .The solution to the dispute should be taken seriously."[97] Besides, the Secretary-General explicitly proposed that "we should deal with the Senkaku Islands dispute in line with the principle of "shelving" required in the Japan-China Joint Statement.[98]

On April 21, Masayoshi Ōhira spoke at LDP's general affairs meeting that "with respect to the Senkaku Islands, firstly we should deal with it from the general situation and solve the dispute through negotiations; secondly, the solution should not involve the sovereignty problem."[99] On the same day, the Yomiuri Shimbun published an article titled with "Prime Minster Should Deal With the Senkaku Islands Issue from the general situation". The article said that "When in 1972 China-Japan relations came into normalization, the dispute over the Senkaku Islands was handled in line with the principle of "not involving" sovereignty issue." It can thus be seen that the "shelving" method was generally recognized by the Japanese media. On April 27, Prime Minister Takeo Fukuda had a meeting with the Secretary-General. They both agreed to deal with the issue according to the diplomatic guideline.[100]

On 10th August, 1978, Chinese vice-premier Deng Xiaoping received Japanese Foreign Affairs Minister Sunao Sonoda who visited China for negotiating the China-Japan Treaty of Peace and Friendship. In their meeting, Sonoda mentioned that "I have to express my opinion on the incident. You must know Japan's position on the Senkaku Islands. We hope that there will be no such incidents any longer." In terms of Sonoda's hope, Deng showed the basic attitude and said that "I have to say a word. We should shelve the dispute. Our generation didn't find a decent solution. But, our next generation and the later generations will work this out."[101]

---

96   "Masayoshi Ōhira Agreed Solution without Touching Territory", Evening edition of The Asahi Shimbun, 20 April, 1978.

97   "Politically Solve the Senkaku Islands Problem: Masayoshi Ōhira is confident in the Adjustment Within the Party", Evening edition of The Asahi Shimbun, 20 April, 1978.

98   Masaya Itokoki, LDP's History From 1964 to 1980, The Asahi Sonorama, November, 1982, p.366.

99   Masayoshi Ōhira Will Handle the Senkaku Islands Issue by Considering the Overall Situation", The Yomiuri Shimbun, 22 April, 1978.

100   "Handling the Senkaku Islands Issue in a Diplomatic way", The Yomiuri Shimbun, 27 April, 1978

101   Zhang Xiangshan, 30 Years of China-Japan Diplomatic Normalization, translated by Eiji Suzuki, Sanwa Co., September 2002, pp. 157-158.

Deng also suggested "shelving the dispute for 20 or 30 years". In respond to Deng's words, Sonoda said "Your Excellency, I understood your point and there is no need to talk more about the issue."[102] Years later, in his memoir, Sonoda cited an old saying "If you induce a snake out of its hole, you will gain nothing."[103] Namely, if you "insist asking for the truth, you will get nothing."

On October 22, Vice-premier Deng Xiaoping visited Japan to attend the ceremony of exchanging the documents of ratification of the China-Japan Treaty of Peace and Friendship. On October 25, at the 2nd round Summit Meeting with Prime Minister Takeo Fukuda, Deng made it clear that "there are all sorts of problems between China and Japan. The Diaoyu Islands is one problem. In Japan, you might call it the Senkaku Islands. With respect to this sort of problems, we should not discuss them during the negotiation this time. I have told your Secretary-General that our generation wasn't wise enough to solve the problem, but our next generation, wiser than us, could figure out a good solution." Takeo Fukuda replied as this: "It is my honor to frankly exchange views on the problems of the world and the problems between China and Japan. I appreciate your frankness. To my point of view, only frank communication could facilitate the development of our relations. Above all, we must stick to the spirits in the China-Japan Treaty of Peace and Friendship."[104] Thus the Summit Meeting re-confirmed the "shelving" method.

On the same day, Deng held a press conference at Japan National Press Club. According to results of the Summit Meeting, he disclosed the "shelving method" to the reporters and said that "The Senkaku Islands is called the Diaoyu Islands by us. The different names show the different views of Japan and China. When the two countries discussed the issue of diplomatic normalization, we promised not to discuss such dispute. This time, we also promised not to touch the problem during the negotiation, since this problem is difficult to make it clear. However, some people intends provoke discords on the issue so as to hinder the development of China-Japan relations. We think that it is wise for both governments to put aside the Diaoyu Islands dispute. .... The next generation will be wiser than us to find a solution that could be accepted by both."[105] In a confidential document, Ministry of Foreign Affairs commented on Deng Xiaoping's words as this: "Although Japan didn't mention the Senkaku Islands dispute at the Summit Meeting, Premier Deng has demonstrated China's position clearly 'It is better not to mention the Diaoyu

102   Sunao Sonoda, Japan, World, Love, Shinchosha, May, 1981, p. 328.
103   Sunao Sonoda, Japan, World, Love, p. 184.
104   Chinese Affairs Department, "Records of the Meeting between Takeo Fukuda and Deng Xiaoping (TS, Perpetual)" (25 October, 1978), p. 11, Index No.04—1022—4, Diplomatic Records Office.
105   "Reports on the Main Ideas of the Deng's Press Conference at Japan National Press Club" (25 October, 1978), China-Japan Relations Documents Collection: 1970-1922, The Kazankai Foundation, November 1993, p. 197.

Islands issue.' That's why Deng said such words at the press conference: 'those who don't expect good relationship between China and Japan hope to mention the issue at the Summit Meeting. I suggest leaving the issue to the next generation..' So to speak, China has made the best to make their attitude as clear as they can. (Later then, Chinese Ambassador Fu Hao told Koshi Tajima, Chief of Chinese Affairs Department of Foreign Affairs Ministry that 'Shelving the dispute is all that China can do.)"[106]

On 30 May, 1979, when replying to the inquiry in terms of the Senkaku Islands, Japanese Foreign Minister Sunao Sonoda said "If we said any words advocating effective control of the Senkaku Islands, China will be irritated. As a nation, China will show their different position. I hope there will be no such difference." He noted that "the relationship between countries is similar to that between people. If the relationship is good, there will be emotion. Japanese has dignity, so does Chinese. Therefore, I absolutely oppose the words that advocate effective control."[107] Sonoda public opposition effectively pinned Japan's hawks.

On 31 May, Yomiuri Shimbun published an editorial titled with "Don't Make the Senkaku Islands Become the Root of Disputes". The main point of the editorial goes as this: "When negotiating the diplomatic normalization in 1972 and signing the China-Japan Treaty of Peace and Friendship last summer, both China and Japan admitted that there was dispute over the Senkaku Islands sovereignty, but both countries dealt with the dispute in the way of "not touching". In a word, the two governments came to an understanding. That is to say, both claimed the sovereignty of the Senkaku Islands and admitted the actual 'existence' of the dispute, but they agreed to leave the dispute to be addressed in the future. Although the understanding wasn't recorded in the Joint Statement or the Treaty, there is no doubt that it is a government's earnest 'promise' to another government. Now that a promise has been made, it surely has to be kept. Sunao Sonoda's reply at the Congress frankly kept the promise between China and Japan."

3. The Acts of China and Japan In Terms of Co-developing the Oil on the Seabed of the Senkaku Islands

Since the China-Japan Treaty of Peace and Friendship was signed and Ōhira Masayoshi cabinet was in office, there were symptoms and a tendency within both governments to co-develop the oil resources on the seabed of the Senkaku Islands. On August 18, 1978, Foreign Minister Sunao Sonoda made

---

106   Asia Affairs Division of Foreign Affairs Ministry, "Chinese Vice-premier Deng Xiaoping Visited Japan and the Relevant Comments (TS, Perpetual)", 30th October, 1978, pp. 19-20, Index No.04-1022-7, Diplomatic Records Office.
107   Reply to Kazunari Inoue's interpellation, at the meeting of Foreign Affairs Committee of the House of Representatives on 30 May, 1978, Retrieved from Congressional Record: http://kokkai.ndl.go.jp/SENTAKU/syugiin/087/0110/main.html.

such statements in the Congress plea: "Since the Treaty has been signed, it is expected to cooperate in oil exploitation.[108] The statement revealed the possibility of China-Japan co-exploitation. With regard to Japan's stance, Deng Xiaoping replied in his meeting with Parliament Member Zenko Suzuki that "we could co-exploit the oil without involving the sovereignty dispute."[109] The Asahi Shimbun on June 1st reported: "the LDP leader voiced at 31 May that "China and Japan should not argue who owned the Senkaku Islands but should discuss the oil development in Bohai Bay as soon as possible and begin the negotiation of the oil development near the Senkaku Islands'." It was also written in the report that "it is better to further promote Japan-China friendly relations in more realistic ways than dispute over the sovereignty....We noticed that the LDP leader paid more attention to the negotiation of co-developing than to the boundary issues."[110]

Besides, Foreign Minister Sunao Sonoda and Transport Minister Kinzi Moriyama spoke at the cabinet council on July 10 that "Sovereignty is another matter. It is hoped to promote the co-development of oil with China." Their words showed their intention of actively turning to co-develop the oil with China near the Senkaku Islands. After the cabinet council, Sonoda immediately instructed the relevant departments of Foreign Ministry to "formal talks with China"[111].

On the same day, Yomiuri Shimbun analyzed in an article on the evening paper: "two ministers' words intended to put aside the sovereignty dispute. It means that the Senkaku Islands could co-develop by China and Japan." The article further introduced the relevant background: "from the point of avoiding international disputes, China and Japan has agreed on shelving the Senkaku Islands dispute. Prime Minister Deng Xiaoping also proposed that 'leave the dispute solved by next generation'." Later, Japan, in order to cope with energy crisis, unofficially suggested China to co-develop the Senkaku Islands while discussing the co-development of Bohai Bay oilfield with China.[112] On that day, Asahi Shimbun commented that "previously, in order to suspend hostilities caused by the dispute, both countries took the measure of 'shelving the Senkaku

---

108   Reply to Haruo Kotan's interpellation, at the meeting of Foreign Affairs Committee of the Senator on August 18, 1978, Retrieved from Congressional Record: http://kokkai.ndl. go.jp/SENTAKU/sangiin/084/1110/main.html.

109   Asia Affairs Division of Foreign Affairs Ministry, "Chronology of China-Japan Co-developing the Oil Near the Senkaku Islands" "Speeches for Summit Meetings During Ōhira Masayoshi's Visit in China—Main Points and References for Replying Questions on China-Japan Disputes (TS. Perpetual)", December of 1979, p. 49, Index No. 052001201, Memorial Hall of Ōhira Masayoshi.

110   "LDP Leaders Stated that Co-developing the Oil Resources is More Sensible than Disputing for Sovereignty", Asahi Shimbun, 1st June of 1979.

111   "PM Sonoda Instructs to Co-develop the Oil Regardless of the Sovereignty", The evening paper of Yomiuri Shimbun, 10 July, 1979.

112   Ibid

Islands dispute' during the negotiation of the China-Japan Treaty of Peace and Friendship. However, a declaration aiming at limiting the oil import for a long time was issued at the Summit Meeting of Major Developed Countries (Tokyo Summit Meeting). To an energy importer country, like Japan the situation was extremely serious. After a thorough consideration, Japan figured that it is impossible to avoid co-developing forever, which manifested Japan's inclination to negotiate with China in terms of co-development.[113]

On 15th July, vice premier Li Xiannian received the press delegation headed by Tetsuo Hiraoka. In their meeting, premier Li expressed agreement with Japan that "Our Japanese friends proposed to co-develop the Senkaku Islands. We agreed the proposal and put aside the territory issue to first develop the resources"[114] On 15th August, PM Ōhira Masayoshi listened to the report from Foreign Affairs Secretary Mass Takajima about that "We will exchange views with China on the basic idea of maritime law in late of this month. We plan to take this as an opportunity to deliver our proposed policy with regard to the co-development of the oil near the Senkaku Islands."[115]

The PM gave his approval. Japan hereby "discussed marine law and other laws with China on 23th August and held an informal negotiation about the marine law with China on 8th and 9th of November."[116]

4. Conclusion

As the above records verified, firstly there is dispute over the Diaoyu Islands sovereignty between China and Japan; secondly the two governments both agreed "shelving the dispute"; thirdly the two countries have ever had the trend to co-develop the resources near the Diaoyu Islands, which is clear and undeniable. The Naoto Kan and Yoshihiko Noda governments made unilateral proposition and action, and then declared "at the time of normalization negotiation, China didn't claim the sovereignty", which upsets the truth and the history. What Japan has done will make it impossible to rationally solve the dispute.

China and Japan are "irremovable neighbors". For the 21st century, the Diaoyu Islands problem is a test of two countries' wisdom. The trade value between China and Japan has increased by 313 times, from the 1.1 billion USD in 1972 to the

---

113 "PM Declares Resource Policy: Emergency Consultation with China for Jointly Exploiting Oil Near the Senkaku Islands", The evening paper of Asahi Shimbun, 10 July, 1979.

114 "Li Xiannian Agrees to Put Aside the Sovereignty Dispute and Cooperate in Oil Developmet Near the Senkaku Islands", Asahi Shimbun, 16 July, 1979.

115 "PM Approves the Negotiation Scheme of the Senkaku Developing", Asahi Shimbun, 16th August of 1979.

116 Asia Affairs Division of Foreign Affairs Ministry, Asia Affairs Division of Foreign Affairs Ministry, "Chronology of China-Japan Co-developing the Oil Near the Senkaku Islands" "Speeches for Summit Meetings During Ōhira Masayoshi's Visit in China—Main Points and References for Replying Questions on China-Japan Disputes (TS. Perpetual)", December of 1979, p. 49, Index No. 052001201, Memorial Hall of Ōhira Masayoshi.

344.9 billion USD with. Besides, the personnel exchanges have grown 599 times, from 9046 times (persons) in 1972 to the 5.4 million times (persons) in 2011. Since 2007, Chinese Mainland (excluding Taiwan, Hong Kong and Macao) has successively became the largest trade partner of Japan for five years. In 2009, China, for the first time, surpassed the US to become Japan's largest export target.

In this context I would like to reanimate the spirits of "seeking common ground while reserving slight differences" advocated during the normalization negotiations. China-Japan relations are expected to obtain further improvement on the basis of "peaceful, friendly, and cooperative" approach.

XIV. The Textual Research on Sovereignty over the Diaoyu Islands by the Historians, Geographers and Jurists in the German-speaking Countries

November, 2012

Liang Zhijian

Editor's note: in order to understand the research on the Diaoyu Islands issue of scholars all over the world, German Research magazine of Shanghai Tongji University Institute of German Research published an article titled The Textual Research on Sovereignty over the Diaoyu Islands by the Historians, Geographers and Jurists such as Kelsen from the German-speaking Countries in 2012. The author is Liang Zhijian, Doctor in Law in Hohai University, Nanjing. He was graduated from Nanjing University (bachelor degree), German Administrative University (master's degree) and University of Vienna, Austria (PhD). After the author's permission, I changed the title into "The Textual Research on Sovereignty over the Diaoyu Islands by the Historians, Geographers and Jurists in the German-speaking Countries."

Abstract: On the basis of the research results of cartographers and scholars of Japanese Studies in the German-speaking region, this paper attempts to analyze the Diaoyu Islands issue from the perspective of jurists in the German-speaking region. The goal is to show the readers the academic contributions to the research on the Diaoyu Islands issue from these cartographers, scholars of Japanese Studies and jurists in the European German-speaking region. The conclusion is that the related facts mentioned by Japan in its "Basic View" have been denied by the research results in the German-speaking region. According to the opinion of Theory of Law in Vienna Circle represented by Kelsen, the Japanese Cabinet's decision on the Diaoyu Islands is illegal. Japan's claim that the "Senkaku Islands" were not ceded to Japan as the affiliated islands of Taiwan by virtue of Treaty of Shimonoseki is not true. The Article 3 of the Treaty of San Francisco is illegal.

1. Foreword

On December 15, 2010, the City Assembly of Ishigaki, Okinawa, Japan submitted a ordinance draft to the legislative assembly of the city, intending to set January 14, as the city's anniversary, "The Pioneering Day of the Senkaku Islands [China's Diaoyu Islands, the same below–editor]". Kyodo News Agency reported that the Cabinet decided on January 14, 1895, to have markers erected on the islands to officially incorporate them into Japan's territory. The aim of this ordinance was to shoe the international community that Senkaku Islands are historically the inherent territory of Japan, and expect to "inspire" domestic public opinions. On December 18, 2010, legislative assembly of Ishigaki passed the ordinance.

The first four paragraphs of Basic Views Concerning the Territorial Title of the Senkaku Islands released by Japanese Ministry of Foreign Affairs summarizes the process of Japan's procession of the sovereignty over the Diaoyu Islands. The Japanese government's subjective opinion is reflected in the five facts in the first three paragraphs.

1. The islands have no traces of the rule of (China's) Qing Dynasty; 2. the Cabinet decided on January 14, 1895, to officially incorporate them into Japan's territory; 3. Japan has treated the "Senkaku Islands" as a part of the Nansei Shoto (Southwest Islands) since January 14, 1895; 4. the "senkaku islands" were not ceded to Japan as the affiliated islands of Taiwan by virtue of Treaty of Shimonoseki which came into effect in May 1895; 5. Japan's "sovereignty" over the "Senkaku Islands" after its surrender in the Anti-Fascist war consisted of two sub facts in two stages.

The first sub fact in the first stage is the Treaty of San Francisco signed on September 8, 1951 and taking effect on April 28, 1952. Article 3 of the treaty incorporated the Senkaku Islands under the administration of the US as a part of Southwest Islands in the Daito Islands; the second one is the treaty concerning Ryukyu Islands and the Daito Islands signed by Japan and the United States on June 17, 1971. Treaty stipulates that the administrative right of the Senkaku Islands should be handed over to Japan.

Under the background that Japan told the world its fives claims through a variety of media, I think it is necessary to record the third party's opinion, especially including cartographers, scholars of Japanese Studies in the German-speaking region. This paper collected maps which reflect the ownership of the Diaoyu Islands drawn by related scholars in German-speaking region and their documents and records as well as related theories of scholars in Vienna Circle represented by Hans Kelsen. Based on these data, I analyze the ordinance of "The Pioneering Day of the Senkaku Islands" and the Basic Views Concerning the Territorial Title of the Senkaku Islands, which were used as facts to prove that the Diaoyu Islands belong to Japan.

After 30 years' of hard works of scholars around the world, the researches on the sovereignty over the Diaoyu Islands comes into a mature stage. We can now see several advanced papers, such as by Austrian cartographer Franz Anton Schrämbl, Philipp Franz von Siebold, the founder of of Japanese Studies in Europe, German scholar Philipp Franz von Siebold, some famous jurists in German-speaking region such as Johann Caspar Bluntschli, Hans Kelsen, Alfred Verdross and Paul Guggenheim, etc. But references given to their works about the Diaoyu Islands, by the domestic and international academic circles is rare. . Therefore, this attempt is beneficial to academic exchanges; at least it can extend the breadth of academic exchanges.

2. International norms of acquiring territory in 1895 and the ordinance of "The Pioneering Day of the Senkaku Islands"

2.1 European customary law of acquiring territory before the Berlin Congo Conference mentioned by jurists in the German-speaking region

As for European international law which contains principles of "discovery and possession", Johann Caspar Bluntschli believes that Europeans began to conduct this practice in the late 15th century: in the era of the Europeans' discovery and occupation of the overseas territories, people thought that the discovery of unknown territory was enough to claim the territorial sovereignty. He cites two examples: 1. in 1496, the fleets under the orders of British Empire discovered and ruled the North America; 2. Spain and Portugal found the South America and Central America and obtain the rights, the new world were distributed to the Spanish and the Portuguese by the Pope Alexander vi in 1493. "International Law" written by Ignaz Seidl-Hohenveldern in 1994 mentioned that the traditional international law in Europe fully developed into the International Law of the world in the 19th century; the European powers went out to discover the European colonies and brought their concept of international law to these places. While in the 19th century, Japan consciously gave up their own traditions, and turned to the European concept of international law. The books concerning International Law written by Peter Fischer and Heribert Franz Kock had the same wording as that of Ignaz Seidl-Hohenveldern: the original territorial occupation (discovery and possession) played a big role until the 19th century.

Bluntschli (1808-1881), the famous Swiss jurist and political scientist, has taught in Zurich, Munich and Heidelberg; he was one of the 11 founders of the world famous International Law Institute which was established in Belgium in September 1873. In 1875, he was the chairman of The Hague Conference of International Law Institute. Mr, Liang Qichao once translated the name "Johann Caspar Bluntschli" as "伯伦知理".

If we generalize the opinions of the four jurists of the German-speaking region—Johann Caspar Bluntschli, Ignaz Seidl-Hohenveldern, Peter Fischer, and Heribert Franz Köck, we can deduct that since as early as the late 15th century to the early 17th century, people gradually accepted the norms of international law, including the original territorial occupation (discovery and possession). As early as the end of the 19th century, namely, as early as 1899, norms of international law began to gradually faded away out of the scope of international communications; reason should be very simple, namely almost all the lands have been found. Since Japan has learned from the European international law when she adoped the legal system of Europe, Japan should obey the stipulations of the international law of Europe during her international communications. In the case of the Diaoyu Islands, Japan should show their learning result because Japan's study of European international law and the Japanese cabinet meeting involving the Diaoyu Island had occurred in the latter half of the 19th century. On January 14, 1895, the Cabinet decided to officially incorporate the islands into Japan's territory, which should conform to the principle of European international law—original territorial occupation (discovery and possession). If before January 14, 1895, no one had argued that Japan's claim regarding the Diaoyu Islands, was legal. contrarily it was seen as illegal. If the principle of European international law—original territorial occupation (discovery and possession) was replaced by the other principles, we should comply with other principles. Therefore, we can find out whether Japan's acquirement of the Diaoyu Islands conformed to the principles of European international law by virtue of the academic research results of jurists in German-speaking region. But this important question was avoided in the documents of the Japanese government.

2.2 The records of the Diaoyu Islands by historians, geographers in German-speaking region from the 18th century to the 20th century

In order to talk about whether Japan's annexation of the Diaoyu Islands on January 14, 1895 conformed to the principles of European international law, we should firstly refer to the maps and documents concerning the Diaoyu Islands before January 14, 1895 in German-speaking region which was the cradle of modern international law; then we compare them with the first fact of Basic Views Concerning the Territorial Title of the Senkaku Islands released by Japanese Ministry of Foreign Affairs: The islands have no traces of the rule of (China's) Qing Dynasty.

In 1800, Atlas map by Schrämb published by the famous Schallbach Press in the Austrian capital Vienna collected the maps published in 1786[117] which mentioned about the Diaoyu Islands. In this map, there is a line German—"Diese Inseln gehören dem König von Likeyo" (these islands belong to Ryukyu) which divided the Yaeyama Islands located in the southwest to Ryukyu from the Diaoyu Island and its affiliated islands of China. It indicates that the Yaeyama Islands south to this line belong to Ryukyu and the islands north to this line belong to China; these islands were marked with Haoyusu, Hoanoeysu, Tscheoey-su (the transliteration of the Diaoyu Island, Huangwei Yu, Chiwei Yu).

That is to say, as early as the 18th century, the cartographers in German-speaking region held that China had the sovereignty over the Diaoyu Islands according to the international law. Compared with the map drawn by Antoine Gaubil, the French missionaries in China based on the records of Xu Baoguang, the map drawn by Schrämb had a major progress that he marked the dividing line between the Diaoyu Islands and the Yaeyama Islands in German, which indicates that the Diaoyu Island and its affiliated islands belong to China rather than the Yaeyama Islands.

In 1843, the German Verlag (Press) Justus Perthes published a colored map entitled "Karte von China and Japan: den Manen d'Anville's und Klapproth's gewidmet". In this map, I. Tiaogu Su (the Diaoyu Island I. Is short for Island in German), I. Haopin Su (Huangwei Yu) and Chiwei Yu (because of its small size, it is marked as Fels which means rock) are mapped within the Chinese territory northwest to the dividing line between China and Ryukyu; their colors are different from that of Ryukyu.

German scholar Siebold enjoys a high reputation in Japan, Germany and even in Europe and the United States. He is the founder and a recognized authority of Japanese Studies. His greatest contribution is Japan Studies compiled by his son. In the 50 years after its publication, 60 kinds of newspapers in Netherlands, Germany, Austro-Hungarian Empire, Britain and the United States published the reviews of this famous book. In 1851, Siebold published an atlas map concerning East Asia, and Northeast Asia, including China and Japan at his own expense. The atlas map were drawn on the basis of original Japanese maps and astronomical observations. On page 5 of the Atlas map, the islands in the south of the Ryukyu Kingdom did not include the Diaoyu Islands. The maps in the book not only prove that the Diaoyu Islands do not belong to the Ryukyu Kingdom, but also are the written records which indirectly prove that the Diaoyu Islands belong to China.

---

117   The German Title of Atlas by Schrämb is the Allgemeiner Grosser Atlas, herausgegeben von F. A. Schrämbl, Wien: Phil. Jos. Schalbacher Verlag, 1800. The publication's information label on the bottom of the page involved Diaoyu Islands reads: MDCCLXXXVI Zu finden in eigenem Verlage in Wien" (published in 1786); this indicates that although the map published in 1800, the page involved Diaoyu Islands was first published in 1786, that is to say , Atlas by Schrämb reprinted 1786 edition of the maps of the Diaoyu Islands .

Another book of Siebold published in 1852 clearly marked the names of the Diaoyu Island and its affiliated islands – Tiaoyusu (the Diaoyu Island), Hoangoùcysu (Huangwei Yu), Tchehoeysu (Chiwei Yu) which used transliteration according to Chinese Southern dialect used by the French missionaries Gaubil in China; In the most right of the table, a column titled "hydrology comments" has the text introduction of the Diaoyu Island and its affiliated islands; the original Japanese map he saw did not mark the Diaoyu Islands; he just wanted to complete the table by adding the whole Diaoyu Island and its affiliated islands.

Siebold has an objective evaluation about Japan's and China's understanding of geography of Ryukyu: in 1609, the Japanese people began to know more about the northern and central Islands of Ryukyu after the invasion of Satsuma the vassal state of Japan. Since, the cause trade between Japan and Ryukyu were mainly done by the Satsuma. It was not very convenient for Japan to sail to Ryukyu, which is why until the end of the 18th century, Japan relatively lacked geographic information of Ryukyu. Besides, the map of Ryukyu in a Japanese book titled as "Sankon tsuran dsuki" were much worse than the map drawn by Xu Baoguang, the Chinese officials and scholars in 1719. In addition, Siebold mentioned China and Japan had known about Ryukyu since the 7th century, but not until in the early 18th century, they knew the detailed information about Ryukyu; People would like to thank the Chinese scholar Xu Baoguang for bringing these most notable information of Ryukyu. Gaubil and (Julius Klaproth) introduced the content with the highest scientific value in Xu Baoguang's records to European; at that time, there were few Japanese documents concerning Ryukyu's history and geography; the Japanese were satisfied with Xu Baoguang's map for a long time. It is worth noting that the Ryukyu's geographical knowledge recorded by Xu Baoguang were obtained by Siebold from Gaubil and were confirmed by the Japanese official map obtained by Siebold in 1826 from Takahasi Sakusaemon, the Japanese court's astronomy officer and astronomer.

Siebold conducted geographic information investigation and study in Japan for 9 years; the first hand results were recognized and used by the U.S. military. and references. As an illustration of Formal Adventure Report, the map of Japan drawn by Lieutenant W. L. Maury and Lieutenant Silas Bent in 1855 clearly mentioned in the attached note that this map is copied the map drawn by Siebold and had several small changes. In Formal Adventure Report, there was a map of Ryukyu which also did not mark the Diaoyu Islands, that is to say, the U.S. military has confirmed that the Diaoyu Islands are not part of the Ryukyu Kingdom's territory.

In 1900, 5 years after the signing of Treaty of Shimonoseki, the company Justus Perthes (founded in 1785), Germany's premier cartographic publisher, has published another map involving the Diaoyu Islands, titled "Asian Political and Military Map Reflecting the Wars between Contemporary China, Korea and Japan: attached caption was: Politics of East Asia from the Perspective of Military". The map title indicates that the map reflects changes in the territories due to wars among China, Japan and Korea till 1900. It not only reflects changes in the territories caused by Treaty of Shimonoseki, but also indicated that China's Taiwan including the Diaoyu Island and its affiliated islands were ceded to Japan according to Treaty of Shimonoseki. To be specific, Taiwan including the Diaoyu Island and its affiliated islands were mapped into Japan's territory; the Diaoyu Island and its affiliated islands were still clearly mapped in the northwest side of the dividing line of Riu Kiu (German of Ryukyu), which indicated that after the Sino-Japanese War, the Diaoyu Island and its affiliated islands still wasn't incorporated in the Ryukyu. This map title indicates that the Diaoyu Island and its affiliated islands were ceded to Japan as a part of Taiwan according to the stipulations of the Treaty of Shimonoseki. In 1953, 40 years after the signing Treaty of Shimonoseki, Columbus-Weltatlas (Columbus World Atlas) published by Columbus-Verlag GmbH (Columbus Press Ltd.) marked the Diaoyu Islands and other main islands (Huangwei Yu and Chiwei Yu) with "Riu-Kiu (Ger. Japanisch) oder Lu-Tschu (ins Chinesische.)" [Riu Kiu Islands (the transliteration of the Japanese name of Ryukyu or Lu–Tschu (the transliteration of the Chinese name of Ryukyu)]. The map mapped the Diaoyu Island, Huangwei Yu and Chiwei Yu into Taiwan northwest to the dividing line between Taiwan and Ryukyu.

In 1950, a year before the signing of the Treaty of San Francisco and 15 years after the publication of Columbus-Weltatlas (Columbus World Atlas) by Columbus-Verlag GmbH (Columbus Press Ltd.), it published the new version of Columbus World Atlas. In the map, the Diaoyu Island and its affiliated islands were mapped in Taiwan sea territories.

From the map of published by the company of Justus Perthes (founded in 1785), Germany's premier cartographic publisher. in 1900, and the maps published by Germany Columbus Press in 1935 and 1950, the atlas drawn by Schrämb in 1786 before the signing of Treaty of Shimonoseki in 1895 and the historical map titled The Map of China and Japan: by the contribution of Julius Klaproth, and the German cartographer Heinrich Karl Wilhelm Berghaus had this map was also published by by the company of Justus Perthes in 1843[118].

In this map we can find that the first fact of the Japanese government— the islands have no traces of the rule of (China's) Qing Dynasty and the third fact—Japan has treated the "Senkaku Islands" as a part of the Nansei Shoto (Southwest Islands) since January 14th, 1895 was untenable.

---

118   The 1843 map's depiction of China was based on Julius Klaproth's ground-breaking Carte de la Chine (Paris, 1842). Julius Klaproth (1783-1835) was a Prussian diplomat, adventurer, cartographer and linguist, who was one of the most intelligent and culturally sensitive Westerners to visit many parts of Asia during his era.

The reason is very simple, because the atlas map drawn by Schrämb in 1786 and the map of published by the company of Justus Perthes (founded in 1785), Germany's premier cartographic publisher in 1843 marks the Diaoyu Islands into China's territory. This is one of the evidence to prove China has the sovereignty over the Diaoyu Islands and it is internationally recognized. It proves that the Diaoyu Islands have traces of the rule of China's Qing Dynasty; the map of published by the company of Justus Perthes in 1900 and the maps published by German Columbus Press in 1935 and 1950 didn't change the name of the Diaoyu Islands into the Senkaku Islands and the name of Ryukyu into Southwest Islands as mentioned in Basic Views Concerning the Territorial Title of the Senkaku Islands released by Japanese Ministry of Foreign Affairs. Moreover, the Diaoyu Islands wasn't included or mapped into Ryukyu in those maps. These five maps published in German-speaking region are undoubtedly the evidence with authenticity from the third party to deny the first and the third subjective opinions of the Japanese government.

We can conclude from Siebold's literature that: Siebold obtained the knowledge of the Diaoyu Islands from the French Jesuit missioner ar Antoine Gaubil and the Chinese official Xu Baoguang; from another perspective, the fact that the Diaoyu Islands were first discovered, named and exploited by the Chinese people and were China's territory based on the effective law at that time was well as those records of Xu Baoguang were confirmed by Siebold's research in Japan for nine years. Moreover, Siebold obtained the Japanese official maps of Ryukyu from those Japanese court astronomers; likewise, those Japanese court astronomers were likely to gain geographic information of the Diaoyu Islands from Siebold. Besides, Philipp Franz von Siebold as the consultant of shogunate, it was of high possibility that he would provided geographic information for Japan's shogunate. After scholars such as Gaubil and Schrämb, the documents left by Siebold also can be the seen as evidence produced by a third party to confirm that China discovered the Diaoyu Islands and achieved the sovereignty of the Diaoyu Island legally. What's more, we are also aware that during Siebold's stay in Japan, the Japanese government might not know the specific location of the Diaoyu Islands, but the Japanese government did know that the territory of the Ryukyu Kingdom didn't include the Diaoyu Islands.

3. Berlin Conference and related dissertations by the jurists of the German-speaking countries

Before I quote the records of Kelsen[119], Alfred Verdross[120] and Paul Guggenheim[121], I will briefly review the Congo Conference (namely General Act of the Berlin Conference). Berlin Conference was held from November 15th, 1884 to February 26th, 1885 in Berlin, Germany. Except for Switzerland and Greece, all major European countries attended this conference. The US has joined in a diplomatic conference together with the European powers for the first time in history. The Article 3 of the General Act stipulated the rules of further occupation of the coasts of West Africa and Congo River Basin for the European powers.

In 1937, Alfred Verdross, the important person of Vienna Circle in German-speaking areas mentioned about the Congo Conference (namely General Act of the Berlin Conference) in a book concerning international law and the acquisition and loss of territories: on February 26th, 1885, Article 34 and Article 35 of General Act of the Berlin Conference stipulated that the occupying power shall have the obligation to inform other countries of the occupation; the purpose was to make other countries able to put forward their protest when necessary. On September 10th, 1919, Treaty of Saint-Germain-en-Lay has repealed this provision. In 1948, Paul Guggenheim combined the Pure Theory of Law of Hans Kelsen with General Act of the Berlin Conference, and drew the same conclusion as that of Alfred Verdross.

---

119   Hans Kelsen (1881-1973) was a professor at the University of Vienna, Austria, Director of School of Law, the Austrian part-time administrative court judge, a professor at the University of Cologne, Germany, the head of the department. He suffered persecution because of his Jewish race during his work in the University of Cologne. Afterwards, he worked in Geneva International Institute of Higher Education, Switzerland, and German University in Prague. His representative masterpiece is Pure Theory of Law and won 3 titles of Emeritus Professor. He obtained 12 honorary doctorate in Holland, the US, Germany, Austria, France, Spain and Mexico. In 1940, Hans Kelsen moved to the United States, and taught in Harvard Law School; in 1945, he became the professor in Department of Political Science at University of California, Berkeley and got American citizenship; he retired in 1951. Hans Kelsen had a significant influence in the fields such as philosophy, constitutional law and international law in the world. He proposed the Pure Theory of Law which provide the scientific law epistemology with frameworks with originality. His theory becomes the thought heights for contemporary legal positivism study and makes great contributions to the development of legal thoughts in the world.

120   Alfred Verdross (1890-1980) together with Kelsen and Adolf Merkl played an active role in the Vienna School of Legal Theory which also greatly influenced today's legal thoughts. Alfred Verdross is a famous scholar of International Law. In 1961, he was the President of Salzburg Conference of Institut of International Law; 1957-1966, he was a member of the United Nations International Law Commission; 1958-1977, he served as a judge of the European Court of Human Rights; 1959-1961, he was the President of Society of International Law.

121   Guggenheim (1899-1977) is a Swiss international law scholar, a former judge in International Court of Justice.

In March 1952, four years after Paul Guggenheim mentioned about General Act of the Berlin Conference, Hans Kelsen mentioned about Article 3 of the Treaty of San Francisco in his book Principles of International Law. Hans Kelsen was the only jurist in German-speaking region to mention about Article 3 of the Treaty of San Francisco before it came into effect on April 28th, 1952. Hans Kelsen wrote: "the islands ruled by Japan will be put under the trusteeship of the United States. We assume after the dissolution of the League of Nations (which means the end of trusteeship), the trusteeship countries and US should extend their sovereignty to related territories after Japan's surrender, this is in accord with the international law. Without this premise, the trusteeship countries and US have no right to deal with these territories.[122]

Most importantly, he added a footnote between the last two sentences— "Japan will concur in any proposal of the United States to the United Nations to place under its trusteeship system, with the United States as the sole administering authority, Nansei Shoto south of 29 degrees, north latitude (including the Ryukyu Islands and the Daito Islands), Nanpo Shoto south of Sofu Gan (including the Bonin Islands, Rosario Island and the Volcano Islands) and Parece Vela and Marcus Island. Pending the making of such a proposal and affirmative action thereon, the United States will have the right to exercise all and any powers of administration, legislation and jurisdiction over the territory and inhabitants of these islands, including their territorial waters."

We can treat this footnote as a hint from Hans Kelsen . He mentioned in this text that there is a clear premise for the legitimacy of the relevant territorial arrangement after the victory of the Anti-Fascist War; that is the US should extend its sovereignty to related territories after Japan's surrender. Without this premise, Japan and the US have no right to deal with these territories. This premise is also applicable to the involved territory in Article 3 of the Treaty of San Francisco. That is to say, there is only one relevant premise pointed out by Hans Kelsen, which is Japan and the US should extend their sovereignty to related territories after Japan's surrender. Without this premise, Japan and the US have no right to deal with these territories.

We can interpret Hans Kelsen's direct quotation of Article 3 of the Treaty of San Francisco as: the legitimacy of the US trusteeship of the Ryukyu Islands and the Nansei Shoto of the Daito Islands depends on whether Japan and the US extended their sovereignty to related territories after Japan's surrender; otherwise, Japan and the US have no right to deal with these territories. The fact is that the surrendered Japan didn't extend its sovereignty to Nansei Shoto, let alone the Diaoyu Island and its affiliated islands which don't belong to the Ryukyu Islands. Similarly, the United States neither extended its sovereignty to Nansei Shoto nor extended its sovereignty to China's Diaoyu Island and its

---

122   See Kelsen, "Principles of International Law," translated by Wang Tieya, Huaxia Press, 1989 , pp. 138-139

affiliated islands. His deduction of Article 3 is the process is unlawful as Japan and the US have no right to deal with these territories. This is the reason why Hans Kelsen treated the Diaoyu Islands as a disputed land

Hans Kelsen's theory of specification can also be used to analyze Japan's opinion that the Diaoyu Islands were not ceded to Japan as a part of Taiwan according to Treaty of Shimonoseki. Hans Kelsen mentioned in his book "General Theory of Specification" that when two logically contradictory statements occurred, one of the statements is not true from the start."[123]

China maintains that the Diaoyu Islands were ceded to Japan as a part of Taiwan according to Treaty of Shimonoseki. While Japan holds that the Diaoyu Islands were not ceded to Japan as a part of Taiwan according to Treaty of Shimonoseki, they were officially "incorporate" them into Japan's territory by the Japanaese Cabinet's decision on January 14, 1895. Given the existence of the "Congo Conference" as the empirical method, the Cabinet's decision on January 14, 1895 was illegal, so in Basic Views Concerning the Territorial Title of the Senkaku Islands, the claim that the Diaoyu Islands were not ceded to Japan as a part of Taiwan according to Treaty of Shimonoseki lost its legality. Based on the related maps and documents in the German-speaking region and the fact that there is no other treaty that ceded the Diaoyu Island and its affiliated islands to Japan, we can draw the only conclusion that: the Diaoyu Islands were ceded to Japan as a part of Taiwan according to Treaty of Shimonoseki; to put it in another way, from the perspective of the Hans Kelsen's Pure Theory of Law, the Diaoyu Islands were ceded to Japan as a part of Taiwan according to Treaty of Shimonoseki, so Japan should return them to China according to the Potsdam Declaration and Armistice Edict of Japanese Emperor Hirohito announced on August 15, of 1945. Therefore, according to Hans Kelsen's point of view, "Japan makes two logically contradictory statements concerning whether the Diaoyu Islands were ceded to Japan as a part of Taiwan according to Treaty of Shimonoseki or not, thus apparently Japan's statement is contradictory from the beginning.

4. Conclusion

We can find that the first fact of the Japanese government—the islands have no traces of the rule of (China's) Qing Dynasty and the third fact—Japan has treated the "Senkaku Islands" as a part of the Nansei Shoto (Southwest Islands) since January 14, 1895 were denied by the historical and geographical literature in German-speaking regions. And, from the perspective of Pure Theory of Law of Vienna Circle, the second fact that the Japanese Cabinet decided on January 14, 1895, to officially incorporate them into Japan's territory is illegal.

---

[123] Hans Kelsen, Allgemeine Theorie der Normen, Wien: Manzsche Verlag und Universitätsbuchhandlung, 1979, S.101.

The fourth fact is that the "Senkaku islands" were not ceded to Japan as the affiliated islands of Taiwan by virtue of Treaty of Shimonoseki which came into effect in May 1895 is untrue. The first sub-fact in the fifth fact that the Treaty of San Francisco signed on September 8, 1951 which took effect on April 28th, 1952. Article 3 of the treaty incorporated the Senkaku Islands under the administration of the US as a part of Southwest Islands in the Daito Islands was deducted as illegal by Kelsen's thesis. Although jurists in Vienna Circle in German-speaking region represented by Hans Kelsen haven't talked much about the Diaoyu Islands, their analyses of the legality of related national behaviors are very insightful and incisive. For example, they have analyzed the two key points in the formation of the Diaoyu Islands dispute—the Japanese cabinet meetings on January 14, 1895 and the Treaty of San Francisco signed on September 8, 1950. Their researches objectively help the deepening of the research on the Diaoyu Islands issue.

Through a brief review of the above, we can conclude that the geographic information of the Diaoyu Islands recorded in Records of Messages from Chong-shan (Zhong Shan Chuan Xin Lu) written by Xu Baoguang in early 18th century was spread to Europe by Gaubil and Klaproth and then was spread to North America by Siebold . This paper cited a lot knowledge of the Diaoyu Island and its affiliated islands from scholars in German-speaking region and used them as the evidences produced by a third party. That is to say, the claim of China and its supporting argument that the Diaoyu Island and its affiliated islets a (except for the 50 years from1895 to 1945 when Treaty of Shimonoseki was effective) have been China's territory since ancient times is confirmed by the evidence from a third party. These information are the evidence to prove China should have sovereign rights over the Diaoyu Islands based on the international law.

In history, Japan has not only studied and adopted the Chinese law system but also the European law system, including the international law. The famous American jurist Prof. Qiu Hongda cited some Japanese literature which mentioned that as early as 1862, Japan began to send students to Europe to study the international law, so at the time (after the second half of the 19th century), Japan should have some scholars who were proficient in Western languages and mastered the concepts and terminology of international law. While China began sending students abroad to study international law after 1872. So from 1862 to 1885, during the 23 years after Berlin Conference, Japan should have fostered a lot of international law scholars and experts proficient in German, English, French. Japan should be aware of the new norms of international law for acquisition of new territories recognized by almost all continental European powers in the Berlin Conference in 1885. If so, on January 14, 1895, 10 years after the General Act of the Berlin Conference came into effect, as a nation which has entered the European Law System, Japan should faithfully perform the obligations stipulated in the General Act of the Berlin Conference in order to meet the premise condition of legal acquisition of a new territory; that is to say, if Japan intended to obtain the islands along the China's coast as Japanese territory, it should notify the Chinese government about its occupation.

According to the research achievements of Inoue Kiyoshi, the famous Japanese scholar, the Japanese government didn't notify the Chinese government about its annexation. Even if the means of communication were backward in those days more than 100 years ago, Japan has failed to notify the Chinese government about its occupation (telegraph services business had already opened between China and Japan at that time), but Japan could tell China about this matter directly in negotiations during the Treaty of Shimonoseki two month after Japanese cabinet meeting on January 14, 1895, if Japan was willing to faithfully perform the obligations stipulated in the General Act of the Berlin Conference. However, Japan did not reveal the related documents concerning the cabinet meeting on January 14, 1895 as a historical archives public until March 1952. Even if Japan did not learn the new norms of international law for acquisition of new territories released by almost all continental European powers in Berlin Conference and was unfamiliar with Hans Kelsen's evaluation of Article 3 of the Treaty of San Francisco, it is never too late for Japan to make up for the missed lesson. The scholars of Germanic Studies in the two countries and scholars in German-speaking region should also take this opportunity to jointly study and communicate with each other.

If we consider the deficit of cultural communication between Asia and Europe, between East Asia and the German-speaking region, we can see that it is by no means a glorious and "pioneering" act by the Ishigaki City of Japan, to surmount this problem. This evaluation is in accordance with the view on norms and values in Hans Kelsen's Pure Theory of Law. That is to say, if one's act doesn't conform to the objective and effective norm, when this act was conducted, this act will be judged as a bad act; so it can provide another kind of "enlightenment" for public opinion. As for those people living in China, Japan or other parts of the world who are unfamiliar with the history of general cultural exchanges between the East and West including the history of international law, I think they should seriously review and learn about this history; they can review those maps in German-speaking region, read about Japan written by Siebold in German and Pure Theory of Law written by Hans Kelsen and other relevant international law works.

Such serious review and understanding is meaningful for the studies and exchanges of Generalized Germanic Studies; I hope they can draw the common and objective conclusion about the sovereignty over the Diaoyu Islands which is also in accord with international law. I don't know to what degree this wish will be realized, but this effort is a reflection of cultural exchanges between China, Japan, and German-speaking region. Furthermore, cultural exchanges between peoples and countries should be one of the important paths to achieve harmony and common prosperity.

Before the end of this article, I want to recall the goodwill statement made by the son of Siebold for the people of Japan who just entered European Law System 112 years ago: "I hope the expectations adjacent to the new era can be achieved. First of all, I wish the Japanese people will never forget that entering into the European Law System not only brings rights, but also brings obligations."

(Originally published in German Research, Section 3, 2012, pp. 62-79, some parts of the article was omitted - editor)

XV. Japan's Misunderstanding on the "Senkaku Islands" Issue

November, 2012

Ukeru Magosaki

Editor's note: Ukeru Magosaki, Former Director of International Intelligence Agency of the Japanese Ministry of Foreign Affairs, published an article "Sekai" (World) magazine in November 2012.

He held that Japan has some misunderstanding on the Diaoyu Islands Issue, which lead to the intensified territorial dispute between China and Japan. Japan should reflect upon its own misunderstanding. According to this article, the Diaoyu Island issue has become increasingly serious. On September 11, the Japanese government decided to spend 2.05 billion yens from its fiscal reserve funds of 2012 for the "nationalization" of the Diaoyu Islands. In response, the Chinese government took strong countermeasures. The situation may be worse and worse.

"Senkaku Islands (Diaoyu Islands in Chinese, the same below–editor) issue are becoming more serious. On September 14, six ocean surveillance ships called "Patrol" of the State Oceanic Administration People's Republic of China's entered into the Japanese territorial waters surrounding the "Senkaku Islands" in succession.

These recent events caught the attention of Shintaro Ishihara, Governor of Tokyo Prefecture. On April 16, 2012, Ishihara, Governor of Tokyo Prefecture addressed in his lecture in the US: "we have been negotiating about using the budget of Tokyo Prefecture to purchase "Senkaku Islands". Afterwards, he called for the Japanese to donate money in order to purchase the "Senkaku Islands".

301 On September 11, the Japanese government decided to spend 2.05 billion yen from its fiscal reserve funds of 2012 for the "purchase" of the "Senkaku Islands". In response, the Chinese government demonstrated a solemn opposition and initiated strong countermeasures. Below the readers can read an important article published in the "the World"—a famous Japanese monthly.

"Is There No Territorial Dispute" over the "Senkaku Islands"

How to view these events?

The key point of the "Senkaku Islands" issue is to choose from the following two cases:

1. The "Senkaku Islands" are inherent territory of Japan, there is no territorial dispute; accordingly, Japan should further consolidate its sovereignty over the Senkaku Islands and take the position applicable for Domestic Law.

2. There is a territorial dispute over "Senkaku Islands" between Japan and China and the two countries should seek for methods to solve this dispute so as to avoid conflicts. I tend to choose the latter.

Japan's territorial issues are closely related to the "postwar problems" we are dealing with after Japan's defeat in the Second World War. On August 14th, 1945, Japan sent a telegraph to the relevant embassies, in which Japan told the United States, Britain, the Soviet Union and China that "Emperor of Japan issued imperial edict that Japan accepts the terms of the Potsdam Declaration". To accept the Potsdam Declaration is the starting point of Japan in the postwar era.

Article 8 of the Potsdam Declaration stipulates: "The terms of the Cairo Declaration shall be carried out and Japanese sovereignty shall be limited to the islands of Honshu, Hokkaido, Kyushu, Shikoku and such minor islands as we determine." While the mentioned Cairo declaration elaborates: "that all the territories Japan has stolen from the Chinese, such as Manchuria, Formosa, and The Pescadores, shall be restored to the Republic of China."

Japan, on the other hand, argues that the process of "Senkaku Islands" being Japan's territory is as follows:

"Since 1885, the Japanese government, through repeated on-site investigations by the authorities of Okinawa Prefecture and other channels, has cautiously confirmed that the Senkaku Islands are not only no-man's islands but also have no traces of the rule of (China's) Qing Dynasty. On this basis, the Cabinet decided on January 14th, 1895, to have markers erected on the islands to officially incorporate them into Japan's territory." (Ministry of Foreign Affairs—Senkaku Islands Q and A)

What's the opinion of China? In 1996, the Section 34 of Beijing Weekly once mentioned: The Diaoyu Islands were first discovered by China and were incorporated into China's territory, since the 16th century, Chinese literature has recorded the Diaoyu Islands". In 1561, an Illustrated Compendium on Maritime Security (Chou Hai Tu Bian) compiled by Hu Zongxian, the supreme commander of the southeast coastal defense of the Ming court, incorporated the Diaoyu Islands into the jurisdiction of the coastal defense of the Ming court.

So we can see that China holds that it has already had the sovereignty over the Diaoyu Islands, so China thinks that the Diaoyu Islands are the territories which Japan has stolen from China . Then we will talk about "the Treaty of San Francisco". On the issue of the "Senkaku Islands", the Treaty of San Francisco stipulates: "Japan renounces all rights, title and claim to Formosa (Taiwan) and the Pescadores (Penghu Islands)." So we wonder whether the "Senkaku Islands" belong to Taiwan or Okinawa?

China has not signed the Treaty of San Francisco. However, we can see the China's talk about the Treaty of San Francisco. On August 15th, 1951, Chinese Foreign Minister Zhou Enlai issued a statement which mentioned about Cairo Declaration, Potsdam Declaration and Yalta Declaration.

What's the opinion of Allies, or the United States? Many Japanese people do not realize that the US does not take a position on the sovereignty of the Senkaku Islands. In this case, the choice that "the "Senkaku Islands" are inherent territory of Japan, there is no territorial dispute" is inappropriate when we consider the international arena.

How to deal with this "dispute"?

The starting point to solve the issue of "Senkaku Islands" should be based on the fact that there is territorial dispute over the Senkaku Islands between Japan and China.

How to deal with this "dispute"?

I think that on the territorial issues, we should consider the following nine aspects:

1. Wee should know China's positions and know the objective composition in our views and China's views so as to avoid unnecessary friction. Most Japanese people don't know and understand China's views regarding the "Senkaku Islands".

2. We should take concrete measures to prevent territorial conflicts. We can refer to the methods adopted by China and ASEAN countries regarding the Spratly Islands. On November 4, 2002, China and ASEAN countries signed Declaration on the Code of Conduct on the South China Sea which mentioned: "The Parties concerned undertake to resolve their territorial and jurisdictional disputes by peaceful means, without resorting to the threat or use of force; The Parties undertake to exercise self-restraint in the conduct of activities that

would complicate or escalate disputes and affect peace and stability including, among others, refraining from action of inhabiting on the presently uninhabited islands, reefs, shoals, cays, and other features and to handle their differences in a constructive manner." It is very important that "the Parties undertake to exercise self-restraint in the conduct of activities that would complicate or escalate disputes and affect peace and stability".

3. We can resort to the International Court of Justice and other means. We should invite a third party to involve in the solving process.

4. We should establish close and multi-level interdependent relationships. Today, no one would imagine that France and Germany would fight against each other because EU countries have established close and multi-level interdependent relationships

5. We can adopt the principles of the UN. The fourth terms of Article 2 of the UN charter stipulates: "All Members shall refrain in their international relations from the threat or use of force against the territorial integrity or political independence of any state, or in any other manner inconsistent with the Purposes of the United Nations."

6. We should all not use military force as a common principle between Japan and China, and we should mention this principle frequently so as to build the atmosphere that we obey this principle with each other. After we signed China-Japan Joint Statement in 1972, we established China-Japan Treaty of Peace and Friendship in 1978, the first Article of which stipulates: "The Contracting Parties affirm that in their mutual relations, all disputes shall be settled by peaceful means without resorting to the use or threat of force."

7. We can shelve this dispute if this generation cannot solve it, meanwhile, we should not resort to force to solve this dispute during the shelving period.

8. We should build a preventive mechanism for engineering in the disputed territories where conflicts may occur. Activities around the disputed territories could be a prelude to a territorial dispute. For example, fishing activities always trigger disputes, so the fishery agreements signed between Japan and the neighboring countries will not only help to negotiate the fishing problems, but also has important significance in ensuring mutual security.

9. When a possible conflict appeared, we should divide it into its several components and find out solutions for each respectively.

The US joining in a possible war

On the issue of the "Senkaku Islands", in 1972, Premier Zhou Enlai and Prime Minister Kakuei Tanaka reached the consensus as "shelving this dispute", so did Vice-Premier Deng Xiaoping and Foreign Minister Sunao Sonoda in 1978.

At present, the Japanese government's position is: "shelving this dispute" is a unilateral wording by China which favors its interests, Japan has never recognized it." Japan is distorting history. Regardless of whether Japan had said any word – which "support the shelving", from the replies of Prime Minister Kakuei Tanaka and Foreign Minister Sunao Sonoda, we can see that they did reach this consensus. The most important point is that the "shelving" is extremely beneficial for Japan. Its reasons are as follows: 1. Japan's jurisdiction is admitted; 2. no military power is needed to change the status quo; 3. Japan can continue its effective control.

On the issue of "shelving", there are some wrong interpretations. For example, some people think that: "in recent years, China's claim of sovereignty over 'the Senkaku Islands' means that China gave up the "shelving the dispute" policy." However, "shelving the dispute" is based on the premise that both countries claim sovereignty over the Senkaku Islands. If both sides claim sovereignty and continue to ignore others claim, it may develop into a military conflict, thus both sides put forward the "shelving the dispute" policy. If both sides claim sovereignty, eventually it may lead to a situation that the issue has to be solved by military force. In the long run, Japan's military force will not be superior.

According to the annual report on China's military in 2011 issued by the United States Department of Defense, China has a total of 1680 Chinese fighter jets, 330 of which are deployed against Taiwan region where the "Senkaku Islands" are also located. In addition, in February 2011, Robert Gates, the US Secretary of Defense, said in his testimony to the US Senate's Armed Services Committee: "in 2025, China will deploy 200 next-generation fighters with stealth performance". If Japan can't develop its ensure air forces, Japan cannot ensure military superiority.

In addition, on November 4th, 2010, the Washington Times published an article titled Chinese Long Range Missiles Can Destroy US Military Bases, which mentioned: "China can destroy U.S. military bases in Japan with 80 medium-range ballistic missiles and 350 Cruise class missiles."

In a possible confrontation with the United States, China can attack the U.S. military bases in Japan with missiles to destroy the runway and command and control facilities. The missile attack can paralyze these bases in seconds.

Even if US has more aircraft forces, but if these bases are paralyzed, none of these jets can play a role. Therefore, it is not easy for the US to take part in a war concerning the "Senkaku Islands".

Here, I also want to demonstrate the US joining in a possible war from the view of treaties.

Article 5 of the Japan US Security Treaty stipulates: Each Party Recognizes that an armed attack against either Party in the territories under the administration of Japan would be a threat to its own peace and safety and declares that it would act accordingly meet the common threat in accordance with its constitutional provisions and processes. "Senkaku Islands" are under the administration of Japan, so they are the object of Article 5. But there is a strategy and controversy embedded in this treaty.

According to the Japan-US Security Treaty, Japan should defend the invasion of its islands on its own. When China attacks "Senkaku Islands", Japanese Self-Defense Forces should perform defensive duties while the US forces won't take part in the war. It's the best option that Self-Defense Forces of Japan can successfully safeguard the "Senkaku Islands", otherwise, the "Senkaku Islands" will be put under China's jurisdiction. In this case, the "Senkaku Islands" will no longer be the object of Japan US Security Treat. This problem is very complicated.

Military means is not a good choice for Japan to defend the "Senkaku Islands" issue. Therefore, Japan should comply with the consensus on "shelving the dispute", which is beneficial to Japan's national interests. To solve the dispute of "Senkaku Islands", Japan should firstly realize the benefits of shelving the dispute, and take measures to support this policy as soon as possible.

Why does the US choose "the third option - the 'Pacific Marine Balance' strategy"?

Finally, we will talk about why "Senkaku Islands" dispute has appeared at this time? It is a good news for the US military officials that the "Senkaku Islands" issue has caused military tensions. Ironically, it was Kevin Maher, former director of the State Department's Office of Japan Affairs who has revealed this view. In the October issue of "National Interest", Maher said: "in order to deal with the threat of China, Japan must take various measures to...... to be specific, in order to gain superiority regarding the air forces, Japan needs to accelerate the implementation and expand purchase plan of the F-35 stealth fighters, and to increase the number of the Aegis equipped warships as well as the development of a missile defense system capable of shooting down intermediate-range ballistic missiles.. Moreover, he also said Japan should expedite plans to build military bases on the Sakishima island chain and on the country's western-most isle of Yonaguni, both part of Okinawa. The Defense Ministry has earmarked ¥6.2 billion in its fiscal 2013 budget request to construct a base on Yonaguni and enhance its defenses, and is also considering building military installations in the Sakishimas. Japan needs to construct self-defense force bases on Miyako Islands to improve the reconnaissance ability of the Coast guard forces, and their detection capabilities etc... when these are achieved, Japan does not need to worry about the Senkaku Islands."

The passage above shows that US military officials make full use of the "Senkaku Islands" dispute in order to sell their weapons to Japan.

At present, faced with China's rise , the United States is re-adjusting its strategy of East Asia. For the US, there are four options: 1. It can attach great importance to the traditional ties between Japan and the US; 2. It can coordinate and cooperate with China according to a global vision; 3. It can take the "Pacific Marine Balance" strategy (using Japan to balance against China); 4.let relevant countries free so that they can establish an international mechanism.

It can be seen that the US policy towards China is a combination of the second and the third option. Here the concept of "Pacific Marine Balance" is not just limited to East Asia.

The so-called "Pacific Marine Balance" refers to those "great powers using their alliances to fight against their enemy countries so as to constrain them". In this way, great powers can be able to maintain their influence without using their own armies.

Historically, the British Empire took full advantage of this policy against the continental European countries. In the 1930s, the United States provided weapons for Britain and other countries, in the early period World War II, the United States did not directly send troops for the war, but indirectly helped the UK who fought against Nazi Germany in the war. The US became a military factory for Democracy, which was also a strategy of "Marine Balance". Today, some Americans put forward the policy of "Marine Balance" in the East Asia. That is to say, faced with the rising China, the United States will not take part in the war, instead, it will support Japan and make Japan fight for the US interests.

If Japan accepts that the effect of "Marine Balance" strategy serves its interests, Japan will make itself China's enemy, which means it is necessary for Japan to conduct military deployment more actively. The "Senkaku Islands" issue is quite suitable for this excuse. Therefore, it is not accidental that those who intend to promote the Japan-US relationships, are keen to issue tough remarks.

(Originally published in Japan Sekai (World) Monthly in November 2012, the author has served as the former head of the Foreign Ministry's Intelligence and Analysis Bureau.)

XVI. Shelving the Diaoyu Islands Dispute Is Advantageous for Japan

July, 2012

Ukeru Magosaki

Editor's note: Ukeru Magosaki, the former head of the Foreign Ministry's Intelligence and Analysis Bureau, published an article in Japan's Asahi Shimbun (comments edition, July 15, 2012), saying that shelving the "Senkaku Islands (the Diaoyu Island and its affiliated islands) dispute is advantageous for Japan".The main contents of Ukeru Magosaki's article includes the following themes:

We should admit there is a territorial dispute over the Senkaku Islands

Ukeru Magosaki: Japan should realize that there is territorial dispute over the Senkaku Islands. I didn't say Japan should make concessions. I just think that Japan should take actions when the situation is advantageous to Japan.

Japan's position is based on the matter that the Cabinet decided on January 14, 1895, to officially incorporate the Senkaku Islands into Japan's territory. Japan holds that the Senkaku Islands are Japan's "inherent territory", but we cannot use "inherent territory" to indicate the territory we only owned for several decades.

On the other hand, China addressed that since the 14th century, the Senkaku Islands have been put under the jurisdiction of China's naval defense. China claims the Senkaku Islands belong to Taiwan and Taiwan belongs to China, thus the Senkaku Islands are China's territory. Because of the Treaty of San Francisco signed in 1951, Japan gave up the sovereignty over Kuril islands and Taiwan. Therefore, we can never say China's claim is unfounded.

Although it is hard for the Japanese to accept, we should firstly admit the Senkaku Islands are not "inherent territory" of Japan, they are "controversial" territory.

In this context, let's take a look at how Japan and China treat this issue.

When the normalization of diplomatic relations between China and Japan was realized in 1972, Prime Minister Kakuei Tanaka hold talks with Premier Zhou Enlai; the two sides decided to "seek common points while reserving difference". In 1978, when negotiating China-Japan Treaty of Peace and Friendship, Vice-Premier Deng Xiaoping commented on the issue of Diaoyu Islands: "It is okay to temporarily shelve such an issue if our generation does not have enough wisdom to resolve it. The next generation will have more wisdom." "Shelving" all kinds of disputes will do good to the friendship between the two countries.

That is to say, the Chinese side actual acquiesces in the effective control of Japan, and suggests that we don't have to resort to force to solve the problem. Shelving the "Senkaku Islands" dispute is advantageous to Japan.

Resources issue is another matter

Japan collided with Chinese fishing boats in 2010 when the Senkaku Islands began to receive attention. I think it is wrong to use Japan's domestic law to deal with this incident. Japan should have driven away those Chinese fishing boats in accordance with the bilateral Fishery Agreement, leaving the punishment rights to China. It is the same with sea resources. As resources are easily linked with territorial disputes, so we should deal with them separately is the wisdom of the international community.

Unfortunately, both the Japanese politicians and citizens believe that it is the right choice to adopt tough attitudes towards China. But, diplomacy which just aims to please public opinions would damage the interests of the state. If Japan is tough, China also has to be tough. If developed into a military conflict, the power of China's self-defense forces has overwhelming advantage. Japan may face complete failure.

It is naive thought that the United States would defend Japan according to the Treaty of San Francisco. The United States has no chance to win If it fought against China in the far east which has no topographic advantages. Will the United States declare total war just for Japan? In addition, the US is always cautious of Japan getting close to China who has already become a superpower. Although the United States takes a "neutral" position on the Senkaku Islands issue, to the United States, it is not a bad thing that between Japan and China keep moderate strained relations.

Japan's claim is not recognized internationally, because the common sense of the international community is not to escalate territorial disputes. Japan is bound to be isolated by the international community if it uses the domestic theories to challenge China.

The present situation of the Senkaku Islands issue is unfavorable for Japan. Shelving the dispute is not to give the impression of weakness, which should be rationally recognized by Japanese politicians and citizens.

(Originally published in in "Asahi Shimbun", July 15, 2012.)

Interview given by Magosaki Ukeru to the Reporter of "Global Times": The US Troops in Japan Can't Safeguard the Diaoyu Islands

On July 24, Ukeru Magosaki, the former head of the Foreign Ministry's Intelligence and Analysis Bureau, spoke to "Global Times": "We must avoid the war for the Diaoyu Islands between Japan and China. This is my biggest concern." (July 2012). Not long ago, this former senior diplomat who researches on East Asian for a long time published an article in Asahi Shimbun, saying "the Diaoyu Islands are not inherent territory of Japan". On July 24, when receiving the interview of our newspaper, Ukeru Magosaki addressed astonishing remarks: I believe some force of the United States hope to see tensions between Japan and China, so Japan and China should jointly fight against this force; fundamentally, the Japan US Security Treaty doesn't aim to defend Japan's interests".

Some Japanese people do ponder over my opinions

Global Times: when did you begin to study the Diaoyu Islands issue?

Ukeru Magosaki: my earliest research focused on the Sino-Soviet territorial disputes. ...... After the establishment of diplomatic relations between Japan and China relations, the two sides decided to shelve the Diaoyu Islands issue. Therefore, we faced no big problems. Then, I lived in Iran for a long time. Iran and Iraq fought against each other for borders division. Territorial disputes once again became my main research direction.

In 1985, when I returned home, I became the chief of Intelligence Analysis Division. China once again became my important research content. Since then, my work has been focused on the relation between China and Japan. But from a historical perspective, I want to know what on earth the Diaoyu Islands dispute is. Therefore, I start studying historical materials. As a result, I wrote a book titled On Japan's Territory–Senkaku Islands, Liancourt Islands and Kuril Islands.

Global Times: why do you think "the Diaoyu Islands are not inherent territory of Japan"?

Magosaki Ukeru: I didn't say the Diaoyu Islands are a part of China. I think the main problem is that a lot of people think that the Diaoyu Islands are Japan's "inherent territory". China claims that the Diaoyu Islands are China's islands, which is not groundless, because these islands have a territorial dispute. ...... If the premise is that the islands are inherent territory of Japan, we should take a tough attitude; if there is a territorial dispute over these islands, we should think about how to avoid disputes. I think it is a bad idea to expand the disputes in order to fight for the territory. Years ago, Iran and Iraq fought for the border demarcation. Unfortunately, at present, China and Japan faced the same dilemma. I think we must avoid the war of the Diaoyu Islands between Japan and China. This is my biggest concern.

After my article had published, many people abuse me on Twitter: when did you become a Chinese; get back to China! But my article also has a good influence on society. The media such as Asahi Shimbun and Sankei Shimbun may not agree with my point of view, but they still published my claims; maybe they think the Japanese also need to listen to this kind of comments. More surprisingly, it produced a social effect, by virtue of which, Japan began to think about Diaoyu Islands issue seriously.

The Japanese garrison cannot safeguard the Diaoyu Islands

Global Times: what's your comments on Shintaro Ishihara's plan of purchasing the islands?

Ukeru Magosaki: I don't think it is a wise idea. There are two reasons: 1. if Mr. Ishihara successfully bought the Diaoyu Islands, he would continue to take some actions. Then, China will surely make corresponding responses which could be a diplomatic one or military one. Mr. Ishihara may not take any measures because he is not a diplomat nor has fighters. What he did is to ignite the Diaoyu Island issue and doesn't make any sense; 2. how to treat the disputed territory? I think the two sides should not increase tensions; it is wise for them to think about how to avoid disputes.

Global Times: Is there any possibility of a military conflict between Japan and China about the islands? what will be the result if it happens.

Ukeru Magosaki: if there is a military conflict between Japan and China, Japan is bound to lose. The Diaoyu Islands nears Taiwan, and the Taiwan issue is one of the most important issues of China, so there is also in the forefront of the China's defense. If there is a military conflict, it is of high possibility that China will take the Diaoyu Islands. However, in my opinion, although China has a strong military power, it will not take the initiative to seize the Diaoyu Islands, because China's priority is the guarantee of the Chinese people's life, which needs the international market. China lives in peace with the people all over the world so as to safeguard China's need of the market. This situation will not change in the next 20 years.

Global Times: what's the mutually beneficial solution of the Diaoyu Islands issue?

Ukeru Magosaki: When the normalization of diplomatic relations between China and Japan was realized in 1972, Premier Zhou Enlai told Prime Minister Kakuei Tanaka that the two sides decided to "seek common points while reserving minor difference". The Diaoyu Islands issue undoubtedly belong to "small difference". Japan and China have more important things to do. Whether the Diaoyu Islands belong to China or Japan, the close relations between Japan and China are beneficial to the development of both countries, which is a common opinion of Premier Zhou Enlai and Mr. Deng Xiaoping. It is important that the citizens in two countries should also have the same understanding that the close relations between Japan and China and mutually help of economic development will bring a better life for the people in the two countries. Therefore, if you can't find the best solution to solve the issue of the Diaoyu Islands, it is perhaps the best policy that we shelve the dispute as Premier Zhou Enlai and Mr. Deng Xiaoping suggested.

Global Times: currently China-Japan relations are kind of strained. What do you think about the China-Japan relations at present and in the future?

Ukeru Magosaki: Japan and China should know clearly that which the most important country is for itself. Obviously, For Japan, China is Japan's largest trading partner , while the United States is no longer the most important country for Japan. It is necessary for Japan to seriously consider this. There is no doubt that for China, it is beneficial to improve relations with Japan. If the two countries are aware of this matter, they will seek solutions through dialogue.

Japan-China relations, of course, are not only the relationship between the two countries; the United States is also behind this relation. There are forces out there in the United States who do not want Japan and China to get close to each other. East Asia has been discussed how to establish an East Asian community. Europe has established the European Union, Asia has Association of Southeast Asian Nations (ASEAN). The close relationship between each other can avoid many disputes. But the relationship between regions is not merely economic and trade relations, but also the security issues. With the increase of China's military power in the future, the United States plans to fight against China with together with Japan. If Japan and China are Indifferent to each other, the mentioned forces in the US will play its role. In the future Japan and China should attach great importance to contend against these forces.

After another five or ten years, the Japanese people will understand the importance of China; so how to avoid disputes in the next five years is very important for the two countries. Taiwan is a good example: people in Taiwan used to demand "independence", but now this kind of voices faded away. At present, if we ask the ordinary Japanese people—which is the largest exporting country of Japan, most of them would say the United States. The Japanese have not understand the importance of China. In five or six years, after the Japanese understand it, they will take more cautious moves.

Global Times: What's your comments on the US strategy of "Returning to Asia" as well as the future situation in Asia?

Ukeru Magosaki: the US strategy of "Return to Asia" is actually a strategy to fight against the increasingly powerful China. Although some people think that China is strong and the US should keep good relations with China, but the attitude of the U.S. military is to restrain the power of China, just as it did to the Soviet Union. Of course, The current status of the United States cannot be compared with its past, so it can only ally with those countries such as Japan, South Korea, Vietnam and Philippines to contend against China.

I think there is no sense in the Japan-US alliance. For example, China has nuclear weapons, but it will not launch them to Japan. This is not because the Chinese fear the nuclear weapons of the US, but because this action is of no meanings and only brings negative influence to China. Diaoyu island issue is similar to this one. I don't think the Japan-US Security Treaty aims to protect the interests of Japan.

In the future, China will become the world's superpower. It is worth noting that in the past when Britain and the US were the world's superpowers, their national standard of living was also the first in the world. But looking to the future of China, for example, in 2020, will China's standard of living be the world's first? I think this is the most important problem facing China.

(Originally published in "Global Times" on July 26, 2012, abridged by the editor.)

XVII. China-Japan cooperation is more valuable than the fight and contest for the sovereignty over Diaoyu Islands

Interview of Ukeru Magosaki by reporter of "Reference News"

Editor's note: Ukeru Magosaki, the former head of the Foreign Ministry's Intelligence and Analysis Bureau, published an article in Asahi Shimbun, which argued that the Diaoyu Islands are not inherent territory of Japan, but the disputed islands and held that shelving the dispute is the most favorable choice for Japan. The interview of Ukeru Magosaki by the reporter of "Reference News" in Tokyo on July 18, 2012 is as follows:

"Japan should not lost in its own claim"

Reporter: in an interview with the Japanese media, you said that the Diaoyu Islands can hardly be seen as the "inherent territory" of Japan, sovereignty over the Diaoyu Islands is disputable, which is different from the diplomatic language of the Japanese government.

Magosaki: the "inherent territory" generally refers to the territory ruled by one country for hundreds of years. The Diaoyu Islands were occupied by Japan after the 1895, so they are not inherent territory of Japan?

Japan paid great attention to the issue of the Diaoyu Islands, but if we ask the Japanese people about the claims of China, almost no one could answer. I think Japan's claims about the Diaoyu Islands have defects.

Of course, it doesn't mean that Japan should give up their claims and standpoint. I just want to tell the Japanese, Japan's claim is not one hundred percent correct. From my perspective, China's position on this issue is tenable as since the Ming Dynasty, the Diaoyu Islands have been put under the jurisdiction of China's naval defense.

The reason why I insist that the Diaoyu Islands are the inherent territory of Japan is that if we have been emphasizing the Diaoyu Islands are inherent territory of Japan, Japan will form a public opinion atmosphere and political atmosphere to further strengthening the effective control. If Japan take further action, China will take countermeasures; the two countries will fall into a "negative spiral", and there will be a high possibility of conflict, which will be disadvantageous to both China and Japan. Compared with the Diaoyu Islands, China-Japan cooperation is more valuable. So I just want to tell the Japanese: China's claims have some reasons and the Japanese should not lost in its own claims.

"Ishihara pours oil on the flames and intends to flatter the US"

Reporter: Mr. Ishihara's action of purchasing the islands are escalating.

Magosaki: it is Shintaro Ishihara, the Tokyo Governor, who wants to pour oil on the flames. In my opinion, those who support Ishihara are also claim the Diaoyu Islands are Japan's inherent territory.

Reporter: why Ishihara released the purchase of the Diaoyu Islands in the United States

Magosaki: although Ishihara has written a book titled "Japan Can Say No", a lot of people think Mr Ishihara belongs to the Anti-US group, actually his opinion towards the US has changed. The postwar Japanese politicians have long argued that without the support of the United States, their political career can't continue. Ishihara may also want to be the Prime Minister, so he wants to get the support of the United States. He knew that if he confronts with China, he will get the support from the United States, so he Ishihara released the purchase of the Diaoyu Islands in the United States. Now Japan's political atmosphere is that politicians obtain their own political interests by inciting national moods.

Reporter: what is the motive of Mr Ishihara who wants to strengthen Japan's effective control over the Diaoyu Islands?

Magosaki: Japan's national strength is declining. In the 1980s, if you asked the Japanese how their living standard is, they would say they were of average standard. However, at present, most people will say they are below average. After the increase of the consumption tax and restarting nuclear power plant soon after the Fukushima nuclear power plant issue, most Japanese are not positive about their living standard. At this moment, Ishihara put forward China threat theory, Korean threat theory, North Korean threat theory, which is easy to induce people to follow him. Japan's economic situation is increasingly serious now, for politicians, the best way to unite the people is to make foreign enemies. In this era when Japan is looking forward to making enemies, it is unnecessary for China to help the Japanese activists fan the flames.

"The United States makes a move to surround China"

Reporter: is the escalation of Diaoyu Islands dispute accidental or inevitable?

Magosaki: why did former Prime Minister Mr Hatoyama step down from office? It is because he confronted with the United States, so Naoto Kan and Noda learned the lesson of Mr Hatoyama's failure and are trying to fawn over the United States. In the process, they recognized that the United States expects the confrontation with China.

In the United States, there are some people who advocate the policy of being hostile to China with military actions. These people are clear that the United States has financial difficulties, so they should rely on Japan, Korea, Vietnam, Philippines, Australia and other countries. They put forward the China threat theory and then mobilize these countries against China, forming the encirclement of China. Under this big background, the Diaoyu Islands issue has been escalated, so, the Diaoyu Islands issue doesn't become complex suddenly; it is just a move of the United States to build encirclement of China by making Japan actively participate in this process. That is to say, the United States are looking forward to the conflict concerning the Diaoyu Islands issue between the two countries.

Reporter: what should China and Japan learn from the lesson of 2010 fishing trawl incident?

Magosaki: After the incident, some new phenomena appeared in Japan. In the election of Okinawa Governor, Nakaima, who emphasizes on the Chinese threat theory, attaches great importance to the Japan-US agreement, has been elected; "warm budget" (referring to the part of the budget spent on the U.S. military base in Japan shouldered by the Japanese government—noted by reporter) is prolonged for 5 years; the Japanese once actively discussed that Japan should send troops to Afghanistan; "Three principles of arms exports" developed to the direction of revision... A series of new phenomena indicates that the Japan-US alliance steps forward. We can say the 2010 fishing trawl incident helped make these ideas reality.

The creator of the 2010 fishing trawl incident was not China, but Japan. Japan stirred up this incident, which was used by some politicians to strengthen the Japan-US alliance.

Ishihara hopes the Chinese side takes countermeasures. China must recognize that it is a trap set up in advance.

"Shelving the dispute should be a consensus of the two countries"

Reporter: why does Shintaro Ishihara who intensifies the contradiction between China and Japan gain numerous supports?

Magosaki: unfortunately, such radical politicians like Ishihara are supported by 80% of the Japanese people. Therefore, China and Japan should think from the strategic perspective to avoid the conflict so as not to let those radical politicians get what they want.

In fact, shelving the dispute advocated by Zhou Enlai and Deng Xiaoping doesn't mean giving the Diaoyu Islands to Japan, but aims to avoid the conflict between China and Japan, in other words, avoiding the use of force. Because there are more important than the Diaoyu Islands dispute between China and Japan; that is the healthy development of the relations between the two countries. the two countries should re-study the spirit of shelving the dispute. It should become the consensus of the two countries.

China and ASEAN have reached a consensus; China and Japan should also reach a consensus. China and Japan should also sign a similar declaration to Declaration on the Code of Conduct on the South China Sea. The specific contents should include two points: 1. The Parties concerned undertake to resolve their territorial and jurisdictional disputes by peaceful means, without resorting to the threat or use of force; 2. the Parties undertake to exercise self-restraint in the conduct of activities that would complicate or escalate disputes and affect peace and stability.

Reporter: what should the two sides do after shelving the dispute?

Magosaki: when I gave a speech in Japan Bar Association, someone said your advocate of shelving the dispute was not very convincing because you didn't tell us what benefits we would get after shelving the dispute. I think the benefit is that China and Japan can establish a community similar to the European Community in the future, putting aside the territorial dispute and giving up hatred; they can establish further cooperation under the premise of remembering the history. By then, the relations between the two countries will never be affected by a disputed territory. China and Japan should march forward towards this goal, before which they should avoid local conflicts. The East Asian Community will become the destination of the "post-shelving era".

(Ukeru Magosaki, born in 1943, the former head of the Intelligence and Analysis Bureau under Japan's Foreign Ministry, the ambassador to Iran, a professor at National Defense Academy of Japan, etc.; resigned in 2009, the author of "The Truth of the Post-war History". This article was originally carried by Xinhua International on July 23, 2012, abridged by the editors)

XVIII. The Trap of Purchasing the Senkaku Islands

August, 2012

Toyoshita Narahiko

On April 16, Tokyo governor Shintaro Ishihara, gave a speech in Washington; he announced Japan's purchase of affiliated islands of the Senkaku Islands — the Diaoyu Island, Nanxiao Island and Beixiao Island owned by individuals.

I have discussed this matter last year (see my article: "Senkaku Islands Issue" and The Japan US Security Treaty, "World"(Sekai) in January, 2011). According to the regional list provided by "Coast Guard Headquarters in Eleventh District", surprisingly, I found that the Kuba Island and Taisho Island have the Chinese names as "Huangwei Yu" and "Chiwei Yu". The two islands were equipped with shooting and bombing grounds and used by US navy. China mentioned these two islands when it claims to the sovereignty over the Diaoyu Islands; the names of these islands were recorded in the literature of Ming Dynasty. Why does Japan Coast Guard still use them? In a word, without the permission of US army, the Japanese can't land on the islands; they are the exclusive administration area of the US army.

"The inherent territory of Japan", "the Senkaku Islands deciding the fate of the nation" (the wording of Ishihara) have five islands and two of them were used their Chinese names when they were handed over to US army; and sadly, they become the shooting and bombing grounds where no Japanese should enter. Is this the true? Are these two islands used as the training grounds. In October 2010, the "government's written plea" said that since 1978, "more than 30 years they received no notice that US army used the islands."

The vague diplomatic strategy of the United States

When Ishihara revealed his intention of purchasing the Kuba Island, he also inadvertently revealed that the Senkaku Islands issue involved Japan-China relations and Japan-US relations. However, there is a more fundamental issue of the sovereignty over the Diaoyu Islands.

Although when Okinawa were returned to Japan in 1972, the islands were mapped into the handover area. However, before the signing of the Okinawa Reversion Agreement in June 1971, the Nixon government had already decided on such a policy: "US will hand over the administrative right of the Senkaku Islands together with Okinawa; the US does not take a position on the sovereignty of the Senkaku Islands."

The Nixon government adopted the vague strategy on the issue of sovereignty; the reason is that it concerns the position of China and Taiwan; besides, the vague strategy on the Senkaku Islands issue will lead to a heated dispute between China and Japan; as a result, the two countries will be controlled by the United States. All in all, the international community think this issue is indeed "unusual", because the Japanese government, the media, researchers, and public opinions in Japan have repeatedly argued that according to the abundant data in history, the Senkaku Islands are undoubtedly an "inherent territory of Japan". But Japan's only Allies—the United States refuses to admit this "obvious historical fact".

"Inherent territory" and inherent land"

When discussing the Senkaku Islands issue, Japan often use the wording —"inherent territory". "Inherent territory" has been used by Japan on many territories such as the Kuril Islands, Take Island, etc. ...... However, the concept of "inherent territory" does not exist in the international law, but this concept with strong political color has been created by the Japanese government and the Japanese Ministry of Foreign Affairs in order to deal with the territorial disputes Kuril Islands, Take Island and Senkaku Islands.

What is the inherent territory? Its basic concept is not clear so far. For example, when did Okinawa (the Ryukyu Islands) become Japan's "inherent territory"? Obviously, Ryukyu was once an independent country in history. Is it when Japan set up the Okinawa County in 1879 (the 12th year of the Meiji period)? However, the Meiji government once put forward the plan that Miyako Islands and Yaeyama Islands will be cede to the Qing government. Therefore, Okinawa, including the Senkaku Islands became Japan's "inherent territory" for the first time during the Sino-Japanese War 15 years later.

To sum up, the essence of the "inherent territory" became clear at a glance at the end of the Pacific War . In late June, 1945, Showa Emperor Hirohito modified the policy decided in early June and appointed Former Prime Minister Konoe Fumimaro as the envoy of Showa Emperor to hold peace talks with the United Nations. The conditions of the drafted "peace negotiations outline" mentioned that: "regarding the national land, in the case of last resort, Japan will agree as long as Japan can keep its inherent land." The "Explanation" part of the specific instructions mentioned: "the so-called inherent land—the last bottom line is to discard Okinawa, Ogasawara Island and Sakhalin." (see the book "Establishment of Japan US Security Treaty", Iwanami New Book Press).

In other words, Okinawa is not Japan's "inherent land", it is only a condition of peace talks, and can be handed over to the United Nations. We can find that, since the Meiji Restoration, Japan's ruling class had two views of territory: one is "inherent land"; the another is "inherent territory" such as those islands around the "inherent land". In order to ensure the safety of the "inherent land", those "inherent territories" can be "abandoned".

Let's take another look at Mr Ishihara's speech in Washington. He eagerly advocated that we should treat China as the "main rival" and push forward the "nuclear development simulation experiment" which is enough to make the world nervous; then we can use Japan's high technology to develop weapons. He also mentioned about developing Non-nuclear attack missile with China's leaders as the very target. At the end of the speech, he put forward the policy of "purchasing the Senkaku Islands".

Ishihara has long been looking forward to sending the Japan Self Defence Forces rather than Coast Guard so as to cause the conflict between soldiers and "military conflict"; then the US may involuntarily be involved in. In Mr Ishihara's view, the purchase of the Senkaku Islands can create such an opportunity.

An Attempt that surpasses "stupidity"

Then, how should Japan deal with the Senkaku Islands issue which causes the most dangerous situation between Japan, US and China?

Firstly, Japan should throw away the meaningless concept of "inherent territory". The government, the media kept rigorously testing this concept which does not exist in international law and blindly repeating this empty rhetoric, which is bound to hinder Japan's diplomacy.

The concept of "Inherent territory" is connected with the assertion that "there is no territorial dispute". The obvious "neutrality" of the US is that the US did not clear that whether the sovereignty over the Senkaku Islands belongs to Japan or China or Taiwan. The US only mentions "the territorial dispute exists". If the Japanese government adheres to the concept of "inherent territory" in the future, it need to persuade the United States in the first place. Without the agreement from the Allies—the United States, Japan should admit that "the territorial dispute exists" and negotiate this matter with China and Taiwan.

(Toyoshita Narahiko, a professor at Kwansei Gakuin University in Japan, specialized in History of International Politics and Diplomacy. The article was originally published in Sekai, Japan in August 2012)

XIX. The Senkaku Islands/Diaoyu Islands Dispute - Testing the Wisdom of People in the 21st Century

June, 2004

Murata Tadayoshi

Foreword

When discussing the *Diaoyu/Senkaku Islands* dispute between China and Japan, I think it is necessary to recall how our smart predecessors have dealt with the issue during their leadership in the 20th century.

Firstly, during the diplomatic normalization, Premier Zhou Enlai's approach to the Diaoyu Islands issue is worth learning. On 28 July, 1972, at his meeting with Takeiri Yoshikatsu, the chair man of Japan's New Komeito at the time, Zhou noted that "there is no need to mention the Diaoyu Islands issue. Compared with the diplomatic normalization, the issue is much less important." Recently, more details about the Zhou's words recorded in Takeiri's notebook were made public: "Up to now, Mr. Takeiri doesn't pay much attention to the Diaoyu issue, do you? So don't I. However, the oil problem is taken seriously by historians. Mr. Kiyoshi Inoue, one of the Japanese historians, concerns about the issue. But don't treat the issue so seriously."

Here Zhou Enlai specially mentioned Kiyoshi Inoue, the professor of Kyoto University at the time intending to ask Takeiri to realize Inoue's research achievements on the Diaoyu Islands. Mr. Zhou's approach merits attention.

Secondly, we should learn from Deng Xiaoping's treatment of the Diaoyu Islands issue. In the late October of 1978, Deng Xiaoping visited Japan to exchanging the documents of ratification of the *China-Japan Treaty of Peace and Friendship*. Deng held a press conference at Japan National Press Club. When a reporter raised doubt about the *Senkaku Islands* dispute, Deng answered that "The Senkaku Islands is called the Diaoyu Islands by us. The different names show the different views of Japan and China. When the two countries discussed the issue of diplomatic normalization, we promised not to discuss such dispute. This time, we also promised not to touch the problem during the negotiation. It is intelligent to put it aside now, since this problem is difficult to make it clear. However, some people intends provoke discords on the issue so as to hinder the development of China-Japan relations. We think that it is wise for both governments to put aside the Diaoyu Islands dispute. It doesn't matter to put it aside for a time or for ten years. Our generation isn't wise enough to solve the dispute. But our next generation will be wiser than us to find a solution that could be accepted by both."

No matter it was when the China- Japan relations came into normalization or when two countries signed the *China-Japan Treaty of Peace and Friendship*, China proposed "shelving" the dispute, which Japan consented. That's why we adopted the policy that improving the China-Japan relationship and enhancing development is the top priority. It has been a quarter century since Deng uttered such words as "Our generation isn't wise enough to solve the dispute. But our next generation will be wiser than us to find a solution that could be accepted by both". However, are we, who living in the 21st century, wiser? Have we worked out an approach that is more reasonable than Zhou Enlai's and Deng Xiaoping's?

What is the historical truth?

The following are the records of the Diaoyu Islands in Chinese historical documents:

One of the keys to the Diaoyu Islands dispute is whether it is "terra nullius".

Since Ming dynasty (1368-1644), the Diaoyu Islands, the Huangwei Yu, and the Chiwei Yu have been concluded into China's territory in all sorts of maps and documents. Especially during Ming dynasty, in order to guard against the Japanese and the pirates, the Ming government imposed a ban on unofficial trade. Paying great attention to the defense along the coast, the government ordered the Great Clearance, which required the residents in the coastal area of Fujian and Guangdong to compulsorily move to the inland areas. Coastal security was the major task of the government. The defense of the coastal islands included that of the Diaoyu Islands, the Huangwei Yu, and the Chiwei Yu, which has been proved by many scholars. For example, in 1562, Ming people Hu Zongxian and Zheng Ruozeng edited the book *Maps and Plans for the Coastal Defense*, which included a map titled as "Map of Mountain Sands in the Coast of Fujian" and one as "Route from Fujian to Japan Guided by Compass—East of Meihuashan Mountain to Naha", respectively in volume one and volume two. The above two maps were also included in Ju Deyuan's book *Arguments Around the Sovereignty of Diaoyu Islands; the Land-stealing History of Japan Vol. 2*. Similarly, Shi Yongtu concluded a map titled with "Fujian Coastal Defense Map" in the second volume of his book the *Defense Maps* during 1621 and 1628.

Ryukyu was governed as Okinawa by the Meji government after the Meiji Restoration in Japan, before which Ryukyu was independent and has been conferred by Ming government and the Qing government. When a new King of the Ryukyus Kingdom took the throne, the King will be conferred by Chinese Emperor, which is an indispensible ceremony to prove the legitimacy of the King. he Ming government and the Qing government have totally sent 24 Sapposhis (ed. Chinese envoys plural). The Sapposhis would describe the whole process and the status quo of Ryukyu in a report called *the Record of the Imperial Title-Conferring Envoys to Ryukyu (Shi Liu Qiu Lu)* and submitted the report to the Chinese emperors. At that time, Fuzhou (capital of Fujian Province, previously called Quanzhou) was the only passageway between the Chinese inland and Ryukyu. The envoys would make use of the southwester around the Summer Solstice to take the sailing boats, departing from Fuzhou to go to the Naha of Ryukyu. The Diaoyu Islands, the Huangwei Yu, and the Chiwei Yu, and other islands at the edge of the continental shelf could ensure the safety of navigation. That's why there are so many records of the islands in the *Envoys' Records in Ryukyu*. In the records, it has been known that after passing the Chiwei Yu, it came to the "Gumishan" (the present Kume Island) and then it would enter the territory of the Ryukyu. The earliest records were written by Chen Kan in 1934 when he visited the Ryukyu as a Sapposhi, which goes as this: "the Pingchia Hill (now called Pengchia), Diaoyu Islands, Huangmao Yu (now called Huangwei Yu) and Chih Yu (now called Chiwei Yu) were left behind. After the journey of one night plus three days, we haven't arrived yet since the Ryukyu boat was small. Later, on the evening of the 11th, the Gumi Mountain (also called Gumi Mountain, known as Kume Island today) was in sight. It belongs to Ryukyu. The aborigines (Ryukyu people) on board were elated, happy to be home. After a whole night's journey, the wind turned east, which made it difficult to advance. Thus we left the original destination. It took another day to arrive at the hill. Several aborigines shipped to us to inquire. The interpreter talked with them and then they left."

It's worth noting that the aborigines taking the same Ryukyu boat with Chen Kan thought when the Gumi Mountain was in sight, they were home, and that's why they were happy. However, the Ryukyu officers in Gumi Mountain were waiting for the imperial envoy.

In 1606, Xia Ziyang, another imperial envoy of the Ming court, wrote in his *the Record of the Imperial Title-Conferring Envoys to Ryukyu (Shi Liu Qiu Lu)* that "When seeing the Kume Island, the Ryukyu people were happy by thinking that they were home. The headman of the Kume Island went out to welcome the envoy delegation and then offered several conches as the tribute to the Ming emperor.

In 1719, Xu Baoguang, a deputy title-conferring envoy to Ryukyu in the Qing Dynasty, clearly noted in his book *Records of Messages from Chongshan* that "Gumi Mountain is the mountain guarding the southwest border of Ryukyu" and "it took forty nights' shipping from the Wuhumen of Fuzhou to the Gumi Mountain of the Ryukyu". Obviously, Gumi Moutain is the boundary between the Diaoyu Islands and the Ryukyu.

In 1756, Zhou Huang, a deputy imperial envoy of the Qing Dynasty, clearly recorded in his book, the *Complete Map of Ryukyu*, that Ryukyu referred to the islands from the southernmost Younaguni Island, to the northernmost Qijie

Island and Kikaiga Shima. The westernmost of Ryukyu is the Kume Island, while the map of Ryukyu didn't include the Diaoyu Islands, Huangwei Yu, Chiwei Yu and other islands. When introducing Ryukyu's "territory", Zhou described Gumi Mountain as "boundary between China and foreign land when going from Fuzhou".

In 1756, Pan Xiang recorded the journeys of Quan Kui and Zhou Huang into his book *Records of the Experience in Ryukyu*. It described the situation of Ryukyu people's welcome when they were close to Gumi Mountain: "On 12th, the Chiyang (probably referred to the Chiwei Yu) was insight and at the night they shipped by the Gouji Sea. On 13th, Gumi Mountain was in sight. Gumi people climbed on the mountain to make a fire for a signal. They in the ship also fired as a response. On 14th, the heads in Gumi Mountain took tens of small boats, guided them to the west part of the mountain and then they drop the anchors."

It could concluded from the above records that from Ming Dynasty to the Qing, all the Chinese envoys' to Ryukyu clearly knew that the Diaoyu Islands, Huangwei Yu and Chiwei Yu were the targets of the seaway and Gumi Mountain was the boundary of Ryukyu. After passing over the trench between Chiwei Yu and Gumi Moutain, they would be in Ryukyu's territory. Both ancient Chinese government and Ryukyu's knew this point clearly.

Japanese Records on Ryukyu's territory

As it is known to all, the book *Illustrated Outline of the Three Countries* written by Hayashi Shihei in 1768 was the earliest Japanese literature to mention Diaoyu Islands. The three countries referred to were Ezo-chi, Ryukyu and Korea. The Map of the Three Provinces and 36 Islands of Ryukyu in the book put Diaoyu Islands as being apart from the 36 islands of Ryukyu and colored it the same as Fujian and Zhejiang (both are part of the mainland of China), indicating that Diaoyu Islands were part of China's territory.

After unifying the whole nation, during Shoho period (from 1644 to 1647), Tokugawa shogunate ordered all vassal states to make the maps of their own states so as to form the map of the whole nation. The maps were made at the proportion of taking six inches as one foot. The map of Satsuma state and the whole Ryukyu nation were preserved by the secretary of Shimadzu (the Kingof Satsuma state) and now they are kept in the Historical Compilation Institute of Tokyo University. In December 2001, at the activity that celebrated the 100th issue of historical collections, a copy with the same size with the original was publicly exhibited at the Tokyo National Museum. The map of the whole Ryukyu nation consists of three maps, namely the map of the Amami Islands, Okinawa and the Sakishima islands. The three maps are all three to six meters large hand-drawings. The map is unbelievably precise and even the coral reefs at the north of Miyako Island, which is part of the Sakishima islands, were drawn clearly. After Shimadzu's conquering the Ryukyu in 1609, Ryukyu belonged to China and Japan, which clearly indicated the boundary between Ryukyu and Chinese Qing Dynasty. The map no doubt showed Ryukyu and its 36 affiliated islands.

The 36 affiliated islands of Ryukyu didn't include the Diaoyu Islands, Huangwei Yu and Chiwei Yu, which was the common understanding of Ryukyu, China and Japan at that time. From the point of view of geography, the Diaoyu Islands, Huangwei Yu and Chiwei Yu, surrounded by the empiric sea with less than 200 meters deep, were at the edge of the continental shelf. After passing Kume Island, there would be a 1000 to 2000 deep trench as well as Kuroshio Current if keep forward. It was difficult for small boats to cross. Many islands, between the Ryukyu Island and the Sakishima islands, were connected by Empiric Sea. People could come and go by boats and a transport network among the 36 islands was taken its shape. A Spanish businessman at that time recorded: going along the Sakishima islands, "travelers could sleep at land every night." Since there was such a safe path, why must the envoys go to Naha at the path of "Diaoyu Islands-Huangwei Yu-Chiwei Yu-Kume Islands"? That's because envoy, as the representative of a country, must travel along an official path, which implied that people have clear sense of territorial waters. Therefore, it was false to claim the Diaoyu Islands to be "terra nullius".

1. Meji Government's Records: did Japan have the sovereignty

Indeed, the Japanese the Ministry of Internal Affairs has ever ordered Nishimura Sutezo, the governor of Okinawa Prefecture at the time, to "investigate the uninhabited island between Okinawa Prefecture and Fuzhou of Qing Dynasty" so as to set up border marking regarding the islands. On November 22, 1885, Nishimura Sutezo submitted "Report on Kume Islands and Chiwei Yu", in which it said: "the situation of the Diaoyu Islands, Huangwei Yu and Chiwei Yu is the same with that described in Records of Messages from Chong-shan. When conferred the Chong-shan, the emperor of Qing Dynasty has sent boats to control the islands and given them names. The islands are the navigation guide from Qing to Ryukyu. Therefore, similar to the situation of Okidaito-jima, it would cause dispute if we landed on the islands and set up sovereignty marker." Nishimura Sutezo here expressed his worries to the Home Ministry.

Japan's Marquis Inoue Kaoru, the Minister of Foreign Affairs at that time, put forward his advice in the following documents:

"Recently, the newspaper of Qing Dynasty said that our government attempted to occupy the islands that belonged to Taiwan and raised Qing government's attention to the issue. Therefore, on this occasion, I planned not to take action rashly in order to avoid unnecessary dispute."

That is to say, Qing government has been wary of Japan's intention. Field Marshal Prince Yamagata Aritomo, the Minister of Home Affairs, made the following conclusion:

Document of Setting up Sovereignty Markers on the Islands between Okinawa Prefecture and Fuzhou of Qing Dynasty

The document was indexed as Confidential Document No. 128 on Home Affairs. The report on the investigation of the inhabited islands between Okinawa Prefecture and Fuzhou of Qing Dynasty was submitted. However, the issue of setting up markers involved the dispute over the sovereignty of the islands between our nation and Qing. It is not the proper time to mention the issue now. I suggested solving the dispute at an appropriate time. Here, Yamagata Aritomo said: "it is not the proper time". However, if Liu Mingchuan couldn't repel the French army, Qing government's rule over Taiwan would turn to be weak. Then it was probable that Japan would set its national markers on the islands in 1885.

On 13 January, 1890 and 2nd November, 1893, the governor of Okinawa Prefecture twice proposed to place Diaoyu Islands under the jurisdiction of Okinawa Prefecture. Diaoyu Islands. But Meiji government suspended it. In 1984, Japan launched the Sino-Japanese War of 1894-1895 (Jiawu War). On 14 January of 1895, the cabinet council of Japan, being about to win the War, secretly passed a resolution to set up the markers.

Kiyoshi Inoue, in his thesis in *Historical Facts of Senkaku Islands/Diaoyu Islands*, illustrated the confidential document (the volume 23 of Japan Diplomatic Documents compiled by the Japanese Foreign Ministry) sent from the Japanese Minister of Internal Affairs Yasushi Nomura to Foreign Minister Mutsu Munemitsu on December 27th of 1894. The document was Confidential Document No. 133. However, the document cannot be found in portal (http://www.jacar.go.jp) of Center for Asian Historical Records of National Archives of Japan.

Japanese government hasn't launched the war against Qing dynasty no matter in 1890 or in 1893. The time when Koga proposed the willingness to develop Diaoyu Islands in 1894 was either earlier than Jiawu War or at the beginning of Jiawu War. At that time, Japan hasn't achieved the complete victory. At the beginning of December 1894, Japan was sure that they would win. The Island of Formosa (Taiwan) was ceded to Japan as the condition of pacification. The Diaoyu Dao Islands were ceded to Japan as "islands appertaining or belonging to the said island of Formosa". This is the "event" relating the seizure of Diaoyu Islands, which is totally different from the previous situation.

On the part of Qing government, Prince Kung in Ministry of Foreign Affairs in Qing Dynasty has begun to prepare for pacification as early as at early October. At early November, Li Hongzhang, the commissioner of trade for the

Beiyang Ministry, who previously advocated resistance, also suggested making peace as early as possible.

Under such circumstance, it was severe cold winter from the late November to the early December. What sort of strategy did Japan government adopt and what sort of dispute was caused in Japan's supreme headquarters? One suggestion was following up a victory with hot pursuit and the other type of suggestion was stopping attack to consolidate the ruling power over the newly acquired lands during winter and waited until the spring to launch another attack.

Itō Hirobumi, the prime minister, attended the supreme headquarters meeting consisting of army and navy at the command of the Mikado (the emperor of Japan), he was a civil officer at the time, though. On 4th, December, Itō Hirobumi criticized the idea of attacking during winter and put forward his strategic suggestions. The main point of the suggestions was:

Indeed, it is gratified to attack Beijing. But the strategy is infeasible. It is stupid to do nothing but stay at the occupied lands, which is morale consuming. At present, what Japan firstly should rule the occupied lands with a small number of troops while attack Weihaiwei Bohai Bay and wiping out Beiyang Fleet (the Chinese imperial navy) with the principal force under the assistance of our navy. Attacking Weihai Port would ensure the attacks of Tianjin and Beijing in the future. Secondly, we should occupy Taiwan. But England and other countries couldn't interfere in the Taiwan occupation. Recently, the domestic voice that advocates asking China to concede Taiwan when making peace grew louder. In a word, it is the best idea to make military occupation in advance.

The supreme headquarter followed Itō Hirobumi's advice and attacked the Weihai Port from late January of 1895. On 13th February, Japan's army overwhelmingly triumphed. During the attack, Japan was preparing for attacking Taiwan. At the middle of March, 1895, the combined fleet, getting round the south of Formosa [Taiwan], marched into the Penghu Islands and occupied the forts on Penghu. Successively, Japan, taking Penghu Islands as its base, made the preparation for Taiwan attack while Japan and Qing government were negotiation on pacification. Because having made sure that Taiwan would be conceded to Japan by Qing government, the combined fleet returned to Sasebo Station.

To the Mikado (Japan Emperor) government, it was a superior opportunity to usurp Diaoyu Islands. Based on Itō Hirobumi's strategy, the government and the supreme headquarters made their resolutions at the same time when the resolution of occupying Taiwan was made. In 1885, the Japanese government was afraid that Qing government would doubt or dispute if Japan publicly set up national markers at Diaoyu Islands. Now since Japan has beat Qing dynasty, Qing government would have no power to resist if Japan set up the navigation markers on Diaoyu Islands. Even if there was any resistance from Qing government, the resistance was vain. Meji government has already decided to attack

Taiwan so Taiwan was destined to be conceded as the condition of pacification. The domineering Meji government took it for grant that there was no need to occupy the inhabited islands, such as Diaoyu Islands, between Taiwan and Okinawa Prefecture and only a navigation marker was enough.

There was no dispute over the sovereignty of Okinawa (Ryukyu). Since having occupied Taiwan, Japan simply solved the Okinawa problem by means of the war from 1894 to 1895.

2. Sovereignty Dispute Was Taken as Excuse to Arouse Nationalism

On February 5th, 2004 when this book was finished, Yoichi Funabashi, a columnist of *Asahi Shimbun newspaper*, wrote the editorial, "Birth of Armitage Doctrine". Since 1996, Yoichi Funabashi, always concerning the territory dispute between China and Japan, has voiced his views for six times in the column of "View" of *Asahi Shimbun*. He began his second view from the following topic:

"On Feb. 2, U.S. Deputy Secretary of State Richard Armitage held a press conference at the Japan National Press Club, in which he said: "We have the U.S.-Japan Security Treaty. That treaty would require any attack on Japan, or the administrative territories under Japanese control, to be seen as an attack on the United States." There is nothing new in his words because he simply cited the contents of Article 5 of the treaty.

"What is noteworthy, however, is that Mr. Armitage, a State Department East Asia expert, used the expression "administrative territories under Japanese control" instead of "Japan" or "Japanese territories." He used this expression to imply the Senkaku Islands, known as Diaoyu Islands in China. He additionally indicated, "The present US administration has corrected the former administration's ambiguous stance toward that issue. The so-called "attitude in the past" refers that U.S. took neutral stand towards the China-Japan dispute over the *Senkaku Islands* territory. Previously, Clinton's government claimed not to bear the defense obligation, stipulated in the Security Treaty, to the *Senkaku Islands*. This time Armitage corrected this attitude and specifically said if 'Japan's administrative territories' were attacked, U.S. would defend. *Armitage Doctrine* was said to be born here."

At the end of the article, Funabashi wrote: "At the time when Six-Party Talks is going on to solve the North Korea issue, Japan shouldn't take such a bad measure to provoke China. But forbearance should be practiced at a certain degree. As a maritime sate, Japan must clearly realize what should insist and what could make compromise from the perspective of national interest and security. We must think how to obtain co-existence in the maritime world with China. Japan shall indicate its tolerance bottom line. The long-lasting request for 'heart for heart' or 'sense of compassion' might be backfire. China is testing the strength of Japan's determination as a maritime nation."

"Firstly, Japan should make public China's violations in terms of oceanographic survey, which included deeply going into the territorial waters of the *Senkaku Islands*. If China continues going into the waters of *Senkaku Islands*, Japan has to detain the illegally landing boats on *Senkaku*, which must be notified to Chinese government."

It has been broken its defense policy that Japanese government sent troops into Iraq. Now Japan should make such remarks to the East Asian countries. However, I suggested Japan not to be incited by Armitage *and* Yoichi Funabashi. Who will obtain benefits if China and Japan dispute over those inhabited small islands? The answer will be clear after a calm thinking.

XX. The Senkaku Islands/Diaoyu Islands Dispute - Testing the Wisdom of People Living in 21st Century

June 2004

Murata Tadayoshi

To sum up the above analysis, as a solid historical fact, the Islands which is called as the Senkaku Islands by Japan is China's and it wasn't and isn't a part of Ryukyu Islands. Japan's occupation of the islands in 1895 is an ignominious behavior under the cover of pacification for Jiawu War. The islands are no legally possessed by Japan. This is the unchangeable truth which demands a practical and realistic to recognize and a objective scientific attitude to analyze.

We incline to t accept the understandings of government, parties and media as the official understandings. However, these understandings are not always the truth. To us, the most important are truth and fact not the interest of some country. Sometimes, a government, party or media would cover up the facts that might harm the interests of its own part.

The issue of Senkaku/Diaoyu Islands couldn't be considered in isolation, but should be evaluated together with the overall history of the Senkaku Islands problem, Okinawa problem and Taiwan problem. History should be analyzed in combination with truth and fact.

When there are opposite views, people should listen attentively to the opposite and solve the dispute in a calm and peaceful way. It absolutely does no good to let the narrow-minded nationalism and fake patriotism to inflame sentiment. On this issue, we should learn from Zhou Enlai and Deng Xiaoping. We should realize that we are not as wise as they are which should raise our introspection. The national relationship between China and Japan are still in the "primary stage" and it requires the mutual constant effort to enhance the relationship to the "advanced stage".

(MurataTadayoshi, the honorary professor of Yokohama National University is scholar on Chinese issues. He majored in Chinese literature, was gradua-ted from the Literature School of Tokyo University in 1973 and finished his Doctoral program on Chinese philosophy.)

XXI. My Notes on the Senkaku /Diaoyu Islands

October, 1979

Takahashi Sougorou[124]

On January 7, 1980, Takahashi wrote on a Japanese newspaper that: d the book after its publication. earsiversity in 1938. Taka has affiliated islands of Taiwan. At the end of Jiawu War between China Qing government and Japan Meji govern-ment, Senkaku Islands, as a part of Taiwan, was conceded to Japan and became Japan publication. earsiversity in 1938. Taka has affiliated islands of Tainecessary to do the "occupation of terra nullius" since there were no national boundaries between Okinawa and Taiwan because of the concession. When defeated in World War II, Japan accepted the provisions of the Potsdam Declaration. According to the Treaty of San Francisco, Taiwan and its affiliated islands were separated from Japan's territory and Senkaku Islands, of course, should be the owned by China."

1. The Chronology of the Japan-China Relations Which Shelved the Senkaku Islands Dispute

On February 21st, 1972, Nixon arrived at Beijing.

On February 27, U.S.-China Joint Communiques was published in Shanghai. In the Article of "Peaceful Coexistence", President Nixon proposed to conclu-de "Anti-hegemonism". On Taiwan issue, U.S. confirmed that all Chinese pe-ople, no matter those in Taiwan or in Mainland, claimed one China and Taiwan was just part of China. The U.S. government has no objection to the stand.

On March 3, on the meeting of UN Committee on the Peaceful Use of Seabed, China's representative An Zhiyuan made a speech on "China's Principled Stand of Maritime Rights", in which he emphasized that "I, on be-half of the government of the People's Republic of China, reiterate: 'China's Taiwan and all its affiliated islands, including Diaoyu Islands, Huangweiyu,

---

124   Shogoro Takahashi, born in 1915 in Tokyo, graduated from the Literature School of Nihon University in 1938. Takahashi has ever made trade with China for a long time in 1960s and 1970s, as the director of the Japan Association for the Promotion of International Trade and the president of Takahashi Corporation. He has written Notes on Senkaku Islands/Diaoyu Islands, Guides for China- Japan Trades, etc. He finished My Notes on Senkaku Islands/Diaoyu Islands, which was published in October 1979, after 10 years' data collection and reading hundreds of expert specialized books as well as made an academic analysis of Diaoyu Islands' sovereignty in this book. Japan Libraries Association has ever recommended the book after its publication.

Chiweiyu, Nanxiaodao, Beixiaodao, etc., are all China's sacred territory. The waters near those islands and the seabed resources in the shallow sea area near China are fully owned by China and don't allow to be encroached by any foreign invaders.' With regard to An Zhiyuan's speech, Ryo Ogiso, the ambassador of Japan, has ever refuted that no country except Japan could claim the sovereignty of Senkaku Islands/Diaoyu Islands.

On March 8th, Japan Foreign Ministry expressed opinions on Senkaku Islands. The main point was that Japan made "occupation of terra nullius" of Senkaku Islands not plundered the islands from China through war, thus Japan should have the sovereignty of Senkaku Islands, which couldn't return to China according to the Cairo Declaration and the Potsdam Declaration.

On May 5, U.S. returned Okinawa to Japan.

On July 5, 1972, Tanaka Cabinet was formed.

On September 25, Kakuei Tanaka arrived at Beijing.

On September 29, 1972, Japan signed the Japan-China Joint Statement which carried the clause of "anti-hegemonism". China and Japan resumed the diplomatic relations. The diplomatic relations between Japan and "Taiwan" would be ended at September 29. ROC-Japan Peace Treaty of 1952 would be invalid and the Senkaku Islands disputed was put aside.

On September 30, when interviewed by Ezaki, the chief editor of editorial column of Asahi Shimbun, Masayoshi Ōhira answered Ezaki's question on how to deal with Diaoyu Islands dispute as such: "The Diaoyu Islands dispute is a minor issue when compared with the normalization of China-Japan relations. This time, the negotiations didn't involve the issue and focused on the normalization issue from beginning to the end."

On October 1, at the press conference at Japan National Golf Club, Prime Minister Tanaka mentioned that during China-Japan negotiations, when Tanaka had proposed to "make clear the sovereignty problem of the Senkaku Islands", Zhou Enlai had avoided head-on discussion by saying that "we will not discuss now. There is no marker on the maps. Diaoyu Islands becomes a problem because oil is found in the seabed of Diaoyu Islands."

On October 5 and 6, although Japan and South Korea had conflicts in terms of solving the issue of overlapped mining area in the East sea, both authorities unprecedentedly decided to shelve the dispute over the sovereignty of the continental shelf of East Sea so as jointly develop the oil and gas in the East Sea.

South Korea considered the natural prolongation of its continental shelf (advocating the possibility of extending it as far as the Okinawa Trough), while Japan proposed the Median line delimitation of the exclusive economic zones, namely the boundary between Japan and South Korea in terms of the continental shelf of East Sea should be divided according to the "equidistance midline".

Japan and South Korea made a compromise so as to jointly develop the petroleum and gas in East Sea. However, the continental shelf of East Sea is the natural prolongation of China. Japan and South Korea cannot dispose the issue concerning the continental shelf of East Sea without the negotiations with China.

In June 11, in the meeting of Budget Committee of the House of Representatives, Masaki Sera raised the inquiry whether the China-Japan Treaty of Peace and would involve the dispute over sovereignty. Masayoshi Ōhira replied Masaki Sera that: "the Treaty intends to provide guidance to the development of China- Japan relation in the future. Therefore, it will not involve the problems of the past." Ōhira's reply indirectly hinted the "shelving" or "freezing" of the Senkaku Islands dispute.

Treaty on Co-developing the Continental Shelf of East Sea between Japan and South Korea and China's Statement

On January 30, 1974, Japan and South Korea, completely ignoring China, signed the Treaty on Co-developing the Continental Shelf of East Sea between Japan and South Korea in Seoul, which was officially named as Treaty on Co-developing the Continental Shelf on the South of Adjoining Sea between Japan and the Republic of Korea. The signing of the Treaty meant that Japan has recognized the "natural prolongation" proposal of South Korea and took the stand not against China's "natural prolongation" proposal.

On February 3th, the spokesman of Chinese Foreign Ministry was authorized to make the following statement:

Chinese government holds the principle that the continental shelf is the natural prolongation of the Chinese mainland. The dispute over the division of the continental shelf should be solved by China and relevant countries in the way of negotiation. However, now Japan and South Korea, hiding from China, defined the so-call "areas jointly developed by Japan and Korea" on the continental shelf. They have infringed on China's sovereignty and Chinese government will firmly disagree with them. If the authorities of Japan and South Korea recklessly develop that area, they have to bear all the ensuing consequences.

Regarding the matter that Japanese government bulldozed the Treaty through Congress and let the Treaty be acknowledged naturally, Chinese Foreign Ministry made the following statement on June 13:

The continental shelf is the natural prolongation of the Chinese mainland. The People's Republic of China possesses the sacred sovereignty of the continental shelf of East Sea. The way to delimitate the part connected with other countries should be decided through China's negations with other countries.

The Treaty on Co-developing the Continental Shelf of East Sea between Japan and South Korea that Japan, hiding from China, signed with South Korean authority is totally illegal and invalid. Without the permission from Chinese government, any country or person shall not take the liberty of conducting developing on the continental shelf. Or the country or person must bear all the ensuing consequences

On June 3, 1978, Japan and South Korea exchanged the signed documents of ratification of the Treaty on Co-developing the Continental Shelf of East Sea between Japan and South Korea.

On June 26, Chinese Foreign Ministry protested their behavior of exchanging the signed documents of ratification and protested and reiterated that the Treaty was totally illegal and invalid

In order to get the petroleum in East Sea, U.S., Japan and South Korea strived for the delimitation of the continental shelf in East Sea without considering the consequences. Some people in Japan thought that it was because petroleum was found in the Senkaku Islands, China would claim its sovereignty. For instance, an editorial in Nihon Keizai Shimbun of Japan on March 5, 1972, said that:

"The issue lies in the underground resources and the mining rights of the petroleum in the continental shelf that connects the Senkaku Islands. The sovereignty of the continental shelf cannot be delaminated in the same way that the territory sovereignty was demarcated. It might be related to the development of the underground resources that China eagerly claimed the sovereignty of the Senkaku Islands in recent days."

However, the fact is the opposite.

Japan intends to take the Senkaku Islands as the start point to make the way in to the vast continental shelf of East Sea. Sonosuke Hanaoka, Development Office Chief of Ministry of International Trade and Industry Japan, publicly said that: "Even if the Senkaku Islands is inhabited, it still could be the start point when we delimitated the Median line of the continental shelf. This is Japan's standpoint." Although our government and press consider the sovereignty of the Senkaku Islands to be different from that of the continental shelf, it is oblivious that our government attempts to obtain the sovereignty of the Senkaku Islands so as to acquire half of the petroleum deposits probably buried deep under the continental shelf of East Sea, which worth hundreds of trillion yen. With respect to Treaty on Co-developing the Continental Shelf of East Sea between Japan and South Korea, Foreign Minister Ōhira Masayoshi protests against China because he thought that the continental shelf was within the Median line and the dispute was not an issue.[125]

---

125   Shogoro Takahashi, Notes on the Senkaku Islands/Diaoyu Islands, pp. 43-46.

Name of the Senkaku Islands

There hasn't been a definite name for the Senkaku Islands. In May of 1969,under the administration of U.S., the major of Ishigaki ordered to set up markers on all the Senkaku Islands, which were respectively named as Uotsuri-Island, Kuba-Island, Taishō-tō-Minami-koIsland, Kita-koIsland-Oki-no-Kita-iwa, Oki-no-Minami-iwa and Tobise in Japanese. The Chinese name of the 8 islands are respectively Diàoyú Dǎo (the Diaoyu Islands)-Huángwěi Yǔ-Chìwěi Yǔ-Nán Xiǎodǎo-Běi Xiǎodǎo, Dà Běi Xiǎodǎo, Dà Nán Xiǎodǎo and Fēi Jiāo Yán. However, they were still not officially named by Japanese government. Some people thought the official name of one island to be Taishō-tō, whereas it was called kumeaka- Island in Okinawa and Chìwěi Yǔ in China. On July 25, 1921 (namely the tenth year of Taishō period), the island was first taken as the national cadastre and was named as Taishō-tō. In Chinese ancient book, Chìwěi Yǔ was also recorded as ChìYǔ. Geologically, Uotsuri-Island was made of sedimentary rocks and its main body was sandstones layer. Taishō-tō, namely the Kumeaka-Island or Chìwěi Yǔ, with almost no trees and little grasses, was made of hydrogenic rocks. Because of the rocks on the island, Taishō-tō was also called ChìYǔ or Chìwěi Yǔ by China and the Kumeaka-Island by Okinawa. Unlike the Iwo To Island and Okidaito Island, the eight Senkaku islands were not named on edict. Therefore, Chinese government didn't take the names as the evidence of the sovereignty. China claimed Diaoyu Island, Huángwěi Yǔ, Chìwěi Yǔ , Dà Běi Xiǎodǎo and Dà Nán Xiǎodǎo to be the sacred territory of China, whereas Japan authority only generally called the eight islands as the Senkaku Islands. In May of 1972, The Intelligence Bureau of Ministry of Foreign Affairs of Japan listed the names of the eight islands in a brochure titled with About the Senkaku Islands, which was the first time that Japan gave those names, not officially and formally though.

On December 25, 1978, at the meeting with the journalists in Japan National Press Club, Deng Xiaoping replied to the journalist that "The Senkaku Islands is called the Diaoyu Islands by us. The different names show the different views of Japan and China. When the two countries discussed the issue of diplomatic normalization, we promised not to discuss such dispute."

Petroleum made the Senkaku Islands become an issue. The initial problem raised by the scholar who studied China Petroleum was actually about the names. After investigation, it was found that the problem was a big one.

The word (シマ) has the meanings of state (州), continent (洲), island (岛), islet (屿), etc. Reef refers to the hidden rocks. Japanese uses "岛" (means island) not "屿" (means islet) to express (シマ). In Fujian province of China, the Penghu Islands and Taiwan there are as many as 29 (シマ) being called "屿" and more on many ancient maps of China. However, there are islands directly recorded as "屿", such as the Huángwěi Yǔ and Chìwěi Yǔ, in the official document of Ryukyu government when administered by the US. On May 1st, 1969, several islands were written as KumeIsland, kobisima, SekibiSho in the document of "The Location and Area for U.S. Army's Shooting Drill". In addition, on December 23th, 1969, according to the "About Blast Manoeuvre" notice sent from officer of Agricultural and Forestry Bureau of Ryukyu government to the local officer in Yaeyama, the blast site was one sea mile radius around the Huángwěi Yǔ On April 1st, 1970, Huángwěi Yǔ was taken as training area in another notice.

Why did both of the US army in Okinawa and the Ryukyu government use the Chinese names of the islands, namely Huángwěi Yǔ and Chìwěi Yǔ ?

It's easy to understand. After defeat in World War II, the Senkaku Islands that Japan officially submitted to the United Nations Command included Chìwěi Yǔ, Huángwěi Yǔ, Běi Xiǎodǎo, Nán Xiǎodǎo and Uotsuri-Island. The map of the Amphibious Division of the Navy of Japan also showed them as Chìwěi Yǔ and Huángwěi Yǔ.

The Ryukyu government used Yúdiào Dǎo (Uotsuri-shim), Huángwěi Yǔ, Chìwěi Yǔ, Nán Xiǎodǎo and Běi Xiǎodǎo in the official documents, the only difference between which was Yúdiào Dǎo or Diàoyú Dǎo. "Diàoyú" in Chinese is the same with the "Yúdiào in Japanese. In his book Fan of Diàoyú (Fishing) that was published by Iwanami Shoten, Saionji Kinkazu's said he was a fan of Diàoyú (fishing). It is common and normal that the Chinese Diàoyú is said to be the Yúdiào in Japanese.

Higaonna Kanryo (1882-1963), a well-known historian who was born in Okinawa, published a book titled Ryukyu no Rekishi (A Brief Histroy of Okinawa). In the book, Higashionna emphasized the importance of names to the sovereignty. In 1879 (the 12th year of Meiji Period), when Meiji government annexed Ryukyu by force, the Ryukyu King (there was no ruler in Okinawa) has ever sought help from China who conferred the Ryukyu King. In order to help Ryukyu, He Ruzhang, China's envoy in Japan, claimed that Ryukyu was the territory of China. Higashionna Kanjun listed the names of the island to refute He's claim. Higashionna said that "Okinawa (Chong Sheng)" meant "alluvial islands (Chong de Dao)". From the south of the nine islands successively were "Kou zhi ge dao (the islands at the mouth)", "alluvial islands (Chong zhi ge dao)" and "Xian zhi ge dao-Saki Island). Because the southernmost "はての島" equals Hateruma Island, Okinoerabu Island and other islands consisted of the "alluvial islands (Chong zhi ge dao)". That's how the name had originated. Higashionna also said that "it must raise attention that the name of the islands were Yamato-names (Japanese names) not Tang names (Chinese names)."

The names of the islands of Okinawa were initiated with "Chong". Obviously, Island, MinnaIsland, Sesoko, Yonaguni, Iriomote-Island, Kurima-Island, Kudaka, etc. were all Yamato names (Japanese names). Although,

Oki-no-Kita-iwa, Oki-no-Minami-iwa and Tobise were Yamato names, they were the names that the measurement squad of Navy gave to the small reef in 1915 (the 4th year of Taishō period) (cited from Notes of the Waters in 1919), which was two different things from what Higashionna said.

Well, are Huángwěi Yǔ and Chìwěi Yǔ Yamato names (Japanese names) or Tang names (Chinese names). Those inherent names are obviously Chinese and are in the same line with the Huaping Yu, Mianhua Yu and Pengjia Yu, Taiwan's affiliated islands. On June 10th, 1895 (the 28th year of Meji Period), Tatsushiro Koga proposed "borrow the official territory) to the government to borrow the whole Kuba Island. Koga set up a stanchion on Kuba Island. Some words inscribed in the stanchion could be seen from the photo taken at that time that "Koga reclaimed Huángwěi Yu...." (the following words were covered). As far as Koga thought, Kuba Island was the name of Okinawa, while the inherent name of the island should be Huángwěi. It is because Huángwěi Yǔand Chìwěi Yǔ are inherent names of the islands that Ryukyu government used them in official documents.

In a word, although our government claims the ownership of the Senkaku Islands, the names of those islands haven't officially defined which is weird. After a second thinking, Prime Minister Ito Hirobumi, the leader of Meji militarism who flattered himself to be the oriental Bismarck grabbed all the islands from Penghu Islands to Taiwan in the war between Japan and Qing dynasty, therefore he thought the names were minor issue and there was no necessity to give official names. However, it was totally out of his expectation that the Imperial Japan would accept the Potsdam Declaration in 1945 and make unconditional surrender to the United Union. He also didn't foresee that in 1960 the dispute would be centered on the oil resources.

1. Internal Official Correspondence about the Senkaku Islands in Japan

The below documents do not involve any correspondence with the Qing government of China.

The Senkaku Islands was first mentioned in the Japan's Diplomatic Materials Vol. 18, which is now kept in Japan Foreign Ministry. This document was published in March of 1950 (the 25th year of the Shōwa period). Kuroiwa Hisashi, for the sake of convenience, particularly named the islands as the Senkaku Islands in 1900 (the 33rd year of the Meji period). Surely, it wasn't recorded as "the Senkaku Islands" in the historical material. The illustrations in the historical material include the following:

Consultation Documents on the Islands Situated between Okinawa Prefecture and Qing Dynasty

Annex 1: Document submitted to Supreme Minister about Erecting National Markers on Above-mentioned Islands (1885)

Annex 2: Handwritten Copy of the Document that Okinawa Prefecture Magistrate Reported to Internal Minister Yamagata (1885)

The Investigation Reports about the above Islands

Note: Overview of the Issue that Kumeaka Island, Kuba Island and Uotsuri Island were Incorporated within our Territory.

No. 38 of Cabinet Document A

From: Inoue Kaoru, the Foreign Minister

On October 9 of the 18th year of Meiji Period

In terms of investigating the inhabited islands situated between Okinawa Prefecture and Qing Dynasty, I here report to you the Document A submitted by Okinawa Prefecture chief (namely the following Attachment B).Please review and note.

(Annex 1)

Attachment B

To: Prime Minister and Internal Affairs Minister. In regard to the investigations of the two outer islands of the uninhabited Kumeseki-shima spread out between Okinawa Prefecture and Fuzhou, China, the Okinawa Magistrate submitted a petition letter as indicated in the attachment paper. Although the above mentioned islands are the same as those found in the Zhong.shan Mission Records, they were only used to pinpoint direction during navigation, and there are no traces of evidence that the islands belong to China. Also, with respect to the names of the islands, it is merely a matter of difference of nomendenture between them [China] and us Japan]. Therefore, upon completion of Okinawa Prefecture's investigations of the [said] uninhabited islands located in the vicinity of islands Kume, Miyako, and Yaeyama under the jurisdiction of Okinawa Prefecture, it is believed that there is no obstruction to placing national markers. I urgently request that this matter be decided. Enclosed in this petition is the aforementioned attachment paper.

(Annex 2)

Attachment Paper A

No. 350: Petition Regarding Investigations at Kumeseki-shima and Two Outer Islands

Investigation on Kumeaka Island and another Island

From: Nishimura Sutezo, Okinawa Prefecture Chief

To: Yamagata Aritomo, Ministers of Home of Japan

On September 22 of the 18th year of Meiji Period

Regarding Investigations at Kumeseki-shima and Two Outer Islands

In regard to the uninhabited islands spread out between this prefecture and Fuzhou, China, a summary of the surveys conducted at those islands in accordance to the secret order previously conferred to the secretary of our prefecture stationed in the capital is described as follows in the enclosed attachment paper (omitted). Because Kumeseki-shima, Kuba-shima and Uotsuri-shima have since ancient time been the names used by this prefecture to refer to them, and since they are uninhabited islands close to the islands, Kume, Miyako, Yaeyama under the jurisdiction of this prefecture, there should not exist any difficulties hindering their incorporation into this prefecture. Yet, due to their differences in terms of topography from the earlier repotted island Daitojima (situated between this prefecture and Osagawa Islands), the possibility must not be ignored that they are the same islands recorded as Diaoyutai , Huangwei-yu , and Chiwei-yu in the Zhongshan Mission Records. If they truly are the same islands, then it is obviously the case that the details of the islands have already been well-known to Qing envoy ships dispatched to crown the former Zhongshan Wang, and already given fixed [Chinese] names and used as navigational aids en route to the Ryukyu Islands. It is therefore worrisome regarding whether it would be appropriate to place national markers on these islands immediately after our investigations. During the middle of next month, upon the return of the employed survey ship, Izumo-maru, which was dispatched to conduct surveys of the two islands (Miyako, Yayeyama), I will immediately submit a detailed report. In regard to the issue of the placement of national markers, your further instructions are requested.

This was just an ordinary letter from Home Ministry to Foreign Affairs Ministry, while the Foreign Affairs Ministry replied a "Qinzhan" (Personal Correspondence) document.

The document was issued on November 21st of the year 1885 to reply the issue of setting up national markers on the inhabited islands between Okinawa Prefecture and Qing dynasty.

Personal Correspondence No. 38

From: Count Inoue Kaoru, the Foreign Minister

To: Yamagata Aritomo, Home Minister of Japan

In response to your letter Annex A No. 38 received on the ninth of this month, in which you requested deliberation over the matter concerning placing national markers on the uninhabited islands of Kumeseki-shima and two other islands spread out in between Okinawa and Fuzhou [China] after investigating them, I have given much thought to the matter. The aforementioned islands are close to the border of China, and it has been found through our surveys that the area of the islands is much smaller than the previously surveyed island, Daito-jima; and in particular, China has already given names to the islands. Most recently Chinese newspapers have been reporting rumors of our government's intention of occupying certain islands owned by China located next to Taiwan, demonstrating suspicion toward our country and consistently urging the Qing government to be aware of this matter. In such a time, if we were to pub-licly place national markers on the islands, this must necessarily invite China's suspicion toward us. Currently we should limit ourselves to investigating the islands, understanding the formations of the harbors, seeing whether or not there exists possibilities to develop the island's land and resources, which all should be made into detailed reports. In regard to the matter of placing national markers and developing the islands, it should await a more appropriate time. Moreover, the surveys conducted earlier of Daito-jima and the investigation of the above mentioned islands should not be published on the official and other newspapers. Please consider this. The above is my personal opinion."

Inoue Kaoru must considered Yamagata be disobedient and must think that Yamagata forgot the Emperor's rescript and imperial mandate in November of 1882 (the 15th year of Meiji Period) to instruct local officials to expand military forces. Japanese government expands the military forces to remove the power of Qing from Korea and put Korea in the ruling of Japan. At that time, Japan was implanting the plan of "attacking Qing" and must think that it doesn't matter even if setting up national markers on the islands in the territory of China and near Okinawa, namely Kumeaka Island (Chìwěi Yǔ) the Kuba Island (Huángwěi Yǔ) and the Uotsuri-Island (the Diaoyu island). Thus, Japan only presented the issue in ordinary file and Inoue Kaoru felt the issue intrac-table. Inoue Kaoru reminded Yamagata Aritomo of paying attention to the issue and not publishing the issue on the official newspaper and other news paper. From this, it could be seen that Yamagata Aritomo might feel that he didn't do the job very well. The following is the document from Yamagata Aritomo to Inoue Kaoru, which was sent in "Confidential Document":

Report on Setting up National Markers in the Uninhabited Island Instructed by the Governor of Okinawa Prefecture

Esteemed Foreign Minister and Noble Inoue Kaoru,

Appendix: A copy of the request that the governor of Okinawa Prefecture asks for instruction of setting up national markers in the uninhabited island from the Minister of Internal Affairs, Mr. Yamagata Aritomo.

Confidential Article 28, Item 2

As shown in the appendix, the report on setting up national makers in the uninhabited island instructed by the governor of Okinawa Prefecture is presented here for your confirmation. Please send it back along with the appendix after it is published with signature and fingerprint.

Esteemed Minister of Internal Affairs and Noble Yamagata Aritomo

November 30, 1885

The instruction is

We think it is not appropriate to set up any markers at present, in reply for the written report.

The two Ministers (Author's note: Foreign Minister and Minister of Internal Affairs)

(Memo)

(Attached letter to the appendix)

(Appendix)

I've almost accomplished the assignment of investigating on the uninhabited island which is under my jurisdiction and I report all the details in the appendix. The issue of setting up national markers mentioned before has certain relationship with the Qing court. In case of some troubles, please give me some instructions about what should I be supposed to do.

The governor of Okinawa Prefecture, Nishimura Sutezo November 24, 1885

Dispatched on December 4

Reply to the report concerning on setting up national markers in the uninhabited island by the governor of Okinawa Prefecture

Esteemed Minister of Internal Affairs and Noble Yamagata Aritomo,

Referring to your letter on November 30th, I approve of your opinion on the report concerning on setting up national markers in the uninhabited island asked by the governor of Okinawa Prefecture. I will send back the instruction of this issue to you, along with the appendix, fingerprint and attached documents.

The Foreign Minister and Noble Inoue Kaoru

The report that the governor of Okinawa Prefecture submitted to Japanese Minister of Internal Affairs on September 22, 1885 mentioned that "investigation should be made according to the principle directed by Kanmori, the secretary in Okinawa Prefecture who resided permanently in Paris", while the "principle" was not illustrated clearly. Did the militarism in Meiji Restoration want to include a minor uninhabited island in Japanese territory or was Kanmori requested by the Ministry of Internal Affairs to conduct secret facts-finding mission on the uninhabited island which albatross dwelled on when he was questioned by the governor of Okinawa Prefecture personally? Considering that Meiji government regarded being occupied in one's own business as its national policy, the reason might be the latter one.

2. The difference between 1885 and 1895

Apart from documents sent among Japanese Minister of Internal Affairs, Foreign Minister and the governor of Okinawa Prefecture, "the Procedure of Incorporating Taishō-tō, Kuba-Island and Uotsuri-Island to its territory" was also contained in the territory and relevant sundries of the 18th volume of Japan's Diplomatic Documents.

After investigation Taishō-tō (Chiwei Island), no signs were found signifying that it was under the jurisdiction of the Qing court (which is about 70 Nautical miles or 200 Li to the southwest of Fuzhou in China), Kuba-Island (nearly 100 miles to 15° southwest of Kume Island and 60 miles to the Ishigaki Island in Yaeyama Islands) and Uotsuri-Island (the same location as that of Kuba-Island, only ten miles away), which were located between Okinawa Prefecture and Fuzhou. Besides, in order to get closer contacts with those uninhabited islands such as Miyako Island and Yaeyama Islands, the governor of Okinawa Prefecture submitted the issue of setting national markers to the Chancellor of the Realm. However in October 9, 1885, Yamagata Aritomo, the Minister of Internal Affairs, has asked the Foreign Minister Inoue Kaoru for suggestions. After careful consideration, Inoue Kaoru replied in October 21st that "this small island has a short distance with the Qing court. Due to the reason that the press of Qing court holds the rumor of our government coveting on the islands near Taiwan and warning the Qing government at present, we should wait for a better time to engage in such activities as building national markers and embarking on development on the islands." Hereby, the two ministers issued joint instruction to the governor of Okinawa Prefecture that "it was not appropriate to set up at present."

The governor of Okinawa Prefecture submitted the matter for approval to the Minister of Internal Affairs once again on January 13, 1890, saying that "the above-mentioned uninhabited islands have remained under no specific jurisdiction", and that he "intends to place them under the jurisdiction of the Office of Yaeyama Islands owing to the needs of managing aquaculture."

On November 2, 1893, the governor of Okinawa Prefecture submitted to the two ministers once again for setting up sovereignty markers in order to govern fishermen who tried to land on those islands. The Minister of Internal Affairs presented this issue to the Cabinet and consulted with the Foreign Minister on December 27, 1894, and then passed it to be examined by the Cabinet unanimously. Authorized by the Cabinet on January 21, 1985, the two ministers jointly issued instruction to the governor of Okinawa Prefecture on setting up sovereignty markers.

Report on Uotsuri Island and the other two islands under the jurisdiction of Japan

No.1

Report to the Minister of Internal Affairs

I have asked for instructions on Article 384 on November 5, 1885 and got written instructions on December 5th of the same year about placing Uotsuri-Island and the other two islands close to Ishigaki Island under the jurisdiction of the Office of Yaeyama Islands. The above-mentioned uninhabited islands have remained under no specific jurisdiction. I apply for placing them under the jurisdiction of the Office of Yaeyama Islands and setting up sovereignty markers owing to the needs of managing aquaculture. Therefore, I hereby apply for placing them under the jurisdiction of the Office of Yaeyama Islands.

The governor of Okinawa Prefecture January 13, 1890

Hence, the Cabinet made a decision on January 14, 1895 that Senkaku Islands was under the jurisdiction of Japan. On March 8, 1972, Japan's Ministry of Foreign Affairs issued the Basic View on the Sovereignty over the Senkaku Islands claiming that "the Cabinet decided to set up sovereignty markers in the island and officially include it into Japan's territory on January 14th, 1895." The illustration of "View on the Senkaku Islands" made by the Public Information and Cultural Affairs Bureau of Ministry of Foreign Affairs in May, 1972 was of the same kind.

Therefore, what was the decision made by the Cabinet?

The above-mentioned "the Procedure of Incorporating Taishō-tō, Kuba-Island and Uotsuri-Island to its territory" recorded the negotiation reached by the Minister of Internal Affairs and the Foreign Minister on December 27, 1894. The file contents are listed as follows.

File on setting up navigation marks

Confidential Article 133 (Signature)

Received on December 28, 1894

Submitted to

Esteemed Foreign Minister Mutsu Munemitsu,

In regard to setting up navigation marks in Kuba-Island and Uotsuri-Island which are under our jurisdiction, the governor of Okinawa Prefecture already submitted in the Appendix No.1 before and I transmitted instructions after negotiating with your ministry in 1885. The circumstances have now changed, so we should call for a decision by the cabinet on the issue.

Besides, I'm looking forward to receiving your reply along with a separate paper.

Japanese Minister of Internal Affairs and Viscount Yasushi Nomura (seal)

December 27, 1894

Words underlined signify the importance. Although the Minister of Internal Affairs wanted to submit proposal to the Cabinet, negotiations should be made with the Foreign Minister so that the dominant right transferred from the Foreign Minister to the Minister of Internal Affairs. In addition, what's the difference of circumstances between December 27th, 1885 and December 27th, 1894. Why did not the Japanese government care for the fact that China has already named those islands? And why did they transform the international affair to a domestic issue?

As the Foreign Minister approved of the negotiation put forward by the Minister of Internal Affairs, this proposal was submitted to the Cabinet. In addition, Appendix No.1 mentioned in this letter was about "the issue of Taishō-tō and the other two islands" which was submitted to the Minister of Internal Affairs Yamagata Aritomo on September 22, 1885 by the governor of Okinawa Prefecture Nishimura Sutezo. No. 2 was the file that the Minister of Internal Affairs submitted to the Chancellor of the Realm on October 9, 1885.

The proposal submitted to the Cabinet

Esteemed Prime Minister and Noble Ito Hirobumi,

The issue of setting up sovereignty markers should be submitted to the Cabinet.

Japanese Minister of Internal Affairs and Viscount Yasushi Nomura (seal)

January 12, 1895

(Attachment Paper)

The islands, Kuba-shima and Uotsuri-shima, located northwestward of Yaeyama Islands under the jurisdiction of Okinawa Prefecture, have heretofore been uninhabited islands. Due to recent visits to the said islands by individuals attempting to conduct fishing related businesses, and that such matters require regulation, it is desirable to have [the islands] be put under the jurisdiction of [Okinawa] Prefecture as requested in the Okinawa Prefectural Governor's petition. For the purpose of recognizing [the islands] under the jurisdiction of

[Okinawa] Prefecture, markers should be constructed in accordance to the said Petition. It is requested of the Cabinet Meeting to decide on the above matter."

On January 14, 1895, the Cabinet made a decision that "the Minister of Internal Affairs submitted for deliberation- appropriate administration should be carried out because someone intend to fish on uninhabited islands of Kuba-Island and Uotsuri-Island, which are on the northwest of Yaeyama Islands under the jurisdiction of Okinawa Prefecture. The governor of this prefecture submitted for the permission to include those islands to Japan's territory and set up sovereignty markers. If anything is proper, the proposal can be passed." The governor of Okinawa Prefecture was instructed on January 21 that "Your proposal of setting up sovereignty markers has been approved."

Yes, this is the truth that our country preoccupied terra nullius to incorporate Senkaku Islands into our territory. It also verifies the sovereignty our government has claimed according to the international law. The decision made by the Cabinet was not submitted to the Mikado (Japan Emperor) for edict, nor published in official newspaper. It was only instructed to the governor of Okinawa Prefecture without issuing any bulletins in this prefecture, so that Japanese citizens were unaware of the facts, not to mention foreigners.

The governor of Okinawa Prefecture held the doubt that Taishō-tō, Kuba-Island and Uotsuri-Island were equivalent to Diaoyu Dao, Huangwei Yu and Chiwei Yu which were recorded in Records of Messages from Chong-shan (Zhong Shan Chuan Xin Lu). He was also worried that the Qing empire had certain relation and the Foreign Minister Inoue Kaoru had scruple that China had already named those islands. These uninhabited islands (Taishō-tō, Kuba-Island and Uotsuri-Island in Okinawa Prefecture) were, in fact, the same Diaoyu Tai, Huangwei Yu and Chiwe Yu in China.

However, there were some alternations in the decision made by the Cabinet in 1895. The decision changed "national markers" in 1885 to "sovereignty markers". Besides, "uninhabited islands which are located between Okinawa Prefecture and Fuzhou" in 1885, was changed to "uninhabited islands close to Ishigaki Island under the jurisdiction of the Office of Yaeyama Islands" and then "uninhabited islands of Kuba-Island and Uotsuri-Island, which are on the northwest of Yaeyama Islands under the jurisdiction of Okinawa Prefecture" in the document of 1895. This reflects militarism in Meiji period strengthened their confidence by military expansion.

It should be highlighted that the documents related to Senkaku Islands was not published until March, 1950. It was because of the publishing of Japan Diplomatic Documents (18th volume) that citizens had the chance to know the truth. Therefore, in regard to the date of "January 21" in the instruction of "setting up sovereignty markers" to the governor of Okinawa Prefecture,

Dr. Okuhara Toshio[126] must directly refer to the original copy of the Cabinet's decision for confirmation.

2. My Opinions on the Problems in the Arguments Made by the Southern Compatriot Community

1. "The Sovereignty of Senkaku Islands and Japan"

It is unimaginable that Sourthern Compatriot Community, a peripheral community of Premier House, would act so actively in Senkaku Island issue. This community published Senkaku Island Special Issue in its interior magazine Okinawa Prefecture (quarterly) on March 25, 1971, the foreword of which was the article as "Gratitude to the Publishing of the Senkaku Island Special" written by the chairman Ohama.

It has been long time since the so-called tributary trade existed and ships dealings frequently between Okinawa Prefecture and China. Senkaku Islands is scattering in this lane and functioned as navigation mark for navigators at that time. Since ancient times, both documents from Okinawa Prefecture and China have recorded this island. However, before Japan incorporated it into Japan's territory, there was no country claiming this island as its national territory, nor did any country rule this place. Besides, after incorporating it to our territory, no country did ever give any objection.

By the way, in terms of administrative region, Senkaku Islands belongs to Ishigaki in Yaeyama Islands, with its land number as Tonoshiro of Ishigaki in the land register book. At that time, the island was naturally state-owned until Tatsushiro Koga bought this island for resources development in 1896. At present, the owner registered in the book is Zenji Koga- the successor of Tatsushiro Koga.

---

126   Okuhara Toshio, emeritus professor, Kokushikan University. Born in 1932 in the city of Dalian, Liaoning Province (then the Japan-controlled Kwantung Leased Territory). Earned his degree in political economy from Kokugakuin University in 1958, after which he went on to gain his master's and doctoral degrees in international law from Waseda University. Served as a lecturer, assistant professor, and professor in the Faculty of Political Science and Economics at Kokushikan University. He was the first Japanese international legal scholar to argue from the legal standpoint that the Senkaku Islands belong to Japan. His publications include "Senkaku Retto: Rekishi to seiji no aida" (The Senkaku Islands: Between History and Politics), in Nihon oyobi Nihonjin (Japan and the Japanese), January 1970; "Senkaku Retto no ryoyuken mondai" (Territorial Issues of the Senkaku Islands), in Kikan Okinawa (Okinawa Quarterly) 56 (1971); and "Mindai oyobi Shindai ni okeru Senkaku Retto no hoteki chii" (The Legal Status of the Senkaku Islands in the Ming and Qing Dynasties), in Kikan Okinawa 63 (1972). In 1972 he won the first award presented by the Yoshida Shigeru Memorial Foundation for academic endeavor for his research on Senkaku Islands sovereignty issues.

As stated above, there is no doubt that Senkaku Islands is Japanese territory, and its ownership is clear. However, as offshore oilfield was found beside the islands, it was just like a baby being awaken that the government of the Republic China in Taiwan informally claimed its sovereignty. Moreover, the Communist Party of China also began to intervene in this issue especially after the leak of Japan-Taiwan cooperative development plan.

It is hard to determine whether it is a good or bad thing because Senkaku Islands lie in a corner of the so-called continental shelf linked to mainland China. On one hand, it is a solid foothold for Japan; one the other hand, it is possible for others to have excuses by taking advantage of the continental shelf theory. All in all, the issue of offshore submarine resources of Senkaku is bound to involve territorial rights and continental shelf theory, thus leading to international disputes.

Southern Compatriot Community is worried about this. In order to solidify Japan's good position, they also feel the urgency to conduct investigations as soon as possible and give relevant suggestions to the government. In last three years, with a huge sum of fund, it has been a governmental project of Japan to have scientific researches continuously.

In regard to the issue of national territory, Japanese government itself should directly present reasons to verify its sovereignty. However, why did Southern Compatriot Community spend about a year to collect "the literature which can verify the sovereignty of Senkaku Islands"? Why did they found the "Senkaku Islands Research Council"? The afterward in the 56th volume of Okinawa Prefecture (quarterly) gave the answer: Southern Compatriot Community "dispatched the lecturer of Kokushikan University (Author's note: professor at present)–Okuhara Toshio to collect buried literatures" in "Okinawa and Ishigaki Island", and finally got an unexpected number of about 200 literatures, valuable official documents and old files". However, among those precious documents, some are not enough or even of no use to verify sovereignty. (Please refer to the article "Reasons of Senkaku Islands' Sovereignty" in the first issue of Chūōkōron in 1978)

Senkaku Islands Research Council (hereinafter referred to as Research Council) has spent about one year on collecting fundamental literatures. And the Research Council published an article "The Sovereignty of Senkaku Islands and Japan" (published in the 56th volume of Okinawa Prefecture (quarterly) on March 25, 1971), written by Prof. Okuhara Toshio. Therefore, I will conclude the overall content of Prof. Okuhara Toshio's article which was published in Chūōkōron as follows.

The Article on Research Council Report Written by Prof. Okuhara Toshio

The article on Research Council work has mainly included the following parts: the Preface, The Incorporation of Territory, The Process to Verify Sovereignty, Legal Position after World War II, The Administration by United States and Government of the Ryukyu Islands, Conclusion and etc.. Judging by this article, the declaration of "The Sovereignty of Senkaku Islands" made by the Government of the Ryukyu Islands on September 17, 1970 was also written by Prof. Okuhara Toshio.

The findings of the Research Council mainly included the following:

Preface

Senkaku Islands were incorporated into Japan's territory according to the occupation principles of the international law.

The incorporation of Senkaku Islands was smooth without receiving any protests from any countries in the world.

Sovereignty of Senkaku Islands

Japan began to indirectly claim its ownership of Senkaku Islands in 1879, which meant that every island in Senkaku Islands was tagged as Japanese territory in the 1879 English version of Japan Map (edited by Matsui Tadabei). The name of Hoa-pin-san Island (refer to Uotsuri-Island), Kobi sho and Sekibi sho were used in this map, Kita KoIsland and Minami KoIsland along with nearby reefs were tagged as convex islands. Besides, those islands could also be found in Japanese Jurisdiction Map compiled by the geographical department of the Ministry of Internal Affairs in 1881. In 1885, after listening to Oshiro Eiho's report on Senkaku Islands, the governor of Okinawa Prefecture dispatched Izumo Maru to conduct field investigation and again Kaimon warship in 1892.

The Incorporation of Territory

In order to incorporate Senkaku Islands under the jurisdiction of Okinawa Prefecture and set up sovereignty markers, the governor of Okinawa Prefecture has submitted all together three times respectively in 1885, 1890 and 1893. On December 27, 1894, the Minister of Internal Affairs agreed to submit this issue to the Cabinet after discussing with the Foreign Minister. The Cabinet decided on January 14, 1895 that Okinawa Prefecture should have jurisdiction over Senkaku Islands and approved to build sovereignty markers as reported by local governor. And Japanese government informed the governor of Okinawa Prefecture on January 21.

The Process to Legally Verify Sovereignty

The governor of Okinawa Prefecture incorporated Senkaku Islands into the Yaeyama District in April, 1896, thus accomplishing the regulated procedure of international law. Later in December 1902, the Senkaku Islands was incorporated into Ishigaki Island.

After incorporating Uotsuri-Island, Kuba-Island, Kita KoIsland and Minami KoIsland of the Senkaku Islands into Yaeyama District, Japanese government claimed they were state land and registered them in Land Register. Uotsuri-Island and Kuba-Island were under the administration of the Ministry of Agriculture and Forestry, while Kita KoIsland and Minami KoIsland were governed by the Ministry of Internal Affairs. As Taishō-tō is small in size (Note by Masaki: the length of the island is about 200 metres), it had not been claimed as state land until July 25, 1921 when it was administrated by the Ministry of Internal Affairs and renamed as Taisho Island.

(2) In December, 1903, the temporary department of land consolidation in Okinawa Prefecture conducted an initial field measurement and drew maps (Author's note: The outline map of Hoa-pin-san Island published on page 96 of the 56th volume of Okinawa Prefecture (quarterly) was perhaps recently drawn, sketching profile, rivers, houses and harbors in the island. Hoa-pin-san Island is a Chinese name, herein means Uotsuri-Island).

Field measurement was carried out by Japan Hydrographic and Oceangraphic Department in 1915, Marine Hydrographic Department in 1931 and Forestry Department of Okinawa Prefecture in 1931. In 1900, Kuroiwa and Miyajima Konosuke were entrusted by Tatsushiro Koga to carry out academic research who worked in Koga's company office in the Yaeyama Islands. The resources fact-finding mission of the Ministry of Agriculture and Forestry also landed on Senkaku Islands in 1932. All of those investigations were of national or regional level. However, Tatsushiro Koga sent people to collect feathers of albatross and marine products in Senkaku Islands in 1884, which belonged to his individual behaviors.

(3) In September, 1896, Japanese government approved to rent four islands, respectively Uotsuri-Island (i.e. Senkaku Island- Author's note), Kuba-Island (i.e. Kobi sho- Author's note), Minami KoIsland and Kita KoIsland to Tatsushiro Koga free of charge for 30 years. Tatsushiro Koga has invested a large sum of fund to develop Senkaku Islands since 1897. He built houses, water storage facilities, wharf and trestle as well as conducted projects like protecting seabirds, experimental cultivation and tree planting in Uotsuri-Island and Kuba-Island. Therefore, he sent 50 workers each year in 1897 and 1898, 29 workers in 1899, and extra 13 men and 9 women in 1900 to Senkaku Islands. Meanwhile, he was also devoted to collecting feathers and guano of albatross. Owing to his achievement in developing culture, Tatsushiro Koga was awarded Medal with Blue Ribbon in 1909.

(4) After Tatsushiro Koga died in 1918, Zenji Koga followed in his father's footsteps to continue developing engineering. Zenji Koga made dry-cured skipjack and specimens of various seabirds, cut trees, and produced sandfish's fins, shellfish, turtle shell and seabird cans in Uotsuri-Island and Minami KoIsland. In order to produce dried skipjack, 80 fishermen and 70 to 80 peeling workers lived on the two islands at one time. The project of collecting albatross's feathers was shut down in 1915 owing to species extinction and cat damage (Author's note: It was said that the number of pet cats once exceeded 2000.). In regard to guano collection, this project was also suspended due to rising freight and losses caused by World War I.

(5) The free use of four islands which were state-owned expired in 1926, and thus the government changed it into an annual lease contract. However, Tatsushiro Koga insisted on paid transfer; therefore the government sold the state land to Koga on March 31st, 1932 at the selling price of 1825 yen on Uotsuri-Island, 247 yen on Kuba-Island, 47 yen on Minami KoIsland and 31.50 on Kita KoIsland.

(6) In 1919, 31 fishermen from Hui'an country, Fujian Province of China were in danger near the Uotsuri-Island. Zenji Koga and others rescued them and settled them in Ishigaki country, and finally sent them back to China. The Consul of Republic of China in Nagasaki therewith wrote a letter expressing thanks to four people including Ishigaki chief and businessman Koga. In that letter, the site that fishermen met in danger was definitely written as Ocean Island of Senkaku Islands, Yaeyama, Okinawa Prefecture of Japanese Empire. The so-called Ocean Island refers to Uotsuri-Island, also known as Hoa-pin-san Island.

2. Senkaku Islands' Administration by the United States and US Governence over the Ryukyu Islands

(1) According to Article 3 of the Treaty of San Francisco, Senkaku Islands was placed under the administration of the United States and the local government of the Ryukyu Islands was also governed by the United States. Taishō Island, the only state land among the islands, was served as the training area of US army since April 16, 1956. Following, since October, 1955, the US army utilized Kuba-Island as its training area. Taishō Island was employed by United States Navy, while Kuba-Island was used by United States Air Force before October, 1955 and by United States Navy afterwards. In regard to the employment of Kuba-Island, the United States demanded the Government of the Ryukyu Islands as its agent to sign lease contract with Zenji Koga and paid rent and royalties.

(2) In May, 1969, administrative markers were established in five islands of Senkaku Islands under the supervision of the Mayor of Ishigaki City.

(3) In July, 1970, funded by the government of the United States, warning boards to penalize trespassing were set up in five islands including Taishō Island.

(4) The patrol boat Citose began cruising since 1968. Citose began to cruise the area of Minami KoIsland on October 2, 1968 and Kuba-Island on July 11, 1970. At that time, Taiwan workers who were found cutting a wreck were requested to leave. However, the United States authorized them to continue their work, thus Taiwan's operations in this region was acknowledged as legal.

Conclusion

Considering the above situation, I can conclude that, owing to the actual smooth and continuous rule of Japan, the reasons are sufficient to verify Japan's jurisdiction rights over the Senkaku islands according to the international law.

Critique of the Research Council's Arguments

"The Sovereignty of Senkaku Islands and Japan" published by the Research Council is of great importance. I will pinpoint to doubtful points in this report.

Several Questions

About the Occupation

It was stated by the Research Council that "Senkaku Islands was incorporated into Japan's territory according to the occupation principles of the international law."

However, the international law illustrates the following premises about incorporating a territory through a state act.

(1) Cession and annexation are two methods to acquire territory through agreements. For example, Meiji Militarism acquired Taiwan by cession while Korea by annexation.

(2) Conquest and occupation are two unilateral actions to acquire territory. Conquest is the act of defeating an opponent and occupying all of its territory.

(3) Accretion is another method. It describes the geographical process by which new land becomes attached to existing land owing to sedimentation in the coast, river bank and lakeshore.

Occupation is a method of acquiring territory which belongs to no one (Terra Nullius). The European powers made advantage of this principle to seize colonies which were virgin soil outside European territory. Therefore, since early 1800s, American and African Continents were reduced to colonies of great-powers through occupation. This kind of principle was totally applied to conceal their piracy.

The occupation must be intended as a claim of sovereignty and must be effective control over the terra nullius. According to international law, terra nullius refers to territory which has never been subject to the sovereignty of any state. Occupation can be carried out as long as the terra nullius is not subject to the sovereignty of any state even though there are habitants.

The specific requirements of the occupation are listed as follows:

(1) The subject of the occupation is a state, i.e., the occupation must be implemented by a state.

(2) The claim of sovereignty refers to informing other states about incorporating a region into its territory by virtue of declaration, legislative or executive actions and announcement. Generally speaking, as regard to the problem of whether other countries accomplish the requirements of occupation, means other than announcement can be applied to claim its sovereignty.

(3) Effective occupation should be made to terra nullius. It cannot be regarded as effective occupation that incorporating an existing terra nullius into one's territory by merely setting up national flag. According to the United States, the effective occupation refers to physical possession, i.e., the land is applied to actual use and there are habitants. However, the judicial precedent of the International Court of Justice misled people to regard it as regional authority to control land. Therefore, even if there are people dwelling on the land, effective occupation cannot be verified since it is not under the jurisdiction of a state. In contrast, a state can conduct occupation on a terra nullius by sending warships and state vessels to inspect regularly so as to indicate the state's jurisdiction over this land. Occupation can be also applied to Polar Regions on which people are hard to live.

It is clear that the Research Council believed that Senkaku Islands was incorporated into our territory by occupation. They also took pains to find out reasons to satisfy the requirements of occupation regulated by the international law. For example, the governor of Yaeyama Island also took part in the investigation of 1990, which was conducted by Miya Island and privately entrusted by Tatsushiro Koga, so that it was also an official investigation.

As far as I'm concerned, based on the research result of Research Council, our government claimed publicly that Senkaku Islands was incorporated into Japan's territory due to the occupation principle. In other words, our government began to claim the sovereignty according to occupation principle after the Research Council submitted its documents which could verify the preoccupation.

(1) On March 25, 1971, the Research Council published its research result that Senkaku Islands was incorporated into Japan's territory according to occupation principle.

(2) On December 12, 1971, the Prime Minister Sato Eisaku said that Senkaku Islands was not ceded from China based on the Article 2 in the Treaty of Shimonoseki, in reply to the inquiry put forward by Congressman Narazaki Yanosuke.

(3) On March 8, 1972, the Foreign Ministry held a press conference to distribute the printed Basic View on the Sovereignty over the Senkaku Islands, claiming that Senkaku Islands was incorporated into our territory due to occupation principle.

(4) In addition, in May 1972, the Public Information and Cultural Affairs Bureau of Ministry of Foreign Affairs claimed in "View on the Senkaku Islands" that "the Cabinet decided to set up sovereignty markers in the island and officially include it into Japan's territory on January 14, 1895. The acquisition of this land was on the basis of occupation principle of the international law."

Before that, our government claimed repeatedly that Senkaku Islands was part of the Nansei Islands in history so that the sovereignty was of no doubt. This statement was altered into "the territory incorporated according to occupation principle".

The issue of Senkaku Islands is unknown to our people until the emerging topic of its abundant oil reserves. As a matter of course, Meiji government didn't ever claim this island, which was claimed in 18th and 23rd volumes of Japan's Diplomatic Documents, which was edited and collected by the Foreign Ministry and published by the UN association of Japan. The 18th volume was published in December 1950 while the 23rd volume in March 1952. Before that, no one knew the process of the incorporation of Senkaku Islands except those who has access to see the original documents. In addition, even though the documents were published, few could afford the high price of 7000 yen and 8000 yen respectively. The initial monthly wages of temporary college graduates were 7000 to 10000 yen.

The Research Council concluded the occupation reasons from Japan's Diplomatic Documents. The purpose of the Research Council was explicit that all its activities were to "verify Japan's jurisdiction over the Senkaku Islands". The fact of preoccupation should be claimed in order to testify the acquisition in that there was little choice in occupation or cession. If it was cession, the Senkaku Islands has already given back to China on October 25, 1945.

Well, were the preemptive occupation procedures totally implemented or not?

Neither imperial order nor the decision made by the Japanese Cabinet was made public and published. Besides, neither the government nor the Okinawa Prefecture issued any official notes about the instruction of setting sovereignty markers in Uotsuri-Island and Kuba-Island. Therefore, no one was aware of this case. There was only one fact that Tatsushiro Koga along with his son Zenji Koga rented Uotsuri-Island (Senkaku Island), Kuba-Island (i.e. Kobi sho- Author's note), Minami KoIsland and Kita KoIsland from Japanese government and established business in middle Taisho period. This was why Prof. Okuhara Toshio claimed the preoccupation as the most important prerequisite to implement effective governing. However, there's no need to scream at effective governing. After the First Sino-Japanese War, the border between Okinawa and Taiwan did not exist. Besides, Formosa and the islands appertaining or belonging to the said island of Formosa as well as the Penghu Islands were included into Japan's territory. Therefore, Japan implemented effective rule over Senkaku Islands rather than occupation on terra nullius.

The uninhabited Senkaku Islands in 1896 changed into terra nullius again in around 1932. Since then, it had been inhabited for more than 40 years.

Senkaku Islands was called as the second Take Island (known as Dokdo in Korea). No official notice was issued concerning on incorporating TakeIsland into Japan's territory, which was decided by the Cabinet on January 28, 1905. As it was stated in Okuma Ryoichi's Take Island History, "The state sovereignty can be performed immediately after the Cabinet claimed the incorporation through conference decision. There were many similar cases to include terra nullius into Japan's territory." (See, Kiyoshi Inoue's Senkaku Islands, p. 132, Modern Review Press)

However, the Minister of Internal Affairs instructed the Cabinet's decision about Take Island as a government decree to the governor of Islands Prefecture on February 15. The content were that "Take Island, which is on 37°30'N (North Latitude) and 131°55'E (East Longitude), 85 sea miles northwest to Oki Islands, is put under the administration of the Oki Islands officer. This issue should be announced within the region." (refer to Okuma Ryoichi's Take Island History) The governor of Islands Prefecture issued No. 40 notice on February 22, which released the above contents (refer to: Ueji's Senkaku Islands and Take Island, p. 129, Education Institute).

In regard to international law, Japan decided to compromise settlement on the issue of a terra nullius which was southwest to Bonin Island before the incorporation of Senkaku Islands. The Ministry of Internal Affairs informed the Foreign Ministry that they intended to name "three islands- between 24°00'-25°30'N, 141°00'-25°30'E and 141°00'-141°30'E, which are scattered in the southwest ocean of Bonin Island" as Iwo To Island, North Iwo To Island and South Iwo To Island respectively; besides, they were put under the jurisdiction of Bonin Island. Later on, the Cabinet made the decision and thus issued No. 190 imperial order on the government bulletin on September 9, 1891. Of course the imperial order had explicitly stated the location, name and ruling local government. By the way, it was explicitly stated in the document of Concerning on the Jurisdiction of Terra Nullius which was submitted to the Cabinet by the government that the location of terra nullius was identified by longitude and latitude, the name was Oki Daitō and thus Daitō Islands were apportioned to Shimajiri District.

However, the procedures of incorporating preoccupied Senkaku Islands were not the same. Japan adopted complete procedures to include island which had nothing to do with China while the same methods was not applied in regard to Senkaku Islands in fear of deteriorating relationship with China. It was because Japan thought there's no need to do like that. The reason was nothing except that Japan had defeated China in the First Sino-Japanese War (1894-95).

2. About Incorporating Formosa (Taiwan) into the Territory of Japan

In terms of incorporating Formosa (Taiwan) into the territory of Japan, some scholars may defend: "Japan didn't receive any protest from any country and incorporated Formosa in a peaceful way."

Although no country in the world lodged a protest against the incorporation, the point of the problem relies on that no matter in 1895 (the 28th year of Meiji period) or now Taiwan is the problem between China and Japan and is none of the business of either the US or the Soviet Union. Moreover, it is also important how China could look at the fact that Japan was China's most atrocious enemy in the past 50 years, from 1894 to 1945 (the 20th year of Showa period). Because of the Treaty of Shimonoseki, there was no border between Okinawa and Taiwan any longer. Besides, after the Mukden Incident (a bombing act made by Japan in Liutiaohu, northeastern part of China, also known as the "Liutiaohu Incident") in September 18 of 1931, the imperial Japanese Army began a large-scale military invasion of the northeastern part of China; Then after the Marco Polo Bridge Incident (also known as the "Lugouqiao/Lugou Bridge Incident" or the "July 7 Incident") on July 7 of 1937, Japan started the large-scale invasion of China, which is called the Second Sino-Japanese War (1937-1945). Up until now, international Law has never prevented any aggressive war and we have to think that the results of aggression were the cession and annexation of the territory.

About the Meaning of Sovereignty

Some scholarly arguments may refute China by saying that "from 1879 (the 12th year of Meiji period), Japan intended and attempted to obtain the sovereignty of the Senkaku Islands."

There is such a saying because that in 1879 the English version of Map of the Great Japan (edited by Matsui Tadabei) was published, in which every Senkaku island has been marked with names and was shown as the territory of Japan. the so-called names were HéPíng Shān, Huángwěi Yǔ and Chìwěi Yǔ. But the names were all Chinese. HéPíng Shān was marked as Hoapinsu or Hoapinsan on the sea map and navigation route. Japan claimed the sovereignty of the Senkaku Islands only for the excuse of the map, but there was no marker of the Senkaku Islands on the map. Besides, Kitagawa, in the notes of the map, wrote that "A record said that when in March of the 28th year of Meiji period the peace talk between Qing and Japan was held in the Shunpanrō hall of Shimonoseki, Japan set the step into the east sea. Later then on, the map of Japan has been completely changed." On the map, there was the Kuba Island, namely the current Kuba Island of Islandjiri District. With that said, in 1895 Japan abandoned his intention of obtaining the sovereignty of the Senkaku Islands in 1879.

What on earth happened in the 12th year of Meiji period?

In this year, Meiji government abolished the Han (haihan-chiken) system and set up the Prefecture system in Ryukyu by force and China and Japan argued about the partition of Ryukyu. At that time, there was no dispute over the sovereignty of the Senkaku Islands. Some people ignored such a historical and political background and irresponsibly deduced that in that year China has had the intention to acquire the sovereignty over the Senkaku Islands. Such a deduction was totally wrong. Even Professor Okuhara himself said: "we discussed the issue from the perspective of International Law, but that doesn't mean that we could ignore historical fact."

In addition, there was also a saying that in 1881 (the 14th year of Meiji period) Geology Documents Compilation Bureau of Home Ministry published the Map of the Prefectures of the Great Japan, on which HéPíng Shān, Huángwěi Yǔ and Chìwěi Yǔ were marked. As it was, why couldn't it be simply say that the Senkaku Islands was our territory? Why did they say China had the intention to obtain the territory?

About the Measures for Incorporating

In terms of the annexation of the Senkaku Islands, this argument was made: "the cabinet meeting….has made the decision with regard to this" and in April of 1896 (the 29th year of Meiji period) the incorporation was finished according to Japanese domestic law.

Is the argument fair ?

If this argument was fair, it would mean that on January 14 of 1895 (the 28th year of Meiji period), the cabinet meeting approved the three report of setting up national markers on the islands made by the governor of Okinawa prefecture respectively in 1885 (the 18th year of Meiji period), 1890 and 1893; on January 21st of 1895, Meiji government finished the whole procedures of incorporating by issuing order of carrying out the marker set-up to the governor. This is ridiculous!

When the Senkaku islands problem was turned to be significant by the petroleum, many people ever said that the Senkaku Islands has been incorporated into the territory of Japan according to the Edict No. 13, which was issued on March 5th of 1896 (the 29th year of Meiji). That is because that if Japan wants to exercise the right of pre-empting in terms of a terra nullius, Japan must first show the plan and then must implement the plan according to imperial edict, which was formally regulated by the old constitution.

Then Edict No.13 came into being.

(1) Since that the Senkaku Islands were incorporated into Japan in the 29th year of Meiji, not a country, let alone China has ever claimed the sovereignty of the Senkaku Islands and also there was no dispute arised from this (from editorial of The Okinawa Times on September 7 of 1970).

(2) Since Japanese government announced the sovereignty of the Senkaku islands in the 29th year of Meiji, … (from the editorial of Ryukyu News on September 13th of 1970).

(3) In 1896, the Senkaku Islands was incorporated into the territory of our country and was administered by Okinawa prefecture (from the editorial of Daily News on December 6 of 1970).

(4) On January 14th of 1895 (the 28th year of Meiji), the islands were decided to be Japan's territory in the cabinet meeting. Edict No. 13 was issued based on the decision of the cabinet meeting and since then the islands were virtually turned into Japan's and were administrated by Ishigaki village(namely the current Ishigaki city), Yaeyama district of Okinawa prefecture (from "Explication of News about the Senkaku Islands", published on Tokyo Shimbun on April 5 of 1971).

(5) In 1881 (the 14th year of Meiji), the Bureau of Geology of Home Ministry expressed the intention of "sovereignty". After that, the Senkaku Islands were formally incorporated into the territory of Japan in April of 1896 (the 29th year of Meiji) and was administrated by Yaeyama district of Okinawa prefecture (from Socialist Party Monthly on March 24 of 1972).

(6) Japan's claim was based on such a fact: on the cabinet meeting held in 1895 (the 28th year of Meiji) and in the Edict No.13 issued in 1896 (the 29th year of Meiji), the Senkaku Islands, as the territory of Japan, were formally incorporated into Okinawa prefecture (from Minagawa Kou's article titled as "The Senkaku Islands").

(7) In the 29th year of Meiji (1896), Japanese government issued the Edict No. 13, announcing the sovereignty over the Senkaku Islands (from Shinshiro Toshihiko's article of "The Senkaku Islands and the Continental Shelf").

(8) After the cabinet meeting on January 14 of the 28th year of Meiji, the Edict No. 13 was issued on April 1 of the 29th year of Meiji to confirm the Senkaku Islands to be the territory of Japan… (from Kaneshiro Mutsu's article of "Around the Senkaku Islands Dispute", published in the first issue of Legal Times in October of 1970).

(9) On January 14 of 1895 (the 28th year of Meiji), the islands were decided to be Japan's territory in the cabinet meeting issued on April 1 of the 29th year of Meiji (please refer to the declaration About the Sovereignty over the Senkaku Islands made by Ryukyu government's declaration on September 17th of 1970).

Together with the above statements, it was emphasized that Japan incorporated the Senkaku Islands into the territory on the basis of the decision given in cabinet meeting held in 1895. The specific assertions are as the following:

1. Japan's behavior is legal, conforming to the principle of preemptive acts provisioned in International Law. Based on the decision of the cabinet meeting on January 14th of the 28th year of Meiji, the Senkaku Islands, as a part of Okinawa, was incorporated into Japan's territory (Foreign Affairs Ministry).

2. According the preemptive act principle of the International Law, our country, in January of the 28th year of Meiji, confirmed the sovereignty over the Senkaku islands and concluded the islands within the administration of Yaeyama district (said by the Premier Ito Hirobumi and Foreign Affairs Minister Munemitsu Mutsu at that time). From then on, the fact has been recognized internationally since there wasn't any protest against Japan's behavior (please refer to "Sovereignty of the Senkaku Islands—Thermometer of the Economy" published in Asahi Shimbun on May 19 of 1972).

3. Before being incorporated into Japan in the 28th year of Meiji, the Senkaku Islands were in a terra nullius status, so-called in International Law. ... In the 28th year of Meiji, the cabinet meeting took the decision for incorporation (annexation) ... (cited from the editorial of Asahi Shimbun on March 2 of 1972).

4. Based on the actual situation, we thought Japan has won the Qing-Japan war and thus held the cabinet meeting in January of the 28th year of Meiji. The meeting, according to the preemptive principle of the International Law, decided the sovereignty of the Senkaku Islands (please refer to the editorial published in Nikon Keizai Shimbun on May 5 of 1972).

At this point Prof. Toshio Okuhara's argument loses scientific spirit.

Based on the decision of the cabinet meeting, Japan took measures regarding the islands. On April 1 of 1896 (the 29th year of Meiji), the measure, namely Edict No. 3, was taken. Surely the edict was about the division of districts in Okinawa prefecture and defined the administrative scope of the five districts, namely Okinawa prefecture was divided into shimajiri District, Nakagami District, Kunigami District, Miyako District and Yaeyama District. The edict wasn't directly related to the matter of incorporating the Senkaku islands into Japan's territory according to Japan's domestic law. However, the governor of Okinawa prefecture explained that the Senkaku islands were incorporated into the Yaeyama islands in Edict No. 13; and was administrated by

Yaeyama district. As the above mentioned, the governor of Okinawa prefecture took the measure of incorporating the Senkaku islands into Yaeyama districts for the sake of administrative division not for administrative incorporating. Before being administratively incorporated into Yaeyama district, the Senkaku islands have never been incorporated into the territory of Japan according to the domestic law. Therefore, the incorporation into Yaeyama district wasn't a simple administrative incorporation and in the meantime the incorporation measure stipulated into the domestic law was also taken (please refer to Professor Toshio Okuhara's article "The Senkaku Islands and its Legal Status", published on The Okinawa Times on September 4 of 1970).

In Edict No. 13, there was no word of the "Senkaku islands". Before the Edict No. 13 the Senkaku Islands were incorporated into the administration of Daito Island. Based on Edict No. 13, the Senkaku islands were incorporated into the administration of Shimajiri District. Daito Island was the island that was mentioned in Inoue Kaoru's official document on October 21 of 1885 (the 18th year of Meiji) to reply Yamagata Aritomo's consultation. In the official document titled with "Reply to the Request of Setting-up National Marker on the Inhabited Island between Okinawa Prefecture and Qing", Inoue Kaoru asked Yamagata Aritomo not to publish the field survey on Daito Island on the official newspaper or other newspaper. On November 20 of 1891 (the 24th year of Meiji), Tatsushiro Koga obtained the permit to develop the islands from Kanji Maruoka, the governor of Okinawa prefecture.

In his article published on The Okinawa Times what the conservative Professor Okuhara has ignored the matter that the Senkaku islands were not incorporated into the territory of Japan according to Edict No.13. In addition, according to the explanation of the governor of Okinawa prefecture, the Kuba-Island and the Uotsuri-Island weren't incorporated into the territory of Japan because the two islands have been incorporated into the territory of Yaeyama District long ago. However, not like Daito Island, there was no imperial edict issued to deal with the problem of the Kuba-Island and the Uotsuri-Island.

Besides, Professor Okuhara racked his brains in scheming the scope of the Senkaku islands that was incorporated into the territory of Japan.

In January of the 28th year of Meiji, it was decided on the cabinet meeting that the Uotsuri-Island and the Kuba-Island were incorporated into the administration of the Okinawa prefecture. The Senkaku islands included the Senkaku Islands, the Nanxiao Islan, the Beixiao Island, the Oki-no-Minami-iwa, the Oki-no-Kita-iwa, a lithoherm named Tobise and the Kumeaka Island, which were not mentioned in the decision of the cabinet meeting at all. Is that could be understood that the cabinet meeting in January of the 28th year of Meiji has no intention to acquire the territory of those islands and lithoherm (please refer to Okuhara's article mentioned in the above).

While Professor Okuhara was contemplating what on earth belongs to the Senkaku islands, Japan only had 3 miles territorial waters. Professor Okuhara must think the following:

Except the Kumeaka Island, those Yus or lithoherm dispersed at the Uotsuri-Island nearby. Besides, the Nanxiao Island, the Beixiao Island, the Oki-no-Minami-iwa and the Oki-no-Kita-iwa were situated at the place 1 miles to 3 miles in the territorial waters of the Uotsuri-Island (editor's note: here Professor Okuhara refers to sea miles).

Thus, although our country has expressed the intention to acquire the territory of the Uotsuri-Island, this was enough to prove that our country already had the intention to have the territory of the Yus and lithoherm (please refer to Okuhara's article mentioned in the above).

To make it plain, Professor Okuhara meant the following:

(1) Fortunately, there was a lithoherm named Tobise 0.8 miles within the territorial waters of Uotsuri-Island.

(2) Tobise could be seen above the sea level (editor's note: about 3.4 meters above sea level) on the high tide, thus Tobise could be accounted as an island according to the definition of the Island in International Law.

(3) Tobise has a 3 sea miles long territorial waters.

(4) Kita-ko Island was situated in the territorial waters of Tobise, about 2.7 miles away from Tobise. Thus Kita-koIsland was the territory of Tobise.

(5) In the territorial waters of Beixiao Island, it was the Nanxiao Island, about 200 meters away from the Kita-koIsland; it was the Oki-no-Minami-iwa, about 2 miles away from the Kita-koIsland.

(6) in the territorial waters of Oki-no-Minami-iwa, it was the Oki-no-Kita-iwa, about 2 miles away from Oki-no-Minami-iwa.

(7) To conclude, if Tobise was considered to be base point, it could be understood why those Yus and lithoherms could also be counted as the territory of Uotsuri-Island.

However, the problem is the Kumeaka Island (Taisho Island or Chìwěi Yǔ). Professor Okuhara might consider the following:

Kumeaka Island is situated 90 km away from the Kuba-Island (Huángwěi Yǔ), 100 km from Uotsuri-Island and 195 km from Ishigaki port. Although it was decided on the cabinet meeting to set up national markers on "the inhabited islands that were called the Kuba-Island and Uotsuri-Island and were situated at the northwest of the Yaeyama Islands", the fact is that the Kumeaka Island was situated 70 miles away from the northeast of Miyako Island and 105 miles away from the northwest of Ishigaki, not "at the northwest of the Yaeyama

Islands". They referred to the two islands dispersing between the Okinawa prefecture and Fuzhou of Qing government, but not the Kumeaka Island in Japan's diplomatic papers in 1885 (the 18th year of Meiji). in 1890 (the 23rd year of Meiji), they referred to the two islands, but not the Uotsuri-Island. In this case, even if the cabinet meeting didn't specially exclude the Kumeaka Island, it wasn't sure the Kumeaka Island was included in the decision of the cabinet meeting. Hence, according to the explanation of the governor of Okinawa, the whole Senkaku islands, including the Kumeaka Island, have been incorporated into the Yaeyama prefecture and thus into the territory of Japan in Edict No. 13 in 1896 (the 29th year of Meiji). (Please refer to the above-mentioned article by Okuhara.

According to the governor's explanation, Kumeaka Island (Chìwěi Yǔ) was also included into the Yaeyama prefecture. Kumeaka Island was identified to be the territory of Japan (the 10th year of Taishō) and was renamed into the Taishō-tō in 1921. Even if Japan has the intention to incorporate Taishō-tō (Chìwěi Yǔ), there were no conditions for preempting.

Even if a country has intention to obtain the territory of an island, places flag and set up a stele claiming the ownership on the island as well as informs other countries of the intention, the preempting will be invalid before actual incorporation. Especially state agency cannot be set up on a preempted inhabited island or on desert. If any emergency happened on the island or desert, a country can only send the state agency to visit the island but should inform other countries of the preemptive intention. There shouldn't be any opposition from other countries in case of dispute in future (please refer to page 125 to 127 of International Law, written by Ryoichi Okada and published by Keisoshobo).

According to Professor Okuhara's logic, Japan didn't effectively rule the Kumeaka Island, but it was the terra nullius that was preempted by Japan, thus he admits that the Kumeaka Island still possesses the status of terra nullius.

Chìwěi Yǔ (ChìYǔ), Huángwěi Yǔ, the Diaoyu Islands (YúdiàoYǔ and HéPíng Shān) have appeared in the historical papers of China and Okinawa from and have been widely known by the European countries since ancient times. If Japan preempted theose islands, Japan should inform other countries the intention to preempt in advance. However, against the political background at that time, Japan has no need to inform other countries in advance since Japan won the war.

It was in May of 1969 (the 44th year of Showa period) that Japan set up national marker on the Taisho Island for the first time, because that saying that the Senkaku islands were rich in petroleum made a stir. The mayor of Ishigaki, which was under the administration of U.S. at that time, issued the order to set up the national marker. Ishigaki has ever been used as the proving ground and the US has dropped bombs and shot cannons to the island from the air and the sea. Prior to this, Japan has never conducted any valid administration on the island. In March of 1873 (the 6th year of Meiji), Foreign Ministry sent seven large- and medium-sized national maps to Ryukyu Han, being afraid that the Okinawa islands would be grabbed by other countries if the boundary wasn't clearly marked and asking Ryukyu to raising the national map from day to night on the Kume Island, Miyako Island, Ishigaki Island, Iriomote Island and Yonakuni Island. But Japan has never raised maps on any Senkaku island or set up national markers.

However, it might diverge from the topic if we over-detailedly discuss the preemptive principle. After the signing of Treaty of Shimonoseki, the Pescadores Group, Formasa and other islands were pillaged from China and there was no boundary between Okinawa and Formasa anymore. Hence, no matter there was order or not, no matter the governor of Okinawa was informed of setting up national marker or not, it was unnecessary.

With regard to the above, Professor Okuhara wrote the following:

The cabinet meeting Decision, on January 14, (the 28th year of Meiji) was the time when the outcome of Qing-Japan war has been definitely settled and the peace talks was going to start and when Japan was striving to gain western powers' recognition for the incorporation of Taiwan to Japan. Therefrom, in such a background, it wasn't hard to imagine that the Qing government who would soon lose Taiwan had such a political judgment: the ownership of the terra nullius—the most insignificant Senkaku islands would not cause dispute.

However, one point was suspicious: before being incorporated into the territory of our country, the Senkaku islands were China's in the sense of legislation, which should be the premise of the discussion. If it was assumed the Senkaku islands were the territory of China, the stance of our country would be harmed. If the Senkaku islands were taken as the affiliated islands of Formosa, in the article 2 of the peace treaty, Formosa and its affiliated islands have been ceded to Japan. Thus, after World War II, Formosa was returned and naturally the Senkaku Islands was also been returned.

Further, if the Senkaku islands are not acknowledged as the affiliated islands of Formosa (Taiwan), Japan (our country) can acquire the sovereignty of the islands which was China's only through the law. However, some people argue that law basis can only be used under the condition when Qing-Japan war hadn't occurred (but it has occurred). On the premise of the Qing-Japan war, it was logical that our country claimed the sovereignty of the Senkaku islands based on the legal claims, but it has to admit that the claim of our country was vulnerable. That's because before proposing the "prescription" principle, it can only be the result of Qing-Japan war that the land of China was incorporated into our territory.

At least it could be said so long as there was such a premise that the Senkaku islands were China's, no matter the islands were the affiliated islands of Formosa or not, they were first incorporated into the territory of Japan as a condition of peace talk. (Please refer to Okuhara's article "On the Sovereignty over Senkaku Islands", published in July 1978 issue.)

In the previous text, it has been discussed that according to International Law country can acquire the territory by cession, annex, conquest, preemptive occupation and accretion. Because both of the War and the acceptance of the Potsdam Declaration are facts, our country can only take the measure of effective occupation to acquire the sovereignty of the Senkaku Islands. Cession, conquest or annex is impossible. Thus, Professor Okuhara emphasized: "I have study the problem from different perspectives. It could be concluded that no fact or evidence could prove that before being incorporated within our territory the Senkaku Islands were China's. In other words, the islands are the so-called terra nullius in International Law" (please refer to Okuhara's article on Chuokoron, which is cited in the previous text).

Professor Okuhara also said:

In International Law, if a country wants to show the intention to acquire the sovereignty of the preempted terra nullius, the country don't need going through the formalities specified in domestic laws, such as the cabinet meeting decision and public announcement. When acquiring a place according to the principle of preempting, the most important measure is effective administration. Such a fact could fully prove the country's intention to acquire the sovereignty.

Considering the natural environment and the non-livable situation on the Senkaku Islands, even if the islands have been actually occupied, if a country could prove that the country could exercise the right of administration, it will be enough for Japan to claim the sovereignty from the perspective of International Law (see, Toshio Okuhara's article "The Senkaku Islands and its Sovereignty", published in the 2nd issue of Asahi Asian Review in 1972). It can be seen that Prof. Okuhara has changed his opinion. All the other countries clearly knew which islands are the Senkaku Islands. Namely, they are the islands on which Foreign Affairs Minister Inoue Kaoru in 1885 ordered setting up of the national markers on the grounds that China has defined the names and that Nishimura Sutezo, the governor of Okinawa prefecture, was afraid, "could lead to the severing of the relationship between Japan and Qing". In spite of that, Okinawa government didn't actually take the measures of incorporation, so did the Ryukyu government. Our government (Japan) has been using the names of the islands given by China in the diplomatic documents. There was no formal Japanese name. It was ridiculous to purport to preempt the occupation of the islands as the terra nullius without even giving a name. Why didn't Japan take the formal measure of incorporation, such as the cabinet meeting decision or the public announcement? Isn't it necessary? The above opinion was totally different from Professor Okuhara's claim in his article that was published on The Okinawa Times on September 4 of 1970. Okuhara said in the article that was titled with "The Legal Status of the Senkaku Islands": the governor of Okinawa explained that the Senkaku Islands was included within the "Yaeyama islands" mentioned in Edict No. 13 and was administratively divided as part of Yaeyama district. He also said: while taking the measure, the governor also took the measure of incorporation stipulated in the domestic law. Professor Okuhara neither negated the edict nor the measure stipulated in the domestic law. However, in 1972, Okuhara changed his claim by saying that there was necessity to go through the formalities specified in domestic laws, such as the cabinet meeting decision and public announcement. Is that the progress of Okuhara's study? No. If it wasn't the pre-empting right, Japan couldn't claim the sovereignty. But our country (China) didn't go through the formalities of preempting. That's why Okuhara changed his claim. In order to illustrate Japan's effective administration of the Senkaku Islands, Professor Okuhara listed the following activities conducted by the government: in 1932 (the 7th year of Showa) Minister of Agriculture conducted a geological survey; in 1940 (the 15th year of Showa) when the airplane AsoMaru was forced to land at Uotsuri Island during a regular cruse, the police of Yaeyama; in 1943 (the 18th year of Showa) the meteorological observatory of Ishigaki conducted survey; in 1945 (the 20th year of Showa) while being evacuated to Taiwan, some Okinawa residents was attacked by U.S. air force and drifted to Uotsuri Island. At that time, the police and the military has ever rescued; etc. Professor Okuhara listed those examples might intend to prove that Japan has played the role of a country on the inhabited islands. Since the border between Okinawa and Taiwan has been eliminated because of the war, it was unnecessary to take those examples as evidence.

Secondly, they also said that China accepted the Senkaku Islands to be the territory of Japan and they listed such an event to prove their saying: in 1920 (the 9th year of Taisho period), the consul of the Republic of China in Nagasaki sent a Letter of Appreciation to Toyokawa Zensuke, the head of Ishigaki village, Zenji Koga and other two people to thank them for saving the 31 fishermen and –women of Fujian Province. In the letter, there were the dictions of "the Senkakus Islands, Yaeyama District, Okinawa Prefecture of the Imperial Japan". However, the author here repeated it again that after the Qing-Japan war there was no border between Okinawa and Taiwan, in the virtual sense, the Senkaku Islands has been the territory of Japan, if we don't argue it is pre-emptive occupation or concession for the time being. It isn't strange that even if China accepted the situation of the border.

About the Legal Status Brought by the End of the World War II

According to Prof. Okuhara, the geological and geographical situation of Ryukyu Islands were not only decided by the government of Ryukyu, but by Japan and the US, which included the Senkaku islands as part of the Ryukyu Islands, thus it was quite clear that it was Japan who claimed the sovereignty. However, Japan did this to realize its own strategic interests. Hence, this cannot be taken as the basis of claiming the sovereignty.

About the Situation of the Civil Administration of Ryuku Islands by the United States and the Administration by the Ryukyu Government

Professor Okuhara Toshio has stated the following: the U.S. Army took Taisho Island (Chìwěi Yǔ) and Kuba-Island (Huángwěi Yǔ) as the training base and paid rent to Zenji Koga; in May of 1969 (the 44th year of Showa) Japan set up the administration marker of Ishigaki on the Senkaku islands at the witness of Ishigaki. Since 1968 (the 43rd year of Showa) the United States Civil Administration of Ryukyu islands sent military airplanes patrolling the Senkaku islands and in 1970 (the 45th year of Showa) a caution sign to warn the illegal infiltration was erected on the Senkaku Islands; etc. However, these events are not enough to be the basis of the sovereignty claim of Japan. Ishigaki thought it was necessary to define the administrative region and set up its marker on the "Senkaku Islands of Yaeyama", because that the petroleum aroused people's attention on the problem of the sovereighty of the Senkaku Islands. 40 years has passed since the Senkaku Island became the terra nullius again. It has been 74 years since the cabinet meeting decision in January of 1895, which has never been published. Our government has ever asked the US to support our claim of the sovereignty, but the US adopted the following stance: "the administration right has been given to Japan. If there is dispute over the sovereignty, the parties concerned should solve the dispute". That is to say, Japan's intention to ask help from the US to support them was utterly refused.

3. Several Sidelights on the Senkaku Islands

Wokou Pirates, the Senkaku Islands and Okinawa (Ryukyu)

Prof. Kiyoshi Inoue described the following in his book: There is another document to prove that Diaoyu islands have become part of the territory of China as early as the 16th century. (See. the Senkaku Islands, published by Modern Review Press in 1972).

The document is the An Illustrated Compendium on Maritime Security, which was edited by Hu Zongxian almost at the time of Chen Kan and Guo Rulin. Hu Zongxian was a famous general in history and for hundred times, has beaten back the Wokou (the Japanese pirates) who caused troubles along the coastal areas of China. The above document was edited on the basis of his experience. He wrote about the strategy and tactics of defending Wokou, the allocation system of the sentry posts as well as weapons and vessels in the document.

The islands along the coast Luoyuan County and Ningde County of Fujian were marked from the map of Fu Qi (the 7th map of Fujian) to the map of Fu Ba (the 8th map of Fujian), which were concluded in Map of Coastal Mountains and Sands, the first volume of the document. From west to east, Jilong Mountain, Pengjia Mountain, Diaoyu Island, Huaping Mountain, Huangwei Mountain, Ganlan Moutain and Chi Yu were sequentially marked in the document. For now, I haven't studied what the current equivalents of above seven islands are. But those islands are situated among the waters on the south of Fuzhou and extend to the east from the coast of Ji Long, thus there is no doubt that Diaoyu islands are concluded within.

Those maps indicate that Diaoyu islands are one of the Chinese islands situated along the coast of Fujian. Apart from Fujia, the coastal areas of China that Wokou's attacked are fully recorded, from southwest to northeast, in the volume 1 of An Illustrated Compendium on Maritime Security. Since all of the areas recorded are all the territory of China, there is no good reason to prove that only Diaoyu islands didn't belong to China.

Professor Toshio Okuhara published an article called "On the Sovereignty over Senkaku Islands"on the first issue of Chuokoron in July of 1978, to refute the above saying:

Kiyoshi Inoue put forward the first volume of An Illustrated Compendium on Maritime Security, namely the Map of Fujian's Coastal Mountains and Sands, and ed to conclude Diaoyu Island to be China's territory according to the maps.

However, it was more reckless to judge Diaoyu to be the territory of China only according to An Illustrated Compendium on Maritime Security than to make conclusion in accordance with the records of Chen Kan and Guo Rulin. Generally speaking, not all the islands with marks on the maps of a country belong to that country, since the islands or regions near the coast will also be included. For example, the coastal map of Japan also included a part of the south area of Korea and Yonaguni Island and Ishigaki Island were also market on the coastal map of Taiwan. If we really want to refer to Maps and Plans for the Coastal Defense, it seems to be more proper to determine the boundary of Fujian Province according to the 7th map of Map of Fujian in the volume 1 of the book. In Map of Fujian, the boundary of Fujian only extended to Pengjia Mountain, and the Small Ryukyu (Taiwan) and Diaoyutai were not included. Taiwan became the territory of China in 1683, 121 years after Maps and Plans for the Coastal Defense, thus it could be inferred that Taiwan was not part of Fujian at that time. Moreover, if Diaoyutai was not a part of Fujian (China), at least it could be indicated Diaoyutai was not China's at that time.

In history, Wokou was most rampant from 1553 (the 32nd year of Jiajing period) to 1559 (the 38th year of Jiajing period). In 1553, Wang Zhi mustered tens groups of Wokou to become the largest Wokou gang. In order to suppress the Wang Zhi gang, in 1556, Ming government appointed Hu Zongxian as the General of Attacking Wokou. Prior to 1556, Ming government has sent envoys to Japan for several times to request the King of Japan to clamp down Wokou. Yang Yi, the predecessor of Hu, has ever sent Zheng Shungong as envoy to Japan. Zheng stayed in Japan for two years. After being the General, Hu sent Jiang Zhou and Chen Keyuan to Japan to negotiate with Wang Zhi. Hu Zongxian and Wang Zhi shared the same hometown. In 1560 (the 39th year of Jiajing period), Hu Zongxian lured Wang Zhi to the hometown to execute Wang and then began to attack Wokou. However, Wokou didn't disappear. Zheng Shungong wrote a book called An Appraisal of Japan. When Jiang Zhou came back, he gave all the materials of the investigation in Japan to Zheng Ruozeng, who was the greatest geologist in Ming. Then Zheng edited An Illustrated Compendium on Maritime Security. Thus, the genuine author of An Illustrated Compendium on Maritime Security wasn't Hu Zongxian but Zheng Ruozeng.

An Illustrated Compendium on Maritime Security changed Chinese' understanding of Japan. Ryotaro Shiba commented the book to the first work studying Japan in the history of China. In 1621 (the first year of Tianqi period), Mao Yuanyi wrote Military Preparations, in which the contents about Japan were fully copied those in An Illustrated Compendium on Maritime Security. As Fujita Motoharu said, it was because Wokou's invasion of China that there were records about Japan in Chen Kan's work, Maps and Plans for the Coastal Defense and Guangyu Tu (an atlas edited in Ming Dynasty) and previously China took Japan as a desolate place not to pay attention to.

Wokou had a lot of bases in Okinawa. It was widely thought that Shangbiwu Island of Kinoe City, near the east of Miyako Island was the base of Wokou. However, the case was different from the descriptions in Ryotaro Shiba's Walking on the Street. It was said that Shiba has ever read Inamura's Study on the History of Wokou on Ryukyu Islands, which was written in 1957. The author has ever asked Yoshikawakobun Press to be answered Inamura's book has been sold out in 1962 and wasn't printed any more.

Shiba wrote that according to Inamuraga's field investigation there were relics of Wokou in Okinawa, especially that in Yaeyama and other islands of Saki Island there was an astonishing number of the relics. Shiba described: "from the end of Medieval Japan to the Song Dynasty, Yuan Dynasty and even the whole Ming Dynasty of China, Wokou took the East Sea as their living room, in and out at will. The activities of those armed businessmen, or pirates shortened the lifespan of Ming Empire. When reading the documents of China, people can understand that the intensity of the war was out of the imagination of later generations."

Wokou sets up a sentry post on Taketomi Island, 48 metres above the sea level. Okinawa people called Wokou post as "かわら".The name was derived from the こうら, which shared the same meaning with "Wokou". The chief of the sub-group of Wokou was called "Head (かしら)". It was said that the word, かわら, has ever appeared in the congratulatory speech of Konami Honmitake on Taketomi Island.

It was said that in Okinawa many places where Wokou has ever lived were called がーら（かわら）. There was a Han called "がーら原" in the Ueno of Miyako-Island, which was thought to be the village of Wokou's offspring. They called their god as "がーら殿御岳". Many of the children who were tough to be the offspring of Wokou were named as "がーら".

When knowing the situation in the above paragraph, it wasn't difficult to understand why Hu Zongxian listed the Senkaku Islands in the defense areas. Before Chen Kan came, Diaoyu Island, Huángwěi Yǔ and the Chìwěi Yǔ Islands were on the seaway from Fuzhou port to Naha port. China gave names to every island.When Hu Zongxian deployed troops, determining to fight with Wokou; he didn't consider Ryukyu to be crucial for the safety of China. Chinese people studied Wokou's invasion from the perspective of weather, geology, military, etc and found that Wokou launched the war after studying the wind direction and wind power. Wokou would take the island near the mainland as the springboard. During Jiajing period, China took the defense strategy of "setting up joint-posts". "Joint-post" refers to the guarding by warships during sea journeys joined on a certain island in order to guard against Wokou pirates' attacks. Meanwhile, China had built a number of fortresses on the mainland.

2. Miyako-Island and Yaeyama Islands Nearly Became the Territory of Qing

Ryukyu "Co-owned by Japan and China" due to Satsuma Shimazu's Invasion

Since 1372 when the first emperor of the Ming Dynasty issued an edict to Satto (also known as Chadu, a King of Chūzan, one of three kingdoms on the island of Okinawa), the Kings of Beishan (North), Zhongshan (Middle) and Nanshan (South) of Ryukyu began to pay tribute to ancient Chinese Emperors. In 1402, Zhongshan King unified Beishan, Zhongshan and NanShan. In 1404, Ming Taizu sent envoys to Ryukyu. The Senkaku Islands were the channels that connected Ryukyu and China. Ryukyu King widely traded with Siam, Palembang, Malacca, Sumatra, Annan (Vietnam), etc. It could be said that the Senkaku Islands was the Ginza Avenue at sea. Because of the tide, all the vessels back from China and the south would take the Senkaku islands as the destination. The vessels from Ryukyu to China would finally arrive at Fuzhou, thus Ryūkyū-kan was constructed in Fuzhou. In a word, the Senkaku islands were the transit islands between Okinawa and Fuzhou. The trade of Ryukyu Kingdom had flourished due to the tribute relationship with China. Ryukyu's trade with the southern countries also rose. In 1547, the Hosokawa ship from Japan and the Imperial ship from China fought against each other at Ningbo Port of China, thus in the 16th century Chinese trade ships were banned from going to Japan by Ming government and China's tribute trade with Japan was thus prohibited. Hence, Satsuma Shimazu who relied on the trade with China was heavily blown. Since 14th century, Ryukyu kept a tribute relationship with China and generated prosperity because of the trade with China, which was noticed by Shimazu. Shimazu intended to control the trade between Ryukyu and China to make profits so as to "pay back the old debts". In 1609 (the 14th year of Keichyou period), Shimazu, with the permit of Tokugawa Ieyasu, "attacked Ryukyu". He led more than 100 ships and 3000 soldiers to attack the Amami Island, with which Ryukyu affiliated. On March 5, they arrived at Untenkou. On April 3, they approached to Shuri Castle and King Shangning surrendered. After the attack, Shimazu changed Ryukyu into a client state (colony) and monopolized the profits generated by Ryukyu-China trade. From then on, Ryukyu was co-owned by Japan and China. The profits of Ryukyu-China trade were huge. As the saying of "twice as much as that of Tang Dynasty" goes, the profits of Ryukyu-China trade were twice much as those of Tang Dynasty. Some commodities could generated 10 times profits. In order to protect the interest, Shimazu must maintain Ryukyu's tribute relationship with China and meanwhile he should prevent China from knowing the fact that Ryukyu has became a client state of Satsuma Han. Satsuma stipulated 15 strict provisions in Ryukyu and China would not interfere in the domestic affairs of Ryukyu. It was impossible that there was dispute over the sovereignty between Ryukyu and China. There are 36 islands of Ryukyu, according to Ryukyu officers and sea navigators who regularly sailed via Diaoyutai, Huángwěi Yǔ and Chìyǔ, which were located between Ryukyu and Fuzhou (China) and were firstly named by China and certainly belonged to China.

3. Ryukyu Islands Negotiated between China and Japan

The Meiji Restoration Government was established by the overthrowing of the "baku-han"[127] system and by restoring the empire-led system in Japan.

In November of 1868 (the first year of Meiji period), Satsuma clan informed Ryukyu King Shangtai of the restoration of kingdom system. The Ryukyu King knew little about the Mikado (Japan Emperor) and even naively believed that after the restoration the orginal Ryukyu territory from the Amami Island to Yoron Island, which was grabbed by Satsuma Shimazu, would be returned to Ryukyu. In May of 1872 (the 5th year of Meiji period), Meiji government summoned Shangjian, the envoy of Ryukyu, to Tyokyo, conferred Ryukyu seignior on Ryukyu King, thus

---

127   Before the Meiji Restoration, Japan was a centralized feudal economy with a unique system known as Bakuhan Taisei. The *bakuhan taisei* was the prevalent feudal political system in the Edo period of Japan. *Baku* is an abbreviation of *bakufu*, meaning "military government"—that is, the shogunate rule. The han referred to the domains ruled by *daimyō(s)*.

Ryukyu King became the noble of Meiji government but the Ryukyu King sought help from the suzerain China. In order to help Ryukyu, China (Qing) ordered He Ruzhang, Qing's first minister to Japan, to negotiate with Meiji government and formally stated that Ryukyu was the vassal state of China.

On December 15 of 1874 (the 7th year of Meiji period), Home Minister, Ōkubo Toshimichi, illustrated detailedly the situation in his report to Sanjō Sanetomi, Daijo-daijin (Supreme Minister). The report was titled as The Plan of Dividing Ryukyu. In November 1871, 54 Ryukyuan sailors who wandered into the central part of Taiwan (Qing) after their ship was shipwrecked were killed. On May 17 of 1874, Meiji government took this as the excuse and sent 3658 soldiers to invade Taiwan. As the dissatisfaction of the lower ranked samurais under the bakuhan system was intensified, the restoration government felt the Meiji regime at the edge of collapse. On one hand, bowing to the pressure of Russia, Japan retrieved from the Sakhalin area; On the other hand, it was heatedly discussed to attack Korea or Taiwan within the Meiji government. In February of 1874, Japan decided to attack Taiwan. Japan took Taiwan as terra nullius and was fiercely counter attacked by China. Ōkubo Toshimichi was sent to negotiate with China and he recalled the negotiation that he has never so "racked the brain and taken such great efforts to persuade" and "the days will not be forgotten forever". By means of negotiation, Ōkubo Toshimichi asked 500,000 Kuping taels from China. From then on, it was widely thought that the dispute over the sovereignty of Okinawa has been settled. However, the fact was not that simple. In the report, Ōkubo Toshimichi Complained: "it hasn't been decided whether Okinawa belongs to China or Japan. It is not good that the result of the negotiation is still unclear."

Because Ryukyu King continued to keep a tribute relationship with China, in January of 1879, Japan dispatched Matsuda Michiyuki, the first secretary of Home Ministry, to Naha (Ryukyu) and delivered Liability Statement of Supervision to Ryukyu King. Matsuda criticized Ryukyu King for not following the order. However, Ryukyu King clearly refused to take the responsibility and justified that Qing envoy and Japanese government was negotiating the issue and he couldn't follow the order before the end of the negotiation. Matsuda was very annoyed at the attitude of Ryukyu king, warning him to "wait for the punishment in future" and went back to Japan for the time being. On March 27, Matsuda lead 400 infantries and 160 policemen to attack Shuri Castle. Shō Tai was ill at that time and Prince Nakijin was Shangtai's representative. In front of Nakijin, Matsuda read off Sanjō Sanetomi's edict to abolish the Han system of Ryukyu and set up Ryukyu Prefecture, and the edict was no longer than two minutes. Ryukyu King had to yield to the military force of Meiji government. In the past 500 years, Ryukyu kingdom hasn't "set up any military force and used diplomacy to deal with its issues". Now such tradition was ended by Japan. However, the rifts between Japan and the original Ryukyu rulers continued and the problem wasn't actually solved.

4. The Meeting of Emperor Meiji and the General Grant

After leaving the office, Ulysses Grant, the 18th President of U.S., has travelled around the world. Grant met with Prince Kung and Li Hongzhang when he visited China, the emperor (Qing) raised the problem of Ryukyu to him.

On August 10 of 1879, Ulysses Grant met with Emperor Meiji at Hamarikyu. Their conversation was recorded in Notes of the Conversation between his Majesty and Ulysses Grant at Hamarikyu on August 10th of 1879. Ulysses Grant intended to mediate in terms of the sovereignty of Ryukyu. Prior to Ulysses Grant, China has asked Bingham, the US envoy in Japan, to mediate between the two countries. Bingham has ever met with Japanese government for several times. The following was Ulysses Grant's statement to Emperor Meiji:

"After I arrived in Japan, I knew about Japan's opinion and understood your claim, China's thinking should also be considered, though. China has been connected with Ryukyu in history. As far as I'm concerned, this time Japan's disposal of Ryukyu problem went against the principle of peace. In addition, China cannot forget the disgrace of Taiwan (Editor's note: it refers to Japan's invasion to Taiwan in 1874). China doubted that Japan intended to rule Ryukyu so as to re-seize Taiwan and block the channel from China to the Pacific. Please understand China's concern and make concessions. I knew from China that if Japan could draw a boundary among Ryukyu Islands and spare a channel from China to the Pacific, China could accept it."

Based on Ulysses Grant's suggestions and implications, Meiji government planned to hand over the Miyako and Yaeyama islands in exchange to earn the most-favored-nation-treatment from China. In June, 1880, the Mikado (Japan Emperor) appointed Shishido Tamaki, as Japan's Embassy in China, as the Plenipotentiary. In February, 1881, Japan began to talk about handing over the Miyako and Yaeyama islands to China. A borderline was set up at the sea 300 kilometers far away between the Okinawa Islands and the Miyako Islands. China suggested that the Amami Islands that Ryukyu grabbed from the Satsuma Han would belong to Japan, the islands, centered on Okinawa Island, was still owned by Ryukyu King, and the Miyako and Yaeyama islands would be the territory of Chinese Qing. However, the negotiation between China and Japan did not end until 1886 (the 19th year of Meiji period).

5. Who Indeed Discovered the Senkaku Islands?

There is a saying in Okinawa that it was Tatsushiro Koga who has first discovered the Senkaku/Diaoyu. This might just be a saying but it includes a complete misunderstanding. It was also said that after the breakthrough of Qing-Japan War (Editor's note: The First Sino-Japanese War), a report on Kumamoto Nichi Shimbun (Kumamoto Nichi Daily News) said that Ise Yajikita found the

Bird Islands (namely the Senkaku Islands). The report was also a mistake. The so-called "findings" referred to that it was them who first saw the Senkaku Islands. However, the history has proved that the saying and the report were all mistaken.

The elders living on Yaeyama nowadays still call the Senkaku Islands as "イーグン・クバ島" (Iigun Kuba) (Editor's note: イーグン refers to Diaoyu Island and クバ島 refers to Kuba-Island). China has given names to every Senkaku island prior to Koga's and Ise's arrival. The names of the islands were clearly recorded in the ancient documents of China and Ryukyu. On September 22 of 1885 (the 18th year of Meiji period), the governor of Okinawa Prefecture, Nishimura Sutezo, submitted a document to Yamagata Aritomo, the Internal Minister, in which Nishimura used Diaoyutai, Huángwěi Yǔ and Chìwěi Yǔ, namely the names given by China.

In 1372, Ming Taizu published the edict conferring Satto as the King of Zhongshan (Middle). Since then, the Kings of Beishan (North), Zhongshan (Middle) and Nanshan (South) of Ryukyu began to pay tribute to ancient Chinese Emperors. In 1402, Zhongshan King unifed Beishan, Zhongshan and Nanshan. In 1404, Ming Taizu sent envoys to Ryukyu. The Senkaku islands were situated on the sea route from Ryukyu to China. From 15th century, Ryukyu extensively traded with many countries in Southeast Asia (at that time there was no such a name), such as Luzon 呂宋 (the Philippines), Siam (Thailand), Malacca (Malaysia), Borneo, Sumatra, Sunda, Java, Palembang and Pattani (Burma). The neighborhood of the Senkaku islands was like "The Ginza at Sea". The ships from Fuzhou to Naha as well the trade ships passing via the Senkaku islands to the southern countries would sail along the route of "Diàoyú Yǔ (or Diaoyutai)-Huángwěi Yǔ-Chìwěi Yǔ (or ChìYǔ), Kume Island and Naha".. Therefore, the Senkaku islands were widely known by those people who regularly travelled along the route. The vessels from Ryukyu to China would finally arrive at Fuzhou, thus Ryūkyū-kan was constructed in Fuzhou. Ryukyu Kingdom thrived because of the trade. According to Okinawa's records, "among the trade ships from Ryukyu to the south countries, there were 58 from Siam. The total number was 104, but some people also said the actual number was more than 150." (Japanese Culture and Geology, Kodansha Encyclopedia of Japan, vol. 17).

Ryukyu treated China with the utmost courtesy; thus was called by China as "a land of courtesy". Ryukyu paid tribute to China and China conferred titles of nobility on Ryukyu King.In order to obtain the economic rights to trade to China, Shimazu Yoshihisa from Satsuma Vassal Toyotomi has ever reached an agreement with Toyotomi Hideyoshi and later he obtained the permit of "conquering Ryukyu" from Tokugawa Ieyasu. In 1609 (the 14th year of Keich period), Shimazu Yoshihisa began "conquering Ryukyu", changed Ryukyu into a client state (colony) and began to grab the wealth generated by Ryukyu-China trade.

In addition, Shimazu also plundered the products of Ryukyu. Satsuma Han required Ryukyu to contribute more than 9,000 dans of rice, 3,000 pieces of cloth woven from plantain fiber, 60 pieces of top-grade Ryukyu cloth, 10,000 pieces of low-grade Ryukyu cloth, 13,000 jins of ramie, 38,000 pieces of rush mats and 100 palm ropes. The top-grade Ryukyu cloth was a kind of very fine traditional handwork. Women used flax to make threads then dyed the treads. In the evenings, women, watched by officers, united in a sentry post to weave the cloth. During the days, women, together with men, worked in the field and during night they couldn't take a rest. It would take the whole night to weave on ruler of the top-grade cloth. We can say that women's great hatred and resentment were woven into the excellent cloth. The Nihon Zankoku Monogatari (The Cruel Story of Japan) (1963) ... a mondo film in 1963 was the first movie produced by Shin-Tôhô Kôgyô K.K., has clearly displayed these events. Moreover, the Maja clan in Naka villiage of Kume Island was famous for its production of 'Tumugi. The craftmanship of making Tumugi still remains alive today. Ryukyu kingdom delivered Tugumi as tribute to China. (See the article titled: The Isolated Island Attached to Okinawa, published in Asahi Shimbun.)

4. The First Sino-Japanese War (1894-95) and the Senkaku

Island and The Story of the Koga Family and the First Man Who Explored the Islands

According to The Brief History of the Senkaku Islands written by Makino Kyoshi, Tatsushiro Koga was the third son of Duoajiro Koga (Koga family). In 1856 (the 3rd year of Ansei period), Tatsushiro was born in Yamada village of Yame District of Fukuoka Prefecture, where produced the famous green tea "Yae Tea", was produced. From generation to generation, Koga family was tea farmer engaging in tea growing and production. The circumstance of Koga family was medium. In 1879 (the 12th year of Meiji period), Tatsushiro Koga travelled to the far-away-home Naba and lived there as a businessman, where Tatsushiro opened a shop specially selling tea and marine products.

In 1879, Meiji government "punished" Ryukyu by force, because that at that time Meiji government had issued the edict of "restoring the Mikado Empire system" "abolishing the Han system and setting up the Prefecture system" and "abolishing the Han system and setting up the Prefecture system" but Shō Tai from Ryukyu ignored the edict and continued the suzerain relationship with China. Hence, Meiji government sent 400 soldiers and 160 military police to Naha to immediately take over the Shuri Castle which wasn't equipped with military defense.

In Makino's record, in 1884, the year after Tatsushiro opened an outlet on Ishigaki Island, Tatsushiro went to the Senkaku Islands to make exploration. He recognized the prospect of Ishigaki Island and began to develop the industry of feathers, shark fin, shellfish and hawks-bill on the island. Later, Tatsushiro went to Nakanokami-Island and developed such industries there. In a word, everything went well.

It was recorded in The Senkaku Islands and Take Island, written by Uechi, that "after hearing people's talks about the Senkaku Islands in Ishigaki, Tatsushiro sent people to investigate the islands in 1884 (the 17th year of Meiji period) and was determined to develop the uninhabited islands", but Koga himself had never went to the Senakaku islands.

In Daisuke Takaoka's news report of 1968, it was argued: said that "it is difficult to acquire the exact exploitation history of the Senkaku Islands, but we can reach some information about Zenji Koga, who owned the Yaeyama islands and created the history of the islands. Zenji's father was Tatsushiro Koga who opened a shop selling tea in Fukuoka. In 1884 (the 17th year of Meiji period), in order to seek tea in the mountains, Zenji's father explored the uninhabited islands and was the first man who explored them."

The Senkaku Islands was incorporated into Japan after the First Sino-Japanese War

Zenji Koga, the son of Tatsushiro Koga who died at the age of 84 on June 5th, 1978, described the situation in the magazine called Contemporary, (issue June 1972) as follows:

"At that time, it was widely rumored among the fishermen on Yaeyama that there were a lot of seabirds on Yukun Kuba Island and it was very fun. A lot of people said that when passing YukunKuba, many young fishermen would forget to fish and was busy with chasing the seabirds. Probably around the 17th year of Meiji period, my father heard the rumors. He was born to be an explorer and thus considered to take a look on the island. Although there was no record about my father's first exploration of the island, he must have his intention. In the next year, namely the 18th year of Meiji period (1885), my father submitted the application of developing the island to Meiji government, but was not accepted. It was said that because the officials thought the ownership of the island was indefinite.

In the 28th year of Meiji period (1895), namely 11 years later than my father's first exploration, Meiji government announced sovereignty over the Senkaku islands. Meiji government's decision might be related with my father's exploration and Nishimura Sutezo's report. However, in my opinion, the direct factor might be Japan's victory in the First Sino-Japanese War."

However, many people said that Tatsushiro Koga went to the Senkaku Islands in 1884 (the 17th year of Meiji period), where as Tatsushiro himself said it was 1885 and the Vol. 1 of One Hundred Years of Okinawa recorded it was before the First Sino-Japanese War, which means Tatsushiro explored the island between 1893 and 1894. In 1895, Tatsushiro transferred the census registration from Fukuoka to Okinawa. In this year he was settled down in Okinawa and was thinking about doing something big. Prior to this, Tatsushiro was living in Okinawa as a traveler but in 1895 he became a local resident.

In order to develop the tea business, Tatsushiro Koga left Fakuoka to the far-away Okinawa. In Okinawa, Tatsushiro made buttons from the noctilucent shells with the capacity of 180-240 tons per annum, which were all over Okinawa, and sold the buttons to Kobe to make money. Later, he opened outlet on Ishigaki. Tatsushiro paid great attention to the albatross on Yukun Kuba Island and submitted application to the government to explore only to be refused because the officials thought "the ownership of the island was indefinite". Later when Japan won the First Sino-Japanese War, on December 20 of 1894, China delivered a message to Japan through the US minister that China would appoint Zhang Yinheng and Shao Youlian as the plenipotentiaries for peace negotiations. On December 25, China recognized the independence of Korea and Japan fully achieved the goal to initiate the war, namely to ruling Korea and intend to eliminate Chinese power from Korea. Two days later on December 27, Japanese Home Minister and Foreign Affairs Minister negotiated to submit problem of the albatross island to cabinet council for discussing. Home Minister Yasushi Nomura wrote in his consultation text to Foreign Affairs Minister Munemitsu Mutsu: "the situation at that time (in the 18th year of Meiji period) was totally different from that of today." Munemitsu Mutsu didn't object the suggestion itself, but what did occur to the situation? The only answer probably is Japan's victory in the war. From that day, the Senkaku Islands "definitely belonged to Japan." The key point of the dispute—when Tatsushiro Koga arrived at the Senkaku Islands?—now became unimportant. On January 14th of 1895, Ito Hirobumi cabinet discussed the problem of the albatross island and agreed to set up navigation markers on the "inhabited islands, which were called Kuba-Island and Uotsuri Island, situated on the northwest of Okinawa's Yaeyama islands". It was hard to understand why Japanese government (Cabinet) put the problem into the discussion agenda when it was so busy dealing with the war affairs.

From January 1st of 1910 to January 9, Okinawa Daily News serialized the article, Koga's Achievements in Ryukyu Islands, to eulogize Tatsushiro Koga who was rewarded with the Medal with Blue Ribbon. Based on the conclusion of Professor Kiyoshi Inoue (the author didn't read the article in person), the main content of the article is as follows:

In the 27th year of Meiji period (1894), Koga applied to the governor of the Okinawa Prefecture for developing the island (Diaoyu island), but because at that time it was unclear whether the island belonged to Japan or not, Koga's application was rejected. Later, Koga submitted application to Home Minister and Agricultural and Commercial Minister, and meanwhile went to Tokyo to report the actual situation of the island, requesting the permit of developing, only to get no result. In the 27th and 28th year of Meiji period, the Qing-Japan war ended and Taiwan was incorporated within the territory of the Japan Empire. In the 29th year of Meiji period (1896), Edict No. 13 announced the ownership of the Senkaku Islands. Thus, Koga applied to the governor for developing and gained the permission in September 1897. Up until now, Koga realized his years' long wish to develop the island (Studies on Histories, Issue 2, 1972).

However, the true situation was that there was completely no such related record in Edict No. 13. The governor of Okinawa Prefecture might be expecting the publishing of the Edict, but one year has past and the Edict wasn't published. It is speculated that the governor might deliver a note about Koga's application to Home Ministry and the central government might replied: since Taiwan was ours, there is no need to take troubles in the procedures to incorporate Kuba-Island and Uotsuri Island within our territory.

With regard to this, Professor Toshio Okuhara published the article, The Evidence of the Sovereignty of the Senakaku Islands, on Issue 7 of Chuokoron in 1978.

It said that:

Our country Japan, has incorporated the Senkaku Islands within our territory on January 14, 1895, (the 28th year of Meiji period according to the decision of the Cabinet meeting). At that time Japan's victory in the war seemed to be definitely settled and the peace talks were about to begin. Various states have accepted the cession of Japan. It wasn't difficult to imagine that under such circumstance Japanese government recognized the Senkaku Islands within Okinawa out of such a political judgment: Qing government has recognized the lost of Taiwan and they wouldn't dispute with Japan over the sovereignty of the Senkaku Islands, such a not-worth-mentioning terra nullius.

However, even if Japan incorporated the Senkaku Islands in such a delicate period, their behavior still left room for doubt: what was the background, against which our country has ever waived the incorporation of the Senkaku Islands? If we think deeply about the timing, one point worth attention: actually Japan always considered the Senkaku Islands to be the territory of China and was seeking opportunity to grab the islands. Was it possible that Japan dealt with the Senkaku Islands while Japan won the war? It was quite natural that there was such a doubt.

Professor Toshio Okuhara wrote the above article to doubt Kiyoshi Inoue's opinion that "the Mikado (Japan Emperor) government thought it to be the best timing to grab Diaoyu islands when the government and the supreme headquarters had adopted the strategy of Premier Ito Hirobomi to occupy Taiwan" (please refer to Kiyoshi Inoue's book, The Senkaku Islands). The article also intended to question the inference that "under the circumstance that Japan won the war and intended to enlarge the war, Japan ambiguously took the act of preempting. Did it actually pre-take away part of the territory of Taiwan from China?" (See, Shogoro Takahashi's article, Do the So-called Senkaku Islands Belong to Japan, published in the second issue of Asahi Asian Review in 1972). In a nutshell, Professor Toshio Okuhara advocated the Senkaku Islands to be terra nullius from the perspective of international law.

About the Decision of Cabinet Meeting and Edict No. 13 and No. 14

The Decision of Cabinet Meeting in Meiji Constitution

On March 8, 1972, the main point in the document published by Foreign Affairs Ministry of Japan, About the Sovereignty of the Senkaku Islands, is: "on January 14 (the 28th year of Meiji period), it was decided in the Cabinet meeting to set up national markers on the Senkaku island and formally incorporated the island within the territory of our country (the Decision of Cabinet Meeting).

Edict No. 13 and No. 14

The international jurists who advocate the preemption right of the Senkaku island as terra nullius try to combine the decision of Cabinet meeting, which was promulgated on January 14, and the Edict No. 13, which was published on March 5, 1896, thus intending to gain basis of evidence from the perspective of legislation.

Announcement of Permitting the Proposal of the Districts set-up in Okinawa Prefecture

The Imperial Sign and Seal

March 5 of the 29th year of Meiji Period

Premier Marquis Hirobumi Ito

Home Minister Yoshikawa Akimasa

Edict No. 13

Article 1 Okinawa Prefecture was divided into the following districts (excluding Naba and Shuri).

Islandjiri District includes all regions of Islandjiri, Kume Island, Kerama Islands, Tonagi Island, Aguni island, Iheya Islands, Tori Island and Daito Island.

Nakagami District includes all regions of Nakagami.

Kunigami District includes all regions of Kunigami and Ie Island.

Miyako Districtincludes Miyako Islands.

Yaeyama District includes Yaeyama Islands.

Article 2 Home Minister has the power of deciding the changes of the boundary or names.

ANNEXE

Article 3 Home Minister will decide the effective date of the Edict.

Announcement of Permitting the Proposal of the Officers set-up in all districts and islands of Okinawa Prefecture

The Imperial Sign and Seal

March 5 of the 29th year of Meiji Period

Premier Marquis Hirobumi Ito

Home Minister Yoshikawa Akimasa

Edict No. 14

Article 1 A sheriff and a secretary will be set up in each of Islandjiri District, Nakagami District and Kunigami District.

Article 2 A director and a secretary will be set up in each of Miyako District Yaeyama District.

Article 3 A district mayor and several secretaries will be set up in each of Naba and Shuri. The sheriff of Islandjiri District will be the district mayor of Naba; the sheriff of Nakagami District will be the district mayor of Shuri;

Article 4 The stipulation of the set-up of the sheriff will be applied to the district mayors; the stipulation of the set-up of secretary to the sheriff will be applied to district secretaries.

Article 5 The governor could decide the number of the sheriff and sheriff secretary in all the districts of Okinawa prefecture. But the number will be limited to the number of the Magistrates.

Annexe

Article 6 The effective date of this Edict will be decided by Home Minister.

Edict No. 13 was about the division of the counties in Okinawa and Edict No. 14 was about set-up of the posts in the counties, districts and offices of Okinawa. In Edict No. 13, Daito Island, where national marker has been set based on the survey in 1885, was included into Islandjiri District, but there was no mention of Kuba-Island (Huángwěi Yǔ and Uotsuri Island (Diaoyu Island).

The Edict didn't aim at incorporating the Senkaku Islands within the territory of Japan. Therefore, there was nothing about the Edict No. 13 in the basic viewpoints of Foreign Affairs Ministry.

The background of Edict No. 13 and No. 14 is: Meiji government kept the old system wholly intact. However, because that the peasants on Miyako launched the movement to abolish poll tax, the government has to conduct modernization reform in Okinawa, namely reforming the land system. All of the reforms were actually the reform of land tax, which was the reform of land system. The system in Okinawa was quite complicated, thus to save trouble the government only set up the division of districts.

All in all, Edict No. 13 was completely unrelated to the sovereignty of the Senkaku Islands.

Treaty of Shimonoseki and the Hand-over of Taiwan and the Peace Negotiations in Shimonoseki

The peace conference of Qing and Japan began in March 20th of 1895 (the 28th year of Meiji) in the Fujino Hall (Shunpanrō hall) in Shimonoseki city. Prime Minister Hirobumi Ito and Foreign Minister Munemitsu Mutsu were Japan's plenipotentiaries while Li Hongzhang was China. There were seven talks for negotiation.

Japan required: China ceded "the southern portion of the province of Fêngtien (includes all islands appertaining or belonging to the province of Fêngtien)", and "the island of Formosa (Taiwan), together with all islands appertaining or belonging to the said island of Formosa; The Pescadores Group (the Penghu Islands)" to Japan; China also paid an additional indemnity of 30,000,000 taels. With regard to Japan's requirement, Li Hongzhang replied: "at the beginning of the war, Japan didn't declare the war to other countries. Japan coverted Qing's land not the independence of Korea, didn't you?" "About the military expenditure, it was not Qing who launched the war and invaded Japan. Thus, it shall make sense for Qing not pay the war indemnity." Qing also expressed that China has recognized definitively the full and complete independence and autonomy of Korea on December 25 of 1894 and Japan has attained its goal of the war, thus the indemnity should be paid only until December 15th and Japan has no sound reason to ask for more indemnity.

When Japan required China to hand over "the island of Formosa, together with all islands appertaining or belonging to the said island of Formosa and the Pescadores Group of islands", China rejected the requirement by correcting "only the Pescadores group". The following is the records, made by Japan, of the negotiation between Prime Minister Hirobumi Ito and Li Hongzhang:

Li: It is hard to understand why Japan demands Taiwan since Taiwan hasn't been occupied in the war.

Ito: as matter of fact, occupation is not important. Even if Taiwan hasn't been occupied, Japan still can ask for it.

Li: I think it unreasonable to claim the land that you haven't occupied.

Ito: How about when Japan sends troops to Taiwan instantly?

Prime Minister Ito said to sign the peace treaty was our top assignment and thus exerted great pressure on Li Hongzhang by saying: "we have prepared well for battle in Hiro Island. 60 transport ships can set sail at any moment. Actually, from last night to this morning, 20 transport ships have passed the strait and their destination was quite near to Tianjin."

Under the pressure, plenipotentiary Li Hongzhang has to cede Taiwan to Japan. The main points of the hand-over of Taiwan were as following, of which some were about the Senkaku Islands and shall attach great importance to.

Li: When Japan comes to China for exchanging the ratified treaties, could you send a plenipotentiary to fully discuss the provisions for handover the land. It is natural for Japan to send military officer to the land that China cedes but it is also hoped for Japan to send civil official there, so that it would be convenient for both parties when the hand-over details are discussed. In addition, the actual hand-over is wished to be conducted six months after exchanging the ratified treaties.

Ito: Six months is too long. I'm afraid that I cannot accept.

Li: Any way, both parties should send plenipotentiaries so as to discuss the aftermath matters.

Ito: There is a specific stipulation for conducting it in Term 2, Article 2 of the Treaty.

Li: China hopes to discuss this (Editor's note: hand-over) after exchanging the ratified treaties.

Ito: We must decide the hand-over matter today not after exchanging.

Li: As a matter of fact, I have no right to order the governor of Taiwan. That's why I hope to leave the matter after exchanging the treaties and suggest Japan could send plenipotentiary to Beijing so as to discuss the matter of hand-over with Ministry of Foreign Affairs. Then, the Foreign Minister will, according to the result of negotiation, issue order to the governor of Taiwan. Please leave the matter after exchanging the treaties and to be discussed together with Treaty of Commerce and Navigation, Treaty on Road Traffic and Trade and other treaties.

Ito: Japan cannot accept your proposal and the hand-over of the land must be ascertained today, immediately.

Li: But the land cannot be handed-over now if not after exchanging the ratification. The hand-over can only be conducted by plenipotentiaries after exchanging the ratification. It is hoped to make an appointment today.

Ito: An appointment is not enough. I can send plenipotentiary at any time so as to complete the actual hand-over. But it must be done today, immediately.

Li: But I have no power to order the governor of Taiwan. Therefore, today is impossible.

Ito: After exchanging the ratified treaties, Taiwan will be Japan's territory and thus there will be no need to discuss the hand-over.

Li: I hope the conditions for hand-over will be ripe in six months. As a matter of fact, if we don't give the local officers enough time to solve public or private affairs, I'm afraid there will be many incidents.

Ito: Why can you agree the special article today?

Li: It is out of my power to agree the article. Thus, I request you to negotiate the matter after exchanging the ratified treaties.

Ito: Then, what time will you discuss the matter and agree the article?

Li: I can't tell you the specific time.

Ito: I cannot agree your proposal.

Li: Because it will after the establishment of the Treaty, the provisions for handing over shall be discussed by the plenipotentiaries from both countries...

Ito: Then there should be a specific date. Let's discuss the matter one month after exchanging the ratified treaties.

Premier Ito clearly put forward the plan to plenipotentiary Li Hongzhang that "both governments shall send plenipotentiaries in a month after exchanging the ratified Treaties and the hand-over shall be finished in two months after exchanging". With regard to the plan, Li Hongzhang said that since the two countries can restore peace and officers from both countries can hand over friendly, there was no necessity to strictly limit the deadline for handover and actually "you are too hungry". Ito suggested exchanging the ratified 15 days after signature whereas Li insisted one month. Ito made compromise that the treaties shall be exchanged 15 to 20 days after signature, while plenipotentiary Li refuted that 20 days was not enough. Ultimately, it was stipulated in Article 5 of the Treaty: "Each of the two Governments shall, immediately upon the exchange of the ratification of the present Act, send one or more Commissioners to Formosa to effect a final transfer of that province, and within the space of two months after the exchange of the ratification of this Act such transfer shall be completed."

The Treaty was signed at 10 o'clock on April 17th of 1895 and Plenipotentiary Li Hongzhang and his party came back to China in the afternoon.

On April 24, 6 days after signing, ambassadors of Germany, France and Russia in Japan visited the Foreign Minister of Japan and appeal to Lin Dong, Deputy Foreign Minister against the cession by raising the "Significant Objection to Ceding Liaodung Peninsula to Japan", which was the so-called "Tripartite Intervention" or "Triple Intervention". Hence, many voices within the Chinese government asked for revising the Treaty and voices opposing ratification rose. Premier Ito and Foreign Minister Munemitsu Mutsu were totally at a loss. Finally, on April 30, an imperial conference was held to make the decision of permanently waiving Liaotung peninsula. The ceremony of exchanging was held on May 8 and on May 10 the Imperial Prescript was published to return Liaotung.

Taiwan was handed over in a hurry

There is no record about the hand-over of Taiwan neither in the documents that the author has collected, nor in A Comprehensive Chronology of Modern Japan and Chronology of Japan, both published by the Iwanami Book Press, or in the chronology contained The History of Japan (special issue 5), which was published by Chuuoukouron Shinsha. However, there is such record the Diplomatic Chronology of Japan edited by Foreign Ministry of Japan (published by Hara Shobo.

On June 2 of 1895 (the 28th year of Meiji period), Li Jingfang as Qing's plenipotentiary together with Kabayama, the governor of Taiwan, conduced the hand-over of Taiwan and the Penghu islands.

During the negotiation of Treaty of Shimonoseki, plenipotentiary Li Hongzhang indicated that it would take six months to finish the hand-over of Taiwan whereas Premier Ito suggested one month. The final agreement was two months. Nevertheless, the fact is that Taiwan was totally handed-over to Japan only in 25 days beginning from the exchange of the ratified treaties. During the negotiation, Ito said: after exchanging the ratified treaties, Taiwan will be Japan's territory and thus there is no necessary to discuss the hand-over. Besides, the residents on Taiwan who were opposed to the cession of Taiwan launched uprising on May 25. Under such a circumstance, Chinese government had no capacity to deal with the matter after dealing with the Treaty. Later the hand-over of Li Jingfang and Kabayama was quite reckless. They didn't even clearly mark the names of the affiliated islands of Taiwan. In May of 1896, Aranao and Heinosuke Yoshioka issued Notes on Taiwan Geology: Complete (For Remediation of Geology) published in Osaka, in which there was a brief record: "in addition to Taiwan Island, on the west of Taiwan Island there are the Pescadores Group and Small Ryukyu island; on the east there are Hongtouyu and Huoshaoyu; in the sea of northeast, there were Gueishan Island and Pengjia Yu."

Professor Toshio Okuhara emphasized that Taiwan became the territory of Japan in 1683 and Mianhua Yu, Huaping Yu and Pengjia Yu were administratively included into Japan in 1905, after the war. Before that, Pengjia Yu and other islands were legally administrated by China as the affiliated islands of Taiwan even before the end of World War II.

Then, when Taiwan was handed over to Japan according to the Treaty, did the three islands, Mianhua Yu, Huaping Yu and Pengjia Yu, affiliate with Taiwan, or Fujian Province? Or were they terra nullius? Why did Professor Toshio Okuhara want to emphasize that point?

Professor Toshio Okuhara might want to say that: It is because the three islands near Ji Long, Mianhua Yu, Huaping Yu and Pengjia Yu, were included within the territory of Japan that they became the affiliated islands of Taiwan; China never took the three islands as the affiliated islands of Taiwan and let alone the Senkaku Islands. Toshio's emphasizing paved the way for his indication that in any way the Senkaku islands were terra nullius.

Geologically, the three islands were situated between the eye and nose of Ji Long. There is no doubt that they affiliate with Taiwan geologically and historically. Because the residents on Taiwan fought against the cession and the officers that Japan government sent to Taiwan were highly corrupted, Japan's experience on Taiwan was quite hard. And even there was a saying that Japan intended to sell Taiwan to France for 100 million Yen. In this case, Japan government finally concluded the three islands within the administration of Taiwan in 1905, ten years after the end of the war. In a word, the three islands didn't affiliate with time at that time. At that time, even the European and American powers have never regarded the three islands as terra nullius so as to covert them. It is globally recognized that the three islands affiliate with Taiwan, so does the Senkaku Islands. Therefore, it is unnecessary to reiterate the fact in the Treaty of San Francisco and Treaty of Taipei, since the fact is self-evident.

5. My Opinion Differences with Professor Kiyoshi Inoue

1. Military Base Versus Petroleum

Professor Kiyoshi Inoue paid attention to the Senkaku's significant function as the military base both in the 1890s and in 1970s, besides the author has noticed the albatross, petroleum and other resources of the islands. In order to illustrate why the Meiji government attached importance to the islands, Inoue gave the following examples: in the March of 1886 (the 19th year of Meiji period) Yamagata Aritomo, the internal Minister, inspected the Okinawa; In the April of 1887 Fukuhara, the major general of Army Reserve, was appointed as the governor of Okinawa Prefecture; In November of 1887, Premier Ito Hirobumi, accompanied by Oyama Iwaoi the Secretary of State for War Issues and Nire Kagenori, the Chief of Naval Operations, inspected Okinawa for 6 days with three warships; Those were all their preparations for the war; in January of 1895 (the 28th year of Meiji period), the House of Peers (Lords) took the "Suggestions on the Reform of Okinawa Prefecture Administration" by emphasizing that "Okinawa is vital for Japan", and "is vital for military", thus the House of Peers (Lords) endeavored to advocate reforming the administration of Okinawa prefecture so as to "reinforce the coastal defense".

Professor Inoue Kiyoshi further wrote in his book, The Senkaku Islands, that "the islands are important for military. If military base is built upon, it means that we set up a cannon under the nose of China." "Besides, we shall build radio base station on the largest island—the Senkaku Island. There is an island with the periphery of 12 km, the area of 367 hectares and rich resource of drinking water, where we can build a rocket base. We can also build a submarine base upon there."

The author thinks that it is reasonable to pay attention to Okinawa since Okinawa is within the territory. Meiji government answered that they didn't grab the Senkaku Islands as the military base so as to attach importance to them. As a matter of fact, the fishermen on Miyako Island who found the Russian Baltic Fleet and ran to the Ishigaki Island to report the finding by taking the sailboat called "Sabani", didn't send people to the Senkaku Islands to watch the situation.

Moreover, the islands were not significant for military use at that time, since now we can directly went from Misawa base, bombed North Korea and went into the center of the spy ship. Since there is no water on Kuba-Island (Huángwěi Yǔ), the Senkaku Island is impossible to be the submarine base.

In the past, neither U.S. nor Japan took the Senkaku Islands as the military base.

2. Stealing or cession?

Secondly, the Senkaku Islands were ceded to become Japan's land according to the Article 2 of Treaty of Shimonoseki.

In terms of the author's article "The So-called Senkaku Islands is Japan's?" published on the second issue of Asahi Asian Review in 1972, Professor Inoue made a critique against me:

"Takahashi's article arouses my attention on the importance of the names of islands. With regard to his opinion that "the Senkaku Islands were grabbed from Qing according to the Treaty of Shimonoseki", I will answer no. As Takahashi pointed out, the hand-over of Taiwan, the Penghu islands was "actually careless and pro forma", which is doubtless. My opinion in the article published on the Studies on History in February of this year was the same with that of Takhashi. At the present, as the illustrations in the part 12 and 13 of this article (editor's note: this refers to "Japan stole the Senkaku Islands and grabbed Taiwan at the war" and "Japan's ownership of the 'Senkaku' islands was invalid according to the international law"), it could be thought that the stealing of the Senakaku Islands was politically related to the obtaining of Taiwan. To be specific, stealing the Senkaku islands was prior to the grabbing of Taiwan, thus Japan's claim of the Senkaku islands was groundless and illegal. If those islands, together with Japan were ceded to Japan as the affiliates (not at the level of geography) islands of Taiwan, it didn't make sense that why those islands were not under the administration of Taiwan but of Okinawa. Looking the whole process of the Mikado (Japan Emperor) government stealing the islands since the 18th year of Meiji period, although it was related to Japan's victory in the war, it cannot totally be isolated from the Article 2 of Treaty of Shimonoseki.

Thus, I think I should make a counter critique of Prof. Inoue Kiyoshi's opinions. As the objective illustration in the book, the Senkaku Islands has been the affiliated islands of Taiwan in the past. It was only because the Qing-Japan war that they were ceded by China to Japan. It might be over-serious to argue that the islands were ceded to Japan according to the Article 2 of Treaty of Shimonoseki but not under the administration of Taiwan. The Meiji imperialism was what the scholars in the future understood after a thoughtful thinking. If we think about the following facts: Japan set up national markers on the Senkaku Island and Kuba-Island in order to manage aquatic products; it was the Okinawa governor who made proposal to Japan government; it was Tatsushiro Koga, living in Naba, who applied for exploring the island upon which there were albatross, there will be no wonder that why the Senkaku islands were under the administration of Okinawa prefecture not Taiwan. To make it simple, the way chosen to deal with the islands issue was the style of Ito cabinet.

Professor Inoue said Japan "stole the Senkaku Islands and grabbed Taiwan after Qing-Japan war". Looking at the whole process, the fact was as Inoue Kiyoshi said. However, the essence of the matter was "cession" according to the Article 2 of Treaty of Shimonoseki. The Treaty eliminated the boundary between Okinawa and Taiwan. Japan's sovereignty over the Senkaku Islands was ascertained by cession.

(The above part of the book was translated from Takahashi Shogoro's article, "My Notes on the Senkaku/Diaoyu Islands")

XXII. Historical Facts Regarding the Senkaku/Diaoyu Islands

June, 1972

Inoue Kiyoshi

Editor's note: Inoue Kiyoshi, born in Kochi Prefecture, Japan in May 1913, graduated from Tokyo University in 1936. He was a Japanese academic, historian, author and professor emeritus of the Kyoto University. He passed away on November 23, 2001 at the age of 87. He boasts many masterpieces such as History of Japanese (Meiji Restoration), History of Japanese, etc. He has been known as a progressive Japanese historian with conscience.

Historical Facts regarding the Senkaku /Diaoyu Islands was once published in History Studies (periodical of History Research Institute of China) in February 1972; and it was also published by Japan's Modern Review Press in October 1972 and it was published again by Japan's Third-Library with the same title in October 1996. The contents of this paper have been translated by the Beijing China-Japan Journalism Association. During the translation process, we referred to the book Diaoyu Islands: History and Sovereignty published by China Social Sciences Press.

I. Why do we talk about Diaoyu Islands issue

At the beginning of November last year (1971), I traveled to Okinawa Prefecture for the first time, in order to study the modern history of Okinawa and the real situation of Japanese army's decisive battle in Okinawa in World War II. Besides, I also wanted to learn about the historic struggle of local residents to against 20 years' of US Army occupation and try to understand their thoughts and feelings as well as collect some documents.

During my trip, I tried to get some historical documents about the so-called Senkaku Islands, in order to confirm whether they had belonged to the Ryukyu Kingdom since ancient times or not. The islands, located about 120 sea miles off Keelung City in Taiwan, between Okinawa and Fujian Province of the Chinese mainland, have become a disputed territory between Japan and China.

But, due to my poor knowledge of Ryukyu, I haven't found any documents to prove that the Senkaku Islands belonged to Ryukyu Kingdom. So I went to ask local residents.

Thanks to the local people's support, I received evidence to prove that none of the so-called Senkaku Islands had ever belonged to Ryukyu. Instead, they think [the islands] belong to China. Japan took these islands after the Japan-Qing Dynasty war in 1895, and renamed them the Senkaku Islands in 1900 (the 33rd year of Meiji).

I think it is a very serious issue. The Senkaku Islands, the right name of which should be the Diaoyu Islands (I will describe the reasons in the book), were taken by Japan from China during Japan-Qing Dynasty war. When Japan surrendered in World War II, lands it took from China should have been returned automatically, according to the relevant territorial clause of the Potsdam Declaration.

In 1968, large oil fields were discovered in the waters of the Diaoyu Islands; besides, the fishing grounds near the Diaoyu Islands boast the bonito and the flying fish. It is a paradise for economy as well as for military. If a military base is built here, it is equal to pointing a gun at China's nose. As early as October 1955 and April 1956, the US built the bomb shooting proving ground respectively on Huangwei Yu (Kuba Island in Japanese) and on Chiwei Yu (Kumeaka Island or Taisho Island in Japanese). On May 15 this year (1972), the Japanese government decided to put these islands which were returned by the US into Air Defense Identification Zone; besides, it also planned to establish a radio base on the largest of these islands—Diaoyu Island (Uotsuri Island in Japanese). With a circumference of 12 kilometers and an area of about 367 hectares as well as abundant drinking water, the Diaoyu Islands can be used as a missile base as well as a submarine base.

The island's economic value and the military value lured Japan's ambition of occupying these islands. The risk that the Japanese people may be enticed to the false patriotism and to incite militarism will be higher. In fact, these islands are still under the US jurisdiction, but in September 1970, the Japanese government sent Self-Defense Forces to intimidate fishing fleets of China's Taiwan in the waters of the Diaoyu Islands. This year (1972) on May 12, the Japanese government made another decision that after May 15, if the Chinese people in Taiwan or in other parts of China enter the waters, they will be arrested by Japanese Self-Defense Forces and police for violations of real estate in criminal law (Daily News, on May 13, 1972). Thus, the Japanese government has created a fraud that the Chinese enter Japan "illegally" and build a stage in order to force the Japanese to walk on the road of Anti-Chinese and false patriotism.

Therefore, it becomes an urgent event that we should know clearly historical facts of the Diaoyu Islands and related international jurisprudence because it is of vital importance for the peace in Asia and the fight against Militarism. I embarked on the research on the history of the islands after I came back from Okinawa. At the end of the year, according to the Chinese documents since the 16th century, I gained a clear idea that the Diaoyu Islands are not terra nullius, but are China's territory. Basically, I can confirm that Japan looted the islands by the victory of the Sino-Japanese War.

China claims the Diaoyu Island and its affiliated islands are not terra nullius; they were and are still China's territory. Japan arbitrarily denies China's claim without any historical basis and creates an accomplished fact of Japan's occupation. It marks the beginning of Japanese imperialism's invasion of foreign territory and its inciting the false patriotism. We have every reason to say that it is related to the fate of the Japanese people.

The two topics of this article are as follows:

The first one is to confirm that the Diaoyu Islands are not terra nullius. I may be repetitive in my previous paper concerning this topic, but I think I have made this fact clear. This time I will add more convincing historical documents in order to prove that the Diaoyu Islands are China's territory. But I can't avoid repeating the previous paper a bit.

The second one is to figure out the process and facts of Japan's occupation of the Diaoyu Islands. It was not fully discussed in the previous article. According to the document at the time, this time I will elaborate that the Diaoyu Islands are looted by Japan by taking advantage of the victory in the Sino-Japanese War. I will correct some errors in the previous article.

That is to say I was right about the relation between the stealing of the Diaoyu Islands and Japan's victory in the Sino-Japanese War; but I was wrong about the relation between the stealing of the Diaoyu Islands and Article 2 of Treaty of Shimonoseki as I wrote that Taiwan and all its affiliated islands looted by Japan included the Diaoyu Islands; the correct expression should be: Taiwan and Penghu Islands were blatantly looted by Japan through Article 2 of Treaty of Shimonoseki. The Diaoyu Islands were not mentioned in the treaty. They were stolen secretly by Japan by virtue of the victory in the Sino-Japanese War. The looting and stealing have connections of time and are related politically. The second topic of this article will demonstrate this matter.

II. The government of Japan deliberately ignores the historical facts

Japan's first formal claim to its sovereignty over the Diaoyu Islands was in the Decision to Guard Senkaku Islands released by Legislative Court of the Ryukyu government under the supervision of United States Civil Administration of the Ryukyu Islands on August 31, 1970. About Japan's sovereignty over the Diaoyu Islands, the decision mentioned "the Senkaku Islands originally belong to the administrative regions of Utonoshiro in Ishigaki City of Yaeyama Islands; before the war, the islands were used by Koga Shop to do business about logging and fishing. there is no doubt that Japan has the sovereignty over the Diaoyu Islands. Besides this, it didn't provide other evidence.

After this "Decision", on September 10 in the same year, the Ryukyu government released "On Sovereignty over Senkaku Islands and Development Right of Resources on Continental Shelf"; later on September 17, it released

"On Sovereignty over Senkaku Islands". In the second statement, the Ryukyu government claims the sovereignty over Senkaku Islands. It firstly mentioned the United States Civil Administration of the Ryukyu Islands released Geographical Realm of Ryukyu Islands (No. 27 edict) on December 25, 1953, in which mapped the Senkaku Islands under its administration.

The statement mentioned:

(1) The Chinese people knew these islands in the late 14th century, and China appointed imperial envoys to grant honorific title to the kings in Ryukyu in recognition of their rule. The records of imperial envoys going from Fuzhou to the Naha of Ryukyu such as Records of Messages from Chong-shan (Zhong Shan Chuan Xin Lu) and the Annals of Chong-shan (Zhong Shan Shi Jian) all mentioned about the names of these islands; besides, the attached map of A General Guide (Zhi Nan Guang Yi) and Zhongshan Historical Records of Ryukyu Kingdom written by the Ryukyuan also mentioned these islands.

However, since the 14th century, none of the documents of Ryukyu and China mentioned the Senkaku Islands belonged to itself. These documents just treated the islands as sea markers on the routes. They only mentioned these islands in logbooks, charts, or Chinese poetry chanting amorous feelings in journey. The book Illustrated Outline of the Three Countries written by Hayashi Shihei is the local literature of Ryukyu. This book indicates that Diaoyu Island, Huangwei Yu, Chiwei Yu (affiliated islands of the Senkaku Islands—noted by Inoue) were part of China's territory. But Hayashi Shihei said his book was based on Records of Messages from Chong-shan (Zhong Shan Chuan Xin Lu); he compiled Illustrated Outline of the Three Countries by combining The Map of the 36 Islands of Ryukyu with charts. He randomly colored the Diaoyu Island and Huangwei Yu which were not included in Ryukyu by The Map of the 36 Islands of Ryukyu with the same color as that of China. Moreover, in the charts in Records of Messages from Chong-shan (Zhong Shan Chuan Xin Lu), we couldn't find any evidence to prove that these islands are China's territory."

To sum up, these islands didn't belong to any country before the 28th year of the Meiji period (1895), to put it in another way, they were terra nullius according to the International Law.

(2) "In the 20th year of the Meiji period (1879), Okinawa conducted the implementation of the county system. Maps of Provinces and Cities in Japan compiled by Geography bureau under Ministry of Internal Affairs (published in the 14th year of the Meiji period and revised in the 16th year of the Meiji period) didn't mark the names of the Senkaku Islands. At that time, these islands were terra nullius. In the 17th year of the Meiji period (1884), Koga Tatsushiro began to collect the feathers of albatrosses and sea food. In order to adapt to this kind of situation, Okinawa Governor submitted a letter to Internal Ministry, saying that Japan should erect national border marks and requested permission to send Izumo Maru for field exploration."

(3) "In November, 1893 (In the 26th year of the Meiji period), Okinawa Governor once again submitted a letter to Internal Ministry and Foreign Ministry with the same reason. On December 27, 1894 (In the 27th year of the Meiji period), the Internal Minister discussed with Foreign Minister about submitting this proposal to the Cabinet, the Foreign Ministry had no objection." On this basis, the Cabinet decided on January 14, 1895, to have markers erected on the islands.

(4) On this basis, on April 1 in the 29th year of the Meiji period (1896), with the No.13 edict of the Okinawa Governor, Japan had markers erected on the islands to officially incorporate them into Japan's territory.

Then, the Ryukyu government issued a statement to explain in detail about the above the incorporation according to Domestic Law; but I think it is more like a kind of excuses. This statement seems to narrate the original historical facts, but in fact, there are a lot of false and distorted wordings; it even deliberately conceals important facts. I will reveal them one by one.

Since this year (1972), various statements have been declared to claim that the Senkaku Islands are Japan's territory, such as Basic Opinions of Japanese Ministry of Foreign (March 8), Asahi Shimbun (Morning News) editorial (March 20), Draft of Basic Opinions of Socialist Party of Japan (March 25), Opinions of Japanese Communist Party (March 30) and many other parties' opinions and newspapers. All these are almost the same as the above statement without any new or detailed evidence. Moreover, they put emphases on the opinion that the islands are terra nullius before Cabinet decided to claim the sovereignty over these islands in 1895. If they don't hold this opinion but admit these islands are China's territory, they will be unable to apply the preemptive occupation of terra nullius in the International Law favored by modern colonialism and imperialism. However, they still can't provide scientific evidence based on historical facts for their viewpoints.

The Japanese Ministry of Foreign Affairs only mentioned: Since 1885, the Japanese government, through repeated on-site investigations by the authorities of Okinawa Prefecture and other channels, has cautiously confirmed that the Senkaku Islands are not only no-man's islands but also have no traces of the rule of (China's) Qing Dynasty. On this basis, the Cabinet decided on January 14th, 1895, to have markers erected on the islands to officially incorporate them into Japan's territory. In 1885 (in the eighteenth year of the Meiji period), Okinawa magistrate hesitated about the incorporation of the islands into Japan's territory because he believed that these islands might be China's territory. Internal Ministry Yamagata Aritomo tended to occupy these island forcibly. His reason was that the islands were the Diaoyu Islands, Huangwei Yu, Chiwei Yu, etc. which were recorded in the Records of Messages from Chong-shan (Zhong Shan Chuan Xin Lu), but they were only sea markers used by the Qing Empire and had no traces of the rule of Qing Dynasty. (see chapter 11). This is just another version of "the islands have no traces of the rule of (China's) Qing Dynasty" mentioned by the Japanese Ministry of Foreign Affairs.

The "opinion" of Japanese Communist Party is as follows: "the documents of Japan and China all had some records of the Senkaku Islands. But neither Japan nor China makes it clear that the unmanned islands belong to itself." "No document of China recorded the Chinese people ever lived on these islands. The Ming and Qing Dynasties did not claim its sovereignty over the Senkaku Islands in the world. Although the Senkaku Islands were put under the jurisdiction of China's naval defense, this is not the same thing as sovereignty."

The Asahi Shimbun reflected the same opinion: "the Senkaku Islands were known by people as early as the late 14th century. They were recorded in the Ryukyuan and Chinese ancient books as sea markers; but we can't find the specified evidence in the documents that the Senkaku Islands are our country's territory, and no historical facts clearly show the signs of the territorial dispute."

JCP (Japanese Communist Party) and Asahi Shimbun seem very confident to conclude that the Ming and Qing Dynasties did not claim its sovereignty over the Senkaku Islands in the world. But they never did any scientific and detailed investigation of historical facts and just as Sato militarist government imposed the terra nullius, a concept created by Modern Imperialism, on feudal China's territory, trying to remove all the historical facts that are disadvantageous to themselves. None of these scholars served for the government and parties has ever stood out to explain the history; but Okuhara Toshio, the Vice Professor of International Law in Kokushikan University, is an exception.

III. It is well known that the Diaoyu Island and its affiliated islands have been China's territory since Ming Dynasty

Japanese Communist Party's newspaper and also the Asahi Shimbun's editorial article mentioned that the documents of Japan and China all had some records of the Senkaku Islands since ancient times; none of them makes it clear that islands belong to China. It seems they did a comprehensive research on the ancient literature, but in fact they didn't, they just make irresponsible remarks. Needless to say, before the Meiji period, China and Japan had no records of the "Senkaku Islands". The Diaoyu Island and its affiliated islands were only recorded in The Map of the Three Provinces and 36 Islands of Ryukyu in the book—Illustrated Outline of the Three Countries written by Hayashi Shihei in 1785. Just as the Ryukyu government's statement in 1970 that The Map of the Three Provinces and 36 Islands of Ryukyu was compiled on the basis of Records of Messages from Chong-shan (Zhong Shan Chuan Xin Lu) written by Xu Baoguang, this map is of high value. I will make a detailed explanation of it later.

In the literature of Ryukyu, the name of the Diaoyu Islands only appeared twice. One is in Zhongshan Historical Records of Ryukyu Kingdom[128], an authoritative history book of Ryukyu Royal Court compiled under the supervision of Ryukyu Prime Minister Xiang in 1650. The other is in A General Guide (Zhi Nan Guang Yi) witten by the great Ryukyu scholar Cheng Shunze in 1708. Xiang Xiangxian quoted Chen Kan's the Record of the Imperial Title-Conferring Envoys to Ryukyu (Shi Liu Qiu Lu), so the name of the Diaoyu Islands was not originally written by Xiang Xiangxian.

In addition, Cheng Shunze's A General Guide (Zhi Nan Guang Yi) introduced the round-trip sea route from Fuzhou to Ryukyu as well as the history, geography, customs and system of Ryukyu, etc. The records of the Diaoyu Islands in "Route from Fuzhou to Ryukyu" referred to the China's maritime works and records of Chinese imperial envoys. At that time, Cheng Shunze was the retainer of the Qing emperor, so though this book was written by Ryukyuan, from the perspective of society and politics, it is a Chinese book.

To sum up, the records of the Diaoyu Islands in literature of Japan and Ryukyu are all based on Chinese documents. It is not a haphazard matter. To Ryukyu, the islands are only located on the sea routes from Fuzhou, China to Naha. Because of the influence of wind direction and water flow, we go from Fuzhou and Taiwan to the Diaoyu Islands before the wind while we go from from Ryukyu to Fujian and Taiwan against the wind. Therefore, the navigation technology at the time prevented Ryukyuans from sailing to the Diaoyu Islands from Ryukyu, which is why they could only know about the islands from the Chinese. They never recorded the conditions of the islands by themselves and there was no need for them to do that.

Unlike Ryukyu and Japan, China has a lot of records about the Diaoyu Islands. In the periods Ming and Qing Dynasties, the Chinese had to concern about the islands because the imperial envoys passed by them when returning to mainland. Besides, in the 15th century and in the 16th century, the Ming government needed to know clearly about the geography of the East China Sea because they had to guard against the attacks of Japanese pirates.

When did the earliest record of these islands appear? I'm not sure. But at least before the mid-16th century. The earliest historical record of the names of Diaoyu Island can be found in the book Voyage with a Tail Wind (Shun Feng Xiang Song) which is likely written during the late Ming dynasty (1368-1644), contains 127 sailing directions related to capturing weather conditions, topographic features in different parts of the country and voyages to different destinations.

---

128 Ryukyu Historical Books compiled by Iha Fuyū, Higaonna Kanryō, Shigeru Yokoyama, Vol. 5.

What's more, the Records of the Imperial Title-conferring Envoys to Ryukyu (Shi Liu Qiu Lu) written in 1534 by Chen Kan, an imperial title-conferring envoy from the Ming court, recorded: "on May 8, our ship set off from Meihuasuo, Fuzhou to foreign sea in the direction of south east. We turned east at Jilongtou (Keelung, Taiwan); on May 10, we passed the Diaoyu Island."

The Records of the Imperial Title-conferring Envoys to Ryukyu (Shi Liu Qiu Lu) written in 1534 by Chen Kan is the earliest official record of the maritime borders between China and Ryukyu. It clearly records: on the 10th day, the strong southerly wind pushed the ship forward with lightning speed and we passed by Pingjia Mountain, Diaoyu Island, Huangmao Yu and Chi Yu. One day and one night's voyage equals that of three days. The barbarians' boats were so small that they were lagging far behind. At sunset time of the 11th day, we saw the Gumi Mountain (now called Kume Island) which belongs to Ryukyu. The aborigines on board all beat drums and danced to express their joy upon arriving home."

As early as in 1372, the first emperor of the Ming Dynasty appointed Yang Zai as the first imperial envoy to grant honorific title to the King in Ryukyu in recognition of his rule. Chen Kan was the eleventh imperial envoy of the Ming Dynasty. The ten envoys to Ryukyu before him must have shipped from Fuzhou on the same sea route as Chen Kan's (because there is no other routes). If they had written some records, they must have recorded the Diaoyu Islands. Maybe they never wrote any records, or their records were lost afterwards. After Chen Kan, the imperial envoy in 1562 was Guo Rulin. In his book Recompiled Records of the Mission to Ryukyu, he mentioned Chen Kan started the Record of the Imperial Title-Conferring Envoys to Ryukyu (Shi Liu Qiu Lu).

Guo Rulin recorded: On the first day of leap month May, we passed the Diaoyuyu. On the third day we reached Chiyuyan, which is a hill at the local boundary of Ryukyu. After another day's sail, we could see Gumi Mountain (Jiumi Island).

The above are early records of the Diaoyu Islands written by Chen Kan and Guo Rulin. We should also pay attention that Chen Kan stated: "Gumi Mountain comes into sight, that is where the land of Ryukyu begins." and Guo Rulin stated that "Chi Yu is the mountain that marks the boundary of Ryukyu". is one of the most literature. Not only should pay attention to this point, but Chen Kan long said island into "is belong to Ryukyu", and the red island Guo Rulin writing " Between the two islands, there is a trench about 2000 meters deep and there is no island. Therefore, shipping from Fuzhou to Naha, Chen Kan firstly reached Gumi Island of Ryukyu. While Guo Rulin stated that "Chi Yu is the mountain that marks the boundary of Ryukyu". They were talking about the same thing from different angles.

As mentioned earlier, Zhongshan Historical Records of Ryukyu Kingdom compiled under the supervision of Ryukyu Prime Minister Xiang Xiangxian, quotes a lot of records from Chen Kan. In ruling class of Ryukyu at that time, the confrontation between the pro-China faction and pro-Japanese faction was very fierce; Xiang Xiangxian belonged to the pro-Japanese group. Zhongshan Historical Records of Ryukyu Kingdom is more like a history book that aimed to legitimize the position of the pro-Japanese faction than an objective account of the history. However, even this book with very strong political overtones quotes a lot of records from Chen Kan without any modification, which indicates that at the time not only the Chinese but also the Ryukyuan knew Gumi Mountain guarding the border of Ryukyu and the territory west to Chi Yu didn't belong to Ryukyu. The statement of the Ryukyu government mentioned: none of the documents of Ryukyu and China mentioned the Senkaku Islands belonged to itself. But the supervision of Ryukyu Prime Minister Xiang Xiangxian clearly stated Diaoyu Islands were not the territory of Ryukyu, not to mention that of China. Moreover, none of the documents of Ryukyu and China mentioned the Senkaku Islands didn't belong to China.

It is true that Chen Kan's records only show that the Diaoyu Island, Huangwei Yu, Chiwei Yu are not Ryukyu's territory, but which country owned these islands? Although these few lines can't explain it, Guo Rulin mentioned "Chi Yu is the mountain that marks the boundary of Ryukyu". Which country is separated from Ryukyu by this boundary? Guo Rulin set off from Fuzhou and then passed some China's islands such as Huaping Yu and Pengjia Mountain; eventually, he reached Chi Yu; Guo Rulin thought if he went before the wind, he would see Gumi Island the next day. All sorts of feelings well up in his mind when he came back, and he then concluded that "Chi Yu is the mountain that marks the boundary of Ryukyu", in which he indicated the boundary between China and Ryukyu. If we insist that the boundary refers to the boundary between Ryukyu and terra nullius, our understanding of Chinese language is too bad.

In that case, Chen Kan said Gumi island belonged to Ryukyu's territory after he arrived there. We should analyze from the whole situation that he set off from Fuzhou and then passed many China's islands; eventually, he reached Gumi island; in this way, we can see that he thought the territory from Fuzhou to Chi Yu belonged to China, which is axiomatic to him and the Chinese people. Therefore, he didn't clearly record that these were China's territory, but when he arrived Gumi island, he realized that it was not China's territory but Ryukyu's territory, so he recorded this sentence.

The Japanese government claims the Diaoyu Islands were originally terra nullius. It had the same logic as Okuhara Toshio, an associate professor of International Law at Kokushikan University who had published an article titled sovereignty over the Senkaku Islands and Mingpao daily in Chian Magazine in September 1971. He wrote: the records written by Chen Kan and Guo Rulin only indicated that Gumi Island (Kume Island) belonged to Ryukyu and the islands before Gumi Island such as the Diaoyu Island, Huangwei Yu and Chiwei Yu didn't belong to Ryukyu islands, but the records didn't say that they were China's territory. Those Records of the Imperial Title-Conferring Envoys to Ryukyu were written by Chinese imperial envoys, if they realized those islands were China's, they should have written it down. However, they didn't, so neither Chen Kan nor Guo Rulin admitted they were China's territory. Therefore, Diaoyu Islands are terra nullius.

Indeed, Chen Kan and Guo Rulin "should" clearly describe in a positive way that the territory west to Chi Yu belonged to China. It is an ordinary situation that one may think it is unnecessary to make that common sense too clear. Therefore, we couldn't conclude that they didn't realize the islands were China's territory just based on they didn't record what they "should" record; this is ridiculous. Moreover, the meaning of "boundary" recorded by Guo Rulin can be only explained as the boundary between China and Ryukyu.

There is another document which can prove that at least in the 16th century, the Diaoyu Islands were a part of China—An Illustrated Compendium on Maritime Security (Chou Hai Tu Bian) compiled by Hu Zongxian, the supreme commander of the southeast coastal defense of the Ming court, in 1561. Its purpose was to guard against the Japanese pirates, so there are some marks of the times and locations of the Japanese pirates' attacks and the locations of sentry points as well as defense sites.

"Map of Coastal Mountains and Sands" (Yan Hai Shan Sha Tu) in the Vol.1 of this book recorded Jilong Mountain, Pengjia Mountain, Diaoyu Island, Huaping Yu, Huangwei Yu, Ganlan Mountain and Chiwei Yu from the west to east. I haven't confirmed their present names, but they were located on the sea south to Fujian and lined to the east from the sea of Keelung, Taiwan, so these islands include the Diaoyu Islands.

The map shows that the Diaoyu Islands are included into China's islands off the coast of Fujian. Vol.1 of An Illustrated Compendium on Maritime Security (Chou Hai Tu Bian) not only recorded the coast of Fujian, but also recorded maps of China's coasts from southwest to northeast which were attacked Japanese pirates. But those maps didn't include the regions outside China's territory, so I can't find any evidence to prove that the Diaoyu Islands are not China's territory.

On December 30, 1971, Ministry of Foreign Affairs of the People's Republic of China declared: "Since the Ming Dynasty, the Diaoyu Islands have been put under the jurisdiction of China's naval defense." Maybe this declaration was also based on this map. From this map, we can see that the Diaoyu Islands were included in China's naval defense. However, the "opinion" of Japanese Communist Party mentioned that although the Senkaku Islands were put under the jurisdiction of China's naval defense, this is not the same thing as sovereignty." I can say that only the Japanese Self-Defense Forces who put China's Diaoyu Islands into its Air Defense Identification Zone, as well as those modern imperialist countries such as the United States and Japan are shamelessly bold to put islands at least 200 nautical miles away from their territory under the jurisdiction of their naval defense. They randomly put this guilty action on the Ming Dynasty and say the defense area is not the same thing as sovereignty, which is nonsense. They are quibbling for their fallacy that the Diaoyu Islands is not a part of China.

VI. Records of the Qing Dynasty also confirm that the Diaoyu Islands are a part of China

According to the previous discussions, we know that in the middle of the 16th century, there were at least three records that can prove the Diaoyu Islands are China's territory. I don't know about records earlier than that, but whether they existed or not, we are sure that the Chinese found the Diaoyu Islands and named them, treating them as China's territory. Moreover, the largest island—the Diaoyu Island has steep cliffs, the largest flat ground of which could hold few people according to the technical skills at that time; so they might not pay special attention to such a tiny island, but they put the islands under the jurisdiction of China's naval defense, so from this perspective, their specially in its list of coastal defense figure, they didn't think the islands were terra nullius. What's more, in the middle of the 16th century, the three documents clearly distinguish these islands from other countries' territory, which is by no means accidental. At that time, the Chinese southeast coast was often attacked by Japanese pirates, so China had to be very sensitive on their boundaries with foreign territories in the southeast coast.

After Guo Rulin, there were three more imperial envoys who went to Ryukyu respectively in 1579, 1606 and 1633. I have read the records written by the first two imperial envoys, but there were no records concerning the boundary of Ryukyu just like what Chen and Guo recorded. I just found some quoted words in the records of the last imperial envoy, so I am not sure whether he recorded something about the borders. Thereafter, the Ming Empire fell; the Qing Empire ruled the country; the kings of Ryukyu continued to receive honorific titles from the Qing Emperor. The first imperial envoy of the Qing Dynasty went to Ryukyu in 1663, but he didn't record the boundary between China and Ryukyu.

As mentioned before, after Chen and Guo, there was no record about the boundary for a long period of time. Therefore, Okuhara Toshio uses it as the evidence to prove that the Diaoyu Islands are terra nullius. I am puzzled that how he figures out such a reason? I feel. The subsequent imperial envoys would carefully read previous records. Originally the records of the imperial envoys

were written for present as well as successive dynasties and successive imperial envoys, and they have the nature of official reports. They are by no means
the so-called Personal navigation diary described by the Ryukyu government
deliberately. In a word, the imperial envoys were all aware of Chi Yu and Gumi
Island being the boundaries between Ryukyu and China, so they thought it was
unnecessary to written it into their own records.

In 1683, Wang Ji was appointed to grant honorific title to the King in Ryukyu.
He recorded in his book, Miscellaneous Records of a Mission to Ryukyu (Shi Liu
Qiu Za Lu) about offering sacrifices to Ocean God between Chi Yu and Gumi
Mountain. It clearly records the "boundary between China and foreign land".

His records are as follows:

On June 24, we saw Pengjia Mountain. We passed the mountain around 8
a.m. and passed the Diaoyu Islands around 6 p.m.... On June 25, we saw mountains. We should see Huangwei Yu before Chiwei Yu, but we arrived Chiwei
Yu unknowingly without seeing Huangwei Yu. After passing the Hei Shui Gou
(dark trench), the sea was no longer peaceful, we offered sacrifices to Ocean
God by throwing pigs and sheep, pouring rice gruel into the sea, burning paper
vessels and beating drums.. After a long time, the sea recovered in peace.

Wang Ji asked the old sailor: "what does Hei Shui Gou mean?" "Boundary
between China and foreign land", answered the old sailor. Wangji asked:
"why?" and the old sailor said: "it is a lucky guess." Wang Ji added: "you did
the ceremonies for the God of the Sea just on the Hei Shui Gou, it may not be
just a guess."

It is necessary to make a little explanation for the above records. the Diaoyu
Islands are located on the East China Sea continental shelf from the east to
the west. On the north side of the islands are waters with depth of less than
200 meters while on the south side of the islands are waters with a depth of
1000 meters and trench with a depth of more than 2000 meters. Black Current
flows from west to east. Especially the south side of Chi Yu is close to the deep
trench, so the sea are of strong winds and high waves. The blue shallow sea and
dark deep sea formed a contrast of color.

As for water color contrast, in 1606, Records of the Imperial Title-conferring
Envoys to Ryukyu (Shi Liu Qiu Lu) written by Xia Ziyang caught my attention.
It recorded that Addendum to Summarized Record of Ryukyu (Liu Qiu Lu Cuo
Yao Bu Yi) (I haven't see it—noted by Inoue) written by former imperial envoy was right about "from Cang Shui to Hei Shui". In the early Qing Dynasty,
this area was known as the "Gou", or "black trench", "black water trench". It
became a general practice that they offered sacrifices to Ocean God by throwing pigs and sheep, pouring rice gruel into the sea, burning paper vessels and
beating drums. Besides Wang Ji's records, this ceremony was also recorded

in Zhou Huang's the Annals of Ryukyu (Liu Qiu Guo Zhi Lue) in 1756, the Record of the Imperial Title-Conferring Envoys to Ryukyu (Shi Liu Qiu Lu) written by Li Dingyuan in 1800, the Incessant Annals of Ryukyu (Liu Qiu Guo Zhi Lue) written by Qi Kun in1808.

Among all these records, the records of Wang Ji are the most detailed; it describes that shipwrecks always happened around that trench; it is very important that it clearly confirms here was the "boundary" between China and foreign lands. Moreover, the captain or other sailors told Wang Ji, who went through here for the first time that here was the "boundary" between China and foreign lands. Thus, it has become a common understanding of the Chinese seafarers.

In addition, Zhou Huang confirmed some records he was interested in the Vol.16 of the Annals of Ryukyu (Liu Qiu Guo Zhi Lue). He summarized the records of Wang Ji—what does Hei Shui Gou mean?" "Boundary between China and foreign land". That is to say that both he and Wang Ji held that between Chiwei Yu and Gumi Island was the boundary between China and foreign land; the territory west to Chiwei Yu was China's territory. the Annals of Ryukyu (Liu Qiu Guo Zhi Lue) and Records of Messages from Chong-shan (Zhong Shan Chuan Xin Lu) was very popular not only in China but also in Japan and Ryukyu. In 1831, it was translated into Japanese with punctuation marks and Chinese reading style of Kanji in Japanese. Qi Kun recorded when passing Chiwei Yu that "when passing the trench, they offered sacrifices to Ocean God". His book was called A Sequel to Survey of Ryukyu, which means that it is the sequel of Zhou Huang's records. Therefore, as long as he didn't do any criticism or correction on Zhou Huang's records, he agreed with Wang and Zhou that the trench is "Boundary between China and foreign land. Hence, we can't say the territory west to Chi Yu is terra nullius. Neither should we say that none of the documents of China clearly records the Diaoyu Islands are China's territory.

The imperial envoy before Qi Kun was Li Dingyuan. He offered sacrifices to Ocean God near the Diaoyu Island rather than Chi Yu. He also recorded that the captain didn't know the black trench; he himself also denied the existence of the black trench. Li Dingyuan was absolutely a empiricist. when he went to Ryukyu, the weather was very good without any winds or waves. Based on his own experiences, he believed the Ryukyu navigator more than the previous records written by other imperial envoys. Besides, he concerned about the waters where shipwrecks frequently happened, but he recorded nothing about the significant trench—boundary between China and foreign land. Li Dingyuan denied the existence of the trench where shipwrecks frequently happened, but we can't deny the "boundary between China and foreign land" recorded by other imperial envoys just because of only one person's experience. Furthermore, after Wang Ji and before Zhou Huang, in 1719, the imperial envoy—Xu Baoguang wrote the famous Records of Messages from Chong-shan (Zhong Shan Chuan Xin Lu), which can also prove the existence of this boundary.

Xu Baoguang intended to correct some wrong records of the route to Ryukyu as well as the geography, history, national conditions of Ryukyu when he went to Ryukyu. In order to make all kinds of charts, he also invited a Chinese expert to go with him. The minute he entered Shuri Castle where the Ryukyu King lived, he embarked on researches on the literature collected in the Ryukyu Kingdom. He discussed with Tei Junsoku and Cai Wen[129] who was 20 years younger than Tei Junsoku. Cai was also a well-known scholar and one of the most authoritative geologists in Ryukyu. Xu Baoguang successively spent more than eight months Ryukyu in researching Ryukyu.

This was how Records of Messages from Chong-shan (Zhong Shan Chuan Xin Lu) was written. Xu Baoguang's records are highly credible. Soon after it was published, it was introduced into Japan. This book together with the Annals of Ryukyu (Liu Qiu Guo Zhi Lue) become the main source for the Japanese at that time to learn about Ryukyu. By quoting the exposition from A General Guide (Zhi Nan Guang Yi), a book written by an authoritative scholar Cheng Shunze in Ryukyu, it recorded the , shipping line from Fuzhou to Naha. The sea route to Ryukyu is: leaving Fuzhou, then sailing to Jilongtou via Huapingyu, Pengjiashan, Diaoyutai, Huangweiyu and Chiweiyu, sail to Gumi Mountain (the principal island at the sea boundary to the southwest of Ryukyu—annotation). Previously Taiwan scholars and Toshio Okuhara of Japan held that the annotation was added by Tei Junsoku, but I didn't see any annotation in the original book, so I think it was added by Xu Baoguang. This is not important that whether Tei Junsoku or Xu Baoguang added it, because Xu constantly exchanged views with Tei Junsoku during his stay in Ryukyu and after returning home; then he wrote Records of Messages from Chong-shan (Zhong Shan Chuan Xin Lu). We can say that this book was accomplished by both of them.

If Xu Baoguang only wrote the Gumi Island guarding the southwest border of Ryukyu), it would be incorrect, because Yonaguni Island of Yaeyama Islands is located in the most southwest of Ryukyu; hence, the most southwest border of Ryukyu should be Yaeyama Islands. Xu Baoguang knew clearly about it, so he wrote Yaeyama Islands guarding the most southwest border of Ryukyu. But he still added that "the principal island at the sea boundary to the southwest of Ryukyu", so he indicates that Gumi Mountain was taken as a boundary marker between China and Ryukyu.

Setting off from China's Fuzhou, he passed the Diaoyu Islands and then arrived Gumi Island at the sea boundary to the southwest of Ryukyu, so he used "the principal island". The island is located in the southwest of Okinawa, so it is the principal island at the sea boundary to the southwest of Ryukyu.

---

129   Cai Wen studied in Fuzhou for three years, specializing in geography, astronomy, meteorology. He served as consul for Ryukyu and contributed to the development of industries and civil engineering of Ryukyu. See "Historical Series of Ryukyu", Volume 5, "Explanation" of Higashionna Kanjun.

Purely from the geographical perspective, Yaeyama Islands located in the most southwest of Ryukyu guards the most southwest border of Ryukyu. All in all, the principal island at the sea boundary to the southwest of Ryukyu used by Xu Baoguang (or Tei Junsoku) indicates that Gumi Mountain was taken as a boundary marker between China and Ryukyu. This is the same as "Chi Yu is the mountain that marks the boundary of Ryukyu" recorded by Guo Rulin.

V. Japan's predecessors also explicitly specify that the Diaoyu Islands belong to China

In the above 4 parts, I have mainly carried out the textual research with records of Chen Kan, Guo Rulin, Hu Zongxian of the Ming Dynasty and Wang Ji, Xu Baoguang, Zhou Huang, Qi Kun of the Qing Dynasty. We can see that since the 16th century, China has clearly documented the boundary between China and the Ryukyu is between Chi Yu and Gumi Island. Apparently, the Diaoyu Islands are neither the territory of Ryukyu nor terra nullius. They are China's territory. Now, we will analyze with the Japanese literature, then we will be more aware that the conclusion is correct. The so-called Japanese literature is The book Illustrated Outline of the Three Countries written by Hayashi Shihei, which is mentioned earlier.

Illustrated Outline of the Three Countries and five appended drawings were firstly published by Suharaya Ichibee in Akitou in 1785. I saw one in University of Tokyo Libraries. The Map of the Three Provinces and 36 Islands of Ryukyu was drawn on a paper of 54.8 cm long, 78.3 cm wide. This map was color printing. In the Northeast is Japan's Kago Island and Tokara Islands which are colored in grayish-green; the Kikaiga Island, Amami Island, Okinawa, Miyako Islands and Yaeyama Islands (originally the Ryukyu Kingdom[130] are colored in pale brown; in the west, from Shangdong Province to Guangdong Province are colored in light red; in addition, Taiwan and 36 Islands of Penghu are colored in yellow[131]. The map marks the southern and northern routes from Fuzhou

---

130   From the Yoron Island north to Okinawa and to Kikaiga Island with Amami Island as their center were the original Ryukyu Kingdom. However, in 1609, after Shimazuji's conquest of Ryukyu Kingdom, these islands become a duchy of Shimazuji. The author of Records of Messages from Chong-shan (Zhong Shan Chuan Xin Lu) and Hayashi Shihei were very clear about this matter, but they still included these islands into the 36 islands of Ryukyu, which indicates that it is the consensus of scholars in China, Ryukyu and Japan. Cai Wen's father revised Zhongshan Historical Records of Ryukyu Kingdom and Cai Wen made further well-proofreading and modification of his father's book thus having compiled the "History of Chong-shan" (1725). The first volume of this book recorded the names of Ryukyu and place names; it divided Ryukyu into Zhongshan and 36 islands, and incorporated the territory to Kikaiga Island into Ryukyu. Before Hayashi Shihei, Arai Hakuseki did the same in his book Southern Islands Chronicles (1719). Undoubtedly, the Diaoyu Islands were not included into the 36 islands.
131   It is difficult to determine why Hayashi Shihei painted Taiwan in a different color from that of mainland China. But we can make an assumption according to one of the

to Naha. Huaping Yu, Pengjia Mountain, Diaoyu Island, Huangwei Yu and Chiwei Yu on the southern route are colored in light red just as mainland China, let alone those islands on the northern route.

According to the map, we can see that Hayashi Shihei treated the Diaoyu Islands as China's territory. Maps are different from the articles, they don't need far-fetched explanation. In the attached drawings of Illustrated Outline of the Three Countries, one map titled Road maps of of the Three Countries recorded the borders of North Korea, Ryukyu, Ezo and Sakhalin, Kamchatka, Tiger Hunting Island, etc. The drawing, with Japan as the center, marks Kamchatka in the north, Ogasawara in the south and China in the west; it can be the great map of East Asia. In such a map, the Diaoyu Islands are painted in the same color as that of China while those islands much bigger than the Diaoyu Islands haven't been painted. It indicates that identifying the borders of the countries is very important in Illustrated Outline of the Three Countries, so the Diaoyu Islands could not be ignored.

About the map of Ryukyu, Hayashi Shihei wrote in the preface that I don't dare to create the maps of these countries....the map of Ryukyu is draw based on Records of Messages from Chong-shan (Zhong Shan Chuan Xin Lu). However, he didn't totally copy the opinion of Records of Messages from Chong-shan (Zhong Shan Chuan Xin Lu); instead, he researched on Records of Messages from Chong-shan (Zhong Shan Chuan Xin Lu) as well as the Records of Ryukyu written by Arai Hakuseki; besides when writing Illustrated Outline of the Three Countries, he also added his own opinions as Records of Messages from Chong-shan didn't color those territories with different colors while Hayashi Shihei used colors to distinguish them.

The Ryukyu government's statement said: "Records of Messages from Chong-shan records that the territory beside the 36 islands is not Ryukyu's territory, so Hayashi Shihei mechanically colored the Diaoyu Islands as China's territory. The book has no value." However, this excuse is extremely ridiculous. Hayashi Shihei didn't mechanically use colors to distinguish the territories, which can be seen from the map where Taiwan and Penghu Islands which are absolutely China territory are colored in different color from that of mainland China while the Diaoyu Islands are painted with the same color as that of mainland China. Obviously, he didn't mechanically colored the Diaoyu Islands as China's territory. He studied Records of Messages from Chong-shan and based on the record—Gumi Mountain (the principal island at the sea boundary to the southwest of Ryukyu), he thought it is the boundary between China and

---

attached drawings in Illustrated Outline of the Three Countries. This drawing painted Ogasawara Islands in a different color from that of Japan, so we can assume that Hayashi Shihei thought Taiwan belongs to China but it is not the affiliated island of mainland China just as Ogasawara Islands which are not affiliated island of Japan but are Japan's territory. Therefore, they were colored in different colors.

Ryukyu. Besides, he believed in the Diaoyu Islands before this boundary are China's territory, so he deliberately distinguished them with different colors.

In fact, records of Gumi Island in Records of Messages from Chong-shan are the same as what Guo Rulin and Chen Kan recorded. The territory east to Gumi Island belongs to Ryukyu while the territory west to Gumi Island belongs to China.

I have published an article titled History of the Diaoyu Islands in History Studies in February. At that time, I didn't see Illustrated Outline of the Three Countries and its attached drawings; what I used was Hayashi Shihei's Collection published by Tokyo Life Press in 1944. The appended drawings of this book didn't use colors to distinguish the territories, so I just pointed out that on the map there is a difference between the Diaoyu Islands and Ryukyu. Later, I read the original which use colors to mark the territories of China clearly.

In addition, Tanimura library in University of Kyoto Libraries collects two more color copies of The Map of the Three Provinces and 36 Islands of Ryukyu. Although it didn't clearly mention that they were copied from the appended drawings of Illustrated Outline of the Three Countries, if one has a look at the copies, he will know they are copied from drawings of Hayashi Shihei, because one of the copy (A) combined five drawings which were copied on a strong Japanese paper with handwriting by the same person. The five appended drawings are maps of Emishi (Hokkaido), Ryukyu, North Korea, Ogasawara Islands as well as borders of countries with Japan as the center of map. The copies colored Ryukyu in reddish-brown, mainland China and Diaoyu Islands in pale brown, Japan in grayish green, Taiwan and Penghu Islands in yellow.

Another copy (B) colored Ryukyu in yellow, mainland China and Diaoyu Islands in light red, Taiwan in gray, Japan in green.

In addition, Tanimura library collects three copies of Map of Eight Regions of North Korea attached to Illustrated Outline of the Three Countries. One of these copies can be grouped into A; another one can be grouped into B as its paper and handwriting are the same as B; besides both of them have the red seal of the original collector. The last one is the original copy product. It is assumed that accordingly there must be a copy of map of Ryukyu with this copy. If so, beside the original drawings, there are three copies of the appended drawings of Illustrated Outline of the Three Countries.

National History Research Institute of Kyoto University collects a color copy of The Map of the Three Provinces and 36 Islands of Ryukyu.

As is known to all, because of the compilation of Illustrated Outline of the Three Countries and War Strategies of Coastal Nations, Hayashi Shihei was disciplined by bakufu and all his published books were confiscated. Hayashi Shihei was the pioneer whose modern national consciousness was awakened.

The reason why he wrote Illustrated Outline of the Three Countries is that he considered that the defense of Japan urgently needs details about Japan's surrounding geographical conditions. The "defense" here is not the defense for Tokugawa shogunate or various counties or this or that feudal Lord or a feudal group, but the defense for the overall "Japan". In addition, he also thought that the significant geographical knowledge shouldn't be monopolize by the feudal shogunate or various dignitaries of various counties or the samurai class; everyone had the equal right to know the geographical knowledge. He thought it was an issue concerning Japan's defense and the Japanese nation, so he dared to publish this book, and published the attached drawings with color printing in order to make the readers clear about the positions of different countries.

The humble intellectual Hayashi Shihei told the Japanese people Japan's defense consciousness in this way; his modern nationalism thoughts and actions angered feudal rulers of Tokugawa Bakufu. However, Hayashi Shihei represents the pioneer whose modern national consciousness was awakened and he gained wide supports from people. His Illustrated Outline of the Three Countries and War Strategies of Coastal Nations was banned, but people are still reading them and passing them to next generations.

As early as 1832, Illustrated Outline of the Three Countries was translated into French by Heinrich Klaproth, the German orientalist, and published in Europe; The appended drawings are published with color printing132. We can see the international community attached great importance to this book; even the people of Europe know the Diaoyu Islands are China's territory.

Hayashi Shihei was a pioneer whose modern national consciousness was awakened. He studied carefully the masterpiece of great scholars of China, Ryukyu and Japan such as Xu Baoguang, Arai Hakuseki, etc. He compiled this book wholeheartedly in order to tell all Japanese people the national defense consciousness. The book resisted to the repression from feudal rulers of Tokugawa shogunate, and was very popular among the patriotic intellectuals and attracted the international attention. The appended drawings of such a book, clearly record the Diaoyu Islands is a part of China. However, Emperor of Japan, militarists and their offspring–modern imperialists as well as their accomplice—Japanese Communist Party completely ignored the records in this book and unexpectedly put forward that "the Diaoyu Islands are terra nullius".

From the 16th to 18th century, the Chinese, the Japanese, the people of Ryukyu left precious literature concerning the Diaoyu Island and Ryukyu, consistently indicating that the Diaoyu Islands are China's territory. However,

---

132   I haven't see the French translation, but on page 22 in History of Takeshima written by Okuma Ryoichi, there are introductions of Heinrich Klaproth's CV and the translation of Illustrated Outline of the Three Countries. In addition, Vol.6 of Law Reviews of NCCU Taiwan collects the color printing of map of Ryukyu in that book.

some people distort the facts by using the differences of the Chinese expressions and terms in modern laws; in the face of maps which are hard to distort, they brazenly say "the author just mechanically uses colors to distinguish them"; they, with shallow hearts, distorted the masterpieces left by great pioneers. I think this argument is not enough to refute their ridiculous claims, so it is necessary to put forward the second argument–"the principle of preemptive occupation of terra nullius in International Law".

VI. Refutation of "preemptive occupation of terra nullius islets"

Just like the Internal Ministry Yamagata Aritomo, the Supreme Commander and Lieutenant as well as the most fanatic proponent of Mikado (Japan Emperor) militarism who attempted to steal the Diaoyu Islands in 1885, they also ignore the records of the Diaoyu Islands in Ming and Qing Dynasties and made improper claim that the islands have no traces of the rule of China, so China didn't conduct effective control over these islands according to the principle of "preemptive occupation of terra nullius" in the International Law. Therefore, they conclude that the islands are terra nullius.

Then, what on earth is the so-called "International Law"? Shigejiro Tabata, Professor in Kyoto University commented on "International Law" in his book "International Law 1" (Law Collection published by Yuhikaku) which aims to explain the standard International Law of modern Japan. He wrote: modern Western Europe sovereign states launched a fierce power struggle in order to maintain and expand their forces, but they also needed reasonable rules to prevent a endlessly intensified power struggle, so International Law was created ". In my opinion, the so-called "reasonable rule" is the interests of the powers. This is very obvious in the principle of "preemptive occupation of terra nullius". Professor. Tabata added: besides the war, another issue attracted attention from scholars of modern International Law. That is the increasingly intensified colonial plunder between countries for the purpose of monopolizing international trades as the discovery of new lands, new routes." In the face of this intensified colonial plunder, a common norms of behavior (admittedly, it often has special motivations behind it, namely, compared with other countries, our own behaviors are legitimate behaviors)—International Law was a heat topic then. In this case, the principle of occupation as a new right to obtain territories has been raised and approved (see page 19).

The principles based on "compared with other countries' behaviors, our own behaviors being legitimate behaviors" became the "International Law", which actually is good for the powers. The principle of "preemptive occupation of terra nullius" is the typical representative. The Spanish, and the Portuguese had invaded islands in America, Asia, Africa and the Pacific and put them into their territory as their colonies by virtue of the principle of "preemptive discovery". When their competitors—Holland and the UK who were more powerful than them emerged, jurists in Holland created the principle of "preemptive occupati-on of terra nullius" which is a beneficial theory for Holland and the UK. It soon was included into "International Law".

The definition of "terra nullius" can show that the principle of "preemptive oc-cupation of terra nullius" was made for the interests of European and American co-lonialism and imperialism. The predecessor of Tabata—Kisaburo Yokota, a scholar of International Law, the Emeritus Professor of University of Tokyo wrote in his book "International Law 2" (Law Collection published by Yuhikaku): the simplest meaning of terra nullius is the territory without people, But in "International Law", the definition of "terra nullius" is that even there are persons on the territory, they will be terra nullius if the territory doesn't belong to any country. The Western Europe's preemptive occupation of Africa is a good example. It is inhabited by wild natives, but the natives didn't constitute a nation according to the International Law, the land is terra nullius (page 98). This is the random definition created by modern Europe's so-called sovereign states under. With this principle, they were unbridled when invading every nation around the world.

Yokota also added some explanation of the establishment of the "principle": "from the late 15th century to the early 18th century, when discovering the new continent or islands, the country just needed to announce the land was its territory and display the national flag with the cross or markers set up on the land, they could own the territory." But in the 19th century, this was not enough; "many countries advocated preemptive occupation of the land must be practical occupation with ruling, which was gradually became a kind of prac-tice of all countries". " In the late 19th century, International Law confirmed that preemptive occupation must have effectiveness." "So-called effectiveness referred to the actual possession of the land and set up effective ruling power. It was necessary to set up administrative organs. Especially in order to maintain police forces, one country needed the police power and in many cases, it also needed military strength" (see p. 99).

This means that countries with military and police strength were the winners. Hence, the "principle" was carefully created by the modern western powers in order to plunder territories of other countries or nations. Modern imperialism inherited the "principle", and use it as a general international law. Using this "principle" to measure the legitimacy of China's feudal territory is an unreaso-nable action of ignoring history conducted by the modern imperialists.

According to the so-called principle of "preemptive occupation" of the Western Europe, in the 16th or 17th century, the "discoverer" of a new land could be the owner of its sovereignty. If so, the Diaoyu Islands must belong to China. The reason is that the Diaoyu Islands were first discovered and named by the Chinese people; and the names of these islands have been repeatedly recorded in the official documents written by Chinese imperial envoys.

In addition, the chancellor—Xiang Xiangxian of the Ryukyu Kingdom who was not a supporter of China admitted records concerning the Diaoyu Islands in China's documents in his book. Hayashi Shihei, the pioneer of Japanese modern nationalism, also admitted this fact and scholars of Western Europe attached great importance to Hayashi Shihei's masterpieces. That is to say, the international community also admits that the Diaoyu Islands are a part of China. The territory belonging to China since the 16th century had to be applied to the "international principle" of the imperialism in the 20th century and the territory was defined as terra nullius with the excuse of insufficient conditions. This is by no means allowable.

If the Diaoyu Islands had to meet Modern Imperialism's principle that the preemptive occupation must have effectiveness, I think it was impossible and of no meanings for the Ming and Qing Dynasties to set up administrative agencies on this small uninhabited island. As for the modern principle of preemptive occupation, Prof. Yokota comments:

"Depending on the situation of the land, sometimes we can't apply this principle (the principle that the preemptive occupation must have effectiveness—noted by Inoue). For example, it is unnecessary to set up administrative agencies and to place police forces and troops on uninhabited islands. In uninhabited places, one can't set those things."

The Diaoyu Islands in the Ming and Qing Dynasties were uninhabited islets; so it is obviously impossible to find traces of "effective rule". Professor Yokota says: "in this case, the country can set up administrative agencies and police forces on the nearby lands or islands to prevent pirates from settling on the unmanned island; besides, it can conduct patrol frequently to implement administrative ban. If necessary, it can send warships and aircraft there at any time, which will be enough."

It is easy to realize all these conditions at present. It is unimaginable in the past when no country had warships, aircraft, radar or radio communications. Besides, even people couldn't live on the island, how can it be the nest of pirates; hence, there was no need to conduct patrol frequently. So what should the Chinese people in Ming and Qing Dynasties do to meet the requires of modern Japanese imperial government and its accomplice—the JCP? Or how can they leave "traces of effective rule" on the Diaoyu Islands? The Chinese people in Ming and Qing Dynasties determined the position of the islands, named them recorded the routes to get to these islands. What else should they do? "What they had already done is enough!"

In fact, the Ming government did a lot more: the Diaoyu Islands were put under the jurisdiction of China's naval defense; An Illustrated Compendium on Maritime Security (Chou Hai Tu Bian) which systematically expounded the tactics of defense against the Japanese pirates marks the location of the Diaoyu

Islands and its jurisdiction. This is what Professor. Yokota said—"the country can set up administrative agencies and police forces on the nearby lands or islands." It is just the version of the Ming Dynasty.

In the end of this chapter, I think there is no need to illustrate the preemptive occupation of the Diaoyu Islands in Ming and Qing Dynasties with the "international principles" of modern imperialism. The Ming and Qing governments as well as the Chinese could never expect that in hundreds of years after their death, modern imperialist "applied" the "International Law theory" to their territory. I want to point out that they were very sure the islands were their territory, which is the evidence. Even the principle of "preemptive occupation" of the modern imperialism can't deny the Diaoyu Islands are China's territory.

VII. People of Ryukyu knew little about the Diaoyu Islands

From the previous chapters, we know that at least since the Ming Dynasty, the Diaoyu Islands have been China's territory, which is admitted not only by the Chinese, and the Ryukyuan, but also by the Japanese. What's the Ryukyuan's opinion towards the Diaoyu Islands? As mentioned above, there are only two books written by the Ryukyuan that have mentioned about the Diaoyu Islands: Zhongshan Historical Records of Ryukyu Kingdom by Xiang Xiangxian and A General Guide (Zhi Nan Guang Yi) by Tei Junsoku. Both of them used the Chinese name to record the islands, and treated them as China's territory. Beside the two books, it there anything else about Diaoyu Islands in Ryukyu?

Adventure of Senkaku Islands (Volume. 140-141 in Series 12 of Journal of Earth Sciences, August-September in 1900) written by Kuroyiwa Hisashi, a teacher in Okinawa, quoted the report submitted by Oshiro Mizutoki, the deforestation official in Mari Village, to Okinawa county on September 14th, 1885. (in Section 63 of Quarterly, Okinawa in December 1972, there is an article recording that Okinawa Governor agreed with the report submitted by Oshiro Eiho, the deforestation official in Mari Village; Oshiro Eiho came from Okinawa; I am not sure whether Oshiro Eiho and Oshiro Mizutoki are the same).

The report mentioned that "the Uotsuri Island is located to the south west of Gumi Island. The island is 3.5 km long and 1.5 km wide; it is about 175 miles far from Gumi Island."

The location and terrain indicates that it is the Diaoyu Islands. If so, at that time, the Ryukyuan changed the Chinese name—"Diaoyu Islands" into the Japanese—"Uotsuri Island" and in the language of Ryukyu, it should be "Tokon". On September 22 in the same year, Sutezou Nishimura, the Okinawa

Magistrate wrote to Yamagata Aritomo, the Ministry of Internal Affairs133: the names such as Kumeaka Island, Kuba Island and Uotsuri Island are used by us since ancient times..." I will explain with evidence that Kumeaka Island is Chiwei Yu in the Chinese literature; Kuba Island is Huangwei Yu; the Uotsuri Island is the Diaoyu Islands.

The magistrate said the names had been used by them since ancient times; it was the action of officials in the Emperor Government that "Diaoyu Island" was changed into "Uotsuri Island"; the people in Ryukyu called the island as "Yokon" or "Yukun", or "Yigun". Adventure of Senkaku Islands has following records:

The Diaoyu Island is also called the Diaoyutai or Heping Mountain or Hoapin-su in the chart (see notes at the end of this chapter - noted by Inoue). Okinawa called it Kuba Island. According to the adventure of people in Okinawa, in history, people in Okinawa called it "yokon". At that time, Kuba Island was Huangwei Yu in the northeast of the islands. But until recent years, somehow, the names were interchanged that Huangwei Yu was called "yokon" while the Diaoyu Island is known as the Kuba. At present, no one intends to change the names.

The article didn't mention that the Diaoyu Islands were called or written as Uotsuri Island. It only mentioned that the island was called "Yokon" and Huangwei Yu was called "Kuba". Until recent years, somehow, the names were were used interchangeably.

Natural Conditions and Customs of the Southern Islands (1949) written by Higaonna Kanryo, born in Naha, Okinawa who was a great scholar specializing in Ryukyu school also used "the Diaoyu Islands" rather than "Uotsuri Island". The book also mentioned that the fishermen in Okinawa called it "Yukun · kubashima". It is said that 'Yokun' is fish island,' kubashima is koba island. Just seeing from these records, we can't determine the original name of island is "Yukun" (or "Yokon"), or "kubashima".

In addition, Makino Kiyoshi, the local historian of Ishigaki city wrote in "Brief History of Yikun kubashima": "the scholars in Yaeyama Islands still call Senkaku Islands as Yikon kubashima; they used the two names together. Yikon is Uotsuri Island and kubashima is Kuba Island. But they don't separate the names of the islands and only use one name to call the Senkaku Islands." (Section 56 of Okinawa)

Makino said, "Yikon kubashima" is not the name only for the Diaoyu Islands but the name for both the Diaoyu Islands and Huangwei Yu. It is the full name of the so-called "Senkaku Islands". I suspect that this statement should

---

133   "Miscellaneous pieces of the territory" in Vol. 18 of Japanese Diplomatic Documents, see Chapter 11.

be correct. The nearest island to the Diaoyu Islands is the Iriomote Island of Yaeyama Islands, about 90 nautical miles away from the Diaoyu Islands. Okinawa is 230 nautical miles from the Diaoyu Islands. Those who had the chance to get near the Diaoyu Islands were officers and the crew of the ship who returned to Naha from Fuzhou. Only the fishermen of Ryukyu would go to the Diaoyu Islands. From the point of geography relations, I think the fisherman in Yaeyama Islands go to these islands more frequently then the fishermen in Okinawa and they are aware of the shape of these islands.

If Makino is correct, then Higaonna Kanryo is wrong to use Yukun kubashima just to call the Diaoyu Island. Besides, by 1970, scholars in Yaeyama Islands still call Uotsuri Island (Diaoyu Island) "Yikon", and call Kuba Island (Huangwei Yu) "kubashima". But this is contradictory to what Kuroiwa said in 1990—"the Diaoyu Island was originally called Yokon · Yukon · Yikon, while Huangwei Yu was called kubashima, but 'recently' the names of islands were interchanged". How to explain this contradiction? It seems that it can only be interpreted as: Up to a certain period in the 19th century , "the Diaoyu Islands" was "Yokon (Yikon)", "Huangwei Yu" was "Kuba"; and about 1900, "the Diaoyu Islands" began to be called "Kuba", "Huangwei Yu" was called "Yokon (Yikon)"; and later, unknowingly, "the Diaoyu Islands" was again called "Yokon (Yikon)", "Huangwei Yu" was called "Kuba", which has been used till today.

The process is very cumbersome and the names of these islands called by the Ryukyuan were very confusing. Until the 20th century, they had to find a common name for these islands, which means that people in Ryukyu didn't know much about these islands. We assume that the life of the Ryukyuan is closely related to these islands; for example, the Ryukyuan often fish here; if the names of the islands were not unified, it was bound to cause confusion when exchanging information; so they should have find a common name to call these islands.

In fact, the Chinese sea navigators and imperial envoys who regularly passed by these islands all called these islands as "Diaoyu Island", "Huangwei Yu" and "Chiwei Yu". As for the Ryukyuan, their life is not closely related to these island, and they just talk about them in some chitchats; in this case, the names may be mixed up. For them, "Uotsuri Island" is totally a strange official language.

Higaonna Kanryo born in Naha said, "Yokun means fish in Ryukyu language"; but Makino born in Yaeyama Islands said in the "Brief History of Senkaku Islands" that Yikon means harpoon, which might be named according to the shape of the island.

I can't determine who is right, because I don't understand the Ryukyu language. If "Yokon" and "Yikon" have the same meaning, and what Makino said is correct, the "Yikon (Yokun)" created according to the shape of the island should not be mistaken so easily.

The Huangwei Yu is covered by Chinese fan palm (Kuba in Japanese), so it is reasonable to call it Kuba Island and the island is shaped like a huge mound rather than a harpoon.

The Diaoyu Island is short from north to south and long from east to west. In the eastern part of the island, there are a steep rock stabbing into the blue sky, which looks like a harpoon; but the reef in the east side of the Diaoyu Islands is the closest to this description, so the British named it Pinnacle and the Japanese navy translated it into "Senkaku". If "yikon" means harpoon, we can assume that the fishermen in the Yaeyama Islands might drifted to the Diaoyu Island, Pinnacle, Huangwei Yu because of the influence of wind and tide, and the shapes of harpoon and pinnacle left a deep impression on them, so they called them "yikon" which didn't refer to only one island. The Huangwei Yu are covered by Chinese fan palm (Koba), so it is called Koba. On this basis, this is why they use "Yukun·kubashima" to call these islands. (Pinnacle is 3 nautical miles east to the Diaoyu Island and 13 nautical miles south to Huangwei Yu; while Huangwei Yu is 10 nautical miles away from the Diaoyu Island; so they formed an archipelago; because Chiwei Yu is 48 nautical miles east to Huangwei Yu, so it doesn't belong to this archipelago).

But if "Yikon" means "Pinnacle", "Yokon (Yukun)" means "fish", so they are two different words, so I have to use another thinking pattern to explain it, which is beyond my ability range.

Natural Conditions and Customs of the Southern Islands mentioned that A General Guide (Zhi Nan Guang Yi) records that going to Fuzhou from Naha, firstly using Shen Compass (south of southwest) then going towards east (a little bit north) for 45km, the Gumi Island and kubashima will come in sight. Here the "kubashima" refers to the Diaoyu Island. Higaonna Kanryo and other people should not make such mistakes. The "kubashima" is either the Kuba Island or the island mentioned in Records of Messages from Chong-shan (Zhong Shan Chuan Xin Lu); if not so, it is not in accordance with the maps. The normal route from Naha to Fuzhou never uses the Diaoyu Island as markers. Therefore, we can't prove that the Diaoyu Island was called "kubashima" in 1708 when A General Guide (Zhi Nan Guang Yi) was written.

In a word, we can't determine when the Diaoyu Islands were called "kubashima" and when "Yokon (Yukon)" or "Yikon" began to be used. Moreover, we don't know when the Ryukyuan call "Huangwei Yu" "Kuba Island ", and "Chiwei Yu" "Kumeaka Island", neither. But as far as I know, "Kuba Island", and "Kumeaka Island" were mentioned in the records written by imperial envoys in the Qing Dynasty. They can't be found in the documents of Ryukyu.

In 1866, Zhao Xin, an imperial envoy, recorded in his A Sequel to Survey of Ryukyu (Xu Liu Qiu Guo Zhi Lue)[134] about the route of the former imperial envoy: that on May 5 in the 18th year of the reign of Emperor Dao Guang of the Qing Dynasty, he set off from Fuzhou; at around 2 p.m. on May 6th, he arrived the Diaoyu Island; at around 4 p.m., he arrived Kuba Island; at dawn on May 7th, he arrived Kumeaka Island; at dawn on May 8, he arrived Kume Island. He recorded the same about his own route: on June 9 (1866) in the 5th year of the reign of Emperor Tong Zhi of the Qing Dynasty, he set off from Fuzhou; at around 6 p.m. on June 11, he arrived the Diaoyu Island; at around 8 p.m., he arrived Kuba Island; at 2 p.m. on June 12th, he arrived Kumeaka Island. Here, the Kuba Island and Kumeaka Island respectively refer to Huangwei Yu and Chiwei Yu.

We don't know why Zhao Xin used Japanese names instead of Chinese names. Maybe, he heard them from the crew from Ryukyu on the ship. If so, then the time when the Ryukyuan used these names can be traced back to the middle of the 19th century. Although Zhao Xin used Japanese names of Huangwei Yu and Chiwei Yu, he still used the Chinese name of the Diaoyu Island. The reason may be that at that time, the crew from Ryukyu on the ship hadn't name the island with "Yokon", "Yukon" or "Yikon". Or, maybe they had already called like that, but because there was no corresponding Chinese characters, so Zhao Xin still used the Chinese name.

If we analyze this matter by combining what Kuroiwa said with the records of Zhao Xin, we can find that the "recently" mentioned by Kuroiwa refers to some time point after the Meiji Restoration.

Anyway, we can't say the Ryukyuan began to call Diaoyu Islands in the Ryukyu language, in middle of the 19th century according to the literature. They probably had been using the Chinese name for a long time. It is not surprising because only when they were occasionally drifted by the storm or returned from Fuzhou, China to Naha can they met these islands. Generally speaking, the Ryukyuan didn't know much about the Diaoyu Islands. Even the ship of imperial envoys might not pass by the Diaoyu Islands because of the restriction of the wind and tide. It is unthinkable that fishermen in Ryukyu went to fish on the Diaoyu Islands against the wind and the current. Therefore, they got the names and other information of the islands from the Chinese. So they are the names of these islands and related knowledge, should first from the Chinese. Moreover, after the Ryukyuans began to call the Islands in the Ryukyu language after the Meiji Restoration, these names hadn't been fixed yet. All these indicate the life of the Ryukyuan is by no means closely related to these islands.

---

134   This name is the same as that of Qi Kun; but this book was written by another person in a different year.

In the next chapter, I will mention something about the logbook of Balcher, the captain of British warship "Samarang". There is a note recording that they had explored the Huangwei Yu island on June 16, 1845. It mentioned that there are some caves which have living traces of drifted fishermen. Captain Balcher said the beds left by the drifters were made of woods of the canoe and Chinese fan palms; obviously the drifters were not European." Captain Balcher speculated that these drifters drank rain drops on the island and ate eggs of seabirds and birds' meat for survival. We don't know whether these drifters were the Chinese or the Ryukyuans. As they didn't find anybody in the caves, so the drifters must have been saved by someone. The probability that they were saved by some Chinese ship is higher than the probability that they were saved by boats of Ryukyu.

VIII. The so-called "Senkaku Islands" have no fixed names and boundaries

Even after the Ryukyuan began to call the Diaoyu Islands "Yokon (Yikon)" or "Kuba" in the language of Ryukyu, they never call these islands the "Senkaku Islands" before 1900. The name "Senkaku" has originated from the names of some of islands which were given by westerners in the 19th century.

When did the westerners know the Diaoyu Islands? I have done some research, but I will not analyze it in detail here. I am sure that in the middle of the 19th century, the westerners marked the Diaoyu Islands as Hoapin-San (or Su) on the map and marked Huangwei Yu as Tiau-Su. In addition, they also marked the reefs on the east side of the Diaoyu Islands as Pinnacle Groups or Pinnacle Islands.

British warship "Samarang" measured the coordinates of the Diaoyu Islands and explored them for the first time in June 1845. The Captain Sir Edward Balcher wrote in his logbook on June 14, "the warship finished the measurement of Yaeyama Islands and returned to Ishigaki Island in the evening, we were determined to find Hoapin-San Islands on the chart. The Hoapin-San is the Diaoyu Islands."[135]

The next day, "Samarang" measured the Pinnacle Islands, on June 16, it measured Tiau-Su (Huangwei Yu). According to the measure results, they published the chart in 1855. Presumably, this chart and the logbook of Sir Edward Balcher became the base of the records of Hoapin-Su and Tiau-Su in British naval charts and Waterways Chronicles afterwards.[136]

Waterways Chronicles written by the Japanese navy after the Meiji Restoration was based on the Waterways Chronicles of the British navy.

135   "Narrative of the Voyage of War Ship the "HMS. Samarang" During 1843-46", by Captain Sir Edward Balcher: London,p. 184.
136   "The Islands Between Japan and the Adjacent Coast Of China"1855.

World Waterways Chronicles (published in Okinawa in March, 1886) compiled by Waterway Bureau under Navy Ministry of Japan has records about the Diaoyu Islands.

The "compilation reason" mentioned in this book underlined that the tenth part of the book —Islands in the South-was based on the Lab Notes of Navy Colonel Narayoshi Yanagi in 1873, Vol.4 of Sea Needle Routes of China (published by British Navy Waterway Bureau in 1884—noted by Inoue) and the Okinawa Chronicles.

I haven't seen the Lab Notes of Narayoshi Yanagi the Okinawa Chronicles mentioned above. But World Waterways Chronicles marks the Diaoyu Islands, Huangwei Yu and Chiwei Yu as Hoapin-san, Tiau-su and Raleighrock just as the logbook of Sir Edward Balcher. Apparently, they are based on British Naval Waterways Chronicles in 1884.

In addition, Japanese Navy Waterways Chronicles copied in Okinawa magazine mentioned above marks the islands as follows:

Vol. 2 of Japanese Waterways Chronicles issued in July 1894 marks the islands as "ホァピンス島" (Noapin-su), "チャウス島" (Tiau-su)" and "ラレレ岩" (Ralie).

Vol. 2 of Japanese Waterways Chronicles (revision) issued in October, 1908 marks the islands as "Uotsuri Island (Hoapin-su)", "Huangwei Yu (Tiau-su)" and "Chiwei Yu (Raleighrock)". So the Diaoyu Islands was changed into Uotsuri Island and the other two still used the Chinese names and added English names, but it didn't mark Huangwei Yu with Kuba Island or mark Chiwei Yu island with Kumeaka Island, which is a common action afterwards. We can see that Uotsuri Island had a fixed name in the Japanese government, but other islands didn't have fixed names.

Vol. 6 of Japanese Waterways Chronicles issued in July 1919 only marks the islands as "Uotsuri Island", "Huangwei Yu" and "Chiwei Yu" without the English names. Southwest Islands Waterways Chronicles of Taiwan issued in March 1941 also marks the islands as "Uotsuri Island", "Huangwei Yu" and "Chiwei Yu", but we don't why it added "Sekibi" behind Chiwei Yu, maybe the Okinawa magazine added it when transcribing.

At the beginning, Japanese Navy Waterways Chronicles completely copied that of the UK; it didn't use the names of the Diaoyu Islands known by Japan nor the Chinese names or Ryukyu names; instead, it used the English names, and even the passage is almost the same as the blueprint logbook of "Samarang"—of the British Navy Waterways Chronicles".

I excerpted from a passage from the logbook of "Samarang" (page 318) and translated it as follows:

A

"the peak of Heping Mountain is 1181 feet. The south of the island is almost vertical and was cut from the northwest. The rest parts incline to the east and there are many trickles of fine water on the slope. There is no traces of residents or visitors on the island, in fact, the island's land can't hold half a dozen people.

"From the warship, we can see the heavily skewed rock grains towards the northeast, so water will easily flow to its northeast coast. As freshwater fish habitat in natural pond in the island, so the island's fresh water is not temporarily-existed, and almost all of the pools are connected to the sea, covered with lush aquatic plants."

I excerpted from the a passage from Vol. 2 of Japanese Waterways Chronicles issued in June, 1894:

B

The peak of Heping Mountain is 1181 feet. The was cut from the northwest. As freshwater fish habitat on the island, so the island have abundant freshwater, and almost all of the pools are connected to the sea, covered with lush aquatic plants." The island's land can't hold half a dozen people and there is no traces of residents on the island.

If compared A and B, we can say B is a concise and good translation of A.

According to the above situation, after the Meiji Restoration, Japan got almost all the scientific knowledge about Diaoyu Islands from books or maps of the British navy. And the name "Senkaku Islands" were translated from Pinnacle Islands as originally named by the British navy.

World Waterways Chronicles used "Senkaku Islands" to mark the Pinnacle Islands written in Chinese characters and added the Japanese katakana — "ピナクルグロース". As it missed a 'p', so the "グロース" should be "グ ループス" (Groups). Vol. 2 of Japanese Waterways Chronicles issued in 1894 used "ピンナクル诸岛"; Japanese Waterways Chronicles (revision) issued in 1908 used "尖头诸屿" (the Senkaku Islands). "ピナクル" (Pinnacle) refers to the pinnacle of the roof for the Christian church. Due to the reefs on the east side of Diaoyu Islands shape like a small pinnacle, so the British named these rocks as Pinnacle Islands, and it was translated to "Senkaku Islands" by the Japanese navy.

Hisashi Kuroiwa was the first person who called all these islands as Senkaku Islands in 1900. He published an article titled "Senkaku Islands" in 1898 in Vol. 5 of Geology magazine and was collected by Oshiro Masataka in the chronicle of Memorial of Mr. Oshiro Masataka. I haven't seen this article, so I don't know the scope the name refers to. In his report—"Adventure of Senkaku Islands" written in 1900, he wrote:

"Senkaku Islands refer to the islands between Okinawa and Fuzhou. They are about 90 miles from Yaeyama Islands and 230 miles away from Okinawa; they are very close to Fuzhou, and are only 220 miles away from Keelung, Taiwan. Compared with the chart published by the Imperial Navy, the islands are consisted of the Diaoyu Islands, the Pinnacle Islands and Huangwei Yu; they are like a drop in the ocean. The islands don't have a united name, so it is inconvenience when talking about it in geography. Therefore, I name them as the Senkaku Islands."

The Senkaku Islands became popular among scholars in the field of geography because of the article published in Geology Magazine. Before that, people didn't know about this name.

Therefore, Toshio Okuhara cited the article—World Waterways Chronicles and only wrote the "Senkaku Islands". He wanted to give readers the impression that the scope of this "Senkaku Islands" is the same as that said by Kuroiwa. In fact, Toshio Okuhara knew clearly that his "Senkaku Islands" refer to Pinnacle Islands, but he deliberately used equivocation.

Moreover, the statement titled On Sovereignty over the Senkaku Islands released the government of Ryukyu mentioned that:" the Maps of Prefectures and Counties in Japan drawn by the Ministry of Internal Affairs and published in 1881, revised in 1883 didn't mark the name of the Senkaku Islands. In the Maps of Prefectures and Counties in Japan there is no "Senkaku Islands" ("尖阁列岛" on the map), but only the "Pinnacle Islands"("尖阁群岛" on the map). They intended to deceive people that today's so-called name of "Senkaku Islands" was existed at that time. These islands were mapped in Okinawa prefecture on the map. Ryukyu government really loves some pointless tricks.

I discovered a more funny statement than this one, which is Unified View of Socialist Party on sovereignty over the Senkaku Islands issued by International Bureau of Socialist Party of Japan. It indiscriminately accepted the statement of the Ryukyu government and mixed "Senkaku Islands" named by Kuroiwa with Pinnacle Islands and brazenly claimed that the "Senkaku Islands" were incorporated under the administration of Okinawa by Geography Bureau under Ministry of Internal Affairs in 1881; and they repeatedly claimed their sovereignty over the Senkaku Islands. I wonder how the map showed their sovereignty over the Senkaku Islands.

Then, how large are the Senkaku Islands mentioned by Kuraiwa? He made it clear that the Senkaku Islands included the Diaoyu Island, Pinnacle Islands, and Huangwei Yu; Chiwei Yu was not included, which is logical in geography, because Chiwei Yu is 48 nautical miles away from Huangwei Yu, and it doesn't belong to the Diaoyu Islands. The report of Kuroiwa mentioned nothing about Chiwei Yu. On Sovereignty over the Senkaku Islands and Resource Development Rights on Continental Shelf issued by the Ryukyu government published on September 10, 1970 stated that the Senkaku Islands included from 25°N to 26°N, and from 123°20′E to 123°45′E, which was the same as the scope mentioned by Kuroiwa; Chiwei Yu (25°55′N, 124°24′E) is not included.

However, after a week, the Ryukyu government published the document titled "On Sovereignty over the Senkaku Islands" which has been quoted frequently in this book. It mentioned that in January in the 28th year of the Meiji period (1895), the Cabinet decided to only talk about Uotsuri Island (the Diaoyu Island–noted by Inoue) and Kuba Island (Huangwei Yu–noted by Inoue); besides the two islands, the Senkaku Islands also included Nanxiao Islands and Beixiao Islands, Okinokitai Rock (Dabeixiao Island -noted by the translator), Okinominami Rock (Dananxiao Island -noted by the translator), reefs called as Tobize (from Nanxiao Islands to Tobize are called Pinnacle Islands) and Kumeaka Island (Chiwei Yu–noted by Inoue). The Ryukyu government didn't have a fixed statement about the scope of the Senkaku Islands, Chiwei Yu sometimes was included. Then, did the Navy Waterway Department have clear records? The answer is no. The Waterways Chronicles before 1908 didn't mention nothing about whether the name included Chiwei Yu; while the Waterways Chronicles in 1918 marked the Senkaku Islands with "the Senkaku Islands are located between Okinawa and Fuzhou, China...include Huangwei Yu, Uotsuri Island, Nanxiao Islands and Beixiao Islands, Okinokitai Rock (Dabeixiao Island–noted by the translator), Okinominami Rock (Dananxiao Island–noted by the translator), among which, Uotsuri Island is the largest."

From Beixiao Islands to Okinominami Rock are called Pinnacle Islands; the Waterways Chronicles in September, 1908 used "尖头诸屿" (Pinnacle Islands) while the Waterways Chronicles in July, 1894 used "ピンナクル诸屿"; Waterways Chronicles in 1886 used "尖阁群岛" (ピンナツクルグロース) and Waterways Chronicles in 1919 used "尖阁列岛" (the Senkaku Islands) named by Kuroiwa and gave detailed explanation: "because of their position, these islands have been know by the Ryukyuan since ancient times, they have names such as "尖头诸屿", "尖阁列岛" (the Senkaku Islands), Pinnacle Islands, etc. "尖阁列岛" (the Senkaku Islands) was named by Kuroiwa; "Pinnacle Islands" was used by the British navy; "尖头诸屿" was the translation of "Pinnacle Islands". The Waterways Chronicles mixed them up willy-nilly.

Southwest Islands Waterways Chronicles of Taiwan in 1941 used "尖头诸屿" and used the same scope just as Waterways Chronicles in 1919. It claimed that "because of their position, these islands have been know by the Ryukyuan since ancient times, they have names such as "尖阁列岛" (the Senkaku Islands), Pinnacle Islands which is called by foreigners. It seemed that "尖阁列岛" (the Senkaku Islands) used to be called by the Ryukyuan; and they call the islands as "尖头诸屿" (Pinnacle Islands) at present.

The so-called "Basic Views of sovereignty over the Senkaku Islands" issued by the Japanese government on March 9, 1972 stated that the Cabinet decided on January 14, 1895, to have markers erected on the islands to officially incorporate them into Japan's territory. However, Cabinet only decided to have markers erected on Uotsuri Island (the Diaoyu Islands) and Kuba Island (Huangwei Yu), the Pinnacle Islands were not included. But as the Pinnacle Islands are located between the Diaoyu Islands and Huangwei Yu, so even the Cabinet didn't mention it, they were still included into the Senkaku Islands, while Chiwei Yu by no means belongs to the Senkaku Islands. Nevertheless, the government put Chiwei Yu into the "Senkaku Islands" and attempted to steal it from China.

The Ryukyu government, the Japanese Ministry of Foreign Affairs, JCP all tried to incorporate the Senkaku Islands determined by Kuroiwa on the basis of geography and Chiwei Yu which was excluded from the Senkaku Islands by Kuroiwa into Japan's territory. But they also know that the Senkaku Islands including Chiwei Yu never existed, so they couldn't issue a clear statement to claim the scope of the Senkaku Islands; hence, they firstly used the Senkaku Islands named by Kuroiwa and then incorporated Chiwei Yu into the scope secretly.

It is really a shame for imperialists to adopt such shallow tricks to territorial issues.In addition, "尖阁列岛" (Senkaku Islands) named by Kuroiwa was never officially admitted by Japan. That's why "Senkaku Islands" was treated as a used name and "尖头诸屿" which is the translation of Pinnacle Islands was used in Navy Waterways Chronicles which have the highest requirements for the rigor of geographical records. However, at present, the Japanese government and the Ryukyu (Okinawa) prefecture government used this name again and cooked up the scope of the "Senkaku Islands", besides, JCP just blindly follows them.

The Japanese government, the Ryukyu (Okinawa) prefecture government, JCP as well as various media outlets have claimed that the Senkaku Islands have been Japan's territory in history and there is no room for debate". In fact, they even don't know their scope and don't have a fixed name for the islands; sometimes they use "尖阁列岛" (Senkaku Islands), and sometimes "尖头诸屿" (Pinnacle Islands); beside Uotsuri Island, government departments don't have fixed names for other islands; Huangwei Yu was called Kuba Island and sometimes it would be changed to the Diaoyu Island; Chiwei Yu was originally called as Kumeaka Island, but unknowingly, it was called Taisho Island; the Japanese navy only used Huangwei Yu and Chiwei Yu or their English names to record them. This is not only a naming issue, essentially, it is significant in political aspects. This is an inevitable phenomenon when Japan's emperor system claims sovereignty over the Senkaku Islands and steal other countries' territories. I will further discuss in Chapter 13.[137]

---

137   By virtue of maps and records, we can see that the "Hoapin–San" or "HOAPIN–SU" marked on the chart of the British is obviously the Diaoyu Island, while the Tiau–Su is Huangwei Yu. Natural Conditions and Customs of the Southern Islands written by Higaonna Kanryo mentioned that "Hoapin–SU" marked on the chart was the Chinese pronunciation of "Huangwei Yu", which is incorrect. In Mandarin, it pronounced as "HuangWei", while in Hokkien, it is "WengBoe" rather than "Heping".

In addition, Kuroiwa called the Diaoyu Islands "Heping Island"; if so, "Hoapin" is the Chinese pronunciation written in Rome letters. But I never find records of Heping Island from China's ancient literature; so "Heping" here is not an original Chinese name, but the Chinese pronunciation written in Rome letters. The earliest person who used "Hoapin" was the author of the first Waterways Chronicles

I want to speak out my ideas about the origin of naming "Hoapin-Su" island, I guess it is a confusion of one thing with another, a mistake made by westerners, they used the Chinese pronunciation of Huangping Yu to call the Diaoyu Island. In Chapter 3, "Map of Coastal Mountains and Sands" (Yan Hai Shan Sha Tu) in An Illustrated Compendium on Maritime Security (Chou Hai Tu Bian) pointed out that from the west to east there are Pengjia Mountain, Diaoyu Island, Huaping Yu, Huangwei Yu ....; while in Records of Messages from Chong-shan (Zhong Shan Chuan Xin Lu), the order is Huaping Yu, Pengjia Mountain, Diaoyu Island. The Chinese might mixed these islands up, so the westerners mistook the Diaoyu Islands for Huaping Yu (Hoapin-Su); the translator of the Japanese navy used Chinese characters—"Heping" to mark "Hoapin".

In addition, I am afraid that "Tiau-Su" refers to Diao Yu (the Diaoyu Islands). "Tiau-Su" was not used for the Diaoyu Islands; instead it was used for Huangwei Yu in the northeast; likely, the "Hoapin-Su" was used for the Diaoyu Island which is located in the east of Huaping Yu.

IX. The So-called Ending the "Ryukyu Disposal" Issue by the Mikado (Japan) Militarism and the Diaoyu Islands

In the end of the Tokugawa shogunate, the Ryukyuan only knew "Yigunkubashima" (the Diaoyu Islands in Ryukyuan language- noted by the translator); they didn't have daily contact with the islands, let alone the Japanese. Except for some scholars, the ordinary warriors and people were unheard of these islands. At that time, the Japanese could by no means have occupied the Diaoyu Islands.

Even after the end of the unrest of the Tokugawa shogunate, Tokugawa Shogunate still fought for Ogasawara Islands against Britain and the United States. And, in the north, Japan fought for the boundary between Japan and Russia in Karahuto (Sakhalin Island - noted by the translator); officials of the Tokugawa shogunate and Katsura Kogoro (Kido Takayoshi) had planned to invade North Korea. The Tokugawa shogunate paid great attention to territorial borders and was eager to expand territories. If someone or even the shogunate yielded to aliens, the Empire of Japan would beat them (Tokugawa shogunate and Katsura Kogoro) mercilessly. But none of them thought of the annexation of Ryukyu or cutting its relationship with the Qing Dynasty, let alone the unmanned Diaoyu Islands in front of the Ryukyu islands. (see Theory of Occupying Korea and Establishment of Militarism in Japan,written by Inoue Kiyoshi)

The first year of the Meiji period (1868), the forces of the Japan Emperor (Mikado) overthrew the Tokugawa Shogunate and established the Emperor's regime. In 1871, the domains and feudal land system of Japan were entirely abolished and the Emperor became the highest despot, hence a united country with a high level of centralization was established. At that time, the Japanese Emperor government already had the ambition to conquer North Korea, Taiwan and Ryukyu. It had an integrated policy for the occupation of the three regions. Mikado (Japan Emperor) militarism revealed its importance for the first time. Later, the Mikado (Japan Emperor) militarism aimed to occupy the Diaoyu Islands. Therefore, Ryukyu is the central issue when we talk about the relationship between the Japanese Emperor Government and the Diaoyu Islands.

Satsuma prefecture administration domain was also abolished along with the establishment of the new system, Japanese Empire Government incorporated the Ryukyu Kingdom which used to belong to the Satsuma prefecture into its own colonial possession. But the Japan Government didn't prevent the Ryukyu Kingdom from tribute-paying to China and its getting title grants from the Chinese Qing Dynasty and even allowed Ryukyu Kingdom to maintain relationships with the Qing Dynasty.

The following year (1872), Japan Government took advantage of the murder of Ryukyuan sailors by local residents of Taiwan (in November, 1871) and made an excuse that they would revenge for the Ryukyuan, thus invaded Taiwan. They made their invasion reasonable and their foundation was that Ryukyu belonged to Japan and the Ryukyuan were the Japanese people, rather than the subordinate people of the vassal state of the Qing Dynasty. After discussions, Japanese Emperor Government, in September 1872, decided to confer Shangtai of Ryukyu is tai" (rather than the Ryukyu King Shangtai) as the Ryukyu seignior with 30000 yen, belonging to Kazoku (noble class in Japan); meanwhile, all the foreign affairs of Ryukyu were put under the jurisdiction of of the Japanese Ministry of Foreign Affairs. King Shangtai of Ryukyu and his courtiers lodged strong objections, but on the one hand, Japanese Government imposed pressure on them, on the other hand it sent officials in Ministry of Foreign Affairs to make verbal guarantee that Ryukyu can keep its current "polity and regime"; although its foreign affairs were put under the jurisdiction of of the Japanese Ministry of Foreign Affairs, Ryukyu can maintain the relationship between Ryukyu and the Qing Dynasty. Japan Government attempted to temporarily muddle through by deceiving Ryukyu rulers.

Under the strong support and guidance of C.E. de Long, the US ambassador to Japan, and retired General Le Gendre, who was recommended by C.E. de Long, Japanese Emperor Government brazenly invaded Taiwan in July 1874. They made up excuses as follows: 1. the "Japanese people" were killed; 2. The place where the people were killed was wild tribes—terra nullius in International Law; the people in wild tribes were not the Chinese people. Their excuse was the same with that they used in the Diaoyu Islands issue.

In order to make the invasion reasonable, in 1873, Taneomi Soejima, the Foreign Minister went to Beijing on June 9 to meet with the British ambassador to Beijing. At that time, the British ambassador asked: what should you do if the Qing government claimed that Taiwan is their territory and they endow Taiwan with its regime". Soejima replied: "we have evidence to prove that the Qing government doesn't have the right; the Qing government never sent officials to the terra nullius, and the name of the terra nullius was not on the map of the Qing Empire; a few years ago, Americans attacked the wild tribes and fought with the people there without the permission of the Qing government; and wild tribes could sign treaties with the US on their own; if they belonged to the Chinese Qing Empire, how can the Qing Empire allow the wild tribes to fight alone and sign treaties with the US on their own? Therefore, the Qing government doesn't have the sovereignty over the wild tribes.[138]

In addition, on June 21, Soejima and Yanagihara held talks about the murder of the Ryukyuan sailors in Taiwan with Ministry of Foreign Affairs in Qing Dynasty. Yanagihara did all the speech and grasped the guidance of speech. He skillfully made the Chinese representatives speak out that some people in Taiwan like outsiders didn't obey the rules of the Qing Emperor; hence, Yanagihara vaguely asserted that "you mean that Taiwan didn't belong to China for a long time and Taiwan was isolated as wild tribes; so it can be at Japan's disposal. He left immediately after saying this. Yanagihara distorted the wording of the Chinese representatives and insisted that the wild tribes of the Qing Empire was the terra nullius in modern International Law. They used it as the excuse of Japan's invasion. In the next year, the Japan's invasion undoubtedly faced the serious protests from the Qing Dynasty and Japan absurdly argued with the wording that "some people in Taiwan like outsiders didn't obey the rules of the Qing Emperor".

The claim that the Diaoyu Islands are terra nullius is the same. They distorted the concept of the Chinese expressions and the modern logic to explain the records of Chen Kan and Guo Rulin as well as the records of Kume Island (Gumi Island) and Chiwei Yu in Records of Messages from Chong-shan (Zhong Shan Chuan Xin Lu).

---

138 Vol. 6 in Japanese Diplomatic Documents.

In 1874 when Japan invaded Taiwan, its strength couldn't compete with the strength of the Qing Dynasty and the Britain, so it was unable for Japan to adhere to the theory of terra nullius. However, the aggressive ambitions of Japan Government became more inflated. Under the support of the UK, Japan's Emperor Government chose North Korea as the first target of its aggression. But since the Korean Kings were like the Ryukyu Kings, they also paid tribute to the Qing Empire. If Japan still allowed Ryukyu to pay tribute to the Qing Empire, this would be stumbling block for of Japan's grand policy that aimed to completely isolate North Korea from China.

Therefore, in July 1875, the Japan Government ordered Ryukyu to stop paying tribute to China and forced it to reform the vassal state status. At the same time, in order to suppress the resistance of the Ryukyu King, Japan forcibly occupied the land of Ryukyu and established a military base there, the Ryukyu Kings and nobles lodged strong opposition and secretly asked for help from the Qing government. Although the Qing government repeatedly protested against Japan's banning of the tribute-paying and title granting system, it didn't give real concrete aid to Ryukyu.

During this period, Japanese Government sent "Unyo" battleship to illegally invade the Han River near Ganghwa Island of North Korea and provoked the garrison stationed in this island, the defenders were forced to fire. The Japanese Emperor Government immediately sent soldiers of the army and navy into North Korea, claiming that North Korea attacked Japan. Under this pressure, in February of the next year, North Korea was forced to sign the first Provisions of Cordial Relations, and in August it was forced to sign the trade rules.

The treaty was Japan's first unequal treaty imposed to a foreign country. According to "Provisions of Cordial Relations", some port places such as Pusan were set as Japan's trading ports and Japan could set up settlements and enjoy privileges in these places.

The trade rules stipulated that the two countries "temporarily" cancel import and export tariffs, Japanese currency would be used in the trading ports of North Korea and would be able to buy-sell goods on this land. This meant that the Japanese had taken control of the North Korea in terms of politics and the Japanese capitalism began to wantonly plunder the economy of North Korea. But the first article of the harsh unequal treaty reads: "North Korea is an independent state and enjoys equal powers with Japan." This actually means that North Korea no longer belonged to the Qing Empire as a vassal state, which indicates Japan's ambition to incorporate North Korea as the vassal of Japan. Thus 11 years ago, Japan buried the seeds of the Sino-Japanese War.

Taking the advantage of the momentum of successfully bullying the North Korea, the Japanese Emperor ordered to intensify efforts to end the "disposal" of Ryukyu. But in the second year after the Japanese-Korean Provisions of

Cordial Relations was signed, the Japanese Emperor Government put full force into the Southwest War. After the victory, in April, 1879, they sent an army of 450 men and 160 police officers to overwhelm Ryukyu which had no army for 200 years. They forced the seignior to Tokyo, and annulled the vassal state and established Okinawa prefecture.

The so-called "Ryukyu disposal" was ended by a declaration as follows: "the Ryukyuan and the native Japanese are originally the same nation, but they were separated politically. Now, Japan finally became a politically unified nation." Currently, this opinion dominates the public opinion, but I don't agree with it.

Ryukyu initially became a small country in the 12th century; in the 14th century, three nations confronted to acquire the island of Okinawa; in the late 15th century, the countries were united. But these countries were independent states and made equal exchanges with Japan; in the late 14th century, Ryukyu began to pay tribute to China and receive China's title granting; at the beginning of the 17th century, Ryukyu was conquered by Shimazu vassal (Japan) and suffered from its brutal oppression and rule; at that time, the Ryukyu Kingdom was still a separate country, and kept paying tribute to China. The historical content of the so-called end of the "Ryukyu disposal" meant that Ryukyu was completely deprived from its independent state status and was forced to cut off itsrelations with China, becoming the colony of Japanese Empire Government. I have written a detailed dissertation concerning this issue from the perspective of history and national theory, if you are interested, you can have a look at it.[139]

X. Japan has completed its occupation of the Ryukyu Islands in the Sino-Japanese War

During the struggle period which led to the so-called "the ending of the Ryukyu disposal" between 1872-1879, Japanese Emperor Government dealt with the border issues and strove to expand its territory. Besides the issue of "Ryukyu disposal", according to the time order, there were the following events:

From September to October, 1873, within the government, there was a debate on the theory of conquering Korea, people who supported this theory such as Saigo Takamori Korea had failed.

---

139   See "Japan's History," Volume 16 — "modern age" (3) — "Okinawa" by Iwanami Book Press (1962); "Okinawa in History" in Pondering over Okinawa Issue written by Yoshio Nakano (ed. 1968, Tokyo Pacific Press); "What is the Difference between Okinawa" in "Liberation Education compiled by the journal National Liberation Education Research, Issue 1970/3, p. 10.

From February to December, 1874 - the Invasion of Taiwan.

In May 1875, Japan signed exchange treaties with Russia concerning the Kuril Islands and Karafuto. The dispute over the Karafuto on the border between Japan and Russia was ended up with Japan's concession. Japan gave up the rights of the southern half of Karafuto and all the Karafuto Island were mapped into the Russia's territory. Russia gave South Sakhalin Islands which had little value in economy and military to Japan as compensation. All the Kuril Islands had been mapped into Japan's territory as Japan originally owned the territory south to the Etorofu islands.

In February 1876, North Korea was forced to sign "Japanese-Korean Provisions of Cordial Relations" and the attached unequal trade rules. Japan wanted make up the loss through aggression of smaller neighbors in order to retrieve some National prestige. This treaty was closely related to the "Ryukyu disposition".

In October 1876, Japan announced to all over the world that Ogasawara Islands were put under the jurisdiction of the Japanese government. In the end of the Tokugawa shogunate, both Britain and the United States declared that they found the terra nullius first and claimed the sovereignty over the islands, thus there were tensions in their relationship with Japan for a period. From the perspective of modern International Law, reason of Britain and the United States was not worse than Japan's; if they insisted on their rights, Japan was impossible to conduct exclusive occupation of Ogasawara Islands. But there was a popular opinion in the US government at that time that owning a territory away from home land as unfavorable. So in 1873, the United States gave up the ownership claim, and turned to Japan. Britain still insisted on their rights, but they'd rather give up the small islands on the Pacific than cause an impasse in the relations with Japan; hence in 1875, the British acquiesced in Japan's claim; in this way, Japan obtained the possession rights[140], and carried out the above announcement.

Through the above events, we can see that the Japan could not confront with Russia, the United Kingdom and the United States, and only made concessions blindly, as well as picked up small bribes from them. On the other hand, it adopted the policy of high pressure and expansion to North Korea, the Qing Government and the Ryukyu Kingdom, trying to expand its sphere of influence. However, due to the lack of power, the spirit was willing, but the flesh was is weak. Although the Ryukyu Kingdom had to give up relations with China and its territory was annexed by Japan, this was not Japan's original idea that if

---

140 See the documents concerning of Ogasawara Islands in "Japanese Diplomatic Documents" volumes 5-9 (the 5-9 year of Meiji period). Negotiations between Tokugawa Shogunate and the UK and the US (see "History of the Kuril Islands and Ogasawara Islands.")

China put forward certain conditions, they would give up part of the land to the Qing government. Although the Ryukyu issue had no ties with Diaoyu Islands issue, it has important contact with the following passages, so it is necessary to briefly introduce the process.

The Qing government treated the Ryukyu Kingdom as its own vassal state. The Qing government once lodged a protest to Japan's preventing Ryukyu from paying tribute to China. On April 4, 1879, Japan annexed Ryukyu completely; On May 10, the Qing government told Shishido, the Japanese envoy in Beijing that China did not admit Japan's disposal. The two countries negotiated about the ownership of Ryukyu for a year and a half. Meanwhile, Grant, the former President of the United States traveled to East Asia and the Qing government invited him to mediate between Japan and China. China advocated "three divisions" plan: the areas located to the north of Amami Island belong to Japan; the parts of the Ryukyu Kingdom located in Okinawa islands, Miyako Islands and Yaeyama Islands belong to China.

Japan refused this scheme, and intended to bargain with the Qing government by using Ryukyu as the bargaining chip.. Japan put forward that Sino-Japanese Provisions of Cordial Relations established in 1871 should add that the Japanese merchants in China enjoy equal rights to that of the European countries and the United States"; and as the areas located to the north of Okinawa islands belong to Japan; Miyako Islands and Yaeyama Islands belong to China.

The Qing government didn't ratify the "Treaty of Island Division and the Supplementary Provisions" proposed by Japan. Due to the ongoing Ili dispute between China and Russia, the Qing government made concessions to Japan and wanted solve the problem of Ryukyu as soon as possible thus improving the relations between Japan and China so as to isolate Russia. In October 1880, the Qing government and Japan reached consensus on the "Treaty of Island Division and the Supplementary Provisions". But then, due to Beiyang Minister Li Hongzhang's strong opposition, the representative of China failed to sign this treaty. On November 1st, the Chinese side informed the Japan minister Shishido as follows: "after listening to the opinions of Nanyang Minister and Beiyang Minister, we plan to make some modifications in respect to the "Treaty of Island Division and the Supplementary Provisions" and afterwards we will formally inform your side.

Shishido Tamaki condemned that China didn't keep its promise and in the second year (1881) on January 5, he presented a tough-talking historical material to China, the main content of which was that "your country refused our offer, and destroyed the terms negotiated by representatives of the two countries; on the Ryukyu disposal issue, we will never accept any objection from your country." Then, he and his attendants left China in anger.[141]

---

141   See "Japanese Diplomatic Documents ", volume 13 and 14 " — On Ownership of Okinawa between Japan and China"; Wang Yunsheng's "China and Japan in 60 Years", Volume 1.

Talks on Ryukyu issue between Japan and China were split, but the Japanese government certainly did not do as Shishido's historical material. After Shishido's return, Foreign Minister Inoue Kaoru demanded the Japanese consul at Tianjin—Takezoe Shinyichiro to hold informal talks with Li Hongzhang to explore the actual situation. On December 14, 1881, he held talks with Li, and reported to the Japanese Ministry of Foreign Affairs in detail; at the same time, he also expressed his own thoughts: Li's intention was to own Miyako Islands and Yaeyama Islands and assist the RyukyuKingthere; it was not the proper time to change the treaty. On January 18, in the second year (1883), Foreign Minister Inoue Kaoru again demanded the Japanese consul at Tianjin—Takezoe Shinyichiro to inquire about Li's intention and told him the government's view on the issue:

If ceding Miyako Islands and Yaeyama Islands will content Li, we have no objection; if they will grant relatives or children of Shangtai as the King, we have "no objection", neither. But Japan have deposed Shangtai, Japan can no longer grant him as the King.

We can't know the content of the talks between Takezoe Shinyichiro and Li; But from the result, we can know that they didn't hold bilateral talks as Foreign Minister Inoue Kaoru suggested.

In March 1883, the Japanese government required the Qing government to re-sign attached trade rules of Japan-Qing Provisions of Cordial Relations which would be expired on April 29. In May, the Qing government's envoy in Japan asked Foreign Minister Inoue Kaoru whether Japan would put treaty negotiations with Ryukyu issue together. Foreign Minister Inoue Kaoru replied: on the issue of Ryukyu, the previous envoy Shishido sincerely negotiated with your government and turned a blind eye to it. Our government thought this issue had nothing to do with trade regulations; naturally, it should need further negotiations[142].

In this way, Foreign Minister Inoue Kaoru and even the Japanese government held that the issue of Ryukyu was unsolved. In other words, we can't conclude that all the Ryukyu Island belonged to Japan, just because the treaty was not signed and Japan refused to negotiate it with the Qing government. The Japanese government admitted that Ryukyu issue is still unsolved.

Because of the above answer of Foreign Minister Inoue Kaoru, China didn't agree to put aside the Ryukyu issue when revising the articles of the trade regulations, so this problem have been dragged to 1886. This year, Japan was trying to revise the European and American treaty. In order to create favorable conditions for the talks, foreign Minister Inoue Kaoru intended to speed up the revision of the treaty between Japan and the Qing (Chinese) government. In

---

142 See "Japanese Diplomatic Documents" Vol. 16, "Related Matters on Modifying Nissin Provisions of Cordial Relations".

March, he advised Shioda Saburo, the envoy in Beijing how to negotiate with the Qing government about the revision of the treaty and he reminded him not to involve in the Ryukyu issue. On April 22, Shioda began negotiations with the Chinese side to revise the treaty. China repeatedly included the Ryukyu issue in the negotiations, but Japan prevaricated it with blarney.[143]

The dispute over Ryukyu between China and Japan was shelved for 8 years until the Sino-Japanese War 1894-95.

At this point, in order to create favorable conditions for negotiations of the revision of treaty with the Europe and the United States, they wanted to obtain the same position in China just as the Europe and the United States. But what was the reason for Japan to separate the Ryukyu issue from treaty negotiations? In negotiations between Japan and China in 1880, Japan aimed to revise the treaty by virtue splitting Ryukyu, but the Qing government didn't agree; so if Japan wanted to revise the treaty as soon as possible, it should put them together, which was known by Foreign Minister Inoue Kaoru.

But since 1883, they separated the two issues. Originally, Japanese Emperor Government's plan of the Japan-China War was imminent, Japan tried its best to prepare for it[144], so it was impossible that Japan would give China the southern Ryukyu which was nearest to China. If this place was China's territory, it would be a significant basis for China to attack Japan; If Japan had it, Japan could attack the southern China or Taiwan on this land. Therefore, the Japanese would never hand over this land to China. Maybe the government had considered that in the near future, even if China would be reluctant, it had to admit the accomplished fact that Japan occupied Ryukyu exclusively.

---

143   See "Japanese Diplomatic Documents" Vol. 19, "Related Matters on Modifying Trade regulations in Nissin Provisions of Cordial Relations"; the treaty negotiations continued until September, 1888. Japan would like to get the position and rights equal to the Europe in order to override the Qing government, but the Qing government did not give in, so the Japanese side stopped the negotiations.

144   Japanese Emperor Government already planned to annex Korea long before, therefore its relations with China was deteriorated. After the Horse incident in 1882, (Korean soldiers together with anti-Japanese groups in Seoul city had rebelled against the North Korean government and the Japanese military instructors), in order to contest for the control over Korea, Japan began to expand its military , thus increased taxes and prepared for a war against China. In November 1884, the Enlightenment Party with the support of Japan staged a coup (Gapsin Coup) and seized power, but in three days, it was defeated by the attack of Korean conservatives with the support of the Chinese Qing government. Japanese envoy in Seoul fled back to Japan. Afterwards, Japan and China sent troops to Korea twice and it has triggered the war between Japan and China. But at that time, the Japanese government had no confidence to launch war. In April the following year (1885), Prime Minister Ito Hirobumi as full ambassador went to Tianjin, and held talks with Li Hongzhang, concluding the Tianjin Treaty which stipulated that the two countries should retreat from North Korea at the same time and should notice each other when sending troops to North Korea in the future. From then on, Japanese Government developed its national strength in various aspects such as military, politics, diplomacy, finance to prepare for a war against China.

In January 1895, during the Sino-Japanese War, the House of Lords passed "Reform Suggestions for Okinawa County"; in the discussion of proposal reasons, they repeatedly emphasized that "Okinawa is a significance land in the oriental", "a significance land of military", and stressed they should reform coast defense in this county. Accordingly, Okinawa was only important in military.[145]

The government cast a huge shadow in Okinawa for the Sino-Japanese War. In March, 1886, Foreign Minister Inoue Kaoru firmly refused to add the Ryukyu issue into the negotiations about Nissin Provisions of Cordial Relations. At the same time, Yamagata Aritomo, the Ministry of Internal Affairs, who was the supreme commander of "great Japan Empire as well as the enthusiastic supporter of warring against China, led the attendants of the Japenese Emperor to visit Okinawa. In April in the second year (1887), reserve major general Fukuhara was appointed as the Governor of Okinawa. This was the first time that a soldier was appointed Governor of Okinawa. In November, Prime Minister Ito Hirobumi led War Minister Oyama Iwao and Secretary of the Navy Military Nire Kagenori to make a six-day visit to Okinawa with Japan's most advanced warships. Ito Hirobumi also made a poem titled "being ordered to patrol Ryukyu": His poem said: "who knows defense strategy in Japan, who spared no effort to ponder over it." Undoubtedly, the goal of this visit was preparation for the war against China.

Everything was ready in July 1894, with the support of British imperialism, Japan declared the war. On July 25, Japanese navy attacked the fleet of the Qing Dynasty near the Feng Island; On July 29, the army ambushed China's army in Asan Bay and Seonghwan, launching the war against China. Later, on August 1st, Japan formally declared war against China. At that time, China had no preparation for the war against Japan ideologically and politically; military modernization of China had just started.

War cut off the original national relations between the two countries. So at the time of the war, all treaties and shelved problems between the belligerent countries no longer stood. The new national relationship should be re-established based on the post-war peace treaties. Due to Japan's victory in the Sino-Japanese War, Treaty of Shimonoseki was signed, by virtue of which Japan enjoyed privileges it had been craving for over the past few years; Japan also imposed new trade treaties and trade regulations on China.

At the start of the war, Ryukyu issue was no longer the suspended problems between the two countries. Japan and China didn't talk about Ryukyu in the talks in Shimonoseki. Therefore, the peace treaty mentioned the issue of Ryukyu. That is to say, when establishing of new relations between the two

---

145   See "Okinawa History" (4) compiled by the Ryukyu government—"Education" in Section 6 Chapter 2; "Annals of Parliament of Great Japan Empire".

countries, the Qing government didn't mention any objection to Japan's occupation of Ryukyu, thus forming the accomplished fact of Japan's exclusive
occupation of Ryukyu. In other words, it was because of Japan's victory in the
Sino-Japanese War that made the Qing government lose all the historical rights
of Ryukyu and established the Japan's exclusive occupation of Ryukyu.

XI. The Japan Empire had craved for Diaoyu Islands for nine years

In order to intensify the invasion of North Korea and China, Japanese
Emperor Government began to attach importance to Ryukyu. After deciding on
the policy of Japan's exclusive occupation of the islands, in 1885 (in the 18th
year of the Meiji period), Japanese Government for the first time had discovered that the Diaoyu Islands were located between Ryukyu and mainland China.

In 1879, soon after Ryukyu was attached to Okinawa, Koga Tatsushiro, an
industrialist born in Fukuoka City, moved to Nana and began fishing and export business. On the Kuba Island (Huangwei Yu), he discovered albatrosses
which could be sold to Europe, this could bring him a fortune. So in 1885he
applied to the Okinawa authorities for a lease contract concerning leasing the
land of the Diaoyu Islands on the basis of business needs.[146]

The Ryukyu government and the JCP said: "the Senkaku Islands" are Japan's
legitimate territory, because the businessman Koga Tatsushiro developed the
Diaoyu Islands for peaceful economic purposes, thus advocating Japan's possession of the islands. In 1885 the Japanese government had noticed the Diaoyu
Islands mainly due to Koga Tatsushiro's application, but their intention to incorporate the islands into Japan's territory was not because the collection of the
albatross feathers; it was because they noticed the islands had geostrategic significance for China's military. Since 1883, the Japanese government's Ryukyu
policy has started mainly from a military perspective. We can clearly sense it,
from the whole process of Japan's occupation of the Diaoyu Islands after 1885.

The Ryukyu government and JCP said Okinawa Prefectural Office in 1885,
after receipt of Koga Tatsushiro's application, reported to the government to
incorporate the island into Japan's territory, but that is not the case. In order
to possess the islands, the Ministry of Internal Affairs firstly secretly ordered Okinawa Prefectural Office to make an investigation about the islands.
Okinawa magistrate's petition to Count Yamagata Aritomo (Home Minister) on
September 22, in 1885 was as follows:

---

146   It has been widely believed that businessman Koga "discovered" the islands in the 17th
year of the Meiji period (1884); in the following year (1885), he submitted lease application to
the Okinawa Prefectural Office for commercial purposes. However, according to lease application submitted on June 10th, 1895: in the 18th years of the Meiji period, Koga sailed to Kuba
Island 90 nautical miles north to Yaeyama Islands (see "Okinawa" magazine No. 56).

No. 350: Petition

Regarding Investigations at Kumeseki-shima and Two Outer Islands

In regard to the uninhabited islands spread out between this prefecture and Fuzhou, China, a summary of the surveys conducted at those islands in accordance to the secret order previously conferred to the secretary of our prefecture stationed in the capital is described as follows in the enclosed attachment paper (omitted). Because Kumeseki-shima, Kuba-shima and Uotsuri-shima have since ancient time been the names used by this prefecture to refer to them, and since they are uninhabited islands close to the islands, Kume, Miyako, Yaeyama under the jurisdiction of this prefecture, there should not exist any difficulties hindering their incorporation into this prefecture. Yet, due to their differences in terms of topography from the earlier repotted island Daitojima (situated between this prefecture and Osagawa Islands), the possibility must not be ignored that they are the same islands recorded as Diaoyutai , Huangwei-yu , and Chiwei-yu in the Zhongshan Mission Records If they truly are the same islands, then it is obviously the case that the details of the islands have already been well-known to Qing envoy ships dispatched to crown the former Zhongshan Wang, and already given fixed [Chinese] names and used as navigational aids en route to the Ryukyu Islands. It is therefore worrisome regarding whether it would be appropriate to place national markers on these islands immediately after our investigations. During the middle of next month, upon the return of the employed survey ship, Izumo-maru, which was dispatched to conduct surveys of the two islands (Miyako, Yayeyama), I will immediately submit a detailed report. In regard to the issue of the placement of national markers, your further instructions are requested.

September 22, 1885

Through this report, we can can find the following important points:

Firstly, why did the Ministry of Internal Affairs secretly investigate on the unmanned islands between Ryukyu and Fuzhou? Why didn't it make this official command public?

Secondly, "the erection of national markers on the islands mentioned here means the national markers of Japan. Was it put forward by Okinawa Prefecture Chief or the Ministry of Internal Affairs?

These above two problems are connected. It can be seen from the reported that the erection of national markers was put forward by the Ministry of Internal Affairs. Internal Ministry Yamagata Aritomo who was the most ardent agitator of militarism, emphasized only the military status of Ryukyu; at the same time, he had ambitions about the nearby islands and attempted to incorporate them into Japan's territory. To achieve this goal, he ordered the Okinawa prefecture chief to conduct the necessary investigation. But it was a matter of international relations; it was easy to cause trouble if Japan publicly give formal investigation orders when Japan was at daggers drawn with the Qing government, hence they issued "the order" secretly.

Thirdly, the chief of the Okinawa prefecture had hesitated after receiving the secret order, because it might not work, although incorporating the islands into Japan's territory would be a good thing. The reason was that Okinawa prefecture thought that these islands are the Diaoyu Islands which was mentioned in the book Records of Messages from Chong-shan (Zhong Shan Chuan Xin Lu[147]). If they are the same islands, these islands have been clearly known and named by the envoy led by Xu Baoguang, who was conferred by China's Qing Emperor. It was obvious that this envoy had taken Ryukyu as their destination. That is to say, they were a part of Chinese territory. Therefore, they were not the same as the Daito Island which was terra nullius.

Although, Yamagata Aritomo received this reasonable report from Okinawa magistrate, he still tried everything possible to incorporated the islands into Japan. He submitted this issue to Cabinet. On October 9th, he consulted with Foreign Minister Inoue Kaoru. He said in his letter: even if they are the islands recorded in the Records of Messages from Chong-shan, the island group is only used for guiding points for Chinese ships and there is no sign to prove that the island belongs to Chinese Qing Dynasty. Only that we and Qing Dynasty have called them with different names." He added: the islands are quite close to Miyako Island, Yaeyama Islands and other inhabited islands are included in the governing areas of Okinawa prefecture. And he said he planned to erect national markers immediately after this field exploration. The most strong argument of this letter to prove the Diaoyu Islands "belongs to Japan's territory" was that the islands are quite close to Miyako Island, Yaeyama Islands and other inhabited islands that were in the governing areas of Okinawa prefecture. But if the "Island Division Treaty" of 1880-1882 plan was realized, such ideas would not be prposed.

Foreign Minister Inoue Kaoru's letter as a reply:

Sent October 21

Personal Correspondence

No. 38

From: From Inoue Kaoru, the Foreign Minister

To: Yamagata Aritomo, Home Minister of Japan

---

147   In 1719, Xu Baoguang, a deputy title-conferring envoy to Ryukyu, assigned by the Qing Dynasty, clearly recorded in his book Records of Messages from Chong-shan (Zhong Shan Chuan Xin Lu) that the voyage from Fujian to Ryukyu passed Huaping Yu, Pengjia Yu, Diaoyu Dao, Huangwei Yu, Chiwei Yu and reached Naba (Naha) port of Ryukyu via Gumi Mountain (the mountain guarding the southwest border of Ryukyu) and Machi Island.

In response to your letter Annex A No. 38 received on the ninth of this month, in which you requested deliberation over the matter concerning placing national markers on the uninhabited islands of Kumeseki-shima and two other islands spread out in between Okinawa and Fuzhou [China] after investigating them, I have given much thought to the matter. The aforementioned islands are close to the border of China, and it has been found through our surveys that the area of the islands is much smaller than the previously surveyed island, Daito-jima; and in particular, China has already given names to the islands. Most recently Chinese newspapers have been reporting rumors of our government's intention of occupying certain islands owned by China located next to Taiwan, demonstrating suspicion toward our country and consistently urging the Qing government to be aware of this matter. In such a time, if we were to publicly place national markers on the islands, this must necessarily invite China's suspicion toward us. Currently we should limit ourselves to investigating the islands, understanding the formations of the harbors, seeing whether or not there exists possibilities to develop the island's land and resources, which all should be made into detailed reports. In regard to the matter of placing national markers and developing the islands, it should await a more appropriate time. Moreover, the surveys conducted earlier of Daito-jima and the investigation of the above mentioned islands should not be published in the Official Gazette or newspapers. Please pay special attention to this. The foregoing is my opinion on the matter.

Foreign Minister Inoue Kaoru had different opinions from Yamagata, he attached great importance to relations with China. Yamagata said: even if China named these islands, (1) there were no evidence to prove the islands were China's territory; (2) we should worry that we and Qing Dynasty called the islands with different names; (3) The islands are quite close to Yaeyama Islands; (4) the islands are terra nullius, so they could be incorporated into Japan's territory.

Foreign Minister Inoue Kaoru did not agree with the above argument, and he also held that:

(1) The islands are also quite close to mainland China; (2) China has named them and attaches great importance to them; (3) the Chinese are acting suspiciously towards Japan, and they are on guard against Japan's occupation of the Islands near Taiwan (the Diaoyu Islands is one of them). Given these circumstances, he objected to immediately erect the national border markers.

That is to say, Foreign Minister Inoue Kaoru and Okinawa officials all attached great importance to the fact that the Diaoyu Islands are China's territory; they were worried that if they "publicly" put it into Japan's territory immediately, Japan would be strongly protested by the Chinese Qing government. As a result, he told Yamagata Aritomo, the Ministry of Internal Affairs not to release this information in newspapers and to secretly carry out the investigation, and avoid that ordinary citizens and foreign countries, especially China should not learn about it. Although he attempted to incorporate the islands into Japan's territory just like Yamagata , he thought that it was not the correct time. Yamagata Aritomo agreed with him and didn't bring the matter to Cabinet.

On November 24th in the same year, Okinawa magistrate reported to the Ministry of Internal Affairs: the islands may have nothing to do with the Qing government. Please instruct me how to handle it, in case we have dispute with the Qing government." On December 25, the Ministry of Foreign Affairs and the Ministry of Internal Affairs jointly gave the following directive: "We think it is not appropriate to set up any national markers at present, in reply to your written petition."

Through investigating the government documents and letters concerning the Diaoyu Islands in 1885, we can see the following: (1) Ministry of Internal Affairs intended and planned to occupy the Diaoyu Islands and secretly ordered Okinawa to investigate the islands; (2) Okinawa thought the islands might be China's territory and was worried about the incorporation of the islands into Japan's territory; (3) Ministry of Internal Affairs still wanted to forcibly occupy them; (4) Ministry of Foreign Affairs was worried that China would protest, so it didn't agree to occupy the island immediately: (5)At last, Ministry of Internal Affairs gave up the issue.

But the above mentioned "Statement on the Sovereignty over the Senkaku Islands" released by the Ryukyu government mentioned: "Until the early stage of the Meiji period (1877-1882), the Senkaku Islands were uninhabited. Around the 17th year of the Meiji period, the businessman Koga Tatsushiro began to collect albatross feathers, wool hair, carapace and shellfish around the Diaoyu Islands and the Kuba Island. In view of the development of this activity, on September 22 in the 18th year of the Meiji period, the government sent "Izumo Maru" to these islands to do a field survey and ordered submitted to the Ministry of Internal Affairs to set up national markers."

But, this is a great distortion of facts as I will explain below:

Firstly, the above statement hides the Okinawa governor's secret investigation of the Diaoyu Islands; Secondly, Okinawa administration thought that the islands might be China's territory and worried about the incorporation of the islands into Japan's territory; Okinawa administration had submitted this matter; but this statement above distorts the truth, brazenly saying that Okinawa submitted to the Ministry of Internal Affairs to set up national markers after investigating these islands. Thirdly, Koga's application was reason behind the erection of national markers, but at the time, Koga's business was still in the planning stage;

Fourthly; Ministry of Foreign Affairs was worried that China would protest, so it didn't agree to occupy the island immediately; Ministry of Internal Affairs gave up at last; but the statement completely concealed this fact.

Fifthly, Okinawa prefecture government expressed that the islands may not have nothing to do with the Qing government in its report in November after the field survey by "Izumo Maru", which was also hidden by the statement which only mentioned about the field survey in September. This false statement said that Okinawa firstly reported the findings, and thereby applied to establish the national border marks, which was an obvious distortion of the history.

Since then, the relationship between the two countries had deteriorated due to the attitude of Japan. Japan smoothly prepared for the war against China step by step. Koga's business got started on the Diaoyu Islands. On January 30h, in 1890, (Meiji 23th year) the Okinawa Governor submitted a report to the Ministry of Internal Affairs:

The document No. 314, from November 3:

In regard to the uninhabited island, Uotsuri-shima, and two outer islands, close to Ishigaki Island of the Yaeyama Islands Group under the jurisdiction of this prefecture, orders on the matter were conferred [by the Home Ministry and Foreign Ministry] on December 5 the same year in response to Report No. 384 of November 5, 1885. However, since the above mentioned uninhabited islands have heretofore remained under no specific jurisdiction, and due to the recent need to regulate marine products, the Yaeyama Islands Office has requested their [the said islands'] appropriate jurisdiction to be decided. At this time, I intend to place them under the jurisdiction of the Yaeyama Islands Office, and hereby submit this matter for your approval".

The Okinawa's attitude was very different from that in 1885. It didn't mention about the islands' relations with China, and used the excuse of managing Koga's business to incorporate the islands under the administration of Okinawa. Former magistrate Nishimura was also Civil Secretary under the Ministry of Internal Affairs at that time; but Maruoka Kanji was totally different, he was appointed as Okinawa magistrate by Civil Secretary. Maruoka was a fanatic nationalist and forcefully promoted Shinto religion of Japan in Okinawa. Only this kind of governor would brazenly ignore the Diaoyu Islands' relations with China and use the excuse of managing Koga's commercial businesses to incorporate the islands into Japan's territory.

I did not find any negotiated documents of Ministry of Foreign Affairs and Ministry of Internal Affairs; but through the recorded Negotiated documents on December 27th, 1894, we can see that the government did not give any indication.

To our surprise, a year before the Sino-Japanese War, on November 2nd, in 1893, Okinawa Governor Narahara Shigeru (originally named, Satsuma, the notorious militarist who brutally repressed the Okinawa people) reported to the Ministry of Foreign Affairs and the Ministry of Internal Affairs as follows:

"Uotsuri Island (Diaoyu Islands) and Kuba Island (Huangwei Yu) should be incorporated under the administration of Okinawa with national markers erected on them."

The content was almost the same as that in January 1890. But this report also experienced the same situation as that in 1890—two ministers didn't negotiate or talk about it in more than a year.[148]

In addition, at the beginning of the Sino-Japanese War in 1894 (I am not sure it was before the start of the war or after it, but it was before Japan wasn't sure whether it could defeat the Qing Empire) Koga Tatsushiro applied for the lease contract concerning leasing the land of the Diaoyu Islands to the Okinawa authorities, Okinawa refused this application, "because they were not clear about whether the islands belonged to Japan". Koga submitted the application to the Ministry of Internal Affairs form on the interior, Agriculture Business Secretary; at the same time, he went to Tokyo to explain the detailed condition of the islands and begged for approval; but he failed.

This was published in Okinawa Daily News from January 1st to 9th in 1910. The article titled Koga's Contribution to the Ryukyu Islands aimed to flatter the businessman Koga.[149]

If the government was really sure that the Diaoyu Islands were terra nullius they should approve Koga's application at that time. It was because the government knew that the islands were a part of China that they had to take it serious before they defeated China.

In this way, Emperor Government finally got the chance. Japan spent 9 years on the plan of occupying the Diaoyu Islands since 1885.

XII. Japan secretly planned to grab the Diaoyu Islands during a Sino-Japanese War

Shortly after Japanese government's refusal of businessman Koga's application, the best opportunity for grabbing the Diaoyu Islands had finally come. Japanese troops conducted a sudden surprise attack and triggered the Sino-Japanese War. Japan was very sure that it would win the war, and thus grab the

---

148   In Vol. 18 of "Japanese Diplomatic Documents", there is an article titled "Whole Story of the Incorporation of the Kumeaka Island, Kuba Island and Uotsuri Island" and in the "postscript" of the book "Miscellaneous Pieces of Territory", it was mentioned that on November 2nd in the 26th year of the Meiji period, Okinawa Governor reported again to the Ministry of Foreign Affairs and the Ministry of Internal Affairs that some person went to the islands for fishing and that management on the islands should be established, he wrote. I suggest the incorporation of the islands under the administration of Okinawa with national markers erected on them. Therefore, on December 27th in the 26th year of the Meiji period, the Ministry of Internal Affairs negotiated with the Ministry of Foreign Affairs......" but we can see that report from Okinawa was shelved for more than a year.

149   The report was included in History of Naha City, in volume 2.

Diaoyu Islands. When Japanese Emperor Government flatly decided to occupy the Diaoyu Islands. On December 27th, the Ministry of Internal Affairs sent a secret document to the Ministry of Foreign Affairs to negotiate the application submitted by the Okinawa Governor in November of the previous year, and demanded him to erect markers on Uotsuri Island and Kuba Island, the original text is as follows:

File on setting up navigation marks

Confidential Article 133 (Signature)

Received on December 28th, 1894

Sumitted to

Esteemed Foreign Minister Mutsu Munemitsu,

In regard to the matter of constructing jurisdiction markers on Kuba-shima and Uotsuri-shima, and in accordance to Attachment Paper A consisting the petition from the Okinawa Magistrate, and the relating Attachment Paper B, orders [to forego the placement of makers] were conferred after our deliberation with your ministry during the 18th year of Meiji [1885].

However, considering the fact that the situation today has changed relevant to the situation back then, I plan to submit this matter to the Cabinet Meeting for approval in an attachment paper. I therefore request to discuss with you this matter in advance.

December 27, 27th Year of Meiji

[1894]

The petition submitted to the Cabinet

Esteemed Prime Minister and Noble Ito Hirobumi,

The issue of setting up sovereignty markers should be submitted to the Cabinet.

Japanese Minister of Internal Affairs and Viscount Yasushi Nomura (seal)

January 12nd, 1895 and a formal resolution was adopted as follows:

(A separate sheet of paper)

The Home Minister has requested a cabinet decision on the following matter: the islands, Kuba-shima and Uotsuri-shima, located northwestward of Yaeyama Islands under the jurisdiction of Okinawa Prefecture, have heretofore been uninhabited islands. Due to recent visits to the said islands by individuals attempting to conduct fishing related businesses, and that such matters require regulation, it is decided that [the islands] be placed under the jurisdiction of Okinawa Prefecture. Based on this decision, the Okinawa Prefectural Governor's petition should be approved. Since there are no disagreements on the matter, it shall proceed based on the above decision.

The consultation letter was different from that 9 years ago; the "Confidential" marked in red is striking, which indicated that the government was afraid of the problem being leaked out.

The Japanese Ministry of Foreign Affairs had no objection. On January 11st in the second year (1895), Foreign Minister Munemitsu Mutsu replied Nomura, the Ministry of Internal Affairs that we had no objection, you could act on your own will. On January 14th, the Cabinet approved the proposal of the Ministry of Internal Affairs and decided to incorporate the Uotsuri Island and Kuba Island under the administration of Okinawa with markers erected on them. catch the fish island (Diaoyu Islandss) and long island establish peg as Okinawa prefecture. On January 21st, the Ministry of Internal Affairs informed the Okinawa Governor: "the erection of national markers on these islands is approved".

In 1885, due to the concerns on China's protests, with the opposition from the Ministry of Foreign Affairs, Yamagata Aritomo failed to obtain the Diaoyu Islands. In 1890, the Japanese government did not make any reply to Okinawa's application; in 1893, the Japanese government still turned a blind eye to Okinawa's application; but now Okinawa's application was successfully approved by Cabinet. Why? The answer was that the time was different from the past.

What on earth was the so-called different situation in 1885 and 1894. Was it that Koga's career on the Diaoyu Islands got started in 1884 and, in 1894 his career was improved and the government felt it necessary to manage it? It can a different situation. But the main difference was showed in 1890. Okinawa applied to erect markers on the Diaoyu Islands out of this change; but the government didn't reply as long as four years. In November, 1893, Okinawa reported again with the same reason, the government still remained in silence. At the end of December, 1894, Okinawa didn't submit again, but the government suddenly replied to the reports submitted one year age and embarked on the possession of the Diaoyu Islands. To conduct necessary manage on the fishery was not the main reason of the difference. The main "difference" was related with other reasons.

In 1890 and 1893, the Sino-Japanese War was not started. Businessman Koga's application was submitted around the beginning of the Sino-Japanese War in 1894. But early December in the same year, Japan thought it would achieve an absolute war victory, so the government planned to secede Taiwan from the Chinese Qing government as one of the conditions of the peace. This was the main difference.

XIII. Japan's sovereignty over the Senkaku Islands is also void according to the International Law

Some argue that Japan's sovereignty over the Senkaku Islands just occurred in the Sino-Japanese War time, the Senkaku Islands were not ceded to Japan in accord with Treaty of Shimonoseki. Therefore, the islands were not stolen from China by Japan as mentioned in the Cairo Declaration. JCP held this opinion. Admittedly, the islands were not ceded to Japan by virtue of Article 2 in Treaty of Shimonoseki, but it was not a coincidence that Japan just stole the Senkaku Islands in the Sino-Japanese War; instead, the Japanese government consciously planned to steal the islands by taking advantage of the victory in the Sino-Japanese War. The matter was discussed by me in detail in the previous chapter XII, so we can see the process of Japan's occupation of the islands as clear as daylight.

Asahi Shinbun's editorial—"fthe Senkaku Islands and Japan's sovereignty" mentioned that: if the Diaoyu Islands were China's territory, the Qing government should have put forward objection immediately when Japan obtained the Islands; but it must be pinted out that the Qing government did not. If the Chinese side had this thought, they should have raised this issue in Nissin peace negotiations or after the Second World War when dealing with the post-war territories.

However, in Nissin peace negotiations, Japan did not mention that Cabinet had decided to occupy the Diaoyu Islands; as Japan did not mention, so the Qing government had no idea about this matter. Because "cabinet meeting resolution" had not been published, so at that time, Japan hadn't established markers on the Diaoyu Islands and didn't use any other methods to claim that the islands belonged to Japan. Therefore, the Qing government was unable to raise this issue in Nissin peace negotiations.

In addition, in the World War II, when dealing with the post-war territories, truly, China did not mention Japan's occupation of the Diaoyu Islands. But I think the author of the editorial may "forget" territorial dispute between Japan and China hadn't been ended. In the San Francisco peace negotiations, the representative of China was even not invited to attend the meeting. So all the resolution in the meeting don't have any binding upon China. In addition, the so-called "Japan-China Treaty" signed by Japan and Taiwan's Chiang Kai-shek clique couldn't represent the position of China as the People's Republic of China, the only legal government of China had been established. Therefore, the treaty was invalid and have no binding upon the People's Republic of China. That is to say, the territorial dispute between China and Japan has not been fully resolved, and it shall be resolved through peace talks between Japan and China in the future. Therefore, we cannot treat the islands as Japan's territory just because China did not put forward objection at that time.

The Meiji government's stealing the Diaoyu Islands was never known by the Qing government and other countries of the world. The Okinawa magistrate's investigation in 1885 was also secret order of the Ministry of Internal Affairs. In addition, Foreign Minister also reminded the Minister of Internal Affairs not to leak the information. . Even the consultative letter written by the Minister of Internal Affairs to Foreign Minister in December 1894 unusually used the secret documents. In January 1895, the cabinet meeting resolution, of course, were not released. On January 21st, no one had been notified that the government ordered Okinawa prefecture to erect national border marks on Uotsuri Island and Kuba Island. All of these were first made public in Vol. 23 of Japanese Diplomatic Documents published in March, 1952.

Moreover, after having received order from the government, actually, Okinawa did not set up markers on the islands. It didn't have it done before Nissin peace conference, or even the next several years. In fact, on May 5th, 1969, the markers were eventually established. That is to say, when it was reported that the "Senkaku Islands" had rich oil sources in their bottom sea, which made the islands become the object of contention between Japan and China, Ishigaki city finally built a rectangular stone marker on the islands.[150]

On the upper of the marker, from left to right, there was engraved "Yaeyama Senkaku Islands", below which, there was engraved the names of islands (from the right to the left: Uotsuri Island, Kuba Island, Taisho Island and Pinnacle Islands; in the bottom was engraved "erected by Ishigaki City". Looking from the perspective of International Law, Japan, should not follow such kind of act.

That is to say, although the Japanese government said that it would incorporate the Diaoyu Islands into Japan's territory, but it didn't make it public before or after the "Treaty of Shimonoseki" was put inforce, and even till recently, it has never made it public. The "International Law" of the "imperialist" countries regulates: the "preemptive occupation of terra nullius" doesn't need to be declared by an international notice; but Domestic Law regulates that the government must at least notify the location, the name and administrative jurisdiction of the new territory. Since the Japanese government hasn't notified and acknowledge the Japanese public, the islands cannot be deemed as Japan's territory.

The Japanese people have no idea about when the Diaoyu Islands was put under the administration of Okinawa. This is because the Japanese government has not notified them. On Sovereignty over the Senkaku Islands and the Right to Develop the resources on its Continental Shelf released by the Ryukyu government on September 10th, 1970, mentioned: "by virtue of the Cabinet's resolution on January 14 in the 28th year of the Meiji period and according to No. 13 edict on April 1st, in the 29th year of the Meiji period, the area is

---

150   See "Okinawa " magazine — "Report of the erection of markers on the Senkaku Islands".

incorporated under the administration of Yaeyama Ishigaki City, Okinawa as Japan's territory."

But this is not the case. "No. 13 edict on April 1st in the 29th year of the Meiji period" mentioned nothing about this matter. The edict's content is as follows:

Announcement of Permitting the Proposal of the Districts set-up in Okinawa Prefecture

The Imperial Sign and Seal

March 5th of the 29th year of Meiji Period

Premier Marquis Hirobumi Ito

Internal Minister Yoshikawa Akimasa

Edict No. 13

Article 1 Okinawa Prefecture was divided into the following districts (excluding Naba and Shuri).

Islandjiri District includes all regions of Islandjiri, Kume Island, Kerama Islands, Tonagi Island, Aguni island,Iheya Islands, Tori Island and Daito Island.

Nakagami District includes all regions of Nakagami.

Kunigami District includes all regions of Kunigami and Ie Island.

Miyako Districtincludes Miyako Islands.

Yaeyama District includes Yaeyama Islands.

Article 2. Home Minister has the power of deciding the changes of the boundary or names.

ANNEXE

Article 3. Home Minister will decide the effective date of the Edict.

The edict did not mention "Uotsuri Island" and "Kuba Island". At that time, Kuroiwa had not yet named the "Senkaku Islands". The statement published by the Ryukyu government on September 17, 1970, held that "the edict in March came into effect on April 1st; Okinawa Governor explains the Yaeyama Islands in No. 13 included the Senkaku Islands, so it put the islands under the administration of Yaeyama Islands county.... at the same time, the islands were incorporated into our territory according to Domestic Law".

This is detestable and arbitrarily bureaucratic distortion. In the No. 13 edict, the islands under the jurisdiction of Shimajiri County were listed; besides, Tori Island and Daito Island which are separated from the Ryukyu Islands are clearly incorporated into Shimajiri County; while jurisdiction area of Yaesu

County was only Yaeyama Islands in the edict, which indicates that the juris-diction area of Yaesu County is traditionally known area—Yaeyama Islands. All the Ryukyuan are clear that the Diaoyu Islands don't belong to Yaeyama Islands. Therefore, if the government wanted to include Diaoyu Islands into Yaeyama Islands without announcing its name, it should be call a notice. The Ryukyu government was so opinionated that it insisted that the Okinawa go-vernor had "explained" the Diaoyu Islands were included in Yaeyama Islands, but it couldn't deny the fact that the government never notified the Japanese pe-ople about the Diaoyu Islands and Huangwei Yu being included into Yaeyama Islands.

In fact, the edict had had nothing to do with the notification of the Diaoyu Islands being put under the jurisdiction of Okinawa; it is merely a announce-ment of establishment of prefectures in Okinawa for the first time.

When was the Diaoyu Islands put under the jurisdiction of the Okinawa? Perhaps it was on April 1st, 1896. But as long as it was never announced to the Japanese people, the occupation was void, even the current government frantically has admitted that the preemptive occupation of terra nullius act can be deemed as part of an imperialist "International Law".

The Meiji government clearly knew the necessity and the significance of the announcement regarding the position, name and administrative subordinate of a new territory. Four years before Japan's grabbing of the Diaoyu Islands in July 1891, the Ministry of Foreign Affairs and the Ministry of Internal Affairs negotiated about the incorporation of uninhabited islands located in the south-west of the Ogasawara Islands into Japan's territory, as follows:

"In the southwest of Ogasawara Islands, there are three originally uninhabi-ted islands scattered in the sea area from 24°0′N to 25°30′N and from 141°0′E to 141°30′E. Over the years, the mainland people have engaged in mining, fisheries over these islands. We should submit the name and administrative subordinate of the islands to Cabinet separately. What we have written above is a matter of International Law, we need to consult this issue in the government."

And, the "separate" draft submitted to Cabinet clearly stated the longitude and latitude of the island, the name and administrative subordinate of the island: "the islands should be put under the administration of Ogasawara Islands. The name of the island located in the central is Iwo To Island; the one in the South is Minamiiwo Island; the one in the North is Kitaiwo Island." The Ministry of Foreign Affairs agreed with this draft and after the cabinet meeting's resolution, on September 9th, in the 24th year of the Meiji period, No. 160 edict notified by their locations, names and the administrative subordinate. The newspapers of the time also reported this news.

After its grabbing of the Diaoyu Islands, in 1905 (in the 38th year of the Meiji period), Japan incorporated Takeshima (in Japanese) Island into Japan's territory. Takeshima (in Japanese) Island used to be called Matsu Island or Ryoko Island, which was near Ulleungdo in the North Korean territory.[151]

At that time, the Cabinet meeting adopted the resolution on January 28th, and the home secretary informed Hamada, the Shimane Governor: "Takeshima (in Japanese) Island, located in 37°9'30" North latitude and 131°55' East, which is 85 nautical miles northwest of the Oki Island is incorporated under the administration of Oki Island Division. I order you to make an announcement of this matter." Hamada Governor made it public on the February 22.

The LDP investigators led by Okuma Ryoichi, the LDP investigator made a detailed description of the possession of Takeshima (in Japanese) Island as follows: "such announcement of a Cabinet decision concerning the territorial status or possession, (like the possession of the Takeshima (in Japanese) Island)is directly related to national sovereignty of a country. Since the early days of the Meiji period, such formalities have become a normal practice of the Meiji government. There are countless cases of incorporating terra nullius into Japan's territory. The incorporation of uninhabited islands such as Iwo To Island (1891), Minami Tori Island (1898) and Okinotori Island (1925), are similar to the case with the Takeshima (in Japanese) Island. Japan has fulfilled the public announcement rule as promulgated by the international community and local governments have issued county notifications." (Iwo To Island as I have stated earlier, was published by edict–noted by author Inoue)

Even the investigator of the ruling party, i.e., the imperialist Liberal Democratic Party has admited the need to announce an incorporation of a new territory. However, no announcement was made when incorporating the Diaoyu Islands. The Japanese government never announced the names, latitude and longitude, and administrative subordinate of these islands# it completely took advantage of the victory of the Sino-Japan war and occupied the islands illegally. This act is nothing but stealing.

For the above reasons, the Japanese government and even the major newspapers have no idea about the scope of the so-called "Senkaku Islands" issue. Even within the government there were disagreements about the names of these "islands", even differences between the Navy Ministry as well as the Ministry of Internal Affairs and Communication. They all know that the islands belong to the Chinese territory, but they have chosen to distort the facts and insisted that they are terra nullius and illegally incorporated the islands into Japan's territory. Therefore, Japan could not and did not announce the "possession" of

151   North Korea believes that Japan's incorporation of Take Island" was the plunder of North Korea's territory. I haven't adequately studied this issue, I am truly skeptical about "History of Take Island" written by Okuma Ryoichi.

the Diaoyu Islands and even could not explain the time of "annexation" and the geographical scope, location and names of the islets correctly.

Compared with the incorporation of Iwo To (Iwojimo) Island and Takeshima (in Japanese) Island, we can see that the incorporation of the Diaoyu Islands was anything but the preemptive occupation of terra nullius. Because, certainly the Diaoyu Islands are not terra nullius, obviously belong to Chinese territory. The principle of preemptive occupation of terra nullius is not applicable to the islands. Even we assume that the Diaoyu Islands are terra nullius, as Japan did not fulfill the necessary legal procedures, "preemptive occupation of terra nullius" cannot be the legal basis of Japan's incorporation of the islands. Japan did all these just to occupy China's territory by taking advantage of the war victory. No matter what excuse Japan sued, Japan is unable to legalize its possession of the Diaoyu Islands.

In 1895, according to Article 2 of Treaty of Shimonoseki, Japan occupied Taiwan; the Spanish government immediately raised the boundary between Philippines and the south of Taiwan. The two governments negotiated about this issue. On August 7th, the two countries issued a joint declaration, regulating the boundary between Japan in western Pacific Ocean and Spanish is the middle latitude line of sailing waters through Bashi Channel. It clearly determined the boundary between Taiwan and Philippines.[152]

In addition, Treaty of Shimonoseki used the latitude and longitude to ceded the Penghu Islands west to Japan; hence, the boundaries with China were clearly defined from the start.

The above treaty didn't mention about the boundary of the east and north side of Taiwan and its affiliated islands. China and Japan didn't further negotiated about it. After the defeat, besides Taiwan, the Qing government had to cede the important land—Liaodong Peninsula to Japan. Under this situation, the Qing government even lost its historical rights to insisted that it never gave up on Ryukyu. How could it negotiated about the ownership of the small islands between Ryukyu and Taiwan? Japan accidentally picked up an extra advantage—not only wiping out Chin's all historical rights of Ryukyu, but also having grabbed China's Diaoyu Islands and Chiwei Yu.

XIV. The current focus of the struggle against militarism is to oppose to the plundering of the Diaoyu Islands

No matter how the Japanese government and the Japanese Communist Party forged or distorted or covered-up the history, playing with the trick of the "International Law of imperialism", they can't change the fact that Japan stole China's territory.

---

152 See "Japanese Diplomatic Documents" Vol. 28, No. 1, "Declaration about Territorial Waters of Western Pacific between Japan and Spanish".

Then, Japan was defeated in the Second World War, and on August 15th, 1945, it unconditionally accepted the Potsdam Declaration of Allies, including China, and it unconditionally surrendered (the surrender documents formally signed on September 2). Therefore, the Diaoyu Islands should be automatically returned to the original owner—China, like Taiwan, Penghu Islands and "Manchuria", because the Potsdam Declaration stipulates: "the terms of the Cairo Declaration shall be carried out" while the Cairo Declaration pointed out that: "The Three Great Allies are fighting this war to restrain and punish the aggression of Japan....that all the territories Japan has stolen from the Chinese, such as Manchuria, Formosa, and The Pescadores, shall be restored to the Republic of China. (the "Republic of China" should be passed to the sole legal administration of China—the Government of the People's Republic of China)

In 1895, after the theft of Diaoyu Islands, no matter how the Japanese government has legalized it domestically or what kind of facilities it set up on the islands; and the businessman Koga realized his dream in September, 1896 that he "leased " the Diaoyu Islands from the government and did his business on the islands; none of these can be the evidence to prove the islands belong to Japan. Even if China did not raise a protest to Japan's stealing the Diaoyu Islands, it doesn't affect the agreed stipulations of the Cairo Declaration and the legal validity of the Potsdam Declaration.

Although, the U.S. imperialism has occupied the Ryukyu Islands and the Diaoyu Islands after Japan's surrender in August, 1945. Although, the Treaty of Peace with Japan in April 28th, 1952, which stipulated that the US would have control over the Diaoyu Islands. None of these events can change the fact that in history the islands belonged to Chinese territory. Therefore, although today the U.S. Government handed over the "administrative rights" of the Diaoyu Islands and the US administrative rights of the "Southwest Islands" to Japan, the Diaoyu Islands will never become Japan's territory. In a word, the Diaoyu Islands are part of Chinese territory.

In spite of this, Japanese imperialism imposed the name—the Senkaku Islands on the Diaoyu Islands, has ignored the historical facts and international ethics, and attempted again to plunder territory from China. China insists that the Diaoyu Islands have been China's territory since ancient times, and any illegal plunder would not be allowed.

Under the support and agitation of Britain and the United States, the old Japanese militarism of Mikado (Japan Emperor) aimed to invade North Korea and Taiwan; as its extension, they destroyed the Ryukyu Kingdom and made it the Emperor Government's colony, finally dragging it into the Sino-Japanese War. When Japan seized the victory, Japan stole China's Diaoyu Islands across Ryukyu. This was the first foreign territory plundered by Japan. The Japanese Mikado (imperial) militarism like violently developed into Japanese militarism which aims to invade Korea, China and Asia.

The ruling class of the defeated Japanese imperialism, under the impulse, assistance, guidance and command of the U.S. imperialism, are walking on the same track as before. Treaty of Japan and South Korea signed in 1956, the joint statement of the treaty of Sato and Nixon in 1969, Japan-US agreement (the U.S. Government handed over the "administrative right" of the "Southwest Islands" such as Diaoyu Islands, Ryukyu and made the area as Japan-US joint military base) on May 15th in this year (1972) are all the sames tricks used by the Mikado (Japan Emperor) militarism. The Diaoyu Islands were the first foreign territory plundered by Japan's rulers after war, which is almost the same as the action of Mikado (Japan Emperor) militarism.

We should stick to the struggles against the plunder of the Diaoyu Islands, which is the current focus of the struggles against the Japanese militarism and imperialism; we Japanese people should exert ourselves today. If we turn a blind eye to this struggle, we can neither oppose imperialism nor militarism. It is an action of helping the Japanese imperialism that we turn the struggles against the plunder of the Diaoyu Islands against the restoration of diplomatic relations between Japan and China. Let us fight against Japanese imperialism and militarism earnestly and sincerely, let us go all out to fight for the biggest and most immediate focus–struggle against the plunder of the Diaoyu Islands by the Japanese imperialism and militarism.

XV. The addendum part

After I sent my manuscripts to the publishing house, I have seen two interesting magazines with two different perspectives. One is Asahi Asia review in Asahi News Agency, which published the "Senkaku Islands" issue special; Another is an article titled Diaoyutai is China's territory in Vol.II of Chapter 14 of "Learning Essence" compiled by Taiwan's Learning Essence [on February 15th, this year (1972)]. I don't want to judge these articles, I just want to express my own feelings and opinions as the supplement of this book.

Are the so-called Senkaku Islands Japan's Territory? written by Takahashi Sougorou published in Asahi Asia Review quote the argument of Higaonna Kanryo, which proves the Ryukyu Islands are originally Japan's territory. Takahashi used it as evidence to explain "Okinawa" and the Japanese names of other islands; this reasoning method also applies to the Diaoyu Islands, all these islands have Chinese names.

The Diaoyu Islands in the Ming and Qing Dynasties were unmanned islands, but they were by no means terra nullius. The terra nullius in the principle of preemptive occupation in International Law is not only an unmanned island but also an unknown island. The isolated unmanned island in the sea without the name in any language can be difined as terra nullius. But even if it has an official name, it belongs to the country which has named it.

In Ming and Qing Dynasties, sailing from Fuzhou to Ryukyu, the islands the navigation marks, so the positions and names of these islands must be determined. In this way, the Diaoyu Islands were named by the Chinese people and it was recorded in the official Chinese historical materials. Moreover, as these islands are located in China's coast, it is obvious that they are China's territory. Besides, in the distant sea, the far away islands have names in the language in Ryukyu, so it is obvious that they are Ryukyu's territory, unlike the Diaoyu Islands with a Chinese name. In this case, even the Ryukyu people don't think these islands with Chinese names are terra nullius. In addition, as discussed in detail in this book, there are two clear historical records which mention that between Chiwei Yu and Kume Island is the "boundary between China and foreign land"; in the Edo period, Illustrated Outline of the Three Countries, the only historical record of these islands in Japan also pointed out that the islands belong to China in the appended drawings. Therefore, in this sense, it is hard to call them "terra nullius".

Takahashi's article makes me understand the importance of the islands' names. But I don't agree with the argument that the Diaoyu Islands may be grabbed from the Qing government by virtue of Article 2 of Treaty of Shimonoseki. As Takahashi points out that the hand- over of Taiwan, Penghu Islands and its affiliated islands "is really a hasty acceptance". In this case, my article in History Research published in the February had the same idea as that of Takahashi, but as described in Chapter 12 and 13, I think the islands were stolen before the ceding of Taiwan and it had inseparable connections with the ceding of Taiwan in terms of politics; the islands were stolen based on no legal or illegal treaty. If these islands were ceded to Japan as Taiwan's affiliated islands (not geographically) according to Article 2 of Treaty of Shimonoseki, it can't explain why the islands were put under the administration of Okinawa rather than Taiwan. From the whole process of Emperor Government's occupation of the Diaoyu Islands in the 18th year of the Meiji period, we have to say it has close relation with Japan's victory in the Sino-Japanese War and it had no direct relationship with Article 2 of Treaty of Shimonoseki.

I am very interested in The Senkaku Islands and its Sovereignty written by Okuhara Toshio in "Asahi Asian Review". This article fully exposed gangster logic of imperialism that the "Senkaku Islands" are Japan's territory. He wrote: "In International Law, if a country has an intention to preemptively acquire the sovereignty of a terra nullius island, the country doesn't need going through the formalities specified in domestic laws, such as the cabinet meeting decision and public announcement of that decision. When acquiring a place according to the preemptive principle, the most important measure is effective administration. Such a fact could fully prove the country's intention to acquire the sovereignty. Considering the natural environment and the non-livable situation on the Senkaku Islands, even if the islands have been actually occupied, if a country could prove that it could exercise the right of administration, it would be enough for Japan to claim sovereignty from the perspective of International Law."

Okuhara hides behind the excuse that China's feudal dynasties didn't conduct effective control over its territories like the modern sovereign states, so he holds that the said islands are terra nullius. By using distorted wording, Okuhara listed evidence to prove Japan possessed the islands before the 18th year of the Meiji period and Japan ruled the land. He also didn't mention that the islands were terra nullius before the 18th year of the Meiji period. He said as he had already proved it that the records of Chen Kan and Guo Rulin just showed that the Diaoyu Islands were not Ryukyu's territory, but they did not say they were a part of China, so the islands were terra nullius. I refuted his argument in the article I published in Historical Research in February, 1972,   I clearly pointed out that how to correctly explain the records of Chen and Guo; with some historical documents, I further explained that the records of Wang Ji clearly mentioned that the areas west to Chiwei Yu belong to China. But Okuhara has turned a blind eye to my comment and was not able to answer could, as he couldn't refute the truth.

Because the natural environment of the "Senkaku Islands" is not suitable for living, so even if there is no "actual possession" in that area nor the notification of possession, Japan still can claim the islands are Japan's territory without undergoing the domestic law procedures. In short, the land is at Japan's disposal, so it is Japan's territory. How arrogant this imperialism talk is? He is so desperate to play the gangster logic, which just exposed the bankruptcy of the argument that the Diaoyu Islands are Japan's territory.

Okuhara puts forward the excuse that China's feudal dynasties didn't conduct effective control over its territory, as should be done by modern sovereign states, thus he holds that the islands are terra nullius.

If the Diaoyu Islands are not "terra nullius" and are China's territory, any argument of "preemptive occupation of terra nullius" will collapse. I have given a detailed proof of this in this book, more detailed than my article published in Historical Research. The journal of "Learning Essence" which I have mentioned before, had published an article titled "An Appraisal of Japan and the recorded Diaoyu Islands" written by Fang Hao, which can further prove my opinion.

In 1555, Zhen Shungong went to Japan upon order of the Chinese emperor (Ming Dynasty) for a fact finding mission. After three years' investigations in Kyushu, Zhen Shungong wrote an excellent 5 volume book entitled "A Mirror Appraisal Japan" (Accounts on Japan) which includes high-quality maps. In the third volume of the book- "A Guide to Japan's Seas," there is a Gyōki-Type map contains—a song—titled as "Songs of a Long Voyage" and this song clearly records the sea route from Guangzhou, China to Kyushu, Japan: Sailing from Jilong Mountain of Xiaodong Island (Taiwan) .... After some 20 hours' of sailing, heading for Diaoyuyu.... From Xiaodong of Meihuadu to Penghu, further to Ryukyu and finally Japan... Diaoyuyu is a small island of Xiaodong. Many Chinese scholars regard Zheng Shungong's reference of the disputed islands as indisputable evidence that the disputed islands did not belong to the Ryukyus, but in particular, to the island of Taiwan.[153]

Although in those days, the administration of the Ming Dynasty did not actually reach Xiaodong (Taiwan), and it was almost a pirate lair near Keelung, but from the perspective of ownership, Taiwan has been a part of China since ancient times, in the administrative districts of the Ming dynasty, Penghu Islands were under the administration of Fujian Province, the patrol division of Penghu Islands also governed Taiwan. Zheng Shungong explicitly specified the Diaoyu Islands were the affiliated islands of Taiwan; hence we can know that the Diaoyu Islands are a part of China. In the works of Chinese historians and geologists a lot of such historical data should be available.

Special frontispiece of Asahi Asia Review newspaper mentioned "Don't Make the Senkaku Islands Hinder the Normalization of Sino-Japanese Relations". This kills the fact that the "Senkaku Islands" were China's territory in history.

"In the socialist countries, generally, nationalism is stronger than that of Europe and the United States. a sentence in the guide book of Czech Republic— our ancestors once had controlled the Adriatic Sea to the North Sea—is quite surprising.

I felt quite strange, but after the careful reading, the great power was originally Holy Roman Empire; Prague, the capital of the Czech Republic was once the great empire's capital.

"Historicism won the favor; but all countries in the world claim their territories in their heydays, I'm afraid it would cause a chaos.

"Therefore, the Senkaku Island Issue cannot be treated by Historicism."

This text gives readers the impression that China seems to claim this territory in its heyday, when it was strong. An issue of the journal titled as "Historical Annals of Senkaku Islands Issue" compiled by the editorial board of the journal was published in 1872 when the Japanese government granted the Ryukyu King Shangtai as Ryukyu seignior, but this issue never mentioned about China's records regarding of the Diaoyu Islands, which brazenly denies the history.

The "Historical Annals of Senkaku Islands" mentioned that in September in the 18th year of the Meiji period, Okinawa magistrate submitted a report to the Ministry of Internal Affairs, in which he put forward the proposal that the islands should be out under the administration of Okinawa with national markers

---

153   Some records say the above book was written in 1556.

erected on them. This is nonsense. The fact was that in order to establish national markers, the Ministry of Internal Affairs ordered Okinawa magistrate to investigate the islands. The results of the investigation was that Okinawa magistrate delayed the erection of national markers as the islands might belong to China. I have made a detailed explanation about this matter, in the above chapters.

The "Annals" from March, 1886, also mentioned in the article titled "World Waterways Chronicles of Ministry of Navy Waterway mentioned about the survey results regarding the Senkaku Islands". It seems that this is the result of independent surveys by the Japanese navy independent surveys, but in fact it was not, it was only copied from Waterways Chronicles of British Navy as mentioned in this book. The annals further mentioned that on April 1st, 1896, "Okinawa implemented the Edict No. 13, the Okinawa governor included the Senkaku Islands into the Yaeyama Islands and treated them as new territories [Uotsuri Island (Diaoyu Island), Kuba Island (Huangwei Yu), Kominami Island (Nanxiao Island), Kokita Island (Beixiao Island)]

"Asahi Asia Review not only ignored the history, but also distorted the facts saying: "most of the Japanese who are concerned about international issues are reluctant to mention the Senkaku Islands issue. Maybe they are afraid to discredit China or make business losses. But it is dishonest for them not to express their opinions."

It is true that international relations experts and historians in Japan are reluctant to mention the Senkaku Islands issue. Editor-in-chief faced a beleaguer because he published my article concerning the Senkaku Islands in the journal of Historical Research. It is difficult to publish articles with the opinion that the Diaoyu Islands are China's territory in history rather than terra nullius in an academic magazine.

It is not because the Japan opinion leaders do not want to annoy China as the Asahi Asia Review has distorted. Just on the contrary, these experts have to obey Japan's rulers, the press and the right-wing forces and the JCP. From the perspective of history science and international law, they can't say that Diaoyu Islands are not terra nullius and that Japan's occupation is not preemptive occupation of terra nullius. But if they say that Diaoyu Islands are are China's territory, they would have face the slander and persecution such as "damaging the interests of the state" and will be labeled as "traitors". The sharper the territorial dispute is, the easier it is for those who tell the truth to be persecuted. Not to mention in the election, those who tell the truth would never be able to get votes. Those who do not overcome their own false patriotism and think the people's territorial sense is too strong will be frightened to death by the ballot crash caused by telling the truth about the Diaoyu Islands issue. As this is the consensus of those politicians and political parties that want to become parliamentary candidates, so most of them like the JCP, claim that the Senkaku

Islands are Japan's territory, incite the "false patriotism" to win people's votes, while those who are unwilling to be stooped choose to remain in silence. These scholars are not afraid of China, but they scruple about Japanese nationalism and JCP, so they are afraid to act and speak bravely and only choose to remain in silence.

Asahi Asia Review who opposes "the silent nationalism" has completely ignored the history without publishing any historical articles. Even its annals have flatly deleted the fact that the islands are China's territory, and it incites in preface: "Experts, Shouldn't Restrain Themselves by the History and Speak Loudly: They Are Japan's Territory!"

In the face of such a grave situation, I really hope that those friendly Japanese people who are against imperialism and militarism step forward bravely and openly speak out the facts, and reject such excuses as "we don't know the historical issue regarding the Senkaku Islands and which is lawful according to laws, so we choose to remain in silence." It is certainly not an issue which can be fobbed off because of ignorance. Whether or not we oppose Japanese imperialism and militarism in reality will determine the future of our Japanese people and nation.

(Post-notes was published on June 11th, 1972, in the June issue of "China Research Monthly".)

XXIII. A Second Article by Inoue Kiyoshi: The Diaoyu Islands/Senkaku Islands are China's Territory

February, 1972

Part 1

There is no doubt that Diaoyu Islands, which is named as the Senkaku Islands in Japan and is claimed to be owned by Japan, was under China's sovereignty since the ancient times. When Japan won the First Sino-Japanese War, namely the war between Qing Dynasty China and Meiji Japan from 1894 to 1895 (or which is known as the "Jiawu War" in Chinese), Japan has annexed Taiwan and the Penghu Islands. Soon later, Japan incorporated those islands within the administration of the Okinawa Prefecture.

Therefore, according to the Cairo Declaration issued by the United States, the United Kingdom and the Republic of China during World War II as well as the Potsdam Declaration which is a statement of the proclamation defining the terms for Japanese surrender, since from the moment when Japan surrendered to the US and China, all the territories that Japan had grabbed from China, including Taiwan, Manchu and those that Japan grabbed from China during and after the first Sino-Japanese War, should be reverted to China. Taiwan was naturally reverted to China. Likely, those islands should naturally become

China's territory. Thus, the islands should become the sole inviolable territory of the People's Republic of China which was able to represent the whole China.

However, the Japanese reactionary rulers and the militarism force colluded with the US imperialism to clamor that the Senkaku Islands was the territory of Japan. They attempted to drag the public into their troops of imperialism and provoke against China. Their imperialist troops will be further enlarged after the so-called reverting of "the administration right of Senkaku" from the US army to Japan on May 15th of this year (namely 1972). We, who genuinely aspire for Japan's independence, and fight for good relations between Japan and China and strive for the peace in Asia, must hinder the conspiracies of the US and Japan ruling groups. I would like illustrate the historical development of the Senkaku Islands, which is taken as weapon by Japan and the US in their conspiracies. In terms of the specific historical study, the readers can refer to my article and arguments published on the February issue of Historical Researches.

Part 2

The so-called Senkaku Islands was the Diaoyu Island (Diaoyúy or Diaoyutai), Huangwei Yu and other islands which were recorded in China's documents as early as the middle of 16th century. In 1532 when Ming emperor conferred the ruler of Ryukyu, Shangqing, as Zhongshanwang, Chen Kan, the envoy of Ming emperor, has come and gone between Fuzhou and Naba. According to the Record of the Imperial Title-Conferring Envoys to Ryukyu (Shi Liu Qiu Lu), the envoy set sailing from the mouth of the Minjiang River (in Fujian Province) on May 8 of 1532, first sailed southwest with Ji Long as the destination and then turned to the north of east when arrived at the offing. On May 10, 1534, when passing from Diaoyúyǔ, the envoy made the following records:

"On the tenth, the winds heading to the south were brisk and the boat sailed swiftly. Though floating downstream with the current, the boat maintained a steady balance without being vigorously shaken. One after another, Pingjia Hill, Diaoyu Yu, Huangmao Yu [Huangwei Yu], and Chi Yu [Chiwei Yu] were left behind... On the dusk of the eleventh, Kume Hill was in sight—it belongs to the Ryukyus. The aborigines [Ryukyu people on board] rejoiced and were happy to have arrived home."

The first time that Chinese Emperor sent investiture envoys (Sapposhi) to Ryukyu was in the year 1372. Before the Chen Kan's envoy in 1532, there were more than ten envoys between Fuzhou and Naba. Their sailing routes were the same with Chen Kan's, namely they first took Ji Long, Pengjia Yu, Diaoyúyǔ, Huángwěi Yǔ and Chiwei Yu as the destination and arrived at Kume Island , then they sailed into the Naba port through Kerama Islands (when sailing back, they passed over the Kume Island not Diaoyu islands and sailed north). Therefore, we can deduce the following: if there were any envoy records earlier than Chen Kan's record, Diaoyu islands would be recorded in those records. It is a pity that Chen Kan's record of 1534 is the eldest record that was preserved. Besides, when mentioning Diaoyu and other islands, Chen Kan didn't give any illustration to the names, which might prove that those islands have come into being long time ago. Not only the names were Chinese names but also the sailing route they chose was used for a long time in the past.

What's more important, Chen Kan recorded that he set off from Fuzhou, the territory of China, and then passed through several islands, which were also the territory of China. Until when he arrived at Kume Island, Chen Kan wrote that "the island belonged to Ryukyu". Here Chen Kan particularly recorded that Ryukyu was located in the front of Kume Island and clearly said that before this, it was not the territory of Ryukyu.

Later than Chen Kan, Guo Rulin, another envoy, set off from Fuzhou on May 29th of 1561. Guo Rulin wrote in his edition of Records of the Imperial Missions to Ryukyu, the following, "On the first of the fifth intercalary moon we passed by Diaoyu Yu; on the third we reached Chi Yu [Chiwei Yu/Kumeseki-shima]. Chi Yu is a regional hill delimiting Ryukyu territory. With another day of [favorable] wind, Kume Hill will be in sight.

Chinese scholars point to this passage to demonstrate that Chi Yu (Chiwei Yu/Kubaseki-shima) was considered a regional island at the Chinese frontier separating Chinese and Ryukyu territory. Hence, Chi Yu and the islands that came before it (collectively, the Diaoyutai/Senkaku Islands) were well within the perimeters of the Chinese border; while islands that lay beyond it constituted Ryukyu territory, beginning from Kume Island.

From the above two historical documents, it could be concluded that the place ahead of Kume Island was the territory of Ryukyu whereas the land on the west of Chìyǔ belonged to China. However, Toshio Okuhara, the conservative associate professor of international law in Kokushikan University, claimed that in the records of the two envoys, Chen Kan and Guo Rulin, it only noted that ahead of Kume Island was the territory of Ryukyu but noted that the west of Chiwei Yu was the territory of China, thus those islands should be terra nullius[154].

Toshio Okuhara, tended to find excuses by confusing ancient Chinese documents with the current international law provisions, which is based on a completely false reasoning. Indeed, Chen Kan and Guo Rulin didn't clearly record that the west of Chìyǔ was China's territory. However, sailing from Fuzhou, passing Ji Long, which was China's indsiputable territory, passing via Pengjia Yu, which was also China's territory, then passing via Diaoyu Yǔ, Huángwěi Yǔ and arriving at Chiwei Yu, the boundary between China and Ryukyu was at sight. Besides, they also recorded that it was Ryukyu when they saw the Kume Island. Seen from the development and context of the documents, it can be clearly grasped that: from

---

154   Please refer to Thoshio's article titled with "The Sovereignty of the Senkaku Islands and the Article on *Mingbao Weekly*" published on magaizne *China* in Sepetember of 1971.

Taiwan to Diaoyu, Huángwěi, Chìwěi Yu and other islands, which were linked to Pengjia located in the east of Pengjia's east, were all the territory of China.

Toshio Okuhara, also argued as follows: " although Chen's and Guo's records were the eldest records, the envoy records after that of Chen Kan and Guo Rulin didn't mention about that content, thus the information which was only recorded in ancient documents cannot be taken as evidence". Toshio Okuhara's argument was unreasonable and untrue. After Chen Kan and Guo Rulin, in 1719 (the 58th year of Kangxi rule period) , Xu Baoguang, who was the leader of the envoy who wrote the Letters of Zhongshan, recorded the sea route from Fuzhou to Naba by quoting the exposition from A General Guide (Zhi Nan Guang Yi), a book written by an authoritative scholar Cheng Shunze in Ryukyu in 1708. With regard to Kume Island, Xu Baoguang, wrote: "Kume Island was the Zhen (guard) island at the sea boundary to the southwest of Ryukyu". The so-called "Zhen" was the guard that guarded the boundary of a country or a village.

In addition, Xu Baoguang listed the territories of Ryukyu in the Letters of Zhongshan, namely the Okinawa Island and the 36 islands of Ryukyu but not included the west of Chiwei Yu. Moreover, at the end of his illustration of Ishigaki Island, which was one of the Yaeyama Islands, and the eight islands around Ishigaki, Xu Baoguang wrote the eight islands "were the southwest boundary of Ryukyu" (Iriomote Island, one of the Yaeyama Islands, was the territory of Ryukyu islands nearest to Diaoyu).

The Letters of Zhongshan were compiled based on the literary works of Cheng Shunze and many other Ryukyu people, and included the discussions of senior officers in Ryukyu King's mansion when Xu Baoguang met them in Ryukyu. It means that Xu Baoguang's records on Kume Islands and the Yaeyama Islands should be the common view of both Chinese people and Ryukyu people at that time.

Prior to Xu Baoguang, Wang Ji, an imperial envoy of the Qing Dynasty, wrote the Miscellaneous Records of a Mission to Ryukyu in 1683. In this book, when Wang passed via Chiwei Yu and began the activities of sacrifice so as to avoid ill fortune and ward off evil spirits, Wang recorded those places as "outskirt" (Jiao) or "trench" (Gou) and described them as the "boundary between China and Foreign nations." In view of the above, as Toshio Okuhara expected, there were specific diction to clarify the boundary between China and Ryukyu.

From the above, it is sure that at least as early as in the middle of 16th century, the territory of Ryukyu was the east of Kume Island whereas the west of Chiwei Yu along with Huángwěi Yǔ and Diaoyu Yǔ were China's territory. There was no any historical records wrote by Ryukyu and Japan to refute the claim or no doubt was uttered. There also was no information negating the claim in the verbal or written records with regard to the communications between

Ryukyu people and the people on Diaoyu Island and Huángwěi Yǔ from the early days. The jouney from Ryukyu to Diaoyu was against the wind and the tide and was quite difficult. In the middle of 19th century when the Japanese Shogunate rule system was perishing, Ryukyu people called Diaoyu Islands as "yokon" or "yokun", Huángwěi Yǔ as Kuba Shima and Chiwei Yu as Kumeaka Island, which was clearly noted in the records of the last Chinese Dynasty.

However, the fact about the names will not influence the sovereignty issue of the islands. Hayashi Shihei's records in his Records of Messages from Chong-shan (Zhong Shan Chuan Xin Lu), no mattter they were maps or illustrations, were totally cited from the Records of Messages from Chong-shan (Zhong Shan Chuan Xin Lu). The Letters of Zhongshan has been introduced to Japan quite long time ago and there was even a Japanese edition of the Letters of Zhongshan. At the later times of the Edo period, the Letters of Zhongshan. has been the most authoritive material for Japanese people's cognition of the Ryukyu islands.

Part 3

After the Meiji Restoration and during 1872(the 5th year of Meiji period) and in 1879 (the 12th year of Meiji period), Japan Emperor Government forcibly "disposed Ryukyu,"the Ryukyu Kingdom was forcibly demolished and replaced with the Okinawa Prefecture attached to Japan. Thus, Shimadzu's (Japan Satsuma clan) vassal state was turned into that of the Mikado's (Japan Emperor) colony this time. It goes without saying that the Okinawa Prefecture had included the territory of the original Ryukyu Kingdom.

In the year when Ryukyu was annexed to Okinawa, the conflict between Qing Dynasty of China and Japan in terms of the ownership of the island reached its climax. Although Shimadzu conquered Ryukyu Kingdom in 1609 and turned it into a colonial affiliate state, Qing continued to rule it, Ryukyu Kingdom was allowed to continue its existing tributary relation with China. And thus China had good reason to argue with Japan for this territory (Ryukyu) because since from Ming Dynasty to Qing period all the Ryukyu kings in history were conferred by Chinese emperors.

With regard to the dispute over the sovereignty of Ryukyu between Qing Dynasty of China and Japan, Japan's democratic and progressive people have advocated that whether Ryukyu belonged to Japan or Qing should be determined by the Ryukyu people, Ryukyu people should be free to determine their independence. They advocated: if Ryukyu people aspired for independence, Japan should take the lead in assisting them and should widely publicize the principle to the whole world that the big nations should not annex the small ones," ...this will be a step forward, that Japan can also liberate itself from the yoke of occidental powers and achieve complete independence." Should we not inherit and carry forward this principle nowadays?

Ulysses Grant, the former president of the United States, has personally me-diated in the quarrel between Qing Dynasty of China and Japan, and the two countries began to negotiate the issue. Qing Dynasty of China proposed to divide Ryukyu into three parts: the Amami Islands could be deemed within Japan's territory (these islands was Ryukyu's territory before Shimadzu had conquered Ryukyu), the Okinawa Island and its periphery would be the terri-tory of Ryukyu kingdom; the Miyako Island and Yaeyama Islands at the south would be owned by China. With regard to China's proposal, Japan suggested the following: the north of Okinawa islands would be Japan's; the Miyako Island and Yaeyama Islands would belong to China. Because Diaoyu islands were deemed outside of Ryukyu, they were not mentioned in both proposals made by Republic of China and Qing Dynasty of China.

That is to say, Qing government made some concessions. Qing Dynasty of China and Japan agreed on Japan's suggestion. In September of 1880, the ple-nipotentiaries of Qing Dynasty of China and Japan signed a treaty . However, Qing emperor didn't ratify the agreement and instructed the government to further negotiate with Japan, and Japan terminated the negotiations. In 1882, when Takezoe Shinichirou went to Tianjin to undertake theposition as the con-sul, he tried to discuss with the Qing Dynasty of China about the boundary of Ryukyu but no agreement was reached.. The issue was delayed until the Sino-Japan war.

In other words, from Meiji Restoration to the Sino-Japan war, Japan had never claimed the territory of Diaoyu Islands and never thought to argue for China's ownership of Diaoyu Islands. The whole world knew that Diaoyu Islands belonged to Qing Dynasty of China.

During that time, in 1884 (the 17th year of Meiji period), the businessman Tatsushiro Koga, who was born in Fukuoka Prefecture, has moved to Naba since 1879 and lived on seafood fishing and export, found groups of albatrosses on Diaoyu Island. Koga sent people to collect feather and seafood nearby for selling and his business had grown each year. In order to explore the business, in 1894 when Sino-Japan war began (the specific month is unknown), Koga submitted application to the Okinawa Prefecture Governor for renting land from the Diaoyu Islands. Later on January 1st of 1910, Okinawa Daily News published an article to commend Koga for his achievement. The article said that with regard to Koga's application for renting land, the Prefecture Governor didn't approve since "the island wasn't sure to be under the sovereignty of the Empire of Japan." Therefore, Koga, rushed to the capital, directly filed a peti-tion to Internal Affairs Minister and Agricultural and Commercial Minister and told them the current situation of the island, adjuring them for permit. However, Koga was refused because the ownership of the island was "unclear".

In the 27th year of Meiji period when the Sino-Japan war ended, Taiwan was included into the territory of the Empire of Japan. In 1896, the 29th year of Meiji period, "the Imperial Edict No. 13 has declared that the Senkaku Islands to be Japan's territory." Hence Koga immediately submitted the land-renting application to the magistrate of Okinawa Prefecture obtained approval until the beginning of September.

A decisive event is worthy of mentioning here. The time when Koga submitted application to the Okinawa Prefectural and the Central Government for renting Diaoyu Island was unclear. It was not certainbefore 1894, the year when the war began. Before the war, the Okinawa Prefectural Office and the Central Government was still not sure about the territory of the island. If the Japanese government, "in accordance with the International Law", thought the island to be terra nullius, we can say that the Japanese government had no reason to reject Koga's application. This was because the island was obviously not terra nullius but the territory of Qing Dynasty of China which was behind Japanese government's disapproval.

The war ended with Japan's seizure of the Penghu Islands as well as Taiwan and its affiliated islands from the Qing Dynasty of China. At that time, the Diaoyu Islands, Huangwei Yu, Chiwei Yu, etc. which connected Taiwan and Ryukyu, were turned into Japan's territory.

As it was mentioned above, according to Imperial Edict No. 13 in 1896, the Senkaku Island became the territory of Japan. The main content of the edict, published on May 5, was about the establishment of the Okinawa prefecture counties and didn't conclude Diaoyu into the Okinawa Prefecture.

In September of 1970, Ryukyu Government published the On Sovereignty over the Senkaku Islands and the Right to Develop the resources on its Continental Shelf. It included the following: "it was determined in the cabinet meeting held on January 14th of the 28th year of Meiji period and put down in the Imperial Edict issued on April 1st of the 29th year, that the Senkaku Islands was included in Japan's territory and belongs to the Ishigaki village, Yaeyama county of the Okinawa Prefecture." However, the content of Imperial Edict No.13 from 1896 was the same as mentioned above. Does it mean that, based on the Article 2 of the Imperial Edict of March 5th and based on the order of Home Secretary, Diaoyu Island was included into the administrative of Ishigaki village on April 4.

What sort of language was used in the 14 January Cabinet Resolution of 1895, which was mentioned in the previous text ? The resolution was put into effect in May of 1895, when the war ended and the Treaty of Shimonoseki was signed. With the Treaty of Shimonoseki, Taiwan was substantially annexed by Japan in May. However, ten months has passed since then and what happened during thisten months? Although, I haven't done a detailed investigation on this issue, but one point is certain. As it was reported in Okinawa Daily News,

Diaoyu Island was included into the territory of Japan, after the end of Sino-Japan War as the condition of making peace.

Part 4

In addition, those islands began to be called as the "Senkaku Islands" in 1900. Kuroiwa, a teacher in the normal school of the Okinawa Prefecture, did an investigation on Diaoyu Islands and generally named the Diaoyu Islands, Chiwei Islands and the ledges between the two as "Senkaku Islands". This was after the publication of "Adventures on Senkaku Islands" published at No. 140 and 141 of Volume 12 of Geological Magazine. Teacher, Kuroiwa Hisashi had given such a name, because in the map and waterway records of British navy at that time, these islands were named as "Pinnacle islands group" due to the shape of the ledges and reefs between Diaoyu and Huangwei islands, thus teacher Kuroiwa translated this English name into Japan. They were also called as "pinnacle islands" in the waterway records of the Japanese navy, and was translated as "Senkaku Islands". The shape of Diaoyu islands are similar to rocks, therefore Diaoyu Island, Senkaku Island and Huangwei Island were altogether called as the "Senkaku Islands". It is worth noticing that Chiwei Yu isn't included in the "Senkaku Islands" as named by Kuroiwa, but today Japanese government claims that Chiwei Yu island is also included in the Japan's territory.

Japanese government has believed that obviously Chiwei Yu is Japan's territory and that the only dispute, between China and Japan, is about theDiaoyu Islands, thus Japan names the Diaoyu Islands as the "Senkaku Islands"and as to the Chiwei Yu, Japanese government will leave this issue to the chance and will try an opporunism.

As I have already illustrated in detail above, Chiwei Yu island is geologically situated at the rim of the continental shelf of China and forms an island group together with Diaoyu Island and Huangwei Yu. Historically, Chiwei Yu was recorded to be the extension of Chinese land at the same time when Diaoyu Island was identified and recorded as the part Chinese land. Therefore, we cannot only mention the "Senkaku islands" issue, simply forget the Chiwei Yu island and we should also remember that the "Senkaku islands", were named by Japan after Japan had grabbed them from China. Therefore, the only correct name for Diaoyu is Diaoyu Islands, which includes not only Diaoyu Island but also the islands from Diaoyu Island to the east of Chiwei Yu. Besides, from the perspective of Japanese people who are against the Japanese imperialism, Diaoyu Islands is the correct name.

Above we have clearly illustrated the history of Diaoyu Islands As to the ownership or sovereignty, our judgment from the historical aspect is that Diaoyu Islands can only be part of the territory of People's Republic of China.

(The article was translated from Cultural Exchange of Japan and China published by Cultural Exchange Association of Japan and China in February of 1972)

Chapter Three

Visual Evidence, Maps and Documents

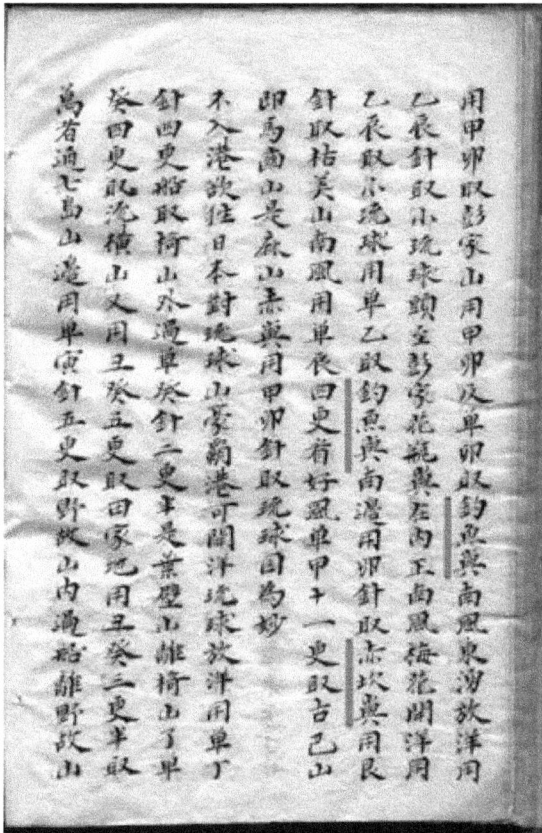

**Voyage with a Tail Wind (Shun Feng Xiang Song) of the Ming Dynasty
Recording the Initial Discovery and Naming of the Diaoyu Islands by China**

Voyage with a Tail Wind (Shun Feng Xiang Song) of the Ming Dynasty written in 1403, includes "compass needle guided routes" drawing" for sailing. The book clearly shows the names of islands regularly passed by Chinese voyagers including "Diaoyu Yu" and "Chikan Yu" (known today as Diaoyu Dao and Chiwei Yu). It proves that the islands along the sea route have been first discovered, named and utilized by China.

This version is an old handwritten copy and has an inscription on the back cover written by the collector in 1639. At present, it has been collected by Bodleian Library of Oxford. (excerpt from The Textual Research on Sovereignty over the Diaoyu Islands before the Sino-Japanese War of 1894-1895 by Wu Tianying)

**The Records of the Imperial Title-conferring Envoys to Ryukyu
(Shi Liu Qiu Lu) of the Ming Dynasty Firstly Recording the Maritime
Border Between China and Ryukyu**

In 1534 during the 13th year of Ming Dynasty Emperor Jia Jing's reign, the imperial envoy to Ryukyu wrote a book titled The Records of the Imperial Title-conferring Envoys to Ryukyu (Shi Liu Qiu Lu, which is the earliest Chinese official document recording maritime boundaries between China and Ryukyu. It clearly records: "On the tenth, the winds heading to the south were brisk and the boat sailed swiftly. Though floating downstream with the current, the boat maintained a steady balance without being vigorously shaken. One after another, Pingjia Hill, Diaoyu Yu, Huangmao Yu [Huangwei Yu], and Chi Yu [Chiwei Yu] , there are too many islands for one's eyes to feast on.... When we arrived at Gumi Mountain which belonged to Ryukyu, aborigines [Ryukyu people on board] rejoiced and were happy to have arrived home."

It indicates that the Diaoyu Islands are China's territory rather than Ryukyu's territory.

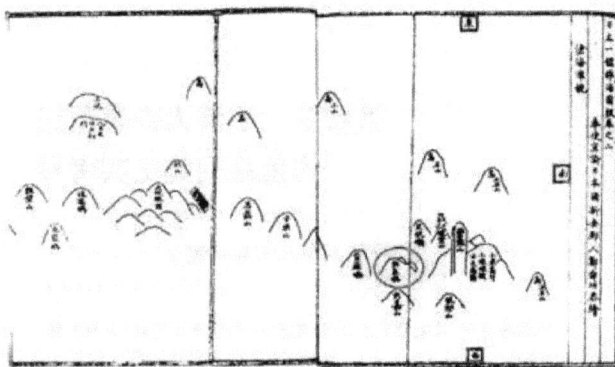

郑舜功所绘台湾、琉球间诸岛屿图

An Appraisal of Japan (Ri Ben Yi Jian) of the Ming Dynasty Recording the Diaoyu Islands Belonging to Taiwan

This picture drawn by Zhen Shungong in 1556 comes from Sea Mirror of An Appraisal of Japan·Across Sea Drawings. In order to fight against the Japanese pirates, in 1552, Zhen Shungong was sent to Japan for exploration under an order by Chinese authorities. Along the route, he passed Taiwan, the Diaoyu Islands, Huangwei Yu. This picture diagrams "Songs of a Long Voyage" and the sea route. Islands such as the Diaoyu Islands are painted in this picture.

After three years' investigations in Kyushu, Zhen Shungong wrote an excellent 5 volume book entitled "A Mirror Appraisal Japan" (Accounts on Japan) which includes high-quality maps.

In the third volume of the book "A Guide to Japan's Seas," there is a Gyöki-Type map contains—a song—titled as "Songs of a Long Voyage" and this song clearly records the sea route from Guangzhou, China to Kyushu, Japan: Sailing from Jilong Mountain of Xiaodong Island (Taiwan) .... After some 20 hours' of sailing, heading for Diaoyuyu.... From Xiaodong of Meihuadu to Penghu, further to Ryukyu and finally Japan. ... Diaoyuyu is a small island of Xiaodong." "Xiaodong" was the name to refer to Taiwan at that time.

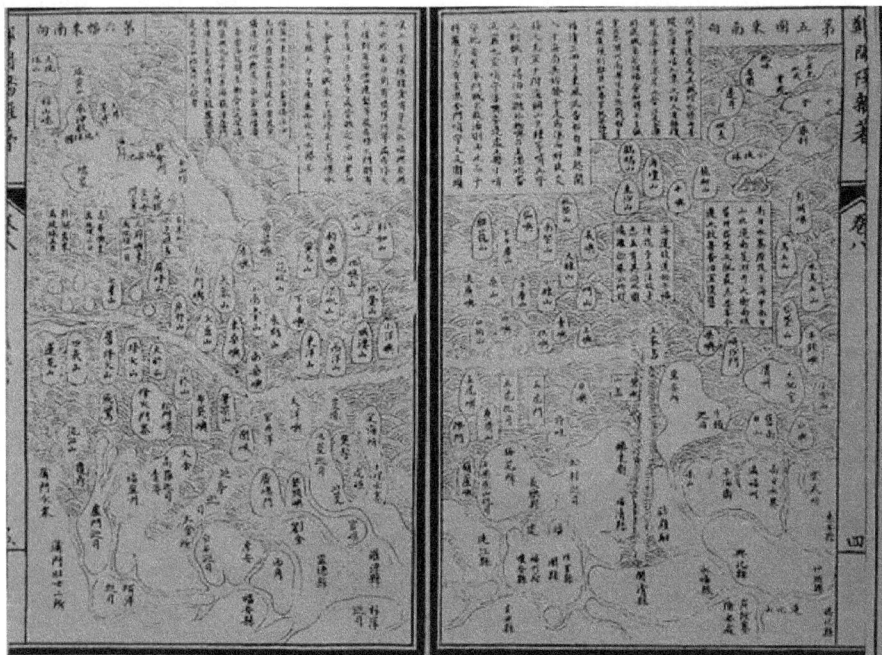

The Great Haiphong Map (Wang Li Hai Fang Tu) of the Ming Dynasty Revealing the Coastline of the East China Sea and Cruise Waters of the Ming Navy

The Great Haiphong Map (Wang Li Hai Fang Tu) drawn by Zhen Ruozeng in 1561 reveals the sea geography of the East China Sea, the naval patrol waters and will post locations, so it includes Taiwan Island, Penghu Islands, Dongsha Mountain, Pingjia Mountain (Zhutai Yu of Taiwan), Jilong Mountain, Pengjia Mountain, Bei Mountain, Huaping Yu, Diaoyu Islands, Huangmao (wei) Mountain, Huangmao Mountain (Ganlan Mountain in An Illustrated Compendium on Maritime Security (Chou Hai Tu Bian), Chiwei Yu, etc..., into the territories within the East China Sea.

Map of Fujian's Coastal Mountains and Sands (Fu Jian Yan Hai Shan Sha Tu) of the Ming Dynasty Revealing the Concrete Measures of Operating the East China Sea in the Ming Dynasty

Map of Fujian's Coastal Mountains and Sands (Fu Jian Yan Hai Shan Sha Tu) drawn up by Zhen Ruozeng in 1562 (the 41th year of the reign of Emperor Jia Jing of the Ming Dynasty) is the revised version of The Great Haiphong Map (Wang Li Hai Fang Tu). It clearly shows the mountains and islands within the East China Sea, which belong to China's maritime territory.

敏繼先陳孔成馬魁道等嚴密
公令張漢若有急即自座守既
卜灣入福清而船始報安焉三
興李君二十五日起行撫按自
港二十六日辰刻至長樂時自
役以二十九日夏至恐風尚未
陝予曰天時難測今已南風又
時乃定且彩長輩皆予所需以
富事在一人信矣遂決而行二
奈海登舟別三司諸君二十九
風大旺瞬目千里長史梁炫舟
球三十日過黃茅閏五月初
馬赤嶼者界琉球地方山也再
矢奈何屏翳絕驅纖塵不動潮
也舟不能行住三日初六日午
土納已山琉球之棻山洋路從
風旺用舵者欲力駕而東勢既
山小姑米山在琉球之西稍過
夷人望見船來即駕小艀來迎

The Records of the Imperial Title-conferring Envoys to Ryukyu (Shi Liu Qiu Lu) of the Ming Dynasty Clearly Recording the Boundary Between China and Ryukyu.

In 1562 during the 41th year of China's Ming Dynasty Emperor Jia Jing's reign, the imperial envoy Guo Rulin in his book Records of the Imperial Title-conferring Envoys to Ryukyu (Shi Liu Qiu Lu) records: "On the first of the fifth intercalary moon we passed by Diaoyu Yu; on the third we reached Chi Yu [Chiwei Yu/Kumeseki-shima]. Chi Yu is a regional hill delimiting Ryukyu territory. With another day of [favorable] wind, Kume Hill will be in sight.

On the first day of leap month May, we passed the Diaoyuyu. On the third day we reached Chiyuyan, which is a hill at the local boundary of Ryukyu. After another day's sail, we could see Gumi Mountain." "The local boundary of Ryukyu" means the boundary between China and Ryukyu. From the above historical document, it could be concluded that the place ahead of Kume Island was the territory of Ryukyu whereas the land on the west of Chìyǔ belonged to China.

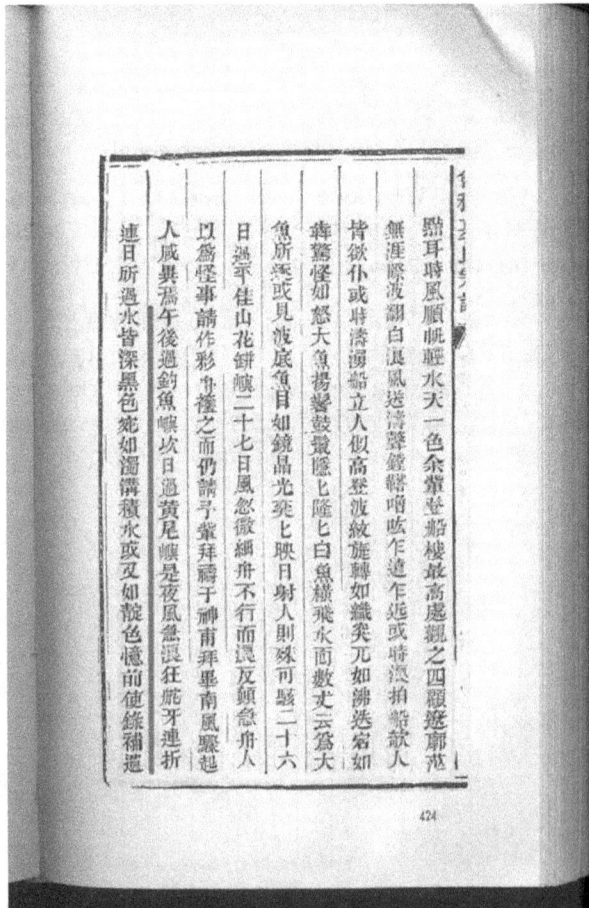

424

令人覘日八處大原猶未見黑影整謂日下有黑影則明日可見山

米山至此七日奚奈何一山裏觀此一飄也不知將所底止乎乃

舟人望山之切誠不啻慢者之于飲食嬰兒之慕慈母也不知將所底止從此數日

必是中國之界未剝舵成風亦稍定亟令安之而風復厲然此數日

九日早隱七望見一艚衆意謂有船則去中國不遠且水離黑入滄

余峰乃為檄告龍王詞用嚴切頃乃波濤稍定舟亦徐風蕩行二十

取各役所帶綿布數百疋於兩艙節七畝之而澳大鳳橫人益恐懼

所以艙水者恃兩瓶耳今艙上床釘顛脫勢必分裂宜連戰之乃集

李美至前曰艙跳入水船倘未裂小人巳令人聖其處幸毋驚但船

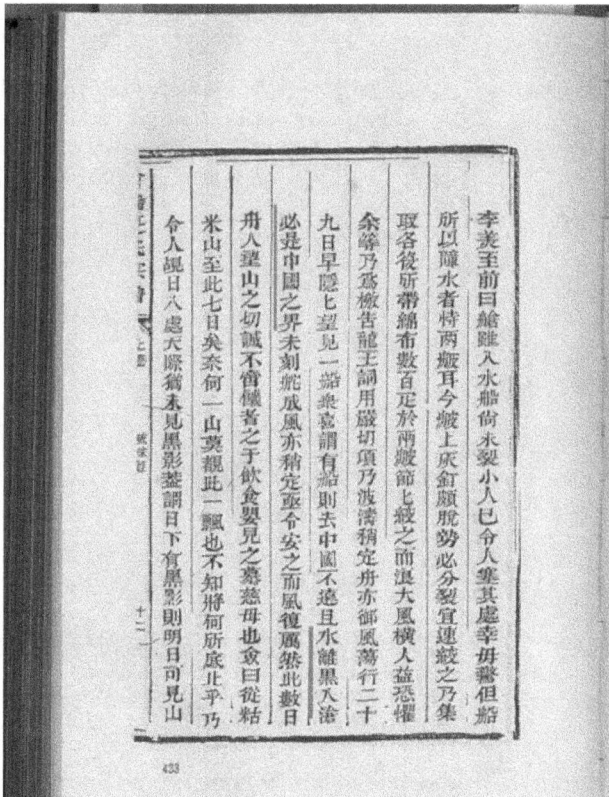

The Records of the Imperial Title-conferring Envoys to Ryukyu (Shi Liu Qiu Lu) of the Ming Dynasty Recording that When the Water Flows From Hei Shui Back to Cang Shui, It Enters the Chinese Territory

In 1606, Xia Ziyang was appointed to grant honorific title to the King of Ryukyu for the 15th time (the 15th imperial envoy). He recorded in his book, Records of the Imperial Title-conferring Envoys to Ryukyu (Shi Liu Qiu Lu) that when he returned to Fuzhou from Naba, what he saw were all dark waters. On October 22 when they passed Gumi Mountain, they encountered hurricane and their ship was wet; On October 29, they saw a ship and everyone cheered as they thought they were close to China; moreover, they crossed the border from black waters to green waters, it must be the boundary of China.... To put it in another way, the Hei Shui Gou is the boundary between Ryukyu and China; green waters belong to China while black waters belong to Ryukyu's waters. "The boundary of China" which is mentioned above is Hei Shui Gou which is the natural maritime boundary between China and Ryukyu. (see "The Records of the Imperial Title-conferring Envoys to Ryukyu (Shi Liu Qiu Lu) of the Xia family"; excerpted from Compiled Documents of Ryukyu in National Library Collection", p. 433.)

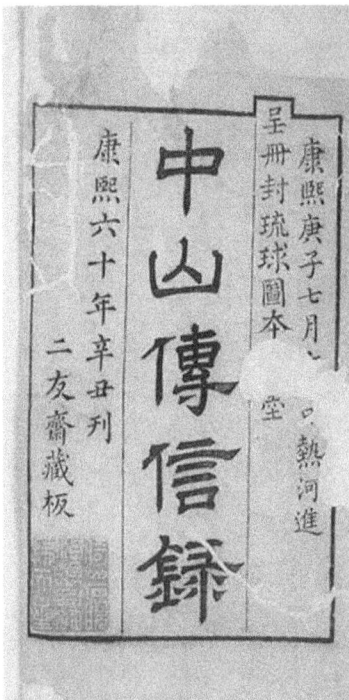

Records of Messages from Chong-shan (Zhong Shan Chuan Xin Lu) of the Qing Dynasty Clearly Recording the Boundary Between China and Ryukyu

In 1719, Xu Baoguang, a deputy title-conferring envoy to Ryukyu sent by the Qing Dynasty, clearly recorded in his book Records of Messages from Chong-shan (Zhong Shan Chuan Xin Lu) that the voyage from Fujian to Ryukyu passed via Huaping Yu, Pengjia Yu, Diaoyu Dao, Huangwei Yu, Chiwei Yu and reached Naba (Naha) port of Ryukyu via Gumi Mountain (the mountain guarding the southwest border of Ryukyu) and Machi Island. "The mountain guarding the southwest border of Ryukyu" refers to the islands on the borders in the southwest waters of Ryukyu. Then he mentioned "nine southwest islands" namely Yaeyama Islands and he concluded: these 8 islands belong to Yaeyama Islands, in China, we call them Yaeyama Islands which guard the most southwestern border of Ryukyu. Cheng Shunze, an authoritative scholar in Ryukyu also mentioned the same conclusion in A General Guide (Zhi Nan Guang Yi). Xu Baoguang quoted the exposition from A General Guide (Zhi Nan Guang Yi): Gumi Mountain (the principal island at the sea boundary to the southwest of Ryukyu). (quote from the Textual Research on Sovereignty over the Diaoyu Islands before the Sino-Japanese War of 1894-1895 written by Wu Tianying, p. 47.). We can see that China and Ryukyu were very clear about their maritime boundaries and related islands at that time.

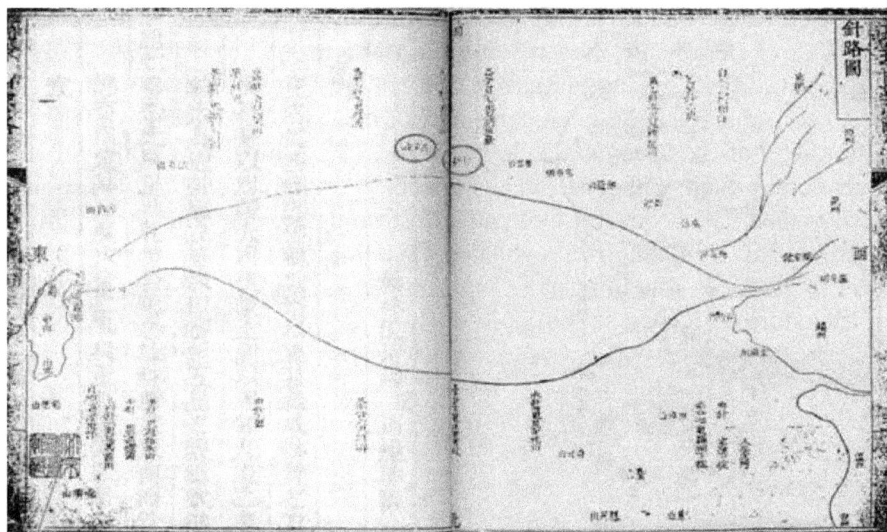

The Annals of Ryukyu (Liu Qiu Guo Zhi Lue) of the Qing Dynasty Recording the Waters Boundary Between China and Ryukyu

In 1756, Zhou Huang, a deputy imperial envoy sent by China's the Qing Dynasty, recorded in his book, the Annals of Ryukyu (Liu Qiu Guo Zhi Lue), that Ryukyu "is separated from the waters of Fujian by Hei Shui Gou to the west; we shipped from Fujian to Ryukyu and went from Cang Shui to Hei Shui. It clearly points out that Hei Shui Gou is the maritime boundary between China and Ryukyu. The Diaoyu Islands within the waters of Fujian are China's territory. The attached "compass needle guided routes" drawing" is also an important evidence to prove the maritime boundary between China and Ryukyu. This is also recorded in p. 899 of Compiled Documents of Ryukyu in National Library Collection published by Beijing Library Press.

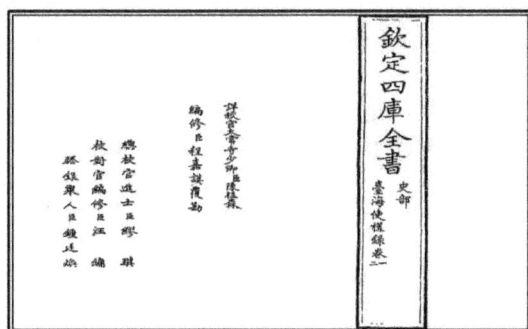

A Tour of Duty in the Taiwan Strait (Tai Hai Shi Cha Lu) of the Qing Dynasty Giving Detailed Accounts Concerning China's Administration Over the Diaoyu

The existing detailed records of China's cruise on the Diaoyu Islands waters is A Tour of Duty in the Taiwan Strait (Tai Hai Shi Cha Lu) written by Taiwan inspection official Huang Shujing in 1722 of the Qing Dynasty. It points out that "there are mountains behind the ocean which is called the Diaoyu Islands. The waters of the Diaoyu Islands can hold tens of ships. This is the official record and ruling symbol of China's effectively administration of its national territory and China's exercise of national sovereignty, this official record is a valuable firm legal empirical evidence. [See Vol. II of A Tour of Duty in the Taiwan Strait (Tai Hai Shi Cha Lu) in Complete Library in the Four Branches of Literature (Si Ku Quan Shu)].

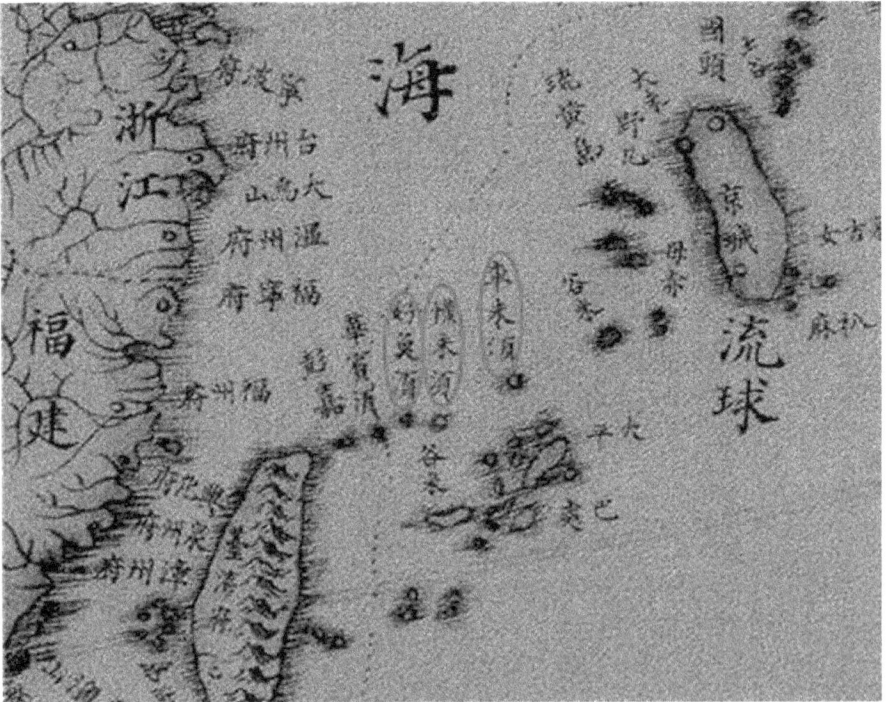

The Great Universal Geographic Map (Kun Yu Quan Tu) Created in the 32nd Year of the Reign of Emperor Qianlong of the Qing Dynasty Marking the Diaoyu Islands as China's Territory

This figure was drawn by Michael Benoist, a French missionary in China in 1767. He colored Huaping Yu, Pengjia Mountain, Diaoyu Island, Huangwei Yu, Chiwei Yu with the same color as that of mainland China and Taiwan. Original names in the picture were written according to the Minnan dialect. The dotted sea lines are the sea routes from Ancient Europe to China , Ryukyu, Japan, etc. (See The Textual Research on Sovereignty over the Diaoyu Islands before the Sino-Japanese War of 1894-1895 written by Wu Tianying, p. 93.)

南過午刻午未風用辰卯鈄至下午行船一
更半入夜行船二更見梅花嶼十三日天明
見釣魚臺從山南過仍辰卯鈄行船二更午
刻見赤尾嶼又行船四更丑過溝祭海申刻
轉西北風夜半轉東北風船猋側危甚十四
日下午轉東南風仍不能進十五日離鳴回
西南鳳仍辰卯鈄十五日黎明見姑米山行

**The Annals of Conferring Titles of Nobility on Ryukyu Emperor
(Ce Feng Liu Qiu Guo Ji Lve) of the Qing Dynasty Recording the Diaoyu
Islands Belonging to China**

During the 13th year of Ming Dynasty Emperor Jia Qing's reign (1808), the great Qing Empire granted honorific title to the King of Ryukyu. Three people, Qi Kun, the imperial envoy, Fei Xizhang, the vice imperial envoy and Shen Fu, as the recorder were appointed to Fujian. On May 2nd, they shipped from Fujian to Ryukyu. On May 2nd, they shipped from Fujian to Ryukyu.

Shen Fu recorded in The Annals of Conferring Titles of Nobility on Ryukyu Emperor (Ce Feng Liu Qiu Guo Ji Lve): On May 11th, we saw the Diaoyu Islands. They looked like penholders. Then we arrived Hei Shui Gou and pra-yed to God. On May 14th, Gumi Mountain comes into sight, that is where the land of Ryukyu begins. On May 15th, we saw mountains shaped like dragons. About 30 to 40 miles away, we gave out three sounds of artillery, and then we saw hundreds of boats coming towards us. The first boat sent us presents and the flag on it read "receive title".

It indicates that the Diaoyu Islands are within China's waters. When they reached Hei Shui Gou, there was still a day's voyage to Ryukyu. Obviously, the border between China and Ryukyu was Hei Shui Gou. Gumi Mountain marks the west border of Ryukyu. On the next day, the imperial envoys saw Gumi Mountain where the land of Ryukyu begins.

According to the textual research, this text can be seen in Vol. 5 of Six Chapters of A Floating Life—The Annals of Conferring Titles of Nobility on Ryukyu Emperor (Ce Feng Liu Qiu Guo Ji Lve) written by Shen Fu. The ori-ginal article was in the Annals of Conferring Titles of Nobility on Ryukyu Emperor (Ce Feng Liu Qiu Guo Ji Lve) in Notepad Beads written by Qian Yong, a famous scholar in the Qing Dynasty (1759-1844, calligrapher) This important historical material is another evidence to prove the Diaoyu Islands belong to China.

Sea Islands Map Drawn by Tei Junsoku from Ryukyu

Tei Junsoku, a famous scholar from Ryukyu drew Sea Islands Map in 1708, which was attached to A General Guide (Zhi Nan Guang Yi). He added the names called by Ryukyu on the islands with Chinese names on the map: Gumi Mountain is called as Kume Island in Ryukyu language; Machi is called as Keromo, it also refers to Chi Yu."

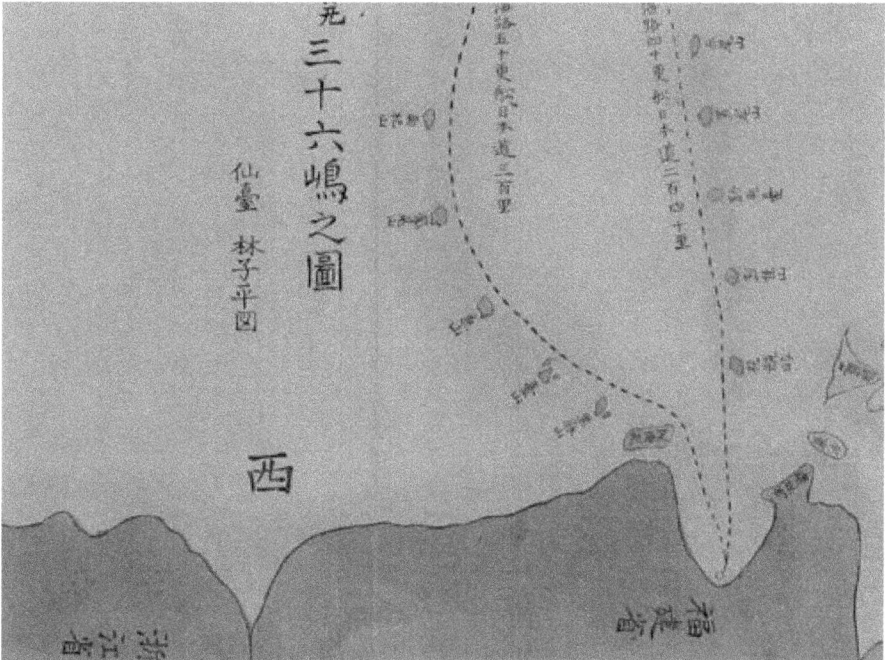

The Book "Illustrated Outline of the Three Countries" Written by Hayashi Shihei in 1785, during Edo period of Japan. The book indicated the Diaoyu Islands as Part of China's Territory by Coloring the Diaoyu Islands with the Same Color as the Mainland of China.

This was the earliest Japanese literature to mention Diaoyu Islands. The three countries referred to were Ezo-chi, Ryukyu and Korea. The Map of the Three Provinces and 36 Islands of Ryukyu in the book put Diaoyu Islands as being apart from the 36 islands of Ryukyu and colored it the same as Fujian and Zhejiang (both are part of the mainland of China), indicating that Diaoyu Dao was part of China's territory. Hayashi Shihei, colored Japan and Ryukyu with another color to show the difference. He agreed with the boundaries between China and Ryukyu recorded by the Chinese imperial envoys and he drew the map which accord with the true boundaries between China and Ryukyu in the maps published by Western countries. It is a honest and fair book without any bias. The book has been collected by the University of Tokyo Libraries.

The Map of East China Sea Littoral States Created by Pierre Lapie (France) in 1809 which marked the Diaoyu Islands, Huangwei Yu, Chiwei Yu and the Taiwan Island with the Same color

The Map of East China Sea Littoral States drawn by French publisher and geographer Pierre Lapie in 1809 painted Diaoyu Island, Huangwei Yu and Chiwei Yu and all Taiwan's affiliated islands in red and painted Ryukyu in green, indicating that the Diaoyu Islands are among Taiwan's affiliated islands and that they belonged to China in the late 19th century.

The Chinese Newspaper Shen-pao Reported in 1885: "The Taiwan Islands Alert" Revealing Japan's Intention to Occupy These Islands

Japan's coveting the Diaoyu Islands aroused China's alertness. The Chinese newspaper Shen-pao reported on September 6th, 1885 an article titled The Taiwan Islands Alert

The Taiwan Islands Alert—"some Japanese people stuck Japan's flag on the sea islands to the north east of Taiwan, revealing Japan's intention to occupy these islands."

The Japanese government scrupled about China's reaction, so it did not dare to make the move immediately.

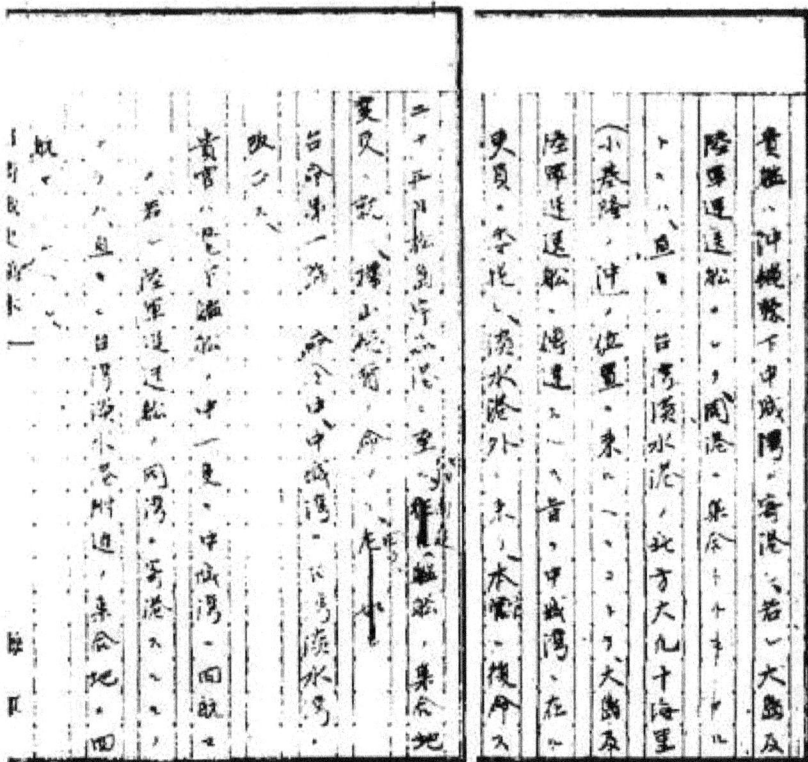

图 38　樺山資紀改定"台湾淡水港　　　　图 39有地海軍中将明言集合地位于
　　　　附近之集合地"　　　　　　　　　　"台湾淡水港北方約九十海里"

Japanese Troops' Occupation of the Diaoyu Islands in May, 1895

In the 28th year of the Meiji period, Conquests of Taiwan Bandits and Thieves of Japan-Qing War History compiled by the Japanese Navy Ministry recorded on May 27th, 1895, Kabayama Sukenori, the Japanese Admiral who was ordered to take over Taiwan, issued a statement, the third of which was the gather point of the transport ships should be 25°20′N, 122°E; namely five nautical miles south of the Senkaku Islands. (note: 122°E was modified to 123°05′E)

The first Japanese Taiwan Governor Kabayama Sukenori occupied the Diaoyu Islands on May 29th, 1895 when he was in the process of taking over Taiwan.

In his statement, he ordered the Japanese troops to gather on Freshwater Harbour, ten nautical miles north of freshwater port of Taiwan (on the sea of Keelung). Freshwater Harbour locates in 25°10′N, so 10 nautical miles north of it is 25°20′N which is the Huaping Yu. It indicates that at that time Japan made the same mistake as Britain that it mistook Huaping Yu for the Senkaku Islands.

"On June 2nd at nine o 'clock in the afternoon, Secretary Shimamura brought the official documents signed and sealed by Kabayama back to Koueki Ship and let Li Jingfang sign and seal on the documents. Then the cession of Taiwan was completed." The Diaoyu Islands were flung in Japan's aggressive abyss. [see Japanese Navy's Conquests of Taiwan Bandits and Thieves in Microfilm Catalog Copy of Selected Archives of Japanese Army, Navy and Other Political Organizations, P. 46113, secret document No.27 and the most secret document No.3; see The Textual Research on Ceding the Diaoyu Islands in Treaty of Shimonoseki by Wu Tianying)

GENERAL HEADQUARTERS
SUPREME COMMANDER FOR THE ALLIED POWERS

AG 091 (29 Jan 46)GS
(SCAPIN - 677)

AG 500
29 January 1946

MEMORANDUM FOR: IMPERIAL JAPANESE GOVERNMENT.

THROUGH : Central Liaison Office, Tokyo.

SUBJECT : Governmental and Administrative Separation of Certain Outlying Areas from Japan.

1. The Imperial Japanese Government is directed to cease exercising, or attempting to exercise, governmental or administrative authority over any area outside of Japan, or over any government officials and employees or any other persons within such areas.

2. Except as authorized by this Headquarters, the Imperial Japanese Government will not communicate with government officials and employees or with any other persons outside of Japan for any purpose other than the routine operation of authorized shipping, communications and weather services.

3. For the purpose of this directive, Japan is defined to include the four main islands of Japan (Hokkaido, Honshu, Kyushu and Shikoku) and the approximately 1,000 smaller adjacent islands, including the Tsushima Islands and the Ryukyu (Nansei) Islands north of 30° North Latitude (excluding Kuchinoshima Island); and excluding (a) Utsuryo (Ullung) Island, Liancourt Rocks (Take Island) and Quelpart (Saishu or Cheju) Island, (b) the Ryukyu (Nansei) Islands south of 30° North Latitude (including Kuchinoshima Island), the Izu, Nanpo, Bonin (Ogasawara) and Volcano (Kazan or Iwo) Island Groups, and all other outlying Pacific Islands [including the Daito (Ohigashi or Oagari) Island Group, and Parece Vela (Okino-tori), Marcus (Minami-tori) and Ganges (Nakano-tori) Islands] and (c) the Kurile (Chishima) Islands, the Habomai (Hapomaze) Island Group (including Suisho, Yuri, Akiyuri, Shibotsu and Taraku Islands) and Shikotan Island.

4. Further areas specifically excluded from the governmental and administrative jurisdiction of the Imperial Japanese Government are the following: (a) all Pacific Islands seized or occupied under mandate or otherwise by Japan since the beginning of the World War in 1914, (b) Manchuria, Formosa and the Pescadores, (c) Korea, and (d) Karafuto.

(1041)

The Supreme Commander for the Allied Powers Instruction (SCAPIN) No.677 Clearly Defining the Japanese Territory, Excluding the Diaoyu Islands

On January 29th, 1946, the Supreme Commander for the Allied Powers Instruction (SCAPIN) No.677 clearly defined Japan's power of administration to "include the four main islands of Japan (Hokkaido, Honshu, Kyushu and Shikoku) and the approximately 1,000 smaller adjacent islands, including the Tsushima Islands and the Ryukyu Islands north of the 30th parallel of North Latitude", but the Diaoyu Islands were not included (Huangwei Yu south of the 30th parallel of North Latitude is located to the most northern part of the Diaoyu Island and its affiliated islands). (this picture is from Wikipedia : Senkaku Islands Dispute)

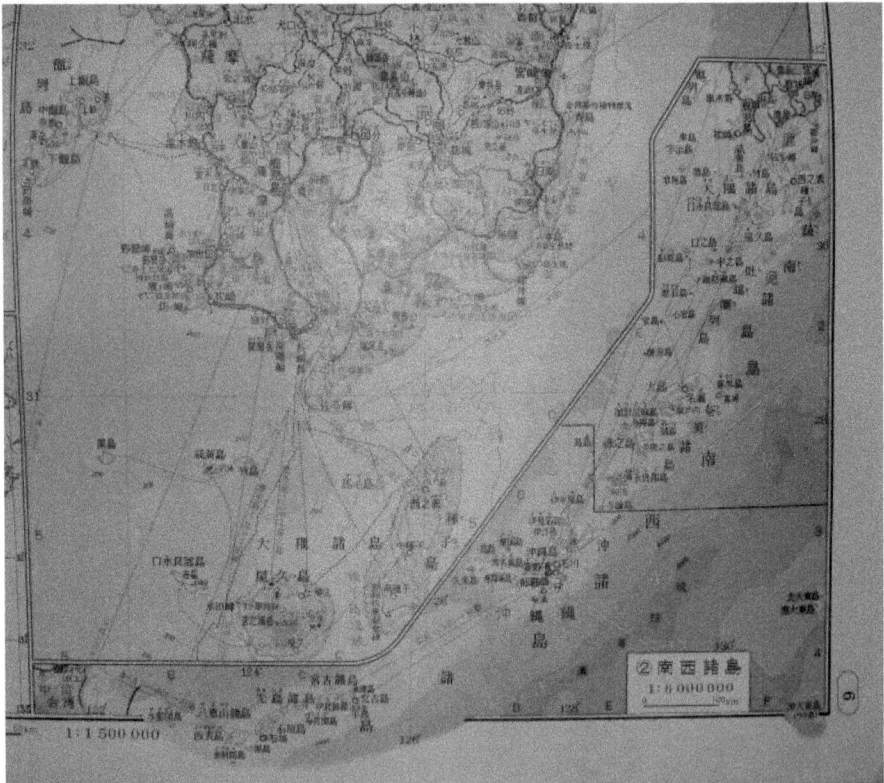

The Map of Japan Published in Japan Excluding the Diaoyu islands

Map of Southwest Islands in the Atlas of Japan published by Imperial Academy Tokyo, Japan, on November 20, 1963, didn't include the Diaoyu Islands into Japan's territory. Neither did The Map of Japan published by Japan on November 25, 1970. (the map is in the Vol.5 of "Shogakukan Japanese Encyclopedia")

According to the study of Chinese scholars, from 1897 to August 1945 before Japan's surrender, Map of Southwest Islands and the Map of Ryukyu Islands in the Kyushu Local Map approved and published by the Japanese authorities didn't map the Diaoyu Islands, Huangwei Yu and Chiwei Yu into Japan's territory. Especially from Japan's surrender in 1945, to March 8th, 1972, none of the maps of Southwest Islands published in Japan included Taiwan's affiliated islands—the Diaoyu Islands, Huangwei Yu and Chiwei Yu.

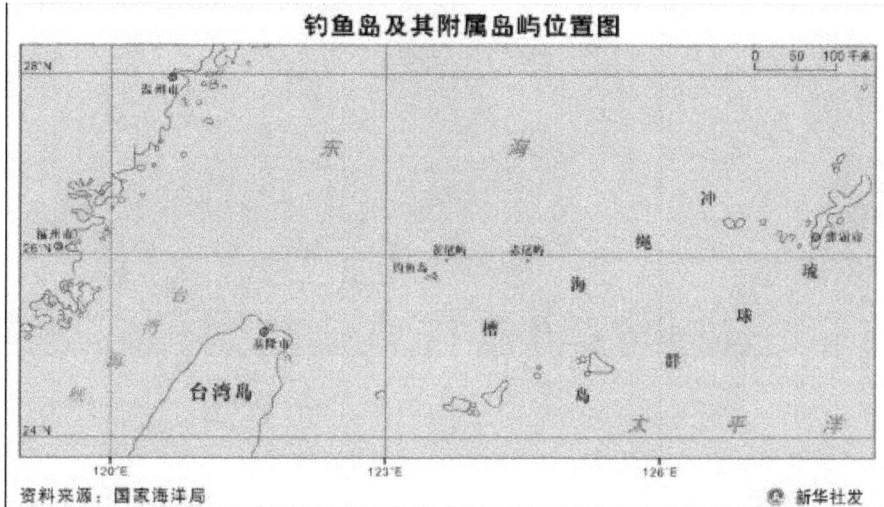

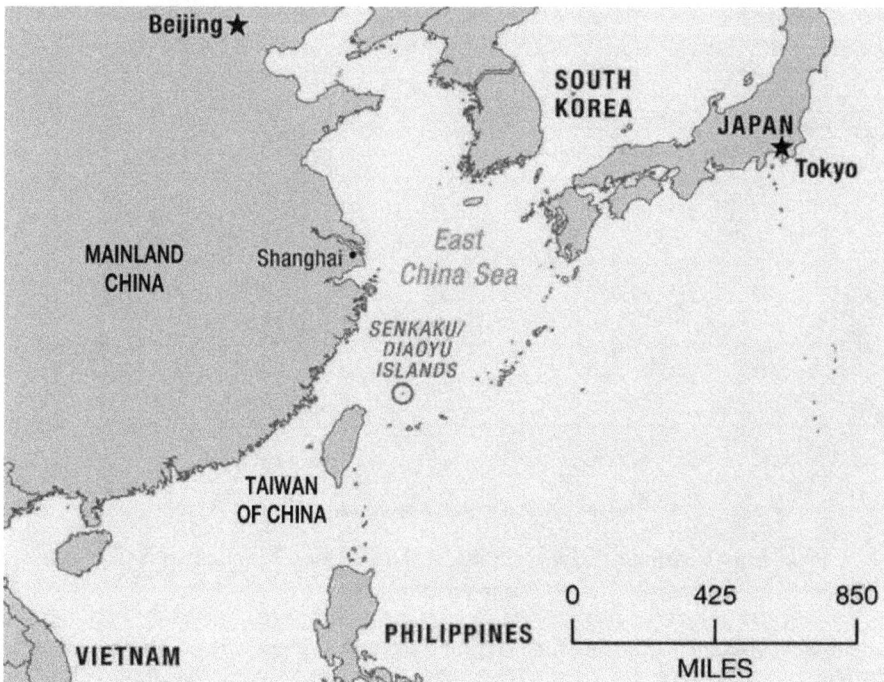

钓鱼岛及其附属岛屿位置图

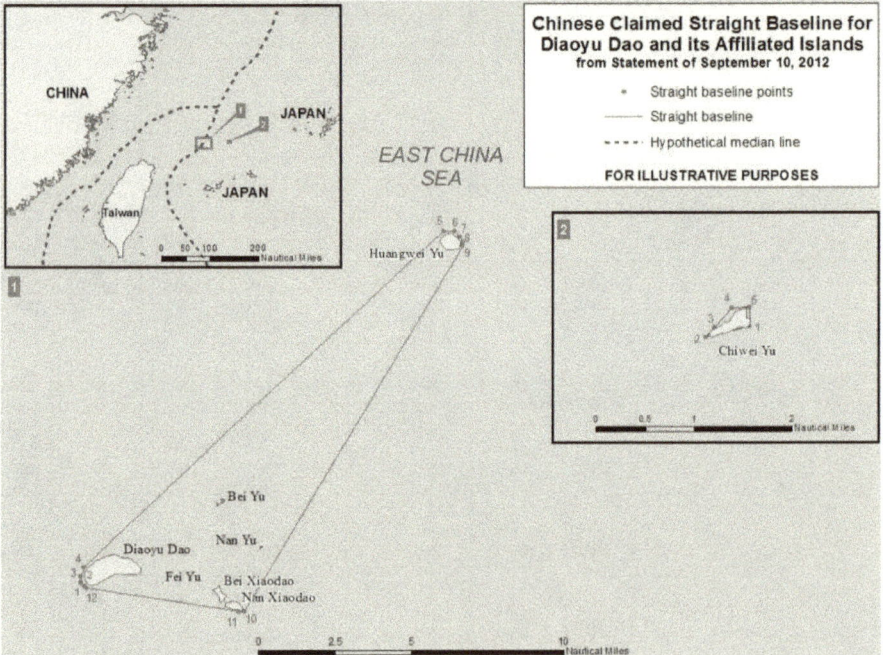

China Has Published the Baselines Map of the Territorial Sea of the Diaoyu Islands

In accordance with the Law of the People's Republic of China on the Territorial Sea and the Contiguous Zone adopted and promulgated on 25 February 1992, the Government of the People's Republic of China announced the baselines of the territorial sea adjacent to Diaoyu Islands and its affiliated islands of the People's Republic of China on September 10th, 2012.

The announced the baselines of the territorial sea of the Diaoyu Islands are delimited by the selected 17 basis points on the Diaoyu Island and its affiliated islands. The territorial sea of the People's Republic of China extends up to 12 nautical miles from its baselines. China will provide necessary facilities and services for ships passing through the waters of the Diaoyu Islands according to relevant provisions of the China's Law and International Law.

In addition, on September 13th EDT, China's UN ambassador Li Baodong made an appointment with the UN Secretary-General Ban Ki-moon. According to the relevant provisions of International Law, Li Baodong submitted the coordinate table and the sea chart of baselines and base points of the territorial sea of the Diaoyu Island and its affiliated islands.

In November, 1943, Generalissimo Chiang Kai-shek, President Roosevelt and Prime Minister Churchill, together with their respective military and diplomatic advisers, met and conferred at Cairo. The following general statement was issued:

"The several military missions have agreed upon future military operations against Japan. They covet no gain for themselves and have no thought of territorial expansion. It is their purpose that Japan shall be stripped of all the islands in the Pacific which she has seized or occupied since the beginning of the First World War in 1914, and that all the territories Japan has stolen from the Chinese, such as Manchuria, Formosa, and the Pescadores, shall be restored to the Republic of China. Japan will also be expelled from all other territories which she has taken by violence and greed. The aforesaid three great powers, mindful of the enslavement of the people of Korea, are determined that in due course Korea shall become free and independent.

"With these objects in view the three Allies, in harmony with those of the United Nations at war with Japan, will continue to persevere in the serious and prolonged operations necessary to procure the unconditional surrender of Japan."

Chapter Four

Related Literature

The Cairo Declaration[1]

December 1st, 1943

[U.S.] Roosevelt, [China] Chiang Kai-shek, [Britain] Churchill

The several military missions have agreed upon future military operations against Japan. The Three Great Allies expressed their resolve to bring unrelenting pressure against their brutal enemies by sea, land, and air. This pressure is already rising.

The Three Great Allies are fighting this war to restrain and punish the aggression of Japan. They covet no gain for themselves and have no thought of territorial expansion. It is their purpose that Japan shall be stripped of all the islands in the Pacific which she has seized or occupied since the beginning of the first World War in 1914, and that all the territories Japan has stolen from the Chinese, such as Manchuria[2], Formosa, and The Pescadores, shall be restored to the Republic of China. Japan will also be expelled from all other territories which she has taken by violence and greed. The aforesaid three great powers, mindful of the enslavement of the people of Korea, are determined that in due course Korea shall become free and independent.

With these objects in view the three Allies, in harmony with those of the United Nations[3] at war with Japan, will continue to persevere in the serious and prolonged operations necessary to procure the unconditional surrender of Japan.

---

1   The famous "Cairo Declaration" published in Washington at 7:50 p.m. December 1st, 1943 (US Eastern War Time) translation released on December 2nd in Chongqing time.
2   Refers to Heilongjiang, Jilin, Liaoning and Rehe, namely the puppet Manchukuo regime controlled by Japan.
3   Refer to the "United Nations"; the customary appellation for the Anti-Fascist Allies.

The Potsdam Declaration

July, 1945

Editor's note: in July 1945, the leaders of the United States, Britain, and China held a conference in Potsdam, Berlin and published "Potsdam Declaration" on the 26th, urging Japan to surrender. The whole article is as follows:

1. We-the President of the United States, the President of the National Government of the Republic of China, and the Prime Minister of Great Britain, representing the hundreds of millions of our countrymen, have conferred and agree that Japan shall be given an opportunity to end this war.

2. The prodigious land, sea and air forces of the United States, the British Empire and of China, many times reinforced by their armies and air fleets from the west, are poised to strike the final blows upon Japan. This military power is sustained and inspired by the determination of all the Allied Nations to prosecute the war against Japan until she ceases to resist.

3. The result of the futile and senseless German resistance to the might of the aroused free peoples of the world stands forth in awful clarity as an example to the people of Japan. The might that now converges on Japan is immeasurably greater than that which, when applied to the resisting Nazis, necessarily laid waste to the lands, the industry and the method of life of the whole German people. The full application of our military power, backed by our resolve, will mean the inevitable and complete destruction of the Japanese armed forces and just as inevitably the utter devastation of the Japanese homeland.

4. The time has come for Japan to decide whether she will continue to be controlled by those self-willed militaristic advisers whose unintelligent calculations have brought the Empire of Japan to the threshold of annihilation, or whether she will follow the path of reason.

5. Following are our terms. We will not deviate from them. There are no alternatives. We shall brook no delay.

6. There must be eliminated for all time the authority and influence of those who have deceived and misled the people of Japan into embarking on world conquest, for we insist that a new order of peace, security and justice will be impossible until irresponsible militarism is driven from the world.

7. Until such a new order is established and until there is convincing proof that Japan's war-making power is destroyed, points in Japanese territory to be designated by the Allies shall be occupied to secure the achievement of the basic objectives we are here setting forth.

8. The terms of the Cairo Declaration shall be carried out and Japanese sovereignty shall be limited to the islands of Honshu, Hokkaido, Kyushu, Shikoku and such minor islands as we determine.

9. The Japanese military forces, after being completely disarmed, shall be permitted to return to their homes with the opportunity to lead peaceful and productive lives.

10. We do not intend that the Japanese shall be enslaved as a race or destroyed as a nation, but stern justice shall be meted out to all war criminals, including those who have visited cruelties upon our prisoners. The Japanese Government shall remove all obstacles to the revival and strengthening of democratic tendencies among the Japanese people. Freedom of speech, of religion, and of thought, as well as respect for the fundamental human rights shall be established.

11. Japan shall be permitted to maintain such industries as will sustain her economy and permit the exaction of just reparations in kind, but not those which would enable her to re-arm for war. To this end, access to, as distinguished from control of, raw materials shall be permitted. Eventual Japanese participation in world trade relations shall be permitted.

12. The occupying forces of the Allies shall be withdrawn from Japan as soon as these objectives have been accomplished and there has been established in accordance with the freely expressed will of the Japanese people a peacefully inclined and responsible government.

13. We call upon the government of Japan to proclaim now the unconditional surrender of all Japanese armed forces, and to provide proper and adequate assurances of their good faith in such action. The alternative for Japan is prompt and utter destruction.

(July 26, 1945)

Joint Statement/Communique between the Government of the People's Republic of China and the Fovernment of Japan

September 29, 1972

At the invitation of Premier Zhou Enlai of the People's Republic of China, Japanese Prime Minister Kakuei Tanaka visited China from Sept 25 to Sept 30, 1972. Chairman Mao Zedong met Japanese Prime Minister Kakuei Tanaka on Sept 27 and had an earnest and friendly conversation.

Japanese Prime Minister Tanaka and Japan's Minister for Foreign Affairs Masayoshi Ohira had an earnest and frank exchange of views with Premier Zhou Enlai and Minister for Foreign Affairs Ji Pengfei in a friendly atmosphere throughout on the question of the normalization of relations between China and Japan and other problems between the two countries as well as on other matters of interest to both sides, and agreed to issue the following Joint Communique of the two Governments:

China and Japan are neighboring countries, separated only by a strip of water with a long history of traditional friendship. The peoples of the two countries earnestly desire to put an end to the abnormal state of affairs that has hitherto existed between the two countries. The realization of the aspiration of the two peoples for the termination of the state of war and the normalization of relations between China and Japan will add a new page to the annals of relations between the two countries.

The Japanese side is keenly conscious of the responsibility for the serious damage that Japan caused in the past to the Chinese people through war, and deeply reproaches itself. Further, the Japanese side reaffirms its position that it intends to realize the normalization of relations between the two countries from the stand of fully understanding "the three principles for the restoration of relations" put forward by the Government of the People's Republic of China. The Chinese side expresses its welcome for this.

In spite of the differences in their social systems existing between the two countries, the two countries should, and can, establish relations of peace and friendship. The normalization of relations and development of good-neighborly and friendly relations between the two countries are in the interests of the two peoples and will contribute to the relaxation of tension in Asia and peace in the world.

1. The abnormal state of affairs that has hitherto existed between Japan and the People's Republic of China is terminated on the date on which this Joint Communique is issued.

2. The Government of Japan recognizes that Government of the People's Republic of China as the sole legal Government of China.

3. The Government of the People's Republic of China reiterates that Taiwan is an inalienable part of the territory of the People's Republic of China. The Government of Japan fully understands and respects this stand of the Government of the People's Republic of China, and it firmly maintains its stand under Article 8 of the Potsdam Declaration.

4. The Government of Japan and the Government of People's Republic of China have decided to establish diplomatic relations as from Sept 29, 1972. The two Governments have decided to take all necessary measures for the establishment and the performance of the functions of each other's embassy in their respective capitals in accordance with international law and practice, and to exchange ambassadors as speedily as possible.

5. The Government of the People's Republic of China declares that in the interest of the friendship between the Chinese and the Japanese peoples, it renounces its demand for war reparation from Japan.

6. The Government of Japan and the Government of the People's Republic of China agree to establish relations of perpetual peace and friendship between the two countries on the basis of the principles of mutual respect for sovereignty and territorial integrity, mutual non-aggression, non-interference in each other's internal affairs, equality and mutual benefit and peaceful co-existence.

The two Governments confirm that, in conformity with the foregoing principles and the principles of the Charter of the United Nations, China and Japan shall in their mutual relations settle all disputes by peaceful means and shall refrain from the use or threat of force.

7. The normalization of relations between China and Japan is not directed against any third country. Neither of the two countries should seek hegemony in the Asia-Pacific region and each is opposed to efforts by any other country or group of countries to establish such hegemony.

8. The Government of Japan and the Government of the People's Republic of China have agreed that, with a view to solidifying and developing the relations of peace and friendship between the two countries, the two Governments will enter into negotiations for the purpose of concluding a treaty of peace and friendship.

9. The Government of Japan and the Government of the People's Republic of China have agreed that, with a view to further promoting relations between the two countries and to expanding interchanges of people, the two Governments will, as necessary and taking account of the existing non-governmental arrangements, enter into negotiations for the purpose of concluding agreements concerning such matters as trade, shipping, aviation, and fisheries.

Premier of the People's Republic of China   Prime Minister of Japan

Zhou Enlai   Kakuei Tanaka

Ji Pengfei

Minister for Foreign Affairs of the People's Republic of China

Masayoshi Ohira

Minister for Foreign Affairs of Japan

September 29, 1972, Beijing

Treaty Of Peace and Friendship Between Japan and The People's Republic of China

August 12, 1978

Japan and the People's Republic of China,

Having recalled with satisfaction that, since the issuance of the joint statement by the Government of Japan and the Government of the People's Republic of China on 29th September 1972 at Beijing, friendly relations between the Governments and the peoples of the two countries have developed extensively on a new basis,

Affirming that the aforementioned joint statement constitutes the basis for relations of peace and friendship between the two countries and that the principles set out in that statement should be strictly observed,

Affirming that the Charter of the United Nations should be fully respected,

Desiring to contribute to the peace and security of Asia and the world,

Seeking to strengthen and develop peaceful and friendly relations between the two countries,

Have decided to conclude a treaty of peace and friendship and have, for this purpose, appointed as their Plenipotentiaries:

For Japan, the Minister of Foreign Affairs, Sunao Sonoda; For China, the Minister for Foreign Affairs, Huang Hua

The Plenipotentiaries of both Parties, having exchanged their full powers, and found them in good and due form, have agreed as follows:

Article 1

1. The Contracting Parties shall develop lasting relations of peace and friendship between the two countries on the basis of mutual respect for the principles of sovereignty and territorial integrity, mutual non-aggression, non-intervention in each other's internal affairs, mutual benefit, and peaceful coexistence.

2. In accordance with the aforementioned principles and the principles of the Charter of the United Nations, the Contracting Parties affirm that, in their mutual relations, they will use peaceful means to settle all disputes and will refrain from the use of force or the threats of the use thereof.

Article 2

The Contracting Parties declare that neither Party will seek hegemony within the Asian and Pacific region or in any other region and that both shall oppose any attempt by any other country or group of countries to establish such hegemony.

Article 3

The Contracting Parties, motivated by the spirit of good neighbourliness and friendship and in accordance with the principles of mutual benefit and non-interference in each other's internal affairs, shall foster contacts and endeavours involving the peoples of the two countries with a view to furthering economic and cultural relations between the two countries.

Article 4

This Treaty shall not affect the relations either Contracting Party maintains with third countries.

Article 5

1. This Treaty is subject to ratification and shall enter into force on the day of the exchange of the historical materials of ratification at Tokyo. This Treaty shall remain in force for 10 years and thereafter until the statement of termination provided for in paragraph 2 of this article is made.

2. Upon the expiration of the initial ten-year period or at any time thereafter, either Contracting Party may terminate this Treaty by informing the other Contracting Party in writing one year beforehand of its intention to do so.

IN WITNESS WHEREOF, the Plenipotentiaries have signed this Treaty and affixed thereto their seals.

DONE at Beijing, 12th August 1978, in duplicate, in the Japanese and Chinese languages, both texts being equally authentic.

For Japan: SUNAO SONODA

For the People's Republic of China: HUANG HUA

China-Japan Joint Declaration On Building a Partnership of Friendship and Cooperation for Peace and Development

November 26, 1998

In response to an invitation extended by the Government of Japan, President Jiang Zemin of the People's Republic of China made an official visit to Japan as a State Guest from Nov 25 to 30, 1998. On the occasion of this historically significant first visit to Japan by a President of the People's Republic of China, President Jiang met with His Majesty the Emperor of Japan, and held an intensive exchange of views with Japanese Prime Minister Keizo Obuchi on the international situation, regional issues and the overall China-Japan relationship.

They attained a broad common view and, based on the success of this visit, declared as follows:

I

Both sides shared the view that as the world in the post-Cold War era continues to undergo great changes toward the creation of a new international order, further economic globalization is deepening interdependence and security dialogue and cooperation are making constant progress. Peace and development remain major issues facing the human society. It is therefore the common wish of the international community to build a new international political and economic order which is fair and rational, and to strive for a peaceful international environment in the twenty-first century that is even more firmly rooted.

Both sides reaffirmed that the principles of mutual respect for sovereignty and territorial integrity, mutual non-aggression, non-interference in each other's internal affairs, equality and mutual benefit and peaceful co-existence, as well as the principles of the Charter of the United Nations, are the basic norms for relations between states.

Both sides positively evaluate the efforts made by the United Nations to preserve world peace and to promote the economic and social development of the world, and believe that the United Nations should play an important role in building and maintaining a new international order. Both sides express support for the reforms of the United Nations including the reform of the Security Council, in order for the United Nations to further embody the common wish and collective will of all Members in its activities and policy decision making process.

Both sides stress the importance of the ultimate elimination of nuclear weapons, and oppose the proliferation of nuclear weapons in any form whatsoever, and furthermore, strongly call upon the nations concerned to cease all nuclear testing and nuclear arms race, in order to contribute to the peace and stability of the Asian region and the world.

Both sides believe that both China and Japan, as nations influential in the Asian region and the world, bear an important responsibility for preserving peace and promoting development. Both sides will strengthen coordination and cooperation in the areas such as international politics, international economy, and global issues, thus actively contributing to the endeavor for the peace and development of the world aimed at the progress of humanity.

II

Both sides believe that, after the Cold War, the Asian region has continued to move toward stability and the regional cooperation has deepened further. In addition, both sides are convinced that this region will exert greater influence on international politics, economics and security and will continue to play an important role in the coming century.

Both sides reiterate that it is the unshakable fundamental policy of the two countries to maintain the peace of this region and to promote its development, and that they will not seek hegemony in the Asian region and settle all disputes by peaceful means, without recourse to the use or threat of force.

Both sides expressed their great interest in the current financial crisis in East Asia and the ensuing difficulties for the Asian economy. At the same time, both sides recognize that the economic foundation of this region is sound, and firmly believe that by advancing rational adjustment and reform based on experiences, as well as by enhancing regional and international coordination and cooperation, the economy of Asia will definitely overcome its difficulties and continue to develop. Both sides affirmed that they would actively meet the various challenges that they faced, and would respectively make their utmost efforts toward promoting the economic development of the region.

Both sides believe that stable relations among the major nations of the Asia-Pacific region are extremely important for the peace and stability of this region. Both sides shared the view that they would actively participate in all multilateral activities in this region, such as the ASEAN Regional Forum, promote coordination and cooperation, and support all measures for enhancing understanding and strengthening confidence.

III

Both sides reviewed the bilateral relationship since the normalization of relations between China and Japan, and expressed satisfaction with the remarkable development in all areas, including politics, economics, culture and personnel exchanges. Further, both sides shared the view that under the current situation cooperation between the two countries is growing in importance, and that further strengthening and developing the friendly and cooperative relations between the two countries not only serve the fundamental interests of their peoples, but also actively contribute to the peace and development of the Asia-Pacific region and the world as a whole. Both sides reaffirmed that the Japan-China relationship is one of the most important bilateral relationships for the respective country, deeply recognized the role and responsibility of both countries in achieving peace and development, and expressed their resolve to establish a partnership of friendship and cooperation for peace! and development toward the twenty-first century.

Both sides restated that they will observe the principles of the Joint Communique of the Government of Japan and the Government of the People's Republic of China, issued on 29 September 1972 and the Treaty of Peace and Friendship between Japan and the People's Republic of China, signed on Aug 12, 1978, and reaffirmed that the above-mentioned documents will continue to be the most important foundation for the bilateral relations.

Both sides are of the view that China and Japan share a history of friendly exchanges spanning more than 2,000 years, as well as a common cultural background, and that it is the common desire of the peoples of the two countries to continue this tradition of friendship and to further develop mutually beneficial cooperation.

Both sides believe that squarely facing the past and correctly understanding history are the important foundation for further developing relations between China and Japan. The Japanese side observes the 1972 Joint Statement between the government of the People's Republic of China and the government of Japan and the Aug 15, 1995 Statement by former Prime Minister Tomiichi Murayama. The Japanese side is keenly conscious of the responsibility for the serious distress and damage that Japan caused to the Chinese people through its aggression against China during a certain period in the past and expressed deep remorse for this. The Chinese side hopes that the Japanese side will learn lessons from the history and adhere to the path of peace and development. Based on this, both sides will develop long-standing relations of friendship.

Both sides shared the view that expanding personnel exchanges between the two countries is extremely important for advancing mutual understanding and enhancing mutual trust.

Both sides confirmed an annual visit by a leader of either country to the other, the establishment of a Tokyo-Beijing hot line between the two Governments, and the further enhancement of personnel exchanges at all levels, in particular among the younger generation who will shoulder the heavy burden of the future development of the two countries.

Both sides shared the view that, based on the principles of equality and mutual benefit, they will formulate long-term, stable, cooperative economic and trade relations, and will further expand cooperation in such areas as high technology, information, environmental protection, agriculture and infrastructure. The Japanese side reiterated that a stable, open and developing China is significant for the peace and development of the Asia-Pacific region and the entire world, and restated its policy of continuing cooperation and assistance for the economic development of China. The Chinese side expressed its gratitude for the economic cooperation extended by Japan to China. The Japanese side reiterated that it will continue to support China's efforts for the early accession to the WTO.

Both sides positively evaluated the beneficial role played by their bilateral security dialogue in increasing mutual understanding, and shared the view that they would further strengthen this dialogue mechanism.

The Japanese side continues to maintain its stand on the Taiwan issue which was set forth in the Joint Communique of the Government of Japan and the Government of the People's Republic of China and reiterates its understanding that there is one China. Japan will continue to maintain its exchanges of private and regional nature with Taiwan.

Both sides affirmed that, based on the principles of the Joint Communique of the Government of Japan and the Government of the People's Republic of China and the Treaty of Peace and Friendship between Japan and the People's Republic of China, and following the spirit of seeking common major benefits while setting aside minor differences, they would work to maximize their common interests and minimize their differences, and, through friendly consultations, appropriately handle the issues, differences of opinion and disputes which currently exist and may arise in the future, thereby avoiding any restraint or obstacle to development of friendly relations between the two countries.

Both sides believe that through establishment of a partnership of friendship and cooperation for peace and development, the bilateral relations will enter a new level of development. To this end, a wide range of participation and sustained effort not only of both Governments, but also of the peoples of both countries, is essential. Both sides firmly believe that, if the peoples of both countries, hand-in-hand, thoroughly demonstrate the spirit shown in this Declaration, it will not only contribute to the friendship of the peoples of both countries for generations to come, but also make an important contribution to the peace and development of the Asia-Pacific region and of the world.

China-Japan Joint Statement on Promoting Strategic, Mutually Beneficial Ties

May 2008

Editor's note: on May 7th, 2008, Chinese President Hu Jintao and Japanese Prime Minister Yasuo Fukuda in Tokyo signed China-Japan joint statement on promoting strategic, mutually beneficial ties in Tokyo. Joint statement reads as follows:

China-Japan joint statement on promoting strategic, mutually beneficial ties

In response to an invitation extended by the Government of Japan, President Hu Jintao of the People's Republic of China made an official visit to Japan as a state guest from May 6th to May 10th, 2008. During his visit to Japan, President Hu met with His Majesty the Emperor of Japan. President Hu also had talks with Prime Minister Yasuo Fukuda, and they reached a common understanding on various points related to the comprehensive promotion of a "mutually beneficial relationship based on common strategic interests" and issued the following joint statement.

The two sides recognized that the Japan-China relationship is one of the most important bilateral relationships for each of the two countries and that Japan and China now have great influence on and bear a solemn responsibility for peace, stability, and development of the Asia-Pacific region and the world. They also recognized that the two countries' sole option is to cooperate to enhance peace and friendship over the long term. The two sides resolved to comprehensively promote a "mutually beneficial relationship based on common strategic interests" and to achieve the noble objectives of peaceful coexistence, friendship for generations, mutually beneficial cooperation, and common development for their two nations.

The two sides again stated that the Joint Communique of the Government of Japan and the Government of the People's Republic of China issued on September 29th, 1972, the Treaty of Peace and Friendship between Japan and the People's Republic of China signed on August 12th, 1978, and the Japan-China Joint Declaration issued on November 26th, 1998, are the political foundation for advancing the Japan-China relationship in a stable fashion and forging the future of the relationship. The leaders confirmed that they would continue to observe the principles enunciated in the three documents. Moreover, both sides confirmed that they would continue to uphold and fully implement the common views enunciated in the Japan-China Joint Press Statements of October 8th, 2006 and April 11th, 2007.

The two sides resolved to face history squarely, advance toward the future, and endeavor with persistence to create a new era of a "mutually beneficial relationship based on common strategic interests" between Japan and China. They announced that they would align Japan-China relations with the trends of international community and together forge a bright future for the Asia-Pacific region and the world while deepening mutual understanding, building mutual trust, and expanding mutually beneficial cooperation between their nations in an ongoing fashion into the future.

The two sides recognized that they are partners who cooperate together and are not threats to each other. The two sides again stated that they would support each other's peaceful development, and they shared the conviction that Japan and China, that uphold the course to peaceful development, would bring great opportunities and benefits to Asia and the world.

(1) The Japanese side expressed its positive evaluation of the fact that China's development since the start of reform and open policy, saying China's development has offered great opportunities for the international community including Japan. The Japanese side stated its support of China's resolve to contribute to the building of a world that fosters lasting peace and common prosperity.

(2) The Chinese side expressed its positive evaluation of Japan's consistent pursuit of the path of a peaceful country and Japan's contribution to the peace and stability of the world through peaceful means over more than sixty years since World War. The two sides agreed to strengthen dialogue and communication on the issue of United Nations reform and to work toward enhancing common understanding with each other on this matter. The Chinese side attaches importance to Japan's position and role in the United Nations and desires Japan to play an even greater constructive role in the international community.

(3) Both sides stated that they would resolve bilateral issues through consultations and negotiations.

Regarding the Taiwan issue, the Japanese side again expressed its adherence to the position enunciated in the Joint Communique of the Government of Japan and the Government of the People's Republic of China.

Both sides resolved to cooperate together while building frameworks for dialogue and cooperation, cooperate together based on the following five pillars:

(1) Enhancement of mutual trust in the political area

The two sides recognized that fostering mutual trust in the political and security area is of great significance to the building of a "mutually beneficial relationship based on common strategic interests" between Japan and China and resolved as follows:

To build a mechanism for the periodic exchange of visits by the leaders of the two countries, with the leader of one country visiting the other country once a year in principle; to convene summit meetings frequently, including holding meetings on the occasion of international conferences; to strengthen the mechanism for exchange and strategic dialogue between the governments, parliaments, and political parties of the two countries; to improve communication regarding the two countries' bilateral relationship, their domestic and international policies, and the international situation; and to endeavor to enhance the transparency of those policies.

To enhance the exchange of high-level visits in the area of security, promote various forms of dialogue and exchange, and further enhance mutual understanding and trust.

To engage in close cooperation to develop greater understanding and pursuit of basic and universal values that are commonly accepted by the international community and to deepen once again understanding of culture that Japan and China have cultivated and shared together over their long history of exchange.

(2) Promotion of people-to-people and cultural exchange as well as sentiments of friendship between the people of Japan and China

The two sides confirmed that persistently promoting mutual understanding and sentiments of friendship between the people and particularly the youth of their two countries would contribute to the strengthening of the foundation of friendship and cooperation between Japan and China over generations and resolved as follows:

To implement a full spectrum of cultural and intellectual interchange by broadly developing exchanges between the two countries' mass media, friendship cities, as well as sports and private organizations.

To promote youth exchange on a continuing basis.

(3) Enhancement of mutually beneficial cooperation

The two sides resolved to engage particularly in the following areas of co-operation so that Japan and China, which have a major influence on the world economy, can contribute to the sustainable growth of the world economy:

To conduct cooperation with particular priority on the areas of energy and the environment, based on the recognition that they have a responsibility to future generations and the international community to engage in such cooperation.

To promote mutually beneficial cooperation and expand common benefits in a wide range of fields, including trade, investment, information and commu-nication technology, finance, food and product safety, protection of intellectual property rights, business environment, agriculture, forestry and fisheries in-dustries, transport and tourism, water, and healthcare.

To strategically and effectively use the Japan-China High-Level Economic Dialogue.

To work together to make the East China Sea a "Sea of Peace, Cooperation and Friendship."

(4) Contribution to the Asia-Pacific region

The two sides agreed that Japan and China, as major countries in the Asia-Pacific region, would maintain close communication and strengthen their co-ordination and cooperation regarding issues in the region. They resolved to promote cooperation with priority on the following:

To jointly do the utmost to maintain peace and stability in the Northeast Asia region and to together promote the Six-Party Talks process. Moreover, both sides shared the recognition that the normalization of Japan-North Korea relations is of great significance to the peace and stability of the Northeast Asia region. The Chinese side welcomes and supports efforts to resolve the outstanding issues of concern between Japan and North Korea and normalize the bilateral relations.

To promote regional cooperation in East Asia based on the three principles of openness, transparency, and inclusiveness and to together promote the reali-zation of peace, prosperity, stability, and openness in Asia.

(5) Contribution to the resolution of global issues

The two sides agreed that, as Japan and China shoulder greater responsibi-lity for the peace and development of the world in the 21st century, they would strengthen coordination regarding key international issues and together pro-mote the building of a world that fosters lasting peace and common prosperity. The two sides resolved to engage in the following cooperation:

To actively participate in the building of an effective post-2012 international framework on climate change based on the Bali Action Plan and the principle of "common but differentiated responsibilities and respective capabilities" under the framework of the United Nations Framework Convention on Climate Change.

To strategically undertake effective cooperation and together make appropriate contribution to promote the resolution of global issues such as energy security, environmental protection, poverty, contagious diseases, and other global issues which are common challenges that the two countries face.

Prime Minister of Japan

Hu Jintao

President of the People's Republic of China

Fukuda Yasuo

Issued in Tokyo on May 7th, 2008

Chapter Five

References

Brief Introduction on Diaoyu Islands (Diaoyu Dao) and the Issue

Xiao Xiaobian

Known as, Diaoyu Island, in Chinese Pinyin Diàoyú Dǎo, and in English as Diaoyu Islands. The official Chinese title is "Diaoyu Islands and its affiliated islands" or "fishing islands", "fishing Leyu". In Hong Kong, Macao and Taiwan region they are called as "Diaoyutai" or "Diaoyutai Lieyu".

Natural Geography and Environment

Diaoyu Dao and its affiliated islands are located between 25°40'–26°00' N (North Latitude) and 123°20'–124°40' E (East Longitude), approximately 356 kilometers from Wenzhou City in Zhejiang Province, 385 kilometers from Fuzhou City in Fujian Province and 190 kilometers from Keelung City in Taiwan Province, the islands enjoy. a subtropical monsoon climate.

Diaoyu Dao and its affiliated islands, which consist of Diaoyu Dao, Huangwei Yu, Chiwei Yu, Nanxiao Dao, Beixiao Dao, Nan Yu, Bei Yu, Fei Yu and other islands and reefs, have approximately a total land mass of 5.69 square kilometers. Diaoyu Dao is the largest, with an area of about 3.90 square kilometers. It is comparatively flat on its northern side but rises steeply on its southeastern side. In shape it resembles a barbed fishing spear because of the jagged reefs to the east and central mountains running from east to west, and terrain is relatively flat in the north, southeast side of the steep are rocky, and looks like a harpoon, the east side of the reef looks like a minaret.

Diaoyu Islands is located in the East China Sea continental shelf, and are geographically part of Taiwan Island and lie in waters ranging from 140 to 180 meters in depth. To the east they are separated from the Ryukyu Islands by the 2,000-meter-deep Okinawa Trough. The turbulent Kuroshio currents that flow from southwest to northeast made it very difficult for ships to approach the islands at the west side of the Okinawa Trough from the east in ancient times. It is no accident, therefore, that the Chinese people were the first to discover and exploit the Diaoyu Dao Islands.

Diaoyu Dao and its affiliated islands are rich in camellia, palm, cactus, sea lotus and rare Chinese medicinal herbs. Many species of seabirds nest on the islands, and they have been called "the islands of flowers and birds." The surrounding waters are the traditional fishing grounds of Chinese fishermen with abundant fishery resources such as mackerel, bonito and lobster. There are also rich oil and natural gas in this area.

Diaoyu Dao (Islands) Has Been China's Inherent Territory since Ancient Times

Diaoyu Island and its affiliated islands have been China's inherent territory since ancient times, and China has indisputable sovereignty over the Diaoyu Islands and its adjacent sea areas. A large number of documents and historical data show that Diaoyu Dao was first discovered, named and exploited by China.

Diaoyu Dao has been part of China's territory since the early years of the Ming Dynasty. Chinese fishermen have exploited the islands and their adjacent waters for generations.

The earliest existent historical record of Diaoyu Dao is in the book Voyage with a Tail Wind (Shun Feng Xiang Song), in 1403 (the first year of the reign of Emperor Yongle of the Ming Dynasty). The book clearly shows the names of islands regularly passed by Chinese voyagers including "Diaoyu Yu" and "Chikan Yu" (known today as Diaoyu Dao and Chiwei Yu).

The imperial courts of the Ming and Qing dynasties sent imperial title-conferring envoys to the Ryukyu Kingdom 24 times. The Records of the Imperial Title-Conferring Envoys to Ryukyu (Shi Liu Qiu Lu) and voluminous materials left by the envoys depict the topography and geography of Diaoyu Dao in detail and clearly state that Diaoyu Dao and its affiliated islands are part of the China's territory. In 1534 (the 13th year of the reign of Emperor Jiajing of the Ming Dynasty), Chen Kan, an imperial title-conferring envoy from the Ming court to Ryukyu, stated in Records of the Imperial Title-Conferring Envoys to Ryukyu: "Diaoyu Yu, Huangmao Yu, Chi Yu, so many islands unfold before my eyes. Then Kume Mountain comes into sight; that is where the land of Ryukyu begins. The Ryukyuans on my ship start singing and dancing excitedly, because they know they have finally returned to their homes." The passage indicates that Ryukyuans believed they had arrived at Ryukyu when they saw Kume Mountain (known as Kumejima Island today) after passing Chi Yu (known as Chiwei Yu today). By 1534, all the major islands in the Diaoyu group had been identified and named by Chen Kanin in his book Shih Liu-Chiu Lu, or Record of the Imperial Envoy to Ryukyu. The Chinese continued to use these islands and considered them part of their kingdom. Chen Kanin's Record of the Imperial Envoy to Ryukyu helps explain the Diaoyu's position in relation to the Ryukyus. The Ryukyus were an independent kingdom up until their annexation by Japan during the late nineteenth century, and they regularly received envoys from the Chinese court on the mainland. These envoys used the Diaoyu as navigational markers during the China-to-Ryukyu voyages. Chen Kanin, sent by the Ming Emperor in 1534, wrote that the Ryukyu natives on board his vessel said nothing about reaching home until the boat neared Kume Island, further north from the Diaoyu.

Nowhere in Chinese records are the Diaoyu considered the territory of Ryukyu. Qing period (1644-1911) records substantiate Chinese ownership of the Diaoyu/Senkaku Islands prior to 1895. Envoy documents indicate that the islands reside inside the "border that separates Chinese and foreign lands." And according to Taiwan gazetteers, "Diaoyu Island accommodates ten or more large ships" under the jurisdiction of Kavalan, Taiwan.

Japan and the International Community Has Recognized Diaoyu Islands as Part of China in Explicit Terms

Until modern times, none of Japan's official historical accounts, national records or academic papers had ever challenged China's territorial sovereignty over Diaoyu Dao, and the Chinese names for the islands were used in all these documents. All Japanese maps published prior to the mid-19th century marked Diaoyu Dao and the mainland of China in the same color.

Accordingly, in 1785, the Japanese scholar Hayashi Shihei wrote the book Illustrated Outline of the Three Countries. An attached Map of the Three Provinces and 36 Islands of Ryukyu depicted Diaoyu Dao in the same color as the mainland of China, indicating that Diaoyu Tai (Diaoyu Dao), Chiwei Mountain (Chiwei Yu) and Huangwei Mountain (Huangwei Yu) were part of China's territory, and clearly separate from Ryukyu.

A Complete Map of the Ryukyu Islands attached to New Annals of Ryukyu which was published in Japan in 1873, A Map of Great Japan with Rectified Prefectures published in 1875, a Map of Great Japan, drawn up in 1876 by the General Staff Office of Japan's Army Ministry, and a Map of Okinawa published in the Annals of Okinawa in 1877 all excluded the Diaoyu Dao Islands. These islands were neither included in the "Maps and Names of Provinces and Cities of Japan" published as late as 1892.

Relevant 19th century documents and maps from Western countries including Britain, France, the United States and Spain also acknowledged that Diaoyu Dao belonged to China. A New Map of China from the Latest Authorities, published in Britain in 1811, marked Diaoyu Dao as part of China's territory. A Map of China's East Coast: Hong Kong to Gulf of Liao-Tung, compiled by the British Navy in 1877, identified the Diaoyu Dao Islands as affiliated to Taiwan Island and clearly separated them from Japan's Nansei Islands. This map was later widely referred to in international exchanges. A map of Asia drawn by the Spaniard J. P. Morales in 1879 marked Diaoyu Dao and Chiwei Yu as China's territory.

Consequently, it can be seen that China's sovereignty over the Diaoyu Islands has been recognized by countries around the world, including Japan.

Japan has grabbed the Diaoyu Islands

Japan's foreign ministry declared in its "Basic View of the Sovereignty over the Senkaku Islands": Since 1885 on, the Japanese government had repeatedly dispatched facts-finding missions to Senkaku İslands through authorities such as its Okinawa Prefecture, and has carefully confirmed that the Senkaku Islands are not only uninhabited islands but also have not been subjected to the rule of the Qing dynasty. Based on this, the Japanese government, on January 14th, 1895, at the Cabinet meeting it was formally decided that a stake should be set up on the island to be officially incorporated into our territory.

However, as mentioned above, historical facts prove that, Diaoyu Islands were not "uninhabited islands", instead the sovereignty of Diaoyu and its affiliated islands clearly belongs to China.

Japan's position is downright "grabbing". From the 1880s onwards, Japan began to soothe the Diaoyu Islands.

Between 1885 and 1893, Okinawa Prefecture three times requested permission from the Japanese government to place Diaoyu Dao under its jurisdiction and erect sovereignty markers. The Japanese government rejected the requests, fearing reaction from the Qing court. According to the Diplomatic Documentation of Japan, On a letter dated September 22, 1885, Okinawa Governor Nishimura Sutezo wrote to the Minister of Internal Affairs Yamagata Aritomo saying that the fact-finding missions, in fact, showed that these "uninhabited islands" were the same Diaoyu Tai, Huangwei Yu and Chiwei Yu that had been recorded in the Records of Messages from Chong-shan and were well known to imperial title-conferring envoys of the Qing court on their voyages to Ryukyu.

Japan started the first Sino-Japanese War in July 1894. Towards the end of November 1894, Japanese forces seized the Chinese port of Lushun (then known as Port Arthur), virtually securing defeat of the Qing court. Against such backdrop, the Japanese Minister of Internal Affairs Yasushi Nomura wrote to Foreign Minister Mutsu Munemitsu on December 27th saying "I am writing to discuss with you about placing sovereignty markers in Kuba-jima and Uotsuri-jima" (Huangwei Yu and Diaoyu Dao). "The circumstances have now changed and it is possible to submit this issue to the cabinet for reconsideration."

On April 17th, 1895, the Qing government was forced to sign the unequal "Treaty of Shimonoseki" with Japan, under which the entire island of Taiwan, together with all its affiliated islands, including Diaoyu Dao, were ceded to Japan. But in fact, at the time, the Japanese government neither set up sovereignty markers on Diaoyu Island and its affliated islands, nor did it include them in an imperial decree on the geographical scope of Okinawa Prefecture. Till the World War II, Japan has never announced that it had annexed the Diaoyu Islands.

Backroom deals between the United States and Japan Concerning Diaoyu Dao are illegal and invalid

During the Second World War, China declared the abolition of all Sino-Japanese treaties, including the Treaty of Shimonoseki.

In December 1943, China, the United States and the United Kingdom issued the Cairo Declaration, which stated in explicit terms that "all the territories Japan has stolen from the Chinese, such as Manchuria, Formosa (Taiwan) and the Pescadores, shall be restored to the Republic of China. Japan will also be expelled from all other territories which she has taken by violence and greed."

In July 1945, China, the US and the UK issued the Potsdam Declaration (The Soviet Union signed the Proclamation in August that year) which stated in Article 8: "The terms of the Cairo Declaration shall be carried out and Japanese sovereignty shall be limited to the islands of Honshu, Hokkaido, Kyushu, Shikoku and such minor islands as we determine." On August 15th, 1945, Japan accepted the Potsdam Declaration and surrendered unconditionally. On September 2nd, in Articles 1 and 6 of the Japanese Historical material of Surrender, the Japanese government pledged to faithfully fulfill the obligations enshrined in the provisions of the Potsdam Declaration. These documents all testify to the fact that Taiwan and its affiliated Diaoyu Dao should have been simultaneously returned to China.

On September 8th, 1951, the United States and a number of other countries, deliberately excluding China, and ignoring Soviet Union's objections signed the Treaty of Peace with Japan (commonly known as the Treaty of San Francisco), which placed the Nansei Islands south of the 29th parallel of north latitude under United Nations' trusteeship, with the United States as the sole administering authority. The islands placed under the administration of the United States in the treaty did not include the Diaoyu Dao Islands.

However, on December 25, 1953, the United States Civil Administration of the Ryukyu Islands (USCAR) issued Civil Administration Proclamation No. 27 defining the "geographical boundary lines of the Ryukyu Islands, including latitude 24°, longitude 122° area", thus arbitrarily expanded its jurisdiction to include China's Diaoyu Islands, reefs, rocks and territorial waters.

On June 17th, 1971, the United States and Japan signed the Agreement Concerning the Ryukyu Islands and the Daito Islands (the Okinawa Reversion Agreement), which provided that any and all powers of administration over the Ryukyu Islands and Diaoyu Dao would be "returned" to Japan.

On September 18, 1951, Zhou Enlai, the then Chinese Foreign Minister, made a solemn statement on behalf of the Chinese government that " the Treaty of Peace with Japan signed in San Francisco is illegal and invalid and can under no circumstances be recognized by the Chinese government since China has been excluded from its preparation, formulation and signing."

On December 30, 1971, the Chinese Ministry of Foreign Affairs issued a statement, saying that "it is completely illegal for the government of the United States and Japan to include China's Diaoyu Dao Islands into the territories to be returned to Japan in the Okinawa Reversion Agreement and that it can by no means change the People's Republic of China's territorial sovereignty over the Diaoyu Dao Islands". The Taiwan authorities and overseas Chinese also expressed strong opposition to the backroom deals between the United States and Japan over the Diaoyu Dao Islands. In the face of strong opposition from the Chinese government and people, the United States had to declare that no agreement or treaty was signed with Japan that included recognition of Japan's sovereignty over Diaoyu Islands. In October 1971, the United States administration publicly stated that "the United States believes that a return of administrative rights over those islands to Japan, from which the rights were received, can in no way prejudice any underlying claims. The United States cannot add to the legal rights Japan possessed before it transferred administration of the islands to us, nor can the United States, by giving back what it received, diminish the rights of other claimants. The United States has made no claim to Diaoyu Dao and considers that any conflicting claims to the islands is an issue to be resolved by the parties concerned."

On September 11, 1996, the United States administration once again declared: "The United States neither recognizes, nor supports the claim of any country to sovereignty over Diaoyu Dao". Till 2012, the US administration still reiterated that it does not take a position on the question of the ultimate sovereignty over Diaoyu Islands.

Thus it can be seen that the "legal basis" formulated by the Japanese government to justify its claim to "sovereignty" over Diaoyu Dao does not hold water.

China Resolutely Claims and Safeguards Its Sovereignty over Diaoyu Islands

The Diaoyu Dao Islands have always been China's inherent territory since ancient times. This is supported by historical facts and jurisprudential evidence. China does not recognize, and resolutely opposes, the unlawful and invalid treaty that Japan used to justify its theft of Diaoyu Islands.

China has always advocated the settlement of territorial disputes through peaceful negotiations. In the negotiations between China and Japan for the resumption of diplomatic relations in 1972, the two sides proceeded from the overall situation of Sino-Japanese friendship and agreed to suspend the issue of fishing islands and decided to wait for later proper conditions, that the issue can be settled then However, Japan did not stop its covert actions on the Diaoyu Islands issue.

Firstly, in recent years, sovereignty-infringing behavior by Japan such as encouraging right-wingers to land on the islands, constructing "lighthouses", leasing the Diaoyu Islands from their "private owners", "naming" the affiliated islands of Diaoyu Island and "purchasing" the islands was initiated by Japan as violations of the Sino-Japanese friendship Agreement, with the view of de facto and fait accompli—gaining control over the islands and makes attempts to gradually get recognition of the international community, for the de facto status of Diayou.

In response to Japan's violation of the territorial sovereignty over the Diaoyu Island, Chinese government has adopted a resolute and vigorous struggle. Diplomatically, the Chinese government made solemn representations to the Japanese government, and initiated a strong countermeasures,

All these show the firm determination and strong will to safeguard the sovereignty over the Diaoyu Islands. Chinese Foreign Ministers and Foreign Ministry spokesmen have, on different occasions, have clearly stated that Diaoyu Dao has always been China's inherent territory. China has solid and sufficient historical and legal basis to support this fact. Any unilateral action by Japan is invalid and will exert no influence on China's sovereignty over Diaoyu Dao. The fact that Diaoyu Dao belongs to China can never be changed and altered.

On September 10th, 2012, at the 20th APEC Informal Leaders' Meeting, Chinese President Hu Jintao said "China's stance on Diaoyu Dao is consistent and clear. Any attempt Japan makes to "purchase" the Diaoyu Islands is illegal and invalid and China resolutely rejects it. The Chinese government is steadfast in its defense of territorial integrity and sovereignty. Japan must be fully aware of the gravity of the situation and retreat from the wrong path. The two countries should join hands to safeguard the overall situation and development of Sino-Japanese relations."

China has adopted a series of legal measures to reaffirm its sovereignty over the Diaoyu Islands: On February 25, 1992, China promulgated the "People's Republic of China territorial waters and its adjoining law" in order to legally reaffirm that the Diaoyu Islands belongs to Chinese territory.

March 3, 2012, China officially announced the standard names of the Diaoyu Islands and its affiliated islands an islets.

On September 10, 2012, the Chinese government issued a statement announcing the baselines of the territorial sea of Diaoyu Dao and its affiliated islands.

On September 13, the Chinese government deposited the coordinates table and chart of the base points and baselines of the territorial sea of Diaoyu Islands and its affiliated islands and submitted the statement to Ban Ki-Moon, the Secretary-General of the United Nations.

China has indisputable territorial sovereignty over the uninhabited islands. China's marine surveillance vessels have been carrying out regular law enforcement patrol missions in the waters of Diaoyu Dao to safeguard sovereignty and exercise jurisdiction. China's fishery administration law enforcement vessels have been conducting regular law enforcement patrols and fishery protection missions to uphold normal fishing order in the waters of Diaoyu Dao.

The relevant departments of the Chinese government have ncorporated Diaoyu Islands and its adjacent waters into the National Sea Area Dynamic Surveillance, Monitoring and Management System, as well as the National Islands Monitoring and Surveillance System. China has also begun releasing weather forecasts and marine environmental forecasts for Diaoyu Dao.

Editor: Xiao Xiao

The Sino-Japanese War

1894-1895

Li Xiaoxiao

The Sino-Japanese War (August 1, 1894 - April 17, 1895) was fought between Qing Dynasty, China and Meiji, Japan, primarily over control of Korea. After the defeat in the Sino-Japanese War, the Qing government was forced to sign the humiliating Treaty of Shimonoseki after the Nanjing Treaty, once again, the Chinese nation fell into abyss of disaster.

Causes of the War and Military Preparations by Two Sides

Japan had already planned this war against China for a long time. As early as in 1868, at the beginning of Meiji period, Japan began to implement and advocate militarism and promoted the basic policy of expansion targeting Korea and China. The Meiji government sped up the military reform and began to implement modern military education and training, and actively expanded militarization for war. Before the outbreak of the Sino-Japanese War, the Japanese army established six field divisions and one Imperial Guard, consisting of 123,000 soldiers. In the Sino-Japanese War, Japan had 240,616 soldiers, among which, there were 174,017 soldiers fighting in the foreign countries. Before the Sino-Japanese War, Japan had 32 navy ships, 24 torpedo warships with displacement amount to 62,000 tons. Japan also sent a large number of agents to China and Korea to gather military intelligence and drew detailed military maps.

The Qing government noticed Japan's ambition of aggression. Li Hongzhang, the Beiyang Minister once pointed out that Japan would be the enemy of China. In 1874, Japan's invasion of Taiwan, especially after the Sino-French War, the Qing government strengthened the construction of coastal defense with Beiyang as the key security space and Japan as the main defense target. The Beiyang navy was formally established in 1888 with 25 naval ships and 4000 officers and soldiers. Before the Sino-Japanese War, three main naval bases in Dagu, Weihaiwei (today's Weihai, Shandong) and Lushun (today's Dalian, Liaoning) were built. But due to the political corruption in the Qing dynasty, the military reform remained in the basic stage and could not be developed further, although total armed forces had increased to 800000 people, due to the improper and backward system, and management drawbacks, and laxity in military training, fighting capacity of the army was low.

In the spring of 1894, Tonghak Uprising broke out in Korea, the Korean government asked China for help on June 3th; the first troops of the Qing government arrived there on June 8. As early as June 2nd, the Japanese Cabinet decided to invade Korea and directly fought against the troops of the Qing government. Japan firstly lured the Oing troops into Korea, but when troops of the Qing Dynasty entered the Korean territory, Japan excused that it wanted to protect its embassy and expatriates in Korea, thus Japan also sent troops into Korea; the Japanese troops quickly seized the strategic positions such as Inchon and Seoul At the same time, it set up a centralized supreme state body to prepare and command the war of aggression. On July 19, Ototi Keisuke, Japan's envoy to Korea, led by Foreign Minister Mutsu Munemitsu forced the Korean government to abolish the China-Korea trade treaty and expel Qing's troops from its territory. On July 23, 1894 the Japanese troops brazenly captured the Korean palace Gyeongbok (the state center) and set up a puppet government headed by Heungseon Daewongun. On July 25, Heungseon Daewongun announced the abolition of all the China-Korea treaties and "authorized" the Japanese troops to expel China's Qing's army in Asan. Japan also cut the Chinese supply lines for its garrison at Asan by a naval blockade, On the same day, Japan Combined Fleet launched the Toshima Battle, it attacked China's troopships and frigates in the nearby waters of Toshima. On July 29, The Japanese army's 9th brigade also attacked the Qing troops in Seonghwan, the Qing troops retreated to Pyongyang. On August 1st, the Qing government was forced to declare war against Japan. On the same day, Meiji Emperor also issued a rescript of war declaration.

Strategies of the Warring Parties

Before instigating this war, Japan's war headquarters had established the "concept of operations"—by overall consideration of navy and ground forces. Its strategic aim was to fight the key battle with Qing's troops in China's Zhili (today's Hebei) and then further defeat Qing's troops in order to oppress the Qing government. Japan thought that the key lay in the outcome of the naval warfare. Therefore, they put forward a two-stage battle plan: firstly, they sent some ground forces to Korea in order to contain Qing's army; if they won the naval battle and seized the control over Yellow Sea, the ground forces would land on Bohai Bay, and fight the decisive battle on Zhili Plains. Reversely, if they lost the naval battle, they would control the Korea Strait with fleets, which would assist the main army to occupy the entire Korea; if they lost the decisive sea battle and China would seize the control over Yellow Sea, they would implement homeland defense with the main ground forces, and defend Japan's coast with naval forces. They would spare no effort to realize the first basic strategy.

While Qing's army hadn't prepared a clear strategy or operational plans before the war. Due to the ambiguous attitudes and inner divisions in the government, the Qing government had neither established the special war operations command headquarter in advance nor had a clear war strategy. At the beginning, China mainly relied on the "peaceful mediation" efforts of other major countries such as Russia and Britain, but in the later stage, it hastily declared war on Japan and ordered Beiyang Ministry Li Hongzhang to send the army to suppress the enemy as rapid as possible", if Li's army would meet the ships of the Japanese army along the Yangtze river or coasts, Li would attack and fight against them. It was actually a strategic plan of defense in the sea and attack on the land. On this basis, the Qing court decided to deploy the army to Korea and gather them in Pyongyang (Korea), there the Chinese army would expel the Japanese army towards south; each naval fleet would defense their protection zones; China's strong Beiyang Fleet would concentrate its forces in the north of the Yellow Sea, and guard the Bohai Strait, and ensuring the safety of the capital city and would support the army which would be fighting in Korea by coordinated actions.

The Process of War

The war lasted almost nine months, according to the changes in regard to battlefields and the strategical situation, it can be roughly divided into three stages.

The first stage: Qing's ground forces had retreat to Yalu river of Korea due to the failure in Pyongyang wars and the Japanese navy seized the control over Yellow Sea. In early August, Wei Rugui, Ma Yukun, Zou Bao, the commander-in-chief and deputy commander-in-chief Feng Shenge led an army of more than 10,000 troops around Pyongyang, while, the Japanese army had a total of more than 8,000 troops.

In mid-August, Japan's supreme headquarter modified its first stage "concept of operation" according to the unpredictable time of the main naval battle and due to its incapacity to develop the decisive battle in Zhili Plain of China. Besides the 5th division, Japan's war headquarter, also sent the 3rd division into the war and the two divisions jointly formed the First Army. Japan's ground forces in Korea aimed to attack rather than to defend and contain, Japan's First Army Group was in charge of the battle in Pyongyang region, and then they would attack Fengtian (today's Shenyang) as planned. At the same time, Japan decided to form the Second Army Group and which would wait for the best opportunity to attack and occupy the Liaodong Peninsula which would be the frontal battles for the decisive battle on Zhili Plain.

In early September, the Japanese 5th Division and 3rd Division set off from Seoul to Pyongyang in four directions in order to surround the Qing's army. The Admiral Ye Zhichao who just lost the battle in Seonghwan was the commander of Qing's army in Pyongyang# but because he was inexperienced in war strategies, the fighting spirit of his army had weakened. On September 15th, the Japanese army attacked Pyongyang from 3 directions, the battles were very fierce. In the afternoon, Xuanwumen district was lost. In the evening, Ye Zhichao abandoned this city and ran away. On September 26th, all the Chinese forces had retreated to the northern borders of China borders, to the banks of the Yalu River.

While the armies were fighting in the Korean Peninsula, Japan's Allied Navy Fleet sailed to the west of the Yellow Sea and even challenged Weihaiwei and Lushun Naval Port of China, and prepared to fight the main battle to topple the strong Chinese Navy, i.e., the Beiyang Fleet. China's Beiyang Fleet stayed between Weihaiwei and Lushun according to the central government's order of "safeguarding the ship to contain the enemy", due this wrong strategy the control of the Yellow Sea passed to Japan after the Toshima Sea Battle. In early September, China's Beiyang Fleet was ordered to defend the army troops who were fighting battles around Pyongyang (Korea). On September 17th, when Beiyang Fleet was retreating to its base, it encountered Japan's Allied Navy Fleet, where the famous Naval Yellow Sea Battle broke out.

The battle lasted 5 hours, wherein Beiyang Fleet lost 5 fleets and 4 was damaged while Japan's Allied Fleet lost ships.

In the first stage, Japan timely adjusted the battle plan of using navy forces and ground forces in a coordinated manner at the same time. In Pyongyang, Japanese forces not only defeated the Qing's army, and pushed the battle to Yalu River, thus directly threatened China's mainland. Since Qing's army was defeated in Pyongyang and its strategic plan of "defense in the seas and attack on the land" had failed; besides, it was too late for them to maneuver for a strong defense, which also determined the second stage the war, thus the Qing's army entered the second stage in a disadvantaged status. And in the naval battles, especially in the Naval Battle of the Yellow Sea, Beiyang Fleet's strength had severely weakened, the Japanese Allied Navy Fleet had achieved its goal of controlling the Yellow Sea, thus Japan's the first strategic plan was achieved.

The second stage: the Japanese forces broke through the defense line of the Yalu River, and landed at Huayuankou; after the battle of Pyongyang and Battle of Yalu River, Japan implemented its plan of the decisive battle in Zhili Plains, accordingly deployed the Second Army Group to land on Liaodong Peninsula to break through the Bohai Bay. First Army Group would attack Qing's defense line at the Yalu River and imposed massive pressure to Fengtian region where lay the mausoleum of the ancestors of the Qing Dynasty, to support the operations of Second Army Group. While the Qing court adopted Li Hongzhang's balanced strategy: "defending the Bohai Sea to save the mainland and Shenyang region which is the critical place in the East". In terms of actual deployment, the Japanese troops were largely deployed around the Yalu River, Fengtian and Shengyang—these regions were Japan's main attack direction—later it proved that Japan's main attack direction, was a wrong judgment—in fact Japan had attached too much importance to the ancestors' mausoleum of the Qing Dynasty. At the same time, to defend Beijing, Li Hongzhang ordered the other provinces to send more troops to defend the land between the Great Wall of Shanhaiguan (Shanhai Pass) and the Qinhuang Island as well as Tianjin, Dagu, Tongzhou, etc. But this led to the shortage of troops in the Liaodong Peninsula which guarded the door of Bohai Sea. There were almost temporary defense troops, along with the Yellow Sea being controlled by Japan,which meant that the Qing Empire was weak against a naval attack by Japan.

The defensive battle of Yalu River began on October 24th. The number of Qing's army defending the north shore of Yalu River was about 30,000. The Sichuan Admiral Song Qing was the commander. The defense line was divided into three sections: middle, east and west, together with Jiulian City as the main defensive position. The deployment of troops was designed as a long line, but the coordination between divisions were weak, and there were no strong reserves deep inside. The Japanese First Army Group successfully broke through the Anping River, the upstream of the Jiulian City, then they built a pontoon over

Yalu River near the Tiger Mountain and planned to attack the Tiger Mountain. Other Chinese divisions heard that Tiger Mountain was lost and fled without a fight. On October 26th, the Japanese army occupied Jiulian City and Anton (today's Dandong). Qing's defensive line of Yalu River had collapsed.

On the same day when the Japanese First Army Group attacked Qing's defensive line of Yalu River, General Oyama Iwao commanded the Japanese Second Army Group with 25,000 troops, with the strong support of Japanese fleets, which had landed at Huayuankou of Lushun. The Japanese landing activity lasted more than 10 days, but Qing's army turned a blind eye to it. On November 6th, the Japanese army invaded Jinzhou (now belonging to Dalian). On November 7th, the Japanese army attacked at the Dalian Bay from three directions, Japan forces observing that Qing's defense forces were too weak, were quite enthusiastic, accordingly, easily and rapidly occupied the Dalian Bay. On November 17th, the Japanese army began to threaten Lushun, but the coordination between the seven generals who were in charge of defending Lushun was weak, so the fighting spirit of 14,000 officers and soldiers was feeble. On November 18th, the vanguard troops of the army attacked Tuchengzi, among the generals only Xu Bangdao, the commander-in-chief, led his forces bravely to fight against the Japanese vanguard troops. On November 22, the Japanese army occupied Lushun (Machuria), killing many adult males who offered resistance. Chinese casualties were officially estimated at 4000 dead. The Japanese lost only 29 men killed, 233 wounded.

The second stage marked, that Qing's army was at an inferior position in the war. Inside the Qing court circles, there was the psychology of making peace with Japan. After the fall of Lushun, the Japanese navy captured the important front base of Bohai Bay. From then on, after the Bohai Bay resistance was defeated, Qing's Beiyang Fleet hid in Weihaiwei, the situation was plummeting.

The third stage: Qing's troops were defeated in the two battlefields of Shandong Peninsula and Liaodong; after the Japan's invasion of Lushun, the Japanese supreme headquarters considered that Bohai Bay would freeze in winter, which would make it difficult for sea manoeuvre, therefore Japan decided to delay the plan of fighting the decisive battle at the Zhili Plain, alternatively, Japan planned to attack Weihaiwei and destroy Qing's Beiyang Fleet, in order to provide a strategic guarantee for the decisive battle at the Zhili Plain. Second Army Group started to train its "combat troops in Shandong" which were around 25000 troops led by Admiral Oyama Iwao, the Allied Navy Fleet planned to cooperate with the troops in Shandong, while First Army Group would undertake a fake attack against Qing's forces in Liaodong forces, so that Qing's army would concentrate its main forces around Liaodong.

The Qing court once again misjudged Japan's main attack direction, it estimated that Japan's First Army Group and Second Army Group would attack Fengtian and break through Jingzhou, pressure Shanhai Pass and prepare to attack Beijing by landing into the Bohai Bay. Therefore, Qing's army with 100,000 troops were deployed around Fengtian, Liaoyang, Tianjin, and Shanhai Pass; but only 30,000 people were deployed around Japan's attack target regions, among which only 14,000 people were sent to defend Rongcheng (today's Jiurongcheng), while Qing's Beiyang Fleet still hid in Weihaiwei in accord with Li Hongzhang's defensive strategy of "Water-land dependency".

On January 20, 1895, Japan's "combat troops in Shandong" landed on the Longxu Island of Rongcheng and occupied Rongcheng. The campaign had begun on 18 January 1895 with a bombardment of the town of Dengzhou, some 100 miles (160 km) to the west of Weihaiwei, by the Imperial Japanese Navy cruisers Yoshino, Akitsushima, and Naniwa. This was a diversion to draw attention away from the landing of the Imperial Japanese Army's Japanese Second Army under the overall command of General Oyama Iwao at Rongcheng, to the east of Weihaiwei. The Japanese forces, which consisted of the 2nd Division under Lieutenant General Sakuma Samata, and the 6th Division (less its 12th Brigade, which was left to garrison Lushunkou) under General Kuroki Tamemoto completed its landing without opposition by 22 January. The Japanese divided into two columns, one following the coastal road, and the other struggling along a path some four miles inland, both departing Roncheng on 26 January. The timing of the attack had been planned to coincide with Chinese New Year, and the invasion encountered no resistance as they converged on Weihaiwei on 29 January. The Japanese launched a three-pronged attack on the landward fortifications to the south and east of the town on 30 January.

On January 30, fortifications in the South of Weihaiwei was destroyed. On February 1st, Japanese troops occupied Weihaiwei. Afterwards, Japan used both navy forces and ground forces to attack Liugong Island and the Beiyang Fleet, people such as Admiral Ding Ruchang committed suicide due to humiliation. On February 17, Weihaiwei naval base was lost and Beiyang Fleet was completely destroyed.

The battle of Liaodong had lasted long. After the Japanese army broke through the defense line of the Yalu River, it occupied Fenghuang City (today's Fengcheng in Liaoning), Xiuyan, Haicheng, etc. In order to change the war situation, the Qing government appointed Liu Kunyi as the Imperial Commissioner and endowed him with the full command of military affairs domestically, and externally, it also appointed governor of Hunan, Wu Dacheng and Song Qing as the deputy of military affairs. On January 17, 1895, Qing's army faced some setbacks when conducting several large-scale counter-offensive attacks around Haicheng. On February 28th, the Japanese army started an attack around Haicheng. On March 4th, Japan occupied Niuzhuang (now the northwest of Haicheng) and on March 7th, it occupied Yingkou; on March 9th, it occupied Tianzhuangtai (today's Dawanan). Within 10 days, more than 100 divisions with 60,000 troops were defeated in Liaodong.

Soon after Japan occupied the Liaodong Peninsula, the Qing court sought ways to strike peace deal with Japan through diplomatic channels. The Qing court was even more eager to make peace with Japan after losing Weihaiwei. Therefore, the Qing court appointed Li Hongzhang as the plenipotentiary to implement the peace negotitaions with Japan. On April 17, Treaty of Shimonoseki was signed and the Sino-Japanese War was ended. Japan had achieved its expectations of aggression without fighting the decisive battle at the Zhili Plain.

The Sino-Japanese War had a profound influence on the Far East's military-political strategic pattern. Japan occupied Taiwan, and won 230 million taels as war reparations, by virtue of which, as a turning point, its monopoly capitalist economy developed rapidly. Japan further expanded it militarization and also became the main source of aggressive wars in the Far East. Moreover, the rise of Japan changed the main original pattern – the opposition and hegemony struggles between Britain and Russia in the Far East. Competition among major powers in the Far East became increasingly fierce, which indicates that the region had ushered in a more turbulent era.

The failure of the Sino-Japanese War has accelerated China's becoming semi-colonial country and China's national crisis become increasingly grave; and at the same time, it also prompted the awakening of the Chinese nation; the bourgeois reform movements and Boxer Rebellion rose rapidly. Under this difficult situation, the Qing government also began to reform its military system and the military reform in modern China began to enter into a full-fledged stage.

The Treaty of Shimonoseki

April 1895

His Majesty the Emperor of Japan and His Majesty the Emperor of China, desiring to restore the blessings of peace to their countries and subjects and to remove all cause for future complications, have named as their Plenipotentiaries for the purpose of concluding a Treaty of Peace, that is to say:

His Majesty the Emperor of Japan, Count ITO Hirobumi, Junii, Grand Cross of the Imperial Order of Paullownia, Minister President of State; and Viscount MUTSU Munemitsu, Junii, First Class of the Imperial Order of the Sacred Treasure, Minister of State for Foreign Affairs.

And His Majesty the Emperor of China, LI Hung-chang, Senior Tutor to the Heir Apparent, Senior Grand Secretary of State, Minister Superintendent of Trade for the Northern Ports of China, Viceroy of the province of Chili, and Noble of the First Rank; and LI Ching-fong, Ex-Minister of the Diplomatic Service, of the Second Official Rank:

Who, after having exchanged their full powers, which were found to be in good and proper form, have agreed to the following Articles:—

Article 1

China recognizes definitively the full and complete independence and autonomy of Korea, and, in consequence, the payment of tribute and the performance of ceremonies and formalities by Korea to China, in derogation of such independence and autonomy, shall wholly cease for the future.

Article 2

China cedes to Japan in perpetuity and full sovereignty the following territories, together with all fortifications, arsenals, and public property thereon:—

(a) The southern portion of the province of Fengtian within the following boundaries:

The line of demarcation begins at the mouth of the River Yalu and ascends that stream to the mouth of the River An-ping, from thence the line runs to Feng-huang, from thence to Hai-cheng, from thence to Ying-kow, forming a line which describes the southern portion of the territory. The places above named are included in the ceded territory. When the line reaches the River Liao at Ying-kow, it follows the course of the stream to its mouth, where it terminates. The mid-channel of the River Liao shall be taken as the line of demarcation.

This cession also includes all islands appertaining or belonging to the province of Fêngtien situated in the eastern portion of the Bay of Liao-tung and the northern portion of the Yellow Sea.

(b) The island of Formosa, together with all islands appertaining or belonging to the said island of Formosa.

(c) The Pescadores Group, that is to say, all islands lying between the 119th and 120th degrees of longitude east of Greenwich and the 23rd and 24th degrees of north latitude.

Article 3

The alignment of the frontiers described in the preceding Article, and shown on the annexed map, shall be subject to verification and demarcation on the spot by a Joint Commission of Delimitation, consisting of two or more Japanese and two or more Chinese delegates, to be appointed immediately after the exchange of the ratification of this Act. In case the boundaries laid down in this Act are found to be defective at any point, either on account of topography or in consideration of good administration, it shall also be the duty of the Delimitation Commission to rectify the same.

The Delimitation Commission will enter upon its duties as soon as possible, and will bring its labors to a conclusion within the period of one year after appointment.

The alignments laid down in this Act shall, however, be maintained until the rectifications of the Delimitation Commission, if any are made, shall have received the approval of the Governments of Japan and China.

Article 4

China agrees to pay to Japan as a war indemnity the sum of 200,000,000 Kuping taels; the said sum to be paid in eight installments. The first installment of 50,000,000 taels to be paid within six months, and the second installment of 50,000,000 to be paid within twelve months, after the exchange of the ratification of this Act. The remaining sum to be paid in six equal installments as follows: the first of such equal annual installments to be paid within two years, the second within three years, the third within four years, the fourth within five years, the fifth within six years, and the sixth within seven years, after the exchange of the ratification of this Act. Interest at the rate of 5 per centum per annum shall begin to run on all unpaid portions of the said indemnity from the date the first installment falls due.

China shall, however, have the right to pay by anticipation at any time any or all of the said installments. In case the whole amount of the said indemnity is paid within three years after the exchange of the ratification of the present Act all interest shall be waived, and the interest for two years and a half or for any less period, if any already paid, shall be included as part of the principal amount of the indemnity.

Article 5

The inhabitants of the territories ceded to Japan who wish to take up their residence outside the ceded districts shall be at liberty to sell their real property and retire. For this purpose a period of two years from the date of the exchange of ratification of the present Act shall be granted. At the expiration of that period those of the inhabitants who shall not have left such territories shall, at the option of Japan, be deemed to be Japanese subjects.

Each of the two Governments shall, immediately upon the exchange of the ratification of the present Act, send one or more Commissioners to Formosa to effect a final transfer of that province, and within the space of two months after the exchange of the ratification of this Act such transfer shall be completed

Article 6

All Treaties between Japan and China having come to an end as a consequence of war, China engages, immediately upon the exchange of the ratification of this Act, to appoint Plenipotentiaries to conclude with the Japanese

Plenipotentiaries, a Treaty of Commerce and Navigation and a Convention to regulate Frontier Intercourse and Trade. The Treaties, Conventions, and Regulations now subsisting between China and the European Powers shall serve as a basis for the said Treaty and Convention between Japan and China. From the date of the exchange of ratification of this Act until the said Treaty and Convention are brought into actual operation, the Japanese Governments, its officials, commerce, navigation, frontier intercourse and trade, industries, ships, and subjects, shall in every respect be accorded by China most favoured nation treatment.

China makes, in addition, the following concessions, to take effect six months after the date of the present Act:—

First.—The following cities, towns, and ports, in addition to those already opened, shall be opened to the trade, residence, industries, and manufactures of Japanese subjects, under the same conditions and with the same privileges and facilities as exist at the present open cities, towns, and ports of China:

Shashih, in the province of Hupeh.

Chungking, in the province of Szechwan.

Suchow, in the province of Kiangsu.

Hangchow, in the province of Chekiang.

The Japanese Government shall have the right to station consuls at any or all of the above named places.

Second.—Steam navigation for vessels under the Japanese flag, for the conveyance of passengers and cargo, shall be extended to the following places:

On the Upper Yangtze River, from Ichang to Chungking.

On the Woosung River and the Canal, from Shanghai to Suchow and Hangchow.

The rules and regulations that now govern the navigation of the inland waters of China by Foreign vessels shall, so far as applicable, be enforced, in respect to the above named routes, until new rules and regulations are conjointly agreed to.

Third.—Japanese subjects purchasing goods or produce in the interior of China, or transporting imported merchandise into the interior of China, shall have the right temporarily to rent or hire warehouses for the storage of the articles so purchased or transported without the payment of any taxes or extractions whatever.

Fourth.—Japanese subjects shall be free to engage in all kinds of manufacturing industries in all the open cities, towns, and ports of China, and shall be at liberty to import into China all kinds of machinery, paying only the stipulated import duties thereon.

All articles manufactured by Japanese subjects in China shall, in respect of inland transit and internal taxes, duties, charges, and exactions of all kinds, and also in respect of warehousing and storage facilities in the interior of China, stand upon the same footing and enjoy the same privileges and exemptions as merchandise imported by Japanese subjects into China.

In the event additional rules and regulations are necessary in connexion with these concessions, they shall be embodied in the Treaty of Commerce and Navigation provided for by this Article.

Article 7

Subject to the provisions of the next succeeding Article, the evacuation of China by the armies of Japan shall be completely effected within three months after the exchange of the ratifications of the present Act.

Article 8

As a guarantee of the faithful performance of the stipulations of this Act, China consents to the temporary occupation by the military forces of Japan of Weihaiwei, in the province of Shantung.

Upon payment of the first two installments of the war indemnity herein stipulated for and the exchange of the ratification of the Treaty of Commerce and navigation, the said place shall be evacuated by the Japanese forces, provided the Chinese Government consents to pledge, under suitable and sufficient arrangements, the Customs revenue of China as security for the payment of the principal and interest of the remaining installments of the said indemnity. In the event that no such arrangements are concluded, such evacuation shall only take place upon the payment of the final installment of said indemnity.

It is, however, expressly understood that no such evacuation shall take place until after the exchange of the ratification of the Treaty of Commerce and Navigation.

Article 9

Immediately upon the exchange of the ratification of this Act, all prisoners of war then held shall be restored, and China undertakes not to ill-treat or punish prisoners of war so restored to her by Japan. China also engages to at once release all Japanese subjects accused of being military spies or charged with any other military offences. China further engages not to punish in any manner, nor to allow to be punished, those Chinese subjects who have in any manner been compromised in their relations with the Japanese army during the war.

Article 10

All offensive military operations shall cease upon the exchange of the ratification of this Act.

Article 11

The present Act shall be ratified by their Majesties the Emperor of Japan and the Emperor of China, and the ratification shall be exchanged at Chefoo on the 8th day of the 5th month of the 28th year of MEIJI, corresponding to the 14th day of the 4th month of the 21st year of Guang Xu.

In witness whereof the respective Plenipotentiaries have signed the same and affixed thereto the seal of their arms.

LI HUNG-CHANG,   [L.S.]

Plenipotentiary of His Majesty the Emperor of China

Senior Tutor to the Heir Apparent

Senior Grand Secretary of State

Minister Superintendent of Trade for the Northern Ports of China

Viceroy of the province of Chili

Noble of the First Rank

LI CHING-FONG

Plenipotentiary of His Majesty the Emperor of China

Ex-Minister of the Diplomatic Service, of the Second Official Rank

Count ITO HIROBUMI,   [L.S.]

Junii, Grand Cross of the Imperial Order of Paullownia

Minister President of State

Plenipotentiary of His Majesty the Emperor of Japan

Viscount MUTSU MUNEMITSU,   [L.S.]

Junii, First Class of the Imperial Order of the Sacred Treasure

Minister of State for Foreign Affairs

Plenipotentiary of His Majesty the Emperor of Japan

Separate Articles to the Treaty of Shimonoseki relating to Weihaiwei

Article 1

The Japanese military forces which are, under Article 7 of theTreaty of Peace signed this day, to temporarily occupy Weihaiwei shall not exceed one brigade; and from the date of the exchange of the ratification of the said Treaty of Peace China shall pay annually one-quarter of the amount of the expenses of such temporary occupation, that is to say, at the rate of 500,000 Kuping taels per annum.

Article 2

The territory temporarily occupied at Weihaiwei shall comprise the islands of Liu-kung and a belt of land 5 Japanese ri wide along the entire coastline of the Bay of Weihaiwei.

No Chinese troops shall be permitted to approach or occupy any places within a zone of 5 Japanese ri wide beyond the boundaries of the occupied territory.

Article 3

The civil administration of the occupied territory shall remain in the hands of the Chinese authorities. But such authorities shall at all times be obliged to conform to the orders which the Commander of the Japanese army of occupation may deem it necessary to give in the interest of the health, maintenance, security, distribution, or discipline of the troops.

All military offences committed within the occupied territory shall be subject to the jurisdiction of the Japanese military authorities.

The forgoing Separate Articles shall have the same force, value and effect as if they had been word for word inserted in the Treaty of Peace signed this day.

In witness whereof the respective Plenipotentiaries have signed the same and affixed thereto the seal of their arms.

Done in Shimonoseki, in duplicate, this 17th day of the 4th month of the 28th year of MEIJI, corresponding to the 23rd day of the 3rd month of the 21st year of Guang Xu.

The Signing Process of Treaty of Shimonoseki

China signed the humiliating treaty in 1895

After the Meiji Restoration, Japan aimed to expand its territory and its strategic targets in the west were Korea and Mainland China. In 1876, Japan forced Korea to sign the first unequal treaty—Jianghua Treaty, by virtue of which, the Japanese invasion forces entered Korea. The Chinese Qing Dynasty and Korea had suzerain-vassal relations which was undermined by Japan who tried to trigger and sharpen conflicts between Korea and China. Signed between China and Japan in March 1885, Special Articles of the Tianjin Treaty between China and Jjapan stipulated equal status to China and Japan over Korea. Then Japan planned further expansion of militarization targeting China.

In the spring of 1894, the Tonghak Rebellion broke out in Korea; the Korea government turned to China for help; initially the Japanese government said it had no objection to China's sending troops; but when troops of the Qing Dynasty entered into Korea, Japan announced an excuse that its aim was to protect its embassy and expatriates in Korea, so Japan also sent its troops into Korea. The Japanese forces attacked China's Beiyang fleet on July 25, which had triggered the Sino-Japanese War. Then, the navies of the two countries fought the Yellow Sea battle. The Armies fought in the broad regions from Korea to Fengtian (today's Liaoning), Japan occupied a large territory of China. In the beginning of 1895, Japan occupied the strategic Weihai in the Shandong Province. The Qing government chose to beg for peace, eventually, The Qing government appointed Li Hongzhang to negotiate a peace treaty with Prime Minister Ito Hirobumi, the Japan's authorized representative and Foreign Minister Mutsu Munemitsu in the Shimonoseki City, of Japan.

On March 20, the two sides met at Sunpanro. Li Hongzhang demanded a truce agreement before the peace negotiations; Japan put forward 4 harsh conditions such as the occupation of Tianjin, which forced Li to give up the cease-fire agreement. After the meeting on March 24, Li was attacked by a ronin (samurai warrior in feudal Japan) when driving back to the Chinese embassy. Japanese governments was worried about a third country's interference, so it rapidly announced its commitment to the cease-fire. On March 30, both parties signed a truce treaty—a truce period of 21 days; the truce scope was limited to the regions of Fengtian, Zhili and Shandong. At that time, the Japanese troops had already occupied the Penghu Islands, and threatened Taiwan, the truce excluded these regions, thus Japan's military activities an pressure remained in this region. On April 1st, Japan put forward harsher terms. Li Hongzhang begged for the revision of these terms. On April 10th, Japan put forward its last amendments and threatened China to make it clear whether it would accept or not, without further discussion. Under the threat of Japan, the Qing government had to accept the terms. On April 17th, Li Hongzhang signed the humiliating Treaty of Shimonoseki.

Treaty of Shimonoseki (also known as Sunpanro Treaty) contained total 11 articles, with "Separate Articles" and "Protocol on Special Articles". The main content of the treaty was as follows:

(1) China recognizes definitively the full and complete independence and autonomy of Korea and Japan's control over Korea;

(2) China cedes Liaodong Peninsula, the island of Formosa (Taiwan), together with all islands appertaining or belonging to the said island of Formosa, and the Pescadores island group to Japan;

(3) China agrees to pay to Japan as the war indemnity, the sum of 200,000,000 Kuping taels;

(4) China opens Shashih, Chungking, Soochow and Hangchow to Japan. Moreover, the Japanese Government shall have the right to station consuls at any or all of the above named places; steam navigation for vessels under the Japanese flag can the convey passengers and cargo;

(5) Japanese subjects shall be free to engage in all kinds of manufacturing industries in all the open cities, towns, and ports of China, and shall be at liberty to import into China all kinds of machinery, paying only the stipulated import duties thereon.

(6) As a guarantee of the faithful performance of the stipulations of this Act, China consents to the temporary occupation by the military forces of Japan of Weihaiwei; and from the date of the exchange of the ratification of the said Treaty of Peace China shall pay annually one-quarter of the amount of the expenses of such temporary occupation, that is to say, at the rate of 500,000 Kuping taels per annum;

(7) Immediately upon the exchange of the ratification of this Act, all war prisoners of war then held shall be freed, and China undertakes not to ill-treat or punish prisoners of war so restored to her by Japan. China also engages to at once release all Japanese subjects accused of being military spies or charged with any other military offenses. China further engages not to punish in any manner, nor to allow to be punished, those Chinese subjects who have in any manner been compromised in their relations with the Japanese army during the war.

The Influence of Treaty of Shimonoseki on the Chinese Society

The Treaty of Shimonoseki was the most serious unequal treaty since after the Treaty of Nanjing; it had brought serious harm to modern China society, it became an important step by the imperialist forces to transform China into the semi-feudal and the semi-colonial society.

(1) large territories were ceded to Japan such as Taiwan, which further inf-ringed the sovereignty of China, stimulated the imperialist ambitions of various powers to dismember China, national crisis of China had deepened.

(2) the huge reparation payment to Japan had increased the economic burden over the Chinese people. At the same time, it accelerated the development of Japanese militarism. The external debt of the Qing government had greatly increased, which gave the major world powers the opportunity to control the lifeblood of China's economy.

(3) the opening of trading ports enabled the imperialist forces to penetrate into mainland China.

(4) allowing the foreign invested production factories in China have serio-usly hindered the development of China's national capitalism.

Treaty of Shimonoseki demonstrated new imperialism based on monopo-listic capitalist trusts, their aggressive attempts to partition the world among themselves through wars. Consequently foreign capitalists' aggression against China has entered a new stage; the degree of China's semi-colonial status was greatly deepened.

(5) Treaty of Shimonoseki has greatly deepened the national crisis of China.

Documents on the Cession of Taiwan to Japan

June 2nd, 1895, Keelung City

Li Xiaoxiao

On the base of Term 2 of Article 5 in Treaty of Shimonoseki, Taiwan was ceded to Japan at the witness of Qing (Chinese) Emperor and Japan's Emperor.

The Qing Emperor sent Li Jingfang (also known as Li Ching-fong), who has the second highest degree in the imperial examinations (the 2nd degree Ding Dai), serving as the Qing minister to Japan.

The Emperor of Japan sent viscount Kabayama Sukenori to be the first Japanese Governor-General of Taiwan. Kabayama Sukenori was a respected Count with the order of the Rising Sun (first class).

Li and Sukenori both were plenipotentiaries and met in Keelung to set the following documented issue:

According to the Article 2 of the agreement reached by the ministers of China and Japan, China will permanently cede Taiwan Island, all the affiliated islands as well as the Penghu Islands to Japan. The administration right of all the islands from 119 °E to 120 °E, from 23°N to 24 °N will be handed over to Japan. In addition, all the fortresses, military works, factories and all of the public objects on those islands, which will be listed on the appendix, will be handed. The two countries sent plenipotentiaries to finish handing over and taking over on the Lunar May 10th of the 21st year of Guangxu Period, namely June 2 of the 28th year of Meiji Period. The two plenipotentiaries signed and sealed on the deed to make the confirmation.

The Lunar May 10 of the 21st year of Guangxu Period

June 2 of the 28th year of Meiji Period

Stipulated in Keelung¹ (Two Copies)

List of the fortresses, military works, factories and all of the public objects on Taiwan Island, all the affiliated islands as well as the Penghu Islands:

1. List of the fortresses, military works, factories and all of the public objects on the whole Taiwan Island, the Penghu Islands, all seaports and all the Prefectures;

2. The treatment to the sea line from Taiwan to Fujian will be decided after China-Japan negotiations.

The Ins and Outs of the Matter

On May 10, 1895, namely the day after exchanging the ratified treaties at Yantai, Japanese government occupied Taiwan by force and ordered and declared that "the Imperial Navy Minister Kabayama Sukenori is here to be promoted to be the admiral appointed as the Governor-General of Taiwan and the military commander. He is ordered to set off for Taiwan immediately." At 10 o'clock of May 13, Japanese government from Tokyo telegrammed Charles Harvey Denby, the United States Ambassador to Beijing, to take a message to Qing government that Japan asked Qing to send an authorized person to finish the hand-over procedures of Taiwan.

The telegraph text was as follows: "Japan has appointed Kabayama Sukenori, Japan's Navy Admiral, as the Governor-General of Taiwan Islands, Penghu Islands and other islands as well as Japan's imperial envoy. The government authorizes Sukenori to handle all the matters according to the last section of Article 5 in Treaty of Shimonoseki. Sukenori will go to his post in two weeks. As soon as he assumes the post, he will finish all the matters that the government authorizes to him. Japanese government hopes that Chinese government could immediately send one or several envoys to meet Sukenori in Taiwan. Please present the name, position of the Chinese envoys to Japan."

---

1 Keelung, officially known as Keelung City, Chinese: pinyin: Jīlóng Shì, is a major port city situated in the northeastern part of Taiwan. It borders New Taipei with which it forms the Taipei–Keelung metropolitan area, the city is Taiwan's second largest seaport (after Kaohsiung).

Ke Shida knew the content of this telegraph in advance and told Li Hongzhang: "We shouldn't hesitate in terms of handing over Taiwan without causing other conflicts or incidents." Li Hongzhang knew that the handover issue was quite intractable, especially at the time when both the military and civilian people in Taiwan were in full of anger and who strongly rejected to hand over of the island. Li Hongzhang figured out a plan that could save his individual prestige by quitting his responsibility. He suggested the imperial court to instruct Tang Ching-sung, the governor-general of Taiwan, to discuss the hand-over issue with the Japanese envoy. However, his suggestion was rejected by the imperial court: "Tang is only the Qing Court's representative in Taiwan and has no right to discuss with Japan's envoy. Please figure out a decent solution and submit to the court."

When Li Hongzhang was worried that there was no solution he could offer, the Ministry of Penalty and Secrets wrote a letter to Privy Counselor Xie Junhang to ask Li Hongzhang and his son to go to Taiwan to solve the handover issue. The letter included the following: "Taiwan issue was mainly created by Li Hongzhang and Li Jingfang. Does it make sense that they should be allowed to detach themselves from the issue when the issue is approaching success or completion? It is believed that since they have the talent to figure out solution of sacrificing Taiwan for peace, they must also have the capability of "assimilating the barbarians with Chinese civilization. Please command Li Hongzhang and Li Jingfang to go to Taiwan in the soonest time in person and finish the handover issue on due date." The Grand Council found the suggestion as reasonable and on May 18th telegraphed the imperial edict to Li Jingfang: "Herewith the court orders the 2nd degree Ding Dai Li Jingfang to set off for Taiwan and finish the handover matter with Japan's envoy."

When receiving this edict, Li Jingfang was shocked. Considering that the issue was difficult to be addressed, Li was afraid to be punished to death and figured out a tricky plan to stay out of the matter.. He asked his father to reply to the court: "Since he came back from Shimonoseki, Li Jingfang fell sick with grievance and toil and has returned to the South to seek medical treatment. Handover issue is quite important. If we send a person who is not familiar with the issue and whose position is not so high. I'm afraid that the result will be negatively affected. Li Jingfang is not qualified for the task. Please withdraw your honor's order and send somebody else to Taiwan."

However, Li Hongzhang's reply didn't work only to be criticized by the emperor. Guangxu issued another imperial edict: "Li Hongzhang shoulders great responsibility and should end the matter in a decent way. How could you stay away from the matter? Now I order Li Jingfang, as my envoy, to Taiwan. Li Jingfang must not dodge difficulty and danger. If there is any problem incurred by Li Jingfang's hesitation, Li Jingfang is the only person who is responsible for the problem. Certainly, Li Hongzhang should also be responsible for that!"

After reading the edict, Li Hongzhang knew very well that it was impossible to act against the imperial edict, thus he requested by telegram the court to send Ke Shida with him to Taiwan. Li Hongzhang sent another telegram to his son who was in Shanghai at that time: "it was difficult for me to resign from the Taiwan issue. As soon as all the envoy members can gather together we are heading for Taiwan." After sending this telegram, Li Hongzhang figured out the idea of handing over the Penghu Islands so as to ensure the safety of his son. Therefore, at the same day, Li Hongzhang cabled a message to the Japanese statesman Ito Hirobumi: "the sovereignty of Taiwan has been handed over to Japan. Japan should dispatch army and navy to repress the reactions and protect the land. Li Jingfang plans to head for Penghu instantly to meet the envoy of Japan."

Reading the text, Ito thought that it would be risky and dangerous if the Chinese envoy would go to Taiwan. Later Ito found out another solution. He asked Chinese envoys first to Nagasaki and then to Taiwan by Japan's boat. On May 22, Ito replied by a telegraph: "It is better for the Chinese envoys first to come to Nagasaki and then travel to Taiwan by a Japanese ship." Li Hongzhang approved the solution. Considering the situation that he is expected to act in accordance with the Japanese authorities, Li Hongzhang thus held a meeting to discuss and check whether he would be taken as a traitor, if he took Ito's advice. After a thorough thinking, Li Hongzhang finally decided to meet the Japanese envoy at the Taiwan port. On May 23, Li Hongzhang's suggestion was accepted by the court.

On May 30, Li Jingfang boarded on a German merchant ship named "the Gerechtigkeit" (Justice) and set the journey from Shanghai, together with Ma Jianzhong, consultant Ke Shida, English interpreter Wu Guangjian, Japanese interpretors Lu Yongming and Tao Dajun, civil officers Zhang Liu and Huangzheng, military officers Lv Wenjing and Gao Xuanchun, as well as 40 guardians. On June 1st, "Gerechtigkeit" entered the Danshui waters. Protected by "Chiyoda", the Japanese naval ship, "Gerechtigkeit" sailed to the neighborhood of Sandiao'ao, the waters east of Keelung. "Hikawa Maru", the ship of the Japanese envoy, dropped the starboard anchor. At half past four of the same day, Li Jingfang sent Tao Dajun to "Hikawa Maru" to tell them that Chinese envoy has arrived and are ready discuss the date of meeting.

At 10 o'clock of June 2, Li Jingfang, with the two Japanese interpreters, took a boat to board on "Hikawa Maru". Kabayama Sukenori welcomed them on the deck and invited them to take seats in the cabin. Sukenori said: "I came to Taiwan by order. Previously I thought the handover issue would be easy since everything was determined in the Treaty. Whereas, out of our expectation, when arriving at the Danshui waters, I sent small military steamboats to the seaport but the small boats were resisted by Qing's cannons. Then we came to Keelung and were targeted by the Chinese cannons again. That's why we have decided to park at Sandiao'ao for the time being. Now an army with 10,000 troops has landed Keelung and we can conquer Keelung in a day."

Li Jingfang replied: "I came here by order to negotiate the matter with your honor. In terms of handover, please explicitly tell me how to do." Sukenori said: "we should wait until the time when we conquer Keelung and discuss the handover in detail in Taipei." Li said: "since the Treaty has been approved by both parties, China has transferred the administration right of Taiwan to Japan. This time, I'm coming to hand over the fortresses, military works, factories and all of the public objects to your honor, based on the Treaty. Now, that Taiwan people have changed their mind. Is it possible to transfer them, one by one on the land? The time will be unknown, if we wait till you land on Taipei. Taiwan is not a small island. The anger of the people cannot be appeased in a day. I'm afraid that the handover will take several years." Sukenori said: "Even so, handover is a major issue and we cannot finish it carelessly." The two envoys discussed until the noon and couldn't reach an agreement. Because of the storms and waves, Li felt quite dizzy. Sukenori proposed: "please return to your ship. I will come to discuss with you."

At 2:00, Sukenori boarded on "Gerechtigkeit" and said: "the Treaty has been approved by both countries. We wish that Japan and China sincerely stick to the peace and not change their mind forever." Li said: "Indeed." Sukenori added: "then, why did the Qing army in Danshui and Keelung attack us? Besides, why is there no explicit notice by the Qing government which ask the military officer and civilians not to resist."

Li Jingfang explained: "after the ratification of the Treaty, the great Qing emperor sent me to Taiwan to do the handover issue and ordered all the military and civilian officers to gradually return to the mainland. These are the evidence of our sincerity for enabling the peace. However, Taiwan people have refused to obey the order and changed their mind and have decided to resist. It's normal that civilians disobey the order from the court. All the resistance and reactions are held by the Taiwan people. Can we argue with them?" Li and Sukenori discussed for a long time, and finally Sukenori said: "we wish that the facts accord with your explanation, and that events are officially backed."

Li Jingfang then asked: "how to deal with the hand-over?" Sukenori replied: "as I have previously suggested." Li sighed: "you are quite obstinate in terms of this point. It seems that Japan has no sincerity to effect the peace." Then Sukenori asked: "what is your opinion?" Li replied: "we can only hand over Taiwan according to the Treaty. There is no other way." Sukenori said: "there must be a list." Li said: "I'm not the local officer in Taiwan. How could I give you the list?" Sukenori said: "the list can be decided by you. If we deal with the issue according to the Treaty, a list is necessary." Li Jingfang then took the pen to make a list and handed it to Sukenori. After reading, Sukenori said: "we solve it in this way for the time being."

In the meantime, the evening time had arrived, Li Jingfang invited the Japanese representative to have dinner at "Gerechtigkeit". After dinner, Mizuno Jun, the newly appointed Director of the Civil Affairs Bureau of Taiwan, discussed the agreement of handover. According to the agreement, "China will permanently cede Taiwan Island, all the affiliated islands as well as the Penghu Islands to Japan. The administration right of all the islands from 119 °E to 120 °E, from 23°N to 24 °N will be handed over to Japan. In addition, all the fortresses, military works, factories and all of the public objects on those islands, which will be listed on the appendix, will be handed. The two countries sent plenipotentiaries to finish the handover and taking over on the Lunar May 10th of the 21st year of Guangxu Period, namely June 2nd of the 28th year of Meiji Period. The two plenipotentiaries signed and sealed on the deed to make the confirmation." Late at night, the agreement was completed in two Chinese copies and two Japanese copies. Sukenori and Li Jingfagn signed and sealed on them.

At 0:30 of June 3, the handover procedures were decided. "Gerechtigkeit" weighed its anchor and sailed off the Taiwan waters. At that time, Chinese consultant Ke Shida wrote down: "at the midnight, the our ship weighed the anchor for leaving. Along with the salute sound from Japanese navy, we are heading for Shanghai. We stayed for 36 hours in the waters of Taiwan. Nobody is happier than Li Jingfang when everything was finished."

(compiled by Li Xiaoxiao)

Roosevelt Proposed to Handover Ryukyu Islands to China's Administration

July, 2005

Wang Xingfu

During Cairo Conference, held from November 22, 1943 to November 26, Chiang Kai-shek has talked with Roosevelt 4 times. At the night of November 23, Chiang Kai-shek, together with Wang Chonghui, had a meeting with Roosevelt. When talking about the issue of depriving Japan of the islands at Pacific Ocean that Japan invaded, Roosevelt came up with the Ryukyu Islands. Roosevelt told Chiang Kai-shek: "Ryukyu Islands is an arc-shaped one consisting of many islands. Japan unjustifiably grabbed the islands and now should be deprived. I'm considering that since the islands are situated close to your country and has intimate relationship with China in history, the islands can be returned to China's administration if China intends to get the islands."

It was totally out of Chiang's expectation that Roosevelt would suggest handing over the Ryukyu islands to China, thus Chiang Kai-shek didn't know how to properly reply. After quite a while, Chiang replied: "as far as I concerned, the islands is better to be occupied by China and the US and then our two countries will co-administer them under the trustee of the UN." With respect to Chiang Kai-shek's reply, Roosevelt, felt that Chiang didn't want the islands and closed the subject.

Ryukyu Islands, with the area of 4600 sq. km., is located between China's Taiwan island and Japan's Kyushu Island, including Sakishima Islands, Okinawa Islands, Amami Islands, Tokara Islands, Ōsumi Islands, etc. During the 12th century, three states were respectively entitled as "middle of the mountain" (Zhongshan), "south of mountain" (Shannan), and "north of mountain" (Shanbei) 山北. In 1372, the three states began to pay tributes to Ming Emperor, were conferred titles of nobility by Ming Emperor and the government and people of the three states frequently contacted with Ming Dynasty. Later, those islands were united to become the Ryukyu Kingdom but continued paying tribute to China's feudal rulers. In 1609, Shimazu, the Satsuma vassal of Japan conquered Ryukyu by force. After then, Ryukyu King began to pay tribute to both Ming Emperor of China and the Satsuma of Japan. However, Ryukyu King was still conferred by Ming Emperor until Qing Dynasty and stressed continued communication with China, which caused Japanese rulers' great dissatisfaction and made Japan worry that Ryukyu would be included into Chinese territory. In 1872, Meiji Government forcibly deposed Ryukyu King and changed Ryukyu into a vassal state without negotiating with China. In 1879, Japan forcibly annexed "Ryukyu" as a vassal state" and included it into Okinawa Prefecture. Japan's embezzlement of Ryukyu prompted the dissatisfaction of many countries and Ryukyu people have resisted and fought against Japan, but failed. Ryukyu Islands has been the east door of China and enjoyed intimate relationships with China in history. Roosevelt has good reasons to offer the administration of Ryukyu to China, but because of Chiang Kai-Shek's hesitation, Roosevelt's offer was rejected in his first attempt.

Chiang Kai-shek Expressed His Intention to Co-administer Ryukyu with the US

On November 25, at the second Chiang Kai-shek-Roosevelt meeting during the Cairo Conference, they talked the Ryukyu islands issue again. Roosevelt said: "Ryukyu islands is located at the northeast of Taiwan and faces the Pacific Ocean. After a thoughtful thinking, I think that Ryukyu is your defense barrier on the east and will be strategically important for you. Taiwan will not be secure if you don't get Ryukyu. What's more important, Ryukyu cannot be occupied for a long time by Japan which is by its origin "naturally" aggressive. Is it Ok that Ryukyu together with Taiwan and the Penghu Islands could be administrated by China?"

Thinking that Ryukyu has been occupied by Japan for long decades and there was nothing about Ryukyu issue in the internal negotiation archive materials, Chiang Kai Shek hesitated and didn't reply for quite a while. Roosevelt thought he didn't express his suggestion very clearly, therefore Roosevelt added: "Will China take over Ryukyu islands? If you will, Ryukyu will be handed over to China when the war is ended." Chiang Kai Shek hesitated again and finally replied: "Ryukyu problem is complicated. I insist my initial suggestion that Ryukyu should be co-administrated by China and the US." Roosevelt now clearly understood that Chiang genuinely didn't want Ryukyu islands, felt that he couldn't persuade Chiang Kai Shek.

Henceforth, Roosevelt and other US leaders didn't mention Ryukyu to Chiang Kai Shek anymore.

Why did Chiang Kai Shek reject Ryukyu at that time? According to the analysis of the KMT officers who accompanied Chiang Kai-shek at Cairo, Chiang Kai Shek went to Cairo mainly to solve the northeastern China issue, plus Taiwan and the Penghu Islands, Ryukyu was not in his agenda. Chiang Kai Shek thought it would be enough to solve the northeastern China issue, Taiwan and the Penghu Islands issues. The other reason was that Japan was powerful in Asia. Chiang Kai Shek was afraid that when China got Ryukyu, Japan would argue with China for Ryukyu so that there would be new dispute between China and Japan.

Because Chiang Kai Shek was determined not to take over Ryukyu, the Cairo Declaration only issued the statement: "All the territories Japan has stolen from the Chinese, such as Manchuria, Formosa, and The Pescadores (the Penghu Islands), shall be restored to the Republic of China", and did not mention a word about Ryukyu.

Chiang Kai-shek strictly Pre-cautioned against Information Leaks

It was until the end of Cairo Conference that Chiang Kai-shek realized it was a mistake not to take over Ryukyu islands and began to regret. Chiang Kai-shek felt it would be a shame for him, he talked about it to Wang Chonghui: "only several people know that Roosevelt planned to hand Ryukyu over to us, so you mustn't tell any other person about it. If someone asks about it, you just tell them that we could not provide solid evidence, and written materials to prove that Ryukyu is ours." Despite of Chiang Kai-shek's repeated pressure, Wang Chonghui, when going back to Chongqing, disclosed about it to few important KMT officials, whom were all Wang's very close friends, that Roosevelt intended to include Ryukyu Islands into China's territory while Chiang Kai-shek didn't accept it. This information could not be kept secret, and many people asked Wang Chonghui about the true story. Frightened to getting into trouble, Wang didn't tell the truth. Later, in all KMT's documents, profiles, magazines and books, the "truth" was mentioned as follows: there was no evidence to show that Ryukyu belonged to China, therefore Ryukyu dispute wasn't mentioned at Cairo Conference.

On March 26, 1945, U.S. started Battle of Okinawa and three months later the US occupied Ryukyu islands. After the World War II, with the foundation of the People's Republic of China and beginning of the Korean War, the U.S. changed his attitudes towards P.R. China and Japan and began to foster Japan to serve his Asia strategy, thus he drastically switched his stance on Ryukyu dispute. In 1962, Kennedy publicly acknowledged that Japan had complete sovereignty over the Ryukyu Islands. In 1972, the U.S. handed over Ryukyu islands to Japan and soon later Japan received complete control over the Ryukyu islands.

On March 19th, When Sima Sangdun, a journalist from Taiwan United Daily News, learned that U.S. government was going to publicly acknowledge Japan's sovereignty over Ryukyu, he felt uneasy and published an article. In the article, Ma Sangdun criticized KMT government's ignorance and recklessness during the Cairo conference and KMT's hiding its mistake of letting the Ryukyu islands go to Japan's sovereignty. Sima Sangdun added, "thus a large defense lock has been created at East Sea." At that time, Sima Sangdun and Taiwan people still didn't know that, the problem was not created due to Chiang Kai-shek's recklessness but that, Chiang Kai-shek was determined not to take over Ryukyu and had refused it twice.

Sima Sangdun's article drew the attention of Taiwan authorities. In order to prevent the matter from going too far, Chiang Kai-shek explained at a KMT senior officers meeting: "as a matter of fact, the positions of Ryukyu and Taiwan were different in the history of our country. At that time (Cairo Conference), Ryukyu was considered to be the defense barrier for us in the East Sea and was militarily important for us. But, we agreed that Ryukyu would be co-administrated by China and the US under UN's trusteeship. Ryukyu issue was thought to be not urgent, therefore we suggested not mentioning it at the conference". However, Chiang Kai Shek didn't utter a word about Roosevelt's offer to handover Ryukyu, in two cases, but refused by him.

Chiang Kai-shek had refused to take over Ryukyu, which had greatly benefitted Japan and the US. Nowadays, the political and military situation and all the disputes over resources in this sea region were caused by the mistakes in the Cairo Conference negotiations.[2]

---

2   Edited by "The Root of Diaoyu Dispute: Chiang Kai-Shek Rejected Ryukyu Twice after World War II" published in Global Times on July 22, 2005. The edited article has been reviewed by the author, Zhang Qixiong.

Supplementary Materials

In his academic article titled as "The Sovereignty of Diaoyu Islands—Demonstrating Japan's Claim from the Perspective of International Law", Mr. Zhang Qixiong, a Taiwan scholar, wrote the following:

On November 23, 1943, during the Cairo Conference, Jiang Zhongzheng has ever expressed to the US President Roosevelt that: China is willing to occupy Ryukyu together with the US. When, Ryukyu is recovered from Japan, China and the US will co-administrate it.

"Ryukyu will be put under international trusteeship and co-administrated by China and the US ", which has been "agreed by both parties" and "recorded" in document. Roosevelt has ever asked Stalin's opinion on China's this claim. On January 12, 1944, at the Pacific Conference held in the White House, Roosevelt expressed to Wei Daoming, the Chinese ambassador in the US that Stalin has agreed to the return of Ryukyu island to China. Roosevelt said: "Stalin is quite familiar with historical issues and he completely agreed that Ryukyu islands should be returned to China."

Soon KMT government lost in the KMT-CPC civil war and KMT escaped to Taiwan. Forced by the situation, KMT government began to depend on the US, politically, diplomatically, militarily and economically, therefore KMT government had no capability to bear the responsibility of co-administrating Ryukyu with the US. Although in such a weak situation, the ROC government kept claiming the sovereignty of the Ryukyu islands and negated Japan's unilateral claim of sovereignty over Ryukyu.

On October 31, 1953, the spokesman of ROC government represented by Ye Gongchao, the "Foreign Minister" of ROC government, has made a speech on the issue, which criticized the negotiation between Japan and the US regarding the return of Great Anmei Island of the North Ryukyu to Japan, which was occupied by the US at that time.

The ROC representative emphasized: "Minister Ye Gongchao, didn't object to the trusteeship of the United Nation, but objects to the transfer of Ryukyu to the administration of Japan." On November 24, the "Foreign Minister" of the ROC government handed a official diplomatic warning note to the US embassy, saying that "the government of China disagrees to thetransfer of Great Anmei Island to Japan". On December 24, "Foreign Minister" Ye Gongchao made a statement criticizing US's illegal transfer. Ye Gongchao emphasized: there is no article in the San Francisco Peace Treaty to authorize the US to transfer the islands to Japan or any other country.

China cannot agree that its suzerain islands, Great Anmei Island and Ryukyu, to be transferred to Japan, let alone its sovereign islands. Japanese Foreign Ministry claimed that "According to the stipulations of the San Francisco

Peace Treaty (1951), the Ryukyu islands and Diaoyu Islands will be administered by the US, which China didn't negate or oppose. This can prove that China doesn't think Diaoyu Islands as part of Taiwan." Whereas the above historical material—San Francisco Peace Treaty (1951)—can also prove that also Japan's claim doesn't exist in this document. Japan has this severe illusion because Japan lacks solid materials to prove its sovereignty, just on the contrary Japan has only referred to those historical documents that have partial meanings. Thus, it is quite reasonable that Japan's claim was wrong.

Once the US Adopted An Ambiguous Position Regarding the Sovereignty of the Diaoyu Islands

Pete Mc Closkey's Statement in September, 1970

Li Xiaoxiao

During World War II, the US had occupied the island as a part of Okinawa Prefecture. Later, the island was also included in the Japan US Security Treaty. On September 10th, 1970, Pete Mc Closkey, the spokesman of U.S. State Council, has ever been asked about U.S.'s stance on the Senkaku Islands and he made the following reply:

According to Article 3 of Peace Treaty with Japan, the US had the right to administer the Senkaku Islands. What the article referred to the islands that were situated at south of 29 degree N. Latitude and was administrated at the end of World War II. However, there were no particular notes about all the islands. The article intended to include the Senkaku Islands (Diaoyu islands, editor's note). According to the Treaty, U.S. government has the right to administer the Senkaku Islands as a part of Ryukyu islands, but considers that residual sovereignty over the Ryukyu remains with Japan. In line with the treaty reached between President Nixon and Prime Minister Sato in September of 1969, the administration right would be returned to Japan in 1972." When Mc Closkey was asked: "if there is clash over the sovereignty of the Senkaku Islands, what will be the attitude of the US?", he answered: "With respect to any conflicting claims, we consider that this would be a matter for resolution by the parties concerned".

For a long time, U.S. remained neutral in the dispute. On March 24, 2004, Ariely, the spokesman of U.S. State Council, pointed out that the administrative control of the islands has been handed over to Japanese government since 1972 on the basis of Ryukyu Returning Treaty. The US knew that there was a dispute over the sovereignty of Diaoyu islands, thus its State Council only said that the islands was the "administrative territory" of Japan, instead of using the term sovereignty. Later on, the US has been very prudent in terms of this issue, and tried to avoid its involvement in the dispute.

However, in 2009, some senators of the US began to support Japan. In September 15, 2009, the Asia-Pacific Division of Foreign Relations Committee held a hearing about the oceanic territory disputes in Asia. Webb, the president of the hearing, criticized China's territorial claims in the South Sea and East Sea and indicated that the US recognized Japan's territory claim of Diaoyu Islands. And later there was no clarification and explanation from the U.S. State Council. On September 7, Japanese Coast Guard's patrol boats collided with China's Fujian fishing trawler, Minjinyu 5179 and Japanese police, captured the the trawler, the captain, and 14 crew members, and took to Ishigaki Island for detention. After the collision, Hilary Clinton, former secretary of the U.S. and Bede, senior director of Asia-Pacific Affairs of the US National Security Council both expressed that the US would not take sides over the Diaoyu Islands, but they added that The Security Treaty Between the United States and Japan could be applied to all the regions and islands under Japan's administration and added that "since after 1972 Diaoyu Islands has been administered by Japan, this is US's consistent stance regarding the dispute."

Annex 1: The report of the News Agency, the meeting between Mr. Xi Jinping and Leon Panetta on September 19 of 2012

Xi Jinping who served as Vice-President of the People's Republic of China and the Vice-Chairman of the Central Military Commission at that time, met Leon Panetta and Leon Panetta said that the US follows the strategy of re-balancing towards the Asia-Pacific with the aim to promote the stability, peace and prosperity of the region and in order to achieve this aim China and the US must develop a constructive relationship. It is delightful that the relationship between the two countries and two armies in recent years has made strides and relations are vigorously developing. The US hopes to enhance strategic dialogue and cooperation with China and establish a new type of relationship between major countries. …, the US is deeply concerned with the recent developments in the East Sea issue. After hearing the historical explanations from China, the US representative said thet US will not take sides in territorial dispute, and calls relevant parties to refrain from taking any provocative actions and that US supports peaceful resolution of international disputes (from people. com.cn on September 20, 2012).

Annex 2: The news report of the program 'Focus Interview' of China Central Television on October 12nd of 2012

At the scholarly seminar held at Woodrow Wilson International Center on October 3rd of 2012, Kissinger, the former Secretary of State of the US, talked about China-Japan dispute over the islands. As a witness of the history, Kissinger indicated that it was the agreement reached by both countries to "shelve" the dispute in 1978. Kissinger added that the US would not interfere in the issue and "deeply hoped" that the Diaoyu dispute to be solved only between China and Japan.

Kissinger had solid information regarding, both Okinawa's return issue and about the diplomatic normalization between China and Japan. In 1971, when the US and Japan were negotiating the Okinawa Reversion Agreement, Kissinger, serving as United States National Security Adviser at that time, was a crucial person who put the principles to distinguish between the "sovereignty" and "right of administration". The "common view" he mentioned this time was understood by Japanese media as: "The Senkaku dispute should be addressed by China and Japan. The United States of America will not involve in it."

Kissinger's attitude was echoed in a report by the Institute of the United States Congress on September 25. The report was a revision of another report titled as the Senkaku Dispute: The US Obligations in Treaty written in 1996. It was said in this report that in term of the Senkaku issue, the US only acknowledged Japan's right of "administration" not its "sovereignty" rights. It was also disclosed in the report that when U.S. government commissioned Congress to ratify the Okinawa Reversion Agreement (1972), the U.S. government said: "the U.S. doesn't have any tendency in terms of Senkaku Sovereignty, even if the right of administration is reversed (passes) to Japan."

Robert Starr, Acting Assistant Legal Adviser of U.S. State Department at that time, at Rodgers' instruction, admitted in a letter on October 21st of 1971: "there is dispute over Senkaku Islands. As far as the US concerned, the right of administration that was reversed to Japan will not impair the sovereignty claim from both sides."

Annex 3: Wu Xianbiao said it was "a mistake out of ignorance" that the US had put Diaoyu Islands under the administration of Ryukyu

According to the news of the Xinhua News Agency on October 9th of 2012, when Dr. Wu Xianbiao, a Chinese American and the lieutenant governor of Delware, was interviewed by Li Dajiu, a Chinese-American journalist, Wu Xianbiao pointed out: "it was the mistake made by an ignorant U.S. military officer at that time to put Diaoyu Islands under the administration of Ryukyu. It was based on such a mistake that Okinawa Reversion Agreement (1972) handed over the administration right of Diaoyu Islands to Japan."

On the Christmas of 1953, D.A.D. Ogden, the deputy chief of U.S. army in all Okinawa islands, publicized the "No. 27 Proclamation of Ryukyu Civil Administration" without any authorization, in which Ryukyu administration region was shown in the map as a hexagon linked by 6 points with longitude and latitude. Diaoyu Islands was mistakenly included into this hexagon.

Dr. Wu Xianbiao has argued that the "No. 27 Proclamation of Ryukyu Civil Administration" re-designed the administration region of Ryukyu, while the "new design" was only the unilateral attitude of the U.S. army and this attitude wasn't based on any international convention, thus it should be taken as legitim.

Dr. Wu Xianbiao is an important figure who participates in the large scale Baodiao Movement initiated by Chinese Americans and overseas Chinese at the beginning of 1970s. In 1971, together with Yang Zhenning and John Fincher, Wu, as the professor of Delware University, was invited by the US Senate or to provide testimony at the hearing for Okinawa Reversion Agreement held by Foreign Relationship Committee of the Senate. Yang, Wu, Fincher, and et,al made a comprehensive illustration of the fact that Diaoyu Islands was within the territory of China from the perspective of history, geology and actuality. On November 2nd, the Foreign Relationship Committee of the Senate passed a resolution about Diaoyu issue by the vote of 16 versus 0, determining to hand over the administration right of Diaoyu Islands to Japan instead of sovereignty.

Records of the Historical Events Related to Ryukyu

September, 2012

Chu Jingtao

1. Independence Movement in Ryukyu Has Lasted for More than 100 Years

In June, 1945, at the time of Japan's dead end, Japan authorities has ever ordered Prime Minister Fumimaro Konoe to visit the Soviet Union as the Mikado's (Japan Emperor) Envoy, attempting to ask Soviet Union's mediation so that Japan would "lose less" in the post-war treaties. Before the peace negotiations, Japan drafted a "Negotiations Outline". It was mentioned in the "Outline" and its "Illustrations" that "as to our territories, we might lose Okinawa (Ryukyu), Ogasawara Islands and Karafuto (Sakhalin Island) at most." The outline reflected Ryukyu's position in the mind of Japanese rulers, namely Ryukyu could be sacrificed and conceded. As a matter of fact, Ryukyu cannot be accounted as the "inherent territory" of Japan. In the history, Ryukyu has been an independent country wherein people have strongly struggled against Japan, during and after its annexation.

Ryukyu's Struggles against Japan's Annexation

In Ancient China, Ming and Qing governments maintained a suzerain–tributary relationship with Ryukyu. In 1870s, Japan successively prevented Ryukyu from paying tribute to Qing dynasty and hindered Ryukyu leadership being conferred by the Chinese Qing government, Japan also changed its reign title, and changed the name into Ryukyu, set up the Okinawa Prefecture and finally included Ryukyu into Okinawa Prefecture. During this, in order to avoid annexation by Japan, the Ryukyu King has ever secretly sent Kôchi Ueekata (namely Xiang Dehong), Lin Shigong and other people to sail across the sea to Fuzhou (China) to demand protection from Qing government so as to save Ryukyu.

In 1877, when He Ruzhang, Qing's first Embassy to Japan, arrived in Kobe (Japan), Ryukyu's chancellor Ma Jian rushed to He Ruzhang's boat. Ma Jian, worrisome and in a unhappy mood, presented him the secret letter written by Ryukyu King. According to the records, from 1879 to 1885, Ryukyu's envoys have totally submitted 28 petition letters to the relevant officers and departments of Qing dynasty. In November of 1880, Lin Shigong has committed suicide for his motherland to attract the concern of the Chinese Qing government to save Ryukyu. But all of these petitions were useless in the end.

In the meantime, Ryukyu people rose up against Japan's brutal rule, besides the officers and aristocrats of Ryukyu were non-cooperative and also resisted Japan. Many aristocrats gathered up and signed the agreement of swearing to fight against Japan's invasion and rule till death, which was the "Blood Agreement" (Xue Pan Shu). There were many such blood agreements signed all over Ryukyu. There were also many armed rebellions. The Miyako Island incident was one typical armed rebellions, by the people:

According to the records, in order to resist Japan's rule, Ryukyu King called upon the Ryukyu people not to obey the orders of Okinawa Prefecture (Japan). The officers of Miyako Island, responded to this call, some local aristocrats and the common people, arranged the signing of the "Blood Agreement" to fight against the Alliance Treaty of Okinawa Prefecture and promised to continue resisting till death. The Blood Agreement stipulated that "if someone died during the resistance struggle, his family will be jointly cared by the co-signatories of the same village." However, a person, who joined the police forces after signing the Agreement, caused the anger of Ryukyu people. Besides, this person hit and arrested a woman who condemned him. Ultimately, about 1200 Ryukyu people crushed into the police station and beat this person to death. Japan was alarmed, when informed about the incident in Miyako Island, the Japanese authorities sent troops the island ro repress the resistance. Many patriots were arrested after the suppression of the incident. Before being beheaded, the patriots cried that "my head will not fall down in front of you. Now, you should clearly see the spirit of the Ryukyu people!".

Assist U.S. Army in the Fight against the Japan Army

In June of 1945, after leading bloody battles against the Japanese forces, the U.S. Army occupied the Ryukyu islands. In the battle of Ryukyu, Japanese troops dispensed hand grenades to Ryukyu people, forced them to commit suicide by jumping off cliffs, and even killed them in order to cope with the problem of lacking food. Several towns of Ryukyu were wiped out and about 200,000 people were dead. Ryukyu people realized that Japan was destined to lose. Actively responding to U.S. Army's attack, some Ryukyu people spontaneously resisted the Japanese order of committing suicide and divulged information to U.S. Army. 3000 Ryukyu students rose up to assist U.S. Army fighting against the Japanese Army and welcome the liberation of Ryukyu.

After the US occupation, in order to eliminate Japan's traces, U.S. advocated and disseminated the use of "Ryukyu", such as "Ryukyu University" and "Ryukyu Newspaper", banned the use of the reign title of Showa, supported a written language distinct from Japanese, used B Yuan as the currency (Originally B Yuan was U.S. military currency and was used by U.S. Army in Ryukyu) and later US Dollar was put in circulation. During the occupation of U.S., being influenced by the world's democratic political atmosphere, national consciousness of Ryukyu people has surged, and they have launched the campaign of national liberation and independence. Brochures and speeches about independence and autonomy spread widely andthe themes of "motherland" and "nation" were propagated. Most people called themselves as part of the Ryukyu nationality, criticized the Japanese government, hoped that they could establish a sovereign state of their own with the help of U.S. In 1947, the press corps of Miyako Island told to the officials of U.S. government and Army: "People on the islands wish to live in a country called Ryukyu and lead an independent country with the protection of U.S."

After their freedom, a number of party organizations emerged. Those parties, according to the Potsdam Declaration, claimed "the liberation of whole Ryukyu nation", "the establishment of Ryukyu's sovereignty", "assisting U.S. Army, who liberated the island, in constructing a democratic Ryukyu" and "setting up a self government" and the Ryukyu independence movement further fermented. Many prestigious figures, such as the Nakasone Genwa of the National Democratic League and the governor of Ryukyu government Shikiya, all hoped for the "independence of the islands".

Against the "Reversion" to Japanese control

However, in order restrict the Soviet Union, U.S. gradually stood in line with Japan. In 19701, the U.S. and Japan reached Okinawa Reversion Agreement, which was firmly opposed by Ryukyu people. Ryukyu people emphasized: "the motherland of Okinawa is Ryukyu, the land that we are standing on. The "reversion" is once more an aggressive act against Ryukyu." Based on the principle of self-determination, Ryukyu people demanded that U.S. should return the administration to Ryukyu people and that they desired to master the future and destiny of the islands by a national referendum. According to the news report by Taiwan press, many Ryukyu people "gathered together and demonstrated in the busy downtown" and assembled during all night to protest U.S. and Japan. Some Ryukyu people decided to go to Taiwan and petitioned Chiang Kai-shek for help. They claimed, in Chinese language, "we belong to the same family", and prepared to petition the United Nation with a report advocating Ryukyu independence or being integrated into China's territory.

At the end of 1971, the so-called 67th "Okinawa Congress" was held to review the "Okinawa Reversion Agreement" and the bill about the "reversion". At the public hall of the "Congress", three members of Ryukyu Youth League Action Team lit the fire cracks and distributed leaflets which wrote: "Japanese has no right to decide Okinawa's destiny".... "we should transcend illusions! The way to liberation relies on the fight against Japan and the US imperialism."

Miyachi Shiro, the president of "China-Ryukyu Association" has ever said that "Ryukyu people felt quite worrisome when learned that the U.S. would 'reverse' Ryukyu to Japan. There is nothing worth celebrating, instead more and more to feel frustrated." Miyachi Shiro argued that Japan and the U.S. reached this "Reverse" agreement, ignored the will and demands of the Ryukyu people. Yamazato, the vice president of the "China-Ryukyu Association" who advocated independence all along, deemed China as the genuine friend and benefactor of Ryukyu and said that "for the last 600 years' of relationship between China and Ryukyu, China has never tried to grab something from Ryukyu and was always been generous, on the contrary Japan, only grabbed and did not give."

After "the reversion of Okinawa" to Japan, some changes occurred in regard to the Ryukyu Independence Movement with the development of Japanese economy and due to Japan's massive assimilation policies, but some Ryukyu people insisted to develop the "Sovereignty Resumption Activities". In 1992, Ryukyu people launched the "Shuri Castle Restoration" movement in order to promote national honor and pride, aimed that people's consciousness of their independent history and culture re-flourishes, and explored the independent future of Ryukyu. In September 1995, Ryukyu FM radio broadcasting station ballot among the local people on "whether Ryukyu should be independent or not", hence the independence demand was raised again. Oyama Chojo, former long-term mayor of Koza/Okinawa City, wrote a best-selling book Okinawa Dokuritsu Sengen (A Declaration of Okinawan Independence), and stated that Japan is not the fatherland of Okinawa, the book reflected Ryukyuan people's voices "we are not Japanese" and criticized the miserable past of the islands. And also, the Okinawa Jichiro (Municipal Workers Union) prepared a report about measures for self-government. Some considered the autonomy and independence of Okinawa to be a reaction to Japanese "structural corruption", and made demands for administrative decentralization.

2. China Ever Tried to Resume the Sovereignty of Ryukyu

The Ryukyu islands group is situated on the Pacific Ocean and in the midst of East Sea, extending from northeast to southwest and lies between Japan's Kyushu Kago Island and the Taiwan Island. In history, Ryukyu and Qing Dynasty have maintained a suzerain-vassal relationship. In 1870s, Japan, pursued the policy of external expansion, sent troops to the islands and included the islands into the administration of Okinawa Prefecture in 1879. In 1945 when Japanese fascism was defeated and surrendered, China strongly voiced for the return of Ryukyu but all the efforts failed due to numerous reasons.

Initially the US Had the Idea of Monopolizing Ryukyu

During World War II, there were about 700 thousand people living on the Ryukyu islands. Although the islands group is small, the affiliated islands scattered all over, which make it significant in terms of military strategy. In 1942, some think-tanks in the US suggested that US should occupy Ryukyu, Taiwan and some other islands situated at the west of Pacific Ocean. In November of 1943, Chiang Kai-shek attended the 3rd China-US-British Summit Meeting in Cairo. According to the US diplomatic archives, during the meeting, Roosevelt, the president of US, suggested that China should resume the sovereignty of Taiwan and also mentioned the Ryukyu issue. "Chiang Kai-shek replied that China would opt to possess Ryukyu together with the US and the two countries should co-administer the islands according to international administration laws." ... Note: Chiang Kai-shek recorded the situation in his diary dated August 16, 1970 as follows:

"Our country didn't waive the sovereignty of Diaoyu Islands. From the perspective of history and politics, no government has ever recognized that Japan owned the sovereignty. What's more, when Japan surrendered at the end of World War II, Japan had renounced all the islands that were apart from Japanese mainland." In addition, on September 10, 1970, U.S. State Council issued a statement that Okinawa would be probably returned to Japan in 1972 and the dispute over the sovereignty of relevant islands should be settled by concerned countries or regions. On September 11, Chiang Kai-shek wrote in his diary: "China didn't agree" with the U.S. on its statement about the Okinawa; "I retain in my right of speak in terms of the US behavior that the US returned Okinawa to Japan without negotiating with China." —Editor)

At that time, some geological scholars were concerned about the destiny of Taiwan and Ryukyu (Ryukyu). At the end of 1944, Hu Huanyong, a geographer, and father of China's population geography edited the book Taiwan and Ryukyu, which was published in Chongqing of China, in which he pointed out: "the territories of Taiwan and Ryukyu must be returned . In the past they were our territories. Six millions of compatriots are waiting to be liberated from Japan's rule. What's more important is that their strategic location is significant for the overall military situation of our country. Our country is situated on the west shore of the Pacific. If Taiwan and Ryukyu wouldn't be returned to us, the offshore naval activities of our country cannot be beyond the Yellow Sea and the East Sea."

In 1945, after a hard fight, the U.S. occupied the Ryukyu islands. Considering the military value of the islands, the U.S. planned to administer them independently for a long time. In April of 1947, the United Nations endorsed the "Agreement on the Islands that Previously Administered by Japan", according to which the Ryukyu islands and Diaoyu Islands, which are situated at the south of 29°N, were given to the administration of the US. The US intended to expropriate Ryukyu and attempted to prohibit the reign title of Showa and to establish a written language distinct from Japanese.

However, due to the Cold War between the US and the Soviet Union getting more intense day by day, in the third phase of the occupation of Japan by the US, towards the end 1940s, the Supreme Commander for the Allied Powers (the West) deemed the political and economic future of Japan firmly established and set about securing a formal peace treaty to end both the war and the occupation of Japan, accordingly the dispute over Ryukyu was delayed. On July 16, 1947, unexpectedly, the U.S. government sent letters to all of the members of Far Eastern Commission of victor major powers, proposing to hold a meeting with Japan on August 19th and asking the 11 countries to attend this meeting which didn't include China. The letters was the mark of the US' preparation of the peace treaty with Japan.

Intellectual Elites Appealed to Take Ryukyu Back

In order to popularize the history of Ryukyu and draw the public's attention, Nanjing Central Daily News published a special issue with the title of "Special Issue on Ryukyu History". The issue included the articles: Ryukyu's Historical Laision with China" (written by historian Ding Shicun), "Textual Research on Ryukyu" (written by Liang Jiabin) and "Notes and the Annexed Tables of Yao Wendong's Postscript to Records of Ryukyu" (written by Chen Zhongmian). These three articles demonstrated Ryukyu's strong historical relations with China by making full use of available historical documents. The editor of the special issue wrote: "the 5th year of Guangxu Period in Qing Dynasty (the year of 1879), Japanese exploited the eventful situation of China to forcefully occupy Ryukyu and ruled the islands for a long time. What's more, Japan has fabricated several documents so as to prove that Ryukyu was not under China's sovereignty, instead all available historical evidence proved that it belonged to Taiwan, especially in the document of Sui Dynasty. Now it is only one year since Japan's surrender. Japanese ambitions germinates again. Japan should give Ryukyu back to Taiwan! The publishing of this special issue aims to raise the attention of all Chinese nation."

As the US had occupied Ryukyu in the war and the Peace Treaty with Japan was close, the army, political, intellectual circles of China frequently voiced their opinions louder. The Geology School of Nanjing Central University gathered a group of famous geologists, such as Hu Yonghuan, Zhang Qijun, Sha Xuequn and Li Xudan. The geologists all demanded the integration of Ryukyu within China's territory. On September 5th, 1947, the newspaper Ta Kung Pao in Tianjin published the essay titled, "Problems about Ryukyu in US-Japan Peace Treaty." which was written by Zhang Qijun who represented Geographical Society of China. The essay pointed out: "Ryukyu's military significance is higher than its economical significance" and the US occupied Ryukyu as it military basis and deployed massive forces there after the World War II, "the US will claim that the islands will belong to US forever". In terms of the solution, Zhang Qijun suggested: "we hope that the Allies could support China in terms of its legitimate demand of resuming the lost territory" and as to the military situation, Zhang Qijun suggested that Ryukyu "can be utilized by international forces to show their respect for the sovereignty and territorial integrity of China".

The government of the Republic of China also began research and discussion. In September, 1947, the Foreign Ministry of the Government of the Republic of China invited a group of senior officials and experts and scholars—three meetings were arranged—and held seminars on the Japan Peace Treaty draft offered by the US. Generally speaking, there were three types of opinions on the ownership of Ryukyu. Geologists such as Zhang Qijun and Hu Huanyong advocated that Ryukyu should be reversed back to China from the perspective of military defense and China's national rejuvenation. Wan Can, Wang Yunsheng, et al. thought it would be illegitimate to ask Ryukyu to be reversed to China and suggested Ryukyu, as a buffer zone, administrated by China. Some experts and scholars proposed that Ryukyu should be administrated by the UN.

Ryukyu Revolutionary Comrades Association of Taiwan Has Generated A Momentum

On 8th October 1947, at the 7th meeting of the Committee of National Political Council, the premier of the ROC, Zhang Qun, Taiwan Executive Yuan presented a proposal arguing that because "as my personal opinion, the solution to Ryukyu dispute is either being retrieved by China, co-administrated by China and the US or administrated by the UN. Our government is paying a close attention to the development of the issue. However, no matter it will be settled in what way, we should object to the claims of Japan. Ryukyu has a special relationship with China the island should be reclaimed." Otherwise, the Taiwan regime intended that a trusteeship be created before the Cairo Conference, as a result of its national favor and the Sino-US relationship, but the trusteeship was not acceptable by the domestic mainstream media. As a result, the Ministry of Foreign Affairs did not find a solution to the Ryukyu problem. The seventh meeting of National Government's Foreign Affairs Committee was held on November 13th, 1947. At this meeting, "the opinions were exchanged and discussed again" regarding the proposal of Committee member Lai Te-Cai's "Recommendations of Ryukyu to be reclaimed to China at the Sino-Japan Peace Conference.

Actually, in 1940s Chiang Kai-shek regime was also closely observing the development of the issue and had the idea of resuming the sovereignty of Ryukyu islands. For this purpose, KMT Central Committee secretly supported the Ryukyu Revolutionary Committee in Taiwan and propagated that Ryukyu people asked Ryukyu to be reversed back to China so as to exert pressure on the US and International society and increase China's say and stakes on the peace treaty negotiations with Japan. On August 14, 1947, Xi Youmi, president of Ryukyu Revolutionary Committee, made a speech in Taiwan that: "no matter from the point of culture, history or nationality, all Ryukyu people are willing to join China as in the past. From the point of military defense, Ryukyu and China are close neighbors and closely interdependent, so China must fight for the return of Ryukyu.

With the changes of internal situation of China and in view of the precarious KMT regime, U.S. tended to be intransigent in terms of Ryukyu's sovereignty, therefore ignored the thoughts of Chiang Kai-shek regime of Taiwan. In September 1951, the conference for Peace Treaty with Japan was convened at San Francisco and U.S. initiated the signing of the peace treaty. With this treaty U.S. began its prolonged occupation of Ryukyu Islands and Diaoyu Islands. It is worth mentioning that the ownership of Diaoyu Islands and Ryukyu Islands are closely related. After being grabbed by Japan in 1895, Diaoyu Islands was put under the administration of Okinawa Prefecture. From 1945 to 1949, the books about Ryukyu Islands published in the Chinese mainland, often referred to the materials published by Japan, and defined the Diaoyu Islands within the territory of Ryukyu Islands. The books were edited in such a way, that it would prepare public opinion to get back the whole Ryukyu group, which naturally would include the Diaoyu Islands at the west of Ryukyu islands.

At the San Francisco Peace Treaty Conference, Chinese people's concern on the future of Ryukyu Islands didn't draw enough attention and enough respect. The ownership of Ryukyu islands and Diaoyu Islands remained as pending issues, which seeded the dispute over East Sea between China and Japan. Since, the Chinese authorities on both sides of the Taiwan Straits didn't attend the conference, the Treaty generated at this conference will not be binding for China. Later, Chiang Kai-shek regime insisted that Ryukyu belonged to China and it was just under the administration of U.S. for the time being and always opposed U.S's reversing it to Japan. When in 1969 the news that the US was planning to give Ryukyu islands and Diaoyu Islands to Japan was exposed to the public, the Chinese people all around the world launched the Baodiao Movement (movement on protecting the Diaoyu Islands).

(The above article was edited by combining the two article published on Global Times, namely "Ryukyu's Independence Movement Since More than 100 Years" published on September 6th. The author was an Associate Research Fellow of Institute of Modern History of the Chinese Academy of Social Sciences. The Article has been checked and approved by the original authors—editor's note.)

Chronicle of Events Regarding the Diaoyu Islands Issue

Introduction

The Diaoyu Islands, is located in the East China sea about 92 nautical miles northeast to Keelung, Taiwan, mainly consist of the Diaoyu island, Huangwei Yu, Chiwei Yu, Nanxiao Island and Beixiao Island and numerous other islets.

The Diaoyu Islands are China's territory since ancient times, they, just like Taiwan, are an inalienable part of China's territory. As early as in the early Ming Dynasty, the Diaoyu Islands were clearly determined as the Chinese territory. Since the Ming Dynasty, the Diaoyu Islands have been put under the control of China's naval defense. Diaoyu Islands are un-inhabited islands, but they were by no means in the terra nullius status. China is the indisputable owner of the Diaoyu Islands. This is supported by historical facts and jurisprudential evidence.

Chronicle of Events

As early as in 1372, the first emperor of the Ming Dynasty appointed Yang Zai as an imperial envoy to grant honorific title to the King of Ryukyu in recognition of his rule in the island. During the trip, they passed by the Diaoyu Islands. Until the Jia Qing Period, there were totally ten imperial envoys who had sailed to Ryukyu to grant honorific title to the King of Ryukyu. However, the records of these imperial envoys were burned by accident.

In 1374 (the 7th year of the reign of Emperor Hongwu of the Ming Dynasty), Marquis of Jinghai, Wu Zhen patrolled seas under order; on the Liushan Sea of Fujian, he encountered Japanese pirates and fought against them around the waters of the Diaoyu Islands andaround the waters of Ryukyu, captured them, the Ryukyuan thought highly of him for a long time.

1403- The earliest historical record of the names of Diaoyu Island, Chiwei Yu and other places can be found in the book of Voyage with a Tail Wind (Shun Feng Xiang Song) published in 1403 (the first year of the reign of Emperor Yongle of the Ming Dynasty). It shows that China had already discovered and named these islands.

1534 - The Records of the Imperial Title-conferring Envoys to Ryukyu (Shi Liu Qiu Lu) written in 1534 by Chen Kan, an imperial title-conferring envoy from the Ming court, clearly stated that "the ship has passed Diaoyu Islands, Huangmao Yu, Chi Yu... Then Gumi Mountain comes into sight, that is where the land of Ryukyu begins." This indicates that the Diaoyu Islands are China's territory and the Gumi Mountain is where the land of Ryukyu begins."

In 1556, Zhen Shungong went to Japan upon order of the government. During the trip, he passed by Taiwan, the Diaoyu Island, Huangma Yu (Huangwei Yu). His drawings of islands between Taiwan and Ryukyu also painted the Diaoyu Islands. In this book an essay entitled "Songs of a Long Voyage" clearly records that Diaoyu Yu is a small island of Xiaodong. "Xiaodong" was a form of addressing Taiwan at that time.

in 1561 (the 40th year of the reign of Emperor Jiajing of the Ming Dynasty), Zheng Ruozeng, "an authority" in coastal geography, wrote Miscellaneous Records by Zheng Kaiyang. The Great Haiphong Map (Wang Li Hai Fang Tu) in Vol. I included the Diaoyu Island, Huangwei Yu, Chiwei Yu. In the same year, the Shi Liu Qiu Lu of another imperial envoy of the Ming Dynasty—Guo Rulin, also stated that "Chi Yu is the mountain that marks the boundary of Ryukyu with mainland China". But we can't find any records of the Diaoyu Islands or the Senkaku Islands in Japan's documents.

In 1562 (the 41th year of the reign of Emperor Jiajing of the Ming Dynasty) An Illustrated Compendium on Maritime Security (Chou Hai Tu Bian) compiled by Zheng Ruozeng under the auspices of Hu Zongxian, the supreme commander of the southeast coastal defense of the Ming court, included the Diaoyu Islands, Huangwei Yu, Chiwei Yu into the jurisdiction of the coastal defense of the Ming court.

In 1562 during the 41th year of Ming Dynasty Emperor Jia Qing's reign, the imperial envoy Guo Rulin was appointed to Ryukyu. His book Records of the Imperial Title-conferring Envoys to Ryukyu (Shi Liu Qiu Lu) records: "On the first day of leap month May, we passed the Diaoyuyu. On the third day we reached Chiyuyan, which is a hill at the local boundary of Ryukyu. After another day's sail, we could see Gumi Mountain. He stated that "Chi Yu is the mountain that marks the boundary of Ryukyu". The subject—China was omitted, so it clearly pointed out the boundary between China and Ryukyu.

In 1605 during the 33rd year of Ming Dynasty Emperor Wanli's reign, Xu Bida, the Secretary for the Ministry of Personnel Management, mentioned the Diaoyu Islands were within China's territory, located in the East China sea about 92 nautical miles northeast to Keelung, Taiwan.

In 1606 during the 34th year of Ming Dynasty Emperor Wanli's reign, the 15th imperial envoy—Xia Ziyang was appointed to grant honorific title to the King of Ryukyu. When he returned to Fuzhou from Naba, he recorded "On October 29th, they saw a ship and everyone cheered as they thought they were close to China; moreover, they crossed the border from black water to green water....on November 1st, the ship arrived Wuhumen. Xia Ziyang clearly recorded that they were in China's waters when they saw the sea waters turned green. To put it in another way, the Hei Shui Gou is the boundary between Ryukyu and China; green waters belong to China while black waters belong to Ryukyu's waters.

In 1609 during the 37th year of Ming Dynasty Emperor Wanli's reign, Japan's vassal in the Satsuma invaded and sent people to do survey on Ryukyu's territory, the Diaoyu Islands were never mentioned in this act. After this event, the Japanese people began to know more about the northern and central Islands of Ryukyu. Since the trade between Japan and Ryukyu were mainly done by the Satsuma. It was not very convenient for Japan to sail to Ryukyu

In 1629 during the 2nd year of Ming Dynasty Emperor Chongzhen's reign, Mao Ruizhi again pointed out in the Record of the Interpreters of August Ming (Huang Ming Xiang Xu Lu) that: "from Fuzhou to [Ryukyu]...the Gumi Mountain is where the land of Ryukyu begins".

In 1640 during the 13th year of Ming Dynasty Emperor Chongzhen's reign, Zhongshan's King Shangfeng pointed out in official communication that: "Ryukyu is adjacent to Fujian; there are clear boundaries between China and Ryukyu".

In 1650 during the 7th year of Qing Dynasty Emperor Shunzhi's reign, Zhongshan Historical Records of Ryukyu Kingdom, an authoritative history book of Ryukyu Royal Court compiled under the supervision of Ryukyu Prime Minister Xiang Xiangxian, quotes Chen Kan as saying that Gumi Mountain comes into sight, that is where the land of Ryukyu begins.

In 1683 during the 22th year of Qing Dynasty Emperor Kangxi's reign, Miscellaneous Records of a Mission to Ryukyu (Shi Liu Qiu Za Lu) written by Wang Ji recorded that Wang Ji asked the old sailor: "what does Hei Shui Gou mean?" "Boundary between China and foreign land", answered the old sailor. It again proves that Hei Shui Gou (Okinawa Trench) is the boundary between China and Ryukyu."

In 1708 during the 47th year of Qing Dynasty Emperor Kangxi's reign, the great Ryukyu scholar Cheng Shunze clearly divided the Gumi Mountain which belongs to Ryukyu and Chiwei Yu which belongs to China in Map of Sea Islands attached in A General Guide (Zhi Nan Guang Yi).

In 1719 during the 58th year of Qing Dynasty Emperor Kangxi's reign, Xu Baoguang, a deputy title-conferring envoy to Ryukyu in the Qing Dynasty, clearly recorded in his book Records of Messages from Chong-shan (Zhong Shan Chuan Xin Lu) that the voyage from Fujian to Ryukyu passed Huaping Yu, Pengjia Yu, Diaoyu Dao, Huangwei Yu, Chiwei Yu and reached Naba (Naha) port of Ryukyu via Gumi Mountain (the mountain guarding the southwest border of Ryukyu) and Machi Island. Gumi Mountain guarding the southwest border of Ryukyu means that Gumi Mountain is the principal island at the sea boundary to the southwest of Ryukyu; he concluded about Yaeyama Islands that the above 8 islands belong to the Yaeyama Islands which are the most southwestern border of Ryukyu".

In 1722 during the 61st year of Qing Dynasty Emperor Kangxi's reign, after patrolling the Diaoyu Islands and Xuepolan (Mount of Olives or Daniao Island, namely Beixiao Island; Dashe Island refers to Nanxiao Island), wrote A Tour of Duty in the Taiwan Strait (Tai Hai Shi Cha Lu) which recorded the condition of the ports and ships and pointed out that there are mountainous islets towards the ocean direction which is called the Diaoyu Islands. The waters of the Diaoyu Islands can hold tens of ships. This is official records and reign marks indicating that the Chinese government conducted effective control over these islands. It has strong international law value.

In 1747 during the 12th year of Qing Dynasty Emperor Qianlong's reign, Re-compiled Annals of Taiwan Prefecture (Chong Zhu Tai Wan Fu Zhi) written by Fan Xian and Modified Annals of Taiwan Prefecture written by Yu Wenyi pointed out the previous version didn't fully record the details of sea defense, so they added some new information about this matter in the two books and transcribed Huang Shujing's records of the Diaoyu Island.

In 1767 during the 32nd year of Qing Dynasty Emperor Qianlong's reign, Michael Benoist, a French missionary in China in 1767 drew the Great Universal Geographic Map (Kun Yu Quan Tu) under the request of the Qing court. He colored Pengjia (Pengjia Mountain), Huabinxu (Huaping Yu), Haoyuxu (Diaoyu Island), Huanweixu (Huangwei Yu), Cheweixu (Chiwei Yu) with the same color to indicate that of mainland China and Taiwan. Original names in this drawing were written with the Minnan dialect.

1785- The Map of the Three Provinces and 36 Islands of Ryukyu in the book—Illustrated Outline of the Three Countries written by Hayashi Shihei in 1785 marked the Gumi mountain guarding the southwest border of Ryukyu and Yaeyama Islands guarding the most southwest border of Ryukyu. He added that the Yaeyama Islands belong to Ryukyu. To the west of the Gumi mountain, he marked Huaping Yu, Pengjia Mountain, Diaoyu Island, Huangwei Yu and Chiwei Yu and colored them with the same color as the mainland of China, indicating that they are part of China's territory.

In 1800, Atlas by Schrämb published by Schallbach Press in the capital of Austria, Vienna collected the map published in 1786 which mentioned about the Diaoyu Islands. In this map, there is a line in German—"Diese Inseln gehören dem König von Likeyo" (these islands belong to Ryukyu) which divided the Yaeyama Islands located in the southwest to Ryukyu from the Diaoyu Island and its affiliated islands of China; it indicates that the Yaeyama Islands south to this line belong to Ryukyu and the islands north to this line belong to China; these islands were marked with Haoyusu, Hoanoeysu, Tsche-oey-su (the transliteration of the Diaoyu Island, Huangwei Yu, Chiwei Yu).

In 1808 during the 13th year of Qing Dynasty Emperor Jiaqing's reign, Qi Kun, an imperial envoy clearly recorded the position of Hei Shui Gou: "on May 13, we saw Chi Yu. After several hours, we offer sacrifices to Ocean God". He also recorded: the "trench" is the Ryukyu coast in the Eight poems of Voyage.

The Map of East China Sea Littoral States drawn by French publisher and geographer Pierre Lapie in 1809 mapped the Diaoyu Islands, Huangwei Yu and Chiwei Yu into China's territory as Taiwan's affiliated islands. Maps such as Latest Map of China published by Britain in 1811, Colton's China published in New York in 1859, A Map of China's East Coast: Hongkong to Gulf of Liao-Tung compiled by British navy in 1877, etc. all have mapped the Diaoyu Islands into China's territory.

1871- Volume 86 of Recompiled General Annals of Fujian (Chong Zuan Fu Jian Tong Zhi), a book compiled by Chen Shouqi and others in 1871 (the 10th year of the reign of Emperor Tongzhi of the Qing Dynasty) included Diaoyu Dao as a strategic location for coastal defense and placed the islands under the jurisdiction of Gamalan, Taiwan (known as Yilan County today).

In 1879 during the 5th year of Qing Dynasty Emperor Guangxu's reign, before Ryukyu Vassal of China was annexed to Japan's Okinawa prefecture, Xiang Dehong, the Grand Master with the Purple-Golden Ribbon suggested China sent soldiers to Ryukyu to defend against the attack of Japan. In his reply to the Japanese Foreign Minister Terashima, he clearly said there were 36 islands in Ryukyu, and the islands between Gumi Island and Fuzhou belonged to China.

In 1879, the Japan annexed Ryukyu. In the same year, the two governments China and Japan negotiated on the ownership of Ryukyu. Japan put forward that Miyako Islands and Yaeyama Islands belong to China; Both sides believed that there were 36 islands in Ryukyu, Diaoyu Islands excluded.

In 1880, October, Japan's envoy Shishido Chi put forward "Miyako Islands and Yaeyama Islands belong to China; then the Chinese Qing government and Japan reached consensus on the "Island Division and Treaty Adding" plan.

On August 21, 1884, after the Japanese government "discovered" the Diaoyu Islands, it asked Okinawa magistrate to make an investigation on the islands. The investigators reported to Sutezou Nishimura. The Okinawa magistrate wrote: "the islands are undoubtedly the Diaoyu islands, Huangwei Yu, Chiwei Yu, etc. which were recorded in the Records of Messages from Chong-shan (Zhong Shan Chuan Xin Lu)." On August 22, 1884, Sutezou Nishimura, the Okinawa Magistrate, reported to Yamagata Aritomo, the Ministry of Internal Affairs: these islands were discovered by the ship of the imperial envoy of the Qing Dynasty who went to grant honorific title to the former Zhongshan King and that they had already been named by China.

In 1885 during the 11th year of Qing Dynasty Emperor Guangxu's reign, Koga Tatsushiro—a Japanese businessman—went to the Diaoyu Island without permission to collect bird feather, pinions and seafood, and applied to rent the islands. In the same year, the Ministry of Internal Affairs gave secret instructions to Kanmori Nagagi, Okinawa Secretary to investigate the islands and establish national border markers.

On September 6, 1885, the Chinese newspaper Shen-pao (Shangai) reported: "some Japanese people stuck Japan's flag on the sea islands to the north east of Taiwan, revealing Japan's intention to occupy these islands".

On October 21, 1885, Inoue Kaoru, the Ministry of Foreign Affairs, wrote to Yamagata Aritomo, the Ministry of Internal Affairs: over the matter concerning placing national markers on the uninhabited islands of Kumeseki-shima and two other islands spread out in between Okinawa and Fuzhou [China] after investigating them, I have given much thought to the matter. The aforementioned islands are close to the border of China, and it has been found through our surveys that the area of the islands is much smaller than the previously surveyed island, Daito-jima; and in particular, China has already given names to the islands. Most recently Chinese newspapers have been reporting rumors of our government's intention of occupying certain islands owned by China located next to Taiwan, demonstrating suspicion toward our country and consistently urging the Qing government to be aware of this matter. In such a time, if we were to publicly place national markers on the islands, this must necessarily invite China's suspicion toward us. Currently we should limit ourselves to investigating the islands, understanding the formations of the harbors, seeing whether or not there exist possibilities to develop the island's land and resources, which all should be made into detailed responds.

In regard to the matter of placing national markers and developing the islands, it should await a more appropriate time."

On August 1, 1894, the Japanese troops in Korea launched a surprise attack against the Chinese army, the Qing government was forced to declare war on Japan. On September 15, the Chinese army was defeated in Pyongyang

(Korea). Later, the Japanese army crossed the Yalu River and captured Jiulian City and Fenghuang City. On September 17th, in the Battle of Yalu River, China's Beiyang Fleet suffered severe losses. Japanese armies occupied Jinzhou, Dalian and Lushun, etc.

1894- In early November, 1894, considering the Qing government's great failure, Li Hongzhang sent De Cuilin, the official in Revenue Division under Tianjin Customs, to Japan to make a peace agreement with Japan, but Japan refused this proposal.

1894- After Japan's victory in the Sino-Japanese War, on December 27th, 1894, Yasushi Nomura, the Ministry of Internal Affairs, sent ciphered text to Foreign Minister Mutsu Munemitsu: "about the arrangement of establishing stakes on Kuba Island and the Diaoyu islands, we hope this matter could be submitted to the cabinet meeting again according to the present situation."

On January 14, 1895, the Cabinet made a decision that "the Minister of Internal Affairs submitted for deliberation- appropriate administration should be carried out because someone intended to fish on uninhabited islands of Kuba-Island and Uotsuri-Island, which are on the northwest of Yaeyama Islands under the jurisdiction of Okinawa Prefecture. The governor of this prefecture submitted a permission to include those islands to Japan's territory and set up sovereignty border markers. If it is proper, the proposal can be passed." The governor of Okinawa Prefecture was instructed on January 21st: "Your proposal of setting up sovereignty markers has been approved."

In March, 1895, the Japanese army captured Niuzhuang. In April, the Japanese army captured Penghu Islands.

On April 17, 1895, China was forced to sign Treaty of Shimonoseki. Japan occupied Taiwan, and imposed 230 million taels as war reparations, by virtue of which, as a turning point, Japanese capitalist economy developed rapidly; Japan further expanded militarization t and also became the main source of war in the Far East region.

On May 8, 1895, China and Japan exchanged ratification of the Treaty of Shimonoseki in Beijing. The people in Taiwan opposed to the ceding of Taiwan and held the armed uprising.

On May 27, 1895, Kbatama Sukenori who was in charge of receiving Taiwan's administration ordered the Japanese navy to gather on the waters about 5 nautical miles way from the Senkaku Islands and wait for instructions. This was the first time that the Japanese army invaded the Diaoyu Islands waters.

1895—On June 2, "the handover of Taiwan was completely ended". Since then, Taiwan became Japan's colony. It was after the victory of War of Resistance against Japanese Aggression in 1945, Taiwan was returned to the bosom of motherland.

On June 10th, 1895, Koga Tatsushiro took advantage of the Treaty of Shimonoseki and advocated that Japan should incorporate the Ryukyu and Diayou islands into Japan's territory. In September, 1896, Koga's application of lending the islands was "approved".

In May 1900, "Adventure of Senkaku Islands" written by Kuroyiwa Hisashi, a teacher in Okinawa referred to "Pinnacle Islands" in the British chart and used the name "Senkaku Islands" to call the Diaoyu Island group, Huangwei Yu. But "Senkaku Islands" named by Kuroiwa Hisashi was never officially admitted by Japan. Until 1995, the documents of Japan Defense Agency still used the Chinese name "Huangwei Yu" and "Chiwei Yu". In addition, Kuroiwa didn't arrive Chiwei Yu, so the "Senkaku Islands" didn't include Chiwei Yu.

On December 9, 1941, the Chinese government officially declared war against Japan, announced the abolition of all treaties between China and Japan.

On December 1, 1943, the governments of China, the United States and Britain issued the "Cairo Declaration" which stipulated: "all the territories Japan has stolen from the Chinese, such as Manchuria, Formosa, and the Pescadores, shall be restored to the Republic of China. Japan will also be expelled from all other territories which Japan has taken by violence and greed."

In July, 1945, the meeting by the leaders of the United States, Britain, and China held in Potsdam, Berlin and published "Potsdam Declaration" on the 26th, urging Japan to surrender. In Article 8 of the Potsdam Declaration stipulates: "The terms of the Cairo Declaration shall be carried out and Japanese sovereignty shall be limited to the islands of Honshu, Hokkaido, Kyushu, Shikoku and such minor islands as we determine."

On September 2, 1945, the Japanese government signed the Japan's agreement of Surrender; Japan accepted the Potsdam Declaration and pledged loyalty to fulfill the provisions of the Potsdam Declaration.

On October 25, 1945, the Chinese government recovered Taiwan formally. China has always stressed that Japan should obey the "Cairo Declaration" and "Potsdam Declaration" and all the territories Japan has stolen from the Chinese should be returned to China, including the Diaoyu Islands.

On January 29, 1946, the Supreme Commander for the Allied Powers Instruction (SCAPIN) No.677 clearly defined Japan's power of administration to "include the four main islands of Japan (Hokkaido, Honshu, Kyushu and Shikoku) and the approximately 1,000 smaller adjacent islands, including the Tsushima Islands and the Ryukyu Islands north of the 30th parallel of North Latitude", but the Diaoyu Islands were not included (Huangwei Yu south of the 30th parallel of North Latitude is located to the most northern part of the Diaoyu Island and its affiliated islands).

On February 2, 1946, Mac Arthur, in the name of Supreme Headquarters of the Allies issued a statement that Japan's power of administration to "include the four main islands of Japan (Hokkaido, Honshu, Kyushu and Shikoku) and the approximately 1,000 smaller adjacent islands, including the Tsushima Islands and the Ryukyu Islands north of the 30th parallel of North Latitude". Based on the Article 8 of Potsdam Declaration, Supreme Headquarters of the Allies in Japan printed and distributed maps of the jurisdiction areas.

On December 4, 1950, as for the Treaty of Peace with Japan, the Central People's Government of the People's Republic of China authorized Foreign Minister Zhou Enlai to issue a statement, emphasizing the main basis of peace treaty with Japan should be the Cairo Declaration, the Yalta Declaration, Potsdam Declaration and the related provisions in regard to Japan; after its surrender to the Far Eastern Commission on June 19th, 1947.

On August 15, 1951, Chinese Foreign Minister Zhou Enlai issued a statement about the draft of Treaty of Peace with Japan and the San Francisco Conference: the Central People's Government of the People's Republic of China holds that the draft of Treaty of Peace with Japan proposed by the US and the UK governments violates international agreements and cannot be accepted. Moreover, the San Francisco Conference which will be forcibly held by the US government without China's participation on September 4th also violates international agreements and can not be accepted. Therefore, it completely contradicts the UN declaration on January 1st, 1942, which stipulates no country should sign peace treaty with Japan alone.

The Central People's Government of the People's Republic of China has always advocated that those countries that fought against Japan should take part in the preparation and establishment of a shared rather than separated, fair and reasonable peace treaty with Japan, rather than forcing an exclusive treaty, truly peaceful rather than aggressive peace treaty with Japan as soon as possible based on major international agreements and documents such as the UN Declaration, the Cairo Declaration, the Yalta Declaration, the Potsdam Declaration and related provisions in regard to Japan after its surrender to the Far Eastern Commission.

On September 8, 1951, Japan, the United States and a number of other countries signed the Treaty of Peace with Japan—commonly known as the Treaty of San Francisco—with China excluded from it. The treaty placed Ryukyu under United Nations' trusteeship, defined the United States as the sole administering authority.

On September 18, 1951, Foreign Minister Zhou Enlai once again said hard facts proved that the Chinese people suffered the greatest sacrifice and made the most contribution for the longest time in the great war against the Japanese imperialism. However, regardless of the international agreements, the

US Government excluded and rejected the People's Republic of China flagrantly. On September 4th, 1951, the US Government unilaterally held the San Francisco Conference where it signed Treaty of Peace with Japan on September 8th. The Treaty of Peace with Japan signed in the San Francisco Conference has been a unilateral treaty without the participation of China. It is by no means a comprehensive treaty or valid.

On February 29, 1952, No. 68 edict (Article 1 in Chapter I of Code Chapter of Ryukyu government) of U.S. military headquarters which was in charge of taking over Ryukyu expanded the scope of its jurisdiction and control in contradiction with the above Article. It mapped the Diaoyu Island and its affiliated islands based on the longitude and latitude division method. The United State made this decision in accordance with its Cold War interests, and sowed the bane of the Diaoyu Islands issue.

In March 1952, the famous International Law scholar Hans Kelsen (1881-1973) underlined the Article 3 of the Treaty of San Francisco in the book "Principles of International Law"; he held that the islands ruled by Japan were all put under administration of the United States. The United States only has the sovereignty right over the islands under the condition that the countries assigned for trusteeship will refrain from their trusteeship status over the islands and Japan surrendered, which conforms to International Law. "Otherwise, the United States has no right to deal with these islands. According to Potsdam Declaration and Armistice Edict signed by Emperor Hirohito on August 15th, 1945, Japan's sovereignty didn't include the Southwest Islands, let alone the Diaoyu Islands which don't belong to Ryukyu, likewise, the United States can't claim sovereignty over Southwest Islands, neither, let alone the Diaoyu Island and its affiliated islands. Therefore, Japan and the United States have no legal right to control these territories."

1963- The Map of the Southwest Islands in the Atlas of Japan published by Imperial Academy Tokyo, Japan, on November 20, 1963, didn't include the Diaoyu Islands into Japan's territory. Neither did The Map of Japan published by Japan on November 25, 1970, (the map is in the Vol. 5 of "Shogakukan Japanese Encyclopedia") especially from Japan's surrender to March 8th, 1972, none of the maps of Southwest Islands published in Japan including maps related to Taiwan's affiliated islands—the Diaoyu Islands, Huangwei Yu and Chiwei Yu, prove this point

In June 1967, US Marine Geology Professor Shepard Emery and Japanese Professor. Niino in Japan's Tokai University jointly published a paper titled "Undersea Formations and Oil Outlook of East China Sea and Korea". The United States in 1967 began to investigate the oil reserves in this sea region. In June 1968, the US confirmed that the continental shelf of East China Sea may contain abundant oil reserves.

In the autumn of 1968, under the support of ECAFE, Prof. Emery together with an expert from Japan, South Korea, Taiwan, China conducted exploration again and confirmed that the waters off the Diaoyu Island had oil fields, hence, Japan and the United States insisted to commandeer the Diaoyu Islands.

On May 15, 1969, with the order of the United States administration, the Japanese government instigated Ishigaki City of Okinawa to erect national border markers in regard to Diaoyu Island. Certain words were carved on the markers such as "Diaoyu Island of Senkaku Islands in Yaeyama" in the front, "markers established by the Ishigaki City", etc.

July 7-16, 1970, United States Civil Administration of the Ryukyu Islands decided to erect billboards which included "Prohibit illegal entry" written in in English, Chinese and Japanese on the five Islands (the Diaoyu Island, Nanxiao Island, Beixiao Island, Huangwei Yu, Chiwei Yu). They have named Huangwei Yu as Kuba Island and Chiwei Yu as Taisho Island. But the official work reports still used their Chinese names.

On August 17, 1970, the Japanese government as the "potential sovereignty subject" put forward three principles for Okinawa: 1. the Senkaku Islands (or Diaoyu Islands) together with Okinawa island group which are under the administration of the United States should be returned to Japan; 2. the Ryukyu administrative government claims sovereignty over the Diaoyu Islands; 3. Okinawa should apply for extraction rights of the oil resources development company to the Ryukyu government and so that Ryukyu government will recognize this company's oil investigation rights as soon as possible.

In August, 1970, the article titled "The Ocean Development—Who Is the Owner of the Seabed" published in Japan's Yomiuri Weekly mentioned: "the East China Sea continental shelf extends from the mainland China's continental shelf, and is separated by Okinawa trench with the Ryukyu Islands. The Senkaku Islands, Danjo Islands are in the front of the continental shelf; although they are closer to Japan (the Ryukyu Islands), since they are on the continental shelf extended from China's continental shelf, we can't say they belong to Japan."

On September 10, 1970, as for the question concerning the US position on the Diaoyu Islands, Pete McCloskey, the spokesman of US Department of State answered: "according to Article 3 of San Francisco Treaty of Peace with Japan the United States has the administrative rights of Southwest Islands. The treaty only mentioned the territory south of 29 degrees north latitude line would put under the jurisdiction of Japan at the end of Second World War. But the treaty never mentioned all the islands in detail. According to the treaty, the US government claims the administrative rights of the Senkaku Islands because the Senkaku Islands (Diayou) are a part of the Ryukyu Islands, but also the treaty holds that potential sovereignty the Senkaku Islands belongs to China. When being asked "what position the United States will take, if there is a dispute over the sovereignty of the Senkaku Islands, he answered "in order to respect all the demands of sovereignty, we think it should be solved by the states which are directly involved."

On September 10, 1970, Foreign Minister of Aichi, Japan replied in Foreign Relations Committee of House of Representatives: there is no need to negotiate about the sovereignty over the Senkaku Islands, as Japan has the absolute sovereignty over the Senkaku Islands."

On September 17th, 1970, the Ryukyu government issued "On Sovereignty over the Senkaku Islands" and said that by virtue of preemptive occupation of terra nullius, the Senkaku Islands has become the Japanese territory, thus declared the fundamental argument and the "Official View" of the Japanese government, for the future.

On December 22, 1970, the Xinhua News Agency reported: "Japanese reactionaries and Chiang Kai-shek group and Park Chung-hee clique have brazenly decided to ally and engage in robbing China's undersea resources together with the US imperialists".

On December 29, 1970, Commentator of the People's Daily published an article We Will Never Allow US and Japanese Reactionaries to Plunder China's Seabed Resources.

On April 9, 1971, United States Department of State said: "the administrative right of the Senkaku Islands together with Okinawa will be returned to Japan in 1972." the position of the United States on this issue is that it should be solved by the states directly involved; if they agree, they can resort to third-party solutions.

On April 9, 1971, United States Department of State accepted China's formal negotiations and will suspend its oil investigations in the East China Sea.

On April 10, 1971, 2500 Chinese-Americans held the parade against Japan's occupation the Diaoyu Islands in Washington. They shouted "the Diaoyu Islands are ours, we will defend the Diaoyu Islands. Fight against the Japanese militarism!" The parade team marched till the front gate of the Japanese embassy in Washington. On the same day, Chinese-Americans also gathered around the Japanese Consulate in Los Angeles for demonstrations.

On June 17, 1971, Japan and the United States signed Okinawa Reversion Agreement in order to handover Okinawa to Japan, and the Diaoyu Islands were also mapped into the handover area. The Chinese all over the world held large-scale Baodiao campaigns (safeguarding the Diaoyu Islands). Under the pressure of public opinion, the United States and Japan announced on the same day: the United States only allows the handover of the administrative jurisdiction rights of the Diaoyu Islands rather than their sovereignty.

On October 26, 1971, in the United Nations General Assembly the People's Republic of China recovered its lawful seat in the United Nations with overwhelming votes of 76 yes to 35 no.

On November 2, 1971, Committee on Foreign Affairs of US Senate passed the Okinawa Reversion Agreement and at the same time declared that the agreement had nothing to do with the sovereignty over the Diaoyu Islands.

On December 30, 1971, the statement of Ministry of Foreign Affairs of the People's Republic of China on the sovereignty over the Diaoyu Islands mentioned that the United States Congress and Japanese Diet passed the Okinawa Reversion Agreement, wherein the Diaoyu Islands were mapped into the handover region. "It is a flagrant and intolerable violation of China's territorial sovereignty. The Diaoyu Island and its affiliated islands have been China's sacred territory since ancient times. Since the Ming Dynasty, the Diaoyu Islands have been put under the jurisdiction of China's naval defense. They are the affiliated islands of Taiwan rather than Ryukyu (Okinawa). The boundary between China and Ryukyu is between the Chiwei Yu and Kume Island. Chinese fishermen in Taiwan had always been engaged in fishing and production activities in regard with the Diaoyu Islands. The Japanese government stole these islands during the Sino-Japanese War (1894-1895). In April 1895, Japan forced the Chinese Qing government to sign the Treaty of Shimonoseki – ceded Taiwan and all its affiliated islands as well as the Penghu Islands to Japan. At present, Japan's Sato government uses these Japan's occupation of China's territories as the proof of Japan's sovereignty over the Diaoyu Islands, which is nothing but an obvious gangster logic."

On March 3, 1972 in The United Nations Committee led Conference regarding "the Peaceful Use of Seabeds", An Zhiyuan, the representative of China argued: "on behalf of the government of the People's Republic of China, I reiterate that Taiwan and its affiliated islands, including the Diaoyu Island, Huangwei Yu, Chiwei Yu, Nanxiao Island, Beixiao Island, are China's sacred territory. The waters and sea resources all belong to China. China will never tolerate any foreign invaders."

On March 8, 1972, the Japanese Ministry of Foreign Affairs issued the Basic Views Concerning the Senkaku Islands" which insisted that it is in the framework of preemptive occupation of terra nullius islands. The islands were not obtained in the Nissin war, thus Japan has the sovereignty over the Diaoyu Islands, the islands cannot be returned to China in accordance with the "Cairo Declaration" and "Potsdam Declaration".

On May 5, 1972, the United States mapped the eight islands such as the Diaoyu Island as part of Okinawa Reversion Agreement and allowed handover of them to Japan illegally. Japan flagrantly sent coast guard patrol boats to the Diaoyu Island and clamored that "Japan will claim sovereignty over the Diaoyu Islands with actions."

On May 20, 1972, China's UN ambassador Huang Hua wrote to the UN secretary-general Kurt Waldheim, and to Presidency of the UN Security Council: "the US and Japan has made secret dealings regarding the Diaoyu Islands, which is totally illegal and invalid; China will never accept it."

The son of Koga Tatsushiro who was the first Japanese businessman who landed on the Diaoyu Islands in 1972, expressed his opinion in a Japanese magazine "Modern" in June: "the Meiji government announced the Senkaku Islands as Japan's territory in 1895, 11 years after my father's adventure. Maybe father's adventure was associated with the application of the Magistrate Nishimura, I think this application was because Japan had won the War (1894-95) and obtained Taiwan."

On September 29, 1972, the government of the People's Republic of China and the Japanese government issued a joint statement. The Government of the People's Republic of China reiterates that Taiwan is an inalienable part of the territory of the People's Republic of China. The Government of Japan fully understands and respects this stand of the Government of the People's Republic of China, and it firmly maintains its stand under Article 8 of the Potsdam Declaration. Premier Zhou Enlai suggested to shelve the Diaoyu Islands issue and solve it later at a convenient time. Both sides have reached a consensus.

On September 30, 1972, in the interview with Asahi Shinbun, Japanese Foreign Minister Ohira when discussing the questions about how to handle the Diaoyu Islands, he answered: "our negotiations with China did not involve the trivial matters, we have focused on the important question of recovering Japan-China diplomatic ties."

In October 1972, the famous Japanese historian Inoue Kiyoshi published Historical Facts of Senkaku/Diaoyu Islands, with the conscience of a fair historian, he explained why the Diaoyu Islands belong to China and revealed the process, how Japan grabbed the Diaoyu Islands, which played an important role in the research on the issue of Diaoyu Islands.

On November 6, 1972, Japanese Foreign Minister Ohira answered Masaki Yoshiaki's question — the Japanese are confused whether Japan-China Treaty of Peace and Friendship involves the territorial issues, please comment on this issue. Foreign Minister Ohira answered: "we have already solved the past issues, Japan-China Treaty of Peace and Friendship aims to enhance the friendly relations between the two countries." His answer indirectly indicated the consensus on the policy of "freezing" or "shelving" the Senkaku Islands issue.

On January 30, 1974, in Seoul, Japan and South Korea signed an agreement between Japan and the Republic of Korea, to jointly develop the continental shelf in the south linking the two countries. Chinese Foreign Ministry Spokesperson issued an authorized statement on February 3rd as follows: the Chinese government, based on the principles that the continental shelf is a natural extension of the mainland, stresses that the division of the East China Sea continental shelf should be determined between China and relevant countries. The Japanese government and the South Korean authorities delimited so-called "common development area" in the East China Sea continental shelf without China's permission and consent, which violates China's sovereignty, the Chinese government firmly opposes this agreement.

On June 13, 1974, Chinese Foreign Ministry Spokesperson issued an authorized statement: the East China Sea continental shelf is a natural extension of mainland China, so People's Republic of China has inviolable sovereignty over the East China Sea continental shelf. The Japanese government and the South Korean authorities signed the agreement between Japan and the Republic of Korea to jointly develop the continental shelf in the south sea, linking the two countries, bur without China's permission, which is totally illegal and invalid. Without the permission of the Chinese government, no country can develop the East China Sea continental shelf.

On June 26, 1974, when Japan and South Korea exchanged ratification of the, the Ministry of Foreign Affairs of China issued a statement: "China opposes to Japan's exchange of ratification without China's permission, which violates China's sovereignty, China reiterates that the agreement between Japan and the Republic of Korea to jointly develop the continental shelf in the south linking the two countries is totally illegal and invalid."

In 1978, a Japanese youth club built the first lighthouse on the Diaoyu Islands.

On August 12, 1978, China and Japan signed the China-Japan Treaty of Peace and Friendship. The 2 sides confirmed the joint statement of China-Japan in 1972 as the basis of peaceful and friendly relations between the two countries. The two sides agreed the following: two sides should follow the principles in the the joint statement of China-Japan in 1972. The 1978 China-Japan Treaty stipulated the Government of Japan and the Government of the People's Republic of China agree to establish relations of perpetual peace and friendship between the two countries on the basis of principles of mutual respect for sovereignty and territorial integrity, mutual non-aggression and non-interference. Both in 1972 and 1978 negotiations about China-Japan Treaty of Peace and Friendship, leaders of two sides have reached a consensus on "shelving the dispute".

In October 1978, Vice-Premier Deng Xiaoping visited Japan for the ratification of the Sino-Japanese Treaty of Peace and Friendship. Commenting on the issue of Diaoyu Island at the press conference, Deng Xiaoping said, "When China and Japan normalized relations, both countries agreed not to involve this issue. When we negotiated the Sino-Japanese Treaty of Peace and Friendship, we also agreed not to deal with this issue at the moment. We believe that it would be wiser to set the issue aside for a while if we couldn't bridge our difference in the current time. It is okay to temporarily shelve such an issue if our generation does not have enough wisdom to resolve it. The next generation will have more wisdom, and I am sure they will eventually find a way acceptable to both sides." No one from the Japanese side made any objection to Deng Xiaoping's comment.

In October 1979, Shogoro Takahashi, the director of the Japan Association for Promotion of International Trade, published Notes on Senkaku Islands/ Diaoyu Islands, which is an expert book, discussing the Diaoyu Islands' ownership. Japan Libraries Association has ever recommended the book after its publication. On January 7, 1980, the author Takahashi wrote an article in a Japanese newspaper: "Historically and geographically speaking, Senkaku Islands are affiliated islands of Taiwan. At the end of the Jiawu War (1894-95) between Chinese Qing government and Japan Meji government, Senkaku Islands, as a part of Taiwan, was ceded to Japan and became Japan's "territory". What important is that at that time Japan didn't think that there was any need to use the argument of "terra nullius" for occupying the Seankaku Islands, because there were no national boundaries between Okinawa and Taiwan due to compromise in the Treaty of Shimonoseki. When defeated in the World War II, Japan accepted the provisions of the Potsdam Declaration. According to the Treaty of San Francisco (1951), Taiwan and its affiliated islands were excluded from Japan's territory, therefore Senkaku Islands, certainly, should be owned by China."

In 1979, Japan built a temporary helipad on the Diaoyu Islands, people of mainland China and Taiwan lodged solemn representations and strong protests targeting the Japanese government.

On November 19th, 1990, the People's Daily published the statement of Foreign Ministry Spokesperson Li Jinhua, he pointed out that the Japanese right-wing political forces set beacon light on the Diaoyu Islands, which seriously violated China's sovereignty.

On February 25, 1992, China promulgated the Law on the Territorial Sea and the Contiguous Zone People's Republic of China which stipulated: the land territory of the People's Republic of China includes the mainland of the People's Republic of China and its coastal islands, Taiwan and all islands appertaining thereto including the Diaoyu Islands, the Penghu Islands, the Dongsha Islands, the Xisha Islands, the Zhongsha Islands and the Nansha Islands; as well as all the other islands belonging to the People's Republic of China. This Law was promulgated by Order No. 55 of the President of the People's Republic of China. Japan lodged strong protest against the law. The Ministry of Foreign Affairs of China reiterated that the Diaoyu Islands group belongs to China.

On July 14, 1996, Japanese right-wing political groups organized and provoked the "Japanese youth club" to illegally build a solar lighthouse again on the Beixiao Island. After that event, the Japanese right-wingers made two illegal landing on the islands.

On September 22, 1996, Chen Yuxiang, the leader of Global Chinese Diaoyu Islands Alliance, together with other 16 people went to the Diaoyu Islands to declare the sovereignty over the Diaoyu Islands. On September 26, when Chen Yuxiang was landing on the island, Japanese patrol ships intercepted him and he was drowned. On October 17, composed of 50 boats, the Hong Kong fleet had fierce confrontation with 60 Japanese patrol boats.

Published on November 26, 1998, China and Japan released the "China-Japan Joint Declaration On Building a Partnership of Friendship and Cooperation for Peace and Development". Both sides agreed the following: squarely facing the past and correctly understanding history are the important foundation for further developing relations between China and Japan. The Japanese side agrees to follow the spirit of the 1972 Joint Statement between the government of the People's Republic of China and the government of Japan and the Statement made by former Prime Minister Tomiichi Murayama on the Aug 15, 1995. The Japanese side is keenly conscious of the responsibility for the serious distress and damage that Japan had given to the Chinese people through its aggression against China during a certain period in the past and expresses deep remorse for this. The Chinese side hopes that the Japanese side will learn lessons from the history and adhere to the path of peace and development. Based on this, both sides will develop long-standing relations of friendship."

In October 2002, the Japanese government leased three unmanned islands including the Diaoyu Island to the Japanese citizens with the price of about 22 million yen per year. On January 2, 2003, Chinese Foreign Ministry Spokesman commented on the above matter, as follows: the Diaoyu Island and its affiliated islands have been China's inherent territory since ancient times. The unilateral actions taken by Japan are totally invalid.

On March 24, 2004, Feng Jinhua and other 6 Chinese citizens landed on the Diaoyu Islands, but were illegal arrested by the Japanese coast guards.

On February 9, 2005, Japanese youth club handed over the beacon to the Japanese government, Japanese government immediately appointed the coast guard to land on the Diaoyu Islands, to set up national border markers.

In February 2008, Japan delivered "Japan's Territorial Sea Chart, to UN Secretary-General, which included the Diaoyu Islands. On May 7th, 2008, China and Japan signed the China-Japan joint statement on promoting strategic, mutually beneficial ties in Tokyo. The two sides again reiterated the following: the Joint Communique of the Government of Japan and the Government of the People's Republic of China issued on September 29, 1972, the Treaty of Peace and Friendship between Japan and the People's Republic of China signed on August 12th, 1978, and the Japan-China Joint Declaration issued on November 26th, 1998, are the political foundations for advancing Japan-China relationships in a stable fashion and forging the relationship towards future. The leaders of the two sides confirmed that they would continue to observe the principles enunciated in the past three documents. Both sides stated that they would resolve bilateral issues through consultations and negotiations. Both sides will enhance the mutually beneficial cooperation and work together to make the East China Sea a "Sea of Peace, Cooperation and Friendship.

May 15th, 2008, the Chinese government submitted an oppositional inquiry letter against Japan's delivery of the "Territorial Sea Chart" which included the Diaoyu Islands to UN Secretary-General. On December 8th, 2008, "Chinese patrol 46" and "Chinese patrol 51" cruised within 12 nautical miles to the co-asts of Diaoyu Islands, which was the first time Chinese official ships passed the 12 nautical miles border regarding the Diaoyu Islands.

On September 6, 2010, the Japanese coast guard patrol ships offended a Chinese trawler in the waters of the Diaoyu Islands. Japan sent two patrol bo-ats to track the Chinese trawler. Around 13 PM, 22 maritime security officers of the Japanese patrol boat boarded the Chinese fishing boat and ordered the fishing boat to stop sailing, with the argument that Chinese trawler violated Japan's "fishery law".

On September 7, 2010, two Japan Coast Guard patrol ships and a Chinese trawler named as "Fujian Fishing Boat 5179" collided in the waters of Diaoyu Islands. On the following day, the Japan Coast Guard illegally seized the Chinese trawler and detained the trawler's captain Zhan Qixiong.

On September 10, 2010, Foreign Minister Yang Jiechi summoned Japanese Ambassador to China Uichiro Niwa and lodged a solemn representation to him. Besides, he lodged a strong protest with Japan over the illegal detaining of the Chinese fishing boat and fishermen in the waters of Diaoyu Islands. He stressed that the Chinese government's determination to defend the sovereignty of the Diaoyu Islands and the interests of Chinese people would continue uns-wervingly. He urged the Japanese side to release the Chinese fishermen inclu-ding its captain and the Chinese fishing boat, unconditionally.

On September 12, State Councilor Dai Bingguo summoned Japan's Ambassador Uichiro Niwa for the fourth time and warned Tokyo not to make a wrong judgment on the situation and urged Japan to make a "wise political resolution". He urged Japan to immediately release the Chinese fishermen and the Chinese fishing boat.

On September 13, Foreign Ministry spokesperson Jiang Yu declared that the 14 Chinese fishermen were freed by Japan, and returned home with a charter flight and the trawler, which was "illegally detained by the Japanese side", had also set off for home on the morning of September 13th. But, Japan continued to hold the captain. China again urged Japan to immediately release the captain.

On September 25, 2010, the captain of the Chinese fishing boat, Zhan Jixiong who was illegally arrested by the Japanese side was freed by Japan, and returned to Fuzhou with a charter flight. Chinese Deputy Foreign Minister Hu Zhengyue and vice governor of Fujian province Hong Jiexu welcomed him at the airport. On the same day, Ministry of Foreign affairs made the following statement: on 7 September 2010, Japan illegally arrested and detained fifteen Chinese fishermen and their fishing boat in the waters off the Diaoyu Island. The captain was detained by Japan till 24 September. These actions have seriously violated China's territorial sovereignty and the human rights of the Chinese citizens. The Chinese government hereby expresses its strong protest. The Diaoyu Island and its affiliated islands have been China's territory since ancient times. China has indisputable sovereignty over these islands. Japan's detention and investigation of the Chinese fishermen and fishing boat and all forms of its related judicial measures are illegal and invalid. Japan must offer China its apology and compensation for this incident."

On September 28, 2010, Chinese Foreign Ministry Spokesperson Jiang Yu held a regular press conference where he expressed hopes that the Japanese will make due efforts to improve China-Japan relations. As for the question — It is reported that Chinese fishery administration boats will carry out regular patrols in the waters of the Diaoyu Island, he said the waters of the Diaoyu Island are traditional fishing waters for the Chinese fishermen. China dispatches official fishery law-enforcement boats to maintain fishing order and protect the safety of lives and properties of Chinese fishermen, in the framework of fishery administration activities in accordance with China's relevant laws and regulations. We hope Japan stop tracking and disrupting China's official fishery law-enforcement boats.

On September 29, 2010, "China's official fishery administration boat 201" sailed to the most eastern end of the Diaoyu Islands — Chiwei Yu.

On March 2, 2011, Japanese F-15J fighters intercepted Chinese Y-8 surveillance planes about 30 nautical miles from the Diaoyu Islands, reportedly the closest distance Chinese military aircraft have been detected to cross the "median line" between Japan and China and passed over the Diaoyu Islands, later the Chinese planes flew towards the west, to their bases in mainland China. Japan's air self-defense force, declared: "our F-15J fighters aimed to hinder Chinese planes from infringing our airspace".

On December 17, 2011, the City Assembly of Ishigaki, in Japan's Okinawa Prefecture, designated January 14th as the "pioneering" day of the "Senkaku Islands," known as the Diaoyu Islands which belong to China

In the morning of January 3, 2012, four Japanese members of the local legislative body in Ishigaki landed on the Diaoyu Islands. On this issue, the Chinese Government lodged solemn representations and protested the Japanese side for the incident. Chinese Government has reiterated that the Diaoyu Island and its affiliated islands have been China's inherent territory since ancient times and China has indisputable sovereignty over them. The Chinese government resolutely defends its territorial sovereignty over the Diaoyu Islands.

On March 2, 2012, based on Island Protection Law of the People's Republic of China, The State Oceanic Administration has issued the list of standardized names of islands and islets in China's territorial waters. The list was approved by the State Council of the People's Republic of China. The State Oceanic Administration and Ministry of Civil Affairs of the People's Republic of China published the standard names (totally 71) including the Diaoyu Island and its affiliated islands and islets.

On the same day, Integrated Maritime Policy Division under Japan's ruling Cabinet announced 39 names of the unmanned islands. Japan's Kyodo News Agency report said that the named islands included the 4 Islands such as North West Island near the Diaoyu Islands in Ishigaki, Okinawa.

On August 15, 2012, the Japanese coast guard "illegally" arrested 14 Hong Kong Baodiao activists for "illegal entry" to waters of Japan. According to NHK's report, they arrived the waters of the Diaoyu Island in local time at 16 PM on August 15 (15 PM in Beijing time), seven people boarded the Diaoyu Islands and demonstrated the Chinese national flag. Japan's coast guard detained five of them; they shouted: "this is the Chinese territory, we don't need a passport!" Afterwards, the Baodiao ship intended to leave, but Japan's coast guard stopped them and investigated the ship, nine people on board were arrested for "illegal entry".

On August 15, 2012, Chinese foreign minister Fu Ying made solemn representations and lodged strong protest with Japan. Fu Ying reiterated China's sovereignty over the Diaoyu Island and its affiliated islets, and demanded the Japanese side guarantee the safety of the 14 Chinese citizens and free them immediately and unconditionally.

On the same day, Chinese foreign ministry spokesperson Qin Gang said: Japan detained 14 Chinese nationals and their vessel on the Diaoyu Islands and its adjacent waters, which is a gross violation of China's territorial sovereignty. The Chinese Government expresses strong condemnation and protest over the dangerous actions such as converging attack made by Japanese ships to obstruct the Chinese vessel.

On August 18, 2012, after repeated solemn representations and various efforts by the Chinese government, on August 17th, Japan released the 14 Chinese citizens who were illegally arrested in the waters of the Diaoyu Islands, unconditionally. Seven of them flew to Hong Kong by a flight from Okinawa Naha Airport in the evening. The other seven went to Ishigaki, Okinawa to check and confirm the condition of their boat and returned by their ship.

On September 10, 2012, in accordance with the Law of the People's Republic of China Regarding the Territorial Seas and the Contiguous Zone which had been promulgated on 25 February 1992, the Chinese government made the following statement: we hereby announce the baselines of the territorial seas adjacent to Diaoyu Island and its affiliated islands of the People's Republic of China. On the same day, the Japanese government announced the "purchase" of the Diaoyu Island and its affiliated Nan Xiaodao and Bei Xiaodao islets to a Japanese citizen, also Japan declared the so-called the "nationalization" of the islands.

On September 10, 2012, the same day, the Ministry of Foreign Affairs of the People's Republic of China issued a statement that the Chinese government and people express firm opposition to and strongly protest against the Japanese move. It pointed out that the Diaoyu Island and its affiliated islets have been China's sacred territory since ancient times. This truth is supported by historical facts and jurisprudential evidence. The Japanese government's so-called "purchase" of the Diaoyu Islands group is totally illegal and invalid. It does not change, not even in the slightest way, the historical fact of Japan's occupation of Chinese territory, nor will it alter China's territorial sovereignty over the Diaoyu Island and its affiliated islands.

On September 11, 2012, the People's Daily published an article titled "How Could Japan "Buy" Chinese-owned Diaoyu Islands?" which expounded China's principled position in detail.

On the anniversary of the September 18 Incident, citizens in Beijing and other cities in the mainland held large scale demonstrations, protesting the Japanese authorities' "nationalization" of the China's Diaoyu Islands. On September 16th, also massive anti-China demonstrations broke out in Japan. Under the incitement of the Japanese right-wing forces, antagonism between people in the two countries became increasingly acute.

The year 2012 marked the 40th anniversary of the normalization of diplomatic relations between China and Japan. However, a series of celebratory meetings were postponed or suspended. Chinese foreign ministry spokesperson Hong Lei held a press conference on September 28th, 2012. He expressed: "this year marks the 40th anniversary of the normalization of China-Japan diplomatic ties and should be a year of opportunity for the two sides to push the bilateral relations, forward. However, a lot of celebratory activities have been sabotaged by Japan's erroneous actions, thus these activities were either canceled or put off. This is what we didn't want to see. The grim situation facing China-Japan relations is totally caused by Japan's blatant infringement of China's territorial sovereignty, outright denial of the outcome of the victory of the World Anti-Fascist War and gross challenge to the post-war international order. We urge the Japanese side to take concrete measures to correct mistakes and stop all activities that violate China's territorial sovereignty so as to get China-Japan relations back on the track of sound development."

On December 13, 2012, Chinese marine surveillance plane B–3837 arrived in the Diaoyu Islands' airspace in order to carry out a joint air-sea patrol with Chinese patrol ships in the area. The patrol teams announced China's territorial claim and told the Japanese ships to leave the area, This was the first time China sent its plane into the Diaoyu Islands' airspace to declare China's indisputable sovereignty over the Diaoyu Islands and its affiliated islets.

On December 16, 2012, Shinzo Abe, Japan's Liberal Democratic Party leader, won the Japanese general elections and became the government head of Japan. When he accepted the media interview for the first time, he declared that "Japan will never make a concession on the Diaoyu Islands issue". Abe claimed that his government is committed to enhance the strength of Japan's "Self Defence Forces" and and Japan "will achieve a comprehensive military power".

In September 2012, Chinese Marine Surveillance Agency launched the mechanism of surveillance cruises and deployed sailing nearby the Diaoyu Islands, which effectively broke down Japan's so-called "actual control" and defended China's maritime rights and interests. According to the news from State Oceanic Administration, China ocean surveillance ship fleet has entered the territorial sea of the Diaoyu Islands for cruise for more than 20 times, and the nearest distance from the Diaoyu Islands was 1.55 nautical miles.

On January 11, 2013, Japanese Prime Minister Shinzo Abe held a press conference in Tokyo, and argued that there is no room for negotiation on the Diaoyu Island issue. He put forward "Japan will absolutely reject a concession and won't make the Senkaku/Diaoyu Islands a negotiating object".

On January 25, 2013, Xi Jinping, general secretary of the Communist Party of China (CPC) Central Committee, met with Natsuo Yamaguchi, the leader of the New Komeito party of Japan at the Great Hall of the People. Xi Jinping said China and Japan are important neighbors to each other, and bilateral cooperation in various fields has reached an unprecedented level in terms of both depth and breadth since the normalization of diplomatic relations 40 years ago, which has given a strong impetus to the development of the two countries. The Chinese government attaches importance to developing relations with Japan and such policy remains unchanged. Facts prove that the 4 political documents between the two countries are the ballast stone of bilateral relations, which should be abided by. Xi Jinping stressed that in order to maintain long-term healthy and stable development of China-Japan relations, both sides must focus on the overall situation, grasp the direction, promptly and properly handle sensitive issues between the two countries. China's position on the Diaoyu Islands issue is consistent and clear. He, added: the Japanese side should face the history as well as the reality and make joint efforts with China through real action to seek effective methods for appropriately controlling and resolving the issue through dialogue and consultation, both sides should take history as a mirror, and look into the future. Xi Jinping urged Japan to respect the national feelings of the Chinese people and correctly handle the historical issues.

On February 10th, 2013, China ocean surveillance ship fleet realized the normalized cruise sail in the waters of the Diaoyu Islands so as to safeguard the sacred territory of the motherland and national marine rights and interests.

(Compiled by Dongming)

Postscript

This book is compiled by the Beijing China-Japan Journalists Association. It has collected various literature, academic papers, and newspapers commentaries, maps cartography and other relevant evidence, regarding the issue.

Given that the Diaoyu island issue has gradually become a serious obstacle for the healthy development of the China-Japan relations, the public needs to know more about the history and background of the dispute. Based on journalism ethics and standards we have tried our best to include, scholars' debates, documents, government statements, speeches by leaders, cartography, maps, news reports and other relevant materials in this book. Accuracy, fairness, affinity, objectivity and relevancy have been our motto when compiling this book. And we have especially included the important literature concerning the over 40 years of normalization period of China-Japan diplomatic relations, which is bygone currently.

In order to enable readers, learn more about the academic arguments made by experts and scholars about the Diaoyu Islands issue, I have selected the comments and papers of the renowned Chinese scholars, including those of Hong Kong and Taiwan. As there are numerous works debating the Diaoyu Islands issue, it has been a difficult task to choose from among them. Due to limitation of length and space, I have extracted several chapters from some masterpieces. These papers, on the basis of facts and jurisprudence, which embody a high sense of responsibility and historical conscience, can tell us the truth of history.

I have translated and collected masterpieces of the famous Japanese historians such as Prof. Inoue Kiyoshi, Mr. Takahashi Sougorou, Mr. Murata Tadayoshi and others. This is one of the most valuable aspects of this book. They have fairly evaluated the history, and used their pen to refute the distortions made by the Japanese government.

The Beijing China-Japan Journalists Association, established in 1994, is an association established by the Chinese news media editors and reporters who once lived in Japan for a long time. Mr. Shao Huaze, the former president of People's Daily and honorary president of our association still serves as the president. As experienced journalists with abundant knowledge of the issues between Japan-China, our association has always been concerned with promoting positive relations and exchanges between the two countries and have contributed to deepening of the mutual understanding between them.

The Diaoyu Islands issue is a sensitive issue which determines whether China-Japan relations can develop healthily. The dispute is rooted in the grave contemporary confrontation between the two countries. The Diaoyu island issue concerns territorial sovereignty and national feelings of the two peoples. Due to historical reasons, though 70 years have passed since the World War II, the issue is not properly solved yet. In the foreseeable future, the issue will still be an important factor affecting the China-Japan relations. We sincerely hope this book can help to deepen mutual lenience on the issue and give play to the wisdom of the Chinese and Japanese people, by virtue of which, the issue can finally be solved in a mutually favorable way.

First of all, we owe the publication to the support and encouragement of our member authors and concerned scholars. When they have learned about our book project, they all have found it meaningful, and affirmed the significance such a valuable informative book concerning the Diaoyu Islands. Some scholars have taken initiative to send me their works, and some even provided their most recent papers, which they have not yet published. We have pleasantly included some of these papers, and grateful for their contributions to our country with their articles, we are all moved by their actions.

At the same time, we owe great thanks for the support of several officials and leaders of civil associations whose work involves Japan, and who have done much for mutual friendship. In the process of compiling this book, we got encouragement from Tang Jiaxuan, the President of the China-Japan Friendship Association. Mr. Shao Huaze, the former president of People's Daily has shown personal concern for the publication of the book, and suggested the title for it. We have also received enthusiastic guidance from Wang Taiping (the counselor of our association), who had been former Consul General of China in Osaka, Japan; Mr. Wu Xuewen (the counselor of our association), who is also the honorary chairman of the China Association of Sino-Japanese Relations History, plus Mr. Liu Jiangyong and Mr. Tang Zhongnan, who are famous scholars on the issue. We have also received from the international department of the People's Daily, People's Daily Press, Global Times.

In the process of preparation numerous newspaper editors have dedicated themselves to collect documents, information, have arranged them, have made translation and editing work, etc, whose names are: Ma Yuan, Wang Xiaoyan, Wang Yuhua, Wang Qingying, Liu Shuiming, Sun Dongmin, Zhu Fulai, Su Haihe, Li Shouzhen, Li Ande, Gao Haikuan, Zhang Ningbin, Zhang Zhe, Yue Linhui, Tang Hui, Zhu Yikai. Besides, Mr. Lin Guoben did a careful proofreading of translations. I want to express my heartfelt gratitude: Thank you all, for the "hard work".

With the publication of the book, our association wants to express our deep respects and gratitude to the people who have supported us!

Except for the official statements, speeches of the leaders, academic papers, newspaper reviews and other articles only represent the author's views. Finally, meticulous efforts were paid for the accuracy of the material and literature included in the book, but we know that mistakes can never be avoided, wherein we sincerely hope our readers can inform us.

The Beijing China-Japan Journalists Association
February 2013, Beijing

www.ingramcontent.com/pod-product-compliance
Lightning Source LLC
Chambersburg PA
CBHW031136020426

42333CB00013B/397